The Nicene-Constantinopolitan Creed

πιστεύομεν εἰς ἕνα Θεὸν πατέρα, παντοκράτορα, ποιητὴν οὐρανοῦ καὶ γῆς, ὁρατῶν τε πάντων καὶ ἀοράτων.	Credo in unum Deum Patrem omnipotentem; factorem coeli et terrae, visibilium omnium et invisibilium.	We believe in one God, the Father, the Almighty, maker of heaven and earth, of all that is, seen and unseen.
καὶ εἰς ἕνα κύριον Ἰησοῦν Χριστόν, τὸν υἱὸν τοῦ Θεοῦ τὸν μονογενῆ, τὸν ἐκ τοῦ πατρὸς γεννηθέντα πρὸ πάντων τῶν αἰώνων, φῶς ἐκ φωτός, Θεὸν ἀληθινὸν ἐκ θεοῦ ἀληθινοῦ, γεννηθέντα, οὐ ποιηθέντα, ὁμοούσιον τῷ πατρί· δι' οὗ τὰ πάντα ἐγένετο· τὸν δι' ἡμᾶς τοὺς ἀνθρώπους καὶ διὰ τὴν ἡμετέραν σωτηρίαν κατελθόντα ἐκ τῶν οὐρανῶν καὶ σαρκωθέντα ἐκ πνεύματος ἁγίου καὶ Μαρίας τῆς παρθένου καὶ ἐνανθρωπήσαντα,	Et in unum Dominum Jesum Christum, Filium Dei unigenitum, et ex Patre natum ante omnia saecula Deum de Deo, Lumen de Lumine, Deum verum de Deo vero, genitum, non factum, consubstantialem Patri; per quem omnia facta sunt; qui propter nos homines et propter nostram salutem descendit de coelis, et incarnatus est de Spiritu Sancto ex Maria virgine, et homo factus est;	We believe in one Lord, Jesus Christ, the only Son of God, eternally begotten of the Father, God from God, Light from Light, true God from true God, begotten, not made, of one Being with the Father. Through him all things were made. For us and for our salvation he came down from heaven: by the power of the Holy Spirit he became incarnate from the Virgin Mary, and was made man.
σταυρωθέντα τε ὑπὲρ ἡμῶν ἐπὶ Ποντίου Πιλάτου, καὶ παθόντα καὶ ταφέντα, καὶ ἀναστάντα τῇ τρίτῃ ἡμέρᾳ κατὰ τὰς γραφάς, καὶ ἀνελθόντα εἰς τοὺς οὐρανούς, καὶ καθεζόμενον ἐκ δεξιῶν τοῦ πατρός, καὶ πάλιν ἐρχόμενον μετὰ δόξης κρῖναι ζῶντας καὶ νεκρούς· οὗ τῆς βασιλείας οὐκ ἔσται τέλος.	crucifixus etiam pro nobis sub Pontio Pilato, passus et sepultus est; et resurrexit tertia die, secundum Scripturas; et ascendit in coelum, sedet ad dexteram Patris; et iterum venturus est, cum gloria, judicare vivos et mortuos; cujus regni non erit finis.	For our sake he was crucified under Pontius Pilate; he suffered death and was buried. On the third day he rose again in accordance with the Scriptures; he ascended into heaven and is seated at the right hand of the Father. He will come again in glory to judge the living and the dead, and his kingdom will have no end.
καὶ εἰς τὸ πνεῦμα τὸ ἅγιον, τὸ κύριον, καὶ τὸ ζωοποιόν, τὸ ἐκ τοῦ πατρὸς ἐκπορευόμενον, τὸ σὺν πατρὶ καὶ υἱῷ συμπροσκυνούμενον καὶ συνδοξαζόμενον, τὸ λαλῆσαν διὰ τῶν προφητῶν·	Et in Spiritum Sanctum, Dominum et vivificantem, qui ex Patre Filioque procedit; qui cum Patre et Filio simul adoratur et conglorificatur; qui locutus est per Prophetas.	We believe in the Holy Spirit, the Lord, the giver of life, who proceeds from the Father and the Son. With the Father and the Son he is worshiped and glorified. He has spoken through the Prophets.
εἰς μίαν, ἁγίαν, καθολικὴν καὶ ἀποστολικὴν ἐκκλησίαν· ὁμολογοῦμεν ἓν βάπτισμα εἰς ἄφεσιν ἁμαρτιῶν· προσδοκῶμεν ἀνάστασιν νεκρῶν, καὶ ζωὴν τοῦ μέλλοντος αἰῶνος. Ἀμήν.	Et unam, sanctam, catholicam et apostolicam ecclesiam. Confiteor unum baptisma in remissionem peccatorum; et expecto resurrectionem mortuorum, et vitam venturi saeculi. Amen.	We believe in one holy catholic and apostolic Church. We acknowledge one baptism for the forgiveness of sins. We look for the resurrection of the dead, and the life of the world to come. Amen.

Consulting Editors

Bishop Kallistos Ware, Oxford

Bishop Stephen Sykes, Durham

Prof. Augustine DiNoia, Rome

Prof. James I. Packer, Vancouver

ANCIENT CHRISTIAN DOCTRINE

5

We Believe in One Holy Catholic and Apostolic Church

EDITED BY
ANGELO DI BERARDINO

SERIES EDITOR
THOMAS C. ODEN

An imprint of InterVarsity Press
Downers Grove, Illinois

©2010 by Institute for Classical Christian Studies (ICCS), Thomas C. Oden and Angelo Di Berardino.

All rights reserved. No part of this book may be reproduced in any form without written permission from InterVarsity Press.

InterVarsity Press® is the book-publishing division of InterVarsity Christian Fellowship/USA®, a movement of students and faculty active on campus at hundreds of universities, colleges and schools of nursing in the United States of America, and a member movement of the International Fellowship of Evangelical Students. For information about local and regional activities, write Public Relations Dept., InterVarsity Christian Fellowship/USA, 6400 Schroeder Rd., P.O. Box 7895, Madison, WI 53707-7895, or visit the IVCF website at <www.intervarsity.org>.

The Scripture quotations quoted herein are from the Revised Standard Version of the Bible, copyright 1946, 1952, 1971 by the Division of Christian Education of the National Council of the Churches of Christ in the U.S.A. Used by permission. All rights reserved.

Selected excerpts from Edward Yarnold, The Awe-Inspiring Rites of Initiation: Baptismal Homilies of the Fourth Century, ©1972; Robert Murray, Symbols of Church and Kingdom: A Study in Early Syriac Tradition, ©2006. Reprinted with the permission of the publisher, The Continuum International Publishing Group, London and New York..

Selected excerpts from Fathers of the Church: A New Translation, ©1947-, used by permission of The Catholic University of America Press, Washington, D.C.

Selected excerpts from New Testament Apocrypha, edited by Wilhelm Schneemelcher, English translation edited by R. McL. Wilson, 2 vols., ©1991-1992. Reprinted by permission of James Clarke, Cambridge, England, and Westminster John Knox, Louisville, Ky.

Selected excerpts from Carolyn Osiek, The Shepherd of Hermas: A Commentary, Hermeneia, ©1999. Reprinted by permission of Fortress Press, Minneapolis, Minn.

Selected excerpts from Ernest Evans, ed. and trans., Tertullian: Adversus Marcionem, 2 vols., ©1972. Reprinted by permission of Oxford University Press.

Selected excerpts from Ernest Evans, trans., Tertullian's Treatise on the Resurrection, ©1960; Ernest Evans, trans., Tertullian's Homily on Baptism, ©1964. Reprinted by permission of SPCK, London.

Selected excerpts from The Works of Saint Augustine: A Translation for the 21st Century, edited by John E. Rotelle, ©1990-. Used by permission of the Augustinian Heritage Institute.

Design: Cindy Kiple
Images: The Adoration of the Trinity by Albrecht Dürer, at Kunsthistorisches Museum, Vienna, Austria. Erich Lessing/Art Resource, NY

ISBN 978-0-8308-2535-6

Printed in the United States of America ∞

 InterVarsity Press is committed to protecting the environment and to the responsible use of natural resources. As a member of Green Press Initiative we use recycled paper whenever possible. To learn more about the Green Press Initiative, visit <www.greenpressinitia tive.org>.

Library of Congress Cataloging-in-Publication Data

We believe in one holy Catholic and Apostolic Church/edited by Angelo Di Berardino.
  p. cm.—(Ancient Christian doctrine; 5)
  Includes bibliographical references and indexes.
  ISBN 978-0-8308-2535-6 (hardcover: alk. paper)
  1. church—Marks.   I. Di Berardino, Angelo.
BV601.W4 2009
262'.72—dc22
                        2009032098

| P | 24 | 23 | 22 | 21 | 20 | 19 | 18 | 17 | 16 | 15 | 14 | 13 | 12 | 11 | 10 | 9 | 8 | 7 | 6 | 5 | 4 | 3 | 2 | 1 |
| Y | 31 | 30 | 29 | 28 | 27 | 26 | 25 | 24 | 23 | 22 | 21 | 20 | 19 | 18 | 17 | 16 | 15 | 14 | 13 | 12 | 11 | 10 |

Contents

A Guide to Using the Commentaries in the Ancient Christian
    Doctrine Series vii

Abbreviations ix

Introduction xiii

*We Believe in One Holy Catholic and
    Apostolic Church: The Church* 1

*We Believe in One Holy Catholic and Apostolic Church:
    One Holy Catholic and Apostolic* 54

We Acknowledge One Baptism 87

For the Forgiveness of Sins 112

We Look for the Resurrection of the Dead 139

*And the Life of the World to Come:
    Blessedness and Condemnation* 175

*And the Life of the World to Come:
    Christ's Return, the Judgment and Eternal Life* 214

Conclusion of the Ancient Christian Doctrine Series 269

Outline of Contents 276

List of Ancient Authors and Texts Cited 279

Biographical Sketches & Short Descriptions of Select
    Anonymous Works 283

Timeline of Writers of the Patristic Period 304

Author/Writings Index 310

Scripture Index 312

A Guide to Using the Commentaries in the Ancient Christian Doctrine Series

Several features have been incorporated into the design of this commentary series. The following comments are intended to assist readers in making full use of each of the volumes.

Sections of the Creed

The five commentaries are first and foremost a phrase-by-phrase commentary on the Nicene-Constantinopolitan Creed. The portion of the Creed for each individual volume has been set in three languages—Greek, Latin and English—with the appropriate phrase under consideration highlighted in bold font in each language. Numerous English translations have been developed in recent years; we have used the ICET version of 1975 because of its current wide use.

Historical Contexts and Overviews

Following each section of the Creed is a short section labeled HISTORICAL CONTEXT. Where wording of the Creed reflects the culmination of discussions of highly controverted issues, readers are offered a brief summary of the controversy and the issues at stake in order for them to make more sense of the selections set forth. Where doctrine developed harmoniously without much controversy, that fact is noted and a brief description of the development of the doctrine is supplied. Following the historical context is a section labeled OVERVIEW, designed to provide a précis of the ensuing section's excerpts. It tracks a reasonably cohesive thread of argument among patristic comments, even though they are derived from diverse sources and generations.

Topical Headings

An abundance of varied patristic comment is available for each phrase of the Creed. At the same time the Creed itself forms a skeleton for supporting the larger doctrinal convictions of the church. Thus the commentary on the Creed can show the full range of the church's systematic theological concerns. For this reason we have broken the sections of the Creed into two levels. First are subsections that group common themes within the patristic comments. Then each individual patristic comment is tagged by a key phrase, metaphor or idea that suggests the essence of the excerpt.

Identifying the Patristic Texts

Following the topical heading of each excerpt, the name of the patristic commentator is given. An English translation of the patristic comment is then provided. This is immediately followed by the title of the patristic work in English and the appropriate textual reference—usually book, section and subsection. If the notation differs significantly between the English-language source footnoted and other sources, alternate references appear in the notes.

The Footnotes

Readers who wish to pursue a deeper investigation of the patristic works cited in this commentary will find the footnotes especially valuable. A footnote number directs the reader to the notes at the bottom of the right-hand column, where in addition to other notations (clarifications or biblical cross references) is found information on English translations (where available) or standard original language editions of the work cited. An abbreviated citation (normally citing the book, volume and page number) of the work is provided. A key to the abbreviations is provided in the front matter. Where there is any serious ambiguity or textual problem in the selection, we have tried to reflect the best available textual tradition. Where original language texts have remained untranslated into English, we provide new translations. Wherever current English translations are already well rendered, they are utilized, but where necessary they are stylistically updated. A single asterisk (*) indicates that a previous English translation has been updated to modern English or amended for easier reading. A double asterisk (**) indicates either that a new translation has been provided or that some extant translation has been significantly amended.

Outline of Contents, List of Ancient Authors and Texts Cited, and Index

In lieu of a subject index, a full outline of the sections and subsections has been included in the back matter of each volume. This should aid readers in finding specific theological content and make the volumes all the more useful for the study of historical and systematic theology. Each volume contains a list of ancient authors and texts cited, as well as a full Scripture index.

Biographical Sketches and Timeline

Many readers will find helpful brief biographical sketches of the patristic writers as well as a timeline placing them within the proper century and geographical location. Rather than repeating the sketches and timeline in each volume, we have decided to gather them at the conclusion of volume five. Similarly, we have supplied the general introduction to the series only in volume one. For any readers who have not purchased the whole set, the general introduction, sketches and timeline may be found online at www.ivpress.com by searching for the series information and following the appropriate links.

Abbreviations

ACCS	*Ancient Christian Commentary on Scripture*. Edited by Thomas C. Oden. 29 vols. Downers Grove, Ill.: InterVarsity Press, 1998-2010.
ACW	*Ancient Christian Writers: The Works of the Fathers in Translation*. Mahwah, N.J.: Paulist Press, 1946-.
AIRI	Edward Yarnold. *The Awe-Inspiring Rites of Initiation: Baptismal Homilies of the Fourth Century*. Slough, U.K.: St. Paul Publications, 1972.
ANF	A. Roberts and J. Donaldson, eds. Ante-Nicene Fathers. 10 vols. Buffalo, N.Y.: Christian Literature, 1885-1896. Reprint, Grand Rapids: Eerdmans, 1951-1956. Reprint, Peabody, Mass.: Hendrickson, 1994.
BTAM	T. Herbert Bindley, trans. *Tertullian's Address to Martyrs*. Oxford: Clarendon, 1891.
CCL	*Corpus Christianorum. Series Latina*. Turnhout, Belgium: Brepols, 1953-.
CER	Origen. *Commentarii in Epistulam ad Romanos*. Edited by T. Heither. 5 vols. Freiburg im Breisgau: Herder, 1990-1995.
CSCO	*Corpus Scriptorum Christianorum Orientalium*. Louvain, Belgium, 1903-.
CSEL	*Corpus Scriptorum Ecclesiasticorum Latinorum*. Vienna, 1866-.
DACL	*Dictionnaire d'archéologie chrétienne et de liturgie*. Edited by Fernand Cabrol. Paris: Letouzey et Ané, 1907-1953.
DAP	Irenaeus. *The Demonstration of the Apostolic Preaching*. Translated by J. Armitage Robinson. London: SPCK, 1920.
DLSB	*The Divine Liturgy of Our Father Among the Saints Basil the Great: Hē Theia Leitourgia ton en hagiois patros hēmōn Vasileiou tou Megalou: A New Translation by Members of the Faculty of Hellenic College/Holy Cross Greek Orthodox School of Theology*, edited with additional translation by Fr. Nomikos M. Vaporis (Brookline, Mass.: Holy Cross Orthodox Press, 1988). Available at <www.goarch.org/en/chapel/liturgical_texts/basil.asp>.
DSG	Gregory the Great. *The Dialogues of Saint Gregory*. Translated by P[hilip] W[oodward] and printed at Paris in 1608. Reedited with an introduction and notes by Edmond G. Gardner. London: P. L. Warner, 1911.
ECS	Everett Ferguson. *Early Christians Speak: Faith and Life in the First Three Centuries*. 3rd. ed. Abilene, Tex.: ACU Press, 1999.
ESHS	Thomas Joseph Lamy, ed. *Sancti Ephraem Syri hymni et sermones*. 4 vols. Mechelen, Belgium, 1882-1902.
FC	Fathers of the Church: A New Translation. Washington, D.C.: Catholic University of America Press, 1947-.

FEF	*The Faith of the Early Fathers: A Source-book of Theological and Historical Passages from the Christian Writings of the Pre-Nicene and Nicene Eras.* Edited and translated by W. A. Jurgens. 3 vols. Collegeville, Minn.: Liturgical Press, 1970-1979.
GMDD	Alan Garrow. *The Gospel of Matthew's Dependence on the Didache.* London: T & T Clark, 2004.
HC	Thomas Halton, ed. *The Church.* MFC 4. Wilmington, Del.: Michael Glazier, 1985.
HPO	André de Halleux. *Patrologie et oecuménisme: Recueil d'études.* Bibliotheca Ephemeridum theologicarum Lovaniensium 93. Leuven: Leuven University Press; Leuven: Peeters, 1990.
ILCV	*Inscriptiones latinae christianae veteres.* Edited by Ernst Diehl. 2nd ed. Berlin: Apud Weidmannos, 1925-1967.
LAF	Kirsopp Lake, ed. and trans. *Apostolic Fathers.* LCL. New York: Macmillan, 1912.
LCC	J. Baillie et al., eds. Library of Christian Classics. 26 vols. Philadelphia: Westminster Press, 1953-1966.
LCL	Loeb Classical Library. Cambridge, Mass.: Harvard University Press; London: Heinemann, 1912-.
LF	Library of Fathers of the Holy Catholic Church. Oxford: John Henry Parker, 1838-1881.
ME	F. Ledegang. *Mysterium Ecclesiae: Images of the Church and Its Members in Origen.* Leuven: Leuven University Press; Leuven: Peeters, 2001.
MFC	Message of the Fathers of the Church. Wilmington, Del.: Michael Glazier. 1983-1988. Collegeville, Minn.: Liturgical Press, 1992-.
NPNF	P. Schaff et al., eds. A Select Library of the Nicene and Post-Nicene Fathers of the Christian Church. 2 series (14 vols. each). Buffalo, N.Y.: Christian Literature, 1887-1894. Reprint, Grand Rapids: Eerdmans, 1952-1956. Reprint, Peabody, Mass.: Hendrickson, 1994.
NTAbh 15	K. Staab, ed. *Pauluskommentare aus der griechischen Kirche: Aus Katenenhandschriften gesammelt und herausgegeben* (Pauline Commentary from the Greek Church: Collected and Edited Catena Writings). NT Abhandlungen 15. Münster in Westfalen: Aschendorff, 1933. (Commentators: Didymus the Blind of Alexandria, pp. 6-44; Severian of Gabala, pp. 225-98; Theodore of Mopsuestia, pp. 172-200; Theodoret of Cyr, pp. 226-460; Gennadius of Constantinople, pp. 118-19; Oecumenius, pp. 432-46.)
NTAp	*New Testament Apocrypha.* Edited by Wilhelm Schneemelcher. English translation edited by R. McL. Wilson. 2 vols. Cambridge: Clarke; Louisville, Ky.: Westminster John Knox Press, 1991-1992.

OCC	Origen. *Contra Celsum*. Translated by Henry Chadwick. 1953. Reprint, Cambridge: Cambridge University Press, 1965.
OPF	Melito of Sardis. *On Pascha and Fragments*. Edited by Stuart George Hall. Oxford Early Christian Texts. Oxford: Clarendon, 1979.
PCR	Theodore De Bruyn, ed. *Pelagius's Commentary on St. Paul's Epistle to the Romans*. Oxford: Clarendon, 1993.
PG	J.-P. Migne, ed. Patrologiae cursus completus. Series Graeca. 166 vols. Paris: Migne, 1857-1886.
PL	J.-P. Migne, ed. Patrologiae cursus completus. Series Latina. 221 vols. Paris: Migne, 1844-1864.
PME	Joseph C. Plumpe. *Mater Ecclesia: An Inquiry into the Concept of the Church as Mother in Early Christianity*. Washington, D.C.: Catholic University of America Press, 1943.
Quasten	Johannes Quasten, ed. *Patrology*. 3 vols. Utrecht: Spectrum Publishers; Westminster, Md., Newman Press, 1950-1960. Vol. 4: *The Golden Age of Latin Patristic Literature from the Council of Nicea to the Council of Chalcedon*. Edited by Angelo Di Berardino. Westminster, Md.: Christian Classics, 1986.
SCK	Robert Murray. *Symbols of Church and Kingdom: A Study in Early Syriac Tradition*. 1975. Reprint, Cambridge: Cambridge University Press 2006.
SHC	Carolyn Osiek. *The Shepherd of Hermas: A Commentary*. Hermeneia. Minneapolis: Fortress, 1999.
TA	Tertullian. *Apologeticus*. The text of Oehler, annotated, with an introduction, by John E. B. Mayor, with a translation by Alexander Souter. Cambridge: Cambridge University Press, 1917.
TAM	Ernest Evans, ed. and trans. *Tertullian: Adversus Marcionem*. 2 vols. Oxford Early Christian Texts. Oxford: Clarendon, 1972.
TAT	G. Gregory Dix, ed. *The Treatise on the Apostolic Tradition of St. Hippolytus of Rome*. London: Alban, 1992.
THB	Ernest Evans, ed. and trans. *Tertullian's Homily on Baptism*. London: SPCK, 1964.
TOTS	Tertullian. *On the Testimony of the Soul and On the "Prescription" of Heretics*. Translated by T. Herbert Bindley. New York: E. S. Gorham, 1914.
TTP	Ernest Evans, ed. and trans. *Tertullian's Tract on the Prayer*. London: SPCK, 1953.
TTR	Ernest Evans, trans. *Tertullian's Treatise on the Resurrection*. London: SPCK, 1960.
WSA	*Works of Saint Augustine: A Translation for the 21st Century*. Edited by John E. Rotelle. 3 parts. Numbered vols. Hyde Park, N.Y.: New City Press, 1990-.

INTRODUCTION

When was the church founded? Jesus spoke of the kingdom of God and not of a religious organization subsequently called the church, for we do not find in the Gospels expressions that make reference to the foundation of a new religious community, a new and distinct community of followers of Jesus. Many parables (the miraculous catch of fish, the sower, the seed and the plant, for example) talk about the growth of the kingdom of God. Jesus perceived his mission as an instrument for the conversion of the people of Israel. Jesus said to the Canaanite woman, "I was sent only to the lost sheep of the house of Israel."[1] But after the resurrection of Jesus, his followers, as a result of his command, turned not only to the people of Israel but to all men and women. Before the ascension, the apostles asked Jesus, " 'Lord, will you at this time restore the kingdom to Israel?' He said to them, 'It is not for you to know times or seasons which the Father has fixed by his own authority; but you shall receive power when the Holy Spirit has come upon you; and you shall be my witnesses in Jerusalem and in all Judea and Samaria and to the end of the earth.' "[2]

The narration of the inauguration of this universal mission, addressed also to the Gentiles, is concretized by two crucial episodes: the action of Peter with Cornelius and the first missionary journey of Paul. There was a major change in perspective that the first Christians found it difficult to accept; in fact, Acts speaks of opposition and arguments. Some accepted Gentiles into the new covenant on the condition that "unless you are circumcised according to the custom of Moses, you cannot be saved."[3] The baptism of the centurion Cornelius (Acts 10–11) expressed the action of the universal mission of evangelization, amply explained by Peter in his preaching to the Jerusalem community. The baptism was administered without requiring that Cornelius and his family be circumcised. Peter further clarified this universal opening in the council referred to in Acts 15: "After there had been much debate, Peter stood up and said to them, 'Brethren, you know that in the early days God made a choice among you, that by my mouth the Gentiles would hear the word of the gospel and believe.' "[4] Relations with the Gentiles changed, in that they were no longer considered impure and to be avoided, and it was no longer forbidden to eat with them. It was an important and solemn moment when Peter entered the house of Cornelius, who "was expecting them [Peter and some brethren] and had called together his kinsmen and close friends."[5] "When Peter entered, Cornelius met him and fell down at his feet

---

[1] Mt 15:24.
[2] Acts 1:6-8; see also Mt 28:19; Mk 16:15; Rom 10:18; Col 1:23.
[3] Acts 15:1; cf. Acts 15:5.
[4] Acts 15:7.
[5] Acts 10:24.

and worshiped him. But Peter lifted him up, saying, 'Stand up; I too am a man.' And as he talked with him, he went in and found many persons gathered; and he said to them, 'You yourselves know how unlawful it is for a man who is a Jew to associate with or to visit any one of another nation; but God has shown me that I should not call any man common or unclean.' "[6] Peter, on hearing Cornelius recount his vision, exclaimed, "Truly I perceive that God shows no partiality, but in every nation any one who fears him and does what is right is acceptable to him."[7] Peter understood and established the will of God, who wants all nations to be saved, without distinction or preference; all nations from now and for the future can be members of the new covenant. Having seen that Cornelius and the others had received the Spirit, Peter baptized them: " 'Can any one forbid water for baptizing these people who have received the Holy Spirit just as we have?' And he commanded them to be baptized in the name of Jesus Christ."[8] Peter then stayed at the house of Cornelius for some days.

The other determining event came from the missionary activity of Paul and Barnabas, which met strong opposition in the community of Antioch.[9] "And when Paul and Barnabas had no small dissension and debate with them, Paul and Barnabas and some of the others were appointed to go up to Jerusalem to the apostles and elders about this question."[10] The decisions taken by the meeting (council) at Jerusalem[11] facilitated the universal opening but did not eliminate the opposition, which continued in the second century, as Justin tells us: there were Christians who observed the law of Moses and wanted to impose it on all; others were more tolerant in that they observed it themselves but did not require that it be observed by all; others gave no importance to the ritual prescriptions of the law.[12] We see from the accounts in Acts that the apostles and the elders officially recognized the evangelization of the Gentiles and their full admission to the new community of the new covenant. This new community was now officially different from that which preceded it and was more distant from its Jewish roots. Luke mentions Peter for the last time on the occasion of the meeting at Jerusalem; from then on, the center of attention was Paul, who continued the mission among the Gentiles.

Let us now return to the question: When was the Christian church founded? One cannot establish a precise moment of its founding. Instead, its birth was slow and continuous. All the premises were there already from the death of Jesus, because the group of the Twelve had been established as the first pillars of a community. In that group a special preeminence was given to Peter. It was the Twelve who took part in the Last Supper and accompanied Jesus to Gethsemane. Immediately after the death and resurrection of Jesus, the Twelve and the other disciples were present in Jerusalem, together with Mary; they united to pray together and break bread.

---

[6] Acts 10:24-28.
[7] Acts 10:34-35.
[8] Acts 10:47-48.
[9] Acts 15:1.
[10] Acts 15:2.
[11] Acts 15:12-35.
[12] Justin *Dialogue with Trypho* 47.

Introduction

The church, as a praying assembly distinct from the Jewish community, became an autonomous entity in the post-Easter period. There is a certain sense in which its consecration came about on the day of Pentecost, with the descent of the Holy Spirit. The consciousness of being a new entity, distinct from its Jewish roots, developed slowly among the disciples; the new community came to be called the Way in the Acts of the Apostles.[13] Paul said, "I persecuted this Way to the death, binding and delivering to prison both men and women."[14] The Way was a doctrine lived by a community. With the entry of Gentiles into this Way, the Christian community opened itself to a new and universal world without limits of language or race. The fact itself of calling themselves Christians increased their awareness of themselves as a new community. So the new community, as the church, was born and grew around the celebration of the Eucharist, where the memorial of Christ was celebrated and where a new identity in the Spirit of Christ was created. The praying community was the concrete and visible manifestation of the church.

The Christian community, from the beginning, was considered to be the people of God, which is an effective and powerful idea for creating a religious and social identity. This idea also gave a strong sense of cohesion and buoyancy in belonging. However, as such it could be viewed too narrowly in an exclusive sense. In reality, other peoples also considered themselves to be the people of God, in particular the people of Israel, tied to their descent from Abraham and chosen by God. So then, in what sense was the Christian community the people of God? Certainly not in the traditional Judaic sense, because all of humanity is in some sense the people of God, who sent his Son for its salvation through his death. That part of humanity which constitutes the church was chosen by God to be at the service of the message of salvation, of the gospel of Jesus Christ, for the good of all, because God wants all people to be saved.[15] The salvation brought by Christ was present in his person, in his ministry and especially in his death: Christ "died for all";[16] Jesus was and is "the Savior of the world";[17] Jesus "gave himself as a ransom for all."[18] The church has the obligation to see that "every tongue [shall] confess that Jesus is Lord"[19] to bring about the "reconciliation of the world."[20] "For there is no distinction between Jew and Greek; the same Lord is Lord of all and bestows his riches upon all who call upon him. For 'every one who calls upon the name of the Lord will be saved.' But how are men to call upon him in whom they have not believed? And how are they to believe in him of whom they have never heard? And how are they to hear without a preacher? And how can men preach unless they are sent? As it is written, 'How beautiful are the feet of those who preach good news!' "[21]

Whoever preaches the gospel is committed to the service of Jesus Christ for all humankind;

---

[13] E.g., Acts 9:2; 19:9, 23; 22:4; 24:22.
[14] Acts 22:4; 24:22.
[15] 1 Tim 2:4.
[16] 2 Cor 5:15.
[17] Jn 4:42; 12:47; 5:36; 12:32; 1 Jn 4:14.
[18] 1 Tim 2:6.
[19] Phil 2:9-11.
[20] Rom 11:15.
[21] Rom 10:12-15.

that person is a minister (the word comes from the Latin *minus*, which means "inferior for service"); all Christians are in the service of the gospel, because they bring, through the Word of God and the sacraments, salvation for themselves and for others. But according to the command of Jesus there are specialized forms of ministry: bishops, elders, deacons and other ministers are in charge to serve God's purpose for humankind. They must be the instruments of God's love in this world for the salvation of all those who believe and love, to communicate the gifts of God to all people. Christian communities, inspired by the Holy Spirit, do not live in chaos. They need some kind of order and structure. Augustine exhorts us to accept this ministry: "If the church should request your services, do not accede to this request out of a desire to get ahead, nor refuse it moved by pleasurable idleness. Obey God, rather, in simplicity of heart, submitting yourselves humbly to him who directs you. Neither should you prefer your peaceful leisure to the needs of the church. If there were no people to minister to the church as she gave you birth, not even you would have found a way to have been born."[22] "Those are your best servants who wish to shape their life on your answers rather than shape your answers on their wishes."[23]

The Nicene Creed and the Church

In the Nicene Creed, after professing the Christian faith in God the Father, his work in our Lord Jesus Christ and his life, and in the Holy Spirit and his sanctification, we say that we believe "in one, holy, catholic and apostolic church." Christians profess faith in the church. What does this mean? Do we believe in the church in the same way as we believe in the Father, in the Son and in the Holy Spirit? The English translation is in some ways confusing and misleading, because in Latin we say, *Credo in unum Deum Patrem omnipotentem . . . et in unum Dominum Iesum Christum . . . et in Spiritum Sanctum . . . et unam, sanctam, catholicam et apostolicam ecclesiam.* We believe in the divine Persons, but the Latin text does not include "in" before the church. When we say "we believe in God, the Father . . . in one Lord, Jesus Christ, the only Son of God, . . . and in the Holy Spirit, the Lord, the giver of life," we profess the work of salvation of the Father, the Son and the Holy Spirit. We put our confidence and faith in God; we trust him and commit ourselves to him, our rock and hope. But we do not believe in the church in the same way we believe in God, because we cannot commit ourselves to an institution, such as the church, which is a work of God's creation.

The word *church* has two main meanings for us: a special building or a community of believers. The building may be very old or quite new, small or a great cathedral, where people go to meet other members of the same faith or to have some moments of peace and dialogue with God. In Europe and in many other countries, the church used to be the core of the population; it marked the lives and the history of each component of a society. This landscape has changed in Western Christian societies; other buildings compete for our attention, and the expression of Christian faith is more and more personal and intimate. We will not talk of the church as a material edi-

---

[22] Augustine *Letter* 48.2.
[23] Augustine *Confessions* 10.26.37.

fice, built with stones, cement, wood or glass, having doors and windows. We will talk of the church as an edifice built with living stones, believers, who are the temple of God, the gathering of the people of God[24] in the service of God and of all humanity in the name of Jesus Christ. Our profession of faith, the creed, is about that spiritual, mystical and universal edifice.

The creed is the synthesis of the revelation of the saving action of the triune God on behalf of the human race (creation, redemption, sanctification); but, while revealed, these Christian truths are beyond full human comprehension, and so they remain mysteries that may be both believed and investigated. Thus the church also comes under the economy of salvation, like the other divine works; it also is a mystery. It is not an exclusively human institution but falls within the plan of God for the salvation of humanity. When and why was the expression "I believe in the church" introduced into the formulas of faith?

The final part of the profession of faith was developed later than the confession in God the Father and Christ the Savior. After the mention of the Holy Spirit, the creed talks of the church, of baptism, of the resurrection and of eternal life. The expression was introduced in the course of the second century, because in the third century it was already common in the baptismal formulas. The reason for the introduction of the reference to the church seems to have been both as a reaction against and an opposition to the Gnostic sects who professed a superior and secret knowledge. By contrast, the great church teaches the visibility of the community of believers and the authorization of the teaching of Jesus through an episcopal succession historically verifiable. No secret teaching exists that should not be manifested to all. Irenaeus of Lyon writes:

> For in the church, it is said, God had set apostles, prophets, teachers,[25] and all the other means through which the Spirit works; of which all those are not partakers who do not join themselves to the church but defraud themselves of life through their perverse opinions and infamous behavior. For where the church is, there is the Spirit of God; and where the Spirit of God is, there is the church, and every kind of grace; but the Spirit is truth.[26]

Irenaeus joins the church with the Holy Spirit.[27] The first mention of the church in a profession of faith is found in the *Epistula Apostolorum*[28] and in the apostolic symbol. The so-called *traditio apostolica* is expressed in the following way: "Glory to you Father and Son with the Holy Spirit in the holy church, now and forever through all ages." The church is put in relationship to the three persons of the Trinity, to whom the community of believers give glory. This is the heavenly city, the new Jerusalem, which lives on earth with all other people

---

[24]Various peoples in history understood themselves to be people of God. Christians are the people of God because they are committed to "the gospel implications of the service of Jesus Christ for all mankind" (G. M. Newlands, *The Church of God* [Basingstoke, U.K.: Marshall, Morgan and Scott, 1984], p. 4).
[25]See 1 Cor 12:28.
[26]Irenaeus *Against Heresies* 3.24.1.
[27]Irenaeus *Against Heresies* 5.20.1.
[28]"What do these five loaves mean? They are the symbol of our faith concerning the great Christianity, and that is the Father, the rule of the entire world, and in Jesus Christ our Savior, in the Holy Spirit the Paraclete, and in the holy church, and in the forgiveness of sins" (chap. 5).

but has something different; it is the soul of the world.

> For the Christians are distinguished from other human beings neither by country, nor language, nor the customs which they observe. For they neither inhabit cities of their own, nor employ a peculiar form of speech, nor lead a life which is marked out by any singularity. The course of conduct which they follow has not been devised by any speculation or deliberation of inquisitive persons; nor do they, like some, proclaim themselves the advocates of any merely human doctrines. . . . They dwell in their own countries, but simply as sojourners. As citizens, they share in all things with others, and yet endure all things as if foreigners. Every foreign land is to them as their native country, and every land of their birth as a land of strangers. . . . They pass their days on earth, but they are citizens of heaven. They obey the prescribed laws, and at the same time surpass the laws by their lives. They love all, and are persecuted by all.[29]

How can we become citizens of heaven, of the new Jerusalem? Not by natural birth, but by spiritual birth. Tertullian says, *Fiunt non nascuntur christiani* ("people become Christians, they are not born such").[30] Believers applied for citizenship in heaven because it was a voluntary choice. Their request was accepted by the bishop after close and long public examination and scrutiny: they were questioned about their life, their jobs, their progress. They had to show the change in their conduct through severe initiation rites and a strong fight against the devil.[31]

Still, almost all Christians of all denominations today profess the same expression: we believe "in one holy catholic and apostolic church." These have been considered throughout the ages the characteristics of the church, which are often referred to as the four marks or notes of the church. They are inseparable and intrinsically linked to each other. Meanwhile, each church has a different ecclesiology, which constitutes a difficulty for Christian unity. What do we mean by the word *church*? What do we mean by professing the oneness, holiness, catholicity and apostolicity of the church? We shall try to give an answer with the help of the fathers of the church, which is the background for Christians of the Nicene-Constantinopolitan creed.

We talk about the Christian church, which, according to some liberal theologians, was not founded by Christ. The sentence is true in the sense that the historical Jesus was a member of the Jewish community, which he intended to reform, to renew Israel. He worked and preached within the boundaries of the land of Israel and in his traditional faith: "Think not that I have come to abolish the law and the prophets; I have come not to abolish them but to fulfill them."[32] But Luke reports this sentence too: "The law and the prophets were preached up until John: since then the good news of the kingdom of God is preached."[33] But the sentence is not correct since the church is the consequence of the life, the teaching and the message of Jesus, who also

---

[29]*Letter to Diognetus* 5.
[30]*Apology* 18.4; *On the Testimony of the Soul* 1.
[31]See Augustine *Sermon* 216.6.
[32]Mt 5:17.
[33]Lk 16:16.

claimed that the time of salvation has come with him and that the law has been fulfilled. He chose the Twelve to be with him, to be sent out to preach and to cast out demons.[34] After the resurrection, Jesus appeared to ten of them and sent them out: "When he had said this, he showed them his hands and his side. Then the disciples were glad when they saw the Lord. Jesus said to them again, 'Peace be with you. As the Father has sent me, even so I send you.' And when he had said this, he breathed on them, and said to them, 'Receive the Holy Spirit. If you forgive the sins of any, they are forgiven; if you retain the sins of any, they are retained.' "[35] In the first years they made decisions about the government of the new community in Jerusalem.[36] Many parables can be understood correctly only if their original core contains a universal perspective that speaks to all peoples. "I tell you, many will come from east and west and sit at table with Abraham, Isaac, and Jacob in the kingdom of heaven."[37]

The Greek term *ekklēsia* means "assembly," "meeting" or "gathering" in classical Greek, and in the Greek cities it had political significance.[38] It comes from the word *ek-kaleō*, made up of *kaleō* ("call," "convoke," "invite") and the prefix *ek* ("from," "out"): therefore, "to call someone out from someplace for something." So, only those expressly called can take part in a meeting. In the Septuagint the term *ekklēsia* is used to translate the Hebrew word *qāhāl*—which at times is used with "synagogue" and signifies "to gather together"—and indicates the totality of the people of God irrespective of its greatness, the people united in assembly especially on particular occasions.[39] We also speak of "the assembly of the Lord."[40] The whole people are united without distinction. The Greek term has a more limited meaning: only those who are called, that is, the best representatives of the city. In the Old Testament sense we find *ekklēsia* employed by Stephen in the book of Acts: "This is the Moses who said to the Israelites, 'God will raise up for you a prophet from your brethren as he raised me up.' This is he who was in the congregation in the wilderness with the angel who spoke to him at Mount Sinai, and with our fathers; and he received living oracles to give to us."[41] In Judaism, *ekklēsia* was synonymous with "synagogue." Both terms signify the "assembly of Israel" and were subsequently used by the Jews.[42]

From the time of Paul, *ekklēsia* becomes a specific and technical term to indicate the people of God of the new covenant, redeemed through Christ: "And God has appointed in the church first apostles, second prophets, third teachers, then workers of miracles, then healers, helpers, administrators, speakers in various kinds of tongues."[43] Sometimes the word is specified with

---

[34]Mk 3:14-15.
[35]Jn 20:20-23.
[36]Acts 6:2-6.
[37]Mt 8:11; cf. Lk 13:29.
[38]"An assembly of citizens summoned by the crier at the public place, the legislative assembly," R. Scott and H. G. Liddell, *A Greek-English Lexicon*, p. 206.
[39]Ezra 2:64.
[40]Deut 23:2-4.
[41]Acts 7:37-38.
[42]Emil Schürer, *The History of the Jewish People in the Age of Jesus Christ (175 B.C.-A.D. 135)*, rev. and ed. Geza Vermes and Fergus Millar, (Edinburgh: T & T Clark, 1973), 2:429-30.
[43]1 Cor 12:28; cf. Mt 16:18; Eph 1:22; 3:10, 21.

other indications, such as "of God" or "of Christ" to express the idea of belonging or origin: "I persecuted the church of God violently and tried to destroy it";[44] "For you, brethren, became imitators of the churches of God in Christ Jesus which are in Judea; for you suffered the same things from your own countrymen as they did from the Jews";[45] "The church of God which is at Corinth";[46] "Give no offense to Jews or to Greeks or to the church of God";[47] "I was still not known by sight to the churches of Christ in Judea";[48] "Greet one another with a holy kiss. All the churches of Christ greet you."[49] Jesus will build his church upon Peter, on the ground of his believing confession: "On this rock I will build my church."[50] In the following verse[51] it is employed with "the kingdom of heaven": the words *church* and *kingdom* are not perfectly synonymous, but closely related. The apostolic and postapostolic writers abandoned the word *kingdom*, which expressed specific Jewish conceptions. They used the word *church* since it was more understandable in conveying a new conception.

The word *ekklēsia* is employed in three different senses. Paul used it in general to denote all local communities in a city[52] or the body of Christians in a particular city.[53] He used *ekklēsia* in the local sense[54] and to refer to small groups in households.[55] A second sense of *ekklēsia* finds Paul using the term in a more universal way, as he does in his first letter to the Corinthians and his letter to the Ephesians.[56] In the same letter to the Corinthians, it also means the eucharistic assembly at Corinth: "What! Do you not have houses in which to eat and drink? Or do you despise the church of God and humiliate those who have nothing?"[57] In Ephesians and Colossians we find yet a third use of the word *ekklēsia*: the church as the body of Christ, who is the head.[58] The church is the bride of Christ, the heavenly bridegroom, who loved her and gave himself up for her cleansing and sanctification.[59] This is not the visible world church, which still has divisions, blemishes and a paucity of faith and love. This church is the medium of the manifestation of the hidden mystery: "That through the church the manifold wisdom of God might now be made known to the principalities and powers in the heavenly places. This was according to the eternal purpose which he has realized in Christ Jesus our Lord."[60] The church has to preserve

---

[44] Gal 1:13.
[45] 1 Thess 2:14.
[46] 1 Cor 1:2.
[47] 1 Cor 10:32; cf. 1 Cor 11:22; 15:9.
[48] Gal 1:22.
[49] Rom 16:16.
[50] Mt 16:18.
[51] Mt 16:19.
[52] Acts 8:1; 9:31; Rev 1:4.
[53] E.g., Acts 5:11; 8:1; 13:1; 15:22; Rev 1:11, 20; 2:1, 8, 12, 18; 22:26.
[54] 1 Thess 1:1; 1 Cor 1:2; 2 Cor 1:1.
[55] Rom 16:5; Philem 1:2.
[56] 1 Cor 10:32; 12:28; Eph 1:22.
[57] 1 Cor 11:22.
[58] Eph 1:22; Col 1:18, 24.
[59] Eph 5:25-27.
[60] Eph 3:9-11; cf. 1 Tim 3:15.

the true doctrine. It is the "church of the living God, the pillar and bulwark of the truth."[61] And through the church "to him be glory in the church and in Christ Jesus to all generations, for ever and ever."[62] "Christ loved the church and gave himself for her, that he might sanctify her, having cleansed her by the washing of water with the word, that he might present the church to himself in splendor, without having spot or wrinkle or any such thing, that she might be holy and without blemish."[63] "Now I rejoice in my sufferings for your sake, and in my flesh I complete what is lacking in Christ's afflictions for the sake of his body, that is, the church, of which I became a minister according to the divine office which was given to me for you, to make the word of God fully known, the mystery hidden from ages and generations but made manifest to his saints."[64]

In these texts, *ekklēsia* indicates something that goes beyond the historic and earthly community to transcend the purely human dimension. In addition, the Greek term expresses an essential characteristic of the new community of believers in Christ, in so far as they are "the called" (from *ek-kaleō* ["to call out"]) who form part of the new people of God: "the church of God,"[65] "the churches of Christ."[66] On the one hand *ekklēsia* indicates the earthly community, visible, historical—be it local or universal; on the other hand it implies a nonterrestrial dimension. For this reason *ekklēsia* is a mystery in the Pauline sense of the term.

To designate the church, whose prehistory for Christians goes back to the Old Testament, many images are used:[67] "Israel of God";[68] Christians are "fellow citizens with the saints and members of the household of God, built upon the foundation of the apostles and prophets, Jesus Christ himself being the chief cornerstone, in whom the whole structure is joined together and grows into a holy temple in the Lord; in whom you also are being built into it for a dwelling place of God in the Spirit";[69] the church is the "flock,"[70] whose shepherd is Christ as Messiah;[71] a "vineyard," where the prophets and the apostles are sent as workers;[72] Christ is the "true vine," and his followers are the branches.[73] The church is "the holy city, new Jerusalem, coming down out of heaven from God, prepared as a bride adorned for her husband";[74] "the household of God, which is the church of the living God,"[75] a spiritual building, and believers are "living stones . . .

---

[61] 1 Tim 3:15; cf. Tit 1:9.
[62] Eph 3:21.
[63] Eph 5:25-27.
[64] Col 1:24-26.
[65] 1 Cor 10:32; 11:16; 15:19; Gal 1:13, etc.
[66] Rom 16:16.
[67] Paul S. Minear, *Images of the Church in the New Testament* (Philadelphia: Westminster Press, 1960; rev. ed., Louisville, Ky.: Westminster John Knox, 2004).
[68] Gal 6:16; cf. Rom 9:6.
[69] Eph 2:19-22.
[70] Lk 12:32; Acts 20:28-29; 1 Pet 5:2-3; Jn 10:1-16; 21:15-17.
[71] Jn 10:11-16; 1 Pet 2:25-26; 5:4.
[72] Mt 20:1-16; Mk 12:1-12; Rev 14:17-20.
[73] Jn 15:1-6.
[74] Rev 21:2; cf. 3:12.
[75] 1 Tim 3:15.

built into a spiritual house."⁷⁶ The church is the bride of Christ, who takes care of her.⁷⁷ Marriage is a symbol of this great mystery of love between Christ and the church.⁷⁸

The image of the body has great importance in Paul, because the body was the symbol of the church as a living being composed of a plurality of members: different organs connected and dependent among them in a unity of life and activities.⁷⁹ This conception of the body intends to express the precept of the unity of Christians. The image of the body seeks to inculcate the union of Christians with Christ, the head of the body, the church.⁸⁰ In the letter to the Ephesians we read that God "has made him the head over all things for the church, which is his body, the fulness of him who fills all in all";⁸¹ in Colossians, "he is the head of the body, the church."⁸² These two sentences seem not only a symbol but also a definition of the church.

Some of those images used in the New Testament indicate the church as a community for salvation. Others underscore the close relationship of Christians and the whole community with Christ. This conception constitutes precisely the mystery of the church, which is the *plerōma* of Christ, as the *Didache* will say: *mystērion kosmikon ekklēsias*⁸³ (translated by Lightfoot "visible mystery of the church"). The church has its origins in the sacrifice of Christ on the cross.⁸⁴ Tertullian writes, "For as Adam was a figure of Christ, Adam's sleep foreshadowed the death of Christ, who was to sleep a mortal slumber, that from the wound inflicted on his side might, in like manner (as Eve was formed), be typified the church, the true mother of the living."⁸⁵ The expression "the body of Christ" has three meanings: the physical body of Christ during his historical life, the glorified body in heaven and the sacramental body in the Eucharist—the mystical body.

With the images used by the New Testament and the Fathers we have some help toward an understanding of the church, which remains for them a mystery. John Chrysostom gives this explanation:

> Nothing is more abiding than the church: she is your salvation; she is your refuge. She is more lofty than the heavens; she is more far-reaching than the earth. She never grows old; she always stays in bloom. And so Scripture indicates her permanence and stability by calling her a virgin; her magnificence by calling her a queen; her closeness to God by calling her a daughter; her barrenness turned to fecundity by calling her "the mother of the seven." A thousand names try to spell out her nobility. Just as the Lord is called by many names— Father, Way, Life, Light, Propitiation, Foundation, Gate, Sinless, One, Treasure, Lord, God Son, Only-Begotten, Form of God, Image of God, since one name could not hope to describe

---

⁷⁶1 Pet 2:5.
⁷⁷2 Cor 11:2; Eph 5:22-33.
⁷⁸Eph 5:32.
⁷⁹1 Cor 12:12, 14-26; Rom 12:4-5; cf. Eph 4:16.
⁸⁰Eph 1:22-23; 4:15-16.
⁸¹Eph 1:22-23.
⁸²Col 1:18.
⁸³*Didache* 11.11.
⁸⁴Col 1:20-22; Eph 2:13-16; 5:25-33.
⁸⁵Tertullian *On the Soul* 42.

the Omnipotent, and many names give us some small insight into his nature, so the church goes by many names.[86]

The term *ekklēsia (tou theou)* became the technical term in Christian circles, used also by pagans, to indicate the Christian church. Celsus, in the second century, distinguished the "great church" from the many sects fighting among themselves.[87] Some pagan authors also used the term *thiasos*, which indicates an association with worship.[88] Sometimes Christians, but only rarely, used the term *synagogue*.[89] The Greek term *ekklēsia* was not translated into Latin but only transliterated as *ecclesia*. This term existed already in the Latin language to indicate an assembly.[90] Tertullian once used the term *curia* in the sense of a reunion (*coitio Christianorum*).[91] In Latin the terms *comitia* and *convocatio* are used to designate this called-out people. Augustine would use the famous expression *civitas Dei*.

Already in Tertullian, *ecclesia* indicated a place of prayer.[92] The term, therefore, came to indicate either the local or the universal community or the place where the Christian assembly came together. To this term adjectives were added to better define it, such as *holy, catholic, one* or *apostolic*, to distinguish it from the many separated Christian communities.

The patristic testimonies concerning the church are widespread, but especially in the first three centuries they are only partial, in that many were lost and others are fragmentary. The early Christian generations did not develop an extensive theory of the church or ecclesiology. They left a series of writings that contain indications and brief references to the church, to its lived life and to its organization which is still in the early stages of development.

The essential elements of the church are the confession of faith, the communion between all the faithful scattered in the various churches of the time, church ministers, the body of writings considered canonical and therefore normative, a certain discipline, the baptismal rite and the eucharistic assembly. Many of the prescriptions, precious to us, regarding the life lived by Christians were passed on orally in the various communities. They emerged from time to time according to current needs. They were developed and adapted to the new situations that emerged with the growth of the communities and with the missionary and geographic expansion in different cultures. In early times, since the faithful were united in the one faith in Christ, the Son of God incarnate, who died and rose, there was not a continuous preoccupation with creating homogeneity of organization and discipline in time and space.

The individual churches jealously guarded their own disciplinary and liturgical traditions, but with time there was a greater level of coordination, at least at the regional level. Also the expressions of the profession of faith were checked against the traditions of other communities so as to

---

[86]Chrysostom *Homily on the Fall of Eutropius* (PG 52:402).
[87]Origen *Against Celsus* 5.59-65.
[88]Lucian *The Death of Peregrinus* 11; Eusebius *Ecclesiastical History* 10.1.8; cf. 1.3.12.
[89]Epiphanius *Adversus Haereses* 30.18.2.
[90]Plinius *Epistle* 10.110.
[91]Tertullian *Apology* 39.
[92]Tertullian *On Modesty* 1.8; 1.20; 3.5; 4.5; 13.7; *On Repentance* 7.10; *On the Veiling of Virgins* 13.1-2.

avoid deviations. The oral tradition was vital for the assessment of a new text or doctrine. Two examples are the following: Serapion of Antioch refused a Gospel of Peter, belonging to the Rhossos community, because it was not in accord with the traditional faith of the Antiochian church.[93] A second example is found in Origen in the introduction to *On First Principles*, where he writes:

> Since many, however, of those who profess to believe in Christ differ from each other, not only in small and trifling matters but also on subjects of the highest importance, as, e.g., regarding God, or the Lord Jesus Christ or the Holy Spirit . . . it seems on that account necessary first of all to fix a definite limit and to lay down an unmistakable rule regarding each one of these and then to pass to the investigation of other points . . . after we had come to believe that Christ was the Son of God and were persuaded that we must learn it from himself. We are aware that there are many who think they hold the opinions of Christ, and yet some of these think differently from their predecessors who received the teaching of the church as transmitted in orderly succession from the apostles and have been preserved in the churches to the present day. That alone is to be accepted as truth which differs in no respect from ecclesiastical and apostolic tradition.[94]

In the different traditions there was a strong consciousness of belonging to a new reality, a living and catholic church, as Paul expressed it: "The cup of blessing which we bless, is it not a participation in the blood of Christ? The bread which we break, is it not a participation in the body of Christ? Because there is one bread, we who are many are one body, for we all partake of the one bread."[95] All the churches formed one body; hence the preoccupation with solidarity and helping the needy and the weak: "They [Peter, James and John] would have us remember the poor, which very thing I was eager to do."[96] For this reason Paul received a collection in all the churches to help the saints in Jerusalem: "Now concerning the contribution for the saints: as I directed the churches of Galatia, so you also are to do. On the first day of every week, each of you is to put something aside and store it up, as he may prosper, so that contributions need not be made when I come. And when I arrive, I will send those whom you accredit by letter to carry your gift to Jerusalem."[97] In the Roman churches it was customary to have collections for other Christian communities in the centuries that followed.

The church of the first three centuries understood itself through a series of images: the ark of the new covenant, the house, the body, the bride, the flock, the vine, the city of Jerusalem, the dove, the moon, the seamless tunic. Female personalities of the Old Testament symbolized the church: Eve, the wife of Lot, Sarah.[98] The church was also called the *verus* ("true") Israel. The richness of the images expresses the different facets of the church, but they are not taken too

---

[93] Eusebius *Ecclesiastical History* 6.12.
[94] Origen *On First Principles* preface 2.
[95] 1 Cor 10:16-17.
[96] Gal 2:10.
[97] 1 Cor 16:1-3.
[98] See Origen *Commentary on the Song of Songs* 1.2.

literally, because each image describes one particular aspect of it.

Christians today may easily accept Jesus and his message but may find it difficult to accept the church institution as it is at present. They have difficulty recognizing the gospel message in the church. The study of the Fathers helps us to see many ecclesial institutions in their historical setting and to see the development and evolution of the organization of the ecclesial community so as to better respond to particular times and places. We find in the early centuries a creative fidelity but also a transforming one with respect to the church's beginnings. The primitive model has an influence on every reform of the church. Belonging to one Christian confession can influence the reading of the ancient documents. This can be a difficulty, but it can also be a help toward grasping the version that best corresponds to the ancient model. For this reason there is need for vigilance so as to reach maximum objectivity in situating documents in their historical context.

The church, as the community of those who are called, is a new *politeia* (a city-state), made up of citizens, or rather, brothers, and not of strangers: "So then you are no longer strangers and sojourners, but you are fellow citizens with the saints and members of the household of God."[99] Its members, coming "from every nation,"[100] are united by love: "And above all these put on love, which binds everything together in perfect harmony."[101] In this community of citizens there is no difference of race, sex or social status: "There is neither Jew nor Greek, there is neither slave nor free, there is neither male nor female; for you are all one in Christ Jesus."[102] In the church there is a variety of services inspired by the Spirit: "There are varieties of working, but it is the same God who inspires them all in every one. To each is given the manifestation of the Spirit for the common good. . . . All these are inspired by one and the same Spirit, who apportions to each one individually as he wills."[103]

Entry into the church, the body of Christ, is through baptism: "For by one Spirit we were all baptized into one body—Jews or Greeks, slaves or free—and all were made to drink of one Spirit."[104] With baptism the converted are incorporated into this body of Christ, obtaining the remission of sins and the gift of the Spirit: "Repent, and be baptized every one of you in the name of Jesus Christ for the forgiveness of your sins; and you shall receive the gift of the Holy Spirit."[105] The gift of the Spirit is received after baptism but presupposes baptism. Baptism associates us with the death and resurrection of Christ: "Do you not know that all of us who have been baptized into Christ Jesus were baptized into his death? We were buried therefore with him by baptism into death, so that as Christ was raised from the dead by the glory of the Father, we too might walk in newness of life. For if we have been united with him in a death like his,

---

[99]Eph 2:19.
[100]Acts 2:5.
[101]Col 3:14.
[102]Gal 3:28; cf. 1 Cor 12:13; Rom 10:12; Col 3:11.
[103]1 Cor 12:6-7, 11.
[104]1 Cor 12:13.
[105]Acts 2:38; 3:19.

we shall certainly be united with him in a resurrection like his."[106] In this way we participate in the body of Christ. This participation will find its fulfillment in the eschatological reality—the final events on earth. "If children, then heirs, heirs of God and fellow heirs with Christ, provided we suffer with him in order that we may also be glorified with him."[107]

Sometimes the newly baptized changed their name to show their new life in Christ through baptism. An inscription in the catacombs in Rome is an example of this thinking. A child who died in the middle of the fifth century (457-463) was born at Easter, changed his name at the time of baptism and died the following Sunday: "Here lies Paschasius, born with the name Severus, in Eastertide, Thursday, the 4th of April [the name of the consuls of the year 457] lived 6 years, received the grace [of baptism] on the 21st of April and left his white baptismal vestments in the sepulcher on the Octave of Easter."[108]

The church is on pilgrimage on earth, its temporary abode, because it is destined for full participation in the kingdom of God: "Beloved, I beseech you as aliens and exiles to abstain from the passions of the flesh that wage war against your soul."[109] Its true citizenship is in heaven: "But our citizenship is in heaven, and from it we await a Savior, the Lord Jesus Christ, who will change our lowly body to be like his glorious body, by the power which enables him even to subject all things to himself."[110] The church is in this world but not of this world.[111] The task of the church in this world is that of preaching the gospel so as to liberate the world from the devil. Its principal task is offering God's saving action through the sacraments.

One Baptism for the Forgiveness of Sins

In the Nicene Creed, after professing belief in the church, members of the Christian community say, "We acknowledge one baptism for the forgiveness of sins." After the coming of the Holy Spirit on the Jewish feast of Pentecost, Peter gave a long public speech explaining, in the light of the Bible, the meaning of the life and death of Jesus of Nazareth. The people asked, "Brethren, what shall we do?"[112] Peter said to them, "Repent, and be baptized every one of you in the name of Jesus Christ for the forgiveness of your sins; and you shall receive the gift of the Holy Spirit. For the promise is to you and to your children and to all that are afar off, every one whom the Lord our God calls to him."[113] The people knew a baptism of repentance, like that of John the Baptist; according to the Synoptic Gospels, Jesus was baptized,[114] and, according to John, occasionally he baptized.[115] The resurrected Christ said to his disciples, "Go into all the world

---

[106] Rom 6:3-5.
[107] Rom 8:17.
[108] *ILCV* 1541.
[109] 1 Pet 2:11.
[110] Phil 3:20-21.
[111] Jn 17:14-16.
[112] Acts 2:37.
[113] Acts 2:38-39.
[114] Mk 1:9-11 and parallel texts.
[115] Jn 3:22; 4:1. However, John also clarifies that it was not Jesus who baptized but his disciples (Jn 4:2).

and preach the gospel to the whole creation. He who believes and is baptized will be saved,"[116] because "repentance and forgiveness of sins should be preached in his name to all nations, beginning from Jerusalem."[117] Baptism is so important as to be a condition for salvation.

What significance did Christian baptism have? Not precisely the same as that of John or of the baptismal ritual of the Mandeans. John said that he baptized with water but then pointed to the One who was coming after him and identified him as "he who baptizes with the Holy Spirit."[118] "He will baptize you with the Holy Spirit and fire."[119] The Holy Spirit is linked with Christian baptism,[120] and water is the sign and the seal. The baptism administrated by the followers of Jesus is not just for repentance, but it has a deeper and more radical meaning through its connection with the Holy Spirit. When Paul went to Ephesus, he found people who had received only John's baptism. And Paul said, "John baptized with the baptism of repentance, telling the people to believe in the one who was to come after him, that is, Jesus."[121] Then they were baptized in the name of Jesus and received the Holy Spirit. Moreover, Paul helps us to understand this further when he writes, "We were buried therefore with him by baptism into death, so that as Christ was raised from the dead by the glory of the Father, we too might walk in newness of life."[122] According to this explanation, baptism is the personal participation of the believer in the death and resurrection of Jesus. It is a rebirth to a new life. We are incorporated into the life of Christ and have a new existence. We "have put on Christ,"[123] and one who "is in Christ . . . is a new creation."[124] Christ and his baptism establish the foundation of the unity of all the members of the church.

The Christians of the first centuries had many tensions and had to work hard to develop their own communal structure—a *koinōnia* between the members of the same community and between those communities. They strove to have unified governance, a shared belief system and a group of sacred writings. Worshiping and believing communities, in different regions inside and outside of the Roman Empire, were and felt and saw themselves as one body of Christ:

> The church, though dispersed through the whole world, even to the ends of the earth, has received from the apostles and their disciples this faith: [she believes] in one God, the Father Almighty, Maker of heaven, and earth, and the sea and all things that are in them; and in one Christ Jesus, the Son of God, who became incarnate for our salvation. . . . As I have already observed, the church, having received this preaching and this faith, although scattered throughout the whole world, yet, as if occupying but one house, carefully preserves it. She also

---

[116] Mk 16:15-16; cf. Mt 28:19.
[117] Lk 24:47.
[118] Jn 1:33.
[119] Mt 3:11.
[120] Jn 3:5; Acts 2:38; 9:17-18; 10:47; 1 Cor 12:13; 2 Cor 1:22.
[121] Acts 19:4.
[122] Rom 6:4.
[123] Gal 3:27.
[124] 2 Cor 5:17.

believes these points [of doctrine] just as if she had but one soul and one and the same heart, and she proclaims them, and teaches them and hands them down, with perfect harmony, as if she possessed only one mouth. For, although the languages of the world are dissimilar, yet the import of the tradition is one and the same. For the churches which have been planted in Germany do not believe or hand down anything different, nor do those in Spain, nor those in Gaul, nor those in the East, nor those in Egypt, nor those in Libya nor those which have been established in the central regions of the world. But as the sun, that creature of God, is one and the same throughout the whole world, so also the preaching of the truth shines everywhere and enlightens all who are willing to come to a knowledge of the truth. Nor will any one of the rulers in the churches, however highly gifted he may be in point of eloquence, teach doctrines different from these (for no one is greater than the Master); nor, on the other hand, will he who is deficient in power of expression inflict injury on the tradition. For the faith being ever one and the same, neither does one who is able at great length to discourse regarding it, make any addition to it, nor does one who can say but little diminish it.[125]

This one baptism is for the remission of sins—any kind of sins. The church had the mission to preach the gospel for the remission of the sins of people from all nations, because all are sinners and must be reconciled to God. Paul talked about the time when the message of Christ would be announced to all people of every race and culture, so that through repentance they can obtain forgiveness of sins and salvation. "All this is from God, who through Christ reconciled us to himself and gave us the ministry of reconciliation; that is, in Christ God was reconciling the world to himself, not counting their trespasses against them, and entrusting to us the message of reconciliation. So we are ambassadors for Christ, God making his appeal through us. We implore you on behalf of Christ, be reconciled to God. For our sake he made him to be sin who knew no sin, so that in him we might become the righteousness of God."[126] The church serves to reconcile the world to God through the preaching and the witness of its members. It loses the meaning of its existence if it forgets the reason for its foundation. That message of repentance and pardon was almost incomprehensible to the entrenched pagan mentality. Pagan thinkers accused Christians of accepting any kind of sinners and derided them for the practice of penance. Julian, the emperor, said, "Those who are corrupt, murderers, those cursed and rejected by all, come here confident that by being washed in this water they will be immediately rendered pure. And when they recommit the same offenses, all they have to do is beat their breasts and bow their head so as to become pure again."[127] Augustine made reference to these criticisms: "Among the pagans there is the habit of criticizing the Christians regarding the practice of penance in use in the church. In regard to this truth, to be able to do penance, the catholic church has always held firm against some heresies."[128] " 'Be responsible,' the pagan says, 'when offering people the

---

[125]Irenaeus *Against Heresies* 1.10-11.
[126]2 Cor 5:18-21.
[127]*Caesares* 10:38 (336AB, ed. C. Lacombrade [Paris: Les Belles Lettres, 1964], pp. 70-71).
[128]Augustine *Sermon* 352.9.

possibility of repentance, promising them impunity for all their crimes: people do evil because they are sure that once they are converted all will be pardoned.'"[129]

The Resurrection of the Dead

The next confession of the Nicene Creed is "We look forward to the resurrection of the dead." According to Paul, the resurrection of Christ is the basis of our belief in the resurrection of the body. This shows the importance of the body for the wholeness of the human being in Christian teaching. The well-attested resurrection of Christ from the dead is the foundation of the belief in the resurrection of human beings. It is the reason for Christian belief and preaching. Paul writes to the Corinthians:

> For I delivered to you as of first importance what I also received, that Christ died for our sins in accordance with the scriptures, that he was buried, that he was raised on the third day in accordance with the scriptures, and that he appeared to Cephas, then to the twelve. Then he appeared to more than five hundred brethren at one time, most of whom are still alive, though some have fallen asleep.... Last of all, as to one untimely born, he appeared also to me.... Now if Christ is preached as raised from the dead, how can some of you say that there is no resurrection of the dead?... If Christ has not been raised, your faith is futile and you are still in your sins.... But in fact Christ has been raised from the dead, the first fruits of those who have fallen asleep.... Come to your right mind, and sin no more. For some have no knowledge of God. I say this to your shame. But some one will ask, "How are the dead raised? With what kind of body do they come?" You foolish man! What you sow does not come to life unless it dies. And what you sow is not the body which is to be, but a bare kernel, perhaps of wheat or of some other grain.... So is it with the resurrection of the dead.... For the trumpet will sound, and the dead will be raised imperishable, and we shall be changed. For this perishable nature must put on the imperishable, and this mortal nature must put on immortality. When the perishable puts on the imperishable, and the mortal puts on immortality, then shall come to pass the saying that is written: "Death is swallowed up in victory." "O death, where is thy victory? O death, where is your sting?" The sting of death is sin, and the power of sin is the law. But thanks be to God, who gives us the victory through our Lord Jesus Christ.[130]

The resurrection of the dead (or of the flesh) is a central theme in ancient Christianity, beginning with Paul, preaching in a Gentile context that had enormous difficulty in accepting it. Paul was scorned and derided when he spoke of it at the Areopagus of Athens: "'Because he has fixed a day on which he will judge the world in righteousness by a man whom he has appointed, and of this he has given assurance to all men by raising him from the dead.' Now when they heard of the resurrection of the dead, some mocked; but others said, 'We will hear you again about

---

[129] Augustine *Expositions of the Psalms* 1 (on Ps 101:10).
[130] 1 Cor 15:3-57.

this.'"[131] In nearby Corinth, Paul had to insist on the resurrection with a long chapter in his letter.[132] The foundation of faith is the resurrection of Christ. The resurrection of the flesh is attributed to the Holy Spirit. It is important to follow the catechesis of the fathers who explain the symbol of the faith, because they offer that which is the common faith and not theological discussions. The apostolic fathers and the apologists had to defend the faith against pagans as well as affirming it for Christians. Many works on the resurrection, some lost, came to be written in these two centuries. A strict link between the resurrection of Christ and the resurrection of the dead through the work of the Spirit is established. The resurrection is linked to the eschatological judgment of the living and the dead. Christian salvation, announced by Christ and brought forward by the faith of the church, is that of the salvation of the whole person, in his totality of soul and body with the total victory over death. Eternal life is the consummation of the resurrection.

Paleochristian art expresses in various ways, through numerous symbols, the faith of the communities in salvation and the resurrection. The idea of death and of the afterlife of Christians was very different from that of the pagan world. For this reason, since the second century, Christians preserved some traditional pagan rites yet adopted practices quite distinct from those of the pagans. In the first century, Christians were buried with all the other dead, like Peter in the Vatican and Paul on the *Via Ostiense*. In the second century, they started separate communal burial places and special rites that were more suitable for their living faith. They called the communal burial places *koimētēria*, a word not used by pagans, which means "dormitory" (*koimaō* ["to sleep"]). For pagans, the *koimētēria* was a place to sleep during the night, not a burial place. For Christians, the *koimētēria* was a burial place, where they fell asleep waiting for the resurrection and the afterlife. They used to write on tombs the word *deposition*, which meant "something given for deposit": the body was deposed in the grave, like a seed in the soil, and in the future it would be restored in a new life.

The Life of the World to Come

The last part of the Nicene Creed says that we look forward to "the life of the world to come." This sentence does not use the word *paradise*; rather, it speaks of the life of human beings extending to the age or world to come. Sometimes the Fathers speak about the "eternal glory": "In the exercise of his grace, may he confer immortality on the righteous and holy, and those who have kept his commandments and have persevered in his love, some from the beginning [of their Christian course] and others from [the date of] their repentance, and may he surround them with everlasting glory."[133] Eternal life is the end of the work of the redemption of Christ in the church, which gives meaning to the incarnation. The resurrection of the dead is for eternal life in the new world: "a new heaven and a new earth; for the first heaven and the first earth had passed away . . . the holy

---

[131] Acts 17:31-33.
[132] 1 Cor 15:3-12.
[133] Irenaeus *Against Heresies* 1.10.1 (ANF 1:331).

city, new Jerusalem, [came] down out of heaven from God, prepared as a bride adorned for her husband; and I heard a loud voice from the throne saying, 'Behold, the dwelling of God is with men. He will dwell with them, and they shall be his people, and God himself will be with them; he will wipe away every tear from their eyes, and death shall be no more, neither shall there be mourning nor crying nor pain any more, for the former things have passed away.'"[134] The martyr Ignatius of Antioch (d. ca. 111) writes, "Bear with me, brothers. Do not hinder me from living; do not desire my death. Bestow not on the world one who desires to be God's, neither allure him with material things. Suffer me to receive the pure light. When I arrive there, then shall I be a man."[135]

The expression "the communion of saints" is not found in the Nicene-Constantinopolitan Creed, but it comes from the Roman symbol (or apostolic symbol); it is absent in the oriental professions of faith but is found in Basil of Caesarea.[136] Initially it indicated communion with the holy things (*sanctorum* is neuter), that is, with the Eucharist, but it makes reference to persons, as Niceta of Remesiana says: "After the confession of the blessed Trinity, you profess faith in the holy catholic church. The church is simply the community of all the saints. All who from the beginning of the world were or are or will be justified. . . . You must believe, therefore, that in this one church you are gathered into the communion of saints."[137]

The apostle Simon received a second name from Jesus;[138] this new name was Peter (*kephas* ["stone, rock"]): "You are Simon the son of John? You shall be called Cephas."[139] Why did Jesus give the second name only to Simon and not to the other apostles? Why that special word *kephas*, which was not known as a personal name previously? This change seems clear from the Gospel of Matthew: "And I tell you, you are Peter, and on this rock I will build my church, and the powers of death shall not prevail against it. I will give you the keys of the kingdom of heaven, and whatever you bind on earth shall be bound in heaven, and whatever you loose on earth shall be loosed in heaven."[140] Peter, during the earthly life of Jesus, had a special and unique role among all his disciples: first to be called, member of the small group around the Master, the spokesman for the Twelve and their representative in Caesarea Philippi; he was present at the transfiguration; personally he received a visit of the risen Lord; he was the rock of the church and the first of the apostles, to whom Jesus solemnly bestowed, by the Sea of the Galilee, the burden to "feed his lambs."[141] According to Paul, Peter was the first eyewitness to Christ's resurrection.[142] Simon Peter was designated to be leader of the people of God, and to him were entrusted his followers. In this way the survival of the new people of God was assured, whose destiny is entrance into the kingdom of God. The Acts of the Apostles shows Peter as the guide of the new community. Paul

---

[134]Rev 21:1-4.
[135]Ignatius *To the Romans* 6.2; cf. ANF 1:76**.
[136]Basil of Caesarea *Homilies on the Psalms* 45.4 (PG 29:421).
[137]Niceta of Remesiana *Exposition of the Faith* 10 (FC 7:48).
[138]Jn 1:42; Mk 3:16; Mt 16:18.
[139]Jn 1:42.
[140]Mt 16:18-19.
[141]Jn 21:16.
[142]1 Cor 15:5.

went to visit Cephas in Jerusalem and "remained with him fifteen days."[143]

Jesus remained within Palestine and did not cross its boundaries, except on a few occasions. Within one generation of his death the tiny community of Jerusalem exploded and scattered in many directions, because we encounter local churches in many cities in Palestine, in Asia Minor, in Greece and in Rome. The followers of Jesus, called Christians in Antioch, presented themselves as witnesses of the life of Jesus Christ, the suffering and crucified Messiah. Because of this witness, they were killed. They knew from Christ and from early personal experience that their future was uncertain and perilous: "Beware of men, for they will deliver you up to councils, and flog you in their synagogues, and you will be dragged before governors and kings for my sake, to bear testimony before them and the Gentiles. When they deliver you up, do not be anxious how you are to speak or what you are to say; for what you are to say will be given to you in that hour; for it is not you who speak, but the Spirit of your Father speaking through you."[144] The followers of Jesus have to take into account the fact that they will meet with persecutions and death in Jesus' name along the way, but they will be blessed: "Blessed are you when men revile and persecute you and utter all kinds of evil against you falsely on my account. Rejoice and be glad, for your reward is great in heaven, for so men persecuted the prophets who were before you."[145] The outlook is not one of triumph in this world: "Remember the word that I said to you, 'A servant is not greater than his master.' If they persecuted me, they will persecute you; if they kept my word, they will keep yours also."[146] Following Christ entails suffering and the cross.[147] Matthew says that in the perspective of every Christian there is a potential vocation to martyrdom.[148] "For whoever would save his life will lose it, and whoever loses his life for my sake will find it."[149] The letters of the apostles already speak about a persecution taking place.[150] Paul writes, "While we live we are always being given up to death for Jesus' sake."[151] For Clement of Rome, already death for Christ was part of daily experience.[152] Martyrdom, in the first centuries of Christianity, was the highest form of witness to the faith.

In these concise phrases, the creed sums up the baptismal and eucharistic confession on the church, the future and human destiny.

---

[143]Gal 1:18.
[144]Mt 10:17-20.
[145]Mt 5:11-12.
[146]Jn 15:20.
[147]Mk 8:31-38.
[148]Mt 16:24-28: "Then Jesus told his disciples, 'If any man would come after me, let him deny himself and take up his cross and follow me. For whoever would save his life will lose it, and whoever loses his life for my sake will find it. For what will it profit a man, if he gains the whole world and forfeits his life? Or what shall a man give in return for his life? For the Son of man is to come with his angels in the glory of his Father, and then he will repay every man for what he has done. Truly, I say to you, there are some standing here who will not taste death before they see the Son of man coming in his kingdom.'" See Mk 8:31-38.
[149]Mt 16:25; cf. Mk 8:35.
[150]Rom 8:33-39; 2 Tim 1:6-8; 4:5-8; 1 Pet 4:12-19.
[151]2 Cor 4:11.
[152]Clement of Rome *Epistle to the Corinthians* 5.1–6.2.

WE BELIEVE IN ONE HOLY CATHOLIC AND APOSTOLIC CHURCH

WE BELIEVE IN ONE HOLY CATHOLIC AND APOSTOLIC CHURCH

The Church

εἰς μίαν, ἁγίαν, καθολικὴν καὶ ἀποστολικὴν ἐκκλησίαν· ὁμολογοῦμεν ἓν βάπτισμα εἰς ἄφεσιν ἁμαρτιῶν· προσδοκῶμεν ἀνάστασιν νεκρῶν, καὶ ζωὴν τοῦ μέλλοντος αἰῶνος. Ἀμήν.	*Et unam, sanctam, catholicam et apostolicam ecclesiam. Confiteor unum baptisma in remissionem peccatorum; et expecto resurrectionem mortuorum, et vitam venturi saeculi. Amen.*	We believe in one holy catholic and apostolic Church. We acknowledge one baptism for the forgiveness of sins. We look for the resurrection of the dead and the life of the world to come. Amen.

HISTORICAL CONTEXT: In our profession of faith we proclaim, "We believe in . . . the church" (*et . . . ecclesiam*). Rufinus explains why in Latin we say, "We believe the church" and not we believe "in the church." He writes:

> "We believe the holy church," not as God but as the church gathered together to God. And we believe that there is "forgiveness of sins"; we do not say "We believe in the forgiveness of sins." And we believe that there will be a "resurrection of the flesh"; we do not say, "We believe in the resurrection of the flesh." By this monosyllabic preposition, therefore, the Creator is distinguished from the creatures and things divine are separated from things human.[1]

The understanding of the Fathers of the significance and the nature of the church is grounded on Scripture, especially on the New Testament. The strong images of Paul support their explanation: the Christian community as the body of Christ, as his bride, as mother. Because she is a bride, she can generate sons and daughters for the Father. Paul, in describing the nature of the Christian community, introduces the image of the church as the body of Christ[2] and expounds it in the Pastoral Letters.[3] Christ is the head of that body: "He is the head of the body, the church. . . . Now I

---

[1] Rufinus *Commentary on the Apostles' Creed* (NPNF 2 3:557). In other words, we believe in God and things divine. We do not believe in things human; we simply believe them.
[2] 1 Cor 12:27-31: "Now you are the body of Christ and individually members of it. And God has appointed in the church first apostles, second prophets, third teachers, then workers of miracles, then healers, helpers, administrators, speakers in various kinds of tongues. Are all apostles? Are all prophets? Are all teachers? Do all work miracles? Do all possess gifts of healing? Do all speak with tongues? Do all interpret? But earnestly desire the higher gifts." [3] Eph 5:23, 29-32: "For the husband is the head of the wife as Christ is the head of the church, his body, and is himself its Savior. . . . For no man ever hates his own flesh, but nourishes and cherishes it, as Christ does the church, because we are members of his body. 'For this reason a man shall leave his father and mother and be joined to his wife, and the two shall become one flesh.' This mystery is a profound one, and I am saying that it refers to Christ and the church."

rejoice in my sufferings for your sake, and in my flesh I complete what is lacking in Christ's afflictions for the sake of his body, that is, the church."[4] There is a mystical identification between believers and Christ, as is shown in the conversion of Paul: "As he journeyed, he approached Damascus, and suddenly a light from heaven flashed about him. And he fell to the ground and heard a voice saying to him, 'Saul, Saul, why do you persecute me?' And he said, 'Who are you, Lord?' And he said, 'I am Jesus, whom you are persecuting.'"[5]

To belong to Christ, to have a personal relationship with him, to have union with him, implies the result of union with other believers. "Do you not know that your bodies are members of Christ? . . . But he who is united to the Lord becomes one spirit with him."[6] Individuals are unified by the same faith and love in Christ: "So we, though many, are one body in Christ, and individually members one of another."[7] According to Paul, believers are members of a body and are connected, serving different functions. It is not only a visible unity, a society with all members in harmony; the unity is of a higher order. It is not only a social or a moral unity but a mystical body. "Mystical" does not mean something strange or hidden; it means that Christ binds, guides, ties, unites us to himself. It is a reality that is not obvious to our intelligence and is beyond our senses and involves a special union of all the members with Christ, who is the head. John uses the image of the vine and the branches:

> I am the vine, you are the branches. He who abides in me, and I in him, he it is that bears much fruit, for apart from me you can do nothing. If a man does not abide in me, he is cast forth as a branch and withers; and the branches are gathered, thrown into the fire and burned. If you abide in me, and my words abide in you, ask whatever you will, and it shall be done for you. By this my Father is glorified, that you bear much fruit, and so prove to be my disciples.[8]

The members are bound through faith, love and sacraments to Christ, who endows us with his gifts: "holding fast to the Head, from whom the whole body, nourished and knit together through its joints and ligaments, grows with a growth that is from God."[9] In the force of this union the church is the fullness or complement (*plerōma*) of Christ: the Father "has put all things under his feet and has made him the head over all things for the church, which is his body, the fulness of him who fills all in all."[10] It forms one whole with him: "For just as the body is one and has many members, and all the members of the body, though many, are one body, so it is with Christ."[11] This body is nourished by the Eucharist: "Because there is one bread, we who are many are one body, for we all partake of the one bread."[12]

The visible church is a human, mixed company, with shadows and spots. We still are not yet "spiritual men, but . . . men of the flesh, . . . babes in Christ."[13] But the church is more than that. It is the visible sign of the presence of the kingdom of God among human beings, sustained by hope, whose soul is the Holy Spirit. Augustine described the Holy Spirit's role in the mystical body of Christ.[14]

In the thinking of the Fathers, both the Eucharist and the church are *corpus Christi*. Augustine brings together the two images in the same expression.[15] There exists a concrete and real continuity between Christ, the head, and the Christian community, the church: the two constitute only one body. This connection is expressed symbolically in the Eucharist. Other similar expressions convey the same doctrine: just as the church consecrates the bread and

---

[4]Col 1:18, 24. [5]Acts 9:3-5. [6]1 Cor 6:15, 17. [7]Rom 12:5. [8]Jn 15:5-8. [9]Col 2:19. [10]Eph 1:22-23. [11]1 Cor 12:12. [12]1 Cor 10:17. [13]1 Cor 3:1. [14]Augustine *Sermon* 267.4 (PL 38:1231D). [15]See Augustine *Sermon* 227.1.

wine, so participation in the Eucharist consecrates those who receive it. One becomes part of the body of Christ through baptism, a new birth.[16] Augustine precisely distinguishes the church, the body of Christ and the city of God from the visible church that is contained within the limits of geographical space and historical time. The church in time is still a *corpus permixtum*; for this he prays for the forgiveness of sins.[17] The church here below is not composed of only saints, as the rigorists wanted (e.g., Novatian), but also of sinners. It is identified only partially with the kingdom of God, but it is still on the way; it is the way, but it is also the means, visible and invisible; it lives in time but is also eternal, sinner and saint. The symbol of the moon expresses this ambivalence of the church. The moon receives light from the sun but changes continually in this life in expectation of being the "perfect moon for eternity."[18]

The church was born on the cross: "There came out blood and water,"[19] which is Christ's church, and it is built on him, just as Adam's wife was taken from his side. The rib of Adam was his wife, and the blood of our Lord, his church. From the rib of Adam came death, and from the rib of our Lord, life. The olive is the symbol of Christ, for from him spring milk, water and oil; milk for babes, water for the young and oil for the sick. Likewise the Olive gave these also, water and blood, in his death, and gave oil in or by his death.[20]

OVERVIEW: Some Fathers talk about the preexistence of the church (HERMAS). This implies the church is a mystery and more than what is seen by the eyes. The church has its existence before the beginning of time; it is the ancient one (IGNATIUS, CLEMENT OF ALEXANDRIA). It exists from the time of Abel (AUGUSTINE) and is later manifested in the flesh of Christ (PSEUDO-CLEMENT). Its creation precedes everything else, however (HERMAS, ORIGEN). The people who lived righteously before the time of Christ belong to the church as members of the spiritual church (JUSTIN, AUGUSTINE, LEO). The ancient law foretold the characteristics of the church in figure and shadow. The church, in turn, represents the new dispensation that is yet to come (METHODIUS). It was previously designated by many figures and hidden mysteries (CAESARIUS). Concretely, the existence of the church is the consequence of historical happenings and of decisions taken by people at particular times in human history (ORIGEN, AUGUSTINE). But from a theological perspective it comes from the eternal will of the Father for salvation, which is manifested in history (IRENAEUS). Paul's letters explain this concept when they speak of eternal election in Christ before the creation of the world:[21] "The mystery hidden for ages in God who created all things; that through the church the manifold wisdom of God might now be made known to the principalities and powers in the heavenly places";[22] "the mystery hidden for ages and generations but now made manifest to his saints"[23] (AUGUSTINE). This is the universal church, the one church of Christ, which exists and coexists in the particular churches. This church remains for all generations to come (CLEMENT OF ALEXANDRIA). Christ, a whole and perfect man, is both head and body of this church, of the local church here and there and of the church throughout the whole world (AUGUSTINE).

The Fathers do not discuss ecclesiology as a formal subject. Instead, they describe the church as a living assembly of faithful called together by the Lord. They use many images to express the different aspects of that assembly. These images convey the idea of the mystery of the church, which is more than an institution or a visible society. Sociological study of the church does not grasp its internal life and

---

[16]Augustine *On Baptism* 3.4.8. [17]Augustine *On Continence* 25; *Sermon* 47.6; Hippolytus *Elenchos* 9.7. [18]Augustine *Expositions of the Psalms* 88.32; *Letter* 55.10; cf. Ps 89:37. [19]Jn 19:34. [20]SCK 125. [21]Eph 1:3-14. [22]Eph 3:9-10. [23]Col 1:26.

spirit. The language of many images, by contrast, shows the nuances of the complexity of the church. No one of the images, as such, can convey the complete idea of the essential nature of the church. Some biblical personalities and things are symbols of the church, many of which are promised and prefigured in the Old Testament and find their fulfillment in the New (Augustine): Eve, Sarah, Rebekah, the ark of Noah, dove, field, house, temple, tower and moon. The church, like the ark of Noah, provides refuge and salvation (Tertullian, Lactantius, Cyprian, Augustine). It is an enclosed garden and a sealed fountain (Firmilian), the tabernacle built by Moses (Ephrem), the spiritual temple of God (Cyprian, Origen, Lactantius, Chrysostom), a spiritual tower built of stones (Hermas) and founded on the rock (Victorinus). It is the fountain of truth (Lactantius), the house of God (Didymus, Augustine), a vineyard that produces as many saints as shoots (Gregory the Great). The church is the resplendent garment that Rebekah presented to her son Jacob (Ambrose) or it is the city of the living God. The teachers of the church cast out and kill those "who work iniquity" (Origen). The church is the pillar of the world (Chrysostom). It is the queen in clothing embroidered with gold adorned with diverse colors (Pacian); the Queen of Sheba was a type of the church. Mary Magdalene was the first to run to the tomb and, like the church, brought to Simon the good news and told him what she had seen: that our Lord had risen and was raised up (Ephrem).

In the Pastoral Letters of Paul we find the word *ekklēsia* ("church") expressed as the body of Christ, who is the head.[24] The image of the body has great importance in the ecclesiology of Paul, because the body is the symbol of the church as a living being composed of a plurality of members: the human body is composed of different organs connected and dependent in a unity of life and activities.[25] This conception of the body intends to express the concept of unity among Christians and of the unity Christians have with Christ, the head of the body, the church. To the Romans, Paul writes that Christians are many, yet one body in Christ, and members of one another. This strong image was used by the Fathers to underline the unity of all Christians and union with Christ, the true giver of life. This teaching thus was for the edification of the body of Christ, who gathers around its head; Christ is the only member of the body who is perfect in righteousness (Clement of Alexandria). The body of Christ, which consists of those who are believers, is animated by the Son of God to be the whole church of God, and it is the house of God and the house of the Son of God. It follows then that this church is the house of the Bridegroom and the bride (Origen). Tertullian underlines the unity of Christ with each believer, because they as believers are the body of Christ (Tertullian).

The church, the wife of Christ for the receiving of the spiritual and blessed seed that is sown by him, increases daily in greatness and beauty and number; she can conceive believers and give them new birth by the washing of regeneration (Methodius). The different members of the body are equal and are only one body, just as the church and Christ are one (Chrysostom). The church has only one body and is adorned and formed of many members (Theodoret): it has real eyes (teachers and leaders) who see in sacred Scripture the mysteries of God. It has real hands, shown in people who get things done and are powerful in the godly works they do. It has feet, those who travel on its behalf to places far and near (Jerome). The explanation Didymus gives is a little different from that of Jerome; he says that the eyes are those who have opted for the

---

[24]Eph 1:22; Col 1:18, 24. [25]1 Cor 12:12, 14-26; Rom 12:4-5; cf. Eph 4:16.

contemplative life, as likewise its hands are for action, performing the deeds of virtue, the body's ears being the name for the intelligent listeners. For Theodore, the members of Christ rise with him because they have been united to him by being born again of the Spirit. The church is the whole body of Christ (*totus Christus*), but at present it is a mixed body, where the flesh still fights against the spirit (Jerome, Augustine) because it has within it strong and weak members; it has those who are being fed on solid bread and those who still need to be reared on milk. The Eucharist changes the faithful into the body of Christ and binds them together, in order not to seem undervalued in their own estimation. The Holy Spirit is to the church what the soul is to the human body. It was born from the suffering Christ on the cross and includes all generations (Augustine).

A feminine metaphor used by Scripture to describe the church is the metaphor of Christ's bride, which conveys other strong and fascinating ideas on love, intimacy and the trust between Christ and his church. The image of marriage used for the relationship between God and his people had a long history in the Old Testament. The prophets describe Israel as God's bride or wife.[26] John the Baptist, in the Gospel of John,[27] talks of himself as the best man and of Christ as the bridegroom. Many texts in the New Testament use the imagery of the bride or wife (church) and the husband (Christ).[28] The marriage between a man and woman is a symbol of the depth of love Christ has for his church[29] and is a great mystery (Gregory of Nazianzus via Jerome).

Who is this bride of Christ? There are two lines of presentation: she is the earthly church (the orthodox, not the heretical one)[30] and the New Jerusalem.[31] The Fathers, following the New Testament and especially Paul, use the metaphor of marriage to explain the church's understanding of itself and the depth of the love between man and woman in marriage. The awareness of the ecclesiological importance of the metaphor started with Irenaeus, Tertullian and Clement. Another source, besides the text in Ephesians, for the theology of the marriage of Christ and the church, was the Song of Songs. It was used first by Hippolytus and after him by Origen. For Origen, Christ is the Bridegroom, the shepherd of the church; he feeds his bride, and she will reign with him. She, as bride, will listen to his voice.

The elders of the church have to take care of the spouse of Christ and preserve her chastity (Pseudo-Clement). The church, as the bride of Christ, cannot be adulterous in faith and living; she must be pure and chaste. The unity between Christ and his church must not be broken, because they are bound together by indissoluble bonds (Fulgentius, Cyprian). Because she is the bride and the unspotted spouse of Christ (Novatian), the church becomes a mother who is able spiritually to conceive and to bear children to God (Cyprian). Christ alone is the bridegroom of the church (Ambrose), and he is jealous of its love (Ephrem). Christ suffered death for the church, that he might present it to himself glorious and blameless, having cleansed it by washing, for receiving the spiritual and blessed seed that is sown by him who with whispers implants it in the depths of the mind. The one who responds in faith is then conceived and formed by the church, as by a woman (Methodius). Christ, as the second Adam, slept on the cross, for his side was struck with a lance and there flowed out the saving mysteries from which the church was born. The earthly church is called to be worthy of that Bridegroom, who now is in heaven, and to remain chaste as Mary did (Augustine). Her tears as the bride of Christ are offered on behalf of

---

[26]See Is 54:5. [27]Jn 3:29; Mt 9:15. [28]2 Cor 11:2; Eph 2; Rev 21. [29]Eph 3:18. [30]2 Cor 11:1-3; Eph 5:15-32. [31]Rev 21:1-11.

her family, who she one day will usher into the heavenly realms (CHRYSOLOGUS).

The church is also known in Scripture as a virgin mother who bears children to the heavenly kingdom as each new generation is regenerated in the Holy Spirit. As a chaste mother (AUGUSTINE) the church is concerned when her children sin. She wants them to imitate the piety and chastity of the virgin mother, and she is rejuvenated when they are converted with all their heart (AUGUSTINE, CHRYSOLOGUS, HERMAS). She is happy for Christians who are faithful during persecution (CYPRIAN), and "our lady mother, the church" helps martyrs to endure persecution (TERTULLIAN, GREGORY THE GREAT). Those who do not partake of Christ are neither nourished into life from the mother's breasts, nor do they enjoy that most limpid fountain that issues from the body of him (IRENAEUS). The mother church is young and does not know old age; she draws her children to herself and kindly takes care of them, the feeble and tender ones. The universal Father is one, as is the universal Word; and the Holy Spirit is one and the same everywhere, and one is the only virgin mother (CLEMENT OF ALEXANDRIA). We can call Father and Son only in the mother church, not outside (TERTULLIAN); the church guides the prayer of the newly baptized. Tertullian refers to the church with the highest respect when he calls it "our lady mother, the church." For Cyprian too, it is possible to call God Father only if we can call the church mother. There is his famous dictum: "If one is to have God for Father, he must first have the church for mother." Only the catholic church, not the heretics, is the bride of Christ and mother, because there is only one true mother in the faith who provides for our rebirth. The church gives birth to the faithful through the waters of baptism (METHODIUS). Those who are born through those waters, as children of Mother Church, must then learn to distinguish truth from falsehood in the sacred Scriptures (VINCENT, MUNNULUS). Then, when they leave this world, the heavenly Mother Church will receive her faithful dead (FUNERAL INSCRIPTIONS), as children who will come to her with all speed, running home to her at the resurrection (METHODIUS).

The ship was another great metaphor used by the Fathers to explain the mystery of the church in the earthly world. This imagery comes from the New Testament (the apostles are called to be fishers of souls) and from the ark that saved Noah's family during the flood[32] (AUGUSTINE). The church as a ship, piloted by the Logos, brings believers to the shores of salvation; the ship is made of wood, however, which means it is fragile. The small boat of Noah, the ark, saved only a few people; the wood of the cross will save many people. Hippolytus was the first one to use the symbol of the ship tossed in the deep but not destroyed, for it has the skilled pilot, Christ. Therefore the passengers remain quiet (LETTER OF CLEMENT TO JAMES). The little ship in Matthew 8:24 is a type of the church, because on the sea, which means this present world, it is being tossed about by the waves, which means persecutions and temptations, while our Lord in his long-suffering is as it were asleep (TERTULLIAN). The leader of the church is the commander, who appoints the assemblies to be made with all possible skill, charging the deacons as mariners to prepare places for the brothers and sisters of Christ as for passengers, with all due care and decency (APOSTOLIC CONSTITUTIONS). The church is propelled through the sea by its sails, which hang from masts that are in the shape of crosses (JUSTIN). The church, like the ark of Noah, sails through the seas of this wicked world as it is tossed about (AUGUSTINE, CHRYSOLOGUS) and shaken by the waves that lash against this ancient vessel (GREGORY THE GREAT).

---

[32] 1 Pet 3:20-21.

The Preexistent Church and Its Visible Foundation by Christ

THE CHURCH AS PREEXISTENT. HERMAS: While I slept, a revelation came to me, brothers and sisters, from a handsome young man who said to me, "The elder lady from whom you received the little book—who do you think she is?" I answered, "The Sibyl." "Wrong," he said, "that is not who she is." "Then who is she?" I asked. "The church," he said. I said to him, "Then why is she elderly?" "Because," he said, "she was created before everything. That is why she is elderly, and for her the world was established." Later, I saw a vision in my house. The elder lady came and asked me if I had already given the book to the elders. I replied that I had not. "You have done well," she said. "I have words to add. When I have finished them all, they will be communicated through you to all the elect. So you will write two little books and send one to Clement and one to Grapte. Clement will send his to the other cities, for he is charged with this responsibility. Grapte will admonish the widows and orphans. But you will read it in this city with the presbyters who preside in the church." SHEPHERD, VISION 2.4.[33]

PREDESTINED BEFORE THE BEGINNING OF TIME. IGNATIUS OF ANTIOCH: Ignatius, who is also called Theophorus, to the church which is at Ephesus, in Asia, deservedly most happy, being blessed in the greatness and fullness of God the Father and predestined before the beginning of time, that it should be always for an enduring and unchangeable glory, being united and elected through the true passion by the will of the Father and Jesus Christ, our God: Abundant happiness through Jesus Christ and his undefiled grace. EPISTLE TO THE EPHESIANS 1.[34]

CHOSEN BEFORE THE FOUNDATION OF THE WORLD. CLEMENT OF ALEXANDRIA: We too are firstborn children, who are reared by God. We are the genuine friends of the Firstborn, who first of all others attained to the knowledge of God, who first were wrenched away from our sins, first severed from the devil. Now, the more benevolent God is, the more impious we are; for he desires us from slaves to become children, while they scorn to become children. O the prodigious folly of being ashamed of the Lord! He offers freedom; you flee into bondage. He bestows salvation; you sink down into destruction. He confers everlasting life; you wait for punishment and prefer the fire that the Lord "has prepared for the devil and his angels."[35] And the Lord, with ceaseless assiduity, exhorts, terrifies, urges, rouses, admonishes; he awakes from the sleep of darkness and raises up those who have wandered in error. "Awake," he says, "O sleeper, and arise from the dead, and Christ shall give you light"[36]—Christ, the Sun of the resurrection, he "who was born before the morning star"[37] and with his beams bestows life. Let no one then despise the Word, lest he unwittingly despise himself. EXHORTATION TO THE GREEKS 9.[38]

CHRIST IS THE HEAD OF THE CHURCH. AUGUSTINE: Our Lord Jesus Christ is, as it were, a whole and perfect man, both head and body. We recognize the head in that man who was born of the Virgin Mary, suffered in the time of Pontius Pilate, was buried, rose again, ascended into heaven, sits at the right of the Father. Therefore we await him as judge of the living and the dead. He is the head of the church. The body belonging to this head is the church: not the local church here, but both the local church and the church throughout the whole world; not the church that belongs to the present time but that which exists from the time of Abel even to all those who will ever be born, even to the end, and who will believe in

---

[33]*SHC* 58. [34]ANF 1:49*. [35]Mt 25:41. [36]Eph 5:14. [37]Ps 109:3 LXX. [38]ANF 2:195*.

Christ. It is the whole population of the saints who belong to but one city. This city is the body of Christ, and Christ is the head of this body. There the angels too are our fellow citizens; but because we are yet on pilgrimage, we labor. They, however, await our arrival in that city. And from that city to which we journey, letters come to us: those letters are the Scriptures, which exhort us to live properly. Expositions of the Psalms 90.2.1.[39]

Stages in the Life of the Church. Augustine: The church is of ancient birth. The church has been on earth ever since saints have been called "saints." At one time the church was in Abel only . . . at one time in Enoch alone . . . at one time in the house of Noah . . . at one time . . . in Abraham alone. Expositions of the Psalms 128.2.[40]

The First Church Is Spiritual. Pseudo-Clement of Rome: So, then, if we do the will of our Father God, we shall be members of the first church, the spiritual—that which was created before sun and moon. But if we shall not do the will of the Lord, we shall come under the Scripture that says, "My house became a den of robbers."[41] So, then, let us elect to belong to the church of life, that we may be saved. I don't think you are ignorant of the fact that the living church is the body of Christ—for the Scripture says, "God created man male and female";[42] the male is Christ, the female the church. You also surely know that the books and the apostles teach that the church has not only existed in the present but also exists from the beginning. For it was spiritual, as was also our Jesus, and was made known at the end of days in order to save us. The church, being spiritual, was made known in the flesh of Christ, signifying to us that if any one of us shall preserve it in the flesh and not corrupt it, he shall receive it in the Holy Spirit. For this flesh is the type of the spirit; no one, therefore, having corrupted the type will receive afterward the antitype. Therefore he says, "Preserve the flesh, that you may become partakers of the spirit." If we say that the flesh is the church and the spirit Christ, then it follows that he who shall offer outrage to the flesh is guilty of outrage on the church. Such a person, therefore, will not partake of the spirit, which is Christ. Such is the life and immortality which this flesh may afterward receive, the Holy Spirit cleaving to it. No one can either express or utter what things the Lord has prepared for his elect. 2 Clement 14.1-4.[43]

The First Foundations of the Church. Origen: For you must please not think that she is called the bride of Christ or the church only from the time when the Savior came in the flesh. She is so called this from the beginning of the human race and from the very foundation of the world—indeed, if I may look for the origin of this high mystery under Paul's guidance—even before the foundation of the world. For this is what he says: . . . "as he chose us in [Christ] before the foundation of the world, that we should be holy and blameless before him. He destined us in love to be his sons through Jesus Christ, according to the purpose of his will."[44] And in the Psalms too it is written: "Remember your congregation, O Lord, which you have gathered from the beginning."[45] And indeed the first foundations of the congregation of the church were laid at the beginning. And for this reason the apostle says that the church is built on the foundation not of the apostles only but also of the prophets. And among the prophets Adam too is reckoned, who prophesied the great mystery in Christ and in the church. . . . For how could he have loved it, if it did not exist? Undoubtedly he loved it who did exist; it existed in all the saints who have been since time began. So, loving it, he came to it. . . . They themselves were

---

[39]*WSA* 3 18:330. [40]*WSA* 3 20:117. [41]Jer 7:11; Mt 21:13. [42]Gen 1:27. [43]ANF 7:521*. [44]Eph 1:4-5. [45]Ps 74:2 (73:2 LXX).

the church whom he loved to the intent that he might increase it in multitude and develop it in virtue and translate it through the love of perfectness from earth to heaven. The prophets, then, ministered to it from the beginning; so also did the angels. COMMENTARY ON THE SONG OF SONGS 2.8.[46]

RIGHTEOUS PEOPLE LIVING BEFORE CHRIST BELONGED TO THE CHURCH. JUSTIN MARTYR: We have been taught that Christ is the firstborn of God, and we have declared above that he is the Word of whom every race of people were partakers. And those who lived with the Word are Christians, even though they have been thought atheists. Such are found among the Greeks, as Socrates and Heraclitus, and men like them among the barbarians,[47] Abraham and Hananiah and Azariah and Mishael and Elijah,[48] and many others whose actions and names we now decline to recount because we know it would be tedious. So that even they who lived before Christ, and lived without reason, were wicked and hostile to Christ and killed those who lived reasonably. But he who, through the power of the Word, according to the will of God the Father and Lord of all, was born of a virgin as a man, and was named Jesus, and was crucified, and died, and rose again and ascended into heaven, an intelligent man will be able to comprehend from what has been already so largely said. FIRST APOLOGY 46.[49]

ALL SAINTS BELONG TO CHURCH. AUGUSTINE: Now by *church* you must understand not only those who began to be saints after the Lord's advent and nativity but all who have ever been saints belong to the same church. You can't say that our father Abraham does not belong to us just because he lived before Christ was born of the virgin and we have become Christians such a long time afterward, that is, after Christ's passion; after all, the apostle says that we are the children of Abraham[50] by imitating Abraham's faith. If then we are admitted to the church by imitating him, are we going to exclude the man himself from the church? It is this church that was represented by Rebekah, the wife of Isaac. It is this church that was also to be found in the holy prophets who understood the Old Testament, realizing that its material promises signified something or other spiritual. If it was spiritual, then all spiritual people belong to the younger son, because first comes the material one and afterward the spiritual. SERMON 4.11.[51]

JUSTIFIED BY FAITH. LEO THE GREAT: All the saints who preceded the time of our Savior were justified by this faith and were made the body of Christ by this sacrament, awaiting the universal redemption of the faithful. SERMON 30.7.[52]

THE LAW FORETOLD CHARACTERISTICS OF THE CHURCH. METHODIUS OF OLYMPUS: For the law is indeed the figure and the shadow of an image, that is, of the gospel; but the image, namely the gospel, is the representative of truth itself. For the ancient people and the law foretold to us the characteristics of the church, and the church represents those of the new dispensation that is to come. Thus we, having received Christ, who said, "I am . . . the truth,"[53] know that shadows and figures have ceased, and we hurry on to the truth, proclaiming its glorious images. For now we know "in part," and as it were "through a glass," since that which is perfect has not yet come to us; namely, the kingdom of heaven and the resurrection, coming when "that which is in part shall be done away."[54] For then will all our tabernacles be firmly set up, when again the body shall rise, with bones again joined

---

[46]ACW 26:149-50*. [47]*Barbarians*, here, means non-Greeks and is in no way meant as a pejorative. [48]Justin included these names because they all had denounced idolatry and, in Justin's eyes, were persecuted because of this. [49]ANF 1:178. [50]Gal 3:7. [51]WSA 3 1:191. [52]MFC 4:36. [53]Jn 14:6. [54]1 Cor 13:10.

and compacted with flesh. Then shall we celebrate truly to the Lord a glad festal day, when we shall receive eternal tabernacles, no more to perish or be dissolved into the dust of the tomb. Now, our tabernacle was at first fixed in an immoveable state but was moved by transgression and bent to the earth, God putting an end to sin by means of death, lest man immortal, living a sinner, and sin living in him, should be liable to eternal damnation. Therefore he died, although he had not been created liable to death or corruption, and the soul was separated from the flesh, that sin might perish by death, not being able to live longer in one dead. Thus sin being dead and destroyed, again I shall rise immortal. I praise God who by means of death frees his children from death, and I celebrate lawfully to his honor a festal day, adorning my tabernacle, that is, my flesh, with good works, as did the five virgins with the five lighted lamps. SYMPOSIUM OR THE BANQUET OF THE TEN VIRGINS 9.2.[55]

THE CHURCH EXISTED IN MANY SAINTLY PEOPLE. CAESARIUS OF ARLES: The catholic church was not only preached after the coming of our Lord and Savior, beloved, but from the beginning of the world, it was designated by many figures and rather hidden mysteries. Indeed, in holy Abel the catholic church existed, in Noah, in Abraham, in Isaac, in Jacob, and in the other saintly people before the time of our Lord and Savior. SERMON 139.[56]

THE CHURCH RECEIVES ITS PATTERN OF LIFE FROM CHRIST. ORIGEN: And the fact that the church is the aggregate of many souls and has received the pattern of its life from Christ may lead us to suppose that it has received that pattern not from the actual deity of the Word of God—and this obviously is far above those actions and dispositions in respect of which people ought to be given a pattern—but rather that it was the soul that he assumed and in which was the utmost perfection, that was the pattern displayed to people. It will then be the likeness of the same soul that he here calls "my neighbor," that the church—and this is the aggregate of those many souls that were formerly under Pharaoh's yoke and among his chariots and now are called the company of the Lord's horsemen—ought to bear. COMMENTARY ON THE SONG OF SONGS 2.4.[57]

THE CHURCH LOVED CHRIST. AUGUSTINE: Though Christ is the founder of the heavenly and eternal city, yet it did not believe him to be God because it was founded by him, but rather it is founded by him in virtue of its belief.... Death itself, the most formidable of all, could not prevent an immense multitude of martyrs throughout the world from not merely worshiping but also confessing Christ as God. The city of Christ, which, although as yet a stranger on earth, had countless hosts of citizens, did not make war on its godless persecutors for the sake of temporal security but preferred to win eternal salvation by abstaining from war. They were bound, imprisoned, beaten, tortured, burned, torn in pieces, massacred, and yet they multiplied. It was not given to them to fight for their eternal salvation except by despising their temporal salvation for their Savior's sake. CITY OF GOD 22.6.[58]

THE NATURE OF THE CHURCH IN HISTORY AND IN ETERNITY. AUGUSTINE: Let me recall with you, then, those two hauls of fish that the apostles gathered in at the bidding of the Lord Jesus Christ: one before the passion; the other after the resurrection. In these two catches of fish, therefore, the whole church is represented, both as it is now and as it will be in the resurrection of the dead. For now it has multitudes without number, both good and bad; after the resurrection, however, it will have only the good in a fixed number. Recall,

---

[55]ANF 6:345*. [56]MFC 4:37; CCL 103:571. [57]ACW 26:143. [58]NPNF 1 2:483.

then, that first netting of fish[59] where we see the church such as it is at this time. The Lord Jesus found his disciples fishing when he first called them to follow him. At that time they had taken nothing during the whole night. When he appeared, however, they heard him say: "Lower the nets." And they answered: "Master, throughout the whole night we have taken nothing, but behold, at your word we are lowering the net." At the bidding of the Almighty they lowered the nets. What else could happen except what he had wished? Nevertheless, by that very incident he determined to point out to us something advantageous for us to know. The nets were lowered. At that time the Lord had not yet suffered; he had not yet risen. The nets were lowered; they took so many fish that the two boats were filled and the nets themselves were breaking from the large number of fish. Then he said to them: "Follow me, and I will make you fishers of men."[60] They received from him the nets of the word of God; they cast them into the world as though into a deep sea; they took the great multitude of Christians that we perceive and marvel at. Moreover, the two boats signified the two peoples, the Jews and the Gentiles, the members of the synagogue and of the church, the people marked by circumcision and by uncircumcision. For, of those two ships, as of two walls coming together from different directions, Christ is the cornerstone.[61] But what have we heard? There the ships were sinking because of the great number of fish. Now the same thing is happening. Many Christians who live evil lives are pulling the church down. It is not enough for them to crush it; in addition, they are breaking the nets. For if the nets were not broken schisms would not have taken place. Let us pass, therefore, from that fishing in which we now take part and come to that which we ardently desire and faithfully long for. . . . But now, after the resurrection, hear, perceive, rejoice, hope and understand what is the nature of the church. "Cast the nets to the right side," he said.[62] Only those on the right side are being taken in; let us not fear those who are evil. For you know he said he would separate the sheep from the goats; that he would place the sheep on the right side and the goats on the left; that he would say to those on the left, "Go into everlasting fire,"[63] and to those on the right, "Receive the kingdom."[64] SERMON 248.1-3.[65]

GOD THE FATHER ALWAYS EXERCISED HIS PROVIDENCE. IRENAEUS: For it was not merely for those who believed on him in the time of Tiberius Caesar that Christ came, nor did the Father exercise his providence for those only who are now alive, but for all people altogether who from the beginning, according to their capacity, in their generation have feared and loved God, and practiced justice and piety toward their neighbors and have earnestly desired to see Christ and to hear his voice. Therefore he shall, at his second coming, first rouse from their sleep all persons of this description and shall raise them up, as well as the rest who shall be judged, and give them a place in his kingdom. For it is truly one God who directed the patriarchs toward his dispensations and "has justified the circumcision by faith and the uncircumcision through faith." For as in the first we were prefigured, so, on the other hand, are they represented in us, that is, in the church, and receive the recompense for those things that they accomplished. AGAINST HERESIES 4.22.2.[66]

GOD THE FATHER HAS ENTRUSTED THE SPIRIT OF LIFE. IRENAEUS: But it has . . . been shown that the preaching of the church is everywhere consistent, and continues in an even course and receives testimony from the prophets, the apostles, and all the disciples—as I have proved—through those in

---

[59]Lk 5:4-8. [60]Mt 4:19. [61]See Eph 2:11-22. [62]Jn 21:6. [63]Mt 25:41. [64]Mt 25:34. [65]FC 38:300-302*. [66]ANF 1:494.

the beginning, the middle and the end, and through the entire dispensation of God. It is that well-grounded system that tends to humanity's salvation, namely, our faith. Having been received from the church, we preserve it, and so by the Spirit of God ever renew its youth, as if it were some precious deposit in an excellent vessel that causes the vessel itself containing it to renew its youth also. For this gift of God has been entrusted to the church, as breath was to the first created man for this purpose: that all the members receiving it may be vivified. This means of communion with Christ has been distributed throughout the church by the Holy Spirit—the earnest of incorruption, the means of confirming our faith and the ladder of ascent to God. "For in the church," it is said, "God has set apostles, prophets, teachers,"[67] and all the other means through which the Spirit works. Those are not partakers who do not join themselves to the church but defraud themselves of life through their perverse opinions and infamous behavior. For where the church is, there is the Spirit of God; and where the Spirit of God is, there is the church and every kind of grace. But the Spirit is truth. Those, therefore, who do not partake of him are neither nourished into life from the mother's breasts, nor do they enjoy that crystal-clear fountain that issues from the body of Christ. Instead, they dig for themselves broken cisterns[68] out of earthly trenches and drink putrid water out of the mire, fleeing from the faith of the church lest they be convicted. Those who reject the Spirit may not be instructed. AGAINST HERESIES 3.24.1.[69]

THE CHURCH AS EDEN. IRENAEUS: Those, therefore, who desert the preaching of the church call into question the knowledge of the holy presbyters. They take no consideration of how much greater consequence a religious person is, even in a private station, than a blasphemous and impudent sophist. Now this is what all the heretics are, and those who imagine that they have hit on something more beyond the truth. They follow those things already mentioned, proceeding on their various ways as though they were all in agreement, foolishly, not however always maintaining the same opinions with regard to the same things. They are like blind people led by the blind, and they shall deservedly fall into the ditch of ignorance lying in their path, ever seeking and never finding out the truth. It behooves us, therefore, to avoid their doctrines and to be careful lest we suffer any injury from them. Rather we flee to the church, and are brought up in her bosom and nourished with the Lord's Scriptures. For the church has been planted as a garden (*paradisus*) in this world. Therefore says the Spirit of God, "You may freely eat of every tree of the garden,"[70] that is, "You may eat from every Scripture of the Lord, but you shall not eat with an uplifted mind or touch any heretical discord. For these people do profess that they have themselves the knowledge of good and evil, and they set their own impious minds above the God who made them. They therefore form opinions on what is beyond the limits of understanding. This is also why the apostle says, "Do not be wise beyond what it is fitting to be wise, but be wise prudently,"[71] that we not be cast forth by eating of the supposed knowledge of these people (that knowledge that knows more than it should) from the paradise of life. Into this paradise the Lord has introduced those who obey his call, "summing up in himself all things which are in heaven, and which are on earth,"[72] but the things in heaven are spiritual, while those on earth constitute the dispensation in human nature (*secundum hominem est dispositio*). These things, therefore, he recapitulated in himself: by uniting humankind to the Spirit and causing the Spirit to dwell in people, he is

---

[67]1 Cor 12:28. [68]Jer 2:13. [69]ANF 1:459. [70]Gen 2:16. [71]Rom 12:3. [72]Eph 1:10.

himself made the head of the Spirit and gives the Spirit to be the head of humankind. For through the Spirit we see and hear and speak. AGAINST HERESIES 5.20.2.[73]

CHRIST FOREKNEW WHO WOULD BELIEVE IN HIM. AUGUSTINE: Do you not see that my desire was, without any prejudgment of the hidden counsel of God and of other reasons, to say what might seem sufficient about Christ's foreknowledge, to convince the unbelief of the pagans who had brought forward this question? For what is more true than that Christ foreknew who would believe in him and at what times and places they should believe? But whether by the preaching of Christ to themselves by themselves they were to have faith, or whether they would receive it by God's gift—that is, whether God only foreknew them or also predestinated them—I did not at that time think it necessary to inquire or to discuss. Therefore what I said was, "Christ willed to appear to people at that time and that his doctrine should be preached among them when he knew and where he knew, that there were those who would believe on him." I could have also said it this way: "Christ willed to appear to people at that time and that his gospel should be preached among those whom he knew and where he knew, that there were those who had been elected in himself before the foundation of the world." But since, if it were so said, it would make the reader desirous of asking about those things that now by the warning of Pelagian errors must of necessity be discussed with greater copiousness and care, it seemed to me that what at that time was sufficient should be briefly said, leaving to one side, as I said, the depth of the wisdom and knowledge of God and without prejudging other reasons, concerning which I thought that we might more fittingly argue, not then but at some other time. PREDESTINATION OF THE SAINTS 18.1.[74]

THE BLESSED LAUGHTER OF THE CHURCH REMAINS. CLEMENT OF ALEXANDRIA: Isaac also, delivered from death, laughed, sporting and rejoicing with his spouse, who was the type of the helper of our salvation, the church, to whom the stable name of endurance is given for this reason: because she alone remains to all generations, rejoicing ever, subsisting as she does by the endurance of us believers, who are the members of Christ. The witness of those that have endured to the end and still rejoice on this account—this is the mystic sport. It is the salvation accompanied with decorous solace that brings us aid. The King, then, who is Christ, beholds from above our laughter, and looking through the window, as the Scripture says,[75] views the thanksgiving and the blessing and the rejoicing and the gladness and furthermore the endurance that works together with them and their embrace. Thus he views his church, showing only his face, which before was hidden to the church, which is made perfect by her royal head. CHRIST THE EDUCATOR 1.5.27.[76]

THE RISEN CHRIST IS THE BRIDEGROOM. AUGUSTINE: So there you have the church's bridegroom. Moses was not silent about him, and neither were the prophets; they foretold that Christ would rise from the dead on the third day, that he would suffer and rise again. We were given a picture of the Bridegroom to save us from going astray. But there are some people, people who appear to hold the same faith about the Bridegroom as we do, who, on seeing that we do not stray from him, try to draw us away from the Bridegroom's members. They say to us, "Yes, he in whom you believe is indeed the bridegroom; we too believe in him. But the bride is not the church to which you belong." So who is? "The Donatist party." So you say, but does the Bridegroom back you

---

[73]ANF 1:548*. [74]NPNF 1 5:507*. [75]It is unclear to what Scripture Clement is referring. [76]ANF 2:214-15*; PG 8:281B.

up? You tell us this, but is this what God tells us through Moses? It is because of the witness borne by Moses that I hold fast to the church, for through Moses we have God's promise, "In your seed shall all the nations of the earth be blessed."[77] You tell us that the Donatist party is the bride, but is that what the Spirit of God tells us through the prophets? The church to which I hold is guaranteed by the prophets, for through a prophet it was foretold that "all the ends of the earth will be reminded and will turn to the Lord."[78]

You see, then, that I hold to the witness of the law and the witness of the prophets. Now let us listen also to him who rose from the dead. He showed himself to be the bridegroom, and we hold fast to him. He confirmed it by demonstrations, he provided proofs. Just as Moses had foretold, just as the prophets had foretold, "it was necessary for Christ to suffer and to rise from the dead on the third day."[79] So far, then, we both hold fast to the Bridegroom on the basis of his words, and I think you are even beginning to agree with me in believing in the words of Moses and the prophets. So let us believe also in what he said, he who rose from the dead. EXPOSITIONS OF THE PSALMS 147.18.[80]

THE IDENTITY OF BRIDE AND BRIDEGROOM. AUGUSTINE: Take the next step. The prayer of a believer must be, "O Lord, I already see that Christ is the bridegroom. That much is done. But let no one entice me away from the members of your bride. Do not be the head for me, unless I am among your members. Tell me something about the church, for I am no longer in any doubt about her bridegroom." Listen, then, to what he says about the church. He continues, "And for repentance and forgiveness of sins to be preached in his name."[81] Nothing can be truer than that: "For repentance and forgiveness of sins to be preached in his name." But where? Some say, "Here, look!" or "Look, there!" But what does Christ say? "Do not believe them. False Christs and false prophets will arise. And say, Here he is! There he is!"[82] They do not say now about the Head, "Here he is! There he is!" for everyone knows Christ is in heaven. They say it about the church where Christ is, the church to which he promised, "Lo, I am with you throughout all days, even to the end of the ages."[83] But the Lord insists, "Do not believe them: Anyone 'Here, look!' or 'Look, there!' is pointing to parts. I purchased the whole." Let the gospel tell me this. But, Lord, tell me the same yourself from the gospel, because you are now risen from the dead, so that those who believe Moses and the prophets may believe you as well. Tell me this yourself. I am listening. "It was necessary for Christ to suffer and to rise from the dead on the third day, and for repentance and forgiveness of sins to be preached in his name throughout all nations, beginning from Jerusalem."[84]

So now where do we stand, heretic? When I was reading from Moses, and when I was reading from the prophets, you wanted to put off a decision until you heard from one who was to rise from the dead. Very well: he has risen, and he has spoken. There is no more room for doubt now about the church of Christ and the wife of Christ than there is about the body of Christ, displayed to the eyes of the disciples and felt by their hands. He who rose from the dead manifested both: he showed the head, and he showed the members; he pointed to the bridegroom, and he pointed to the bride. Either join me in believing in both or believe in one only to your own condemnation. What use is it to believe that he rose from the dead, that he rose again in the same body? You believe that he displayed his scars and that, as he had been crucified and buried, so he returned to them alive and proved that it was truly he. Fine: you do well to believe this. But the one

---

[77]Gen 22:18. [78]Ps 22:27 (21:28 LXX). [79]Lk 24:46. [80]*WSA* 3 20:462. [81]Lk 24:47. [82]Mt 24:23-24. [83]Mt 28:20. [84]Lk 24:46-47.

whom you believe is speaking, so you had better listen: "For repentance and forgiveness of sins to be preached in his name." Where? Throughout the whole wide world. If I wanted to make this point, I who am wrestling with heretics, I who am in the thick of the fight with them and am even now in dispute with them about this vital question, I could not put it as effectively against heretics in the present as he put it against those who would arise in the future. What more do you ask? Forgiveness of sins is being preached in Christ's name. Where? "Throughout all nations." Where? "Beginning from Jerusalem." You need to be in communion with this church. Why should we quarrel? This church began from the earthly Jerusalem, so that it might come to rejoice in God in the heavenly Jerusalem. It begins from the earthly city and ends in the heavenly city. In the heavenly Jerusalem will be the whole church that drew the beginning of its faith from the earthly Jerusalem. EXPOSITIONS OF THE PSALMS 147.18.[85]

Images of the Church

BOTH TESTAMENTS ATTEST THE CHURCH. AUGUSTINE: The Old Testament is the promise in figure and symbol; the New Testament is the promise spiritually understood. Thus, while the Jerusalem that was on earth belongs to the Old Testament, it bears the image of the Jerusalem that is in heaven and that belongs to the New Testament. Material circumcision of the flesh belongs to the Old Testament; circumcision of the heart belongs to the New Testament. The people, according to the Old Testament, are liberated from Egypt; the people, according to the New Testament, are liberated from the devil. The Egyptian persecutors and Pharaoh pursue the Jews as they make their exodus from Egypt; the Christian people are pursued by their own sins and by the devil, the high chief of sins. Just as the Egyptians pursue the Jews as far as the sea, so Christians are pursued by their sins as far as baptism. Observe, and see; through the sea the Jews are liberated, in the sea the Egyptians are overwhelmed. Through baptism Christians are liberated and quit of their sins, while their sins are destroyed. Those ones come out after the Red Sea and journey through the desert; so too Christians after baptism are not yet in the promised land but live in hope. SERMON 4.9.[86]

REPRESENTED IN MANY WAYS. AUGUSTINE: One thing can be signified in many ways. That is, the church that is represented by those two children [Esau and Jacob] is also represented by this garment, because one thing can be signified in many ways, though it is none of them in obvious reality and all of them symbolically. A lamb cannot be a lion; a lion cannot be a lamb. But our Lord Jesus Christ could be both lion and lamb—neither lion nor lamb in obvious reality, both lion and lamb symbolically. So children cannot be a garment, and a garment cannot be children. But the church, since it is neither children nor garment in the obvious way, is both children and garment symbolically. SERMON 4.25.[87]

THE GLORY OF THE CHURCH SIGNIFIED. AUGUSTINE: Behold before our eyes the statement that follows: "Be exalted, O God, above the heavens! Let thy glory be over all the earth!"[88] Let one who does not grasp the second part not believe the first part. For what is the significance of "and your glory be over all the earth," except that your church is above all the earth, your lady is above all the earth, your spouse, your beloved, your dove, your bride is above all the earth? She is your glory, as the apostle says: "A man ought not to cover his head, since he is the image and glory of God; but woman is the glory of man."[89] If woman

---

[85]WSA 3 20:462. [86]WSA 3 1:189. [87]WSA 3 1:199*. [88]Ps 57:5. [89]1 Cor 11:7.

is the glory of man, the church is the glory of Christ. Sermon 262.5.⁹⁰

An Ark of Refuge. Tertullian: We will see to it, if, after the type of the ark, there shall be in the church a raven, kite, dog and serpent. At all events, an idolater is not found in the type of the ark: no animal has been fashioned to represent an idolater. Let not that be in the church that was not in the ark. On Idolatry 24.⁹¹

The Dove Brings Peace from Heaven. Tertullian: By the same divine ordinance of spiritual effectiveness the dove who is the Holy Spirit is sent forth from heaven, where the church is, which is the type of the ark, and flies down bringing God's peace to the earth, which is our flesh, as it comes up from the washing after the removal of its ancient sins. On Baptism 8.⁹²

No Salvation Apart from the Ark. Cyprian: Peter also, showing this, set forth that the church is one and that only they who are in the church can be baptized. He said, "In the ark of Noah few, that is, eight souls, were saved by water; in a similar way even baptism shall save you,"⁹³ proving and attesting that the one ark of Noah was a type of the one church. If, then, in that baptism of the world thus expiated and purified, one who was not in the ark of Noah could be saved by water, one who is not in the church, to which alone baptism is granted, can also now be enlivened by baptism. Letter 75.2.⁹⁴

God Is Building the Church. Augustine: So then, brothers and sisters, even now the ark is being built, and those hundred years are these times; this whole stretch of time is signified by the number of years. So if those people deserved to perish, who took no notice of Noah building the ark, what do those deserve who take no notice of the salvation offered while Christ is building the church? . . . Christ, God, man for our sakes, is building the church. He has placed himself as the foundation for this ark; every day timbers immune to decay, faithful men and women who renounce this world, are entering into the structure of the ark. Sermon 361.21.⁹⁵

Ark and Garden. Firmilian of Caesarea: But neither must we pass over what has been necessarily remarked by you, that the church, according to the Song of Songs, is a garden enclosed and a fountain sealed, a paradise with the fruit of apples.⁹⁶ They who have never entered into this garden and have not seen the paradise planted by God the Creator, how shall they be able to afford to another the living water of the saving washing from the fountain that is enclosed within and sealed with a divine seal? And as the ark of Noah was nothing else than the sacrament of the church of Christ, which then, when all without were perishing, kept only those who were within the ark safe, we are clearly instructed to look to the unity of the church. Even as also the apostle Peter laid down, saying, "Thus also shall baptism similarly save you";⁹⁷ showing that as they who were not in the ark with Noah not only were not purged and saved by water but at once perished in that deluge; so now also, whoever are not in the church with Christ will perish outside, unless they are converted by penitence to the only and saving washing of the church. Letter 74.15, to Cyprian.⁹⁸

A Tabernacle Built by Moses. Ephrem the Syrian:
> Moses built a tabernacle
>   in the desert for the Godhead;
> because he dwelled not in their hearts,
>   he shall dwell in the holy of holies.

---

⁹⁰FC 38:391. ⁹¹ANF 3:76. ⁹²THB 19. ⁹³Cf. 1 Pet 3:20-21. ⁹⁴ANF 5:398*. ⁹⁵WSA 3 10:239. ⁹⁶Song 4:12-13. ⁹⁷1 Pet 3:21. ⁹⁸ANF 5:394.

For the Gentiles the church was built,
   a gathering for prayers;
In our souls dwells the Power
   which guides all things.
By the baptism of the Holy Spirit
   we share in the forgiveness of sins,
   and by his power, which has come to dwell
      in the bread,
   he enters and rests in us.
Hymn 48.13-24.[99]

Temple of God. Cyprian: If it is possible for a person born outside the church to become a temple of God, why should it not also be possible for the Holy Spirit to be poured out on that temple? One who, having cast off his sins in baptism, has been sanctified and formed spiritually into a new person, has certainly been made fit for receiving the Holy Spirit. As the apostle says, "All of you who have been baptized in Christ have put on Christ."[100] Letter 74.5.2.[101]

The Church as Spiritual Edifice. Origen: All of us who believe in Christ Jesus are said to be "living stones" according to what Scripture proclaims, saying, "'But you are living stones, having been built a spiritual house in a holy priesthood, so that you may offer spiritual sacrifices acceptable to God through Jesus Christ."[102]

As in those earthly stones, we certainly know it is observed that those stones that are stouter and stronger are cast first into the foundation so that the weight of the total edifice can be committed to them and set upon them. . . . So now, understand that even some of the living stones are in the foundation of this spiritual edifice. But who are those who are placed together in the foundation? "The apostles and the prophets." Indeed, Paul says these things. "You are built," he says, "on the foundation of the apostles and the prophets, with Christ Jesus our Lord himself as the cornerstone."[103]

That you may prepare yourself more quickly, O hearer, for the construction of this edifice, that you may find yourself to be a stone nearer to the foundation, learn that Christ is the foundation of this building that we are now describing. For thus the apostle Paul says, "No one can lay another foundation except that which has been laid, which is Christ Jesus."[104] Blessed therefore are those who build devout and holy structures on so noble a foundation.

But in this edifice of the church, there must also be an altar. From this I think that whoever of you "living stones" are suited for this, and are inclined to devote yourselves to prayers and, day and night, to offer entreaties to God and sacrifice victims of supplications, you yourselves are the ones from which Jesus builds the altar. Homilies on Joshua 9.1.[105]

Except the Lord Build the House. Lactantius: Solomon was never called the son of God, but the son of David. And the house that he built was not firmly established, as the church, which is the true temple of God which does not consist of walls but of the heart and faith of those who believe in him and are called faithful. But that temple of Solomon, inasmuch as it was built by hand, fell by the hand. Lastly, his father . . . prophesied in this manner respecting the works of his son: "Unless the Lord builds the house, those who build it labor in vain; unless the Lord watches over the city, the watchman stays awake in vain."[106] Divine Institutes 4.13.[107]

Approaching the Shrine of the Temple. Lactantius: It is evident that all the prophets declared concerning Christ . . . that, being born with a body of the race of David, he should build an eternal temple in honor of God. This temple is called the church and as-

---

[99]SCK 79. [100]Gal 3:27. [101]ACW 47:73. [102]1 Pet 2:5. [103]Eph 2:20. [104]1 Cor 3:11. [105]FC 105:96-97. [106]Ps 127:1 (126:1 LXX). [107]ANF 7:113.

sembles all nations to the true worship of God. This is the faithful house, this is the everlasting temple; and if anyone has not sacrificed in this, he will not have the reward of immortality. And since Christ was the builder of this great and eternal temple, he must also have an everlasting priesthood in it. And there can be no approach to the shrine of the temple, and to the sight of God, except through him who built the temple. DIVINE INSTITUTES 4.14.[108]

VARIOUS STONES, DIFFERING FUNCTIONS. CHRYSOSTOM: The church is nothing else than a house built of the souls of us human beings. Now this house is not of equal honor throughout, but of the stones that contribute to it, some are bright and shining, while others are smaller and more dull than they and yet superior again to others. There we may see many who are in the place of gold also, the gold that adorns the ceiling. Others again we may see who give the beauty and gracefulness produced by statues. Many we may see standing like pillars. For he is accustomed to call people also "pillars"[109] not only on account of their strength but also on account of their beauty, adding as they do much grace and having their heads overlaid with gold. We may see a multitude, forming generally the wide middle space and the whole extent of the circumference; for the body at large occupies the place of those stones of which the outer walls are built. Or rather we must go on to a more splendid picture yet. This church, of which I speak, is not built of these stones, such as we see around us, but of gold and silver and of precious stones, and there is abundance of gold dispersed everywhere throughout it. HOMILIES ON EPHESIANS 10.[110]

BUILT WITH DIFFERENT STONES. HERMAS: She said to me: "Look, do you not see in front of you a large tower being built on water with shiny square stones?" The tower was being built in a square by the six young men who had come with her. But about ten thousand other men were carrying stones, some from the depth of the sea, some from land, which they were delivering to the six young men who were taking and building with them. All the stones that were dragged from the depths they placed in the building, for they were shaped to fit right into joint with the other stones, so they adhered to one another so well that the joints did not show. The building of the tower seemed to be of one stone. Of the other stones brought from dry ground, some they threw away and some they put in the building. Still others they broke up and threw away far from the tower. But there were many other stones lying around the tower that they did not use for the building. Some were scaly, others had cracks, others were broken off, others were white and round and did not fit into the building. I saw other stones cast far away from the tower that fell on the road and did not stay there but rolled off onto rough ground. Others were falling into fire and burning up; others were falling near water and could not roll into the water even though they wished to keep rolling into the water. SHEPHERD, VISION 3.2.4-9.[111]

THE CHURCH AS A TOWER. HERMAS: "And the tower," I asked, "what does it mean?" "This tower," he replied, "is the church." "And these virgins, who are they?" "They are holy spirits, and men cannot otherwise be found in the kingdom of God unless these have put their clothing on them: for if you receive the name only and do not receive from them the clothing, they are of no advantage to you. For these virgins are the powers of the Son of God. If you bear his name but possess not his power, it will be in vain that you bear his name. Those stones," he continued, "which you saw rejected bore his name but did not put on the clothing of the virgins." "Of what nature is their clothing, sir?" I asked. "Their very names," he

---

[108]ANF 7:113. [109]Gal 2:9. [110]NPNF 1 13:101. [111]*SHC* 60-61.

said, "are their clothing. Everyone who bears the name of the Son of God ought to bear the names also of these; for the Son himself bears the names of these virgins. As many stones," he continued, "as you saw [come into the building of the tower through the hands] of these virgins, and remaining, have been clothed with their strength. For this reason you see that the tower became of one stone with the rock. So also they who have believed on the Lord through his Son and are clothed with these spirits shall become one spirit, one body, and the color of their garments shall be one. And the dwelling of such as bear the names of the virgins is in the tower." "Those stones, sir, that were rejected," I inquired, "on what account were they rejected? for they passed through the gate and were placed by the hands of the virgins in the building of the tower." "Since you take an interest in everything," he replied, "and examine minutely, hear about the stones that were rejected. These all," he said, "received the name of God, and they received also the strength of these virgins. Having received, then, these spirits, they were made strong and were with the servants of God; and theirs was one spirit and one body and one clothing. For they were of the same mind and wrought righteousness. After a certain time, however, they were persuaded by the women whom you saw clothed in black, and having their shoulders exposed and their hair disheveled, and beautiful in appearance. Having seen these women, they desired to have them, and clothed themselves with their strength and put off the strength of the virgins. These, accordingly, were rejected from the house of God and were given over to these women. But they who were not deceived by the beauty of these women remained in the house of God. You have," he said, "the explanation of those who were rejected." SHEPHERD, SIMILITUDE 9.13.[112]

BAPTISM AND THE UNITY OF THE CHURCH. HERMAS: "I understand, sir," I replied. "Now, sir," I continued, "explain to me, with respect to the mountains, why their forms are various and diverse." "Listen," he said, "these mountains are the twelve tribes, which inhabit the whole world.[113] The Son of God, accordingly, was preached to them by the apostles." "But why are the mountains of various kinds, some having one form and others another? Explain that to me, sir." "Listen," he answered, "these twelve tribes that inhabit the whole world are twelve nations. And they vary in prudence and understanding. As numerous, then, as are the varieties of the mountains that you saw are also the diversities of mind and understanding among these nations. And I will explain to you the actions of each one." "First, sir," I said, "explain this: why, when the mountains are so diverse, their stones, when placed in the building, became one color, shining like those also that had ascended out of the pit." "Because," he said, "all the nations that dwell under heaven were called by hearing and believing on the name of the Son of God. Having, therefore, received the seal, they had one understanding and one mind; and their faith became one and their love one, and with the name they bore also the spirits of the virgins. On this account the building of the tower became of one color, bright as the sun. But after they had entered into the same place and became one body, certain of these defiled themselves, and were expelled from the race of the righteous and became again what they were before, or rather worse." SHEPHERD, SIMILITUDE 9.17.[114]

FOUNDED ON THE ROCK. VICTORINUS OF PETOVIUM: Christ is the Rock by which and on which the church is founded. And thus it is overcome by no traces of maddened people. Therefore the heretics are not to be heard who assure themselves that there is to be an earthly reign of a thousand years; who think, that is to say, on the same wavelength with

---

[112]ANF 2:48. [113]Rev 7:4. [114]ANF 2:49-50.

the heretic Cerinthus. For the kingdom of Christ is now eternal in the saints, although the glory of the saints shall be made known after the resurrection. COMMENTARY ON THE APOCALYPSE 16.[115]

THE FOUNTAIN OF TRUTH. LACTANTIUS: Therefore it is the catholic church alone that retains true worship. This is the fountain of truth, this is the abode of the faith, this is the temple of God into which if anyone shall not enter, or from which if any shall go out, he is estranged from the hope of life and eternal salvation. DIVINE INSTITUTES 4.30.[116]

THE HOUSE OF GOD. DIDYMUS THE BLIND: Now, the Lord's ways are his virtues practiced in keeping with the observance of his commandments, of which the holy one says to God, "Make me to know your ways, O Lord; teach me your paths."[117] The one who walks and treads a well-worn path in them will gain divine rewards, receiving from the Lord the role of judging his house and guarding his divine halls. The house in this text is to be understood not as a place or a building but as the assembly of those occupying it, as the apostle suggests in saying, "Christ over his house as a son, we being his house";[118] and to Timothy he writes, "If I am delayed, you may know how one ought to behave in the household of God, which is the church of the living God, the pillar and bulwark of the truth."[119] Now, this house is judged by Jesus, who has appointed in the church "apostles, prophets, shepherds, teachers, for perfecting the saints"[120]—not casually but with careful judgment and discernment, for one person to be appointed in the role of an apostle, another in the place of a prophet, while others are for pastoring Christ's flock and developing the divine teaching for those with a holy disposition for learning. Resembling these people is what occurs in the Psalms: "God has taken his place in the divine council; in the midst of the gods he holds judgment."[121] COMMENTARY ON ZECHARIAH 3.[122]

LOST SHEEP RETURNED. AUGUSTINE: Now, however, the true shepherd has come looking for you. You have been lovingly hoisted onto his shoulders and brought back to the sheepfold, that is, to the house of God, which is the church, where Christ is your shepherd and the sheep stay together in one flock. SERMON 366.1.[123]

THE FIELD OF GOD. AUGUSTINE: He smelled his clothes and said, "Behold, the smell of my son is as the smell of an abundant field, which the Lord has blessed."[124] This field is the church. Let's prove that the church is a field. Listen to the apostle telling the faithful: "You are God's field, God's building."[125] Not only is the church a field, but also God is the tiller of the field. Listen to the Lord: "I am the vine, you the twigs, and my Father is the vinedresser."[126] Toiling in this field as a laborer and hoping for an eternal reward, the apostle claims no credit for himself, except a laborer's due. "I planted," he says, "Apollos watered, but God gave the growth. So neither he who plants nor he who waters is anything, but only God who gives the growth."[127] Notice how he safeguards humility to make sure of belonging to Jacob, to that field that is the church, and of not losing the robe whose smell was as the smell of an abundant field or passing over to the pride of Esau, materialistic in thought and abounding in arrogance. SERMON 4.26.[128]

THE CHURCH AS VINEYARD. GREGORY THE GREAT: In the reading of the holy Gospel much elucidation is required that I wish, if I may, to deal with summarily lest I burden you with unduly long and prolix exposition. The kingdom of heaven is said to resemble a prop-

---

[115]ANF 7:360. [116]ANF 7:133. [117]Ps 25:4. [118]Heb 3:6. [119]1 Tim 3:15. [120]Eph 4:11; 1 Tim 3:15; Heb 3:6. [121]Ps 82:1. [122]FC 111:74*. [123]WSA 3 10:289. [124]Gen 27:27. [125]1 Cor 3:9. [126]Jn 15:1, 5. [127]1 Cor 3:6-7. [128]WSA 3 1:199.

erty owner who brought hired workers to tend his vineyard. Who more closely resembles this vineyard owner than the Creator, who rules his creatures and possesses his elect in this world as a master does his slaves in his household, that is, the universal church, which from Abel the just to the last chosen one who will be born at the end of the world? The church produces as many saints as the vineyard shoots. The owner of the vineyard brings workers to cultivate it at dawn and at the third, sixth, ninth and eleventh hours, because from the beginning of the world to the end he does not cease to assemble preachers for the instruction of the people, his faithful. For the dawn of the world was from Adam to Noah, the third hour from Noah to Abraham, the sixth hour from Abraham to Moses, the ninth hour from Moses to the coming of the Lord, the eleventh hour from the coming of the Lord to the end of the world. HOMILIES ON THE GOSPELS 19.[129]

A RESPLENDENT GARMENT. AMBROSE: Accordingly, Jacob received his brother's clothing[130] because he excelled his brother in wisdom. . . . Rebekah presented this clothing as a symbol of the church. She gave to the younger son the clothing of the Old Testament, the prophetic and priestly clothing, the royal Davidic clothing, the clothing of Kings Solomon, Hezekiah and Josiah, and she gave it too to the Christian people, who would know how to use the garment they had received, since the Jewish people kept it without using it and did not know its proper adornments. This clothing was lying in a shadow, cast off and forgotten. It was disfigured by a deep haze of impiety and could not be unfolded further in their narrow hearts. The Christian people put it on, and it became resplendent. They made it shine with the brightness of their faith and the light of their good works. Isaac recognized the familiar fragrance that attached to his people; he recognized the clothing of the Old Testament, but he no longer recognized the voice of the people of old. Accordingly he knew that it had been changed. Even today the same clothing remains, but the confession of a people of greater devotion resounds harmoniously; Isaac was right to say, "The voice is Jacob's voice, but the hands are the hands of Esau."[131] JACOB AND THE HAPPY LIFE 2.2.9.[132]

THE CITY OF GOD. ORIGEN: For if "the city of the Lord" is understood to be the church of the living God, the teachers of the church cast out and kill those "who work iniquity"—the opposing demons and antagonistic powers that drive humans to sin—by teaching, by building up, and by unlocking mysteries and secrets from the sorts of places in the divine letters in which we are now. Or if we understand "the city of the Lord" to be the soul of each of us that is built by the Lord from "living stones,"[133] that is, from various and diverse virtues, anyone holy and diligent also casts out sinners from that city, that is, he destroys in the morning the most wicked thoughts and distorted desires. HOMILIES ON JOSHUA 8.7.[134]

THE CHURCH IS A MYSTERY. CHRYSOSTOM: Here he speaks of the dispensation in our behalf. Do not tell me of the bells or of the holy of holies or of the high priest. The church is the pillar of the world. Consider this mystery, and you will be awestruck. For it is indeed "a great mystery" and a "mystery of godliness,"[135] and it is "undoubtedly great" because it is beyond question. Since in his direction to the priests he had stipulated nothing like the regulations in Leviticus, he refers the whole matter to a higher being, saying, "God was manifest in the flesh." The Creator appeared incarnate. He was "justified in the Spirit." As it was written, "Wisdom is justified by her deeds,"[136] or because he practiced no guile, as the prophet says, "He had

---

[129]MFC 4:36. [130]See Gen 27:15. [131]Gen 27:22. [132]FC 65:150-51. [133]1 Pet 2:5. [134]FC 105:93. [135]Cf. 1 Tim 3:16. The Greek in 1 Tim 3:16 for "piety" is *eusebeia* and may also be translated as "godliness" or "religion." [136]Mt 11:19.

done no violence, and there was no deceit in his mouth,"[137] he was "seen of angels." Angels together with us saw the Son of God, not having seen him before. Great, truly great, was this mystery. He calls the dispensation on our behalf a mystery, and well may it be called so, since it is not made known to everyone. Indeed, it was not made known to the angels, for how could it, since "it was made known by the church"?[138] Therefore he says, "Undoubtedly, great is the mystery of piety." Great indeed it was. For God became man, and man became God. HOMILY 11, ON 1 TIMOTHY.[139]

MANY IMAGES FOR THE CHURCH. PACIAN OF BARCELONA: You indeed correctly state that the church is a people born again of the water and the Holy Spirit, free from denial of the name of Christ; the temple and the house of God; "the pillar and bulwark of the truth";[140] a holy virgin with the purest feelings; the spouse of Christ "from his bones and flesh";[141] "without spot or wrinkle";[142] observing the laws of the Gospels in their entirety. Who among us denies this? But we add moreover the church is "the queen in clothing embroidered with gold adorned with diverse colors";[143] "a fruitful vine on the walls of the house of the Lord";[144] the mother of "maidens without number";[145] "the one beautiful and perfect dove, the chosen of her mother";[146] the very mother of all, "built on the foundations of the apostles and prophets, Christ Jesus himself being the cornerstone";[147] and "a great house" made sumptuous with a diversity of every kind of vessel.[148] LETTER 3.2.[149]

THE QUEEN OF SHEBA. EPHREM THE SYRIAN: "The queen of the South will arise at the judgment with this generation and condemn it."[150] For she is a type of the church. For she came to Solomon; so has the church come to our Lord. And as she condemns it, so does the church also. For if she, who desired to see wisdom that has passed away and a king who has perished, judges the synagogue, how much more the church, which desires to see the King who does not pass away and the wisdom which cannot err? For "if we suffer with him, . . . we may also be glorified with him."[151] EPHREM'S COMMENTARY ON TATIAN'S DIATESSARON 11.4.[152]

MARY MAGDALENE A TYPE OF THE CHURCH. ATTRIBUTED TO EPHREM THE SYRIAN:

He drew Mary Magdalene
  to come and see his resurrection.
And why was it first to a woman
  that he showed his resurrection, and
    not to men?
Here he showed us a mystery
  concerning his church and his mother.
At the beginning of his coming to earth
  a virgin was first to receive him,
and at his raising up from the grave
  to a woman he showed his resurrection.
In his beginning and in his fulfillment
  the name of his mother cries out and is
    present.
Mary received him by conception
  and saw an angel before her;
and Mary received him in life
  and saw angels at his grave.
Again, Mary is like the church,
  the Virgin, who has borne the firstfruits
    by the gospel.
In the place of the church, Mary saw him.
  Blessed be he who gladdened the church
    and Mary!
Let us call the church itself "Mary,"
  for it befits her to have two names.
For to Simon, the foundation,
  Mary was first to run,
and like the church, brought him the good
    news
  and told him what she had seen

---

[137]Is 53:9. [138]Eph 3:10. [139]MFC 4:37*; cf. NPNF 1 13:442. [140]1 Tim 3:15. [141]Eph 5:30. [142]Eph 5:27. [143]Ps 45:12. [144]Ps 128:3. [145]Song 6:8. [146]Song 6:9. [147]2 Tim 2:20. [148]Eph 2:20. [149]FC 99:40. [150]Mt 12:42. [151]Rom 8:17. [152]SCK 137.

that our Lord had risen and was raised
up.
Fittingly did she come to Simon
and bring him the good news that the
Son was risen,
For he was the rock and foundation
of the church of the Gentiles, the
elect.
MEMRE OF HOLY WEEK.[153]

The Church as the Body of Christ

THE BODY OF CHRIST. CLEMENT OF ALEXANDRIA: Directly in point is the instance of the apostle, who says, writing to the Corinthians, "For I betrothed you to Christ to present you as a pure bride to her one husband,"[154] whether as children or saints, but to the Lord alone. And writing to the Ephesians, he has unfolded in the clearest manner the point in question, speaking to the following effect: "Till we all attain to the unity of the faith, and of the knowledge of God, to a perfect man, to the measure of the stature of the fullness of Christ: that we be no longer children, tossed to and fro by every wind of doctrine, by the craft of men, by their cunning in stratagems of deceit; but, speaking the truth in love, may grow up to him in all things"[155]—he says these things in order to edify the body of Christ, who is the head and man, the only one perfect in righteousness. And we who are children guarding against the blasts of heresies that fill us with hot air and not putting our trust in fathers who teach us otherwise—we are then made perfect when we are the church, having received Christ the head. CHRIST THE EDUCATOR 1.5.[156]

PRAISING THE EDUCATOR. CLEMENT OF ALEXANDRIA: Belonging to the church is union with Christ. When the Educator brought us over into his church, he united us to himself as the teaching and all-encompassing Word. It is only right, then, that, having gotten to this point, we should offer to the Lord the reward of due thanksgiving—praise suitable to his fair instruction. CHRIST THE EDUCATOR 3.12.[157]

THE CHURCH AS BODY. ORIGEN: We say that the holy Scriptures declare the body of Christ, animated by the Son of God, to be the whole church of God. The members of this body—considered as a whole—consist of those who are believers. Now a soul enlivens and animates the body, which of itself has no natural power of motion like a living being. In the same way, the Word arouses and moves the whole body, the church, to appropriate action. The Word awakens, moreover, each individual member belonging to the church, so that they do nothing apart from the Word. AGAINST CELSUS 6.48.[158]

THE CEDAR BEAMS AND RAFTERS OF THE HOUSE OF GOD. ORIGEN: It is plain, however, that Christ is describing the church, which is a spiritual house and the house of God, even as Paul teaches, saying, "But if I am delayed, you may know how one ought to behave in the household of God, which is the church of the living God, the pillar and bulwark of the truth."[159] So, if the church is the house of God, then—because all things that the Father has are the Son's—it follows that the church is the house of the Son of God.

There is, however, frequent mention of "churches" in the plural. This is the case, for instance, in the passage that says, "We recognize no other practice, nor do the churches of God."[160] And again, Paul writes to the churches of Galatia, and John to the seven churches. The church or the churches, then, are the houses of the Bridegroom and the bride, the houses of the soul and the Word. There are beams of cedar in them. We read of

---

[153]SCK 147. [154]2 Cor 11:2. [155]Eph 4:13-15. [156]ANF 2:213. [157]ANF 2:295**. [158]ANF 4:595**. [159]1 Tim 3:15. [160]1 Cor 11:16.

some cedars of God on which the vine that was brought out of Egypt is said to have spread out its boughs and branches. This is what it says in the Psalms: "The shadow of it covered the hills and the branches thereof the cedars of God."[161]

Obviously, then, there are in the church some things that are called cedars of God. So, when the Bridegroom says, "the beams of our houses are cedars," we must understand the cedars of God to be those who protect the church. Among them there are some who are stronger ones that are called rafters. And I think that those who faithfully discharge the office of a bishop in the church may appropriately be called the rafters, by which the whole building is sustained and protected, both from the rain and from the heat of the sun. And I think that, in the next place after these, priests are called beams. Moreover, the rafters are said to be a cypress. This tree possesses a greater strength and sweetness of smell, thus denoting a bishop as being at once sound in good works and fragrant with the grace of teaching. And in the same way the beams are said to be a cedar, to show that priests ought to be full of the virtue of incorruption and the fragrance of the knowledge of Christ. COMMENTARY ON THE SONG OF SONGS 3.3.[162]

MEMBERS OF THE BRIDE. ORIGEN: As for her speaking of "our bed," in the sense of the place of her body that she shares with the Bridegroom, you must understand this in the light of the figure that Paul also uses when he says that our bodies "are members of Christ."[163] For when he says "our bodies," he shows that these bodies are the body of the bride, but when he mentions the "members of Christ," he indicates that these same bodies are also the body of the Bridegroom. If, then, these bodies are shady, as we said just now, in the sense that they are full of good works and leafy with the abundance of spiritual perception, then we can truly say of them that "the sun shall not smite you by day, nor the moon by night."[164] . . . Think, moreover, whether we may not also call the body that Jesus took a bed that is shared by himself and the bride. Through it the church has been allied to Christ and has been enabled to become a partaker in the Word of God. COMMENTARY ON THE SONG OF SONGS 3.2.[165]

THE CHURCH IS CHRIST. TERTULLIAN: Even in a company of two the church exists.[166] The vitality of the church is Christ. When, then, you cast yourself at the brothers' knees, you are handling Christ, you are entreating Christ. In a similar way, when they shed tears over you, it is Christ who suffers, Christ who prays to the Father for mercy. What a child asks is ever easily obtained. Grand indeed is the reward of modesty that the concealment of our fault promises us! Even if we hide it somewhat from human knowledge, shall we equally conceal it from God? ON REPENTANCE 10.[167]

WE ARE MEMBERS OF THE BODY OF CHRIST. METHODIUS OF OLYMPUS: You seem to me, O Theophila, to excel in action and in speech over everyone else and to be second to none in wisdom. For there is no one who will find fault with what you're saying, however contentious and contradictory that person might be. Yet, while everything else seems rightly spoken, one thing, my friend, distresses and troubles me, considering that that wise and most spiritual man—I mean Paul—would not vainly refer to Christ and the church the union of the first man and woman if the Scripture meant nothing higher than what is conveyed by the mere words and the historical sense. For if we are to take the Scripture as a bare representation referring exhaustively to the union of man and woman, why should the apostle—calling these things to remembrance and guiding us into the way of the Spirit, as

---

[161]Ps 80:10 (79:11 LXX). [162]ACW 26:175-76*. [163]1 Cor 6:15. [164]Ps 121:6. [165]ACW 26:173-74. [166]See Mt 18:20. [167]ANF 3:664*.

I opine—allegorize the history of Adam and Eve as having a reference to Christ and the church? For the passage in Genesis reads thus: "Then the man said, 'This at last is bone of my bones and flesh of my flesh: she shall be called Woman, because she was taken out of Man.' Therefore a man leaves his father and his mother and cleaves to his wife: and they become one flesh.'"[168] But the apostle, when considering this passage, by no means, as I said, intends to take it according to its mere natural sense, as referring to the union of man and woman, as you do. For you, explaining the passage in too natural a sense, laid down that the Spirit is speaking only of conception and births, that the bone taken from the bones was made into another person and that living creatures coming together swell like trees at the time of conception. But he, more spiritually referring the passage to Christ, thus teaches: "He who loves his wife loves himself. For no man ever hates his own flesh, but nourishes and cherishes it, as Christ does the church, because we are members of his body. 'For this reason a man shall leave his father and mother and be joined to his wife, and the two shall become one.' This is a great mystery, and I take it to mean Christ and the church."[169] SYMPOSIUM OR THE BANQUET OF THE TEN VIRGINS 3.1.[170]

THE BODY IS ONE. CHRYSOSTOM: And how is it possible that they should be one? When throwing out the difference of the members, you must consider the body. For the foot is the same thing that the eye is in regard to its being a member and constituent part of the body. For there is no difference in this respect. Nor can you say that one of the members makes a body of itself but another does not. For they are all equal in this, for the very reason that they are all one body. But having said this and having shown it clearly from the common judgment of all, he added, "so it is with Christ."[171] And when he might have said, "so also is the church," for this was the natural consequent, he does not say it but instead of it places the name of Christ, carrying the discourse up on high and appealing more and more to the hearer's reverence. But his meaning is this: "So also is the body of Christ, which is the church." For as the body and the head are one, so he said that the church and Christ are one. Therefore he also spoke of Christ instead of the church, giving that very name to his body. Just as he said, "Your body is one thing though it be composed of many, so also in the church we all are one. For though the church be composed of many members, yet these many form one body."[172] HOMILIES ON FIRST CORINTHIANS 30.1.[173]

EVERY MEMBER NECESSARY. THEODORET OF CYR: Paul is pointing out that just as the body has many members, some of which are more important than others, so it is with the church also. But every member is necessary and useful. COMMENTARY ON THE FIRST EPISTLE TO THE CORINTHIANS 12.12.[174]

EYES, HANDS AND FEET NEED EACH OTHER. JEROME: "If your hand or your foot is an occasion of sin to you."[175] Since he here is speaking to the apostles, and on them he has established the church, in whatever he says to them he is saying to the church, for it has only one body but many members. The apostle expresses this same concept in his letter to the Corinthians where he treats of spiritual gifts:[176] there are prophets, teachers, priests, miracle workers and those possessing other powers. It is there that he says, "Can the eye say to the hand, 'I do not need your help'; nor again the hand to the feet, 'I have no need of you'?"[177] He says this by way of example, but the passage is much too long to reproduce. The point he makes, however, is that the one body

---

[168]Gen 2:23-24. [169]Eph 5:28-32. [170]ANF 6:316-17*. [171]1 Cor 12:12. [172]1 Cor 12:12. [173]NPNF 1 12:176*. [174]PG 82:326. [175]Mt 18:8. [176]See 1 Cor 12. [177]1 Cor 12:21.

of the church is formed from many members. The church has real eyes: its teachers and leaders see in sacred Scripture the mysteries of God.... It also has hands, practical people who, of course, are not eyes but hands. Do they plumb the mysteries of sacred Scripture? No, but they are powerful in works. The church has feet: those who make official journeys of all kinds. The foot runs that the hand may find the work it needs to do. The eye does not scorn the hand, nor do the eye or hand scorn the belly as if is it were idle and unemployed. Often, it happens that the apparently less honorable members are actually the more useful. And so, the apostle also says, "Our less honorable members have more abundant honor."[178] Why do I say all this? Because the church, the body of the Lord, is adorned and formed of many members. If, therefore, it should happen that the eye of the church is a stumbling block to you, the hand a scandal to you, the foot an occasion of sin, it is better for you to be without that faculty and go with the rest of them into the kingdom of heaven; better to have a blind eye and a lame foot than to go into everlasting hellfire. A bishop has wandered from the truth; a priest has fallen into sin; a deacon has transgressed. Do not say that he is greater in rank, but let the eye be plucked out, the hand cut off, the foot amputated, that the rest of the members may be saved. HOMILY 85 ON MATTHEW 18.7-9.[179]

THE COORDINATION OF THE BODY OF CHRIST. PACIAN OF BARCELONA: But come now, proceed with the rest. "The church is the body of Christ."[180] Without doubt, it is the body, not merely a member. It is the body composed of many parts and members, made into one, just as the apostle says: "For the body does not consist of one member but of many."[181] Therefore the church is the full body, solid and spread over the entire world, like a state, I would say, whose parts are all united. Not like you Novatians are, some very small and insolent portion and a mere tumor that has swelled up and separated from the rest of the body. "The church is the temple of God." A truly magnificent temple, "a great house," having assuredly "vessels of gold and silver but also of wood and earthenware, and some for noble use,"[182] many, indeed, excellent ones destined for the manifold functions of various tasks. "The church is a holy virgin with the purest feelings, the spouse of Christ." A virgin, it is true, but also a mother. A spouse, it is clear, but also a wife and a mate, "taken from her husband,"[183] and for that reason, "bone of his bones and flesh of his flesh."[184] For about her, David says, "Your wife will be like a fruitful vine within your house; your children will be like olive shoots around your table."[185] Abundant, therefore, is the progeny of this virgin, and without number are her offspring, by which the whole world is filled, by which the populous colony invariably swarms the encircled hives. Great is the care of that mother for her children, and tender is her affection. The good are honored, the haughty are chastised, the sick are cared for; no one perishes, no one is despised, the young are kept safe under the indulgent protection of the mother. The church is "without spot or wrinkle."[186] LETTER 3.4.1-4.[187]

THE CONJOINED MEMBERS OF CHRIST'S BODY. DIDYMUS THE BLIND: What is thus styled God's house is in another sense Christ's body composed of and furnished with many limbs: its eyes are those who have opted for the contemplative life, as likewise its hands are for action, performing the deeds of virtue, the body's ears being the name for the intelligent listeners, who will individually say, "The Lord's instruction opens my ears." In an appropriate sense "those not wanting in zeal" might be called the feet of Christ's body. It

---

[178]1 Cor 12:23. [179]FC 57:196-97*. [180]Eph 5:23. [181]1 Cor 12:14. [182]2 Tim 2:20. [183]Gen 2:23; Eph 5:30. [184]Gen 2:23. [185]Ps 128:3. [186]Eph 5:27. [187]FC 99:42-43.

follows that judging the house of the Lord is judging the divine body, so that one person is the eye (as mentioned above), another the hand for performing what is good to do and put into practice, and similar comment will be made on the remaining limbs as well. In a way resembling the judgment of God's house he also guards his divine halls, of which the Holy Spirit cries aloud to those eager to live in them, "Adore the Lord in his holy halls."[188] COMMENTARY ON ZECHARIAH 3.[189]

THE MEMBERS RISE WITH CHRIST. THEODORE OF MOPSUESTIA: You are all members of Christ because you have been united to him by being born again of the Spirit. You have the hope that you will rise again, just as he rose. FRAGMENT ON 1 CORINTHIANS 6.15.[190]

THE CHURCH IS NOW A MIXED BODY. AUGUSTINE: There's another point, because the whole Christ (*totus Christus*), as Scripture presents him to us, is both head and body. Just as Christ is the head of the church, so the church is the body of Christ. And it isn't such indeed by itself; it is together with its head that it constitutes the whole Christ. So the church has within it strong members, it has weak ones; it has those who are being fed on solid bread, it has those who still need to be reared on milk. I will add something else, which has to be admitted; in the very companionship of the sacraments, in fellowship of baptism, in the sharing at the altar, the church has just members and it has unjust ones. Now, after all, the body of Christ, which you know about, is the threshing floor; later on it will be the granary. Still, as long as it is the threshing floor, it does not refuse to put up with straw. When the time comes for storing, it will separate the wheat from the straw. SERMON 364.3.[191]

THE BODY, NOT THE FLESH, OF CHRIST. JEROME: Note that the church is never called the flesh but always body of Christ. Whatever lives according to the flesh must necessarily be embodied. That is true. But it is not true that whatever is body is consequently living according to the flesh. COMMENTARY ON THE EPISTLE TO THE EPHESIANS 3.5.22-23.[192]

THE FLESH AND SPIRIT STILL STRUGGLE. AUGUSTINE: But, they say, how is the flesh by a certain likeness compared with the church? What! Does the church lust against Christ? The same apostle said, "The church is subject to Christ."[193] Clearly the church is subject to Christ, because the spirit lusts against the flesh so that on every side the church may be made subject to Christ. But the flesh lusts against the spirit, because the church has not yet received that perfect peace that was promised. This is why the church is made subject to Christ for the pledge of salvation, and the flesh lusts against the spirit from the weakness of sickness. For those to whom he spoke were nothing other than members of the church when he said, "Walk by the Spirit, and do not gratify the desires of the flesh. For the desires of the flesh are against the Spirit, and the desires of the Spirit are against the flesh; for these are opposed to each other; to prevent you from doing what you would."[194]

These things were most assuredly spoken to the church, which if it were not made subject to Christ, the spirit would not be lusting in it against the flesh through continence. This is why they were indeed able not to perfect the lusts of the flesh, but through the flesh lusting against the Spirit they were not able to do the things they wanted to, that is, not even to have the very lusts of the flesh. And finally, why should we not confess that in spiritual people the church is subject to Christ but that carnal people still lust against Christ? Did not they lust against Christ to whom it was said, "Is

---

[188]Is 50:5; Rom 12:11; Ps 29:2. [189]FC 111:74. [190]NTAbh 15:181. [191]WSA 3 10:277. [192]PL 26:530-31. [193]Eph 5:24. [194]See Gal 5:16-17.

Christ divided?"[195] ... Thus the holy church, so long as it has these kinds of members, is not yet without spot or wrinkle. To these are added those other sins also, for which the daily cry of the whole church is, "Forgive us our debts."[196] Nor should we think that spiritual persons are exempt from these either. Not only carnal persons but spiritual persons as well are included, as he who lay on the breast of the Lord and whom our Lord loved before others says, "If we say we have no sin, we deceive ourselves, and the truth is not in us."[197] But in every sin, more in what is greater, less in what is less, there is an act of lust against righteousness. And it is written about Christ: "Whom God made our wisdom, our righteousness and sanctification and redemption."[198] In every sin therefore without doubt there is an act of lust against Christ. But when he who "heals all our sicknesses" leads his church to the promised healing of sickness, then in none of its members will there be any trace of a spot or wrinkle.... We should therefore look forward to the perfect health of our flesh when it will no longer experience any opposition at that time in the church of Christ when we will be safe and secure without any fear. ON CONTINENCE 25.[199]

THE WHOLE BODY OF CHRIST. AUGUSTINE: So Christ is preaching Christ, the body preaching its head and the head looking after its body. And that's why the world hates us, as we have heard from the Lord himself. It wasn't, you see, just to a few apostles that he said this, that the world would hate them and that they ought to "rejoice when people belittled them and uttered every kind of evil against them, because this would make their reward greater in heaven."[200] The Lord wasn't speaking to them alone when he said these things; but he was speaking to his whole body, speaking to all his members. Any who wish to be in his body and be his members mustn't be surprised that the world hates them. SERMON 354.1.[201]

TRANSFORMED INTO THE BODY OF CHRIST. AUGUSTINE: And therefore receive and eat the body of Christ, yes, you that have become members of Christ in the body of Christ; receive and drink the blood of Christ. In order not to be scattered and separated, eat what binds you together; in order not to seem cheap in your own estimation, drink the price that was paid for you. Just as this turns into you when you eat and drink it, so you for your part turn into the body of Christ when you live devout and obedient lives. He himself, you see, as his passion drew near, while he was keeping the Passover with his disciples, took bread and blessed it and said, "This is my body which is for you."[202] Likewise he gave them the cup he had blessed and said, "This is my blood of the covenant, which is poured out for many for the forgiveness of sins."[203] You were able to read or to hear this in the Gospel before, but you were unaware that this Eucharist is the Son. But now, your hearts sprinkled with a pure conscience and your bodies washed with pure water, "approach him and be enlightened, and your faces will not blush for shame."[204] Because if you receive this worthily, which means belonging to the new covenant by which you hope for an eternal inheritance, and if you keep the new commandment to love one another, then you have life in yourselves. You are then, after all, receiving that flesh about which Life itself says, "The bread which I shall give is my flesh for the life of the world," and, "Unless people eat my flesh and drink my blood, they will not have life in themselves."[205] So then, having life in him, you will be in one flesh with him. This sacrament, after all, doesn't present you with the body of Christ in such a way as to divide you from it. This, as the apostle reminds us, was foretold in holy Scripture: "They shall be two in one flesh."[206] "This,"

---

[195]1 Cor 1:13. [196]Mt 6:12. [197]1 Jn 1:8. [198]1 Cor 1:30. [199]NPNF 1 3: 389-90**. [200]Mt 5:11-12. [201]*WSA* 3 10:156. [202]1 Cor 11:24. [203]Mt 26:28. [204]Ps 34:5. [205]Jn 6:51, 53.

he says, "is a great sacrament; but I mean in Christ and in the church."²⁰⁷ And in another place he says about this Eucharist, "We who are many are one body,"²⁰⁸ one loaf. So you are beginning to receive what you have also begun to be, provided you do not receive unworthily; else you would be eating and drinking judgment on yourselves. SERMON 228B.3-4.²⁰⁹

THE CHURCH UNDERGOES WHAT CHRIST'S BODY UNDERWENT. AUGUSTINE: This kind of bodily absence and powerful presence of his among all the Gentiles was also signified in that woman who had touched the hem of his garment, when he wanted to know and said, "Who touched me?" As though absent, he wants to know; as though present, he heals. "The crowds are crushing you," say the disciples, "and you can ask, 'Who touched me?'"²¹⁰ He said, "Who touched me?" as though he were walking free touched by nobody at all, and they point out, "The crowds are crushing you." And it's as though the Lord were saying, "I'm looking for someone who touched me, not for someone who crushed me."

It's the same even now with his body, that is, his church. She is touched by the faith of a few, jostled by the throng of the many. That the church is the body of Christ, you as her children have certainly been taught, and if you will, that is what you are yourselves. The apostle says this in several places: "For his body," he says, "which is the church."²¹¹ And again, "But you are the body of Christ and its members."²¹² So if we are his body, his church undergoes now what his body underwent then in the crowd. It is crushed by crowds; it is touched by a few. Flesh crushes it, faith touches it. So lift up your eyes, I beg you, those of you who have eyes to see with. You certainly have something you can see. Lift up the eyes of faith, touch the outer hem of the garment, that will be enough for your salvation. SERMON 62.5.²¹³

CHRIST AND HIS CHURCH ARE THE WHOLE BODY. AUGUSTINE: What a tremendous honor, my brothers and sisters! In the Lord's words we are to recognize ourselves. Who could still be persecuting Christ, when he was seated in heaven at the right hand of the Father? But while the head was reigning there, the members were still toiling away here. The teacher of the nations,²¹⁴ the blessed apostle Paul, has taught us what we are in relation to Christ: "But you," he says, "are the body of Christ and his members."²¹⁵ So the whole Christ is head and members. Look at our own bodies, grasp the comparison. If you happen to be hurt in a crowd, and someone treads on your foot, the head yells for the foot. And what does it yell? "You're treading on me." "Saul, Saul, why are you persecuting me?"²¹⁶

When Saul, you see, was persecuting the preachers of the gospel, through whom the Lord was being carried throughout the world, Christ's feet were being trampled on by him; it was on them, after all, that Christ was going out to the nations, on them that Christ was running all over the place. The future foot was trampling on Christ's feet. The man who was going to carry the Lord's gospel throughout the whole wide world was trampling on what he himself was going to be. "How beautiful are the feet," as the prophet says, and this very teacher reminds us, "of those who bring news of peace, who bring good news!"²¹⁷ There was also this that we sang in the psalm: "Their voice goes out through all the earth." Do you want to see where Christ has gotten to on those feet? "And their words to the end of the world."²¹⁸ SERMON 299C.2.²¹⁹

THE BODY OF CHRIST PRAYS FOR FORGIVENESS. AUGUSTINE: The whole body of Christ, diffused through the entire world, that is, the whole church, practices penance as that

---

²⁰⁶Gen 2:24. ²⁰⁷Eph 5:31-32. ²⁰⁸1 Cor 10:17. ²⁰⁹WSA 3 6:262. ²¹⁰Lk 8:45; Mk 5:30-31. ²¹¹Col 1:24. ²¹²1 Cor 12:27. ²¹³WSA 3 3:158. ²¹⁴See 2 Tim 1:11. ²¹⁵1 Cor 12:27. ²¹⁶Acts 9:4. ²¹⁷Is 52:7; Rom 10:15. ²¹⁸Ps 19:4. ²¹⁹WSA 3 8:251.

corporate unity that says in the psalm, "To you have I cried from the ends of the earth; when my heart was in anguish." Thus, light begins to dawn on us as to why the Lenten season was inaugurated as the solemnity of this humiliation. For the united church that cries from the ends of the earth when its heart is in anguish cries from those four regions of the earth that even the Scriptures often mention, that is, from the east and west, from the north and the south. Through the entire area the Decalogue of the Law has been promulgated, not merely to be feared in its literal expression but to be fulfilled in the grace of charity. Thus, when four has been multiplied by ten, we see the number forty rounded out. Sermon 210.6.[220]

Believers Are Members of the Body of Christ. Augustine: We heard the apostle, when he was read, rebuking and curbing human lusts and saying, "Do you not know that your bodies are members of Christ? Shall I therefore take the members of Christ and make them members of a prostitute? Never!"[221] So he said our bodies are the members, or parts, of Christ; since Christ is our head in that he became man for our sakes, the head of which it is said, "He is the Savior of our body,"[222] his body, though, is the church. So if our Lord Jesus Christ had only taken on a human soul, only our souls would be his members. But in fact he also took on a body and thus is a real head for us, who consist of soul and body; and therefore our bodies too are his members.

So if any of you were longing so intensely for a little fornication that you were ready to undervalue yourself and in yourself to despise yourself, at least don't despise Christ in yourself; don't say, "I'll do it, I'm nothing; 'all flesh is grass.'"[223] But your body is a member of Christ. Where were you off to? Come back. Over what precipice, so to say, were you so keen to throw yourself? Spare a thought for Christ in yourself, recognize Christ in yourself? "So shall I take the members of Christ, and make them the members of a harlot?" The harlot, you see, is the woman who agrees to commit adultery with you; and perhaps she is a Christian and is also taking the members of Christ and making them the members of an adulterer.

Together you are despising Christ in yourselves and not recognizing your Lord or giving a thought to your price, your true value. What sort of Lord is that, do you think, who makes his slaves into his brothers and sisters? Brothers and sisters, though, wasn't enough; he also had to make them into his members. Has such great worth, such tremendous dignity, really grown so cheap? Because it was bestowed so graciously, is it not to be treated with respect? If it hadn't been bestowed, it would be desired; because it has been bestowed, is it to be despised? Sermon 161.1.[224]

The Holy Spirit Is the Soul of the Church. Augustine: So none of you must say, "I have received the Holy Spirit; why am I not speaking with the tongues of all nations?" If you want to have the Holy Spirit, consider this, my dear brothers and sisters: our spirit, by which every person lives, is called the soul; our spirit, by which every single human being lives, is called the soul. And you can see what the soul does in the body. It quickens all its parts; it sees through the eyes, hears through the ears, smells through the nostrils, speaks with the tongue, works with the hands, walks with the feet. It's present simultaneously to all the body's parts, to make them alive; it gives life to all, their functions to each. The eye doesn't hear, the ear doesn't see, the tongue doesn't see, nor do ear and eye speak. But they're alive all the same; the ear's alive, the tongue's alive; different functions, life in common.

That's what the church of God is like; in

---

[220]FC 38:104. [221]1 Cor 6:15. [222]Eph 5:23. [223]Is 40:6. [224]WSA 3 5:135.

some of the saints it works miracles, in other saints it proclaims the truth, in other saints it preserves virginity, in other saints it preserves married chastity; in some this, in others that. All doing their own thing but living the same life together. In fact, what the soul is to the human body, the Holy Spirit is to the body of Christ, which is the church. The Holy Spirit does in the whole church what the soul does in all the parts of one body. But notice what you should beware of, see what you should notice, notice what you should be afraid of. It can happen in the human body—or rather from the body—that one part is cut off, a hand, a finger, a font; does the soul follow the amputated part? When it was in the body, it was alive, cut off, it loses life. In the same way too Christian men and women are Catholics while they are alive in the body; cut off, they have become heretics, the Spirit doesn't follow the amputated part. So if you wish to be alive with the Holy Spirit, hold on to loving-kindness, love truthfulness, long for oneness, that you may attain to everlastingness. SERMON 267.3.[225]

WHOEVER HAS THE HOLY SPIRIT. AUGUSTINE: So whoever has the Holy Spirit is in the church, which speaks the languages of all people. Whoever is outside this church hasn't got the Holy Spirit. The reason, after all, why the Holy Spirit was prepared to demonstrate his presence in the tongues of all nations was so that those who are included in the unity of the church that speaks all languages might understand that they have the Holy Spirit. One body, says the apostle Paul, "one body and one spirit."[226] Consider our own bodies and their parts. The body consists of many parts, and one spirit quickens all the parts. Look here, by the human spirit, by which I am myself this human being, I bind together all parts of my body; I command the limbs to move, I direct the eyes to see, the ears to hear, the tongue to talk, the hands to work, the feet to walk. The functions of the different parts vary, but the unity of the spirit coordinates them all. Many things are commanded, many things are done; but it's just one who commands and one who is served. What our spirit, that is, our soul, is to the parts or members of our body, that the Holy Spirit is to the members of Christ, to the body of Christ. That's why the apostle, after mentioning one body, in case we should take it as a dead body—"one body," he says.

But I ask you, is this body alive?

It's alive.

With what?

With one spirit. And one spirit.

So consider, brothers and sisters, the case of our own bodies, and grieve for those who cut themselves off from the church. With our parts or members, as long as we're alive, while we're in good health, all the members carry out their functions. If one member is hurt in any way, all the other members sympathize with it. And yet, because it's in the body, while it can feel pain, it can't expire. What, after all, does it mean to expire, but to lose the spirit? But now, if a member is cut off from the body, the spirit doesn't follow, does it? And yet the member can be recognized for what it is; it's a finger, a hand, an arm, an ear. Apart from the body it retains its shape, it doesn't retain life. So too with persons separated from the church. You ask them about the sacrament, you find it; you look for baptism, you find it; you look for the creed, you find it. That's the shape or form; unless you are quickened inwardly by the Spirit, any boasting you do about the outward form is meaningless. SERMON 268.2.[227]

THE HEAD AND BODY TOGETHER. AUGUSTINE: Well now, this is what I have told you frequently, and now tell you once more. (For, as the apostle said, "To keep writing the same things to you is not irksome to me, and is safe for you."[228]) Our Lord Jesus Christ consists of

---

[225]WSA 3 7:276. [226]Eph 4:4. [227]WSA 3 7:278-79.

head and body, as a perfect man. We recognize the head in the man who was born of the Virgin Mary, suffered under Pontius Pilate, was buried, rose again, ascended into heaven and is seated at the Father's right hand, from where we expect him to come again as judge of the living and the dead. He is the head of the church. The church is the body that belongs to this head. By this we do not mean just the church present in this place but the church both here and throughout the whole world; and not the church of our own day alone but that which began with Abel and extends to all who will be born and will believe in Christ to the very end, the whole people of the saints who belong to the one city. That city is the body of Christ, and Christ is its head. There the angels are our fellow citizens; but while we are still toiling along on our pilgrimage, they, at home in the city, look forward to our arrival.

From that city from which we are still exiles, letters have reached us; these letters are the Scriptures, which exhort us to live good lives. But why speak merely of letters? There is more than that; the king himself came down and made himself the way for us on our pilgrimage, so that by walking in him we may not go astray, or faint on the journey, or fall in with robbers or stumble into the traps that are set alongside the path.

We know him thus as the whole Christ, which means Christ in this universal sense, Christ with his church. But he alone was born of the Virgin, and he alone is the church's head, he who is the mediator between God and humankind, Christ Jesus. A mediator he had to be, in order to reconcile through himself those who had gone far away from God; for mediation implies two parties. We had gone far away from God's majesty and offended him by our sin; so God's Son was sent as mediator to destroy by his blood the sins that had estranged us from God. He placed himself in between, to restore us and reconcile us to God, for by turning away from him we had become prisoners of our sins and trespasses. He is our head, he who is God, equal to the Father, the Word through whom all things were made; but though as God he is our creator, he became man to re-create us. He is God to make us, but man to make us anew.

Let us keep him before our eyes as we listen to the psalm. Pay close attention, beloved, for it is the discipline and teaching of our school, and it will empower you to understand not this psalm only but many others, if you hold onto this rule. Sometimes a psalm—and indeed not only a psalm but any prophecy—speaks of Christ in such a way that it clearly refers to the head alone; but sometimes it passes from the head to the body, by which I mean the church, apparently without any change of person. This happens because the head is not separated from the body, so Scripture speaks of them as one sole person. I will give you an example of what I am talking about, dearly beloved. There is a psalm where Christ's passion is described in a manner plain to everyone: "They dug holes in my hands and my feet; they numbered all my bones. They shared out my garments among them, and cast lots for my tunic."[229] Even the Jews are embarrassed when they hear these verses, so very obvious is it that the prophecy refers to the passion of our Lord Jesus Christ. Yet though our Lord Jesus Christ was free from sin, at the opening of that same psalm he says, "O God, my God, why have you forsaken me? The tale of my sins leaves me far from salvation."[230] You can distinguish between what is said in the person of the head and what in the person of the body. The sins belong to us; the suffering undergone for our sake belongs to the head. But in virtue of the passion he endured for us, the sins that belong to us are blotted out. The same principle holds for our present psalm. EXPOSITIONS OF THE PSALMS 90.2.1.[231]

---

[228]Phil 3:1. [229]Ps 22:16-18 (21:17-19 LXX). [230]Ps 22:1 (21:1 LXX). [231]WSA 3 18:330-31.

THE CHURCH WAS BORN FROM THE CROSS.
AUGUSTINE: Now our Lord Jesus Christ sometimes speaks through the prophets in his identity as our head, for he is Christ, our savior. He is seated at the right hand of the Father, but for our sake he was also born of the Virgin and suffered under Pontius Pilate. You know how he suffered: his innocent blood was poured out as our ransom. He redeemed us, guilty prisoners that we were in the devil's clutches, and forgave us our transgressions, using his own blood, our ransom price, to blot out the record of our debt. He is the ruler, the bridegroom and the redeemer of the church, and he is our head. Now, if he is the head, obviously he must have a body. His body is holy church, and she, to whom the apostle says, "You are Christ's body, and his members,"[232] is also his bride. The whole Christ, head and body together, constitute a perfect man. Women are included in this, for woman was formed from man and belongs with him. Of the first marriage it was written, "They will be two in one flesh,"[233] and the apostle interprets this saying in the light of the mystery, for the statement was made about those two original humans only because in them the marriage of Christ and the church was prefigured. This is how the apostle explains it: "They will be two in one flesh. This is a great mystery, but I am referring it to Christ and the church."[234] He tells us elsewhere that Adam foreshadowed Christ: "Adam . . . was a type of the one who was to come."[235] And, as Adam was a type of Christ, so too was the creation of Eve from the sleeping Adam a prefiguration of the creation of the church from the side of the Lord as he slept, for as he suffered and died on the cross and was struck by a lance, the sacraments that formed the church flowed forth from him. By Christ's sleeping we are to understand his passion. This image is used in another psalm, which says in his name, "I rested and fell asleep, and I arose because the Lord will uphold me."[236] As Eve came from the side of the sleeping Adam, so the church was born from the side of the suffering Christ.

As you know, our Lord Jesus Christ speaks through the prophets sometimes with his own voice and at other times with ours, because he makes himself one with us; as Scripture says, "They will be two in one flesh."[237] Indeed, the Lord referred to this himself when, speaking about marriage in the Gospel, he emphasized, "So they are two no longer, but one flesh."[238] One flesh, because Christ took flesh from our mortal stock, but not one Godhead, because he is the creator and we are creatures. Yet because of our union with him, whatever the Lord says in virtue of the fleshly nature he assumed can be taken as said both by the head who has now ascended into heaven and by the members who still struggle along on their earthly pilgrimage. EXPOSITIONS OF THE PSALMS 138.2.[239]

THE CHURCH INCLUDES ALL GENERATIONS.
AUGUSTINE: All of us together are the members of Christ and his body, not only those of us who are in this place but throughout the whole world; and not only those of us who are alive at this time, but what shall I say? From Abel the just right up to the end of the world, as long as people beget and are begotten, any of the just who make the passage through this life, all that now—that is, not in this place but in this life—all that are going to born after us, all constitute the one body of Christ; while they are each individually members of Christ. So if all constitute the body and are each individually members, there is of course a head, of which this is the body. "And he himself," it says, "is the head of the body, the church, the firstborn, himself holding the first place."[240] And because it is also says of him that "he is always the head of every principal-

---
[232]1 Cor 12:27. [233]Gen 2:24. [234]Eph 5:31-32. [235]Rom 5:14. [236]Ps 3:5 (3:6 LXX). [237]Gen 2:24. [238]Mt 19:6. [239]WSA 3 20:256-57. [240]Col 1:18.

ity and power,"[241] this church that is now on its pilgrimage is joined to that heavenly church where we have the angels as fellow citizens, with whom we would be quite shameless in claiming equality after the resurrection of our bodies, unless Truth had promised us this, saying, "They shall be equal to the angels of God,"[242] and there is achieved one church, "the city of the great King."[243] SERMON 341.11.[244]

The Church as Bride of Christ

A GREAT MYSTERY. JEROME: Gregory of Nazianzus, a very eloquent man and outstandingly versed in the Scriptures, used to say while discussing this passage with me:[245] See how great the promise in this passage is! The apostle, interpreting it as an analogy of Christ and the church, does not himself even profess to have expounded it as the dignity of the idea demanded. He is in effect saying, "I know that this analogy is full of ineffable promises. It requires a divine heart in its interpretation. But in the weakness of my understanding I can only say that in the meantime it should be interpreted as Christ in relation to the church. Even all that is said of Adam and Eve is to be interpreted with reference to Christ and church." COMMENTARY ON THE EPISTLE TO THE EPHESIANS 3.5.32.[246]

CHRIST SUMMONS THE BRIDE. TERTULLIAN: He accounts the church as in himself, and concerning it the same Spirit says to him, "You shall clothe yourself with them all, as an ornament upon a bride."[247] This bride Christ also summons to himself by the mouth of Solomon, if indeed you have found this written, "Come, my bride, from Lebanon,"[248] pleasantly introducing the mention of Lebanon, the mountain, which among the Greeks is the word for incense: for it was out of idolatry that he made the church his bride. Now deny, if you can, your utter madness, Marcion: you go so far as to assail the law of your own god. He contracts no marriages nor recognizes them when contracted, refuses baptism except to the celibate or the eunuch, keeping it back until death or divorce. How then can you call his Christ a bridegroom? This title belongs to him who has joined together male and female, not to one who has put them asunder. AGAINST MARCION 4.11.[249]

CHRIST THE TEACHER IS THE BRIDEGROOM. CLEMENT OF ALEXANDRIA: And now, in truth, it is time for me to cease from my instruction and for you to listen to the Teacher. And he, receiving you who have been trained up in excellent discipline, will teach you the oracles. To noble purpose has the church sung, and the Bridegroom also, the only Teacher, the good Counsel, of the good Father, the true Wisdom, the Sanctuary of knowledge. CHRIST THE EDUCATOR 3.12.[250]

CHRIST IS THE SHEPHERD WHO LEADS HIS BRIDE. ORIGEN: It is plain from these words that this Bridegroom is also a shepherd. We had already learned that he is also a king, for the undoubted reason that he rules over people. But he is a shepherd, because he feeds the sheep; he is the Bridegroom, because he has the bride, who is to reign with him, even as it is written: "The queen stood at your right hand in gilded clothing."[251] These are the elements in the drama, as far as the historical sense goes.

Let us now search out the mystical meaning, and, if it is necessary to anticipate somewhat matters that we shall have to deal with later, in order to show what sort of people these companions are, let us remember that it is written that "there are threescore queens" but "only one dove" among them, "only one perfect one" who shares the kingdom. But the others are of

---

[241]Col 2:10. [242]Lk 20:36. [243]Mt 5:35. [244]WSA 3 10:26. [245]Eph 5:31. [246]PL 26:535-36. [247]Is 49:18. [248]Song 4:8. [249]TAM 2:307, 309. [250]ANF 2:294-95. [251]Ps 45:9.

lower rank, those who are called the "fourscore concubines"; yet "the young maidens, who are without number," come after the concubines in point of dignity.[252] Now all these represent different classes of believers in Christ, associated with him in different relationships; so that, for instance, taking another figure, we call the whole church the body of Christ, as the apostle does; but in that body, so he tells us, there are diverse members, some of them eyes, some hands, some even feet, and all them coordinated in the members of this body according to the merit of their several functions and work. COMMENTARY ON THE SONG OF SONGS 2.4.[253]

CHRIST'S BRIDE LISTENS TO THE SHEPHERD'S VOICE. ORIGEN: Christ, to begin with, is recognized by his church by his voice alone. For he first sent his voice in advance through the prophets, and so, although he was not seen, he was heard. And he was heard through the things that they proclaimed about him. The bride, that is, the church that was gathered together from the beginning of time, heard his voice only, until such time as she saw him with her eyes and said, "Behold, here he comes." COMMENTARY ON THE SONG OF SONGS 3.11.[254]

THE BRIDEGROOM IS THE WORD. ORIGEN: The bride of the Word, the soul who abides in his royal house—that is, the church—is taught by the Word of God, who is her Bridegroom, whatever things are stored and hidden within the royal court and the king's chamber. COMMENTARY ON THE SONG OF SONGS 3.13.[255]

CHRIST'S DISCIPLES TEACH HIS BRIDE. ORIGEN: Now we understand the moon and the stars to be analogous to the bride, the church and the disciples, who have their own light or a light acquired from the true sun to illuminate those who have not been able to provide a source of light in themselves. COMMENTARY ON THE GOSPEL OF JOHN 1.25(24).[256]

CHURCH LEADERS MUST TAKE CARE OF CHRIST'S BRIDE. PSEUDO-CLEMENT OF ROME: Wherefore do you, as elders of the church, exercise the spouse of Christ to chastity (by the spouse I mean the body of the church); for if she is apprehended to be chaste by her royal Bridegroom, she shall obtain the greatest honor; and you, as wedding guests, shall receive great commendation. But if she is caught having sinned, she herself indeed shall be cast out; and you shall suffer punishment, if at any time her sin has been through your negligence. EPISTLE TO JAMES 7.[257]

CLEAVING TO CHRIST. FULGENTIUS OF RUSPE: Any soul that cleaves faithfully to Christ is like a wife living faithfully with her husband. Even in chaste wedlock she may grieve the mind of her husband. But she preserves the faith of the marriage bed with chaste purity. Prudently and temperately she orders the husband's household. Even while she falls short meeting his seed she lives chastely and faithfully with him. Though human infirmity often causes her to transgress against him, conjugal chastity makes her cleave with pleasure to her husband. ON THE INCARNATION 41.[258]

THE SPOUSE OF CHRIST CANNOT BE ADULTEROUS. CYPRIAN: The spouse of Christ cannot be adulterous; she is uncorrupted and pure. She knows one home; she guards with chaste modesty the sanctity of one couch. She keeps us for God. She appoints the children whom she has borne for the kingdom. Whoever is separated from the church and is joined to an adulteress is separated from the promises of the church; nor can one who forsakes the church of Christ attain to the rewards of Christ. He is a stranger; he is profane; he is an enemy. He can no longer have God for his Father who has

---

[252]Song 6:8-9. [253]ACW 26:119-20. [254]ACW 26:208. [255]ACW 26:231. [256]ME 141. [257]ANF 8:219. [258]CCL 91:346.

not the church for his mother. If anyone could escape who was outside the ark of Noah, then he also may escape who shall be outside of the church. The Lord warns, saying, "He who is not with me is against me, and he who gathers not with me scatters."[259] One who breaks the peace and the concord of Christ does so in opposition to Christ; one who gathers elsewhere than in the church scatters the church of Christ. The Lord says, "I and the Father are one";[260] and again it is written of the Father, and of the Son and of the Holy Spirit, "And these three are one."[261] And does any one believe that this unity that thus comes from the divine strength and coheres in celestial sacraments can be divided in the church and can be separated by the parting asunder of opposing wills? One who does not hold this unity does not hold God's law, does not hold the faith of the Father and the Son, does not hold life and salvation. ON THE UNITY OF THE CHURCH 6.[262]

THE FAITHFUL MUST BE WITH CHRIST AND HIS CHURCH. CYPRIAN: Now the apostle Paul says, "For this reason a man shall leave father and mother, and they will be two in one flesh. This is a great mystery: but I speak concerning Christ and the church."[263] These are the words of the blessed apostle: with his own holy voice he testifies to the unity between Christ and his church, bound together as they are by indissoluble bonds. How then can a man abide with the bride of Christ and within his church? LETTER 51.1.2.[264]

EVIL DAYS. CYPRIAN: The church of God, the bride of Christ, has fallen on such evil days that she is now to follow the example of heretics! In order to celebrate the heavenly sacraments, light has to borrow moral guidance from darkness; Christians are now to imitate the actions of antichrists. LETTER 74.4.1.[265]

A VIRGIN BRIDE. NOVATIAN: May purity, then—that purity that goes above and beyond the will and that we should will always to possess—be also given to us for the sake of redemption, so that what has been consecrated by Christ cannot be corrupted. If the apostle states that the church is the bride of Christ, I ask you now to reflect just what purity is required of you, when the church herself is given in marriage as a virgin bride. IN PRAISE OF PURITY 2.[266]

THE CHURCH IS UNSPOTTED. CYPRIAN: But if . . . the fear of God is to be found among us, if we persevere in upholding the faith, if we stand watch over the precepts of Christ, if we guard the sanctity of his bride unspotted and undefiled, if there are impressed on our minds and hearts the words of the Lord, who says, "And when the Son of Man comes, do you think he will find faith on earth?"[267] then, as faithful soldiers of God, campaigning for God with faith and wholehearted dedication, let us protect courageously and faithfully the encampment that God has entrusted to our charge. LETTER 74.9.[268]

THE JEALOUS LOVE OF THE BRIDEGROOM. EPHREM THE SYRIAN:
Be jealous for me, for I am yours,
   and to you, Lord, am I betrothed!
The apostle who betrothed me to you
   told me that you are the jealous One.
A bulwark to chaste wives
   is the jealousy of their husbands.
CARMINA NISIBENA 6.12.[269]

CHRIST ALONE IS THE BRIDEGROOM OF THE CHURCH. AMBROSE: Christ alone, then, is the bridegroom to whom the church, his bride, comes from the nations and gives herself in wedlock. She was previously poor and starving but is now rich with Christ's harvest,

---

[259]Mt 12:30. [260]Jn 10:30. [261]1 Jn 5:8. [262]ANF 5:423. [263]Eph 5:31-32. [264]ACW 44:83. [265]ACW 47:72. [266]FC 67:166. [267]Lk 18:8. [268]ACW 47:75. [269]SCK 141*.

gathering in the hidden bosom of her mind handfuls of the rich crop and gleanings of the Word. In this way she may nourish with fresh food her, who is worn out, bereaved by the death of her Son and starving, she, mother of the dead, but not abandoning the widow and destitute in her search for new children. Christ, then, alone is the bridegroom, begrudging not even the synagogue the sheaves of his harvest. Would that the synagogue had not voluntarily excluded herself! . . . Who indeed but Christ could dare to claim the church as his bride, whom he alone, and no other, has called from Lebanon, saying, "Come hither from Lebanon, my bride, come hither."[270] Or of whom else could the church have said, "His throat is sweetness, and he is altogether desirable"?[271] . . . To whom else but the Word of God could these words apply: "his legs are pillars of marble, set upon bases of gold"?[272] For Christ alone walks in the souls and makes his path in the minds of his saints, in which, as on bases of gold and foundations of precious stone, the heavenly Word has left his footsteps ineffaceably impressed. Clearly we see, then, that both the man and the type are pointing to the mystery of the incarnation. ON THE CHRISTIAN FAITH 3.10.72-75.[273]

FORMED OF THE BONES AND FLESH OF CHRIST. METHODIUS OF OLYMPUS: For humanity, having been composed, like water, of wisdom and life, has become identical with the very same untainted light that poured into him. Thus it was that the apostle directly referred to Christ the words that had been spoken of Adam. For thus will it be most certainly agreed: that the church is formed out of his bones and flesh. And it was for this reason that the Word, leaving his Father in heaven, came down to be "joined to his wife,"[274] and slept in the trance of his passion and willingly suffered death for her, that he might present the church to himself glorious and blameless, having cleansed her by the water of baptism,[275] for the receiving of the spiritual and blessed seed, which is sown by him who with whispers implants it in the depths of the mind. New life is conceived and formed by the church, as by a woman, so as to give birth and nourishment to virtue. For in this way, too, the command, "Increase and multiply,"[276] is duly fulfilled, the church increasing daily in greatness and beauty and multitude, by the union and communion of the Word who now still comes down to us and falls into a trance by the memorial of his passion. Otherwise the church could not conceive believers and give them new birth by the laver of regeneration, unless Christ, emptying himself for their sake, that he might be contained by them, as I said, through the recapitulation of his passion, should die again, coming down from heaven, and being "joined to his wife," the church, should provide for a certain power being taken from his own side, so that all who are built up in him should grow up, even those who are born again by the laver, receiving of his bones and of his flesh, that is, of his holiness and of his glory. For he who says that the bones and flesh of Wisdom are understanding and virtue says most rightly; and that the side is the Spirit of truth, the Paraclete, of whom the illuminated receiving are rightly born again to incorruption.

For it is impossible for anyone to be a partaker of the Holy Spirit and to be chosen a member of Christ unless the Word first came down on him and fell into a trance, in order that he, being filled with the Spirit and rising again from sleep with him who was laid to sleep for his sake, should be able to receive renewal and restoration. For it is only right to call him the side of the Word, even the sevenfold Spirit of truth, according to the prophet. God took him, in the trance of Christ, that is, after his incarnation and passion, and prepared a helper for him—I mean the souls that are

---

[270]Song 4:8. [271]Song 5:16. [272]Song 5:15. [273]NPNF 2 10:253*. [274]Eph 5:31. [275]Eph 5:26-27. [276]Gen 1:28.

betrothed and given in marriage to him. For it is frequently the case that the Scriptures thus call the assembly and mass of believers by the name of the church, the more perfect in their progress being led up to be the one person and body of the church. For those who are the better and who embrace the truth more clearly, being delivered from the evils of the flesh, become, on account of their perfect purification and faith, a church and helper of Christ, betrothed and given in marriage to him as a virgin, according to the apostle, so that receiving the pure and genuine seed of his doctrine, they may cooperate with him, helping in preaching for the salvation of others. And those who are still imperfect and beginning their lessons are born to salvation and shaped, as by mothers, by those who are more perfect, until they are brought forth and regenerated to the greatness and beauty of virtue; and so these, in their turn making progress, having become a church, assist in laboring for the birth and nurture of other children, accomplishing in the receptacle of the soul, as in a womb, the blameless will of the Word. SYMPOSIUM OR THE BANQUET OF THE TEN VIRGINS 3.8.[277]

THE HONORED BRIDE. METHODIUS OF OLYMPUS: In hymns, O blessed spouse of God, we attendants of the bride honor you, O undefiled virgin church of snow-white form, dark-haired, chaste, spotless, beloved. SYMPOSIUM OR THE BANQUET OF THE TEN VIRGINS 11.2.[278]

THE CHURCH WAS BORN FROM THE SIDE OF CHRIST. AUGUSTINE: Perhaps you still wanted to ask, "When do we rise up? We are hidden to sit down now, but when will our rising up be?" Ask yourself: When was the Lord's rising up? Wait for him who has gone ahead of you. If you do not wait for him, you are wasting your labor in rising up before the light. Think now: when was Christ exalted? After his death. That means that you too must hope for your rising up after death. Hope for the rising up of all the dead, because he has risen and ascended. But where did he sleep? On the cross. When he slept on the cross, his sleep was a sign, or rather, a fulfillment of the sign given in Adam. When Adam slept, a rib was withdrawn from him[279] and Eve was created; so it was with the Lord also when he slept on the cross, for his side was struck with a lance and there flowed out the saving mysteries from which the church was born.[280] The church is the bride of the Lord, made from his side, as Eve was made from Adam's; and as Eve could be made from the man's side only when he slept, so was the church made only from the side of a man who died. And if Christ rose only after he had died, can you hope for exaltation, unless it be after this life?

But perhaps you wanted to press the question further: "When shall I rise up? Couldn't it be before I have sat down?" The psalm takes care to enlighten you: "After I have given sleep to his beloved," it says. God gives this gift after his beloved have fallen asleep, for then his beloved—Christ's beloved, that is—will rise. All will rise, in fact, but not all in the same way as Christ's beloved. There will be a rising up for all the dead, but what does the apostle say about it? "Though we shall all indeed rise again, we shall not all be changed."[281] Some rise for punishment, but we rise as our Lord rose, provided that we are his members, so that we may follow our head. If we are his members, we are also his beloved, and then the rising that initially was real only in the Lord will be ours also. The light rose before us, and we rise after the light. It is a waste of time for us to rise before the light—to seek exaltation before our death, I mean—for Christ our light was not exalted as to his flesh until after he had died. The same is true for us who are built into him as his members and, being his members, are his beloved. After we have accepted

---

[277]ANF 6:319-20**. [278]ANF 6:353*. [279]See Gen 2:21-22. [280]See Jn 19:34. [281]1 Cor 15:51.

our sleep, we shall rise again at the resurrection of the dead.

One man, and one only, rose never to die again. Lazarus rose,[282] but he was to die again later. The widow's son rose[283] only to die once more. The daughter of the synagogue's president rose,[284] but she too would die again. Christ rose, but he would never die any more. Listen to the apostle: "Rising from the dead, Christ will never die again, nor will death ever again have the mastery over him."[285] EXPOSITIONS ON THE PSALMS 126.7.[286]

A BRIDE WORTHY OF SUCH A BRIDEGROOM. AUGUSTINE: Thus it is then that sometimes in the Scriptures Christ is presented in such a way that you are to understand him as the Word equal to the Father; in such a way sometimes that you are to understand him as the mediator, since "the Word became flesh to dwell among us."[287] . . . Sometimes, though, in such a way that you are to understand the head and the body, with the apostle himself expounding as clearly as may be what was said about husband and wife in Genesis: "They shall be two," it says, "in one flesh."[288] Notice his exposition, because I don't want to give the impression of having the nerve to say something I've cobbled up myself. "For they will be two," he said, "in one flesh"; and he added, "This is a great sacrament." And in case anyone should still think that this is to be found in husband and wife according to the natural joining of the sexes and their bodily coming together, "but I mean," he went on, "in Christ and the church."[289] So this is how we take as referring to Christ and the church what is said elsewhere: "They shall be two in one flesh; they are not now two, but there is one flesh."[290]

And just as bridegroom and bride, so also head and body, because "the head of the woman is the man."[291] So whether I say head and body, or whether I say bridegroom and bride, you must understand the same thing.

And that's why the same apostle, while he was still Saul, heard the words, "Saul, Saul, why are you persecuting me,"[292] because the body is joined to the head. And when as a preacher of Christ he was now suffering from others what he had done himself as a persecutor, "that I may fill up," he said, "in my flesh what is lacking from the afflictions of Christ,"[293] thus showing that what he was suffering was part and parcel of the afflictions of Christ. This can't be understood of the head, which now in heaven is not suffering any such thing; but of the body, that is, the church; the body, which with its head is the one Christ.

So present yourselves to such a head as a body worthy of him, to such a bridegroom as a worthy bride. That head can only have a correspondingly worthy body; and such a great husband as that can only marry a correspondingly worthy wife. "To present himself," it says, "with a glorious church, not having stain or wrinkle, or any such thing."[294] This is the bride of Christ, without stain or wrinkle. Do you wish to have no stain? Do what is written: "Wash yourselves, be clean, remove the wicked schemes from your hearts."[295] Do you wish to have no wrinkle? Stretch yourself on the cross. You see, you don't only need to be washed but also to be stretched, in order to be without stain or wrinkle; because by the washing, sins are removed, while by the stretching, a desire is created for the future life, which is what Christ was crucified for.

Listen to Paul, once he was washed: "Not," he says, "because of the works of justice which we have done, but according to his own mercy he has saved us, by the washing of rebirth."[296] Listen to him as he is stretched: "Forgetting," he says, "what lies behind, stretched out to what lies ahead, according to intention I follow

---

[282]See Jn 11:44. [283]See Lk 7:15. [284]See Mk 5:42. [285]Rom 6:9. [286]WSA 3:20:89-91. [287]Jn 1:14. [288]Gen 2:24. [289]Eph 5:31-32. [290]Mt 19:5-6. [291]1 Cor 11:3. [292]Acts 9:4. [293]Col 1:24. [294]Eph 5:27. [295]Is 1:16. [296]Tit 3:5.

after to the palm of God's calling from above in Christ Jesus."[297] SERMON 341.12-13.[298]

CHASTE LIKE MARY. AUGUSTINE: To the same church the apostle says, "For I have promised you to one spouse, that I might present you as a chaste virgin to Christ."[299] ... The church, then, like Mary, has inviolate integrity and incorrupt fecundity. What Mary merited physically, the church has guarded spiritually, with the exception that Mary brought forth one Child, while the church has many children destined to be gathered into one body by one. SERMON 195.2.[300]

TEARS THROUGH SUPPLICATION. PETER CHRYSOLOGUS: How he will be roused through and through at the constant tears of his church, at the blood and sweat of his bride! For the church pours forth continual tears through those who make supplication, and she sweats sacred blood through her martyrs, until Christ returns and, to the eternal joy of this heavenly Mother, ushers from the mortal bier to everlasting life her only son, that is, the Christian people, whom so many ages bear off to their death.

But since the time of Christ's birth is coming, and virginity is about to bring to light the heavenly miracle of producing a child, and it is no longer a star that announces the birth of the divine King, but the very ascent of the sun, let us all hasten to offer adoration, and with holy gifts let us acknowledge that our God and King has come forth from the temple of the Virgin. Let us offer gifts, because a public offering is always made at the birth of a king. Let us offer gifts, because utterly irreverent is the one who adores with empty hands. The magi attest to this, who were weighed down with gold, aflame with frankincense and hallowed with myrrh when they bent down before Christ's cradle. SERMON 103.5-6.[301]

The Church as Mother

THE SPOUSE OF CHRIST IS OUR MOTHER. AUGUSTINE: This is the Lord our God; this Man, our Savior, is the mediator between God and humankind. Born of the Father, he created his Mother; formed as man in his mother, he glorified his Father. He is the only Son of the Father without woman's parturition; the only son of his mother, without man's cooperation. Surpassing all the sons of men in beauty,[302] he, the Son of holy Mary and the spouse of holy church, has made the church like to his mother, since he made it a mother for us and he kept it a virgin for himself. To the same church the apostle says, "For I have betrothed you to one spouse, that I might present you as a chaste virgin to Christ."[303] SERMON 195.2.[304]

HOW THE CHURCH SEEKS TO IMITATE THE VIRGIN MOTHER. AUGUSTINE: Now, that which follows pertains to us: "I believe in the holy church." We constitute the church, but I do not say "we" in such a way as to include only those who are here, who now hear me. I include as many faithful Christians as are here, by the grace of God, in this church, that is, in this city, as many as are in this region, as many as are in this province, as many as are across the sea, as many as are in the whole world, since "from the rising of the sun unto the going down of the same, the name of the Lord is worthy of praise."[305] Thus, the catholic church, our true mother, true bride of her spouse, exists today. Let us honor her because she is the bride of so great a Lord. And what shall I say? Great and unique is the condescension of her spouse; he found her a courtesan and made her a virgin. She should not deny that she was a courtesan, lest she forget the mercy of her liberator. How was she not a courtesan when she committed fornication in the pursuit of

---

[297]Phil 3:13-14. [298]WSA 3 10:27-28. [299]2 Cor 11:2. [300]FC 38:42. [301]FC 110:126. [302]See Ps 45:2 (44:3 LXX). [303]2 Cor 11:2. [304]FC 38:42 [305]Ps 113:3.

idols and demons? Fornication of heart was in all; of the flesh in a few, but of the heart in all. And he came and made her a virgin; he made the church a virgin. She is a virgin in faith. He has a few nuns, virgins in the flesh; he ought to have all, women and men alike, virgins in the faith. For there chastity, purity and holiness ought to exist. SERMON 213.7.[306]

VIRGIN BRIDE AND MOTHER. AUGUSTINE: Do you wish to know how the church is a virgin? Hear the apostle Paul; hear the friend of the Bridegroom who is zealous, not for himself but for the Bridegroom: "I betrothed you to one spouse." He spoke to the church. To which church? To all, wherever his letter could reach. "I betrothed you to one spouse, that I might present you a chaste virgin to Christ. But I fear lest," he said, "as the serpent seduced Eve by his guile. . . ."[307] That serpent never physically defiled Eve, did he? Yet he did destroy her virginity of heart. On that account Paul said, "I fear lest . . . your minds may be corrupted from that chastity which is in Christ." Therefore, the church is a virgin; she is a virgin, may she be a virgin. Let her beware of the deceiver, lest he turn out to be a corrupter. The church is a virgin. Are you, perhaps, going to say to me, "If the church is a virgin, how does she bring forth children? Or, if she does not bring forth children, how did we give our names so that we might be born of her?" I answer, "She is a virgin, and she also brings forth children." She imitates Mary, who gave birth to the Lord. Did not the holy Mary bring forth her Child and remain a virgin? So, too, the church both brings forth children and is a virgin. And if you would give some consideration to the matter, she brings forth Christ, because they who are baptized are his members. "You are," said the apostle, "the body of Christ and his members."[308] If, therefore, the church brings forth the members of Christ, she is very like to Mary. SERMON 213.7.[309]

THE NEW GENERATION. IRENAEUS: He will judge also the Ebionites. For how can they be saved unless it was God who wrought their salvation on earth? Or how shall humanity pass into God, unless God has first passed into humanity? And how shall humanity escape from the generation subject to death, if not by means of a new generation, given in a wonderful and unexpected manner (but as a sign of salvation) by God—I mean that regeneration that flows from the virgin through faith? Or how shall they receive adoption from God if they remain in this generation, which is naturally possessed by humanity in this world? AGAINST HERESIES 4.33.4.[310]

THE CHURCH AS CHASTE MOTHER. AUGUSTINE: In that church that the apostle Paul calls a virgin, the minds of all should be undefiled. "For I betrothed you to one spouse, that I might present you a chaste virgin to Christ."[311] The church, therefore, imitating the mother of her Lord in mind, though not in body, is both mother and virgin. Since the virginity of his mother was in no way violated in the birth of Christ, he likewise made his church a virgin by ransoming her from the fornication of demons. You holy virgins, born of her undefiled virginity, who, scorning earthly nuptials, have chosen to be virgins in the flesh, rejoice now and celebrate with all solemnity the fecundity of the "virgin on this day. . . . I address all here present; I speak to all; I include in my exhortations the whole church, that chaste virgin whom the apostle speaks of as espoused to Christ.[312] SERMON 191.2-3.[313]

THE TRUE MOTHER OF THOSE WHO EMBODY LOVE. AUGUSTINE: Who cannot see that those who dare to speak thus against the Christian Scriptures, though they may not be

---

[306]FC 38:126-27. [307]2 Cor 11:2-4. [308]1 Cor 12:27. [309]FC 38:127. [310]ANF 1:507. [311]2 Cor 11:2. [312]See 2 Cor 11:2. [313]FC 38:30-31.

what they are suspected of being, are at least not Christians? For to Christians this rule of life is given, that we should love the Lord our God with all the heart, with all the soul and with all the mind, and our neighbor as ourselves; for on these two commandments hang all the law and the prophets. Rightly, then, the catholic church, you who are most true mother of Christians, not only teaches that God alone (whom to find is the happiest life) must be worshiped in perfect purity and chastity, bringing in no creature as an object of adoration whom we should be required to serve. From that incorrupt and inviolable eternity to which alone humankind should be made subject, in cleaving to which alone the rational soul escapes misery, excluding everything made, everything liable to change, everything under the power of time, without confounding what eternity and truth and peace itself keeps separate or separating what a common majesty unites. Not only do you teach this, but you also possess love and charity to our neighbor in such a way, that for all kinds of diseases with which souls are for their sins afflicted, there is found with you a medicine of prevailing efficacy. . . .

So we must understand the words of the apostle: "Christ loved the church, and gave himself for it; cleansing it with the washing of water by the word, that he might present it to himself a glorious church, not having spot, or wrinkle, or any such thing."[314] For in this world there is the washing of water by the word that purifies the church. But as the whole church, as long as it is here, says, "Forgive us our debts,"[315] it certainly is not while here without spot or wrinkle or any such thing; but from that which it here receives, it is led on to the glory that is not here, and to perfection, and, "I have come to send fire on the earth."[316] These two utterances of one God stamped on both Testaments exhibit with harmonious testimony the sanctification of the soul, pointing forward to the accomplishment of that which is also quoted in the New Testament from the Old: "Death is swallowed up in victory."[317] OF THE MORALS OF THE CATHOLIC CHURCH 30.62-64.[318]

THE BEE AS NATURE'S MODEL OF CHASTITY. PETER CHRYSOLOGUS: Let no one be surprised if the holy church, the virgin and mother, propagates numerous offspring with heavenly fruitfulness, generates her shepherds on her own and gives birth on her own to her rulers, since a bee, which does not know intercourse, is unacquainted with lewdness and free from immorality, provides a pattern of purity, an example of chastity and a sign of virginity. The bee conceives solely through her mouth from the dew that comes from the heavens, gives birth through her mouth, molds chaste offspring with her mouth, forms her leaders with her mouth and generates and produces her kings herself with her mouth. Thus the church, like the bee, in being subject to her own progeny can manifest charity, demonstrate obedience, hand down an ordered way of life, establish a discipline for conduct and show her affection for her glorious work. I said that she is subject to her own progeny, because freedom remains when servitude is voluntary; but power that is out of control loses all semblance of freedom. SERMON 130A.1.[319]

SIGNS OF REPENTANCE REJUVENATE MOTHER CHURCH. HERMAS: When she finished talking to me, the six young men who were building came and took her away to the tower, and another four took up the couch and took it to the tower as well. I did not see the faces of these men because they were turned away. But as she was leaving I asked her to give me a revelation about the three forms in which she had appeared to me. She answered, "You must ask someone else to reveal this to you." For at first, last year, brothers and sisters, I

---

[314]Eph 5:25-27. [315]Mt 6:12. [316]Lk 12:49. [317]1 Cor 15:54. [318]NPNF 1 4:58*. [319]FC 110:198.

had seen her rather old and sitting in a chair. In the next vision, her face was younger but her flesh and hair were older and she spoke to me standing. She looked more joyful, though, than before. In the third vision, she was much younger, very lovely, and only her hair looked older. She was completely joyful and seated on a couch. I was quite depressed about this, wanting to understand the revelation. In a night vision, I saw the elder lady say to me, "Every request requires humility. So fast, and you will receive what you ask from the Lord." . . . "Listen," he said, "about the three forms you [sing.] seek. Why did she first appear to you older and seated in a chair? Because your [pl.] spirit is older and already fainting away and has no power because of your softness and double-mindedness. Just as older people, no longer having any hope of rejuvenation, look forward to nothing but their sleep, so you too who have become softened by everyday concerns have given yourselves over to apathy and have not cast your cares on the Lord. Your intent has been shattered, and you have grown old in your sadness." "Then I would like to know why she was sitting in a chair, sir." "Because every weak person sits out of weakness in order to support the bodily weakness. You [sing.] have the meaning of the first vision. In the second vision you saw her standing with a younger-looking face and more joyful than before, but her flesh and hair were older. Listen," he said, "to this parable as well. Someone who is older has already abandoned hope because of weakness and poverty and looks forward to nothing but the last day of life. Then, this person suddenly received an inheritance, and on hearing of it, rose up, rejoiced and got stronger. Such a one no longer lies prone but stands up, is renewed in the very spirit previously destroyed by the former deeds and no longer sits but takes on courage. So too you [pl.], hearing the revelation. Because the Lord had compassion on you and renewed your spirits, you have put aside your soft ways, and strength has entered into you, and you were empowered in the faith. The Lord, seeing you made strong, rejoiced. This is why he showed you the building of the tower and will show you other things if you remain at peace among yourselves with all your heart. In the third vision, you [sing.] saw her young, happy and lovely in appearance. It is as if some good news should come to someone living in sadness, and this person at once forgets the former sadness and focuses on nothing but the news just heard and is strengthened from then on for doing good. Such a person's spirit is renewed because of the joy received. So too you [pl.] have received renewed spirits by seeing these good things. You [sing.] saw her sitting on a couch, a secure position, for a couch has four legs and thus stands securely. So too the world is supported by four elements. Those who are converted will become completely new and securely founded—those who are converted with all their heart. You have the entire revelation; do not ask anything more about a revelation. If anything else is needed, it will be revealed to you." SHEPHERD, VISION 3.10-13.[320]

THE CHURCH DURING PERSECUTION.

EUSEBIUS OF CAESAREA: But the intervening time was not wasted or fruitless to them,[321] for by their patience the measureless compassion of Christ was manifested. For through their continued life the dead were made alive, and the witnesses showed favor to those who had failed to witness. And the virgin mother had much joy in receiving alive those whom she had brought forth as dead. ECCLESIASTICAL HISTORY 5.1.45.[322]

THE CHURCH HELPS THE MARTYRS.

TERTULLIAN: Among the provisions for the body that not only our lady mother, the church, from her own bosom but also individ-

---

[320]*SHC* 83-84. [321]Eusebius is referring to the martyrs of Lyons. [322]NPNF 2 1:216.

ual brothers from their own private resources supply to you in your prison, blessed martyrs designate, accept something from me too, which may serve to nourish your spirit also. For it is not good for the body to be filled and for the spirit to hunger. Surely if that which is weak receives attention, that which is weaker ought still less to be neglected. Not that I have any claims to address you; yet to the most skilled gladiators, not only experts and their own trainers give advice, but even nonprofessionals and any chance onlookers from outside the ring, so that hints suggested from the very crowd have often proved profitable. To the Martyrs 1.[323]

The Role of Leaders. Gregory the Great: We should therefore act in such a way that we appeal to them with reason and kindness so that they want to follow us instead of fleeing from us. And, when we prove to them from their own Scriptures what we tell them, we may be able, with God's help, to convert them to the bosom of Mother Church. Letter 13.12.[324]

The Church Is Always a Young Mother. Clement of Alexandria: In contradistinction, therefore, to the older people, the new people are called young, having learned the new blessings; and we have the exuberance of life's morning prime in this youth that knows no old age, in which we are always growing to maturity in intelligence, are always young, always mild, always new: for those must necessarily be new who have become partakers of the new Word. And that which participates in eternity is likely to be assimilated to the incorruptible: so that to us appertains the designation of the age of childhood, a lifelong springtime, because the truth that is in us, and our habits, saturated with the truth, cannot be touched by old age; but Wisdom is ever blooming, ever remains consistent and the same and never changes. "Their children," it is said, "shall be borne upon their shoulders, and fondled on their knees; as one whom his mother comforts, so also shall I comfort you."[325] The mother draws the children to herself; and we seek our mother the church. Whatever is feeble and tender, as needing help on account of its feebleness, is kindly looked on and is sweet and pleasant, anger changing into help in the case of such: for thus horses' colts, the little calves of cows, and the lion's whelp, the stag's fawn and the child of humans are looked on with pleasure by their fathers and mothers. Thus also the Father of the universe cherishes affection toward those who have fled to him; and having begotten them again by his Spirit to the adoption of children, knows them as gentle, and loves those alone, and aids and fights for them; and therefore he bestows on them the name of child. Christ the Educator 1.5.[326]

The Shepherd of the Church. Clement of Alexandria: But we are God-taught and glory in the name of Christ. How then are we not to regard the apostle as attaching this sense to the milk of the babes? And if we who preside over the churches are shepherds after the image of the Good Shepherd, and you the sheep, are we not to regard the Lord as preserving consistency in the use of figurative speech, when he speaks also of the milk of the flock? And to this meaning we may secondly accommodate the expression, "I have given you milk to drink, and not given you food, for you are not yet able," regarding the meat not as something different from the milk but the same in substance. For the very same Word is fluid and mild as milk, or solid and compact as meat. And entertaining this view, we may regard the proclamation of the gospel, which is universally diffused, as milk; and as meat, faith, which from instruction is compacted

---

[323]*BTAM* 51. [324]NPNF 2 13:97*. [325]Is 66:12-13. [326]ANF 2:214.

into a foundation, which, being more substantial than hearing, is likened to meat and assimilates to the soul itself nourishment of this kind. Elsewhere the Lord, in the Gospel according to John, brought this out by symbols, when he said, "Eat my flesh, and drink my blood," describing distinctly by metaphor the drinkable properties of faith and the promise, by means of which the church, like a human being consisting of many members, is refreshed and grows, is welded together and compacted of both, of faith, which is the body, and of hope, which is the soul; as also the Lord of flesh and blood. CHRIST THE EDUCATOR 1.6.[327]

ONE FATHER, ONE SON, ONE HOLY SPIRIT AND THE VIRGIN MOTHER. CLEMENT OF ALEXANDRIA: But the Lord Christ, the fruit of the Virgin, did not pronounce the breasts of women blessed or select them to give nourishment; but when the kind and loving Father had rained down the Word, himself became spiritual nourishment to the good. O mystic marvel! The universal Father is one, and one the universal Word; and the Holy Spirit is one and the same everywhere, and one is the only virgin mother. I love to call her the church. This mother, when alone, had no milk, because alone she was not a woman. But she is once virgin and mother—pure as a virgin, loving as a mother. And calling her children to her, she nurses them with holy milk, namely, with the Word for childhood. Therefore she had not milk; for the milk was this child fair and comely, the body of Christ, which nourishes by the Word the young brood, which the Lord himself brought forth in throes of the flesh, which the Lord himself swathed in his precious blood. O amazing birth! O holy swaddling bands! The Word is everything to the child, both father and mother and tutor and nurse. "Eat my flesh," he says, "and drink my blood." Such is the suitable food that the Lord ministers, and he offers his flesh and pours forth his blood, and nothing is wanting for the children's growth. O amazing mystery! We are enjoined to cast off the old and carnal corruption, as also the old nutriment, receiving in exchange another new regimen, that of Christ, receiving him if we can, to hide him within; and that, enshrining the Savior in our souls, we may correct the affections of our flesh. CHRIST THE EDUCATOR 1.6.[328]

THE FATHER AND SON ONLY IN MOTHER CHURCH. TERTULLIAN: Happy are they that acknowledge the Father. This it is that Israel is reproached with: because the Spirit calls heaven and earth to witness, saying, "I have begotten sons and they have not acknowledged" me.[329] But when we say "Father" we also give God a name: this form of address involves both affection and authority. Also in the title "Father" we call on the Son, for he says, "I and the Father are one."[330] Even our mother the church is not omitted, seeing that in "son" and "father" there is a recognition of "mother": for the name of both father and son has its actuality from her. Thus under one generic term we both honor God, along with those that are his, and are mindful of the commandment and pass censure on those who have forgotten the Father. ON PRAYER 2.[331]

THE LIVING MOTHER CHURCH. TERTULLIAN: For our one Father, God, lives, and our mother, the church; and neither are we dead who live to God, nor do we bury our dead, inasmuch as they too are living in Christ. ON MONOGAMY 7.[332]

THE HOLY SPIRIT BUILDS THE CHURCH. TERTULLIAN: The light of the truth has shone forth through Christ, and the human race has thrown away its idols; observe whether what follows has not been fulfilled: "For the Lord

---

[327]ANF 2:219. [328]ANF 2:220. [329]Is 1:2. [330]Jn 10:30. [331]*TTP* 5-7. [332]ANF 4:64.

of hosts hath taken away from Judea and from Jerusalem," besides other matters, "the prophet and the wise master builder," namely, the Holy Spirit, who is building the church, which is the temple and home and city of God. AGAINST MARCION 3.23.[333]

CHRISTIANS ARE CHILDREN OF THE FREE WOMAN. TERTULLIAN: For if "Abraham had two sons, one by a bondmaid and the other by a free woman, but he that was by the bondmaid was born after the flesh, while he that was by the free woman was by promise: which things are allegorical." This means they indicate something else: "for these are two testaments"—or two revelations, as I see they have translated it—"the one from Mount Sinai," referring to the synagogue of the Jews, "which," according to the law entails bondage;[334] the other, above all principality, power, and domination and every name that is named not only in this world but also in that which is to come, is "our mother,"[335] that holy church, in whom we have expressed our faith. And consequently he adds, "So then, brothers, we are not children of the bondwoman, but of the free."[336] AGAINST MARCION 5.4.[337]

A HOLY VIRGIN FOR THE BRIDEGROOM. TERTULLIAN: And if his purpose is to present the church as a holy virgin to Christ, evidently as bride to bridegroom, the metaphor cannot be made to apply to one hostile to the actuality of the institution referred to. AGAINST MARCION 5.12.[338]

CHRIST HAS LOVED THE CHURCH. TERTULLIAN: Christ has loved the flesh no less than the church: for no man can fail to have affection even for the portrait of his bride but in fact will keep it safe and pay it respect and put a garland on it. The likeness of a thing has partnership in honor with the thing itself. Need I now make heavy weather of it to prove that there is the same God of the man and of Christ, of the woman and the church, of the flesh and the spirit, when the apostle himself cites and even expounds the Creator's ruling? "For her sake shall a man leave his father and mother . . . and the two shall be in one flesh: this is a great mystery."[339] Enough meanwhile if the Creator's mysteries are great in the apostle's sight, though of low esteem among the heretics. "But I speak," he continues, "with reference to Christ and the church." You have there an interpretation, not a setting aside, of the mystery: his words prove that the type and figure of the mystery were set forth of old by him to whom also the mystery belonged. AGAINST MARCION 5.18.[340]

THE PRAYER OF THE NEWLY BAPTIZED. TERTULLIAN: Therefore, you blessed ones, for whom the grace of God is waiting, when you come up from that most sacred washing of the new birth and when for the first time you spread out your hands with your brothers in your mother's house, ask of your Father, ask of your Lord, that special grants of grace and apportionments of spiritual gifts be yours. ON BAPTISM 20.[341]

FATHER AND MOTHER. CYPRIAN: Thus the Spirit cannot be received unless the person who is to receive it already exists. Now the birth of Christians is in baptism; and the generation and sanctification of baptism are with the one bride of Christ. She alone is capable of spiritually bearing and giving birth to children to God. This being so, where and of what mother and to whom is one born who is not a child of the church? If one is to have God for Father, he must first have the church for mother. LETTER 74.7.2.[342]

---

[333]*TAM* 1:243. [334]See Gal 4:21-24. [335]Gal 4:26. [336]Gal 4:31. [337]*TAM* 2:531*. [338]*TAM* 2:589. [339]Eph 5:31-32. [340]*TAM* 2:627. [341]*THB* 43. [342]*ACW* 47:74*.

VIRGINS INCREASE THE JOY OF MOTHER CHURCH. CYPRIAN: My address is now to virgins, whose glory, as it is more eminent, excites the greater interest. This is the flower of the ecclesiastical seed, the grace and ornament of spiritual endowment, a joyous disposition, the wholesome and uncorrupted work of praise and honor, God's image answering to the holiness of the Lord, the more illustrious portion of Christ's flock. The glorious fruitfulness of Mother Church rejoices by their means and in them abundantly flourishes; and in proportion as a copious virginity is added to her number, so much the more it increases the joy of the mother. To these I speak, these I exhort with affection rather than with power; not that I would claim—last and least and very conscious of my lowliness as I am—any right to censure. Rather, because I am always careful to be on guard, I fear more from the onslaught of Satan. THE DRESS OF VIRGINS 3.[343]

TO BREAK UNITY IS A SACRILEGE. CYPRIAN: I have learned that you . . . have given consent to the appointment of another bishop—contrary to the ordinance of God, contrary to the law of the gospel, contrary to the unity established for the catholic church. You have allowed a second church to be established—that is a sacrilege, that is forbidden; you have agreed that Christ's members should be wrenched apart, that the Lord's flock, which has but one body and soul, should be torn into pieces by lacerating rivalry. LETTER 46.1.2.[344]

RETURN TO MOTHER CHURCH. CYPRIAN: I do beg you that, at least so far as you are concerned, this unlawful rending of our brotherhood should not persist. Rather, we beg that, being mindful of your confession and of God's teaching handed down to us, you should return to your mother from whom you have departed, from whom you went forth to win glory of your confession, bringing such jubilation to your same mother. LETTER 46.1.3.[345]

THE TRUE BRIDE OF CHRIST. CYPRIAN: How can they possibly assert and maintain that one may become a child of God without having been born within the church? For it is in baptism that the old person dies and the new person is born, as the blessed apostle makes manifestly clear and proves when he says that God has saved us through the washing of rebirth. Now if rebirth is in the washing, that is to say, in baptism, how can heresy, which is not the bride of Christ, give birth to children, through Christ, to God? It is the church alone, being joined and united to Christ, who spiritually gives birth to children. . . . And so, if she is his beloved, the bride who alone is sanctified by Christ and alone is cleansed by his washing, then obviously heresy, being no bride of Christ and incapable of being cleansed or sanctified by his washing, is also incapable of giving birth to children of God. LETTER 74.6.2.[346]

THE ONE MOTHER CHURCH IS FRUITFUL. CYPRIAN: The church's fruitful abundance spreads her branches over the whole world. She broadly expands her rivers, liberally flowing, yet her head is one, her source one; and she is one mother, plentiful in the results of fruitfulness, from her womb we are born, by her milk we are nourished, by her spirit we are animated. ON THE UNITY OF THE CHURCH 5.[347]

REJOICING IN THE FIDELITY OF CONFESSORS. CYPRIAN: How joyously does your Mother Church receive you in her bosom, as you return from the battle! How blissfully, how gladly, does she open her gates, that in united bands you may enter, bearing the trophies from a prostrate enemy! With the triumphing men come women also, who, while contending

---

[343]ANF 5:431*. [344]ACW 44:73. [345]ACW 44:73. [346]ACW 47:73-74. [347]ANF 5:423.

with the world, have also overcome their sex; and virgins also come with the double glory of their warfare, and boys transcending their years with their virtues. Moreover, also, the rest of the multitude of those who stand fast follow your glory and accompany your footsteps with the insignia of praise, very near to, and almost joined with, your own. In them also is the same sincerity of heart, the same soundness of a tenacious faith. Resting on the unshaken roots of the heavenly precepts and strengthened by the evangelical traditions, the prescribed banishment, the destined tortures, the loss of property, the bodily punishments, have not terrified them. THE LAPSED 2.[348]

THE CHURCH AS A MOTHER. CYPRIAN: Will not they, when the day of judgment comes, say, "We have done nothing; nor have we forsaken the Lord's bread and cup to hasten freely to a profane contact. The faithlessness of others has ruined us. We have found our parents our murderers. They have denied to us the church as a mother; they have denied God as a Father. Thus, while we were little, unforeseeing and unconscious of such a crime, we were associated by others to the partnership of wickedness, and we were ensnared by the deceit of others"? THE LAPSED 9.[349]

THE CHURCH GIVES BIRTH TO THOSE BAPTIZED. METHODIUS OF OLYMPUS: Let us then go over the ground again from the beginning, until we come in course to the end, explaining what we have said. Consider if the passage seems to you to be explained to your mind. For I think that the church is here said to give birth to a male; since the enlightened (the baptized) receive the features and the image and the manliness of Christ, the likeness of the form of the Word being stamped on them and begotten in them by a true knowledge and faith, so that in each one Christ is spiritually born. And, therefore, the church swells and travails in birth until Christ is formed in us,[350] so that each of the saints, by partaking of Christ, has been born a Christ. According to which meaning it is said in a certain Scripture, "Touch not mine anointed, and do my prophets no harm,"[351] as though those who were baptized into Christ had been anointed by communication of the Spirit, the church contributing here their clearness and transformation into the image of the Word. And Paul confirms this, teaching it plainly, where he says, "For this cause I bow my knees unto the Father of our Lord Jesus Christ, of whom the whole family in heaven and earth is named, that he would grant you, according to the riches of his glory, to be strengthened, I with might by his Spirit in the inner man; that Christ may dwell in your hearts by faith."[352] For it is necessary that the word of truth should be imprinted and stamped on the souls of the regenerate. SYMPOSIUM OR THE BANQUET OF THE TEN VIRGINS 8.8.[353]

BORN OF CHRIST AND THE CHURCH. JEROME: The same allegorical interpretation applies both to Christ and to the church, that Adam is to prefigure Christ and Eve the church. For the last Adam was made a life-giving spirit.[354] Just as the whole human race is born from Adam and his wife, so a whole multitude of believers has been born of Christ and the church. COMMENTARY ON THE EPISTLE TO THE EPHESIANS 3.5.31.[355]

CHILDREN OF THE CHURCH DISTINGUISH TRUTH FROM FALSEHOOD. VINCENT OF LÉRINS: But it will be said, if the words, the sentiments, the promises of Scripture, are appealed to by the devil and his disciples, of whom some are false apostles, some false prophets and false teachers, and all without exception heretics, what are Catholics and the

---

[348]ANF 5:437. [349]ANF 5:439*. [350]Gal 4:19. [351]Ps 105:15. [352]Eph 3:14-17. [353]ANF 6:337. [354]1 Cor 15:45. [355]PL 26:535B.

children of Mother Church to do? How are they to distinguish truth from falsehood in the sacred Scriptures? They must be very careful to pursue that course which, in the beginning of this Commonitory, we said that holy and learned men had commended to us, that is to say, they must interpret the sacred canon according to the traditions of the universal church and in keeping with the rules of catholic doctrine, in which, moreover, they must follow universality, antiquity, consent. And if at any time a part opposes itself to the whole, novelty to antiquity, the dissent of one or a few who are in error to the consent of all or at all events of the great majority of Catholics, then they must prefer the soundness of the whole to the corruption of a part; in which same whole they must prefer the religion of antiquity to the profaneness of novelty; and in antiquity itself in like manner, to the temerity of one or of a very few they must prefer, first of all, the general decrees, if such there be, of a universal council, or if there is no such, then, what is next best, they must follow the consentient belief of many and great masters. Which rule having been faithfully, soberly and scrupulously observed, we shall with little difficulty detect the noxious errors of heretics as they arise. COMMONITORY 27.[356]

THE TRUTH OF THE CATHOLIC CHURCH.
MUNNULUS OF GIRBA: Munnulus of Girba said, "The truth of our mother the catholic church, brothers, has always remained and still remains with us, and even especially in the Trinity of baptism, as our Lord says, 'Go and baptize the nations, in the name of the Father, of the Son and of the Holy Spirit.'"[357] Since, then, we manifestly know that heretics have not either Father or Son or Holy Spirit, they ought, when they come to the church our mother, truly to be born again and to be baptized; that the cancer that they had, and the anger of damnation and the witchery of error, may be sanctified by the holy and heavenly washing." THE SEVENTH COUNCIL OF CARTHAGE UNDER CYPRIAN.[358]

MOTHER CHURCH RECEIVES A LITTLE BOY.
MACUS: Innocent boy, so soon have you begun to dwell among the innocent. For you how enduring this new life is! What a joy is yours to have Mother Church receive you on your return from the world! Let us repress the narrow in our hearts, let us restrain the tears in our eyes. FUNERAL INSCRIPTION FROM ROME.[359]

THE CHILDREN OF THE CHURCH COME TO HER. METHODIUS OF OLYMPUS: The woman who appeared in heaven clothed with the sun, and crowned with twelve stars, and having the moon for her footstool, and being with child and travailing in birth, is certainly, according to the accurate interpretation, our mother the church, O virgins, being a power by herself distinct from her children; whom the prophets, according to the aspect of their subjects, have called sometimes Jerusalem, sometimes a bride, sometimes Mount Zion and sometimes the temple and tabernacle of God. For she is the power that is desired to give light in the prophet, the Spirit crying to her: "Arise, shine; for your light is come, and the glory of the Lord is risen upon you. For, behold, the darkness shall cover the earth, and gross darkness the people: but the Lord shall arise upon you, and his glory shall be seen upon you. And the Gentiles shall come to your light, and kings to the brightness of your rising. Lift up your eyes round about, and see; all they gather themselves together, they come to you: your sons shall come from far, and your daughters shall be nursed at your side."[360] It is the church whose children shall come to her with all speed after the resurrection, running to her from all quarters. She rejoices receiving the light that never goes down and clothed with the bright-

---

[356]NPNF 2 11:152. [357]Mt 28:19. [358]ANF 5:567. [359]ILCV 2500B (cf. DACL 4.2236); PME 88. [360]Is 60:1-4.

ness of the Word as with a robe. For with what other more precious or honorable ornament was it becoming that the queen should be adorned, to be led as a bride to the Lord, when she had received a garment of light and therefore was called by the Father? Come, then, let us go forward in our discourse and look on this marvelous woman as on virgins prepared for a marriage, pure and undefiled, perfect and radiating a permanent beauty, wanting nothing of the brightness of light; and instead of a dress, clothed with light itself; and instead of precious stones, her head adorned with shining stars. For instead of the clothing that we have, she had light; and for gold and brilliant stones, she had stars; but stars not such as those which are set in the invisible heaven, but better and more resplendent, so that those may rather be considered as their images and likenesses. SYMPOSIUM OR THE BANQUET OF THE TEN VIRGINS 8.6.[361]

The Church as a Ship

LIKE A SHIP TOSSED IN THE DEEP. HIPPOLYTUS: But we who hope for the Son of God are persecuted and trodden down by those unbelievers. For the "wings of the vessel" are the churches; and the sea is the world, in which the church is set, like a ship tossed in the deep but not destroyed; for she has with her the skilled pilot, Christ. And she bears in her midst also the trophy which is erected over death; for she carries with her the cross of the Lord. For her prow is the east and her stern is the west, and her hold is the south, and her tillers are the two Testaments; and the ropes that stretch around her are the love of Christ, which binds the church; and the net that she bears with her is the layer of the regeneration that renews the believing, from which too are these glories. As the wind the Spirit from heaven is present, by whom those who believe are sealed. She has also anchors of iron accompanying her, namely, the holy commandments of Christ, which are strong as iron. She has also mariners on the right and on the left, assessors like the holy angels, by whom the church is always governed and defended. The ladder in her leading up to the sail yard is an emblem of the passion of Christ, which brings the faithful to the ascent of heaven. And the topsails aloft on the yard are the company of prophets, martyrs and apostles, who have entered into their rest in the kingdom of Christ. TREATISE ON CHRIST AND ANTICHRIST 59.[362]

THE PILOT IS CHRIST. PSEUDO-CLEMENT OF ROME: Let therefore the passengers remain quiet, sitting in their own places, lest by disorder they occasion rolling or careening. Let the midshipmen give heed to the fare. Let the deacons neglect nothing with which they are entrusted. Let the presbyters, like sailors, studiously arrange what is needful for each one. Let the bishop, as the mate, wakefully ponder the words of the pilot alone. Let Christ, even the Savior, be loved as the pilot and alone believed in the matters of which he speaks; and let all pray to God for a prosperous voyage. Let those sailing expect every tribulation, as traveling over a great and troubled sea, the world—sometimes, indeed, disheartened, persecuted, dispersed, hungry, thirsty, naked, hemmed in; and, again, sometimes united, congregated, at rest; sometimes also seasick, giddy, vomiting, that is, confessing sins, like disease-producing bile—I mean the sins proceeding from bitterness and the evils accumulated from disorderly lusts. By their confession, as by vomiting, you are relieved of your disease, attaining healthful safety by means of prudence. EPISTLE TO JAMES 15.[363]

THE SHIP ON THE SEA OF GALILEE. TERTULLIAN: Others make the obviously forced suggestion that the apostles underwent

---

[361]ANF 6:336. [362]ANF 5:216-17. [363]ANF 8:221.

a substitute for baptism on that occasion when they were sprinkled and covered with the waves in the little ship:[364] also that Peter, when he walked on the sea, was sufficiently immersed.[365] But it is one thing, I imagine, to be splashed or to be cut off by the violence of the sea and quite another to be baptized by the discipline of religion. Also that little ship presented a type of the church, because on the sea, which means this present world, it is being tossed about by the waves, which means persecutions and temptations, while our Lord in his long-suffering is as it were asleep,[366] until when things reach their final extremes he is awakened by the prayers of the saints[367] to calm the world and restore tranquility to his own. ON BAPTISM 12.[368]

ORDERING WORSHIP. APOSTOLIC CONSTITUTIONS: When you call an assembly of the church as commander of a great ship, appoint the assemblies to be made with all possible skill, charging the deacons as mariners to prepare places for the brothers as for passengers, with all due care and decency. And first, let the building be long, with its head to the east, with its vestries on both sides at the east end, and so it will be like a ship. In the middle let the bishop's throne be placed, and on each side of him let the presbytery sit down; and let the deacons stand near at hand, in close and small garments, for they are like the mariners and managers of the ship; with regard to these, let the laity sit on the other side, with all quietness and good order. And let the women sit by themselves, they also keeping silence. In the middle, let the reader stand on some high place: let him read the books.... In the next place, let the presbyters one by one, not all together, exhort the people, and the bishop in the last place, as being the commander. Let the porters stand at the entries of the men and observe them. Let the deaconesses also stand at those of the women, like shipmen.... But if anyone be found sitting out of his place, let him be rebuked by the deacon, as a manager of the foreship, and be removed into the place proper for him; for the church is not only like a ship but also like a sheepfold. CONSTITUTIONS OF THE HOLY APOSTLES 2.57.[369]

THE HUMAN FORM SUGGESTS THE CROSS. JUSTIN MARTYR: For no one crosses the sea without a sail. No one plows the earth without an instrument. Diggers and mechanics do not do their work without tools that have the proper shape. And the human form differs from that of the irrational animals in nothing else than in its being erect and having the hands extended and having on the face extending from the forehead what is called the nose, through which there is respiration for the living creature. This shows no other form than that of the cross. And so it was said by the prophet, "The breath before our face is the Lord Christ."[370] FIRST APOLOGY 55.[371]

THE CHURCH IS LIKE NOAH'S ARK. AUGUSTINE: Speaking of Noah, our unerring Scriptures tell us that he "was a just and perfect man in his generation,"[372] meaning that he was perfect as far as citizens of the City of God can be perfect during the pilgrimage of this present life, not, of course, as perfect as they are to be in that immortal life in which they will be as perfect as the angels of God. Now, it was this Noah whom God ordered to make an ark in which, along with his family—his wife, sons and daughters-in-law—and also the animals that, at God's bidding, joined him in the ark, Noah would be saved from the devastation of the deluge.

---

[364]See Mt 8:24. [365]Mt 14:29. [366]See Mt 8:24. [367]See Rev 6:10. [368]ANF 3:675**. Tertullian is arguing here against those who said the disciples were not baptized with John's baptism but nonetheless received a baptism of another sort, as when they crossed the Sea of Galilee. See further discussion elsewhere in this volume where we deal with baptism. [369]ANF 7:421. [370]Lam 4:20. [371]ANF 1:181**. [372]Gen 6:9.

Undoubtedly the ark is a symbol of the City of God on its pilgrimage in history, a figure of the church that was saved by the wood on which there hung the "Mediator between God and men, himself man, Christ Jesus."[373] Even the very measurements of length, height and breadth of the ark are meant to point to the reality of the human body into which he came as it was foretold that he would come. . . . As for the door in the side, that surely symbolizes the open wound made by the lance in the side of the Crucified—the door by which those who come to him enter in, in the sense that believers enter the church by means of the sacraments that issued from that wound. It was ordered that the ark be made out of squared timbers—a symbol of the foursquare stability of a holy life, which, like a cube, stands firm however it is turned. So it is with every other detail of the ark's construction. They are all symbols of something in the church. . . .

Biblical interpretations, of course, can vary in value—and I do not claim that mine is the best—but any interpretation that is to catch the mind of the writer who described the flood must realize the connections of this story with the City of God which, in this wicked world, is ever tossed like the ark in the waters of a deluge. Anyone is free to reject the interpretations I gave in the work against Faustus. I said, for example, that the words "with lower, middle chambers, and third stories shall they make it" can be applied to the church. The church is gathered from all nations and is two-storied because it has room for two kinds of men, the circumcised and the uncircumcised, or the Jews and the Greeks, as the apostle calls them. But the church is also three-storied because after the flood the whole world was repeopled with descendants from the three sons of Noah.

Now, anyone is entitled to say something else, so long as what he says is in harmony with the rule of faith. Thus, God wanted the ark to have rooms not only in the lower story but also in the middle story—the "middle chambers"—and even in the top story—the "third stories"—so that there should be living space from the bottom to the top. These stories may well be taken to imply the three virtues praised by the apostle: faith, hope and charity. CITY OF GOD 15.26.[374]

TOSSED BY THE STORM OF THIS WORLD. PETER CHRYSOLOGUS: "But when morning had broken Jesus stood on the shore,"[375] so that the church above all, in which the disciples were then being tossed about by the waves of the sea, he might lead back to firmness of faith in him. And so because he had found them destitute of any power of faith and thoroughly lacking any manly strength, he scolded them, such as they were, by calling them "children," when he addressed these words to them: "Children, do you have anything to eat?"[376] For there they were: Peter, who had denied; Thomas, who had doubted; and John, who had fled. . . . The others arrive by boat and haul along their catch of fish, in order to bring with them to the Lord the results of their faithful labor, namely, the church tossed about by the storms of this world and those whom they catch with the net of the gospel and raise out of the deep to the light from above. "They were not far from the land,"[377] it says. They were not far from "the land of the living," since the end of the present order had already made them very close to the future. "But only about two hundred cubits." From the Jews and the Gentiles he doubles the number one hundred, he who by being the Lord of the two peoples joins together the life and salvation of them both for glory. SERMON 78.4, 7.[378]

SHAKEN BY THE WAVES. GREGORY THE GREAT: For in this position I am being shaken

---

[373]1 Tim 2:5. [374]FC 14:477-79. [375]Jn 21:4. [376]Jn 21:5. [377]Jn 21:8. [378]FC 110:32, 34.

by such great waves of this world that I can in no way direct my ship into port, a ship old and rotting, which I undertook to control through God's hidden plan. LETTER 1.41.[379]

PRAY FOR THE ENDANGERED VESSEL.
GREGORY THE GREAT: But because, while unworthy and infirm, I have taken on an old and very broken-down ship (for the waves pour in from all sides and the rotten planks, shaken by daily and powerful storms, suggest a shipwreck), I ask by our almighty Lord that in this danger of mine you [John, the bishop of Constantinople] stretch forth the hand of your prayer. LETTER 1.4.[380]

---

[379]CCL 140:47-48. [380]CCL 140:4.

WE BELIEVE IN ONE HOLY CATHOLIC AND APOSTOLIC CHURCH

One Holy Catholic and Apostolic

εἰς μίαν, ἁγίαν, καθολικὴν καὶ ἀποστολικὴν ἐκκλησίαν·	*Et unam, sanctam, catholicam et apostolicam ecclesiam.*	We believe in one holy catholic and apostolic Church.
ὁμολογοῦμεν ἓν βάπτισμα εἰς ἄφεσιν ἁμαρτιῶν·	*Confiteor unum baptisma in remissionem peccatorum;*	*We acknowledge one baptism for the forgiveness of sins.*
προσδοκῶμεν ἀνάστασιν νεκρῶν, καὶ ζωὴν τοῦ μέλλοντος αἰῶνος. Ἀμήν.	*et expecto resurrectionem mortuorum, et vitam venturi saeculi. Amen.*	*We look for the resurrection of the dead and the life of the world to come. Amen.*

HISTORICAL CONTEXT: In the Apostolic Symbol (Apostles' Creed) the profession of faith is personal: "I believe" (*credo*), while in the Nicene-Constantinopolitan Creed it is "we believe" (*credimus*).[1] The community expresses its faith together. At the last part of the creed, after the profession in the Holy Spirit and his work, we say we believe "in one holy catholic and apostolic church." These four notes are constitutive for the definition of the church as the church of Christ, and they enable its recognition by all the baptized.

Holiness has always been the first characteristic of the church to be recognized. Already from the beginning of the second century, in the *Epistula apostolorum* we find the saying the "holy church." Beginning from here, the texts of the Fathers repeatedly and incessantly define the church as holy, up to the Nicene-Constantinopolitan profession of faith. The biblical foundation for its use leaves us in no doubt. Jesus, the holy one of God, is the center of the new community chosen and consecrated to raise up to God true spiritual worship. This church is the holy temple of God, and the death of Christ makes it holy and immaculate. The baptized are called holy ones to indicate their belonging to God and the consecration brought about by the baptismal water. The celebration of the Eucharist highlighted for all believers the state of holiness in which they participated and to which they were called. This was so deeply experienced that the apostle felt obliged to write about the necessity for a serious examination of conscience before approaching the celebration of the banquet.[2] The holiness of the church is founded on the presence and action in it of the Holy Spirit. It is, therefore, an original holiness that has no analogy in previous history; it is objective and full, fount and source of every other personal holiness that is born in the church and is developed. If the church were not holy, it could not proclaim as holy those who give testimony to true evangelical life. The history of the church, then, is above all and before all a history of holiness. It is not possible to ignore or not recognize this dimension without misinterpreting the sacred texts and two thousand years of the history of the church. If the church is holy, then it cannot, because of its nature, sin or have sins. This poses another problem that must be faced: the presence of sinners.

The affirmation of the unity of the church

---

[1] The standard forms of the creed as printed in this series are first-person plural in Greek and English but singular (*credo*) in Latin. [2] See 1 Cor 11:30-32.

finds its root in the great high-priestly prayer placed on the lips of Jesus in the Gospel of John: "that they may all be one; even as thou, Father, art in me, and I in thee, that they also may be in us, so that the world may believe that thou hast sent me."[3] Paul many times exhorts readers to attain to this unity by using the powerful image of the body of Christ, where all members are connected. The unity of the church was affirmed not only in rhetoric but in organization: each local church was led by a bishop in communion (*koinōnia*) with other bishops, according to the principle of one bishop for one city and his territory. His office was primarily liturgical and one of guidance. He presided over the liturgical assemblies and was aided by presbyters and deacons. Unity was expressed by the celebration of the Eucharist. The bishop decided who would be admitted to catechesis, who admitted catechumens to baptism, who baptized and who celebrated the Eucharist, who admitted or excluded people from the Eucharist, who gave penance to sinners and pardoned them.

The church of the early centuries elaborated different systems to preserve, favor and develop unity among the churches. The lack of centralization and the absence of strong cohesion, in the institutional sense, constituted a weakness of the Christian communities, in relation to the whole church. Certainly, it was a strength in that all the churches were involved and felt responsible, but it was also a weakness, especially at a time when doctrine was being refined and discipline was being constituted. This was true both in the relations between churches and inside a particular community because of the sense of participation of all the components.

The affirmation that the church is holy comes from Scripture, as does that of unity. The New Testament often calls Christians holy ones.[4] The church is "without spot or wrinkle or any such thing, that she might be holy and without blemish."[5] The first letter of Peter says, "But you are a chosen race, a royal priesthood, a holy nation, God's own people, that you may declare the wonderful deeds of him who called you out of darkness into his marvelous light."[6] The holy nation is the new community constituted of Christians; its holiness does not mean that in the church there are not sinners, but the church participates in the holiness of God, the only holy one.

The term *catholic*, not much used before, acquired a new significance in the mouth of Christians. Pacian of Barcelona wrote that during the time of the apostles no one used to be called catholic. But when heretics had appeared and were striving under various names to tear apart the communities, the apostolic people required a name of their own by which they would mark the unity of an uncorrupted people. Ignatius of Antioch (d. 111) was the first to attribute the adjective *catholic* to the church to warn Christians against the celebration of the Eucharist by schismatics.[7] The meaning of this term in Ignatius is not very clear.[8]

The final description that the creed uses in referring to the church is the adjective *apostolic*. This term, not present in the New Testament, refers directly to the apostles as a historical reality. In early Christianity, the apostles enjoyed a privileged position in that they were bearers of the message of Jesus and about Jesus. That message could be transmitted only by people legitimately chosen and invested with that authority proper to Jesus. The first bearers of the message in turn sent other messengers. Its communication was oral. At the beginning of the second century, Papias of Hierapolis considered the oral reception more profitable than the written. Also, Tertullian made reference to the methodology of reading Scripture within the oral tradition. The apostolic authority, in the

---

[3]Jn 17:21. [4]1 Cor 1:2; Phil 1:1; Col 1:1. [5]Eph 5:27. [6]1 Pet 2:9.
[7]*To the Smyrneans* 8.2. [8]André de Halleux, "'L'Église catholique' dans la lettre ignaciennes aux Smirniotes," in HPO, 90-109 ("Le Symbole de la foi," 1-110).

course of the second century, was found in written texts that went under the names of the apostles. All appealed to the apostles and their teaching, even the Gnostics, who made reference to a secret teaching of Jesus and the apostles. From this came the necessity of a public and documented succession from the apostles onward through the drawing up of the lists of bishops.

The terminology of succession is not present in the New Testament. The preoccupation with assuring the continuity and fidelity to the deposit and to sound doctrine is present in the Pastoral Letters and in the Acts of the Apostles to preserve an identity in time and space.[9] For this reason, the priesthood was instituted.[10] The succession was assured through the imposition of hands and the invocation of the grace of God: "Do not neglect the gift you have, which was given you by prophetic utterance when the council of elders laid their hands upon you";[11] "Hence I remind you to rekindle the gift of God that is within you through the laying on of my hands; for God did not give us a spirit of timidity but a spirit of power and love and self-control."[12] Clement of Rome was the first to elaborate the terminology of succession. Tertullian confronted the issues of churches not founded by the apostles. Over time, apostolicity came to carry the weight of institutional and doctrinal importance with regard to the catholicity of the church.

One could write the history of the ancient church as a continuous battle against swarms of heresies and schisms. It was a church in continuous tension between unity and division, which it overcame partially through the centralization of power in the hands of the bishops. From this arose the necessity to celebrate numerous conciliar assemblies, at various levels (diocesan, provincial, regional or more than one geographical area, or of the whole empire). In the councils, for example, there was the African practice of rereading the canons of the previous meetings. Why? This rereading was also a sign of continuity. The councils, then, were a model of collegiality at various levels, both geographically and through time.

This continuity was very important for the faith and life of the church. As J. N. D. Kelly says, when Christians inserted the title of apostolicity in the creed, they wanted to affirm the historic and verifiable continuity of the faith, of the church, of the individual believers and of the church's ministerial organization.[13] The two terms *apostolic* and *catholic*, complement each other, in that the first explains the present unity and continuity with its origins while the second explains present *koinōnia*. Since in the fourth century, during the Arian controversy, some of the churches of apostolic foundation accepted the doctrine of Arius, the expression "apostolic churches" had begun to lose its apologetic character; already the emphasis was being put on the teaching that derived from the apostles. In fact, Vincent of Lérins, at the beginning of the fifth century, no longer used such a notion. While the expression "apostolic church" in the singular is used to refer to the whole church, which is and must remain on the foundation of the apostles, it is often used together with the adjective "catholic." The Roman church, though not exclusively, was normally referred to as the apostolic see.

Christians of the early centuries found and practiced different ways of preserving and promoting communion, unity of faith and discipline between the numerous communities spread throughout the Roman Empire especially, in the first centuries, and in the autonomous political entities in the succeeding centuries. Such methods, more or less effective and useful, were indispensable because of the great variety that was very notable. Further-

---

[9] 1 Tim 6:20; 2 Tim 4:3. [10] 1 Tim 5:17, 22; Tit 1:5; Acts 14:23; 20:17. [11] 1 Tim 4:14; cf. 1 Tim 5:22. [12] 2 Tim 1:6-7; cf. Acts 14:23. [13] J. N. D. Kelly, "'Catholique' et 'Apostolique' aux premiers siècles," *Istina* (1969): 33-45.

more, communication and circulation of ideas was problematic. Still, the organizations that were formed to ensure unity evolved strongly and sometimes assumed permanent forms. In the process of ensuring ecclesial *pax*, the laity became more and more marginalized, when they, in fact, had exercised a significant role in early times. For example, in the third century, the councils took place in public assembly; also, the laity traveled with *litterae communionis* to be welcomed by other communities; the laity were vigilant about the orthodoxy of their bishop. Contact with other Christian communities served to maintain and develop a consciousness of being a unity of many communities, like a federation of churches in which there exists a hierarchy of importance, of reference and of coordination. In the East, the seats of reference were those of Alexandria, of Antioch of Syria and, from the end of the fourth century, of Constantinople, which more and more became the center of attention and acquired a type of primacy, which was challenged by the other eastern sees. The presence of the emperor in the capital attracted many bishops there who, during their stay in the city, were able to form a type of permanent council.

There had to be a close system of communication, especially since at that time there was no canon law, only norms and local and regional traditions. The conciliar canons, not excluding those of the ecumenical councils, had a rather limited circulation, and knowledge of them was poor. A well-defined biblical canon did not exist either at that time. The Bible, a fundamental part of Christianity, was the constant point of reference in the life of Christian communities, in particular, in antiquity. Biblical exegesis was at the basis of preaching, of catechesis, of doctrinal elaboration, of ethics, of the institutions and the liturgy, and of the controversies. It was the source of unity but also of division because of the different possible interpretations, depending on different theologies. For this reason, discussion and communication, and not imposition from above, created real communion between the churches.

OVERVIEW: Ignatius, early in the second century, exhorts the Christians of Ephesus to harmonious unity as a choir composed of many voices. This unity is visible in the prayer around the altar, where we receive of the bread of God (IGNATIUS). The church, like a tower, is built by many stones that become one with the Rock (HERMAS). The community of brothers and sisters is spread all over, and they partake of the same bread and the same cup (IRENAEUS, CYPRIAN). The foundation of unity is the same faith received from the church, because the gift of God has been entrusted to the church; it, having its origin firm from the apostles, perseveres in one and the same opinion with regard to God and his Son (IRENAEUS), and it alone remains to all generations, rejoicing ever, subsisting as it does by the endurance of believers, who are the members of Christ (CLEMENT OF ALEXANDRIA). The sacrament of unity is expressed by the undivided coat of the Lord Jesus Christ, which is not cut but is received as an entire garment (CYPRIAN): one God, one Christ, one hope, one faith, one church, one baptism and one chair (one bishop in each local church). The bishop of Carthage is a great and passionate defender of the unity of the church. The unity comes from one bread, one cup and one Holy Spirit (LITURGY OF BASIL). The church, as only one body of Christ, is formed by the faithful throughout the whole world, which are, and which have been and which shall be (CHRYSOSTOM). The bread on the altar, sanctified by the Word of God, is the body of Christ; the cup, or rather what the cup contains, is the blood of Christ. If we receive them well, we are ourselves what we receive, the body of Christ, many though we be. At Pentecost, the unity of the church, which is the fruit of the Holy Spirit, was represented in the tongues of all nations. The earthly church is made one by the harmony of charity (AUGUSTINE).

The church, through communion with the Holy Spirit, is the place of holiness in view of its source and its destination. The holy churches are lovers of the truth and harbors of anchorage (THEOPHILUS). The church is holy because it is made for the honor of God and is sacred to him (CLEMENT OF ALEXANDRIA). Our most holy Mother Church is troubled by heresies (TREATISE ON REBATISM). The Fathers make particular observations on the word *holy* when they explain this sentence of the creed to catechumens. This name is peculiar to her, the mother of us all and the spouse of our Lord Jesus Christ, the only-begotten Son of God (CYRIL OF JERUSALEM). Life everlasting is given through the one, true and holy catholic church, which has the keys of the kingdom of heaven (AUGUSTINE). There is one holy catholic church in contrast to those who have departed from the faith (RUFINUS). The holiness of the church comes from Christ (CHRYSOLOGUS).

Both the local church and the universal church are catholic (MARTYRDOM OF POLYCARP). In the local sense, it is the true and authentic church, but all the other churches that are in communion with one another are true and authentic. The catholic church is spread throughout the world in the geographical sense (APOSTOLIC CONSTITUTIONS). The church is called catholic because it extends over all the world, from one end of the earth to the other, and because it teaches universally and completely one and all the doctrines that ought to come to human knowledge (CYRIL OF JERUSALEM). The church is the community of all the saints: all who from the beginning of the world were, are or will be justified (NICETA). The heretics inflict injury on the faith itself, while the schismatics break off from brotherly charity: they do not belong to the church catholic (AUGUSTINE). The true and genuine Catholic loves the truth of God and loves the church. He or she loves the body of Christ, esteems divine religion and the catholic faith above every thing, holding it as the highest authority and in the highest regard as being above our genius, eloquence or any philosophy we might hold (VINCENT).

The apostles provided for succession knowing there would be strife in the church (CLEMENT OF ROME). There are three grades of hierarchy—bishops, priests *(presbyterium)* and deacons—where bishops represent the Lord himself (IGNATIUS). Hegesippus, wanting to be sure of orthodoxy, undertook a journey, leaving from the East (Palestine?) and going as far as Rome, visiting the principal churches to verify their teaching; to this end he established an episcopal succession through which one can go back to the teaching of the apostles. The apostolicity of the churches and episcopal succession is historically verifiable against heretics who appeal to a secret tradition (IRENAEUS).

The apostles founded the churches and were themselves taught by God through Christ, thus assuring the transmission of true doctrine (TERTULLIAN). Meetings between the bishops—contact through letters, journeys and especially the synods—are the means by which *koinōnia* is exercised between the churches, with the purpose of remaining faithful to the traditions, in spite of the diversity of new situations and new disciplinary problems that have to be faced. The church of Rome exercises its role in that it "presides in charity" (IGNATIUS) and is founded by Peter and Paul, whose tombs it preserves (IRENAEUS).

The ancient church assigned a preeminent role to the criterion of historic apostolicity, as an irrevocable and necessary criterion to censure the unity and ecclesial communion of the one church of Christ. All the churches have to be apostolic, but the mother churches, those that founded or preceded others temporally, had greater responsibility also for their organization. Apostolicity is something historical and demonstrable from the lists of the bishops of the different churches; such lists are a chain of transmission of the original and faithful deposit and allow verification of its authenticity (IRENAEUS, TERTULLIAN, CLEMENT OF ALEXANDRIA, ORIGEN).

Very early on the adjective *apostolic* assumed a doctrinal and institutional significance in relation to the term *catholic* (TERTULLIAN, ORIGEN). The catholic church is the authentic one because it goes back to the apostles and faithfully transmits the teaching of the apostles, the first and the true witnesses of the teaching of the Lord and furthermore because it is founded by the apostles who made decisions regarding its future ministerial organization (TERTULLIAN, EPHREM, ALEXANDER, ATHANASIUS). The mission received by Christ from the Father is entrusted to his disciples, who are called to be faithful witnesses through succession from the apostles to those who will take their place in the mission of announcing the kingdom of God and preserving the faith once for all delivered to the saints (AUGUSTINE).

The Unity of Christians and of the Whole Church

CHRISTIANS MUST LIVE IN CONCORD. IGNATIUS OF ANTIOCH: I do not issue orders to you as if I were some great person. For though I am bound for the name of Christ, I am not yet perfect in Jesus Christ. For now I begin to be a disciple, and I speak to you as fellow disciples with me. For it is necessary for me to have been stirred up by you in faith, exhortation, patience and long-suffering. But inasmuch as love will not allow me to be silent in your regard, I have therefore taken on myself first to exhort you that you would all run together in accordance with the will of God. For even Jesus Christ, our inseparable life, is the manifested will of the Father; as also bishops, settled everywhere to the utmost bound of the earth, are so by the will of Jesus Christ.

Therefore it is fitting that you should run together in accordance with the will of your bishop just as you already do. For your justly renowned presbytery, worthy of God, is fitted as exactly to the bishop as the strings are to the harp. Therefore in your concord and harmonious love, Jesus Christ is sung. And I ask you, individual by individual, to become a choir, that being harmonious in love and taking up the song of God in unison, you may with one voice sing to the Father through Jesus Christ, so that he may both hear you and perceive by your works that you are indeed the members of his Son. It is profitable, therefore, that you should live in a blameless unity, that thus you may always enjoy communion with God. EPISTLE TO THE EPHESIANS 3-4.[14]

THE UNITY OF THE COMMUNITY. IGNATIUS OF ANTIOCH: For if in this brief space of time I have enjoyed such fellowship with your bishop—I mean not of a mere human but of a spiritual nature—how much more do I consider happy those of you who are joined to him just as the church is to Jesus Christ, and as Jesus Christ is to the Father, so that all things may agree in unity! Let no one deceive himself: If anyone is not within the altar, he is deprived of the bread of God. For if the prayer of one or two possesses such power, how much more that of the bishop and the whole church! He, therefore, who does not assemble with the church has even by this manifested his pride and condemned himself. For it is written, "God resists the proud."[15] Let us be careful, then, not to set ourselves in opposition to the bishop, in order that we may be subject to God. EPISTLE TO THE EPHESIANS 5.[16]

THE CHURCH AS ONE TOWER. HERMAS: For this reason you see that the tower became

---

[14]ANF 1:51*. [15]Prov 3:34; Jas 4:6; 1 Pet 5:5. [16]ANF 1:51*.

of one stone with the rock. So also those who have believed on the Lord through his Son and are clothed with these spirits shall become one spirit, one body, and the color of their garments shall be one. And the dwelling of such as bear the names of the virgins is in the tower. "Those stones, sir, that were rejected," I inquired, "why were they rejected? For they passed through the gate and were placed by the hands of the virgins in the building of the tower." "Since you take an interest in everything," he replied, "and examine minutely, hear about the stones that were rejected. These all," he said, "received the name of God, and they received also the strength of these virgins. Having received, then, these spirits, they were made strong and were with the servants of God; and theirs was one spirit, and one body and one clothing, for they were of the same mind and did what is right. After a certain time, however, they were persuaded by the women whom you saw clothed in black, having their shoulders exposed and their hair disheveled and were beautiful in appearance. Having seen these women, they desired to have them, and clothed themselves with their strength and put off the strength of the virgins. These, accordingly, were rejected from the house of God and were given over to these women. But they who were not deceived by the beauty of these women remained in the house of God. You have," he said, "the explanation of those who were rejected." SHEPHERD, SIMILITUDE 9.[17]

A GREAT COMMUNITY OF BROTHERS AND SISTERS. ABERCIUS: The citizen of an eminent city, I made this tomb in my lifetime, that I might have here a resting place for my body. Abercius by name, I am a disciple of the chaste shepherd who feeds his flocks of sheep on mountains and plains, who has great eyes that look on all sides. He taught me . . . faithful writings. He sent me to Rome to behold a kingdom and to see a queen with golden robe and golden shoes. There I saw a people bearing the splendid seal. And I saw the plain of Syria and all the cities, even Nisibis, having crossed the Euphrates. And everywhere I had associates. Having Paul as a companion, everywhere faith led the way and set before me food, the fish from the spring mighty and pure whom a spotless Virgin caught. He gave this to friends to eat, always having sweet wine and giving the mixed cup with bread. These words, I, Abercius, standing by, ordered to be inscribed. In truth, I was in the course of my seventy-second year. Let him who understands and believes this pray for Abercius. But no man shall place another tomb on mine. If one does so, he shall pay to the treasury of the Romans two thousand pieces of gold, and to my beloved fatherland Hieropolis, one thousand pieces of gold. ANCIENT ROMAN FUNERAL INSCRIPTION.[18]

WHERE THE CHURCH IS, THERE IS THE SPIRIT OF GOD. IRENAEUS: It has been shown that the preaching of the church is everywhere consistent and continues in an even course and receives testimony from the prophets, the apostles and all the disciples—as I have proved—through those in the beginning, the middle and the end, and through the entire dispensation of God and that well-grounded system that tends to humankind's salvation, namely, our faith. This faith, having been received from the church, we do preserve, and by the Spirit of God, it is always renewing its youth as if it were some precious deposit in an excellent vessel, causing the vessel itself containing it to renew its youth also. For this gift of God has been entrusted to the church, as breath was to the first created man, for this purpose, that all the members receiving it may be vivified. And the means of communion with Christ has been distributed throughout it, that is, the Holy Spirit, the guarantee of incorrup-

---

[17]ANF 2:48. [18]Quasten 1:172.

tion, the means of confirming our faith and the ladder of ascent to God. For in the church, it is said, God has set apostles, prophets, teachers[19] and all the other means through which the Spirit works. Of this all those are not partakers who do not join themselves to the church but defraud themselves of life through their perverse opinions and infamous behavior. For where the church is, there is the Spirit of God; and where the Spirit of God is, there is the church, and every kind of grace; but the Spirit is truth. . . . [Those who do not join themselves to the church] flee from the faith of the church, lest they be convicted, and reject the Spirit, that they may not be instructed. AGAINST HERESIES 3.24.1.[20]

UNITY COMES FROM THE APOSTLES. IRENAEUS: The church throughout all the world, having its origin firmly from the apostles, perseveres in one and the same opinion with regard to God and his Son. AGAINST HERESIES 3.12.7.[21]

THE SAME FAITH. IRENAEUS: But the path of those belonging to the church circumscribes the whole world, as possessing the sure tradition from the apostles, and allows us to see that the faith of all is one and the same, since all receive one and the same God the Father, and believe in the same dispensation regarding the incarnation of the Son of God, and are attentive to the same gift of the Spirit, and are conversant with the same commandments, and preserve the same form of ecclesiastical constitution, and expect the same advent of the Lord and await the same salvation of the complete person, that is, of the soul and body. And undoubtedly the preaching of the church is true and steadfast, in which one and the same way of salvation is shown throughout the whole world. For to it is entrusted the light of God, and therefore the wisdom of God, by means of which it saves all—a wisdom that is declared in its going forth; it speaks faithfully in the streets, is preached on the tops of the walls and speaks continually in the gates of the city.[22] For the church preaches the truth everywhere. It is the seven-branched candlestick that bears the light of Christ. AGAINST HERESIES 5.20.1.[23]

FOR ALL GENERATIONS. CLEMENT OF ALEXANDRIA: For what other employment is fitting for a wise and perfect person than to sport and be glad in the endurance of what is good and order what is good, holding festival with God? That which is signified by the prophet may be interpreted differently—namely, of our rejoicing for salvation, as Isaac. He also, delivered from death, laughed, sporting and rejoicing with his spouse, who was the type of the helper of our salvation, the church. To her the stable name of endurance is given, because she alone remains to all generations, rejoicing ever, subsisting as she does by the endurance of us believers, who are the members of Christ. CHRIST THE EDUCATOR 1.5.[24]

THE ONE CHURCH IS SPREAD FAR AND WIDE. CYPRIAN: The church also is one, which with increasing fecundity is spread abroad far and wide into a multitude, just as there are many rays of the sun but one light; and many branches of a tree but one strength based in its tenacious root. And since from one spring flow many streams, although the multiplicity seems diffused in the liberality of an overflowing abundance, yet the unity is still preserved in the source. Separate a ray of the sun from its body of light; its unity does not allow a division of light. Break a branch from a tree and, when broken, it will not be able to bud. Cut off the stream from its fountain, and that which is cut off dries up. Thus also the church, bathed in the light of the Lord, sheds forth its rays over the whole world, yet

---

[19]See 1 Cor 12:28. [20]ANF 1:458. [21]ANF 1:433. [22]See Prov 1:20-21. [23]ANF 1:548*. [24]ANF 2:214.

it is one light that is everywhere diffused, nor is the unity of the body separated. Its fruitful abundance spreads its branches over the whole world. It broadly expands its rivers, liberally flowing, yet its head is one, its source one. It is one mother, plentiful in the results of fruitfulness: from its womb we are born, by its milk we are nourished, by its spirit we are animated. ON THE UNITY OF THE CHURCH 5.[25]

THE SACRAMENT OF UNITY. CYPRIAN: This sacrament of unity, this bond of a concord inseparably cohering, is set forth where in the gospel the coat of the Lord Jesus Christ is not at all divided or cut but is received as an entire garment and is possessed as an uninjured and undivided robe by those who cast lots for Christ's garment, who rather might have put on Christ. Holy Scripture speaks, saying, "But of the coat, because it was not sewed, but woven from the top throughout, they said one to another, 'Let us not rend it, but cast lots whose it shall be.'"[26] That coat bore with it a unity that came down from the top, that is, that came from heaven and the Father, which was not to be at all rent by the receiver and possessor, but without separation we are given its whole and substantial entireness. He cannot possess the garment of Christ who parts and divides the church of Christ. On the other hand, again, when at Solomon's death his kingdom and people were divided, Abijah the prophet, meeting Jeroboam the king in the field, divided his garment into twelve sections, saying, "Take ten pieces; for thus says the Lord, 'Behold, I will rend the kingdom out of the hand of Solomon, and I will give you ten scepters; and two scepters shall be unto him for my servant David's sake, and for Jerusalem, the city which I have chosen to place my name there.'"[27] As the twelve tribes of Israel were divided, the prophet Abijah rent his garment. But because Christ's people cannot be rent, his robe, woven and united throughout, is not divided by those who possess it. Undivided, united, connected, it shows the coherent concord of our people who put on Christ. By the sacrament and sign of his garment, he has declared the unity of the church. ON THE UNITY OF THE CHURCH 7.[28]

ONE ALTAR, ONE CHURCH. CYPRIAN: God is one, and Christ is one: there is one church and one chair founded, by the Lord's authority, on Peter. It is not possible that another altar can be set up or that a new priesthood can be appointed, over and above this one altar and this one priesthood. Whoever gathers elsewhere, scatters. Whatever is so established by humankind in its madness that it violates what has been appointed by God is an obscene outrage; it is a sacrilege. LETTER 43.5.[29]

THE MYSTERY OF UNITY. CYPRIAN: And the tradition handed down to us is that there is one God and one Christ, one hope and one faith, one church and one baptism appointed only in that one church. Whoever departs from that unity must be found in company with heretics; and in defending heretics against the church, he is launching an attack on the sacred mystery of this divine tradition. The sacred mystery of this unity we also see expressed in the person of Christ, who says in the Song of Songs, "An enclosed garden is my sister, my bride, a sealed fountain, a well of living water, an orchard of fruits." Now if this church is an enclosed garden and a sealed fountain, how is it possible for anyone who is not within the church to enter that garden or to drink from its fountain? LETTER 74.11.[30]

ONLY ONE CHURCH. CYPRIAN: Between us we have but one church; we are united in heart; we are inseparable in concord. What bishop would not, therefore, rejoice in the honors of his brother bishop as if they were his very

---

[25]ANF 5:423*. [26]Cf. Jn 19:23-24. [27]Cf. 1 Kings 11:31. [28]ANF 5:423. [29]ACW 44:64. [30]ACW 47:77.

own? Where is a community of brothers who would not take delight in the joy of their fellows? LETTER 60.1.[31]

UNITY MUST BE PRESERVED. CYPRIAN: With us unanimity and concord should not on any account be broken. For our part we are unable to forsake the church, to go outside it and come over to you; therefore, it is rather up to you to return to the church, your mother, and to your brothers. And we exhort, urge and beg you to do so with all our might. LETTER 46.2.[32]

THE UNITY OF THE CHURCH IS WITH THE BISHOP. CYPRIAN: Speaking there is Peter, on whom the church had been built, and in the name of the church he is teaching and revealing that even when a whole host of proud and presumptuous people may refuse to listen and go away, the church itself does not go away from Christ, and in his view the church consists of the people who remain united with their bishop; it is the flock that stays by its shepherd. But you ought to realize that the bishop is in the church and the church is in the bishop, and whoever is not with the bishop is not in the church. You must understand that it is to no avail that people may beguile themselves with the illusion that while they are at peace with the bishops of God they may still worm their way in and surreptitiously hold communion with certain people. Whereas, in truth, the church forms one single whole; it is neither rent nor broken apart but is everywhere linked and bonded tightly together by the glue of the bishops sticking firmly to each other. LETTER 66.8.[33]

ONLY ONE BAPTISM WITHIN THE CATHOLIC CHURCH. CYPRIAN: I cannot imagine what foolhardy supposition induces some of our colleagues to think that there is no need for those who have been bathed among heretics to receive baptism when they come over to us—on the grounds that, so they contend, there is only one baptism. Of course there is only one baptism, but it is to be found within the catholic church, for the church itself is one, and there cannot be baptism outside of that church. There cannot be two baptisms: hence, if heretics genuinely baptize, they must be the ones who have the power of baptism. Anyone who uses the weight of his authority to offer to heretics this sort of advocacy is capitulating to them; he is agreeing that an enemy and adversary of Christ would appear to have the power of cleansing, purifying and sanctifying humankind.[34]

But what we say is this: Those who come from heresy are not being rebaptized with us; they are being baptized. They cannot receive anything there, where there is nothing; rather, they come to us so that here they may receive, where all grace and truth belong (for grace and truth are one). Even so, some of our colleagues would rather give honor to heretics than agree with us; they refuse to baptize those who come to them, asserting the oneness of baptism. And yet by so doing they are themselves in effect creating two baptisms in that they affirm that baptism is also to be found among heretics. Or else—clearly the more grievous offense—they are doing their best to give precedence and superiority to the foul and unholy washing of heretics over the one and only, the true and lawful baptism of the catholic church. They fail to heed the words of Scripture: *If a man is baptized by one who is dead, what does his washing avail him?*[35] Now it is evident that those who are not in the church of Christ are reckoned among the dead and that one man cannot be given life by another man who himself does not have life; there is only the one church, which has obtained the grace of eternal life, and it not only has life itself for

---

[31]ACW 46:88. [32]ACW 44:73. [33]ACW 46:121-22. [34]See, however, Augustine's comments concerning Cyprian and his call to rebaptize those baptized by heretics. Augustine's comments can be found in the section on baptism in this volume. [35]Sir 34:25.

eternity but also gives life to God's people. LETTER 71.1.[36]

ONLY ONE. CYPRIAN: And the tradition handed down to us is that there is one God and one Christ, one hope and one faith, one church and one baptism appointed only in that one church. Whoever departs from that unity must be found in company with heretics; and in defending heretics against the church, he is launching an attack on the sacred mystery of this divine tradition. LETTER 73.11.1.[37]

BAPTISM FOUND ONLY IN THE CHURCH. CYPRIAN: What blindness of soul can this be, what perverseness, to refuse to acknowledge the unity of faith that proceeds from God the Father and from the tradition of Jesus Christ our Lord and God. For if it is the case that the church is not with heretics for the reason that the church is one and cannot be divided, and if the Holy Spirit is not with them for the reason that the Spirit is one and cannot be with outsiders and aliens, then it indeed follows that baptism cannot be with heretics either, for baptism is to be found only within that same unity. Baptism can be separated neither from the church nor from the Holy Spirit. LETTER 74.4.2.[38]

ONE BREAD, ONE CUP, ONE HOLY SPIRIT. LITURGY OF SAINT BASIL: And unite us all to one another who become partakers of the one bread and the cup in the communion of the one Holy Spirit. Grant that none of us may partake of the holy body and blood of your Christ to judgment or condemnation but that we may find mercy and grace with all the saints who have pleased you: ancestors, patriarchs, prophets, apostles, preachers, evangelists, martyrs, confessors, teachers and every righteous spirit made perfect in faith. Especially for our most holy, pure blessed and glorious lady, Theotokos [mother of God] and ever-virgin Mary. LITURGY OF SAINT BASIL.[39]

UNITY IS FROM CHRIST. EPHREM THE SYRIAN: Blessed are you, O church, for Isaiah also exulted in you in his prophecy: Behold, a virgin shall conceive and bear a child whose name is a mighty symbol. O the meaning revealed in the church! Two names, which have united and become one, Emmanuel, God with you at all times, since he united you with his members. HYMNS ON THE NATIVITY 25.5.[40]

THE CHURCH ONE BODY. CHRYSOSTOM: "One Lord, one faith, one baptism."[41] Now what is this one body? The faithful throughout the whole world, both which are, and which have been and which shall be. And again, they that before Christ's coming pleased God are one body. How so? Because they also knew Christ. When does this appear? "Your father Abraham," he says, "rejoiced that he was to see my day; he saw it and was glad."[42] And again, "If you believed Moses," he says, "you would believe me, for he wrote of me."[43] And the prophets too would not have written of one, of whom they knew not what they said; they both knew him and worshiped him. Thus then were they also one body. . . . Now why am I saying this? There are great numbers in the church; there are those who, like the head, are raised up to a height; who, like the eyes that are in the head, survey heavenly things, who stand far aloof from the earth and have nothing in common with it, while others occupy the rank of feet and tread on the earth; of healthy feet indeed, for to tread on the earth is no crime in feet, but to run to evil. "Their feet," says the prophet, "run to evil."[44] HOMILIES ON EPHESIANS 10.[45]

THE UNITY AND SANCTITY OF THE CHURCH. CHRYSOSTOM: While our Father's house is burning, we are sleeping, as it were, a deep and stupid sleep. And yet who is there whom this

---

[36]ACW 46:49. [37]ACW 47:77. [38]ACW 47:72. [39]DLSB. [40]SCK 149*. [41]Eph 4:5. [42]Jn 8:56. [43]Jn 5:46. [44]Is 59:7. [45]NPNF 1 13:99*.

fire does not touch? Which of the statues that stand in the church? For the church is nothing else than a house built of the souls of us. Now this house is not of equal honor throughout, but of the stones that contribute to it, some are bright and shining, while others are smaller and more dull than they, and yet superior again to others.... We see around us, but of gold and silver and of precious stones, and there is abundance of gold dispersed everywhere throughout it. But, oh, the bitter tears this calls forth! For all these things the lawless rule of vainglory has consumed—that all-devouring flame that no one has yet got under. And we stand gazing in amazement at the flames but no longer able to quench the evil. As to the cause, it has devoured the supports of the very pillars of the church. Those of us who supported the roof and who formerly held the whole building together it has enveloped in the flame.... Thus is it also at this moment with the church: the fire has laid hold on every part. We seek human honors, we burn for glory, and we do not pay attention to Job when he says, "If like Adam [or, after the manner of men] I covered my transgressions by hiding my iniquity in my bosom, because I feared the great multitude."[46] ... We are no longer able to rebuke those who are under our rule, because we ourselves also are possessed with the same fever as they. We, who are appointed by God to heal others, need the physician ourselves. What further hope of recovery is there left, when even the very physicians themselves need the healing hand of others?

I have not said these things without an object, nor am I making lamentations to no purpose but with the view that one and all, with our women and children, having sprinkled ourselves with ashes and clothed ourselves about with sackcloth, may keep a long fast, may beseech God to stretch forth his hand to us and to stay the peril. For need is there indeed of his hand, that mighty, that marvelous hand. HOMILIES ON EPHESIANS 10.[47]

A NAME OF UNITY. CHRYSOSTOM: "To the church of God."[48] Not "of this or of that man," but of God. "Which is at Corinth." You see how at each word Paul puts down their swelling pride; training their thoughts in every way for heaven? He calls it, too, the church of God, showing that it ought to be united. For if it is of God, it is united, and it is one, not in Corinth only but also in all the world, for the church's name is not a name of separation but of unity and concord. HOMILIES ON 1 CORINTHIANS 1.1.[49]

THE BODY IS ONE. CHRYSOSTOM: And how is it possible that they should be one? When distinguishing the differences of the members, consider the body. For the same thing that the eye is, this also is the foot in regard to its being a member and constituting a body. For there is no difference in this respect. Nor can you say that one of the members makes a body of itself but another does not. For they are all equal in this, for the very reason that they are all one body. But having said this and having shown it clearly from the common judgment of all, he added, "so also is Christ." And when he should have said, "so also is the church," for this was the natural consequent, he does not say it but instead speaks the name of Christ, carrying the discourse up on high and appealing more and more to the hearer's reverence. But his meaning is this: "So also is the body of Christ, which is the church." For as the body and the head are one person, so he said that the church and Christ are one. Therefore also he indicated Christ instead of the church, giving that name to his body. "As then," he says, "our body is one thing though it is composed of many: so also in the church we all are one thing. For though the church is composed of many members, yet these many form one body." HOMILIES ON 1 CORINTHIANS 30.1.[50]

---

[46]Cf. Job 31:33-34. [47]NPNF 1 13:101*. [48]1 Cor 1:1. [49]NPNF 1 12:3*. [50]NPNF 1 12:176.

UNITY FROM THE EUCHARIST. AUGUSTINE: That bread that you can see on the altar, sanctified by the Word of God, is the body of Christ. That cup, or rather what the cup contains, sanctified by the Word of God, is the blood of Christ. It was by means of these things that the Lord Christ wished to present us with his body and blood, which he shed for our sake for the forgiveness of sins. If you receive them well, you are yourselves what you receive. The apostle says, "We who are many are one body."[51] That's how he explained the sacrament of the Lord's table; one loaf, one body, is what we all are, many though we be.

In this loaf of bread you are given clearly to understand how much you should love unity. I mean, was that loaf made from one grain? Weren't there many grains of wheat? But before they came into the loaf, they were all separate; they were joined together by means of water after a certain amount of pounding and crushing. Unless wheat is ground, after all, and moistened with water, it can't possibly get into this shape that is called bread. In the same way you too were being ground and pounded, as it were, by the humiliation of fasting and the sacrament of exorcism. Then came baptism, and you were, in a manner of speaking, moistened with water in order to be shaped into bread. But it's not yet bread without fire to bake it. So what does fire represent? That's the chrism, the anointing. Oil, the fire feeder, you see, is the sacrament of the Holy Spirit. SERMON 227.1.[52]

THE VALUE OF UNITY IMPRESSED ON US. AUGUSTINE: My dearest friends, there's so much God does in order to emphasize the importance of unity. What he did at the very beginning of creation should make you think; when God established the universe, he made the constellations in the sky, while on earth he made the plants and trees. He said, "Let the earth produce," and the trees and all green plants were produced; he said, "Let the waters produce things that swim and fly," and it happened like that; he said, "Let the earth produce the living soul of all cattle and beasts,"[53] and it happened like that. Did God make all the other birds from one bird? All fishes from one fish? All horses from one horse? All beasts from one beast? Didn't the earth produce many of them simultaneously and together, completing the requisite numbers with multiple births?

We come now to the making of man, and only one was made, and the human race from that one. He wasn't even willing to make two separately, a male and a female, but just one man, and from the one man one woman. Why so? Why is the human race begun from one person, if not because the importance of unity is being impressed on the human race? The Lord Christ too was from one. SERMON 268.3.[54]

ONE CATHOLIC CHURCH THROUGHOUT THE WORLD. AUGUSTINE: While these things belong to both sorts, all the nations belong only to Augustine: the spiritual sort because these in turn belong to the church, which has filled the whole world. Pay careful attention, brothers, and see the different as far as you can, as far as the Lord grants you. All spiritual people see that the church throughout the whole world is one, true and catholic. SERMON 4.32.[55]

THE UNITY OF THE CHURCH REPRESENTED. AUGUSTINE: It is because of the coming of the Holy Spirit that this is a solemn day for us, the fiftieth after the Lord's resurrection, coming after seven weeks. But count the days of seven weeks, each of seven days, and you will find there are forty-nine of them; one is added to impress on us the importance of unity. What about the actual coming of the Holy Spirit, what did that do? How did he make his

---

[51]1 Cor 10:17. [52]*WSA* 3 6:254. [53]See Gen 1:11, 20, 24. [54]*WSA* 3 7:279-80. [55]*WSA* 3 1:202.

presence known, how did he demonstrate it? They all spoke with the tongues of all nations. Actually, there were 120 people in one place— the symbolically sacred number twelve of the apostles multiplied by ten.

So what, then? Did each single person, of those on whom the Holy Spirit came, speak in a single tongue of all the nations, these speaking one language, and those another, and did they somehow or other divide up the languages of all nations between them? Not like that; but each person, one person, was speaking in the languages of all nations. One person was speaking in the tongues of all nations; the unity of the church in the tongues of all nations. So there you are; here too the unity of the catholic church is being impressed on us as it is spread throughout the whole world. SERMON 268.1.[56]

UNITY IS FRUIT OF THE HOLY SPIRIT. AUGUSTINE: You appear in your own eyes to say, "Jesus is Lord." And perhaps, without understanding it rightly, you are paying attention to what the apostle says, "No one can say 'Jesus is Lord' except by the Holy Spirit."[57] But when he says "can say," he puts it emphatically, and means it in a special sort of sense. Yes, nobody can say "Jesus is Lord" except in the Holy Spirit—but provided you say it in deeds, not just in words. After all, "Jesus is Lord" can be said even by the people of whom he says, "Do what they say, but do not do what they do."[58] All the heresies, which you people also condemn of course, they all say, "Jesus is Lord." And he's not, of course, going to eliminate from the kingdom of heaven those whom he finds to be in the Holy Spirit; and yet he did say, "Not every one who says to me, 'Lord, Lord,' shall enter the kingdom of heaven."[59] But nobody can say "Jesus is Lord" except in the Holy Spirit; nobody at all, evidently; but in the sense in which it was meant, that is, in deeds. Which is why the Lord went on to add, "But he who does the will of my Father who is in heaven," that one will enter the kingdom of heaven.[60] The same apostle, you see, also says of some people, "They profess to know God, but they deny him by their deeds."[61] As it can be denied by deeds, so it can be said by deeds. In this manner of saying things, nobody can say "Jesus is Lord" except in the Holy Spirit.

So if you don't accede to the unity but continue to set yourselves apart, you will be worldly, not having the Spirit. If, though, you accede under false pretenses, the Holy Spirit of discipline will put to flight false pretenses.[62] So then, the time you can be sure you have the Holy Spirit is when you consent through sincere charity firmly to attach your minds to the unity. That's the sort of answer we must give them when they say, "What are we going to receive?" As for ourselves, brothers and sisters, let us present them with the example of good works, neither being proud because we happen to stand firm ourselves nor despairing of those who are still lying flat on their faces. SERMON 269.4.[63]

ESTABLISHED IN THE UNITY OF THE CHURCH. AUGUSTINE: The glad day has dawned, brothers and sisters, on which holy church is resplendent in the faces of the faithful and warm in their hearts. This day that we are celebrating, of course, is the one on which the Lord Jesus Christ, glorified after the resurrection by his ascension, sent the Holy Spirit. That, after all, is what was written in the Gospel, when he said, "If anyone thirsts, let him come to me and drink. He who believes in me, . . . 'Out of his heart shall flow rivers of living water.'" The Evangelist went on to explain, "Now this he said about the Spirit, which those who believed in him were to receive; for as yet the Spirit had not been given, because Jesus was not yet glorified."[64] So it remained,

---

[56]*WSA* 3 7:278. [57]1 Cor 12:3. [58]See Mt 23:3. [59]Mt 7:21. [60]Mt 7:21. [61]Tit 1:16. [62]Cf. Wis 1:5. [63]*WSA* 3 7:285-86. [64]Jn 7:37-39.

once Jesus was glorified when he had risen from the dead and ascended into heaven, for the Holy Spirit now to be given, sent by him as it had been promised by him; and that indeed is what happened.

The Lord, you see, spent forty days with his disciples after the resurrection and then ascended into heaven; and on the fiftieth day, which we are celebrating today, he sent the Holy Spirit, as it is written, that "suddenly a sound came from heaven like the rush of a mighty wind, and it filled the house where they were sitting. And there appeared to them tongues as of fire, distributed and resting on each one of them. And they were all filled with the Holy Spirit and began to speak in other tongues, as the Spirit gave them utterance."[65] That gust was purging their hearts of worldly chaff; that fire was consuming the straw of ancient lusts; those tongues they were speaking in, filled by the Holy Spirit, were prefiguring the church of the future through the languages of all nations.

I mean, just as after the flood the ungodly pride of people built a high tower against the Lord and the human race was deservedly divided by languages, so that each nation would speak its own language and thus not be understood by the others; so in a similar way the devout humility of the faithful has brought to the unity of the church the variety of their different languages, so that what discord had dissipated charity might gather together, and the scattered members of the human race, as of one body, might be attached to their one head, Christ, and so reunited and fused together into the unity of the holy body by the fire of love. And so it is that those people have absolutely no share in this gift of the Holy Spirit who hate the grace of peace, who do not hold on to the fellowship of unity. . . . You, though, my brothers and sisters, members of the body of Christ, seedlings of unity, sons and daughters of peace, keep this day joyfully, celebrate it without anxiety. Among you, after all, is being fulfilled what was being prefigured in those days, when the Holy Spirit came. Because just as then, whoever received the Holy Spirit, even as one person, started speaking all languages, so too now the unity itself is speaking all languages throughout all nations; and it is by being established in this unity that you have the Holy Spirit; you that do not break away in any schism from the church of Christ, which speaks all languages. SERMON 271.[66]

MADE ONE BY THE HARMONY OF CHARITY. AUGUSTINE: Listen very briefly to the apostle, or rather to Christ speaking through the apostle. To what he says about the sacrament of the Lord's table: one loaf, one body, is what we, being many, are.[67] There you have it all; I said it in a moment. But you must weigh the words, don't count them. If you count the words, it's short enough; if you weigh them, it's tremendous. One loaf, he said. However many loaves may be placed there, it's one loaf, however many loaves there may be on Christ's altars throughout the world, it's one loaf. But what does it mean, one loaf? He explained very briefly: one body is what we, being many, are. This is the body of Christ, about which the apostle says, while addressing the church, "you are the body of Christ and individually members of it."[68] What you receive is what you yourselves are, thanks to the grace by which you have been redeemed; you add your signature to this when you answer "Amen." What you see here is the sacrament of unity. . . . But just as one loaf is made from single grains collected together and somehow mixed in with each other into dough, so in the same way the body of Christ is made one by the harmony of charity. And what grains are for the body of Christ, grapes are for his blood; because wine

---

[65]Acts 2:2-4. [66]*WSA* 3 7:298-99. [67]See 1 Cor 10:17. [68]1 Cor 12:27.

too comes out from the press, and what was separated one by one in many grapes flows together into a unity and becomes wine. Thus both in the bread and in the cup there is the mystery, the sacrament, of unity. SERMON 229A.1-2.[69]

The Church, a Community of Believers, Is Holy

THE CHURCH IS HOLY. THEOPHILUS OF ANTIOCH: To the world which is driven and tempest-tossed by sins, God has given assemblies—holy churches, in which survive the doctrines of the truth. They are like island harbors of good anchorage; and into these run those who desire to be saved, being lovers of the truth, and wishing to escape the wrath and judgment of God. TO AUTOLYCUS 2.14.[70]

CONSTRUCTED BY THE WILL OF GOD. CLEMENT OF ALEXANDRIA: And *sacred* has a twofold application, designating both God and the structure raised to his honor; how shall we not with propriety call the church holy, through knowledge, made for the honor of God, sacred to God, of great value and not constructed by mechanical art or embellished by the hand of an impostor but by the will of God fashioned into a temple? For it is not now the place, but the assemblage of the elect, that I call the church. This temple is better for the reception of the greatness of the dignity of God. For the living creature, which is of high value, is made sacred by that which is worth all, or rather which has no equivalent, in virtue of the exceeding sanctity of the latter. Now this is the gnostic, who is of great value, who is honored by God, in whom God IS enshrined, that is, the knowledge respecting God is consecrated. STROMATEIS 7.5.[71]

OUR MOST HOLY MOTHER CHURCH. TREATISE ON REBAPTISM: It is the very greatest disadvantage and damage to our most holy mother church, now for the first time suddenly and without reason to rebel against former decisions after so long a series of so many ages. For not for any other reason Peter—who had already been baptized and had been asked what he thought of the Lord by the Lord himself, and the truth of the revelation of the Father in heaven being bestowed on him had confessed that Christ was not only our Lord but was the Son of the living God—was shown subsequently to have withstood the same Christ when he made announcement of his passion and therefore was depicted as being called "Satan." TREATISE ON REBAPTISM 6.[72]

HOLY CATHOLIC CHURCH. CYRIL OF JERUSALEM: But the word *ecclesia* is applied to different things. It is written of the multitude in the theater of the Ephesians, "And when he had said this, he dismissed the assembly."[73] Similarly, one might properly and truly say that there is an assembly (*ecclesia*) of evildoers that would conceivably include the meetings of the heretics, the Marcionists and Manichaeans, and the rest. Thus the faith has securely delivered to you now the article, "and in one holy catholic church," that you may avoid their disgraceful meetings and ever abide with the holy church catholic in which you were regenerated. And if ever you are visiting in cities, do not ask simply where the Lord's house is (for the other sects of the profane also attempt to call their own dens houses of the Lord), nor merely where the church is, but where is the catholic church. For this is the peculiar name of this holy church, the mother of us all, which is the spouse of our Lord Jesus Christ, the only-begotten Son of God. For it is written, "As Christ loved the church and gave himself up for her,"[74] and all the rest, and is a figure and copy of Jerusalem above, "which is free, and she is our mother,"[75] which before was bar-

---

[69]WSA 3 6:269-70. [70]ANF 2:100. [71]ANF 2:530. [72]ANF 5:670*. [73]Acts 19:41. [74]Eph 5:25. [75]Gal 4:26.

ren but now has many children.

For when the earlier assembly was cast off, in the second, which is the church catholic, God has set, as Paul says, "first apostles, second prophets, third teachers, then miracles, then gifts of healings, helps, governments, various kinds of tongues,"[76] and every sort of virtue, I mean wisdom and understanding, temperance and justice, mercy and lovingkindness and patience unconquerable in persecutions. She, "by the armor of righteousness on the right hand and on the left, by honor and dishonor,"[77] in former days amid persecutions and tribulations crowned the holy martyrs with the varied and blooming chaplets of patience. Now in times of peace by God's grace she receives her due honors from "kings and those who are in high places"[78] and from every sort of human tribe. And while the kings of particular nations have bounds set to their authority, the holy church catholic alone extends her power without limit over the whole world; for God, as it is written, "has made her border peace." But I should need many more hours for my discourse, if I wished to speak of all things which concern her. CATECHETICAL LECTURE 18.26-27.[79]

THE HOLINESS OF THE CHURCH. AUGUSTINE: The creed goes on, after presenting us with the Trinity, to the holy church. God has been pointed out to you, and his temple. For the temple of God, says the apostle, which is what you are, is holy.[80] That is the holy church, the one church, the true church, the catholic church, fighting against all heresies; it can fight, but it cannot be outfought. All heresies have emerged from it, like useless twigs pruned from a vine, while it remains itself in its root, in its vine, in its love. SERMON 398.14.[81]

LIFE EVERLASTING. AUGUSTINE: You undoubtedly see, my dearly beloved, how even in the very words of the holy creed, as a conclusion to all the beliefs that pertain to the mystery of faith, a certain addition has been made so that the words "through the holy church" might be used. Avoid, therefore, as much as possible, the various separated deceivers whose sects and names, in view of their large number, would take too long to mention now. As a matter of fact, I have many things to say to you, but you are not able to bear them just now. One thing I commend to your prayers, namely, that you turn away your mind and your attention in every respect from one who is not catholic, so that you may be able to gain remission of sins, resurrection of the body and life everlasting through the one, true and holy catholic church, in which the Father, Son and Holy Spirit are presented as one God to whom be honor and glory forever. SERMON 215.9.[82]

THE KEYS OF THE KINGDOM OF HEAVEN. AUGUSTINE: Also the holy church; honor, love, proclaim her as your mother, the Jerusalem that is above, the holy city of God. She it is who, in this faith that you have heard, bears fruit and grows in the whole world, "the church of the living God, the pillar and bulwark of the truth,"[83] who tolerates the wicked in the communion of the sacraments, knowing that they are due to be separated from her at the end and withdrawing from them meanwhile in the dissimilarity of her morals. This church has received "the keys of the kingdom of heaven"[84] for the sake of her grains of corn now groaning among the chaff but destined to be piled manifestly in the granaries at the final winnowing. This is so that in her, through the blood of Christ, by the working of the Holy Spirit, there may be had the forgiveness of sins. In this church the soul that had been dead in its sins comes to life again, in order to be made alive with Christ, by whose grace we have been saved. SERMON 214.11.[85]

---

[76]1 Cor 12:28. [77]2 Cor 6:7-8. [78]1 Tim 2:2. [79]NPNF 2 7:140-41*. [80]1 Cor 3:17. [81]*WSA* 3 10:454. [82]FC 38:149-50. [83]1 Tim 3:15. [84]Mt 16:19. [85]*WSA* 3 6:157.

WE BELIEVE ONE HOLY CHURCH. RUFINUS OF AQUILEIA: We come next in the order of belief to the holy church. We have mentioned already why the creed does not say here, as in the preceding article, "in the holy church." They, therefore, who were taught already to believe in one God, under the mystery of the Trinity, must believe this also, that there is one holy church in which there is one faith and one baptism, in which is believed one God the Father and one Lord Jesus Christ, his Son, and one Holy Spirit. This is that holy church that is without spot or wrinkle. For many others have gathered together so-called churches, as Marcion, and Valentinus, and Ebion, and Manichaeus, and Arius, and all the other heretics. But those churches are not without spot or wrinkle of unfaithfulness. And therefore the prophet said of them, "I hate the church of the malignants, and I will not sit with the ungodly."[86] But of this church that keeps the faith of Christ in its wholeness, hear what the Holy Spirit says in the Song of Solomon, "My dove is one; the perfect one of her mother is one."[87] One then who receives this faith in the church, let him not turn aside in the council of vanity, and let him not enter in with those who practice iniquity.

For Marcion's assembly is a council of vanity in that he denies that the Father of Christ is God, the creator, who by his Son made the world. Ebion's is a council of vanity since he teaches that, while we believe in Christ, we are still to observe the circumcision of the flesh, the keeping of the sabbath, the accustomed sacrifices and all the other ordinances according to the letter of the law. Manichaeus's is a council of vanity in regard to his teaching, first in that he calls himself the Paraclete; then that he says that the world was made by an evil God; denies God the creator; rejects the Old Testament; asserts two natures in God, one good, the other evil, mutually opposing one another; affirms that people's souls are coeternal with God; that, according to the Pythagoreans, they return through multiple circles of birth into cattle and animals and beasts; denies the resurrection of our flesh; maintains that the passion and nativity of the Lord were not really of flesh, but only apparently. It was the council of vanity when Paul of Samosata and his successor Photinus afterward taught that Christ was not born of the Father before the world but had his beginning from Mary alone and did not believe that being God he was born man, but rather that of man he was made God. It was the council of vanity when Arius and Eunomius taught as their explicit opinion that the Son of God was not born of the very substance of the Father but was created out of nothing, and that the Son of God had a beginning and is inferior to the Father. Moreover, they affirm that the Holy Spirit is not only inferior to the Son but is also a ministering angelic spirit. Theirs also is a council of vanity who confess indeed that the Son is of the substance of the Father but distinguish and separate the Holy Spirit, while yet the Savior shows in the Gospel that the power and Godhead of the Trinity are one and the same, saying, "Baptize all nations in the name of the Father, and of the Son and of the Holy Spirit." It is plainly impious for humankind to put asunder what God has has joined together. That also is the council of vanity that a stubborn and wicked contention formerly gathered together, affirming that Christ assumed human flesh indeed, but not a rational soul, since Christ conferred one and the same salvation on the flesh, and the animal soul and the reason and mind of humankind. That also is the council of vanity that Donatus drew together throughout Africa, by charging the church with delivering up the sacred books, and with which Novatus disturbed people's minds by denying the grant of repentance to the lapsed and condemning second marriages, though contracted possibly of necessity. All

---

[86]Ps 26:5. [87]Song 6:9.

of these then avoid as congregations of malignants. Those also who are said to assert that the Son of God does not see or know the Father, as himself is known and seen by the Father; or that the kingdom of Christ will have an end; or that the flesh will not be raised in the complete restoration of its substance. Likewise those who deny that there will be a just judgment of God in respect of all and affirm that the devil will be absolved from the punishment of damnation due to him. To all these, I say, let the believer turn a deaf ear. But hold fast by the holy church, which confesses God the Father Almighty and his only Son, Jesus Christ our Lord, and the Holy Spirit of one well-balanced and harmonious substance, believes that the Son of God was born of the Virgin, suffered for people's salvation, rose again from the dead in the same flesh in which he was born, and, lastly, hopes that he will come the judge of all, through whom also both the forgiveness of sins and the resurrection of the flesh are preached. A COMMENTARY ON THE APOSTLES' CREED 39.[88]

HOLY BECAUSE IT IS IN CHRIST. PETER CHRYSOLOGUS: And the holy church, as though united to Christ, in order to be conveyed to the full glory of divinity. . . . And the holy church. We also believe in the church, which we believe and profess has been received and confirmed into Christ's glory. . . . We believe in the holy church, which Christ took to himself in such a way as to make it a sharer in his divinity. . . . We believe in the holy church: because the church is in Christ, and Christ is in the church. The one who confesses the church has professed that he has believed in the church. SERMONS 58.11; 59.14; 60.14; 62.15.[89]

The Church Is Catholic, Bringing Salvation to All

WHERE JESUS CHRIST IS. IGNATIUS OF ANTIOCH: Let that be deemed a proper Eucharist which is administered either by the bishop or by one to whom he has entrusted it. Wherever the bishop shall appear, there let the multitude of the people also be; even as, wherever Jesus Christ is, there is the catholic church. It is not lawful without the bishop either to baptize or to celebrate a love feast; but what he shall approve of, that is also pleasing to God, so that everything that is done may be secure and valid. EPISTLE TO THE SMYRNEANS 8.2.[90]

IN EVERY PLACE. MARTYRDOM OF POLYCARP: The church of God that sojourns at Smyrna, to the church of God sojourning in Philomelium and to all the congregations of the holy and catholic church in every place: Mercy, peace, and love from God the Father and our Lord Jesus Christ be multiplied. MARTYRDOM OF POLYCARP 1.[91]

THROUGHOUT THE WORLD. MARTYRDOM OF POLYCARP: Now, as soon as he had ceased praying, having made mention of all that had at any time come in contact with him, both small and great, illustrious and obscure, as well as the whole catholic church throughout the world, the time of his departure having arrived, they set him on a donkey and conducted him into the city, the day being that of the great sabbath. MARTYRDOM OF POLYCARP 8.[92]

THE CHURCH CATHOLIC IN SMYRNA. MARTYRDOM OF POLYCARP: At length, when those wicked men perceived that Polycarp's body could not be consumed by the fire, they commanded an executioner to go near and pierce him through with a dagger. And on his doing this, there came forth a dove and a great quantity of blood, so that the fire was extinguished. And all the people wondered that there should be such a difference between the

---

[88]NPNF 2 3:558-59*. [89]FC 109:224, 228-29, 236; FC 110:245. [90]ANF 1:89-90. [91]ANF 1:39. [92]ANF 1:40.

unbelievers and the elect, of whom this most admirable Polycarp was one, having in our own times been an apostolic and prophetic teacher and bishop of the catholic church that is in Smyrna. For every word that went out of his mouth either has been or shall yet be accomplished. MARTYRDOM OF POLYCARP 16.[93]

A SHEPHERD OF THE CHURCH THROUGHOUT THE WORLD. MARTYRDOM OF POLYCARP: He was not merely an illustrious teacher but also a preeminent martyr, whose martyrdom all desire to imitate, as having been altogether consistent with the gospel of Christ. For, having through patience overcome the unjust governor and thus acquired the crown of immortality, he now, with the apostles and all the righteous in heaven, joyfully glorifies God, even the Father, and blesses our Lord Jesus Christ, the savior of our souls, the governor of our bodies and the shepherd of the catholic church throughout the world. MARTYRDOM OF POLYCARP 19.[94]

THE LOAVES AS SYMBOLS OF THE FAITH. EPISTULA APOSTOLORUM: What do these five loaves mean? They are the symbol of our faith concerning the great Christian faith in the Father, the rule of the entire world, and in Jesus Christ our Savior, in the Holy Spirit the Paraclete, and in the holy church and in the forgiveness of sins. EPISTULA APOSTOLORUM 5.[95]

THE HOLY CHURCH IN EVERY PLACE. APOSTOLIC CONSTITUTIONS: God and Father of our Lord Jesus Christ, Father of mercies and God of all consolation, you who live in the highest but regard the lowest, you who know all things before they are, you who gave the rules of the church through the word of your grace, who predestined from the beginning the race of the righteous through Abraham, who instituted princes and priests and did not leave your sanctuary without a minister; who from the beginning of the world has been pleased to be glorified by those whom you have chosen, pour out on him the power that is from you, the princely Spirit, which you gave to your beloved Son Jesus Christ, which he gave to your holy apostles, who founded the church in every place as your sanctuary, for the glory and endless praise of your name. Grant, Father who knows the heart, to your servant whom you chose for the episcopate, that he will feed your holy flock, that he will wear your high priesthood without reproach, serving night and day, incessantly making your face favorable and offering the gifts of your holy church; in the spirit of high priesthood having the power to forgive sins according to your command; to assign lots according to your command; to loose any bond according to the authority that you gave to the apostles; to please you in mildness and a pure heart, offering to you a sweet scent, through your Son Jesus Christ, through whom to you be glory, power and honor, Father and Son, with the Holy Spirit, in the holy church, now and throughout the ages of the ages. Amen. CONSTITUTIONS OF THE HOLY APOSTLES 8.2.5.[96]

HERE AND EVERYWHERE. LITURGY OF THE BLESSED APOSTLES: Divided, sanctified, completed, perfected, united and commingled have been these renowned, holy, life-giving and divine mysteries, the one with the other, in the adorable and glorious name of your glorious Trinity, O Father, Son and Holy Spirit, that they may be to us, O Lord, for the propitiation of our offenses and the forgiveness of our sins; also for the grand hope of a resurrection from the dead and of a new life in the kingdom of the heavens, for us and for the holy church of Christ our Lord, here and in every place whatsoever, now and always, and forever. LITURGY OF THE BLESSED APOSTLES 16.[97]

---

[93]ANF 1:42. [94]ANF 1:43. [95]*NTAp* 1:253. The original was composed in Greek, it seems, in Egypt in the middle of the second century. This is one of the first times we find the words "holy church." [96]ANF 7:482*. [97]ANF 7:566*.

ONE HOLY CATHOLIC CHURCH. CYRIL OF JERUSALEM: Now then let me finish what still remains to be said for the article, "in one holy catholic church," on which, though one might say many things, we will speak but briefly.

It is called "catholic" then because it extends over all the world, from one end of the earth to the other, and because it teaches universally and completely one and all the doctrines that ought to come to human knowledge, concerning things both visible and invisible, heavenly and earthly. It is also called "catholic" because it brings into subjection to godliness the whole race of humankind, governors and governed, learned and unlearned, and because it universally treats and heals the whole class of sins that are committed by soul or body and possesses in itself every form of virtue that is named, both in deeds and words and in every kind of spiritual gifts.

And it is rightly named *ecclesia* because it "calls forth" and assembles together all people, according to what the Lord says in Leviticus, "And assemble all the congregation at the door of the tent of meeting."[98] And it is to be noted that the word *assemble* is used for the first time in the Scriptures here, at the time when the Lord puts Aaron into the high priesthood. And in Deuteronomy also the Lord says to Moses, "Gather the people to me, that I may let them hear my words, so that they may learn to fear me."[99] And he again mentions the name of the church when he says concerning the tablets, "And on them were all the words which the LORD had spoken with you on the mountain out of the midst of the fire on the day of the assembly";[100] as if he had said more plainly, in the day in which you were called and gathered together by God. The psalmist also says, "Then I will thank you in the great congregation; in the mighty throng I will praise you."[101]

Of old the psalmist sang, "Bless God in the great congregation, the LORD, O you who are from Israel's fountain!"[102] But after the Jews were cast away from his grace for the plots that they made against the Savior, the Savior built out of the Gentiles a second holy church, the church of us Christians, concerning which he said to Peter, "And on this rock I will build my church, and the powers of death shall not prevail against it."[103] And David, prophesying of both these, said plainly of the first that was rejected, "I hate the company of evildoers,"[104] but of the second that is built up he says in the same psalm, "LORD, I love the habitation of your house";[105] and immediately afterward, "In the great congregation I will bless the LORD."[106] For now that the earlier assembly one church in Judea is cast off, the churches of Christ are increasing over all the world. Of them it is said in the Psalms, "Sing to the LORD a new song, his praise in the assembly of the faithful."[107] . . . The Lord says, "From the rising of the sun even unto the going down of the same, my name is glorified among the Gentiles."[108] Concerning this holy catholic church Paul writes to Timothy, "you may know how one ought to behave in the household of God, which is the church of the living God, the pillar and bulwark of the truth."[109] CATECHETICAL LECTURE 18.22-25.[110]

ESTABLISHED THROUGHOUT THE WORLD. NICETA OF REMESIANA: After the confession of the blessed Trinity, you profess faith in the holy catholic church. The church is simply the community of all the saints. All who from the beginning of the world were or are or will be justified—whether patriarchs, like Abraham, Isaac and Jacob, or prophets, whether apostles or martyrs, or any others—make up one church, because they are made holy by one faith and way of life, stamped with one Spirit, made into one body whose head, as we are told,

---

[98]Lev 8:3. [99]Deut 4:10. [100]Deut 9:10. [101]Ps 35:18; Heb 2:12. [102]Ps 68:26. [103]Mt 16:18. [104]Ps 26:5. [105]Ps 26:8. [106]Ps 26:12. [107]Ps 149:1. [108]Mal 1:11. [109]1 Tim 3:15. [110]NPNF 2 7:139-40*.

is Christ. I go further. The angels and virtues and powers in heaven are comembers in this one church, for as the apostle teaches us, in Christ all things, whether on the earth or in the heavens, have been reconciled.[111] You must believe, therefore, that in this one church you are gathered into the communion of saints. You must know that this is the one catholic church established throughout the world, and with it you must remain in unshaken communion. There are, indeed, other so-called churches with which you can have no communion: for example, those of the Manichaeans, the Cataphrygians, the Marcionites, and other heretics and schismatics. These churches ceased to be holy, because they were deceived by the doctrines of the devil to believe and behave differently from what Christ commanded and from the tradition of the apostles. EXPLANATION OF THE CREED 10.[112]

HERETICS AND SCHISMATICS DO NOT BELONG TO THE CHURCH CATHOLIC. AUGUSTINE: Inasmuch, I repeat, as this is the case, we believe also in the holy church, intending thereby assuredly the catholic. For both heretics and schismatics style their congregations churches. But heretics, in holding false opinions regarding God, do injury to the faith itself; while schismatics . . . in wicked separations break off from brotherly charity, although they may believe just what we believe. Therefore neither do the heretics belong to the church catholic, which loves God; nor do the schismatics form a part of the same, inasmuch as it loves the neighbor and consequently readily forgives the neighbor's sins, because it prays that forgiveness may be extended to itself by him who has reconciled us to himself, doing away with all past things and calling us to a new life. And until we reach the perfection of this new life, we cannot be without sins. Nevertheless it is a matter of consequence of what sort those sins may be. ON FAITH AND THE CREED 10.[113]

ONE HOLY, TRUE, CATHOLIC CHURCH. AUGUSTINE: After commendation of the Trinity there follows the phrase "the holy church." God is pointed out, and his temple. "For the temple of God is holy," says the apostle, "which temple you are."[114] This same is the holy church, the one church, the true church, the catholic church, fighting against all heresies. Fight, it can. Be fought down, it cannot. As for heresies, they went all out of it, like unprofitable branches pruned from the vine, but the church itself abides in its root, in its Vine, in its charity. "The gates of hell shall not prevail against it."[115] ON FAITH AND THE CREED 14.[116]

HOLY BECAUSE OF ITS UNION WITH CHRIST. EPHREM THE SYRIAN: This pure love, which was ordained from Adam down to our Lord, was a symbol of our Lord's perfect love. Therefore the church has left idols and possessions, like father and mother; and Christ himself left his Father on high and his mother below and died for his church, so that by his death he might give life to the church, which he loved, and might raise it up and bring it to that kingdom of his. ON EPIPHANY 5.21-23.[117]

STRENGTHEN THE HOLY HOUSE. LITURGY OF SAINT BASIL: Again we pray to you, be mindful of your holy, catholic and apostolic church, which is from one end of the inhabited earth to the other. Grant peace to it which you have obtained with the precious blood of your Christ. Strengthen also this holy house to the end of the ages. LITURGY OF SAINT BASIL.[118]

WE RECOGNIZE THE CONGREGATION BY NAME CATHOLIC. PACIAN OF BARCELONA: But during the time of the apostles, you will say, no one used to be called catholic. So be it. It may have been so. I allow you even that. But when, after the apostles, heresies had

---

[111]See Col 1:20. [112]FC 7:49. [113]NPNF 1 3:331. [114]1 Cor 3:17. [115]Mt 16:18. [116]NPNF 1 3:374*. [117]SCK 138. [118]DLSB.

appeared and were striving under various names to tear to pieces and split apart the dove and the queen of God, did not the apostolic people require a name of their own, by which they would mark the unity of an uncorrupted people, lest the error of some should tear limb from limb the undefiled virgin of God? Was it not right that the original ecclesial source be designated by its own particular appellation?

Suppose that this very day I entered a populous city. When I had found Marcionites, Apollinarians . . . and the rest of that kind who call themselves Christians, by what name should I recognize the congregation of my own people, unless it were called catholic? Come now! Who has conferred so many names on these other groups? Why do so many cities, so many nations, each have their own defining designation? The same one who asks about the name *catholic* will not be ignorant of the origin of his own name if I shall inquire about such. From where was the name *catholic* bequeathed to me? Certainly that which has not fallen for so many ages was not borrowed from a man. This name *catholic* does not ring of Marcion, nor of Apelles nor of Montanus; nor does it take heretics as its originators.

Many things the Holy Spirit, whom God sent from heaven to the apostles as their comforter and guide, has taught us; many things reason teaches us, as Paul declares; and honesty, too, and, as he says, nature itself.[119] And what now? Does the authority of the disciples of the apostles, of the earliest priests, of the most blessed martyr and teacher Cyprian, carry so little weight with us? What about the great number of priests on this, our side, who throughout the entire world were united in a single ecclesial community with this very same Cyprian? What about the great number of venerable bishops, of martyrs, of confessors? LETTER 1.3-4.[120]

THE NAME WAS BESTOWED ON US BY GOD.

PACIAN OF BARCELONA: Concerning the name *catholic* I answered fully and in a conciliatory manner. For I said that it mattered to neither one of us what the other was called. But if you demanded to know the meaning of the name, whatever it might be, it is wonderful—whether it means "one in all" or "one above all"[121] or, an interpretation I have not mentioned previously, "the king's child"—that is, the Christian people.[122] Certainly this name, which has endured for so many centuries, was not bestowed on us by ourselves but by God. And truly I rejoice that, although you may have preferred other names, you agree that the name belongs to us. And what if you were to deny this? Then nature would cry out. Or if you still have doubts, let us say nothing about it. We will both be that which we are called, under the witness of the antiquity of the name. If, however, quite stubbornly you continue to ask, take care lest that "man of might" may exclaim to you, "Why do you ask my name? The name itself is wonderful."[123] I then sensibly added that we ought not to consider from where Catholics acquired this name, because neither was it traditionally considered to represent a charge against the Valentinians if they were named after Valentinus, or against the Phrygians, if from Phrygia, or against the Novatians, if after Novatian. LETTER 2.2.[124]

THE TRUE CATHOLIC LOVES THE TRUTH.

VINCENT OF LÉRINS: This being the case, he is the true and genuine Catholic who loves the truth of God, who loves the church, who loves the body of Christ, who esteems divine religion and the catholic faith above everything, above the authority, above the regard, above the genius, above the eloquence, above the philosophy of every person whatsoever. He sets light by all of these and, continuing steadfast and established in the faith, resolves that he will believe that and that only which he is

---

[119]See 1 Cor 11:14. [120]FC 99:20-21. [121]Cf. Eph 1:4. [122]See *De Baptismo* 6. [123]Cf. Judg 13:18. [124]FC 99:28.

sure the catholic church has held universally and from ancient time. Whatever is new and an unheard-of doctrine, however, he shall find to have been furtively introduced by someone or another, besides that of all or contrary to that of all the saints. This, he will understand, does not pertain to religion but is permitted as a trial, being instructed especially by the words of the blessed apostle Paul, who writes about this in his first epistle to the Corinthians, "There must needs be heresies, that they who are approved may be made manifest among you,"[125] as though he should say, "This is the reason why the authors of heresies are not immediately rooted up by God, namely, that they who are approved may be made known; that is, that it may be apparent of each individual how tenacious and faithful and steadfast he is in his love of the catholic faith." COMMONITORY 20.[126]

The True Catholic Church Is Apostolic

CHRIST WAS SENT BY GOD. CLEMENT OF ROME: The apostles have preached the gospel to us from the Lord Jesus Christ; Jesus Christ has done so from God. Christ therefore was sent forth by God, and the apostles by Christ. Both these appointments, then, were made in an orderly way, according to the will of God. Having therefore received their orders, and being fully assured by the resurrection of our Lord Jesus Christ and established in the word of God, with full assurance of the Holy Spirit, they went forth proclaiming that the kingdom of God was at hand. And thus preaching through countries and cities, they appointed the firstfruits of their labors, having first proved them by the Spirit, to be bishops and deacons of those who should afterwards believe. Nor was this any new thing, since indeed many ages before it was written concerning bishops and deacons. For thus says the Scripture in a certain place, "I will appoint you bishops in righteousness and their deacons in faith."[127] 1 CLEMENT 42.[128]

A SUCCESSION PROVIDED. CLEMENT OF ROME: Our apostles also knew, through our Lord Jesus Christ, that there would be strife on account of the office of the episcopate. For this reason, therefore, inasmuch as they had obtained a perfect foreknowledge of this, they appointed those ministers already mentioned and afterward gave instructions that when these should fall asleep, other approved men should succeed them in their ministry. We are of the opinion, therefore, that those appointed by them or afterward by other eminent men, with the consent of the whole church, and who have blamelessly served the flock of Christ in a humble, peaceable, and disinterested spirit and have for a long time possessed the good opinion of all cannot be justly dismissed from the ministry. For our sin will not be small if we eject from the episcopate those who have blamelessly and holily fulfilled its duties. Blessed are those presbyters who, having finished their course before now, have obtained a fruitful and perfect departure from this world; for they have no fear lest anyone deprive them of the place now appointed them. But we see that you have removed some men of excellent behavior from the ministry, which they fulfilled blamelessly and with honor. 1 CLEMENT 44.[129]

ORAL TRADITIONS BETTER THAN WRITTEN. PAPIAS OF HIERAPOLIS (VIA EUSEBIUS): If, then, anyone came who had been a follower of the elders, I questioned him in regard to the words of the elders—what Andrew or what Peter said, or what was said by Philip, or by Thomas, or by James, or by John, or by Matthew, or by any other of the disciples of the Lord, and what things Aristion and the presbyter John, the disciples of the Lord, say. For I did not think that what was to be gotten from the books would profit me as much as what came from the living and abiding voice.

---

[125] 1 Cor 11:19. [126] NPNF 2 11:146. [127] Cf. Is 60:17 (LXX). [128] ANF 1:16*. [129] ANF 1:17*.

Ecclesiastical History 3.39.4.[130]

We Interpret According to Our Teaching. Tertullian: We do not take our scriptural teaching from the parables, but we interpret the parables according to our teaching. On Modesty 9.1.[131]

An Apostolic Character. Ignatius of Antioch: Ignatius, who is also called Theophorus, to the holy church which is at Tralles, in Asia, beloved of God, the Father of Jesus Christ, elect and worthy of God, possessing peace through the flesh and blood and passion of Jesus Christ, who is our hope, through our rising again to him, which also I salute in its fullness and in the apostolic character and wish abundance of happiness. Epistle to the Trallians 1.[132]

The Bishop Represents the Lord. Ignatius of Antioch: Now the more anyone sees the bishop keeping silence, the more he ought to revere him. For we ought to receive every one whom the master of the house sends to be over his household, as we would do him that sent him. It is clear, therefore, that we should look on the bishop even as we would on the Lord himself. And indeed Onesimus himself greatly commends your good order in God, that you all live according to the truth and that no sect has any dwelling place among you. Nor, indeed, do you pay attention to anyone other than to Jesus Christ, who speaks in truth. Epistle to the Ephesians 6.[133]

Established in the Doctrines of the Lord. Ignatius of Antioch: Study, therefore, to be established in the doctrines of the Lord and the apostles so that anything you do may prosper both in the flesh and spirit; in faith and love; in the Son, and in the Father and in the Spirit; in the beginning and in the end; with your most admirable bishop, and the well-compacted spiritual crown of your presbytery and the deacons who are according to God. Be subject to the bishop, and to one another, as Jesus Christ is to the Father, according to the flesh, and the apostles are to Christ, and to the Father and to the Spirit, so that there may be a union both fleshly and spiritual. Epistle to the Magnesians 13.[134]

In Search of the Apostolic Succession. Hegesippus (via Eusebius): But Hegesippus, who lived immediately after the apostles, gives the most accurate account in the fifth book of his memoirs. He writes as follows: "James, the brother of the Lord, succeeded to the government of the church in conjunction with the apostles. He has been called the Just by all from the time of our Savior to the present day; for there were many that bore the name of James. He was holy from his mother's womb; and he drank no wine or strong drink, nor did he eat flesh. No razor came on his head; he did not anoint himself with oil, and he did not use the bath. . . . And one of them, who was a fuller, took the club with which he beat out clothes and struck the just man on the head. And thus he suffered martyrdom. And they buried him on the spot, by the temple, and his monument still remains by the temple. He became a true witness, both to Jews and Greeks, that Jesus is the Christ. And immediately Vespasian besieged them." These things are related at length by Hegesippus, who is in agreement with Clement. Ecclesiastical History 2.23.[135]

Succession Confirmed and Recorded. Hegesippus (via Eusebius): Hegesippus in the five books of memoirs which have come down to us has left a most complete record of his own views. In them he states that on a journey to Rome he met a great many bishops and that he received the same doctrine from

---

[130]NPNF 2 1:170. [131] ANF 4:82**. [132]ANF 1:66. [133]ANF 1:51-52. [134]ANF 1:64-65. [135]NPNF 2 1:125-27.

all. It is fitting to hear what he says after making some remarks about the epistle of Clement to the Corinthians. His words are as follows: "And the church of Corinth continued in the true faith until Primus was bishop in Corinth. I conversed with them on my way to Rome, and stayed with the Corinthians many days, during which we were mutually refreshed in the true doctrine. And when I had come to Rome I remained a there until Anicetus, whose deacon was Eleutherus. And Anicetus was succeeded by Soter, and he by Eleutherus. In every succession, and in every city that is held which is preached by the law and the prophets and the Lord." ECCLESIASTICAL HISTORY 4.22.1-3.[136]

THE APOSTOLIC SUCCESSION IS KEPT UP.
IRENAEUS: It is within the power of all, therefore, in every church, who may wish to see the truth, to contemplate clearly the tradition of the apostles manifested throughout the whole world. We are in a position to bring to mind those who were by the apostles instituted bishops in the churches and to demonstrate the succession of these men to our own times. They neither taught nor knew of anything like what these heretics rave about. For if the apostles had known hidden mysteries, which they were in the habit of imparting to "the perfect" apart and privately from the rest, they would have delivered them especially to those to whom they were also committing the churches themselves. For they intended that these men should be very perfect and blameless in all things whom also they were leaving behind as their successors, delivering up their own place of government to these men. These men, if they discharged their functions honestly, would be a great boon to the church, but if they fell away, the most dire calamity would result.

Since, however, it would be very tedious, in such a volume as this, to provide a record of the successions of all the churches, we rather have chosen to confound all those who—in whatever manner, whether by an evil self-pleasing, by vainglory or by blindness and perverse opinion—assemble in unauthorized meetings. We do this, I say, by indicating that tradition derived from the apostles, of the very great, the very ancient and universally known church founded and organized at Rome by the two most glorious apostles, Peter and Paul. We also do this by pointing out the faith preached to humanity that comes down to our time by means of the successions of the bishops. For it is a matter of necessity that every church should agree with this church because of its preeminent authority, that is, the faithful everywhere, inasmuch as the apostolic tradition has been preserved continuously by those faithful men who exist everywhere.

The blessed apostles, then, having founded and built up the church, committed into the hands of Linus the office of the episcopate. Of this Linus, Paul makes mention in the epistles to Timothy. To him succeeded Anacletus; and after him, in the third place from the apostles, Clement was allotted the bishopric. This man, as he had seen the blessed apostles and had been conversant with them, might be said to have the preaching of the apostles still echoing in his ears and their traditions before his eyes. Nor was he alone, for there were many still remaining who had received instructions from the apostles. In the time of this Clement, no small dissension having occurred among the brothers at Corinth, the church in Rome dispatched a most powerful letter to the Corinthians, exhorting them to peace, renewing their faith and declaring the tradition that it had lately received from the apostles, proclaiming the one God, omnipotent, the maker of heaven and earth, the creator of human beings, who brought on the deluge and called Abraham, who led the people from the land of Egypt, spoke with Moses, set forth

---

[136]NPNF 2 1:198-99*.

the law and sent the prophets, and who has prepared fire for the devil and his angels. From this document, whosoever chooses to do so may learn that he, the Father of our Lord Jesus Christ, was preached by the churches and may also understand the apostolic tradition of the church, since this epistle is of older date than these men who are now propagating falsehood and who conjure into existence another god beyond the Creator and the Maker of all existing things. To this Clement there succeeded Evaristus. Alexander followed Evaristus; then, sixth from the apostles, Sixtus was appointed; after him, Telephorus, who was gloriously martyred; then Hyginus; after him, Pius; then after him, Anicetus. Soter having succeeded Anicetus, Eleutherius does now, in the twelfth place from the apostles, hold the inheritance of the episcopate. In this order and by this succession, the ecclesiastical tradition from the apostles and the preaching of the truth have come down to us. And this is most abundant proof that there is one and the same vivifying faith, which has been preserved in the church from the apostles until now and handed down in truth. AGAINST HERESIES 3.3.1-3.[137]

WHERE THE TRUTH IS TO BE FOUND. IRENAEUS: Since therefore we have such proofs, it is not necessary to seek the truth among others. It is easy to obtain from the church since the apostles, like a rich man depositing his money in a bank, lodged in its hands most copiously all things pertaining to the truth. In this way, any person who wants to can draw from it the water of life. For the church is the entrance to life; all others are thieves and robbers. On this account are we bound to avoid them but to choose what pertains to the church with the utmost diligence and to lay hold of the tradition of the truth. For how does the case stand? Suppose there arises a dispute relative to some important question among us. Should we not have recourse to the most ancient churches with which the apostles held constant intercourse and learn from them what is certain and clear in regard to the present question? For how should it be if the apostles themselves had not left us writings? Would it not be necessary, in that case, to follow the course of the tradition that they handed down to those to whom they did commit the churches? AGAINST HERESIES 3.4.1.[138]

PERMANENT TEACHING. IRENAEUS: Since, therefore, the tradition from the apostles does thus exist in the church and is permanent among us, let us revert to the scriptural proof furnished by those apostles who did also write the gospel, in which they recorded the doctrine regarding God, pointing out that our Lord Jesus Christ is the truth and that no lie is in him. AGAINST HERESIES 3.5.1.[139]

THE APOSTOLIC SUCCESSION. IRENAEUS: Therefore it is incumbent to obey the presbyters who are in the church—those who, as I have shown, possess the succession from the apostles; those who, together with the succession of the episcopate, have received the certain gift of truth according to the good pleasure of the Father. But it is also incumbent to hold in suspicion others who depart from the primitive succession and assemble themselves together in any place whatsoever, looking on them either as heretics of perverse minds, or as schismatics puffed up and self-pleasing or again as hypocrites, acting thus for the sake of profit and vainglory. For all these have fallen from the truth. . . .

From all such persons, therefore, it behooves us to keep aloof, but to adhere to those who, as I have already observed, do hold the doctrine of the apostles and who, together with the order of priesthood (*presbyterii ordine*), display sound speech and blameless conduct for the confirmation and correction of others. . . .

---

[137]ANF 1:415-16*. [138]ANF 1:416-17. [139]ANF 1:417.

Such presbyters does the church nourish of whom also the prophet says, "I will give you rulers in peace, and you bishops in righteousness."[140] Of whom also did the Lord declare, "Who then shall be a faithful steward (*actor*), good and wise, whom the Lord sets over his household, to give them their meat in due season? Blessed is that servant whom his Lord, when he comes, shall find so doing."[141] Paul, then, teaching us where one may find such, says, "God has placed in the church, first, apostles; second, prophets; third, teachers."[142] Where, therefore, the gifts of the Lord have been placed, there it behooves us to learn the truth, namely, from those who possess that succession of the church that is from the apostles and among whom exists that which is sound and blameless in conduct, as well as that which is unadulterated and incorrupt in speech. For these also preserve this faith of ours in one God who created all things. They increase that love that we have for the Son of God, who accomplished such marvelous dispensations for our sake. They expound the Scriptures to us without danger, neither blaspheming God, nor honoring the patriarchs nor despising the prophets. AGAINST HERESIES 4.26.2-5.[143]

THE SUCCESSIONS OF THE BISHOPS. IRENAEUS: True knowledge is the doctrine of the apostles, and the ancient constitution of the church throughout all the world and the distinctive manifestation of the body of Christ according to the successions of the bishops, by which they have handed down that church that exists in every place and has come even to us, being guarded and preserved without any forging of Scriptures, by a very complete system of doctrine and neither receiving addition nor curtailment. It also requires reading the Word of God without falsification and a lawful and diligent exposition in harmony with the Scriptures, both without danger and without blasphemy. And above all, it requires the preeminent gift of love, which is more precious than knowledge, more glorious than prophecy, and which excels all the other gifts of God. AGAINST HERESIES 4.33.8.[144]

THE APOSTOLIC TRADITION SET FORTH IN THE APOSTOLIC CHURCHES. TERTULLIAN: But if it was after the apostolic age that the truth suffered adulteration as regards the rule of faith in God, it follows that in its own time the apostolic tradition suffered no adulteration as regards God's rule of faith. And we shall be called on to recognize as apostolic no other tradition than that which is today set forth in the apostolic churches. But you will find no church of apostolic origin whose Christianity repudiates the Creator. Or else, if these churches are taken to have been corrupt from the beginning, can any churches be sound? Shall they be those hostile to the Creator? Put in evidence a single one of your churches that is of apostolic origin, and you will have me convinced. Since then it is on all accounts certain that from Christ right down to Marcion no other god than the Creator was included in the statement of this mystery, this gives all necessary protection to my statement of the case by which I prove that the very idea of that heretical god originated with this separation between the gospel and the law, while there is support for my previous postulate that we may not accept as a god one whom a man has constructed out of his own mind—unless of course he is a prophet, and then it would not be of his own mind. Whether Marcion can be so called—well, proof of this will be required. There was no call for discussion: the truth, like a wedge, thrusts out every heresy, while Christ is set forth as the representative of no other god than the Creator. AGAINST MARCION 1.21.[145]

---

[140]Cf. Is 60:17. [141]Mt 24:45-46. [142]1 Cor 12:28. [143]ANF 1:497-98. [144]ANF 1:508. [145]*TAM* 1:55-57.

THE APOSTLES FOUNDED CHURCHES IN EVERY CITY. TERTULLIAN: Christ Jesus our Lord (may he bear with me a moment in thus expressing myself!), whoever he is, of whatever God he is the Son, of whatever substance he is man and God, of whatever faith he is the teacher, of whatever reward he is the promiser, did, while he lived on earth, declare what he was, what he had been, what the Father's will was that he was administering, what the duty of humankind was that he was prescribing. He made this declaration, either openly to the people or privately to his disciples, of whom he had chosen the twelve chief ones to be at his side and whom he destined to be the teachers of the nations. Accordingly, after one of these had been struck off, he commanded the eleven others, on his departure to the Father, to "go and teach all nations, who were to be baptized into the Father, and into the Son and into the Holy Spirit."[146] Immediately, therefore, so did the apostles, whom this designation indicates as "the sent." Having, on the authority of a prophecy, which occurs in a psalm of David, chosen Matthias by lot as the twelfth, in the place of Judas, they obtained the promised power of the Holy Spirit for the gift of miracles and of utterance; and after first bearing witness to the faith in Jesus Christ throughout Judea and the surrounding churches, they next went out into the world and preached the same doctrine of the same faith to the nations. In a similar way, they then founded churches in every city, from which all the other churches, one after another, derived the tradition of the faith and the seeds of doctrine and are every day deriving them, that they may become churches. Indeed, it is on this account only that they will be able to deem themselves apostolic, as being the offspring of apostolic churches. Every sort of thing must necessarily revert to its original for its classification. Therefore the churches, although they are so many and so great, comprise but one primitive church, founded by the apostles, from which they all spring. In this way all are primitive, and all are apostolic, while they are all proved to be one, in unbroken unity, by their peaceful communion, and title of brotherhood and bond of hospitality—privileges that no other rule directs than the one tradition of the selfsame mystery. PRESCRIPTIONS AGAINST HERETICS 20.[147]

THE APOSTLES TAUGHT BY GOD THROUGH CHRIST. TERTULLIAN: From this, therefore, we draw up our rule. Since the Lord Jesus Christ sent the apostles to preach, our rule is that no others ought to be received as preachers than those whom Christ appointed. For "no man knows the Father save the Son, and he to whom the Son will reveal him."[148] Nor does the Son seem to have revealed him to any other than the apostles, whom he sent forth to preach what, of course, he had revealed to them. Now, what that was which they preached—in other words, what it was which Christ revealed to them—can, as I must here likewise prescribe, properly be proved in no other way than by those very churches that the apostles founded in person, by declaring the gospel to them directly themselves, both *vive voce*,[149] as the phrase is, and subsequently by their epistles. If, then, these things are so, it is in the same degree made known that all doctrine that agrees with the apostolic churches—those original formations and sources of the faith must be reckoned for truth, as undoubtedly containing that which these very churches received from the apostles, the apostles from Christ, Christ from God. Whereas all doctrine must be prejudged as false that taste like anything contrary to the truth of the churches and apostles of Christ and God. It remains, then, that we demonstrate whether this doctrine of ours, of which we have now given the rule, has its origin in the tradition of the apostles, and whether all other doctrines do not ipso facto

---

[146]Mt 28:19. [147]ANF 3:252*. [148]Mt 11:27. [149]Lat. "Living voice."

proceed from falsehood. We hold communion with the apostolic churches because our doctrine is in no respect different from theirs. This is our witness of truth. PRESCRIPTIONS AGAINST HERETICS 21.[150]

A GUARANTEE OF THE TRUE DOCTRINE. TERTULLIAN: But if there are any heresies that are bold enough to plant themselves in the midst of the apostolic age, that they may thereby seem to have been handed down by the apostles because they existed in the time of the apostles, we can say: Let them produce the original records of their churches; let them unfold the roll of their bishops, running down in due succession from the beginning in such a manner that their first bishop shall be able to show for his ordainer and predecessor some one of the apostles or of apostolic men—a man, moreover, who continued steadfast with the apostles. For this is the manner in which the apostolic churches transmit their registers. This is the case with the church of Smyrna, which records that Polycarp was placed therein by John. It is also the same with the church of Rome, which makes Clement to have been ordained in a similar way by Peter. In exactly the same way the other churches likewise present their bishops whom, as having been appointed to their episcopal places by apostles, they regard as transmitters of the apostolic seed. Let the heretics contrive something of the same kind. For after their blasphemy, what is there that is unlawful for them? But should they even effect the contrivance, they will not advance a step. For their very doctrine, after comparison with that of the apostles, will declare, by its own diversity and contrariety, that it had for its author neither an apostle nor an apostolic man; because, as the apostles would never have taught things that were self-contradictory, so the apostolic men would not have inculcated teaching different from the apostles unless they who received their instruction from the apostles went and preached in a contrary manner. To this test, therefore will they be submitted for proof by those churches who, although they do not derive their founder from apostles or apostolic men as being of much later date, for they are in fact being founded daily, yet, since they agree in the same faith, they are considered no less apostolic because they are agreed in doctrine. Then let all the heresies, when challenged to these two tests by our apostolic church, offer their proof of how they deem themselves to be apostolic. But in truth they neither are so, nor are they able to prove themselves to be what they are not. Nor are they admitted to peaceful relations and communion by such churches as are in any way connected with apostles, inasmuch as they are in no sense themselves apostolic because of their diversity as to the mysteries of the faith. PRESCRIPTIONS AGAINST HERETICS 32.[151]

THE VOICES OF THE APOSTLES. TERTULLIAN: Come now, you who would indulge a better curiosity, if you would apply it to the business of your salvation, run over to the apostolic churches in which the very thrones of the apostles are still preeminent in their places, in which their own authentic writings are read, uttering the voice and representing the face of each of them severally. Achaia is very near you, in which you find Corinth. Since you are not far from Macedonia, you have Philippi; and there too you have the Thessalonians. Since you are able to cross to Asia, you can reach Ephesus. Since, moreover, you are close to Italy, you have Rome, from which there comes even into our own hands the very authority of the apostles themselves. How happy is its church, on which apostles poured forth all their doctrine along with their blood! Where Peter endures a passion like his Lord's! Where Paul wins his crown in a death like John's. Where the apostle John was first plunged, unhurt, into boiling oil, and then sent to his

---

[150]ANF 3:252*. [151]ANF 3:258*.

island exile! See what it has learned, what it has taught, what fellowship it has had with even our churches in Africa! PRESCRIPTIONS AGAINST HERETICS 36.[152]

TRANSMISSION OF TRUE DOCTRINE. CLEMENT OF ALEXANDRIA: But they, safeguarding the true tradition of the blessed teaching, which comes straight from the apostles Peter, James, John, and Paul and transmitted from father to son has come down to us with the help of God to deposit in us those ancestral and apostolic seeds. STROMATEIS 1.1.[153]

THE MOST EXACT KNOWLEDGE. CLEMENT OF ALEXANDRIA: It is necessary to condescend to questions and to ascertain by way of demonstration by the Scriptures themselves how the heresies failed, and how in the truth alone and in the ancient church is both the most exact knowledge and the truly best set of principles. STROMATEIS 7.15.[154]

THE PROMINENCE IS ITS ONENESS. CLEMENT OF ALEXANDRIA: Such being the case, it is evident, from the high antiquity and perfect truth of the church, that these later heresies, and those yet subsequent to them in time, were new inventions falsified from the truth. From what has been said, then, it is my opinion that the true church, that which is really ancient, is one, and that in it those are enrolled who according to God's purpose are just. For from the very reason that God is one and the Lord one, that which is in the highest degree honorable is praised in consequence of its singleness, being an imitation of the one first principle. In the nature of the One, then, is associated in a joint heritage the one church, which they strive to cut asunder into many sects. Therefore in substance and idea, in origin, in preeminence, we say that the ancient and catholic church is alone, collecting as it does into the unity of the one faith—which results from the peculiar Testaments, or rather the one Testament in different times by the will of the one God, through one Lord—those already ordained, whom God predestined, knowing before the foundation of the world that they would be righteous. But the preeminence of the church, as the principle of union, is, in its oneness, in this surpassing all other things and having nothing like or equal to itself. STROMATEIS 7.17.[155]

TRANSMITTED IN SUCCESSION FROM THE APOSTLES. ORIGEN: For as we ceased to seek for truth (notwithstanding the professions of many among Greeks and barbarians to make it known) among all who claimed it for erroneous opinions, after we had come to believe that Christ was the Son of God and were persuaded that we must learn it from himself; so, seeing there are many who think they hold the opinions of Christ, and yet some of these think differently from their predecessors, yet as the teaching of the church, transmitted in orderly succession from the apostles and remaining in the churches to the present day, is still preserved, that alone is to be accepted as truth that differs in no respect from ecclesiastical and apostolic tradition. ON FIRST PRINCIPLES, PREFACE 2.[156]

THE CHURCH NAMED BY THE APOSTLES. EPHREM THE SYRIAN: Look on the prophets and the apostles, how like they are to each other! The prophets gave the name of God to the flock of God, and the apostles gave the name of Christ to the church of Christ. NISIBENE HYMNS 20.7.[157]

THE APOSTLES ARE STILL THE FISHERMEN. EPHREM THE SYRIAN: But fishermen fish for an unknown catch, for sometimes with fish they catch serpents. So it is here. It was not a single people for which they fished and still fish, to

---

[152]ANF 3:260-61. [153]ANF 2:301. [154]ANF 2:550*. [155]ANF 2:555*. [156]ANF 4:239. [157]SCK 153.

bring them to salvation, but the whole of creation. And as Simon's net drew up all kinds of fish, so the church today is filled with all kinds of nations. And by the power of the words of our Savior, who said to his holy apostles, "Follow me, and I will make you fishers of men,"[158] this is in their hands till the end of the world; and through them, that is, by their hands, he fishes people to life with the net of the gospel, which has been cast into the sea of the world and has gathered fish of every kind. And just as there they chose the good fish and cast them into vessels, so we too shall be chosen at the end, "those who have done good, to resurrection of life, and those who have done evil, to the resurrection of judgment."[159] HOMILY 15.[160]

THE TRUE CHURCH IS FOREVER. ALEXANDER OF ALEXANDRIA: And besides the pious opinion concerning the Father and the Son we confess to one Holy Spirit, as the divine Scriptures teach us; who has inaugurated both the holy men of the Old Testament and the divine teachers of that which is called the New. And besides this we also confess one only catholic and apostolic church, which can never be destroyed, though all the world should seek to make war with it. Instead, it is victorious over every most impious revolt of the heretics who rise up against it. For its Goodman has confirmed our minds by saying, "Be of good cheer, I have overcome the world."[161] EPISTLES ON THE ARIAN HERESY 1.12, TO ALEXANDER, BISHOP OF THE CITY OF CONSTANTINOPLE.[162]

FOUNDED ON THE TEACHING OF APOSTLES. ATHANASIUS: But what is also to the point, let us note that the very tradition, teaching and faith of the catholic church from the beginning was preached by the apostles and preserved by the Fathers. On this the church was founded. If anyone departs from this, he neither is, nor any longer ought to be called, a Christian. LETTER TO SERAPION 1.28.[163]

HANDED DOWN FROM THE BEGINNING. ATHANASIUS: We are proving that this view has been transmitted from father to father, but you, O modern Jews and disciples of Caiaphas, how many fathers can you assign to your phrases? Not one of the understanding and wise, for all abhor you, except for the devil alone. None but he is your father in this apostasy, who both in the beginning sowed you with the seed of this irreligion and now persuades you to slander the ecumenical council, for committing to writing not your doctrines but that which from the beginning those who were eyewitnesses and ministers of the Word have handed down to us. For the faith, which the council has confessed in writing, that is the faith of the catholic church. To assert this, the blessed Fathers so expressed themselves while condemning the Arian heresy. DEFENSE OF THE NICENE DEFINITION 27.[164]

WHAT KEEPS ME IN THE CHURCH. AUGUSTINE: For in the catholic church, not to speak of the purest wisdom the knowledge of which only a few spiritual men attain in this life—and then they only know a small portion of it, indeed, because they are only human, still they know it without any uncertainty (since the rest of the multitude derive their entire security not from acuteness of intellect but from simplicity of faith)—still, even if I do not speak of this wisdom that you do not believe to be in the catholic church, there are many other things that most justly keep me in its bosom. The consent of peoples and nations keeps me in the church. Its authority, inaugurated by miracles, nourished by hope, enlarged by love, established by age also keeps me there. The succession of priests keeps me, beginning from the very seat of the apostle Peter to whom the Lord after his resurrection gave it in charge to feed his sheep, down

---

[158]Mt 4:19. [159]Jn 5:29. [160]*SCK* 177. [161]Jn 16:33. [162]*ANF* 6:296. [163]*FEF* 336. [164]*NPNF* 2 4:168*.

to the present episcopate. And so, lastly, does the name itself of "catholic," which, not without reason, amid so many heresies, the church has thus retained. It does this so that, though all heretics wish to be called Catholics, yet when a stranger asks where the catholic church meets, no heretic will venture to point to his own chapel or house. Such then in number and importance are the precious ties belonging to the Christian name that keep a believer in the catholic church. And it is only right that they should, though from the slowness of our understanding or the small attainment of our life, the truth may not yet fully disclose itself. But with you, where there is none of these things to attract or keep me, the promise of truth is the only thing that comes into play. Now if the truth is so clearly proved as to leave no possibility of doubt, it must be set before all the things that keep me in the catholic church. But if there is only a promise without any fulfillment, no one shall move me from the faith that binds my mind with ties so many and so strong to the Christian religion. AGAINST THE LETTER OF THE MANICHAEANS 4.5.[165]

[165]NPNF 1 4:130.

WE ACKNOWLEDGE ONE BAPTISM

εἰς μίαν, ἁγίαν, καθολικὴν
καὶ ἀποστολικὴν ἐκκλησίαν·
ὁμολογοῦμεν ἓν βάπτισμα
εἰς ἄφεσιν ἁμαρτιῶν·
προσδοκῶμεν ἀνάστασιν νεκρῶν,
καὶ ζωὴν τοῦ μέλλοντος αἰῶνος. Ἀμήν.

*Et unam, sanctam, catholicam
et apostolicam ecclesiam.*
Confiteor unum baptisma
*in remissionem peccatorum;
et expecto resurrectionem mortuorum,
et vitam venturi saeculi. Amen.*

We believe in one holy catholic
and apostolic Church.
We acknowledge one baptism
for the forgiveness of sins.
We look for the resurrection of the dead
and the life of the world to come. Amen.

HISTORICAL CONTEXT: Christian baptism (which means "immersion" or "ablution") goes back to Christ in the sense that it is administered because of his mandate. It is distinct from other previous types of baptism in use among the Hebrews. Regardless of who officiates in baptism, it is considered that it is always Christ who baptizes: "He will baptize you with the Holy Spirit and with fire."[1] In the letter to Titus, baptism is defined as "the washing of regeneration and renewal in the Holy Spirit."[2] It is given that "he might sanctify her [the church], having cleansed her by the washing of water with the word."[3] Already in the New Testament there exists a rich theology about baptism as rebirth, regeneration and purification by the Spirit; as seal of faith, as union with Christ in death and resurrection, making the baptized children of God; and as forgiveness of sins and as a condition for entering the kingdom of God.

Mark and Matthew begin their Gospels with the baptism of John and conclude with the command of Christ to baptize all. The Gospel of Mark ends with the command of Jesus: "Go into all the world and preach the gospel to the whole creation. He who believes and is baptized will be saved; but he who does not believe will be condemned."[4] Peter, on the day of Pentecost, exhorts the people to receive baptism for the remission of sins: "Repent, and be baptized every one of you in the name of Jesus Christ for the forgiveness of your sins; and you shall receive the gift of the Holy Spirit."[5] Thus remission of sins and receiving the gift of the Holy Spirit are closely united. Jesus, however, does not need a baptism of repentance. The connection between the Holy Spirit and baptism emerges also from the baptism of the centurion at Caesarea, when Peter affirms that "if then God gave the same gift to them as he gave to us when we believed in the Lord Jesus Christ, who was I that I could withstand God?"[6]

Perhaps it can be said that the Acts of the Apostles, having been written some decades after the facts it relates, does not mirror the original practice of the church, which in the meantime could have modified the rite of baptism of Jewish proselytes. In fact, Paul attests to the fact that he was baptized; therefore in 33/34 baptism is already a Christian rite, considered necessary for admission to the church[7] with a significance totally different from the rite of purification in use for proselytes. Christian baptism is not of a ritual nature—in which case it would be repeatable. Once received, it does not admit repetition because it is a sign of the forgiveness of sins and of the new birth in Christ. From the beginning it is perceived as a necessary means for salvation, even if it does not seem absolute and necessary as an external ritual. In fact, the fathers

---

[1] Mt 3:11. [2] Tit 3:5. [3] Eph 5:26. [4] Mk 16:15-16. [5] Acts 2:38. [6] Acts 11:17. [7] See Rom 6:3; Acts 9:18; 22:16.

of the church speak also of a baptism of blood (martyrdom for the faith) and of a baptism of desire.

During the New Testament period we do not have liturgical details on the baptismal rite. After a brief preparation, a preliminary profession of faith was necessary, which varied according to the churches. For converts to Christianity from Judaism, such a profession had to be christological in character, while for those coming from paganism the profession included also the mention of God the Father. However, in every case, it had to be in some way trinitarian, as we begin to see more clearly in the second century. It seems also that the profession was articulated in responses that the one being baptized made to the questions of the one baptizing during the baptismal rite, which in general was required to take place through total immersion, in total nudity, in running water. However, considering the circumstances of place and time, baptism could be administered by pouring water on the head (affusion). The *Didache*, a document that came from the countryside of Syria, from the second half of the first century, describes the rite as follows: "Concerning baptism, baptize thus: Having first rehearsed all these things, baptize, 'in the name of the Father and of the Son and of the Holy Spirit,' in running water; but if you have no running water, baptize in other water, and if you cannot baptize in cold water, then use warm water. But if you have neither, pour water three times on the head 'in the name of the Father, Son and Holy Spirit,' and before the baptism let the baptizer and him who is to be baptized fast, and any others who are able. And you shall bid him who is to be baptized to fast one or two days before."[8] This text also gives the formula that accompanied the rite. The formula is trinitarian, but we do not know the exact development of the rite, so it may not have been a true and proper liturgical formula. The *Didache* does not mention other rites, such as anointing and the imposition of the hands. In some texts there is mention of baptism in the name of Jesus, but that signified nothing other than that the one who received baptism was going back to him and with such a baptism Jesus was consecrating us to himself.

From several New Testament texts we note the existence of the imposition of hands,[9] tied to the descent of the Holy Spirit on the neophyte. We have no secure testimony of other rites, such as the renunciation of Satan, exorcism, or anointing with oil, or about times and places and ministers. The anointings are certain from the end of the second century, when already guiding the liturgy was the prerogative of the bishop: "It is not lawful apart from the bishop either to baptize or to hold a love feast," writes Ignatius of Antioch to the Smyrneans at the beginning of the second century.[10] The most notable and precise testimony to the baptismal rite at the beginning of the third century is offered by the so-called *Traditio apostolica (Apostolic Tradition)*, which refers to a preceding tradition and mirrors the liturgy of an urban community, different from the archaic *Didache*. Other documents rich in information are, principally, Hermas, the first *Apology* of Justin Martyr, *On Baptism* by Tertullian, the *Acts of Thomas*, a Syriac apocryphal work, Clement of Alexandria, the *Didascalia syriaca*, Origen and Cyprian. Justin points out the close connection between baptism, which he calls illumination, and participation in the Eucharist. Tertullian gives many details on the ritual and on the time, which normally was Easter, because it was at that time that our Lord's passion was accomplished. Cyprian and an African council defended the baptism of infants, against Tertullian, because "it is not right to deny the mercy and grace of God to any man that is born." The same opinion is accepted by Origen, who also speaks

---

[8]*Didache* 7 (LAF). [9]Acts 19:5-6; 8:14-17. [10]*Letter to the Smyrneans* 8.2.

of the baptism of blood (martyrdom) for the forgiveness of the sins.

On the basis of these texts, we can roughly reconstruct the baptismal rite, which normally took place on Easter night. Its minister was the bishop. Various anointings took place, the number depending on the sources, with different explanations. At least one was connected to the conferring of the Spirit. After the blessing of the water, there came the renunciation of Satan on the part of the one being baptized, to indicate the refusal of the pagan gods; then exorcisms were carried out to explain that Christ has dominion over all things. The renunciation of Satan, the exorcisms and the confession of faith, given the different religious context, were not practiced in the ancient Syro-Palestinian churches.

Baptism, in the normal rite, consisted of a triple immersion: each one following the response of the candidate to the minister who asked questions on the trinitarian faith. The *Apostolic Tradition* describes the central rite as follows:

> Then after these things let him be given over to the presbyter who stands at the water. And let them stand in the water naked. And let a deacon likewise go down with him into the water. As he goes down to the water, let him who baptizes lay hands on him saying thus: Do you believe in God the Father Almighty? And he who is being baptized shall say: I believe. Let him forthwith baptize him once, having his hand laid on his head. And after this let him say: Do you believe in Christ Jesus, the Son of God, who was born of the Holy Spirit and the Virgin Mary, who was crucified in the days of Pontius Pilate, and died, and rose the third day living from the dead, and ascended into the heavens, and sat down at the right hand of the Father, and will come to judge the living and the dead? And when he says: I believe, let him baptize him the second time. And again let him say: Do you believe in the Holy Spirit in the holy church and the resurrection of the flesh? And he who is being baptized shall say: I believe. And so let him baptize him the third time.[11]

The whole ceremony ended with the kiss of peace on the part of the whole community.

In the fourth century, these rites tended to expand in number, in extension, in time and in dramatic power. The greater number of candidates led to some of the rites being anticipated on Good Friday. One rite acquired a strong spiritual and social significance: the newly baptized wore a white garment for the whole week following the baptism.

Around the middle of the third century, there arose a bitter dispute about the validity of baptism administered by heretics outside of the catholic church. The Roman and Alexandrian tradition prevailed in which only the imposition of hands was required, as a sign of reconciliation to those baptized by heretics, and who wished to enter and be part of the catholic church. The best formulation of this theology is found in Augustine, who held that the validity of baptism does not depend on the person of the minister but on Christ. The following expression of Augustine became famous: "Peter may baptize, but this is he [Christ] that baptizes; Paul may baptize, yet this is he that baptizes; Judas may baptize, still this is he that baptizes."[12]

Present research on the baptism of infants has come to a full stop. It is believed that the practice existed from the apostolic period. However, we have explicit evidence only from the following centuries. Baptism of infants becomes more and more common beginning with the fifth century. An adequate period of preparation for baptism is something that

---

[11]*TAT* 35-37. [12]*Tractates on the Gospel of John* 6.7; NPNF 1 7:41.

caught hold only slowly: we find it fully developed only in the third century, and it reached its high point in the fourth century and then began to decline because of the spread of infant baptism. A number of reasons pointed to its necessity and influenced its development: the numerous heresies, the conscious decision to break with the pagan world, the weakening of initial enthusiasm and apostasy in times of persecution.

In the first centuries of Christianity, the three sacraments of baptism, confirmation and the Eucharist were closely tied together, because immediately after the baptismal rites, and only thereafter, was one admitted to the Eucharist. The baptismal liturgy normally closed with the eucharistic celebration, except in the case of clinical baptisms—baptisms out of necessity because of grave illness, or in the case of small babies for whom the Eucharist was deferred. Baptism (pardon of sins and spiritual rebirth) and confirmation (the gift of the Holy Spirit) were strictly united both in theological reflection and in catechetical preaching, and they were conferred by the same minister, the local bishop, during the same liturgy, so it is difficult to determine the specific gestures that referred to confirmation.

In the New Testament, much importance is given to the outpouring of the Holy Spirit on the newly converted. In the case of the centurion Cornelius, that outpouring comes before baptism,[13] but this is an exceptional case. In general the outpouring of the Spirit comes after baptism and by the imposition of the hands by the apostles, and it is a gesture that is necessary for completion of baptism. "Now when the apostles in Jerusalem heard that Samaria had received the word of God, they sent them Peter and John, who came down and prayed for them that they might receive the Holy Spirit; for it had not yet fallen on any of them, but they had only been baptized in the name of the Lord Jesus. Then they began laying their hands on them and they received the Holy Spirit."[14] In fact, to be a full member of the new community, both were necessary, the immersion (ablution) in water and the imposition of hands. Very soon, the rite became one continuous process, with no intervals in between the various parts, which are still nonetheless. All the components ultimately were included together under the one name of baptism. The various terms for baptism were all synonymous: baptismal bath, ablution, rebirth or new birth, illumination, *sphragis* ("seal").

When Christianity spread to the countryside and ceased to be exclusively urban, rural parishes were created far from the populated areas where the bishop resided. For practical and disciplinary reasons in the West, baptism in these parishes could be administered by priests, while confirmation was reserved for the bishop. In the East, however, it was administered by the one who baptized but with oil (the *myron*) blessed by the bishop. By this time we are in a period, however, in which the rites were already extremely significant, and there was full awareness of the distinction between the two sacraments. The same could not be said about the first centuries.

Overview: Before our Lord's passion and resurrection, there were many diverse sacrifices for sin, but now there is only the one sacrifice of Christ, which brings forgiveness through the grace of baptism (Origen). Previously, salvation was by faith yet unclothed, although anyone who tries to assert that the apostles were not baptized neglects the fact that they were most likely baptized with John's baptism. As to the time of year when baptisms should occur, since any day is the Lord's day, a person can be baptized whenever it is appropriate. Traditionally, however, some times were favored over others. Our Lord's passion was considered the most auspicious time for arranging for baptism, since he underwent a baptism by fire for

---

[13] Acts 10:44-48; 11:15-17. [14] Acts 8:14-17; cf. Acts 19:1-6.

us. Another day was Pentecost, since the grace of the Holy Spirit was first given on that day.

That same Holy Spirit hovered over the waters of creation in the beginning, sanctifying all water for use in baptism, whether it is the water of the Tiber or the Jordan that is used (TERTULLIAN). Although it is preferable that living water be used in baptism (i.e., water that is flowing), if such water is not available, then it is appropriate to use other water, preferably cold, but warm water may be used. If water is not available for immersion, water may be poured over the head three times, in the name of the Father, Son and Holy Spirit (DIDACHE). Those who go down into the water are blessed with the remission of sins through the water and the wood of the cross (EPISTLE OF BARNABAS, HERMAS, THEOPHILUS), just as the wood of the ark saved Noah and his family (JUSTIN). From the beginning, mercy has always been associated with water. Thus we who are sinners should flee to the water for that mercy that can put out the fire of sin and punishment (PSEUDO-CLEMENT, ORIGEN). Through the water we are set free to eternal life (TERTULLIAN).

When the baptized person is conducted to the holy pool of sacred baptism, a rebirth occurs (CYRIL OF JERUSALEM), a regeneration accompanied by illumination (JUSTIN). He or she renounces the devil before entering into the water and is immersed three times using the words of our Lord in the gospel, amplified somewhat. Afterward, those who are baptized taste a mixture of milk and honey and then refrain from daily baths for a week. The newly baptized are also invited to partake of the Eucharist (TERTULLIAN, ACTS OF PETER) after they have received the illumination of baptism (JUSTIN) and are enabled to see the truth (CLEMENT OF ALEXANDRIA). Baptism is accompanied by the anointing, or chrism, with which it shares an intimate connection. By virtue of this gift we are called Christians, having received Christ's name and his anointing, which makes us into "christs" (CYRIL OF JERUSALEM). The anointing, baptism and Eucharist are all of a piece in bringing the gift of forgiveness and life (ACTS OF THOMAS). As the unction in baptism flows on our flesh, it brings spiritual cleansing (TERTULLIAN).

In baptism we receive the spiritual cleansing of the forgiveness of sins and new birth (ACTS OF THOMAS, MELITO). We also receive participation in Christ's suffering (CYRIL OF JERUSALEM). In baptism a death occurs, but there is also regeneration (AUGUSTINE) as the old Adam dies and the new Adam is raised from the font in a type of resurrection (AMBROSE). We are created anew to live before God, empowered by the fount of the Spirit (PACIAN) and bathed in the bath of regeneration, which completely renews our nature (CHRYSOSTOM). In baptism our life is regenerated through the Holy Spirit (BASIL), who produces the new person in us (PACIAN). We become the dwelling place for God the Spirit (EPHREM) as we receive the Spirit of Christ (ODES OF SOLOMON, IRENAEUS), having been made clean in the waters of baptism.

As the creed confesses, there is only one baptism (TERTULLIAN), which is to be administered only once. We are washed once by baptism and daily by prayer (AUGUSTINE). All are reborn again through baptism (IRENAEUS), including infants, who also are to be baptized (CYPRIAN, HIPPLOYTUS, ORIGEN), which is the firm tradition of the church (AUGUSTINE, TOMBSTONE INSCRIPTIONS).

Some of the ancient martyrs even baptized themselves (ACTS OF PAUL AND THECLA) in the baptism of fire and blood, which is the baptism of martyrdom. If there is no time for baptism, as in the case of the thief on the cross, martyrdom for the sake of Christ may supply what was wanting of baptism, but also faith and conversion of heart if baptism cannot be performed. The crossing of the Jordan by the Israelites was a type of baptism as they passed through the waters to enter the promised land. We hope to do the same when we pass through the fiery river of cleansing in order to cross over into the paradise of life everlasting (ORIGEN).

Baptism That Occurred Before Christ's Death and Resurrection

ONLY ONE FORGIVENESS OF SINS. ORIGEN: But perhaps the hearers of the church may say, generally it was better with the ancients than with us, when pardon for sinners was obtained by offering sacrifices in a diverse ritual. Among us, there is only one pardon of sins, which is given in the beginning through the grace of baptism. After this, no mercy or any indulgence is granted to the sinner. Certainly it is fitting that Christians, "for whom Christ died,"[15] have a more difficult discipline. For the ancients, sheep, he-goats, cattle and birds were killed and fine wheat flour was moistened. For you, the Son of God was killed. How could it please you to sin again? And yet, lest these things not so much build up your souls for virtue as cast them down to despair, you heard how many sacrifices there were in the law for sins. Now hear how many are the remissions of sins in the gospel. HOMILIES ON LEVITICUS 2.4.[16]

BAPTISM AS CLOTHING FOR THE FAITH. TERTULLIAN: Let us suppose that formerly, before our Lord's passion and resurrection, salvation was by faith unattired: yet now that the faith has been enlarged, for those who believe in his nativity and passion and resurrection the sacrament has been expanded and the seal of baptism added. Baptism is, in some sense, a clothing for the faith that was previously unattired, and faith can no longer save apart from its own law. For there has been imposed a law of baptizing, and its form prescribed: "Go, he says, teach the nations, baptizing them in the name of the Father and the Son and the Holy Spirit."[17] When this law was associated with that well-known pronouncement, "Except a man has been born again of water and the Holy Spirit he shall not enter into the kingdom of heaven,"[18] faith was put under obligation to the necessity of baptism. Consequently from then onward all believers began to be baptized. Later on also, when Paul had believed he was then baptized. Baptism is what the Lord had enjoined on him at that stroke of blindness when he said, "Arise and go into Damascus: there it shall be shown to you what you must do":[19] namely, be baptized, for this alone did he lack. Apart from that, he had well enough learned and believed that the Nazarene is the Lord, the Son of God. ON BAPTISM 13.2.[20]

WHEN AND HOW WERE THE APOSTLES BAPTIZED? TERTULLIAN: Now there is a standing rule that without baptism no one can obtain salvation. It derives in particular from that pronouncement of our Lord, who says, "Except a man be born of water he cannot have life."[21] Because of this, certain persons' overprecise or even audacious discussions have arisen as to how, in view of that standing rule, the apostles can have obtained salvation, when we observe that none of them except Paul were baptized in our Lord. In fact, since Paul is the only one from among them who has put on the baptism of Christ,[22] either we have the case prejudged (they say) concerning those others' peril who are without Christ's baptism, so that the standing rule may be safe, or else, if salvation is appointed even for these unbaptized, the general rule is repealed. God is my witness that I have heard such remarks, that no one may suppose me so low-minded as to invent of my own, by the license of my pen, thoughts calculated to strike others with doubt. So now I shall answer, as well as I can, those who say the apostles had not been baptized.

---

[15]Cf. Rom 14:15. [16]FC 83:46-47. [17]Mt 28:19. [18]Jn 3:5. [19]Acts 9:6; 22:10. [20]*THB* 31. [21]Jn 3:5. [22]Acts 9:18.

If they had obtained John's baptism, what need had they of our Lord's? Our Lord himself had set the limit of one baptism by saying to Peter when he asked to be thoroughly washed, "he who has once bathed has no need to do it again,"[23] and this he would certainly not have said to one unbaptized. This also is an express argument against those who deprive the apostles even of John's baptism, hoping to abolish the sacrament of the water. Nor can it be thought credible that the way for the Lord, meaning John's baptism, had not already been prepared in those persons who were being appointed to open up the way of the Lord throughout the whole world. Our Lord was baptized, though he owed no debt to repentance: did not sinners need to be? That other persons were not baptized—these were not, you see, Christ's companions but enemies of the faith, doctors of the law and Pharisees. Concerning these we might also argue that as our Lord's adversaries refused to be baptized, those who followed the Lord must have been baptized and cannot have thought as his enemies did, especially when the Lord on whom they were attending had testified to John's high importance when he said, "Among those born of women there is none greater than John the Baptist."[24] Others make the obviously farfetched suggestion that the apostles underwent a substitute for baptism on that occasion when in the little ship they were aspersed with the waves. ON BAPTISM 12.[25]

THE TIME OF BAPTISM. TERTULLIAN: The Passover provides the day of most solemnity for baptism, for then was accomplished our Lord's passion, and into it we are baptized. With fairly good reason we could interpret it as a type, that when our Lord was about to keep his last Passover he sent his disciples to make ready, with the remark, "You shall meet a man carrying water."[26] By the sign of water he indicated the place for the Passover to be celebrated. After that, Pentecost is a most auspicious period for arranging baptisms, for during it our Lord's resurrection was several times made known among the disciples, and the grace of the Holy Spirit first given and the hope of our Lord's coming made evident: because it was at that time, when he had been received back into heaven, that angels said to the apostles that he would so come in like manner as he had also gone up into heaven, namely, at Pentecost. Moreover when Jeremiah says, "And I will gather them together from the ends of the earth on the festal day of Passover,"[27] he also indicates the day of Pentecost, which is in a special sense a festal day. For all that, every day is a Lord's day: any hour, any season, is suitable for baptism. If there is a difference of solemnity, it makes no difference to the grace. ON BAPTISM 19.[28]

The Living Water of Baptism

DIFFERENT WATERS OF BAPTISM. TERTULLIAN: But it will suffice that I have made a brief selection of those facts in which the rationale of baptism is in evidence, especially that primary one which even so long ago was by their relative position made a prophetic indication and type of baptism, namely, that the Spirit of God, who since the beginning was borne on the waters, would as baptizer abide on waters. A holy thing in fact was carried on a holy thing—or rather, that which carried acquired holiness from that which was carried on it. Any matter placed beneath another is bound to take to itself the quality of that which is suspended over it. This is especially the case in corporal matter which must take up the spiritual quality which, because of the subtlety of the substance it belongs to, finds it easy to penetrate and inhere. Thus the nature of the waters, having received holiness from the Holy, itself conceived power to make holy.

---

[23]Jn 13:10. [24]Mt 11:11. [25]*THB* 27, 29. [26]Mk 14:13; Lk 22:10. [27]Jer 31:8. [28]*THB* 41.

Let no one on that account object, "But are we then baptized in those same waters which were there in the beginning?" Not those very same—yet still the same, to the extent that the species is one, though there are many individual instances, and that which has become an attribute of the species overflows into the individuals.

Consequently it makes no matter whether one is washed in the sea or in a pond, a river or a fountain, a cistern or a tub: and there is no difference between those whom John baptized in Jordan[29] and those whom Peter baptized in the Tiber—unless perhaps that eunuch whom Philip baptized in casual water in the course of his journeyings obtained a greater, or a less, amount of salvation. Therefore, in consequence of that ancient original privilege, all waters, when God is invoked, acquire the sacred significance of conveying sanctity. For at once the Spirit comes down from heaven and stays on the waters, sanctifying them from within himself, and when thus sanctified they absorb the power of sanctifying—though the simile would equally apply to the simple act, that as we are defiled by sins as though with filth, we are washed clean in water. But as sins are in the flesh yet are not visible (since no one carries on his complexion the stains of idolatry, adultery or embezzlement), so people of this sort are filthy in their spirit, which is where sin begins: for the spirit is the master and the body the servant. Yet each of these imparts guilt to the other, the spirit by its directive, the flesh by service rendered. Thus when the waters have in some sense acquired healing power by an angel's intervention, the spirit is in those waters corporally washed, while the flesh is in those same waters spiritually cleansed. ON BAPTISM 4.[30]

BAPTISM IN LIVING WATER. DIDACHE: Concerning baptism, baptize this way: After reviewing all of this teaching, baptize in the name of the Father, Son and Holy Spirit, in living [running] water. But if living water is not available, then baptize in other water; and cold is preferred, but if not available, in warm. But if neither is available, pour water three times on the head in the name of the Father, Son and Holy Spirit. But before the baptism, let the overseer fast, and also the one being baptized, and all others who are able. Be sure to instruct the one being baptized to fast one or two days before. DIDACHE 7.[31]

BLESSED ARE THEY WHO GO INTO THE WATER. EPISTLE OF BARNABAS: But let us inquire whether the Lord took any care to foreshadow the water and the cross. Now concerning the water it is written in reference to Israel that they would not receive the baptism that brings remission of sins. . . . Note how he pointed out the water and the cross at the same time. For this is the meaning: Blessed are those who set their hope on the cross and go down into the water. He speaks of the reward at his proper season; then, he says, I will repay. But then what does he say? Their leaves shall not fade.[32] This means that every word that comes out of your mouth in faith and love shall tend to bring conversion and hope to many. . . . He says this because we go down into the water laden with sins and filth and rise up from it bearing fruit in the heart, resting our fear and hope on Jesus in the spirit. And whoever shall eat of these shall live forever.[33] This means that whoever, says he, hears these things spoken and believes will live forever. EPISTLE OF BARNABAS.[34]

THE RESURRECTION THROUGH WATER. HERMAS: "Show me still more, sir," I said. "What do you want now?" he said. "Why, sir," I said, "did the stones rise from the depth and were placed into the building of the tower,

---

[29]Cf. Mt 3:6. [30]*THB* 9, 11. [31]Translation by Ivan Lewis from extant Greek manuscripts with consideration given to the Coptic and Latin text <ivanlewis.com/Didache/didache.html>. [32]See Ezek 47:12. [33]See Ezek 47:12. [34]ANF 1:144**.

having borne these spirits?" "They had to rise through water," he said, "in order to be made alive. In no other way could they enter the reign of God, unless they put off the deadliness of their first life. So too those who had fallen asleep received the seal and entered the reign of God. Before bearing the name of the Son of God," he said, "a person is dead. But on receiving the seal, the person puts aside deadliness and takes on life. So the seal is the water. Into the water they go down dead and come up alive. The seal was proclaimed to them, and they profited from it to enter into the reign of God." "Why, sir," I said, "did the forty stones rise with them from the depth already having the seal?" "Because," he said, "these are the apostles and teachers who proclaimed the name of the Son of God, who, having fallen asleep in power and faith of the Son of God, even proclaimed to those who had previously fallen asleep and gave them the seal of the proclamation. They descended with them into the water and came up again, except that these descended alive and came up alive. Because of them, these others were enlivened and came to know the name of the Son of God. This is why these others also arose with them, and together were fashioned into the building of the tower and were made to dwell with them without needing trimming. They fell asleep in justice and great purity, except that they did not have this seal. So you have the explanation of these things." SHEPHERD, SIMILITUDE 9.16.1-7.[35]

THROUGH WATER, THE REMISSION OF SINS. THEOPHILUS OF ANTIOCH: On the fifth day the living creatures that proceed from the waters were produced. The multifaceted wisdom of God is also revealed in these things, for who could count all the many and various kinds of creatures there? Moreover, the things proceeding from the waters were blessed by God, that this also might be a sign that human beings are destined to receive repentance and remission of sins through water and the washing of regeneration—as many as come to the truth, and are born again and receive blessing from God. To AUTOLYCUS 2.16.[36]

REGENERATED BY WATER, FAITH AND WOOD. JUSTIN MARTYR: "You know, then, sirs," I said, "that God has said in Isaiah to Jerusalem: 'I saved you in the deluge of Noah.'"[37] What God meant when he said this was that the mystery of saved humanity appeared in the deluge. For righteous Noah, along with the other mortals at the deluge, that is, with his own wife, his three sons and their wives, being eight in number, were a symbol of the eighth day in which Christ appeared when he rose from the dead, forever the first in power. For Christ, being the firstborn of every creature, became again the chief of another race regenerated by himself through water and faith and wood, containing the mystery of the cross, even as Noah was saved by wood when he rode over the waters with his household. Accordingly, when the prophet says, "I saved you in the times of Noah,"[38] as I have already remarked, he addresses the people who are equally faithful to God and possess the same signs. For when Moses had the rod in his hands, he led your nation through the sea. And you believe that this was spoken to your nation only, or to the land. But the whole earth, as the Scripture says, was inundated, and the water rose in height fifteen cubits above all the mountains, so that it is evident this was not spoken to the land but to the people who obeyed him. He also had before prepared a resting place for them in Jerusalem, as was previously demonstrated by all the symbols of the deluge; I mean, that by water, faith and wood, those who are prepared ahead of time and who repent of the sins that they have committed

---

[35]*SHC* 232-33. [36]ANF 2:101**. [37]See Is 54:9. [38]Cf. 1 Pet 3:20.

shall escape from the impending judgment of God. DIALOGUE WITH TRYPHO 138.[39]

BORN AGAIN FOR GOD. PSEUDO-CLEMENT OF ROME: Come to baptism readily as a child to a parent that God may consider your ignorance as the original cause of your transgressions. But if, after you have been invited, you will not come or delay to do so, then by the just judgment of God you will perish because you have not been willing. And do not believe that you will ever have hope if you remain unbaptized, even if you are more pious than all the pious have been hitherto. Rather, you will then suffer a punishment all the more severe because you have done good works not in a good way. For to do good is good only when it takes place as God has commanded. But if in opposition to his will you will not be baptized, then you serve your own will and despise his decree.

But someone may say, "What good results to piety when someone is baptized with water?" In the first place, you are doing the will of God. And in the second place, when you are born again for God of water, then through fear you get rid of your first birth, which came of lust. In this way you attain to salvation. But this is not possible in any other way. For thus has the prophet appealed to us with an oath: "Truly I say unto you, if you are not born again of living water . . . you cannot enter into the kingdom of heaven."[40] Therefore come! For from the beginning there has been associated with the water something that shows mercy; it knows those who are baptized in the thrice-holy name and delivers them from future punishment, bringing as gifts to God the good works of the baptized done after baptism. Therefore flee to the water, for that alone can quench the violence of fire. One who has not yet been willing to come still bears in himself the spirit of passion and for that reason does not desire to approach the living water for his own salvation. Come then now, be you a righteous or an unrighteous person. For if you are righteous, you need only to be baptized for salvation, but an unrighteous person ought not only to submit to baptism for the forgiveness of the sins he has committed in ignorance but should also do good according to the measure of his past godlessness, as baptism requires. Therefore hurry, whether you are at present righteous or unrighteous, that soon you may be born to God the Father, who begets you of water. PSEUDO-CLEMENTINE HOMILIES 11.25-26.[41]

THE HOLY SPIRIT AND FIRE. ORIGEN: Why do I mention this? Because the baptism with which Jesus baptizes is "in the Holy Spirit and fire."[42] I am mindful of what I said before, and I have not forgotten my earlier explanation.[43] But I also wish to present something new. If you are holy, you will be baptized with the Holy Spirit. If you are a sinner, you will be plunged into fire. One and the same baptism will be turned into condemnation and fire for the unworthy and for sinners. But to those who are holy and have been turned to the Lord in total faith, the grace of the Holy Spirit and salvation will be given. Therefore, he who is said to baptize "in the Holy Spirit and fire" has "a winnowing fan in his hand, and he will cleanse his threshing floor. And he will gather his wheat into a barn, but the chaff he will burn in unquenchable fire."[44] HOMILIES ON THE GOSPEL OF LUKE 25.3.[45]

SET AT LIBERTY TO LIFE ETERNAL. TERTULLIAN: This discussion of the sacred significance of that water of ours in which the sins of our original blindness are washed away and we are set at liberty to life eternal will not be without purpose if it provides equipment for those who are at present under instruction, as well as those others who, content to have

---

[39]ANF 1:268*. [40]Jn 3:5. [41]NTAp 2:537-38*. [42]Jn 3:5. [43]Homily 24.1-2. [44]Lk 3:17. [45]FC 94:110.

believed in simplicity, have not examined the reasons for what has been conferred on them and because of inexperience are burdened with a faith that is open to temptation. And in fact a certain female viper from the Cainite sect, who recently spent some time here, carried off a good number with her exceptionally pestilential doctrine, making a particular point of demolishing baptism. Evidently it was in her nature to do this: for vipers and asps as a rule, and even basilisks, frequent dry and waterless places. But we, being little fishes, as Jesus Christ is our great Fish, begin our life in the water, and only while we abide in the water are we safe and sound. Thus it was that that portent of a woman, who had no right to teach even correctly, knew very well how to kill the little fishes by taking them out of the water. ON BAPTISM 1.[46]

Rebirth, Illumination and Eucharist

BAPTISM, THE TIME OF REBIRTH. CYRIL OF JERUSALEM: Then you were conducted by the hand to the holy pool of sacred baptism, just as Christ was conveyed from the cross to the sepulcher close at hand. Each person was asked if he believed in the name of the Father and of the Son and of the Holy Spirit. You made the confession that brings salvation and submerged yourselves three times in the water and emerged. By this symbolic gesture you were secretly reenacting the burial of Christ three days in the tomb. For just as our Savior spent three days and nights in the hollow bosom of the earth, so you on first emerging were representing Christ's first day in the earth, and by your immersion his first night. For at night one can no longer see, but during the day one has light. In the same way, you saw nothing when immersed as if it were night, but you emerged as if to the light of day. In one and the same action you died and were born. The water of salvation became both tomb and mother for you. What Solomon said of others is opposite to you. On that occasion he said, there is "a time to be born, and a time to die,"[47] but the opposite is true in your case—there is a time to die and a time to be born. A single moment achieves both ends, and your begetting was simultaneous with your death. SERMON 2.4.[48]

REBIRTH, REGENERATION AND ILLUMINATION. JUSTIN MARTYR: I will also explain the manner in which we dedicated ourselves to God when we were made new through Christ, since if we left this out in our exposition we would seem to falsify something. As many as are persuaded and believe that the things we teach and say are true and undertake to live accordingly—these people are instructed to pray and ask God with fasting for the remission of their past sins, while we pray and fast with them. Then they are brought by us where there is water and are born again in the same manner of rebirth by which we ourselves were born again, for they then receive washing in water in the name of God the Father and Master of all, and of our Savior, Jesus Christ, and of the Holy Spirit. For Christ also said, "Except you are born again, you will not enter into the kingdom of heaven."[49] Now it is clear to all that it is impossible for those who have once come into being to enter into their mothers' wombs. And it is said through Isaiah the prophet, as we wrote before, in what manner those who have sinned and repent shall escape from their sins. He thus spoke: "Wash, become clean, put away evil doings from your souls, learn to do good, judge the orphan and plead for the widow, and come and let us reason together, says the Lord. And though your sins be as scarlet, I will make them white as wool, and though they be as crimson, I will make them white as snow. But if you will not listen to me, a sword will devour you; for the mouth of the Lord has spoken these things." And we have learned from the apostles this

---

[46]*THB* 5.　[47]Eccles 3:2.　[48]*AIRI* 76.　[49]Jn 3:5.

reason for this [rite]. Since at our first birth we were born of necessity without our knowledge, from moist seed by the intercourse of our parents with each other, and were brought up in bad habits and wicked behavior; in order that we should not remain children of necessity and ignorance, but of free choice and knowledge, and obtain remission of the sins formerly committed, there is named at the water over one who has chosen to be born again and has repented of his sinful acts, the name of God the Father and Master of all; they who lead to the washing the one who is to be washed call on this name alone. For no one can give a name to the ineffable God; and if anyone should dare say there is one, he raves with a hopeless insanity. And this washing is called illumination, as those who learn these things are illuminated in the mind. And one who is illuminated is washed in the name of Jesus Christ, who was crucified under Pontius Pilate, and in the name of the Holy Spirit, who through the prophets foretold all the things about Jesus. FIRST APOLOGY 61.[50]

THE ELEMENTS OF THE RITE OF BAPTISM. TERTULLIAN: To deal with this matter briefly, I shall begin with baptism. When we are going to enter the water, but a little before, in the presence of the congregation and under the hand of the president, we solemnly profess that we disown the devil and his pomp and his angels. Then we are immersed three times, making a somewhat ampler pledge than the Lord has appointed in the Gospel. Then when we are taken up (as newborn children), we taste first of all a mixture of milk and honey, and from that day we refrain from the daily bath for a whole week. We take also, in congregations before daybreak and from the hand of none but the presidents, the sacrament of the Eucharist, which the Lord both commanded to be eaten at meal times and enjoined to be taken by all alike. THE CHAPLET 3.2-3.[51]

AFTER ILLUMINATION. JUSTIN MARTYR: But we, after thus washing the one who has been convinced and has assented to our instruction, lead him to those who are called brothers, where they are assembled. And we offer prayers in common for ourselves and for the one who has been illuminated and for all others everywhere, that we may be accounted worthy, having learned the truth, by our deeds also to be found good citizens and guardians of what is commanded, so that we may be saved with eternal salvation. Having ended the prayers, we greet one another with a kiss. Then there is brought to the ruler of the brothers bread and a cup of water and a cup of wine mixed with water, and he taking them sends up praise and glory to the Father of the universe through the name of the Son and of the Holy Spirit and offers thanksgiving at some length for our being accounted worthy to receive these things from him. When he has concluded the prayers and the thanksgiving, all the people present assent by saying "Amen." "Amen" in the Hebrew language signifies "so be it." And when the ruler has given thanks and all the people have assented, those who are called by us deacons give to each of those present a portion of the eucharistized bread and wine and water, and they carry it away to those who are absent. FIRST APOLOGY 65.1.[52]

REGENERATION AND DIFFERENT NAMES. CLEMENT OF ALEXANDRIA: Immediately on our regeneration, we attained that perfection after which we aspired. For we were illuminated (baptized), which is to know God. One is not then imperfect who knows what is perfect. And do not reprehend me when I profess to know God, for so it was deemed right to speak to the Word, and he is free.[53] . . . Being baptized, we are illuminated; illuminated, we become children; being made children, we are made perfect; being made perfect, we are made

---

[50]ACW 56:66-67. [51]ANF 3:94. [52]ACW 56:70. [53]See Jn 8:35.

immortal. "I," says he, "have said that you are gods, and all sons of the Highest."[54] This work is variously called grace, illumination, perfection and washing: washing, by which we cleanse away our sins; grace, by which the penalties accruing to transgressions are remitted; and illumination, by which that holy light of salvation is beheld, that is, by which we see God clearly. CHRIST THE EDUCATOR 1.6.[55]

ILLUMINATED TO SEE THE TRUTH. CLEMENT OF ALEXANDRIA: We who are baptized, having wiped off the sins that obscure the light of the divine Spirit, have the eye of the spirit free, unimpeded and full of light, by which alone we contemplate the Divine, the Holy Spirit flowing down to us from above. This is the eternal adjustment of the vision, which is able to see the eternal light, since like loves like; and that which is holy loves that from which holiness proceeds, which has appropriately been termed light. "Once you were darkness, now you are light in the Lord."[56] . . . Knowledge, then, is the illumination we receive, which makes ignorance disappear and endows us with clear vision. Further, the abandonment of what is bad is the adopting of what is better. . . . We are washed from all our sins and are no longer entangled in evil. This is the one grace of illumination, that our characters are not the same as before our washing. CHRIST THE EDUCATOR 1.6.[57]

FAITH, WATER, CONFIRMATION AND EUCHARIST. ACTS OF PETER: But when the ship met with a calm in the Adriatic, Theon remarked on the calm to Peter and said to him, "If you will count me worthy to be baptized with the sign of the Lord, you have the opportunity." For all those aboard the ship were drunk and had fallen asleep. And Peter went down by a rope and baptized Theon in the name of the Father and of the Son and of the Holy Spirit. And he came up out of the water rejoicing with great joy, and Peter also was more cheerful because God had accounted Theon worthy of his name. And it came to pass that at the same place where Theon was baptized, there appeared a young man shining with splendor, saying to them, "Peace be with you." And immediately Peter and Theon went up and entered the cabin; and Peter took bread and gave thanks to the Lord, who had accounted him worthy of his holy service, and because the young man had appeared to them saying, "Peace be with you." And he said, "Most excellent, the only holy one, it is you who have appeared to us, you God Jesus Christ; in your name has this man been washed and signed with the holy sign. Therefore in your name I impart to him your Eucharist, that he may be your perfect servant without blame forever." ACTS OF PETER 2.[58]

BAPTISM IS COMPLETED BY CHRISM. CYRIL OF JERUSALEM: Now that you have been "baptized into Christ" and have "put on Christ," you have become conformed to the Son of God.[59] For God "destined us to be his sons,"[60] so he has made us like to the "glorious body of Christ."[61] Thus, since you "share in Christ,"[62] it is right to call you christs or anointed ones. As God said, referring to you: "Touch not my anointed ones."[63] You have become anointed ones by receiving the sign of the Holy Spirit. Since you are images of Christ, all the rites carried out over you have a symbolic meaning. Christ bathed in the river Jordan, and having invested the waters with the divine presence of his body, he emerged from them, and the Holy Spirit visited him in substantial form, coming to rest on like. In the same way, when you emerged from the pool of sacred waters, you were anointed in a manner corresponding with Christ's anointing. That anointing is the Holy Spirit, of whom the blessed Isaiah spoke when he prophesied in the person of the Lord: "The

---

[54]Ps 82:6. [55]ANF 2:215*. [56]Eph 5:8. [57]ANF 2:216*. [58]NTAp 2:291-92*. [59]Gal 3:27; Rom 8:29. [60]Cf. Eph 1:5. [61]Cf. Phil 3:21. [62]Heb 3:14. [63]1 Chron 16:22.

Spirit of the Lord is upon me because he has anointed me; . . . you love righteousness and hate wickedness; therefore God, your God, has anointed you with the oil of gladness above your fellows."[64]

Just as Christ was truly crucified, buried and raised again, and you are considered worthy to be crucified, buried and raised with him in likeness by baptism, so too in the matter of anointing, Christ was anointed with the spiritual oil of gladness because he is the author of spiritual joy. And you have been anointed with chrism because you have become fellows and sharers of Christ.

But be sure not to regard the chrism merely as ointment. Just as the bread of the Eucharist after the invocation of the Holy Spirit is no longer just bread but the body of Christ, so the holy chrism after the invocation is no longer ordinary ointment but Christ's grace, which through the presence of the Holy Spirit instills his divinity into us. It is applied to your forehead and organs of sense with a symbolic meaning; the body is anointed with visible ointment, and the soul is sanctified by the holy, hidden Spirit.

Now that you are considered worthy of this holy chrism, you are called Christians, and this title you substantiate by your new birth. For before being thought worthy of this grace you did not strictly merit such an address. You were still advancing along the path toward being Christians. SERMON 3.[65]

The Baptismal Seal

THE SEAL OF ETERNAL LIFE. ACTS OF THOMAS: And when Marcia had brought these things, Mygdonia stood before the apostle with her head bare; and he taking the oil poured it on her head, saying, "Holy oil given to us for sanctification, hidden mystery in which the cross was shown to us, you are the straightener of crooked limbs; you are the humbler of hard works; you are he who shows the hidden treasures; you are the shoot of goodness. Let your power come; let it be established on your servant Mygdonia; and heal her through this anointing!" And when the oil had been poured out, he requested the nurse to unclothe her and gird a linen cloth about her. Now there was there a spring of water, and going to it the apostle baptized Mygdonia in the name of the Father and the Son and the Holy Spirit. And when she was baptized and clothed, he broke bread and took a cup of water and made her partaker in the body of Christ and the cup of the Son of God, and said, "You have received your seal and obtained for yourself eternal life." And immediately there was heard from above a voice saying, "Yes, amen." And when Marcia heard this voice, she was startled and besought the apostle that she too might receive the seal. And giving it to her the apostle said, "The zeal of the Lord be about you, as about the others." ACTS OF THOMAS 121.[66]

ANOINTING, BAPTISM AND EUCHARIST. ACTS OF THOMAS: When the apostle had thus prayed for them, he said to Mygdonia, "Unclothe your sisters!"' And she unclothed them, girded them with girdles and brought them. But Vazan had come forward before, and they came after him. And Judas took oil in a silver cup and spoke thus over it: "O fruit fairer than the other fruits, with which no other can be compared at all; altogether merciful; fervent with the force of the word; power of the tree which if people put on they conquer their adversaries; you who crown the victors; symbol and joy of the weary; who has brought to humanity glad tidings of their salvation; who shows light to those in darkness; . . . and let it dwell in this oil over which we name your holy name!" And when the apostle had said this, he poured it first on Vazan's head, then on the heads of the women, saying, "In your name,

---

[64]Is 61:1, 3. [65]*AIRI* 79-80*. [66]*NTAp* 2:388.

Jesus Christ, let it be to these souls for remission of sins, and for the turning back of the adversary and for salvation of their souls!" And he commanded Mygdonia to anoint them [the women], but he himself anointed Vazan. And when he had anointed them, he led them down to the water in the name of the Father and of the Son and of the Holy Spirit.

But when they had come up from the water he took bread and a cup and blessed and said, "Your holy body which was crucified for us we eat, and your blood which was poured out for us for salvation we drink. Let your body, then, become for us salvation, and your blood for remission of sins!" ACTS OF THOMAS 157.[67]

UNCTION IN BAPTISM. TERTULLIAN: After that we come up from the washing and are anointed with the blessed unction, following that ancient practice by which, ever since Aaron was anointed by Moses, there was a custom of anointing them for priesthood with oil out of a horn. That is why the high priest is called a christ, from chrism, which is the Greek for "anointing," and from this also our Lord obtained his title, though it had become a spiritual anointing, in that he was anointed with the Spirit by God the Father: and so it says in the Acts, "For of a truth they are gathered together in this city against your holy Son whom you have anointed."[68] So also in our case, the unction flows on the flesh but turns to spiritual profit, just as in the baptism itself there is an act that touches the flesh, that we are immersed in water, but a spiritual effect, that we are set free from sins. ON BAPTISM 7.[69]

The Remission of Sins

FORGIVENESS OF SINS. MELITO OF SARDIS: Come then, all you families of humanity who are compounded with sins, and receive forgiveness of sins. For I am your forgiveness, I am the Pascha of salvation, I am the lamb slain for you; I am your ransom, I am your life, I am your light, I am your salvation, I am your resurrection, I am your king. I will raise you up by my right hand; I am leading you up to the heights of heaven; there I will show you the Father from ages past. ON PASCHA 103.[70]

BAPTISM IS FOR THE REMISSION OF SINS. CYRIL OF JERUSALEM: No one should think, then, that his baptism is merely for the remission of sins and for adoption in the way that John's baptism brought only remission of sins. We know well that not merely does it cleanse sins and bestow on us the gift of the Holy Spirit—it is also the sign of Christ's suffering. This is why, as we heard just now, Paul cried out, "Do you not know that all of us who have been baptized into Christ Jesus were baptized into his death? We were buried therefore with him by baptism into death."[71] These words he said to those who had assented to the view that baptism confers remission of sins and adoption but not that it further implies a share by imitation in the true suffering of Christ. SERMON 2.6.[72]

Regeneration

THE SACRAMENT OF REGENERATION. AUGUSTINE: The sacrament of baptism is most assuredly the sacrament of regeneration. But just as one who never lived cannot die, and one who has not died cannot rise again, so too one who was never born cannot be reborn. ON THE MERITS AND FORGIVENESS OF SINS AND ON INFANT BAPTISM 2.27.43.[73]

THE NEW PERSON RAISED FROM THE FONT. AMBROSE: In the beginning our Lord made human beings so that they would never die, so long as they never tasted sin. But they committed sin; they became subject to death; they were cast out of paradise. But the Lord, who

---

[67]*NTAp* 2:401. [68]Acts 4:27. [69]*THB* 17. [70]*OPF* 59*. [71]Rom 6:3-4. [72]*AIRI* 77*. [73]*FEF* 3:92.

wished his gifts to last forever and to destroy all the wiles of the serpent and to cancel out all harm it had done, first passed sentence on them: "You are dust and to dust you shall return,"[74] and so he made human beings subject to death. The sentence was divine, and it could not be remitted by humankind. The remedy was found. It was that human beings should die and rise again. Why? So that what had formerly served as a sentence should now serve as a gift. And what is this but death? "How can this be?" you ask. Because death, when it comes, puts an end to sin. . . .

When we die, we do indeed stop sinning. It seemed, then, that the sentence was being served, because human beings, who had been created to live forever as long as they did not sin, now became mortal. But in order that God's gift might continue forever, human beings died, but Christ invented the resurrection in order to restore the heavenly gift that had been lost through the deceit of the serpent. Both death and resurrection, therefore, are to our advantage, for death is the end of sin, and the resurrection is the reformation of our nature.

But to prevent the deceit and tricks of the devil prevailing in this world, baptism has been invented. If you would know the source of baptism, listen to what Scripture, or rather the Son of God, says. The Pharisees refused the baptism of John; they "rejected the purpose of God."[75] Baptism is therefore God's purpose. What grace there must be when God's purpose is in operation!

Listen: to break the hold of the devil in this world as well, a means was found for making a living human being die and a living human being rise again. What does "living" mean? It means living by the life of the body, since the individual can come to the font and be immersed in it. . . . So it is that the font is a kind of grave. . . .

Thus the Father forgives sin, so does the Son and so does the Holy Spirit. Do not be surprised that we are baptized in one name: in the name, that is, of the Father and of the Son and of the Holy Spirit; because Christ spoke of only one name where there is one substance, one divinity, one majesty. This is the name of which it is written: "In this must all find salvation." It is in this name that you have all been saved, that you have been restored to the grace of life.

So the apostle exclaims, as you have just heard in the reading, "Whoever is baptized is baptized in the death of Jesus." What does "in the death" mean? It means that just as Christ died, so you will taste death; that just as Christ died to sin and lives to God, so through the sacrament of baptism you are dead to the old enticements of sin and have risen again through the grace of Christ. This is a death, then, not in the reality of bodily death but in likeness. When you are immersed, you receive the likeness of death and burial, you receive the sacrament of his cross, because Christ hung on the cross, and his body was fastened to it by the nails. So you are crucified with him, you are fastened to Christ, you are fastened by the nails of our Lord Jesus Christ lest the devil pull you away. May Christ's nail continue to hold you, for human weakness seeks to pull you away.

So you were immersed, and you came to the priest. What did he say to you? "God the Father Almighty," he said, "who has brought you to a new birth through water and the Holy Spirit and has forgiven your sins, himself anoints you into eternal life." See where the anointing has brought you: "to eternal life," he says. Do not prefer this present life to eternal life. For example, if an enemy should come against you, wishing to rob you of your faith, if he threatens you with death to make you go astray, consider what choice you should make. Do not choose the life in which you have not been anointed. Choose the one in which you have been anointed. Choose eternal life rather

---

[74]Gen 3:19. [75]Lk 7:30.

than this life. ON THE SACRAMENTS 2.17-19, 22-24.[76]

BAPTISM AS REGENERATION. PACIAN OF BARCELONA: You, indeed, correctly state that the church is a people born again of the water and the Holy Spirit, free from denial of the name of Christ. It is the temple and the house of God; "the pillar and the bulwark of the truth";[77] a holy virgin with the purest feelings; the spouse of Christ "from his bones and flesh";[78] "not having a spot or wrinkle";[79] observing the laws of the Gospels in their entirety.... For the present, let us consider those of yours. "The church is a people born again of the water and the Holy Spirit." Well now, who has closed off the fountain of God to me? Who has snatched away the Spirit? In fact, with us is "the living water,"[80] the very water that gushes from Christ. But you, separated from the everlasting fountain, from where do you receive your birth? And likewise has the Holy Spirit not departed from the original mother; from where did it come to you? Of course, perhaps the Spirit has followed one who engages in strife and, having abandoned so many priests and not content with its consecrated dwelling place, has truly loved the broken cistern of an impure fountain?[81] From where do your people possess the Spirit, those whom an anointed priest has not sealed? From where do they possess the water, those who have withdrawn from their mother's womb? From where do they possess spiritual renewal, those who have lost the cradle of nuptial peace? LETTER 3.2.[82]

NEW CREATURES. CHRYSOSTOM: You heard today that the blessed Paul, who leads the church to Christ as a bride to her spouse, told us in his letter to the Corinthians, "If any man is in Christ, he is a new creature."[83] To prevent us from interpreting the text as applying to a visible creation, he stated "if any man is in Christ," teaching us that if anyone has gone over to the side of those who believe in Christ, he is an example of a new creature. Tell me, if we see new heavens and other portions of his creation, is there a profit in this that can match the benefit we gain from seeing a person converted from evil to virtue and changing from the side of error to that of truth? This is what the blessed Paul called a new creature, and so immediately he went on to say, "The former things have passed away; behold, they are all made new!"[84] By this he showed in brief that those who, by their faith in Christ, had put off like an old cloak the burden of their sins, those who had been set free from their error and been illumined by the light of justification, had put on this new and shining cloak, this royal robe. This is why he said, "If any man is in Christ, he is a new creature: the former things have passed away; behold, they are all made new."[85] BAPTISMAL INSTRUCTIONS 4.12.[86]

BAPTISM IS THE BATH OF REGENERATION. CHRYSOSTOM: If you are willing, let me first tell you the names we give to this mystic cleansing, for it does not have one name but is spoken of in many and varied ways. This cleansing is called the bath of regeneration. He "saved us," says Paul, "through the bath of regeneration and renewal by the Holy Spirit."[87] It is also called an enlightenment, and again it is Paul who calls it this: "But call to mind the days gone by, in which, after you had been enlightened, you endured a great conflict of sufferings."[88] And again: "For it is impossible for those who were once enlightened, and who have tasted the heavenly gift and then have fallen away, to be renewed again to repentance."[89] It is also called baptism. "For all you who have been baptized into Christ, have put on Christ."[90] It is called a burial. "For you were

---

[76]*AIRI* 116-19 [77]1 Tim 3:15. [78]Eph 5:30. [79]Eph 5:27. [80]Jer 2:13. [81]Jer 2:13. [82]FC 99:40*. [83]2 Cor 5:17. [84]2 Cor 5:17. [85]2 Cor 5:17. [86]ACW 31:71. [87]Tit 3:5. [88]Heb 10:32. [89]Heb 6:4-6. [90]Gal 3:27.

buried," says Paul, "with him by means of baptism into death."[91] It is called a circumcision. "In him, too, you have been circumcised with a circumcision not wrought by hand but through putting off the body of the sinful flesh."[92] It is called a cross: "For our old self has been crucified with him, in order that the old body of sin may be destroyed."[93] Many other names could be mentioned, but in order not to spend all the time on the various names of this gift of God's grace, let us now go back to the first of these names and finish our discussion of what it means. But first let us extend the scope of our instruction. The washing that is common to all people is that of the baths, which usually cleanses away the filth of the body. There is also the washing of the Jews, which is more solemn than that of the baths but much inferior to the bath of grace. While this bath cleanses bodily filth, it does not merely remove the uncleanness of the body but also that which clings to a weak conscience. BAPTISMAL INSTRUCTIONS 9.12.[94]

BAPTISM RENEWS OUR NATURE. CHRYSOSTOM: This bath does not merely cleanse the vessel but also melts the whole thing down again. Even if a vessel has been wiped off and carefully cleaned, it still has the marks of what it is and still bears the traces of the stain. But when it is thrown into the smelting furnace and is renewed by the flame, it puts aside all dross, and, when it comes from the furnace, it gives forth the same sheen as newly molded vessels. BAPTISMAL INSTRUCTIONS 9.21.[95]

Baptism and the Holy Spirit

OUR LIFE IS REGENERATED THROUGH THE SPIRIT. BASIL THE GREAT: The dispensation of our God and Savior concerning humankind is a recall from the fall and a return from the alienation caused by disobedience to close communion with God. This is the reason for the sojourn of Christ in the flesh, the pattern of life described in the Gospels, the sufferings, the cross, the tomb, the resurrection; so that the one who is being saved through imitation of Christ receives that old adoption. For perfection of life the imitation of Christ is necessary, not only in the example of gentleness, lowliness and long-suffering set us in his life but also of his actual death. So Paul, the imitator of Christ,[96] says, "being made conformable unto his death; if by any means I might attain unto the resurrection of the dead."[97] How then are we made in the likeness of his death?[98] In that we were buried with him by baptism. What then is the manner of the burial? And what is the advantage resulting from the imitation? First of all, it is necessary that the continuity of the old life be cut. And this is impossible unless a person is born again, according to the Lord's word;[99] for the regeneration, as indeed the name shows, is a beginning of a second life. So before beginning the second, it is necessary to put an end to the first. . . . How then do we achieve the descent into hell? By imitating, through baptism, the burial of Christ. For the bodies of the baptized are, as it were, buried in the water. Baptism then symbolically signifies the putting off of the works of the flesh; as the apostle says, you were "circumcised with the circumcision made without hands, in putting off the body of the sins of the flesh by the circumcision of Christ; buried with him in baptism."[100] And there is, as it were, a cleansing of the soul from the filth[101] that has grown on it from the carnal mind, as it is written, "You shall wash me, and I shall be whiter than snow."[102] On this account we do not, as is the fashion of the Jews, wash ourselves at each defilement but own the baptism of salvation[103] to be one. For there the death on behalf of the world is one, and one

---

[91]Rom 6:4. [92]Col 2:11. [93]Rom 6:6. [94]ACW 31:135-36. [95]ACW 31:138. [96]1 Cor 11:1. [97]Phil 3:10-11. [98]Rom 6:4-5. [99]Jn 3:3. [100]Col 2:11-12. [101]1 Pet 3:21. [102]Ps 51:7. [103]1 Pet 3:21.

the resurrection of the dead, of which baptism is a type. For this cause the Lord, who is the dispenser of our life, gave us the covenant of baptism, containing a type of life and death, for the water fulfills the image of death, and the Spirit gives us the earnest of life. Thus it follows that the answer to our question why the water was associated with the Spirit[104] is clear: the reason is because in baptism two ends were proposed; on the one hand, the destroying of the body of sin,[105] that it may never bear fruit to death;[106] on the other hand, our living to the Spirit and having our fruit in holiness; the water receiving the body as in a tomb figures death, while the Spirit pours in the quickening power, renewing our souls from the deadness of sin to their original life. This then is what it is to be born again of water and of the Spirit, the being made dead being effected in the water, while our life is wrought in us through the Spirit. In three immersions, then, and with three invocations, the great mystery of baptism is performed, to the end that the type of death may be fully figured and that by the tradition of the divine knowledge the baptized may have their souls enlightened. It follows that if there is any grace in the water, it is not of the nature of the water but of the presence of the Spirit. For baptism is "not the putting away of the filth of the flesh but the answer of a good conscience toward God."[107] So in training us for the life that follows on the resurrection, the Lord sets out all the manner of life required by the gospel, laying down for us the law of gentleness, of endurance of wrong, of freedom from the defilement that comes from the love of pleasure and from covetousness, to the end that we may of set purpose win beforehand and achieve all that the life to come of its inherent nature possesses. . . .

Through the Holy Spirit comes our restoration to paradise, our ascension into the kingdom of heaven, our return to the adoption of children, our liberty to call God our Father, our being made partakers of the grace of Christ, our being called children of light, our sharing in eternal glory and, in a word, our being brought into a state of all "fullness of blessing,"[108] both in this world and in the world to come, of all the good gifts that are in store for us, by promise of this, through faith, beholding the reflection of their grace as though they were already present, we await the full enjoyment. If such is the earnest, what the perfection? If such the first fruits, what the complete fulfillment? Furthermore, from this too may be apprehended the difference between the grace that comes from the Spirit and the baptism by water: in that John indeed baptized with water but our Lord Jesus Christ by the Holy Spirit. "I indeed," he says, "baptize you with water unto repentance; but he that comes after me is mightier than I, whose shoes I am not worthy to bear: he shall baptize you with the Holy Spirit and with fire."[109] Here he calls the trial at the judgment the baptism of fire, as the apostle says, "The fire shall try every man's work, of what sort it is."[110] ON THE HOLY SPIRIT 15.35-36.[111]

THE SPIRIT OF GOD PRODUCES THE NEW PERSON. PACIAN OF BARCELONA: Thus Christ engenders life in the church through his priests, as the same apostle states, "And indeed, in Christ I have begotten you."[112] And so the seed of Christ, that is, the Spirit of God, produces through the hands of the priests the new person, conceived in the womb of our spiritual mother and received at birth at the baptismal font, with faith still attending as the nuptial protectress. For neither will someone appear attached to the church who has not believed, nor will someone be born from Christ who has not received his Spirit. We must believe therefore that we can be born

---

[104]Jn 3:5. [105]Rom 6:6. [106]Rom 7:5. [107]1 Pet 3:21. [108]Rom 15:29. [109]Mt 3:11. [110]1 Cor 3:13. [111]NPNF 2 8:21-22. [112]1 Cor 4:15.

again. For Philip asserts thus, "If you believe, it is possible."[113] Christ must be received so that he may beget, for so says the apostle John, "As many as received him, to them he gave the power to become sons of God."[114] But these things cannot otherwise be fulfilled, except by the sacraments of baptism and chrism at the hands of the bishop. For by baptism sins are washed away; by chrism the Holy Spirit is poured out on the individual. Yet both of these are obtained through the action and words of the bishop. And so it is that the whole person is born again and renewed in Christ, "so that just as Christ was resurrected from the dead, so we too may walk in the newness of life."[115] In other words, having put aside the errors of our former life—namely, servitude to idols, cruelty, fornication, licentiousness, and the other vices of flesh and blood—we should, through the Spirit, follow new ways in Christ: faith, modesty, innocence and chastity. And "just as we have borne the image of earthly man, let us also bear his, who is from heaven,"[116] because "the first man was of the earth, the earthly one; the second, from heaven, the heavenly one."[117] If we act in this manner, dearly beloved, we shall die no more. For even if we die in this body, we shall live in Christ, as he himself says, "He who believes in me, although he were dead, shall live."[118] ON BAPTISM 6.2.[119]

A DWELLING FOR GOD. EPHREM THE SYRIAN: Moses built a tabernacle in the desert for the Godhead. Because he did not dwell in their hearts, he shall dwell in the holy of holies. For the Gentiles the church was built, a gathering for prayers. In our souls dwells the Power that guides all things. By the baptism of the Holy Spirit we share in the forgiveness of sins, and by his power, which has come to dwell in the bread, he enters and rests in us. HYMNS PRESERVED IN ARMENIAN 48.13-24.[120]

THE NEW BIRTH OF BAPTISM. ODES OF SOLOMON: From baptism we receive the spirit of Christ, and in the same hour that the priests invoke the Spirit, "she" [the Spirit] opens the heavens and descends and hovers over the waters, and those who are baptized put her on. From all who are born of a body the Spirit is absent until they come to birth by water and then receive the Holy Spirit. ODES OF SOLOMON 24.1; 28.1-2.[121]

BAPTISM AND THE HOLY SPIRIT. IRENAEUS: For so (they said) do the faithful keep when there abides constantly in them the Holy Spirit, who is given by him in baptism and is kept by him who has received him by the practice of truth and holiness and justice and patience. For it is resurrection of this spirit that comes to the faithful, when the body receives once more the soul and along with it is raised by the power of the Holy Spirit and brought into the kingdom of God. PROOF OF THE APOSTOLIC TEACHING 42.[122]

MADE READY FOR THE HOLY SPIRIT. TERTULLIAN: Not that the Holy Spirit is given to us in the water, but that in the water we are made clean by the action of the angel and made ready for the Holy Spirit. Here also a type had come first. As John was our Lord's forerunner, preparing his ways,[123] so also the angel, the mediator of baptism, makes the ways straight for the Holy Spirit, who is to come next. He does so by that canceling of sins that is granted in response to faith signed and sealed in the Father and the Son and the Holy Spirit. ON BAPTISM 6.[124]

One Baptism

ONLY ONE BAPTISM. TERTULLIAN: I do not know if another matter besides is being worked

---

[113]Acts 8:37. [114]Jn 1:12. [115]Rom 6:4. [116]1 Cor 15:49. [117]1 Cor 15:47. [118]Jn 11:25. [119]FC 99:92*. [120]SCK 79*. [121]SCK 143. [122]ACW 16:74. [123]Cf. Mt 3:3; Mk 1:2; Lk 3:4. [124]THB 15.

up into a controversy about baptism. I shall in any event take up again a thing I previously left out, that I may not appear to be deliberately omitting themes that will shortly demand attention. We have one baptism, and one only, on the evidence both of our Lord's gospel and of the apostle's letter, where he says that there is one God and one baptism, and one church which is in heaven.[125] Certainly we have justification for discussing what practice should be observed in respect of heretics. For it was to us that the announcement was made, whereas heretics have no part or lot in our regulations. The very fact of their being deprived of fellowship bears witness that they are outsiders. It is no duty of mine to take cognizance in them of a precept enjoined on me. They do not have the same God as we have, nor do they have the one—that is, the same—Christ. Consequently, they do not have the one—because they do not have the same—baptism. ON BAPTISM 15.[126]

BAPTISM IS GIVEN ONLY ONCE. AUGUSTINE: Cease, then, to bring forward against us the authority of Cyprian in favor of repeating baptism, but cling with us to the example of Cyprian for the preservation of unity. For this question of baptism had not been as yet completely worked out, but yet the church observed the most wholesome custom of correcting what was wrong, not repeating what was already given, even in the case of schismatics and heretics. She healed the wounded part but did not meddle with what was whole. And this custom, coming, I suppose, from apostolic tradition (like many other things that are held to have been handed down under their actual sanction, because they are preserved throughout the whole church, though they are not found either in their letters or in the councils of their successors)—this most wholesome custom, I say, according to the holy Cyprian, began to be amended, as we might call it, already by his predecessor Agrippinus. ON BAPTISM 2.7.12.[127]

IN BAPTISM ALL SINS ARE FORGIVEN, ONLY ONCE. AUGUSTINE: The forgiveness of sins. You have the creed complete in yourselves, when you are baptized. None of you must say, "I did this or that, perhaps it can't be forgiven me." What have you done? How serious was it? . . . Baptism was introduced on account of all sins; on account of the minor sins, without which we cannot exist here, the prayer was introduced. What does the prayer say? Forgive us our debts, just as we too forgive our debtors.[128] We are washed just once by baptism, washed daily by prayer. But don't commit those sins for which you have to be cut off from the body of Christ, which God preserve you from. I mean, those people you can see here doing penance have committed wicked acts, whether adultery or other frightful deeds; that's why they are doing penance. I mean, if their sins were slight, the daily prayer would be sufficient to blot them out. SERMON 398.15.[129]

Infant Baptism

ALL ARE REBORN AGAIN THROUGH BAPTISM. IRENAEUS: For he came to save all by means of himself—all, I say, who through him are born again to God—infants and children, and boys and youths, and old men. AGAINST HERESIES 2.22.4.[130]

INFANTS MUST BE BAPTIZED. CYPRIAN: As far as concerns the case of infants, you expressed your view that they ought not to be baptized within the second or third day of their birth; rather, the ancient law on circumcision ought to be respected and you therefore concluded that the newly born should not be baptized and sanctified before the eighth day. Our council adopted an entirely different conclusion. No one agreed with your opinion on the matter; instead, without exception we all formed the

---

[125]Eph 4:4-5. [126]*THB* 33*. [127]NPNF 1 4:430**. [128]Mt 6:12. [129]WSA 3 10:454. [130]ANF 1:391.

judgment that it is not right to deny the mercy and grace of God to any person who is born. But seeing that the Lord says in his own Gospel, "The Son of man has come not to destroy the souls of men but to save them,"[131] we must do everything we possibly can to prevent the destruction of any soul. We need to ask, What can be lacking to one who has been already formed by the hands of God in his mother's womb? To our way of thinking, indeed, and to our eyes infants after their birth appear to grow and increase as the earthly days go by; but as far as God their Maker is concerned, whatever has been made by him is perfect and complete thanks to his handiwork and almighty power. Moreover, the divine Scriptures in which we put our trust declare to us that all, whether infants or older, enjoy exactly equal shares in the divine bounty.... Now if you think of this action in terms of different ages and bodily sizes, an infant could not possibly have the same dimensions as a fully grown adult, nor could his small limbs match and measure up to an older person's. But in this incident what is being illustrated is divine and spiritual equality, according to which all people are equal and alike because they have all once been made by God; we may be different, so far as the world is concerned, in the development of our bodies depending on our various ages, but there is no difference between us so far as God is concerned. LETTER 64:2-3.[132]

THE BAPTISM OF INFANTS. HIPPOLYTUS: And they shall baptize the little children first. And if they can answer for themselves, let them answer. But if they cannot, let their parents answer or someone from their family. APOSTOLIC TRADITION 21.[133]

BAPTISM TO BE GIVEN TO INFANTS. ORIGEN: What we already have recalled above, "No one is pure from uncleanness even if his life is only one day long."[134] To these things can be added the reason why it is required, since the baptism of the church is given for the forgiveness of sins, that, according to the observance of the church, that baptism also be given to infants; since, certainly, if there were nothing in infants that ought to pertain to forgiveness and indulgence, then the grace of baptism would appear superfluous. HOMILIES ON LEVITICUS 8.5.[135]

THE BAPTISM OF CHILDREN. ORIGEN: Thus it was fitting that those offerings that, according to the law, customarily cleanse stain should be made. They were made for our Lord and Savior, who had been "clothed with stained garments"[136] and had taken on an earthly body. Christian brothers often ask a question. The passage from Scripture read today encourages me to treat it again. Little children are baptized "for the remission of sins." Whose sins are they? When did they sin? Or how can this explanation of the baptismal washing be maintained in the case of small children, except according to the interpretation we spoke of a little earlier? "No man is clean of stain, not even if his life upon the earth had lasted but a single day."[137] Through the mystery of baptism, the stains of birth are put aside. For this reason, even small children are baptized. For "unless a man be born again of water and spirit, he will not be able to enter into the kingdom of heaven."[138] HOMILIES ON THE GOSPEL OF LUKE 14.5.[139]

INFANT BAPTISM ESTABLISHED IN TRADITION. AUGUSTINE: And this is the firm tradition of the universal church, in respect to the baptism of infants, who certainly are as yet unable "with the heart to believe unto righteousness, and with the mouth to make confession unto salvation,"[140] as the thief could do—no, who even, by crying and moaning when the mystery is performed on them, raise their voices in opposition to the mysterious words.

---

[131]Cf. Jn 12:47. [132]ACW 46:110-11. [133]TAT 33. [134]Job 14:4-5 (LXX). [135]FC 83:158. [136]Zach 3:3. [137]Job 14:4-5 (LXX). [138]Jn 3:5. [139]FC 94:58-59. [140]Rom 10:10.

And yet no Christian will say that they are baptized to no purpose. ON BAPTISM 4.23.[141]

THE NECESSITY OF BAPTISM FOR INFANTS. AUGUSTINE: Likewise, if anyone shall say that even infants who depart life without sharing in this sacrament shall be made alive in Christ, he certainly goes counter to the teaching of the apostle and condemns the whole church, which is in great haste to baptize infants, because of the unquestioned belief that otherwise they cannot possibly be made alive in Christ. And of those who are not made alive in Christ we must conclude that they remain under that condemnation of which the apostle speaks: "By the offense of one unto all men to condemnation."[142] . . . Blessed Cyprian, indeed, was not setting up some new decree but affirming the most solid belief of the church in order to correct some who thought that a child should not be baptized sooner than the eighth day after birth, when he said that it was not the body but the soul that was to be saved from destruction. He also agreed with some of his fellow bishops that a child could be validly baptized almost at the instant he or she was born. LETTER 166.21-23.[143]

INFANT BAPTISM IS OF THE APOSTOLIC AGE. AUGUSTINE: The custom of Mother Church in baptizing infants is certainly not to be scorned, nor is it to be regarded in any way as superfluous, nor is it to be believed that its tradition is anything except apostolic. The age of infancy also has a great weight of witness, for it was the infant age that first merited to pour out their blood for Christ.[144] ON THE LITERAL INTERPRETATION OF GENESIS 10.23.29.[145]

GRACE RECEIVED. EARLY INSCRIPTION: Sweet Tyche lived one year, ten months, fifteen days, received [grace] on the eighth day before the Kalends. Gave up her soul on the same day. THIRD CENTURY.[146]

GRACE OBTAINED. EARLY INSCRIPTION: Postumius Eutenion, a believer, who obtained holy grace the day before his birthday at a very late hour and died. He lived six years and was buried on the fifth of Ides of July on the day of Jupiter on which he was born. His soul is with the saints in peace. Felicissimus, Eutheria and Festa his grandmother to their worthy son Postumius. EARLY FOURTH CENTURY.[147]

DEPARTED A BELIEVER. EARLY INSCRIPTION: To the sacred divine dead. Florentius made this monument to his worthy son Appronianus, who lived one year, nine months, and five days. Since he was dearly loved by his grandmother and she saw that he was going to die, she asked from the church that he might depart from the world a believer. THIRD CENTURY.[148]

Blood Baptism

SELF-BAPTISM. ACTS OF PAUL AND THECLA: Then they sent in many beasts, while she stood and stretched out her hands and prayed. And when she had finished her prayer, she turned and saw a great pit full of water and said, "Now is the time for me to wash." And she threw herself in, saying, "In the name of Jesus Christ I baptize myself on the last day!" And when they saw it, the women and all the people wept, saying, "Do not throw yourself into the water!" so that even the governor wept that such beauty should be devoured by seals. So, then, she threw herself into the water in the name of Jesus Christ; but the seals, seeing the light of a lightning flash, floated dead on the surface. And there was about her a cloud of fire, so

---

[141]NPNF 1 4:461. [142]Rom 5:18. [143]FC 30:25. [144]See Mt 2:16. [145]FEF 3:86. [146]ILCV 1:1531 (Quoted in ECS 56). [147]ILCV 1:1524 (Quoted in ECS 56). [148]ILCV 1:1343 (Quoted in ECS 56).

that neither could the beasts touch her nor could she be seen naked. ACTS OF PAUL AND THECLA 34.[149]

BAPTISM BY FIRE. ORIGEN: Jesus has come to bring not only the sword on earth, but also fire. "And what will I," he says, "but that it be kindled?" May this fire therefore be kindled in you also. May it consume your every calculation that is earthly and of the body. May you now with heart and soul submit to that baptism with which Jesus "was straitened until it was accomplished." And you, who have a wife and children, brothers and sisters, remember the words: "If any man come to me and hate not his father and mother and wife and children and brothers and sisters, he cannot be my disciple."[150] And both of you should remember these words: "If any man come to me, and hate not"—in addition—"his own life also, he cannot be my disciple." EXHORTATION TO MARTYRDOM 37.[151]

BAPTISM OF BLOOD. ORIGEN: Let us remember also the sins that we have committed and that except by baptism it is not possible to obtain remission of sins. But according to the laws of the gospel, one cannot be baptized twice in water and the Spirit for the remission of sins.[152] We are given, however, the baptism of martyrdom. Obviously it bears this name from the fact that to the text: "Can you drink of the chalice that I drink?"[153] There is added, "Or be baptized with the baptism wherewith I am baptized?"[154] Elsewhere it is said, "And I have a baptism wherewith I am to be baptized. And how am I straitened until it be accomplished?"[155] Note also that the baptism of martyrdom, as received by our Savior, atones for the world; so too when we receive it, it serves to atone for many. Just as they who assisted at the altar according to the law of Moses seemed to procure for the Jews remission for sins by the blood of goats and oxen,[156] so the souls of believers that "are beheaded for the testimony of Jesus"[157] do not assist in vain at the altar of heaven[158] but procure for them that pray the remission of sins. EXHORTATION TO MARTYRDOM 30.[159]

BAPTISM SUPPLIED BY MARTYRDOM. AUGUSTINE: That the place of baptism is sometimes supplied by martyrdom is supported by an argument by no means trivial, which the blessed Cyprian adduces from the thief, to whom, though he was not baptized, it was yet said, "Today you shall be with me in paradise."[160] On considering this again and again, I find that not only martyrdom for the sake of Christ may supply what was wanting of baptism, but also faith and conversion of heart, if recourse may not be had to the celebration of the mystery of baptism for want of time. ON BAPTISM 4.22.29.[161]

Baptism as Type

CROSSING THE JORDAN IS A TYPE OF BAPTISM. ORIGEN: Lest you marvel when these deeds [the crossing of Jordan] concerning the former people are applied to you, O Christian, the divine word promises much greater and loftier things for you who, through the sacrament of baptism, have parted the waters of the Jordan. . . . Indeed, you who long to draw near to the hearing of the divine law have recently forsaken the darkness of idolatry and are now for the first time forsaking Egypt. When you are reckoned among the number of catechumens and have undertaken to submit to the precepts of the church, you have parted the Red Sea, and placed in the stations of the desert, you daily devote yourself to hearing the law of God and to looking on the face of Moses, through which the glory of the Lord is revealed. But if you also

---

[149]NTAp 2:245. [150]Lk 14:26. [151]ACW 19:180-81. [152]Cf. Mt 3:11; Mk 1:8; Lk 3:16; Jn 1:33. [153]Mk 10:38. [154]Mk 10:38. [155]Lk 12:50. [156]Cf. Lev 16:3-22; Ps 50:13; Heb 9:13; 10:4. [157]Rev 20:4; cf. Rev 6:9. [158]1 Cor 9:13. [159]ACW 19:171. [160]Lk 23:43. [161]NPNF 1 4:460.

have entered the mystic font of baptism and in the presence of priestly and levitical order have been instructed by those venerable and magnificent sacraments, which are known to those who are permitted to know those things, then, with the Jordan parted, you will enter the land of promise by the services of the priests. In this land, Jesus receives you after Moses and becomes for you the leader of a new way. HOMILIES ON JOSHUA 4.1.[162]

PASSING OVER TO PARADISE. ORIGEN: At the Jordan River, John awaited those who came for baptism. Some he rejected, saying, "generation of vipers," and so on.[163] But those who confessed their faults and sins he received. In the same way, the Lord Jesus Christ will stand in the river of fire near the "flaming sword."[164] If anyone desires to pass over to paradise after departing this life and needs cleansing, Christ will baptize him in this river and send him across to the place he longs for. But whoever does not have the sign of earlier baptisms, him Christ will not baptize in the fiery bath. For it is fitting that one should be baptized first in "water and the Spirit."[165] Then, when he comes to the fiery river, he can show that he preserved the bathing in water and the Spirit. Then he will deserve to receive in addition the baptism in Christ Jesus, to whom is glory and power for ages of ages. Amen. HOMILIES ON THE GOSPEL OF LUKE 24.2.[166]

---

[162]FC 105:51-53. [163]Lk 3:7. [164]Acts 1:5. [165]Jn 3:5. [166]FC 94:103-4.

FOR THE FORGIVENESS OF SINS

εἰς μίαν, ἁγίαν, καθολικὴν	Et unam, sanctam, catholicam	We believe in one holy catholic
καὶ ἀποστολικὴν ἐκκλησίαν·	et apostolicam ecclesiam.	and apostolic Church.
ὁμολογοῦμεν ἓν βάπτισμα	Confiteor unum baptisma	We acknowledge one baptism
εἰς ἄφεσιν ἁμαρτιῶν·	**in remissionem peccatorum;**	**for the forgiveness of sins.**
προσδοκῶμεν ἀνάστασιν νεκρῶν,	et expecto resurrectionem mortuorum,	We look for the resurrection of the dead
καὶ ζωὴν τοῦ μέλλοντος αἰῶνος. Ἀμήν.	et vitam venturi saeculi. Amen.	and the life of the world to come. Amen.

HISTORICAL CONTEXT: After his ignominious and shameful death, the friends of Jesus of Nazareth spread the idea that he was the Son of God. The only living God of Israel had a son? The people met him, talked to him, knew his family and parents: he was only a man. But his friends and disciples said that he was the natural Son of God the Father and became man through the virgin Mary; this human birth was referred to as the incarnation, because he took on human flesh (Lat *in* + *caro*). Why? The Nicene Creed answers, "For us and for our salvation he came down from heaven: by the power of the Holy Spirit he became incarnate from the virgin Mary and was made man." The reason for the incarnation is the love of God for humankind: to free women and men from their sins. If they believe in Jesus Christ, are baptized and repent of their previous sinful life, they become sisters and brothers of him, the only true Son. Through him they become the adopted sons and daughters of the Father. The new relationship with God is founded on his fatherly love; we are reborn through the word and the water and participate in his life. As Jesus called God my "Abba! Father,"[1] we too can call him "Abba! Father"[2] as his adopted sons and daughters. "But to all who received him, who believed in his name, he gave power to become children of God; who were born, not of blood nor of the will of the flesh nor of the will of man, but of God."[3]

Thomas Aquinas defines the adoption: "Adoption is the act by which a person lawfully takes for his child or grandchild, and so on, one who does not belong to him."[4] The ancient juridical concept of adoption was used to explain the love of God for human beings, through which he communicates his life to them and transforms them. The main way used was the incarnation of the Son of God, who became the Son of Man, in order that human beings would become children of God the Father. And how do they become children of God? We "were born not of blood, nor of the will of the flesh nor the will of man, but of God."[5] It is the gift of divine adoption through baptism, which is a rebirth. The ancient Christians lived in the spiritual atmosphere of adoption by the Father because they had been reborn of God; they had been called by faith in Christ to sonship. They created new names for the baptized to express their feeling at being adopted by God the Father: Adepta ("Adopted"), Theogonius or Deigenitus ("generated by God"), Regeneratus, ("Regenerated"), Renatus ("Reborn").

The Nicene Creed assumes a close connection between the one baptism and the forgiveness of sins: "We acknowledge one baptism

---

[1] Mk 14:36; Mt 26:39, 42. [2] Rom 8:15; Gal 4:5. [3] Jn 1:12-13.
[4] *Summa Theologica*, supplemental question 57. [5] Jn 1:13.

for the forgiveness of sins." The reception of baptism through God's providence leads to the forgiveness of sins. Meanwhile it also generates the practice of the forgiveness of sins in the church. Jesus died on the cross: "For this is my blood of the covenant, which is poured out for many for the forgiveness of sins."[6] The first predication of the disciples of Jesus was faith in Jesus Christ and pardon of sins through repentance and the reception of baptism, because the announcement of pardon of sins was the mission bestowed on them by Jesus "that repentance and forgiveness of sins should be preached in his name to all nations, beginning from Jerusalem."[7]

From the day of Pentecost on, baptism became the instrument for the forgiveness of sins. Peter, in his first speech on the day of Pentecost, told the crowds, "Repent, and be baptized every one of you in the name of Jesus Christ for the forgiveness of your sins; and you will receive the gift of the Holy Spirit."[8] When Paul believed in Jesus Christ, he was told by Ananias at Antioch, "And now why do you wait? Rise and be baptized, and wash away your sins, calling on his name."[9] And so Peter later wrote, "Baptism . . . now saves you, not as a removal of dirt from the body but as an appeal to God for a clear conscience, through the resurrection of Jesus Christ."[10] Baptism wipes away all kind of sins in connection with repentance: "Repent, therefore, and turn again, that your sins may be blotted out, that times of refreshing may come from the presence of the Lord."[11] In Christ and in our faith in him "we have redemption, the forgiveness of sins."[12] The forgiveness of sins is the condition of being adopted by the Father, because, as we say in the creed, "for us and for our salvation" the Son of God became man.

The first Christians experienced the unfortunate fact that, even after having received the forgiveness of sins in baptism, many still committed grievous sins. Because they were forgiven by God, they were the saints, the elect. What should they do? Is there another pardon after baptism? Yes; if they repent and reject the sin, there is still forgiveness.[13]

OVERVIEW. If the Spirit of Christ dwells in us, his dwelling place will be given back to him and his temple restored. If we have Christ's peace in us, then through the Spirit of peace we have the spirit of Christ (ORIGEN). We do not have to do anything that is not worthy of God and Christ (CYPRIAN). The Lord Jesus Christ gave the power to be made children of God (BASIL). The spirit of God lives in us; the word *God* must be taken to refer to the Holy Spirit (AMBROSIASTER). God's temple is holy, but anyone who has committed fornication is profane. The building does not belong to the worker but to the master (CHRYSOSTOM). The one who believes in Christ receives the Holy Spirit who dwells in him by the washing of rebirth, and thus he is spiritual (THEODORE).

We are in the Spirit because we are occupied with spiritual things. We have been enriched with God's Spirit, for his Spirit has come to dwell in our hearts, and we have taken our place among the children of God (CYRIL OF ALEXANDRIA). The Spirit of Christ, who loved his enemies and prayed for them, is the spirit of humility, patience and all virtues (PELAGIUS). The temple of God is the person in whom charity is dwelling (AUGUSTINE).

Heretics were deprived of the Son's gift, which is eternal life, and they did not receive the incorruptible Word because they remained in mortal flesh. In fact, the Word of God was made man, and he who was the Son of God became the Son of Man, that people, having been taken into the Word and receiving the adoption, might become children of God. The

---

[6]Mt 26:28. [7]Lk 24:47. [8]Acts 2:38. [9]Acts 22:16. [10]1 Pet 3:21. [11]Acts 3:19; see Acts 5:31; 10:43; 13:38. [12]Col 1:14; see Eph 1:7. [13]See Mt 18:22-25; Gal 6:1; 1 Cor 5:1-13; 2 Cor 2:5-11; 2 Thess 3:14; 1 Tim 1:20; Jn 20:21-23; Jas 5:14-16.

father of the human race is the Word of God, and the seed of the Father of all was commingled and united with flesh (Irenaeus). We have received the Spirit to enable us to know the one to whom we pray, the one and only Father of all (Clement of Alexandria). Whoever will become a child of God by the Spirit of adoption will first become a servant of God by the spirit of slavery; we no longer receive the spirit of slavery in fear, but rather, like a mature person, we have received the Spirit of adoption, in whom we cry. The Spirit of adoption bears witness and assures our spirits that we are children of God after we have passed from the spirit of slavery and have come under the Spirit of adoption (Origen). The Spirit of God is the same as the Spirit of Christ and the same as the Holy Spirit. Only one is the Son by nature, the only-begotten of the Father, through whom all the rest are called children (Origen).

When we go down into the water and are, in a fashion, entombed in the water as Christ was in the rock, we may rise again to walk in newness of life. The offenses committed against us are slight and trivial and easily settled, but those which we have committed against God are great and need such mercy as only he has (Cyril of Jerusalem). Baptism is like a death when we go down into water, and when we rise again it is like a resurrection (Ambrose). Set free by the grace of God from fear, we have received the Spirit of sonship so that we might govern our life with great care (Ambrosiaster). We have been born of God, not of blood, such as was the case with the first birth, which occurred in misery from miserable parents. The first birth was from male and female; the second birth is from God and the church. God wanted to be a son of man, and he wanted people to be children of God (Augustine).

God gave them something great and excellent; certainly, insofar as it is possible, he made them equal in honor by giving them the gift of sonship (Theodore). Those who have been called by faith in Christ to sonship with God put off the littleness of their own nature, adorned with the grace of him who honors them as with a splendid robe (Cyril of Alexandria).

Blessed are they who, placing their trust in the cross, have gone down into the water and whoever shall hear you speaking, and believe, shall live forever (Letter of Barnabas). Bishops have the power of binding and loosing (Pseudo-Clement), and we will tell those who preside over the church to direct their ways in righteousness, that they may receive in full the promises with great glory. Our life has been, and will be, saved through the water of grace. Repentance is great wisdom, and one who has sinned understands that he acted wickedly in the sight of the Lord (Hermas).

We were born without our knowledge or choice, by our parents coming together. In order that we may not remain the children of necessity and of ignorance but may become the children of choice and knowledge, we may obtain in baptism the remission of sins. By reason of this water of repentance and knowledge of God we have believed. Wash therefore and be clean now, and rid your souls of sin (Justin).

We have received baptism for the remission of sins, but because faith is the perpetuation of our salvation, we must bestow much care on the maintenance of it (Irenaeus). The Lord ordered baptism of repentance to lead the way, with the view of first preparing, by means of the sign and seal of repentance, those whom God was calling, through grace, to inherit the promise surely made to Abraham. That baptismal washing seals our faith, which is begun and is commended by the faith of repentance. The spirit is the master, and the body is the servant. Yet each of these imparts guilt to the other, the spirit in how it directs the flesh, the flesh by its service rendered; the spirit is in those waters corporally washed, while the flesh is in those same waters spiritually cleansed. Where there are the three, the Father and the Son and the Holy Spirit, there is the church, which is a body of three (Tertullian).

Just as the Son ascended into heaven, we shall also ascend with him, and just as he sits at the right hand of God, we shall also sit with him. Christ rose from the dead by the glory of the Father, and we have died to sin and are buried together with Christ. We shall rightly be said to have risen together with Christ by the glory of the Father. So we must spend some time in good living and keep ourselves clean of all stains and vices (ORIGEN). The sinner and the penitent are not a spot on the church, because as long as such a person sins and does not repent, he is placed outside of the church (PACIAN).

This is the grace by which those who believe in and confess Father, Son and Spirit receive in baptism the remission of all their sins (NICETA). We should not be surprised that we are baptized in one name: in the name, that is, of the Father and of the Son and of the Holy Spirit, because Christ spoke of only one name where there is one substance, one divinity, one majesty (AMBROSE). In fact, baptism is the sign and symbol of resurrection, and just as water cleans the dirt of the body, so we believe that we have been spiritually cleansed by baptism from every sin and have been renewed (AMBROSIASTER). It is faith in this Trinity that gives the grace of remission from sin; it is this confession that gives to us the gift of filial adoption. Baptism has made us dead to sin once for all. Paul says there are two mortifyings and two deaths: one is done by Christ in baptism; the other it is our duty to effect by earnestness afterward. In both, a death occurs, but not that of the same subject.

If you will show care in guarding and managing the gifts that have already been given, how can God fail to judge you worthy again of still greater liberality? Instead of the one who descended into the water, a different person comes forth, one who has wiped away all the filth of his sins, who has put off the old garment of sin and has put on the royal robe (CHRYSOSTOM). Christ, the repairer of our evildoing, assumes manhood in its fullness, saves man and becomes the type and figure of us all. Baptism, then, is a purification from sins, a remission of trespasses, a cause of renovation and regeneration. This gift is not bestowed by the water but by the command of God, and the visitation of the Spirit that comes sacramentally to set us free (GREGORY OF NYSSA).

The charity of God has been poured out in our hearts through the Holy Spirit, who has been given to us, and eternal life is the possession of those who have reached home; the earnest is the reassurance of those who are still on the way there. Our true home is not such that we should put anything else before it. God's purpose is that we should be transformed into something better by losing our sinfulness and mortality. The inheritance he promises us is such that many can obtain it without any of them suffering strained circumstances; that is why he invited the Gentile peoples into his family and why the only Son has innumerable brothers and sisters. Finally, we are promised that whatever is loosed by these keys on earth is also loosed in heaven (AUGUSTINE).

We believe in the forgiveness of sins, since through Christ and the church the one who is born as a new human being will have nothing of the old one (CHRYSOLOGUS). Since we are destined to live in this world where no one lives without sin, on that account the remission of sin depends not solely on the washing in holy baptism but also on the Lord's daily prayer, which you will receive after eight days (AUGUSTINE). Forgiveness results in a change of mind (RUFINUS). Through Christ's death we die to our guilt and learn to live in Christ (CYRIL OF ALEXANDRIA).

His image and likeness and the water by the grace of the Spirit clean the body from sin and deliver it from corruption, the water indeed expressing the image of death but the Spirit affording the promise of life (JOHN OF DAMASCUS).

You Are God's Temple

GOD DWELLS IN THE HEARTS OF BELIEVERS. ORIGEN: He opened, therefore, the wells and taught us that we might not seek God in some one place but might know that "sacrifice is offered to his name in every land."[14] For it is now that time "when the true worshipers worship the Father" neither in Jerusalem nor on Mount Gerizim "but in spirit and truth."[15] God, therefore, dwells neither in a place nor in a land, but he dwells in the heart. And if you are seeking the place of God, a pure heart is his place. For he says that he will dwell in this place when he says through the prophet, "I will dwell in them and walk in them; and they shall be my people and I will be their God, says the Lord."[16] Consider, therefore, that perhaps even in the soul of each of us there is "a well of living water,"[17] there is a kind of heavenly perception and latent image of God. HOMILIES ON GENESIS 13.[18]

THE SPIRIT OF CHRIST RESTORES OUR TEMPLE. ORIGEN: If the spirit of Christ dwells in you, it seems essential that his dwelling place (i.e., your body) will be given back to him and his temple restored. This is how you can know whether you have the spirit of Christ or not. Christ is wisdom,[19] so if you are wise according to Christ and know what is his, then by this wisdom you have the spirit of Christ. Likewise, Christ is righteousness;[20] therefore, if you have the righteousness of Christ, by that righteousness you have the spirit of Christ. Christ is peace;[21] if you have Christ's peace in you, then through the spirit of peace you have the spirit of Christ. So it goes with love, with sanctification and with all that belongs to Christ.[22] The one who has these things may be confident of having the spirit of Christ in him and can hope that his mortal body will be restored to life on account of the spirit of Christ dwelling in him. COMMENTARY ON THE EPISTLE TO THE ROMANS.[23]

WE ARE TO BE GOD'S TEMPLES. CYPRIAN: If we are the children of God, if we have already begun to be his temples,[24] if (after receiving the Holy Spirit) we live in a holy and spiritual way, if we have lifted up our eyes from the earth toward heaven, if we have raised our hearts, full of God and Christ, to supernal and divine things, let us do nothing that is not worthy of God and Christ, as the apostle arouses and urges us. JEALOUSY AND ENVY 14.[25]

THE SOUL CLOTHED WITH CHRIST. BASIL THE GREAT: When the soul has been clothed with the Son of God, it becomes worthy of the final and perfect stage and is baptized in the name of the Father of our Lord Jesus Christ, who, according to the testimony of John, gave the power to be made the children of God. CONCERNING BAPTISM 1.2.[26]

THE TEMPLE IS HOLY. AMBROSIASTER: Paul says this [you are the temple of God] in order to prick the consciences of those who have corrupted their bodies through evil living, especially the man who was having an affair with his father's wife. COMMENTARY ON 1 CORINTHIANS.[27]

THE SPIRIT LIVES IN US. AMBROSIASTER: It is necessarily the case that God lives in his own temple. Note that because he says that the Spirit of God lives in us, the word God must be taken to refer to the Holy Spirit in this verse. COMMENTARY ON PAUL'S EPISTLES.[28]

PROFANING GOD'S TEMPLE. CHRYSOSTOM: God's temple is holy, but anyone who has committed fornication is profane. HOMILIES

---

[14]Cf. Mal 1:11. [15]Cf. Jn 4:20-23. [16]Cf. 2 Cor 6:16. [17]Jn 4:14. [18]FC 71:191. [19]1 Cor 1:24, 30. [20]1 Cor 1:30; 1 Jn 2:1. [21]See Jn 14:26-27; Eph 2:13-17. [22]See Jn 3:16; Eph 3:19. [23]CER 3:310, 314; ACCS NT 6:213. [24]See 1 Cor 3:16. [25]FC 36:304. [26]FC 9:380. [27]CSEL 81 1:38; ACCS NT 7:35. [28]CSEL 81 1:38; ACCS NT 7:35.

on the Epistle of Paul to the Corinthians 9.7.[29]

We Are the Building of God. Chrysostom: The building does not belong to the worker but to the master. If you are a building, you must not be split in two, since then the building will collapse. If you are a farm, you must not be divided but rather surrounded with a single fence, the fence of unanimity. Homilies on First Corinthians 8.6.[30]

The Holy Spirit Dwells in Believers. Theodore of Mopsuestia: The one who believes in Christ receives the Holy Spirit, who dwells in him by the washing of rebirth, and thus he is spiritual. But if such people then turn around and serve worldly passions, in that respect they are carnal. Paul says that those who have become spiritual according to their confession of faith may nevertheless still live as though they were carnal so as to become an insult to the Holy Spirit, who dwells in them. Pauline Commentary from the Greek Church.[31]

The Temple Restored. Pelagius: God will not allow the temple of his Spirit to perish. In the same way as he raised Jesus from the dead, he will also restore your body. Commentary on Romans.[32]

We Are in the Spirit of God. Pelagius: You are in the Spirit because you are occupied with spiritual things. The Spirit of God dwells in those in whom his fruit is manifest, as Paul says to the Galatians: The fruit of the Spirit is love, joy, et cetera.[33] The Spirit of Christ, who loved his enemies and prayed for them, is the Spirit of humility, patience and all virtues. Commentary on Romans.[34]

God's Spirit Dwells in Us. Cyril of Alexandria: We have been enriched with God's Spirit, for his Spirit has come to dwell in our hearts, and we have taken our place among the children of God and yet have not lost being what we are. For we are human according to nature, even though we cry, "Abba! Father." Letter 1.35.[35]

The One Who Loves. Augustine: Nor can there be the slightest doubt that the temple of God is the person in whom charity is dwelling. John too, you see, says God is charity.[36] Now when the apostles said these things and urged on us the absolute primacy of charity, they could only be belching forth what they had themselves eaten. Sermon 350.1.[37]

Adoption into the Family of God

The Son of God Became the Son of Man. Irenaeus: But, being ignorant of him who from the Virgin is Emmanuel, they [the heretics] are deprived of his gift, which is eternal life.[38] Because they do not receive the incorruptible Word, they remain in mortal flesh and are debtors to death, not obtaining the antidote of life. Mentioning his own gift of grace, the Word says to them, "I said, you are all the sons of the highest, and gods; but you shall die like men."[39] He undoubtedly speaks these words to those who have not received the gift of adoption but who despise the incarnation of the pure generation of the Word of God. They defraud human nature of promotion into divinity and prove themselves ungrateful to the Word of God, who became flesh for them. For it was for this end that the Word of God was made man, and he who was the Son of God became the Son of man, that people, having been taken into the Word and receiving the adoption, might become the children of God. For by no other means could we have attained incorruptibility

---

[29]NPNF 1 12:52. [30]NPNF 1 12:46. [31]NTAbh 15:176; ACCS NT 7:35. [32]PCR 108. [33]Gal 5:22. [34]PCR 108. [35]FC 76:31. [36]1 Jn 4:8, 16. [37]WSA 3 4:107. [38]Rom 6:23. [39]Ps 82:6-7.

and immortality, unless we had been united to incorruptibility and immortality. But how could we be joined to incorruptibility and immortality unless, first, incorruptibility and immortality had become that which we also are, so that what is corruptible might be swallowed up by incorruptibility, and the mortal by immortality, that we might receive the adoption of children? AGAINST HERESIES 3.19.1.[40]

THE SPIRIT OF GOD PRODUCED LIVING CHILDREN. IRENAEUS: Now the father of the human race is the Word of God, as Moses points out when he says, "Is not he your father who has obtained you by generation, and formed you and created you?"[41] At what time, then, did he pour out on the human race the life-giving seed—that is, the Spirit of the remission of sins, by means of whom we are quickened? Was it not then, when he was eating with people and drinking wine on the earth? For it is said, "The Son of man came eating and drinking."[42] . . . This whole matter was prefigured through Lot: The seed of the Father of all—that is, of the Spirit of God, by whom all things were made—was commingled and united with flesh—that is, with his own workmanship. By this commixture and unity, the two synagogues—that is, the two churches—produced from their own father living children to the living God. AGAINST HERESIES 4.31.2.[43]

ADOPTION IS THE GIFT OF THE FATHER. IRENAEUS: For the Father bears the creation and his own Word simultaneously, and the Word borne by the Father grants the Spirit to all as the Father wills. To some he gives after the manner of creation what is made, but to others he gives after the manner of adoption, that is, what is from God, namely, generation. And thus one God the Father is declared who is above all and through all and in all. The Father is indeed above all, and he is the head of Christ; but the Word is through all things and is himself the head of the church; while the Spirit is in us all, and he is the living water,[44] which the Lord grants to those who rightly believe in him and love him and know that "there is one Father, who is above all, and through all, and in us all."[45] AGAINST HERESIES 5.18.2.[46]

OUR REAL FATHER. CLEMENT OF ALEXANDRIA: We have received the Spirit to enable us to know the one to whom we pray, our real Father, the one and only Father of all, that is, the one who like a Father educates us for salvation and does away with fear. STROMATEIS 3.11.78(5).[47]

BELIEVERS ARE ADOPTED BY GOD'S GRACE. ORIGEN: It is certain that whoever will become a child of God by the Spirit of adoption will first become a servant of God by the spirit of slavery. For the beginning of service to God is to be filled with the spirit of fear when still a little child [i.e., a new convert], since the fear of the Lord is the beginning of wisdom.[48] . . . As long as we remain children in the inner person, we hold the Spirit in awe until we reach the point at which we can rightfully receive the Spirit of adoption as children and become like the Son and the Lord of all. For Paul says everything is yours,[49] and God has given us everything together with Christ. This is why Paul says that after we have died together with Christ and after his Spirit comes into us, we no longer receive the spirit of slavery in fear (that is, we do not return to the state of children, and we have completed the first stages of faith), but rather, like mature persons, we have received the Spirit of adoption in whom we cry, "Abba! Father!" COMMENTARY ON THE EPISTLE TO THE ROMANS.[50]

---

[40]ANF 1:448-49. [41]Deut 32:6. [42]Mt 11:19. [43]ANF 1:505. [44]Jn 7:37. [45]Eph 4:6. [46]ANF 1:546. [47]FC 85:304. [48]Prov 9:10. [49]1 Cor 3:22. [50]CER 4:36, 38; ACCS NT 6:217.

FELLOW HEIRS OF CHRIST. ORIGEN: The Son of God says to his fellow heirs, "You will also sit on twelve thrones, judging the twelve tribes of Israel."[51] Thus Christ leads his fellow heirs not only into a part of the inheritance but also into a sharing of his power. COMMENTARY ON THE EPISTLE TO THE ROMANS.[52]

ADOPTED CHILDREN OF GOD. ORIGEN: The Spirit of adoption . . . bears witness and assures our spirits that we are children of God after we have passed from the spirit of slavery and come under the Spirit of adoption, when all fear has departed. We no longer act out of fear of punishment but do everything out of love for the Father. It is right too that the Spirit of God should be said to bear witness with our spirits and not with our souls, because the spirit is our better part. COMMENTARY ON THE EPISTLE TO THE ROMANS.[53]

THE SPIRIT OF ADOPTION. ORIGEN: The Spirit of God is the same as the Spirit of Christ and the same as the Holy Spirit. But he is also called the Spirit of adoption, as the apostle makes clear in this passage. David spoke of this Spirit also when he said, "Take not thy Holy Spirit from me."[54] There are many children of God, as Scripture says: "You are gods, sons of the Most High, all of you,"[55] . . . but only one is the Son by nature, the only-begotten of the Father, through whom all the rest are called children. Likewise there are many spirits but only one who truly proceeds from God and who bestows on all the others the grace of his name and his sanctification. COMMENTARY ON THE EPISTLE TO THE ROMANS.[56]

A SHARE OF THE LORD'S DIVINITY. ORIGEN: For, in our view, the Lord has known those who are his because he has been made one with them and has given them a share of his own divinity and has taken them up, as the language of the Gospel says, into his own hand, since those who have believed in the Savior are in the Father's hand. For this reason also, unless they fall from his hand, thereby removing themselves from the hand of God, they will not be snatched away, for no one snatches anyone from the Father's hand. COMMENTARY ON THE GOSPEL OF JOHN 19.25.[57]

BAPTISM AS ADOPTION. CYRIL OF JERUSALEM: For this reason Paul has just now cried out loud, "Are you ignorant that all we who were baptized into Christ Jesus, were baptized into his death? We were buried therefore with him by baptism into his death."[58] These words he spoke to some who were disposed to think that baptism ministers to us the remission of sins and adoption but has not also furthered, by representation, our fellowship in Christ's true sufferings. CATECHETICAL LECTURE 20.6.[59]

NEWNESS OF LIFE. CYRIL OF JERUSALEM: As Jesus died in taking away the sins of the world, that, by putting sin to death, he might rise in righteousness, so too, when you go down into the water and are, in a fashion, entombed in the water as he was in the rock, you may rise again to walk in newness of life. CATECHETICAL LECTURE 3.12.[60]

A COVENANT WITH GOD. CYRIL OF JERUSALEM: "And forgive us our debts as we forgive our debtors."[61] We have many sins. We offend both in word and in thought, and we do very many things worthy of condemnation. And if we say that we have no sin, we lie, as John says: "We deceive ourselves."[62] And we make a covenant with God, entreating him to forgive us our sins, as we also forgive our neighbors their debts. Considering then what

---

[51]See Mt 19:28. [52]CER 4:36, 38; ACCS NT 6:219. [53]CER 4:36, 38; ACCS NT 6:219. [54]Ps 51:11. [55]Ps 82:6. [56]CER 4:32; ACCS NT 6:216. [57]FC 89:173. [58]Rom 6:3. [59]NPNF 2 7:148. [60]LCC 4:96*. [61]Mt 6:12. [62]1 Jn 1:8.

we receive—and in return for what?—let us not put off or delay forgiving one another. The offenses committed against us are slight and trivial and easily settled. But those which we have committed against God are great and need such mercy as only he has. Pay attention, therefore, lest the slight and trivial sins against you cut you off from forgiveness from God for your horrible sins. CATECHETICAL LECTURE 23.16.[63]

THE ADOPTION OF BELIEVERS. AMBROSE: It is not strange that one who puts to death the deeds of the flesh will live, since one who has the Spirit of God becomes a child of God.[64] It is for this reason that he is a child of God, so that he may receive not the spirit of slavery but the spirit of the adoption of children, inasmuch as the Holy Spirit bears witness with our spirit that we are children of God.[65] LETTER 52.[66]

REGENERATED IN THE BAPTISMAL FONT. AMBROSE: Baptism is like a death when you go down into the water and like a resurrection when you rise again. Thus, according to the interpretation of the apostle, just as Christ's resurrection was a regeneration, so the resurrection from the font is also a regeneration. ON THE SACRAMENTS 3.1.2.[67]

WE CAN CALL GOD "ABBA." AMBROSIASTER: Paul says this because once we have received the Holy Spirit we are delivered from all fear of evil deeds, so that we might no longer act in such a way as to be afraid once more.[68] Beforehand we were under fear, because once the law was given everyone was considered guilty. Paul called the law the spirit of fear because it made people afraid on account of their sins. But the law of faith, which is what is meant by the Spirit of sonship, is a law of assurance, because it has delivered us from fear by pardoning our sins and thus giving us assurance.[69] Set free by the grace of God from fear, we have received the Spirit of sonship so that, considering what we were and what we have become by the gift of God, we might govern our life with great care lest the name of God the Father be disgraced by us and we incur all the things we have escaped from. . . . We have received such grace that we can dare to say to God, "Abba! Father!" For this reason Paul warns us not to let our trust degenerate into pride. For if our behavior does not correspond to our voice when we cry, "Abba! Father!" we insult God by calling him Father. Indeed, God in his goodness has indulged us with what is beyond our natural capacity. COMMENTARY ON PAUL'S EPISTLES.[70]

WE RECEIVED THE GRACE OF THE SPIRIT. CHRYSOSTOM: Do not think that it is of small things you are hearing when you hear of this birth, but rouse up your mind and immediately tremble, being told that God has come on earth. For this was so amazing and beyond expectation that because of these things the very angels formed a choir and in behalf of the world offered up their praise for them. And the prophets from the first were amazed at this, that "he was seen upon earth, and conversed with men."[71] Yes, for it is far beyond all thought to hear that God the unspeakable, the unutterable, the incomprehensible, and he who is equal to the Father, has passed through a virgin's womb, and has promised to be born of a woman and to have Abraham and David for forefathers. HOMILIES ON THE GOSPEL OF MATTHEW 2.2.[72]

BECOME CHILDREN OF GOD. AUGUSTINE: And how do they become children of God "who are born not of blood, nor of the will of a man nor of the will of the flesh, but of God"?

---

[63]NPNF 2 7:155. [64]See Rom 8:14; 1 Jn 3:14. [65]See Rom 8:16. [66]FC 26:278. [67]FC 44:290**. [68]See Hag 2:5; 2 Tim 1:7. [69]See Is 32:17-18; 1 Thess 1:4-5; Heb 10:22. [70]ACCS NT 6:217. [71]Bar 3:37. [72]NPNF 1 10:9.

Pay close attention: these here have been born of God, having received power to become children of God. They have been born of God, not of blood, such as is the case with the first birth, the case with the birth in misery coming from miserable parents. But those who have been born of God, what was it that they were first born of? From a mixing of blood, from the blood of male and female, from a mingling of the flesh of male and female, that is what they were born of. But now, how is it they are born of God? The first birth was from male and female; the second birth is from God and the church. SERMON 121.4.[73]

MADE CHILDREN BY GRACE. AUGUSTINE: And how are they born to him? Because they become children of God and brothers and sisters of Christ, they must of course be born. How, I mean, could they be children if they weren't born? But the children of human beings are born of flesh and blood, and of the will of a man and the embrace of spouses. But these, how are they born to him? Not of bloods, as of a man and a woman. "Bloods" isn't Latin, but because the Greek has it in the plural, the translator preferred to keep it and speak what the grammarians would say isn't Latin and still spell out the truth so that it could be heard by the weak and feeble. You see, if he said "blood" in the singular, he would not be spelling out what he wished to; human beings after all are born of the bloods of male and female. So let us say it then and not be afraid of a caning from the grammarians, provided we can get at the sure and solid truth. To find fault with what he understands is to be ungrateful for having understood.

Not of blood, nor of the will of the flesh, nor of the will of the man.[74] He used "flesh" for woman, because Adam said when she had been made from his rib, "This is now bone from my bones and flesh from my flesh,"[75] and the apostle says, "He that loves his wife loves himself; for nobody ever hates his own flesh."[76] So then, "flesh" is used for the wife, just as elsewhere "spirit" is used for the husband. Why? Because he guides, she is guided; he should be commanding, she serving; because where the flesh is in command, the spirit serving, it is an upside-down (*perversa*) household. What could be worse than a household where the woman rules the man? No, the right sort of household is where the man rules, the woman complies. Thus the right sort of person is the one in whom the spirit is in command, the flesh serves.

So then, not of the will of the flesh, nor of the will of man, but of God these were born.[77] That human beings, however, might be born of God, God was first of all born of them. Christ, after all, is God, and Christ was born of human beings. It was indeed only a mother he looked for on earth, because he already had a Father in heaven; he was born of God that we might be fashioned, and he was born of a woman that we might be refashioned. Don't be astonished, then, folks, at being made a child by grace because you were born of God according to his Word. First that very Word chose to be born of a human being so that you might feel no unease at being born of God and might be able to say to yourself, "Not without reason did God choose to be born of a human being; for thus could he regard me of some value such that I might be made immortal and he might be born a mortal for my sake." That's why, after saying of God they were born, as though to save us from being overwhelmed and flabbergasted at such grace, that it might seem incredible to us that human beings were actually born of God, he says, to set your mind at ease, "And the Word was made flesh and took up residence among us."[78] So why be astonished that human beings are born of God? Observe God himself being born of human beings: And the Word was made flesh and took up resi-

---

[73]WSA 3 4:236. [74]Jn 1:13. [75]Gen 2:23. [76]Eph 5:28-29. [77]Jn 1:13.

dence among us. HOMILIES ON THE GOSPEL OF JOHN 2.14-15.[79]

TWO KINDS OF BIRTH. AUGUSTINE: This spirit and this life were not what were being savored by Nicodemus there, who had come to Jesus at night. Jesus says to him, "Unless one is born afresh, one will not see the kingdom of God." And he there, still savoring his own flesh, with as yet no savor of the flesh of Christ in his mouth, says, "How can a man, when he is old, be born a second time? He can't enter his mother's womb a second time, can he, and be born?"[80] This man knew of no birth but the one from Adam and Eve; he didn't yet know about the one from God and the church. He only knew of those parents who produce children for death; he didn't know of those who produce them for life. He only knew parents who produce heirs and successors; he didn't know of those who, living forever themselves, produce children who will remain with them forever.

So then, while there are in fact two kinds of birth, he had an understanding of only one. One is from the earth, the other from heaven; one from the flesh, the other from the Spirit; one from mortality, the other from eternity; one is from male and female, the other from God and church. But both of these two are once and for all events, neither the one nor the other can be repeated. Nicodemus had a correct understanding of birth in the flesh; so you there, just see that you understand birth in the Spirit in the same way as Nicodemus understood birth in the flesh. What did Nicodemus understand? "A man can't enter his mother's womb afresh, can he, and be born?" I have already been born of Adam, Adam can't father me again; I have already been born of Christ, Christ cannot again be my father. Just as the womb cannot be repeated, so neither can baptism. HOMILIES ON THE GOSPEL OF JOHN 11.6.[81]

GOD A SON OF MAN. AUGUSTINE: Hey there, brothers and sisters; God wanted to be a son of man, and he wanted people to be children of God! He himself descended because of us; let us for our part ascend because of him. It was alone, you see, that he both came down and ascended, the one who said, "Nobody has ascended into heaven but the one who came down from heaven." So aren't those then going to ascend into heaven whom he makes sons and daughters of God? They certainly are going to; this is what we have been promised: They shall be the equals of the angels of God.[82] So how in that case does nobody ascend except the one who came down; because just one came down, just one ascended. What about the rest? What are we to understand, except that because they will be his members, he ascends as one man? That's why he concludes, "Nobody has ascended into heaven but the one who came down from heaven, the Son of Man who is in heaven."[83] Does it astonish you that he was both here and in heaven? He put his disciples in the same position. Listen to the apostle Paul saying, "The company we keep is in heaven."[84] If the man Paul the apostle was walking about in the flesh on earth, and was keeping company in heaven, was the God of heaven and earth unable to be both in heaven and earth at the same time? HOMILIES ON THE GOSPEL OF JOHN 12.8.[85]

ADOPTED THROUGH THE SON'S GRACE. AUGUSTINE: But he added, "As many, though, as did receive him." What did he bestow on them? Great kindness; great mercy. Singly born, he did not wish to remain the one and only. Many couples who have had no children adopt ones when advanced in years and realize by choice what nature was unable to provide; that's what human beings do. But someone who has an only son rejoices in him all the more, because he alone will take possession of the whole inheritance and not have anyone else to divide

---

[78]Cf. Jn 1:14. [79]WSA 3 12:65-66. [80]Jn 3:4. [81]WSA 3 12:216-17. [82]Lk 20:36. [83]Jn 3:13. [84]Phil 3:20. [85]WSA 3 12:235.

it with and thus turn out the poorer. Not so God; he sent the very same one and only Son he had begotten, through whom he had created everything, into this world so that he should not be alone but should have adopted brothers and sisters. You see, we were not born of God in the same way as that only begotten Son of his but were adopted through the Son's grace. For the only-begotten Son came to forgive sins, those sins that had us so tied up that they were an impediment to his adopting us; he forgave those he wished to make his brothers and sisters and made them coheirs.

That, after all, is what the apostle says: "If, however, a son, he is also an heir";[86] and again, "Heirs indeed of God, but coheirs of Christ."[87] No, he wasn't afraid of having co-heirs, because his inheritance is not whittled down if many possess it. They, in fact, become the inheritance that he possesses, and he in turn becomes their inheritance. Listen to how they become his inheritance: The Lord said to me, "You are my Son; I today have begotten you. Ask of me, and I will give you nations as your inheritance."[88] How does he, in his turn, become their inheritance? It says in the psalm, "The Lord is my apportioned inheritance and cup."[89] May we possess him and may he possess us; he possesses us as our Lord; we possess him as salvation, we possess him as light. So then, what did he give those who did receive him? He gave them authority to become children of God, those who believe in his name,[90] that they might thus keep hold of the wood and cross the sea. HOMILIES ON THE GOSPEL OF JOHN 2.13.[91]

GOD GIVES THE GIFT OF SONSHIP. THEODORE OF MOPSUESTIA: For those, he says, who received him, their reception was not useless. He gave them something great and excellent; certainly, insofar as it is possible, he made them equal in honor by giving them the gift of sonship. They take advantage of that grace not by being reborn in the body according to the natural order of generation. Rather, they are given birth by divine power through a certain similarity and relationship with him. COMMENTARY ON THE GOSPEL OF JOHN 1.1.12.[92]

CALLED BY FAITH TO SONSHIP OF GOD. CYRIL OF ALEXANDRIA: They who, he says, have been called by faith in Christ to sonship with God put off the littleness of their own nature, adorned with the grace of him who honors them as with a splendid robe—they mount up to a dignity above nature. For no longer are they called children of flesh but rather offspring of God by adoption.

But note how extremely careful the blessed Evangelist is in his words. For since he was going to say that those who believe are begotten of God, he needs to exercise additional caution. He needs to do this in case anyone should suppose that they are in truth born of the essence of God the Father and arrive at an exact likeness with the Only-begotten. Or they might think that "from the womb before the Daystar I begat you"[93] is something less appropriately said of the Son too. If they went down this path, the Son too, at length, would be brought down to the nature of creatures, even though he is said to be begotten of God. This is why he needs this additional caution. For when he had said that power was given to them to become children of God from him who is by nature Son—and thus here for the first time introduces what is by adoption and grace—he avoids danger by adding afterward they were begotten of God. He does this so that he might show the greatness of the grace that was conferred on them, gathering as it were into a kinship of nature that which was alien from God the Father and raising up its connection to the nobility of its Lord through his own heartwarming love for it. COMMENTARY ON THE GOSPEL OF JOHN 1.9.[94]

---

[86]Gal 4:7. [87]Rom 8:17. [88]Ps 2:7-8. [89]Ps 16:5. [90]Jn 1:12. [91]WSA 3 12:64-65. [92]CSCO 4 3:32; ACCS NT 4a:38. [93]Ps 110:3 (109:3 LXX). [94]LF 43:105-6**.

The Forgiveness of Sins

WE DESCEND INTO THE WATER FULL OF SINS. LETTER OF BARNABAS: Let us further inquire whether the Lord took any care to foreshadow the water of baptism and the cross. Concerning the water, indeed, it is written in reference to the Israelites that they should not receive that baptism that leads to the remission of sins but should procure another for themselves. . . . Mark how he has described at once both the water and the cross. For these words imply, blessed are they who, placing their trust in the cross, have gone down into the water. For he says, "They shall receive their reward in due time." Then he declares, "I will reward them." . . . This means that we indeed descend into the water full of sins and defilement but come up bearing fruit in our heart, having the fear of God and trust in Jesus in our spirit. "And whoever shall eat of these shall live forever." This means whoever shall hear you speaking and believe shall live forever. EPISTLE OF BARNABAS 11.[95]

THE BISHOP HAS THE POWER OF BINDING AND LOOSING. PSEUDO-CLEMENT OF ROME: But about that time, when he was about to die, the brothers being assembled together, he suddenly seized my hand, and rose up and said in presence of the church, "Hear me, brothers and fellow servants. Since, as I have been taught by the Lord and teacher Jesus Christ whose apostle I am, the day of my death is approaching, I lay hands on this Clement as your bishop; and to him I entrust my chair of discourse, even to him who has journeyed with me from the beginning to the end and thus has heard all my homilies—who, in a word, having had a share in all my trials, has been found steadfast in the faith; whom I have found, above all others, pious, philanthropic, pure, learned, chaste, good, upright, large-hearted and striving generously to bear the ingratitude of some of the catechumens. Therefore I communicate to him the power of binding and loosing, so that with respect to everything that he shall ordain in the earth, it shall be decreed in the heavens. For he shall bind what ought to be bound and loose what ought to be loosed, as knowing the role of the church. Therefore hear him, as knowing that he who grieves the president of the truth, sins against Christ and offends the Father of all. Wherefore he shall not live; and therefore it becomes him who presides to hold the place of a physician and not to cherish the rage of an irrational beast." EPISTLE TO JAMES 2.[96]

A GREAT JUBILEE OF FORGIVENESS. HERMAS: For after you have made known to them these words that my Lord has commanded me to reveal to you, they will then be forgiven all the sins that in former times they committed, and forgiveness will be granted to all the saints who have sinned even to the present day, if they repent with all their heart and drive all doubts from their minds. For the Lord has sworn by his glory, in regard to his elect, that if any one of them sin after a certain day that has been fixed, he shall not be saved. For the repentance of the righteous has limits. Filled up are the days of repentance to all the saints; but to the heathen, repentance will be possible even to the last day. You will tell, therefore, those who preside over the church, to direct their ways in righteousness, that they may receive in full the promises with great glory. Stand steadfast, therefore, you who work righteousness, and have no doubts so that your passage may be with the holy angels. Happy are you who endure the great tribulation that is coming on, and happy are they who shall not deny their own life. SHEPHERD, VISION 1.2.2.[97]

SAVED THROUGH THE WATER OF GRACE. HERMAS: I asked her, "Why was the tower built on the waters, O lady?" She answered, "I told you before, and you still inquire carefully:

---

[95]ANF 1:144. [96]ANF 8:218. [97]ANF 2:11.

therefore inquiring you shall find the truth. Hear then why the tower is built on the waters. It is because your life has been and will be saved through water. For the tower was founded on the Word of the almighty and glorious name, and it is kept together by the invisible power of the Lord." SHEPHERD, VISION 1.3.3.[98]

REPENTANCE IS GREAT WISDOM. HERMAS: And he answered and said to me, "I am set over repentance, and I give understanding to all who repent. Do you not think," he said, "that it is great wisdom to repent? For repentance is great wisdom. For he who has sinned understands that he acted wickedly in the sight of the Lord. He remembers the actions he has done. He repents and no longer acts wickedly. He does good munificently and humbles and grieves his soul because he has sinned. You see, therefore, that repentance is great wisdom." And I said to him, "It is for this reason, sir, that I inquire carefully into all things, especially because I am a sinner, that I may know what works I should do that I may live. For my sins are many and various." And he said to me, "You shall live if you keep my commandments and walk in them; and whoever will hear and keep these commandments will live to God." SHEPHERD, MANDATE 2.4.2.[99]

REMISSION OF SINS, REGENERATION AND ILLUMINATION. JUSTIN MARTYR: I will also relate the manner in which we dedicated ourselves to God when we were made new through Christ. For if we should omit this, we would be unfair in the explanation we are making. As many as are persuaded and believe that what we teach and say is true and undertake to be able to live accordingly are instructed to pray and to entreat God with fasting, for the remission of their sins that are past. Meanwhile we are praying and fasting with the penitent. Then they are brought by us where there is water and are regenerated in the same manner in which we were ourselves regenerated. For in the name of God, the Father and Lord of the universe, and of our Savior Jesus Christ, and of the Holy Spirit, they then receive the washing with water. For Christ also said, "Unless you are born again, you shall not enter into the kingdom of heaven."[100] Now, that it is impossible for those who have once been born to enter into their mothers' wombs is clear to all. How those who have sinned and repent shall escape their sins is declared by Isaiah the prophet, as I wrote above, "Wash yourselves. Make yourselves clean. Put away from your souls the evil of your deeds. Learn to do well. Judge the fatherless. Plead for the widow. Come, let us reason together, says the Lord. And though your sins are as scarlet, I will make them white like wool; and though they are as crimson, I will make them white as snow. But if you refuse and rebel, the sword shall devour you: for the mouth of the Lord has spoken it."[101]

We have learned from the apostles the reason for this rite. At our birth we were born without our own knowledge or choice, by our parents coming together. We were brought up in bad habits and wicked training. In order that we may not remain the children of necessity and of ignorance but may become the children of choice and knowledge and may obtain in the water the remission of sins formerly committed, there is pronounced over him who chooses to be born again and has repented of his sins the name of God the Father and Lord of the universe. He is the one who leads to the basin the person who is to be washed calling him by this name alone. For no one can utter the name of the ineffable God; and if anyone dares to say that there is a name, he raves with a hopeless madness. And this washing is called illumination, because those who learn these things are illuminated in their understandings. And in the name of Jesus Christ, who was crucified under Pontius Pilate, and in the name of the Holy Spirit,

---

[98]ANF 2:14. [99]ANF 2:22*. [100]Jn 3:5. [101]Is 1:16-20.

who through the prophets foretold all things about Jesus, he who is illuminated is washed. FIRST APOLOGY 61.[102]

THE WATER OF LIFE IN BAPTISM. JUSTIN MARTYR: By reason, therefore, of this water of repentance and knowledge of God, which has been ordained on account of the transgression of God's people, as Isaiah cries, we have believed. We testify that that very baptism that he announced is alone able to purify those who have repented. This is the water of life. But the cisterns that you have dug for yourselves are broken and profitless to you. For what is the use of that baptism that cleanses the flesh and body alone? Baptize the soul from wrath and from covetousness, from envy and from hatred; and, behold, the body is pure. For this is the symbolic significance of unleavened bread, that you do not commit the old deeds of wicked leaven. DIALOGUE WITH TRYPHO 14.[103]

WASHING IN BAPTISMAL WATER. JUSTIN MARTYR: For since you have read, O Trypho, as you yourself admitted, the doctrines taught by our Savior, I do not think that I have done foolishly in adding some short utterances of his to the prophetic statements. Wash therefore, and be now clean and put away iniquity from your souls, as God bids you be washed in this water, and be circumcised with the true circumcision. DIALOGUE WITH TRYPHO 18.[104]

NO OTHER WAY OF FORGIVENESS. JUSTIN MARTYR: It becomes you to eradicate this false hope from your souls and hurry to know in what way forgiveness of sins and a hope of inheriting the promised good things shall be yours. But there is no other way than this— to become acquainted with this Christ, to be washed in the fountain spoken of by Isaiah for the remission of sins; and for the rest, to live sinless lives. DIALOGUE WITH TRYPHO 44.[105]

BAPTISM FOR THE REMISSION OF SINS. IRENAEUS: Now, that we may not suffer anything of this kind, we must hold the rule of faith without deviation, following the commandments of God, believing in God and fearing him as Lord and loving him as Father. Now, this work is produced by faith. For Isaiah says if you do not believe, neither will you understand. And faith is produced by the truth. For faith rests on things that truly are. For in things that are, as they are, we believe. Believing in things that are, as they ever are, we keep firm our confidence in them. Since then faith is the perpetuation of our salvation, we must bestow much care on the maintenance of it, in order that we may have a true comprehension of the things that are. Now faith begets this in us, just as the elders, the disciples of the apostles, have handed down the faith to us. First of all it calls us to bear in mind that we have received baptism for the remission of sins, in the name of God the Father and in the name of Jesus Christ, the Son of God, who was incarnate and died and rose again, and in the Holy Spirit of God. This baptism is the seal of eternal life. It is the new birth to God, that we should no longer be the sons of mortals alone but also of the eternal and perpetual God, in order that what is everlasting and continuing is made godly. God is over all things that are made, and all things are put under him. All the things that are put under him are made his own. For God is not ruler and Lord over the things of another but over his own. All things are God's. Therefore God is almighty, and all things are of God. PROOF OF THE APOSTOLIC TEACHING 3.[106]

THE BAPTISM OF REPENTANCE OF JOHN. TERTULLIAN: By and by, promising freely the grace that in the last times he was intending to pour as a flood of light on the universal world through his Spirit, he ordered the baptism of

---

[102]ANF 1:183. [103]ANF 1:201*. [104]ANF 1:203. [105]ANF 1:217. [106]DAP 71-73.

repentance to lead the way, with the view of first preparing, by means of the sign and seal of repentance, those whom he was calling, through grace, to inherit the promise surely made to Abraham. John does not hold back his peace, saying, "Enter on repentance, for now shall salvation approach the nations"—the Lord, that is, bringing salvation according to God's promise. ON REPENTANCE 2.[107]

BAPTISM IS THE SEALING OF FAITH. TERTULLIAN: Baptismal washing is a sealing of faith. This faith is begun and is commended by the faith of repentance. We are not washed in order that we may cease sinning, but because we have ceased, since in heart we have been bathed already. For the first baptism of a learner is this, an absolute awe. From then on insofar as you have understanding of the Lord, faith is sound, the conscience having once for all embraced repentance. Otherwise, if it is only after baptismal waters that we cease sinning, it is of necessity, not of free will, that we put on innocence. ON REPENTANCE 6.[108]

THE SANCTIFIED WATER OF BAPTISM. TERTULLIAN: Therefore, in consequence of that ancient original privilege, all waters, when God is invoked, acquire the sacred significance of conveying sanctity. For at once the Spirit comes down from heaven and stays on the waters, sanctifying them from within himself. When thus sanctified, they absorb the power of sanctifying. This simile applies quite simply: As we are defiled by sins as though with filth, we are washed clean in water. But as sins are in the flesh yet are not visible (since no one carries on his complexion the stains of idolatry, adultery or embezzlement), so people of this sort are filthy in their spirit, which is where sin begins. For with them the spirit is the master and the body the servant. Yet each of these imparts guilt to the other, the spirit by its direction, the flesh by its service rendered. Thus when the waters have in some sense acquired healing power by an angel's intervention, the spirit is in those waters corporally washed, while the flesh is in those same waters spiritually cleansed. ON BAPTISM 4.[109]

THE TRIUNE GOD. TERTULLIAN: The Holy Spirit does so by that canceling of sins that is granted in response to faith signed and sealed in the Father and the Son and the Holy Spirit. For if in three witnesses every word shall be established, how much more shall the gift of God? By the benediction we have the same mediators of faith as we have sureties of salvation. That number of the divine names of itself suffices for the confidence of our hope. Yet because it is under the charge of three that profession of faith and promise of salvation are in pledge, there is a necessary addition, the mention of the church: because where there are the three, the Father and the Son and the Holy Spirit, there is the church, which is a body of three [the triune God]. ON BAPTISM 6.[110]

REGENERATED IN BAPTISM. TERTULLIAN: Every soul, by reason of its birth, has its nature in Adam until it is born in Christ. In addition, it is unclean as long as it remains without this regeneration and because it is unclean it is actively sinful and infects even the flesh with its shame because of their fusion. ON THE SOUL 40.[111]

BURIED WITH CHRIST IN BAPTISM. ORIGEN: If we have been buried together with Christ in the way we outlined above, that is, because we have died to sin, it follows that just as Christ was raised from the dead, we shall rise together with him. Just as he ascended into heaven, we shall also ascend with him, and just as he sits at the right hand of God, we shall also sit with him, as the apostle says elsewhere: he has made us

---

[107]ANF 3:657-58*. [108]ANF 3:662*. [109]THB 11*. [110]THB 15, 17. [111]ANF 3:220*.

sit with him in the heavenly places in Christ Jesus.[112] Christ rose from the dead by the glory of the Father, and if we have died to sin and are buried together with Christ, and if all who see our good works glorify our Father who is in heaven, "we shall rightly be said to have risen together with Christ by the glory of the Father so that we may walk in newness of life." For newness of life occurs when we have put off the old person with his deeds and put on the new person who has been created according to God[113] and who is renewed in the knowledge of God according to the image of him who created him.[114] COMMENTARY ON THE EPISTLE TO THE ROMANS.[115]

BAPTISM IS PREACHED FOR REMISSION OF SINS. ORIGEN. Then, "Jordan" means "descending." But the "descending" river of God, one running with a vigorous force, is the Lord our Savior. Into him we are baptized with true water, saving water. Baptism is also preached "for the remission of sins." Come, catechumens! Do penance, so that baptism for the remission of sins will follow. He who stops sinning receives baptism "for the remission of sins." For if anyone comes sinning to the washing, he does not receive forgiveness of sins. Therefore, I implore you, do not come to baptism without caution and careful consideration. First show "results worthy of repentance."[116] Spend some time in good living. Keep yourselves clean of all stains and vices. Your sins will be forgiven when you yourselves begin to despise your own sins. Put aside your own offenses, and they will be forgiven you. HOMILIES IN LUKE 21.4.[117]

REPENTANT SINNERS ARE CURED. PACIAN OF BARCELONA: That is, not having heresies. . . . For among these are certain spotted and wrinkled folds, envious of the decorations of the precious vestments of the church.[118] But the sinner and the penitent are not a spot on the church, because as long as such a person sins and does not repent, he is placed outside of the church; when he ceases to sin, he is already cured. On the other hand, the heretic tears, divides, spots and wrinkles the garment of the Lord, which is the church of Christ. "For while there are schisms and quarrels among you," says the apostle, "are you not of the flesh and do you not walk as men?"[119] And moreover, "Their words will gradually spread like a cancer."[120] This is the spot on the church's unity, this is the wrinkle. Lastly, when the apostle speaks of these things, he is bringing to our attention the love and affection of Christ. LETTER 3.4.4.[121]

IN BAPTISM, REMISSION OF OUR SINS. NICETA OF REMESIANA: Next, you believe in the forgiveness of sins. This is the grace by which those who believe in and confess God and Christ receive in baptism the remission of all their sins. We call it a rebirth, because it makes a person more innocent and pure than when he is born from his mother's womb. EXPLANATION OF THE CREED 10.[122]

ALL SINS FORGIVEN IN THE ONE NAME OF THE TRINITY. AMBROSE: Thus the Father forgives sin, so does the Son and so does the Holy Spirit. Do not be surprised that we are baptized in one name: in the name, that is, of the Father and of the Son and of the Holy Spirit; because Christ spoke of only one name where there is one substance, one divinity, one majesty. This is the name of which it is written: "In this must all find salvation." It is in this name that you have all been saved, that you have been restored to the grace of life. ON THE SACRAMENTS 2.22.[123]

SIGN AND SYMBOL OF THE RESURRECTION. AMBROSIASTER: First of all, this means that

---

[112]See Eph 2:6. [113]Eph 4:22-24. [114]Col 3:10. [115]ACCS NT 6:155. [116]Lk 3:8. [117]FC 94:89-90. [118]Cf. Ps 45:12. [119]1 Cor 3:3. [120]2 Tim 2:17. [121]FC 99:43. [122]FC 7:50. [123]AIRI 118.

Christ raised his own body from the dead. For he is the power of God the Father, as he said: Destroy this temple, and in three days I will raise it up."[124] He was saying this about the temple of his own body.... It also means that we now have a new way of life that has been given to us by Christ. For by baptism we have been buried together with Christ in order that we may henceforth live according to the life into which Christ rose from the dead. Therefore baptism is the sign and symbol of the resurrection, which means that we ought to abide in the commandments of Christ and not go back to what we were before. For the person who dies does not sin: death is the end of the sin. This is symbolized by water, because just as water cleans the dirt of the body, so we believe that we have been spiritually cleansed by baptism from every sin and renewed, for what is incorporeal is cleansed invisibly. COMMENTARY ON PAUL'S EPISTLES.[125]

ALL OUR WICKEDNESS LAID ASIDE IN BAPTISM. AMBROSIASTER: Happily Paul says that we can rise again if we have been united with Christ in the likeness of his death, that is, if we have laid aside all our wickedness in baptism and, having been transferred into a new life, no longer sin. In this way we shall be like him in resurrection, because the likeness of his death presupposes a similar resurrection.... The likeness does not mean that there will be no difference at all between us, of course. We will be like him in the glory of his body, not in the nature of his divinity. COMMENTARY ON PAUL'S EPISTLES.[126]

DEAD TO SINS. CHRYSOSTOM: Being dead to sin means not obeying it anymore. Baptism has made us dead to sin once for all, but we must strive to remain in this state of affairs, so that however many commands sin may give us, we no longer obey it but remain unmoved by it, as a corpse does. HOMILIES ON ROMANS 10.[127]

OUR SINS ARE BURIED IN BAPTISM. CHRYSOSTOM: Here then Paul says there are two mortifyings and two deaths. One is done by Christ in baptism. The other it is our duty to effect by earnestness afterward. Our former sins were buried. That came as his gift. But remaining dead to sin after baptism must be the work of our own earnestness, however much we find God here also giving us large help. For this is not the only thing baptism has the power to do, to obliterate our former transgressions. It also secures against subsequent ones. As then in the case of the former, your contribution was faith that they might be obliterated, so also in those subsequent to this, show forth the change in your aims, that you may not defile yourself again. For it is this that he is counseling you when he says, "for if we have been planted together in the likeness of his death, we shall be also in the likeness of his resurrection." Do you observe how he rouses the hearer by leading him straightway up to his Master? He takes great care to show the strength of the analogy. This is why he does not say "in death," lest you should pounce on it, but "in the likeness of his death." For our essence itself has not died, but the man of sins, that is, wickedness. And he does not say, "for if we have been" partakers of "the likeness of his death," but what? "If we have been planted together," so by the mention of planting, he gives us a hint of the fruit resulting from it. For as his body, by being buried in the earth, brought forth the salvation of the world as its fruit. Similarly also ours being buried in baptism bore as fruit righteousness, sanctification, adoption, countless blessings. And it will bear also hereafter in the gift of the resurrection. Since then we were buried in water, as he was buried in earth—and we in regard to sin, he in regard to his body—this is why he did not say, "we were planted together in his death" but "in the likeness of his death." For both the

---

[124]Jn 2:19. [125]ACCS NT 6:155-56. [126]ACCS NT 6:157. [127]NPNF 1 11:405.

one and the other is death, but not that of the same subject. Then he says, "as we have been planted together in his death, we shall be in that of his resurrection." Here he is speaking of the resurrection which is to come. HOMILIES ON ROMANS 11.[128]

BAPTISM IS THE DEATH OF SIN. CHRYSOSTOM: Paul did not say "in death" but "in a death like his." For both the first and the second are death but not the death of the same thing. The first is the death of the body, the second is the death of sin. BAPTISMAL INSTRUCTIONS 10.10.[129]

THE GREAT GIFT OF BAPTISM IS ADOPTION. CHRYSOSTOM: But since you stand at the threshold of the royal palace and are about to approach the very throne where the King sits who apportions the gifts, show every ambition in your requests. Only ask for nothing worldly or human; make your petition worthy of him who grants the gifts. As you come forth from the waters, symbolizing your resurrection by rising up from them, ask him to be your ally, so that you may guard well the gifts he has given you, and that you may not be conquered by the deceits of the wicked one. Beg him for peace among the churches, beseech him for those who are being led astray, prostrate yourselves in behalf of those who are in sin, so that we may be judged worthy of mercy in some degree. "For he has granted you great confidence," he has enrolled you in the front ranks of his friends, and has received into the adoption of sons you who were formerly captives and slaves with no right to speak out. He will not reject your prayers; again imitating in this his own goodness he will grant you everything you ask. BAPTISMAL INSTRUCTIONS 2.29.[130]

THE GREAT GIFT OF GOD IS THE FORGIVENESS OF SINS. CHRYSOSTOM: I urge you to imitate him (Paul). You have deserved now to go under the yoke of Christ and you have enjoyed the benefit of filial adoption; now show forth, right from the beginning, such a fervor and faith in Christ that you may draw to yourselves richer graces from on high, and may make the garment given to you shine more brightly, and may enjoy the abundant favor of the Master. Even though you had never done anything good, even though you had the burden of your sins lying heavy upon you, he imitated his own goodness and judged you worthy of these great gifts. For he not only delivered you from your sins and gave you justification by his grace, but he also showed you forth as holy and made you his sons by adoption. If he has taken the lead in giving you such gifts, if you are eager, after receiving so much, to contribute your fair share, if you will show care in guarding and managing the gifts that have already been given, how can he fail to judge you worthy again of still greater liberality? BAPTISMAL INSTRUCTIONS 4.11.[131]

A DWELLING PLACE FOR THE HOLY SPIRIT. CHRYSOSTOM: After this anointing, the priest makes you go down into the sacred waters, burying the old man and at the same time raising up the new, who is renewed in the image of his Creator. It is at this moment that, through the words and the hand of the priest, the Holy Spirit descends upon you. Instead of the man who descended into the water, a different man comes forth, one who has wiped away all the filth of his sins, who has put off the old garment of sin and has put on the royal robe.

That you may also learn from this that the substance of the Father, Son and Holy Spirit is one, baptism is conferred in the following manner. When the priest says: 'So and so is baptized in the name of the Father, and of the Son, and of the Holy Spirit,' he puts your head down into the water three times, and

---

[128]NPNF 1 11:408-9*. [129]ACW 31:152. [130]ACW 31:54. [131]ACW 31:70.

three times he lifts it up again, preparing you by this mystic rite to receive the Spirit. For it is not only the priest who touches the head, but also the right hand of Christ, and this is shown by the very words of the one baptizing. He does not say: 'I baptize so and so,' but: 'So and so is baptized,' showing that he is only the minister of grace and merely offers his hand because he has been ordained to this end by the Spirit. The one fulfilling all things is the Father and the Son and the Holy Spirit, the undivided Trinity. It is faith in this Trinity which gives the grace of remission from sin; it is this confession which gives to us the gift of filial adoption.

What follows suffices to show us from what those who have been judged worthy of this mystic rite have been set free, and what they have gained. As soon as they come forth from those sacred waters, all who are present embrace them, greet them, kiss them, rejoice with them and congratulate them, because those who were heretofore slaves and captives have suddenly become free men and sons, and have been invited to the royal table. For straightway after they come up from the waters, they are led to the awesome table heavy laden with countless favors, where they taste of the Master's body and blood, and become a dwelling place for the Holy Spirit. Since they have put on Christ himself, wherever they go they are like angels on earth, rivaling the brilliance of the rays of the sun. BAPTISMAL INSTRUCTIONS 2.25-27.[132]

REPENT OF YOUR SIN. CHRYSOSTOM: Have you sinned? Enter into the church and wipe away your sin. The number of times you fall down in the marketplace equals the number of times you rise up. Likewise, as many times as you sin, repent for your sin; do not become discouraged. And if you sin a second time, repent a second time. Do not be completely deprived of the hope for the proposed goods through indolence. And if you are in the depths of old age and you sin, enter into the church and repent, because the church is a hospital, not a court of justice. Here, the priests do not hold you responsible for your sins but grant you forgiveness. Tell your sin solely to God—"Against you only have I sinned and done evil before you"[133]—and your sin is forgiven. HOMILIES ON REPENTANCE AND ALMSGIVING 3.4.19.[134]

BAPTISM ERASES ALL SINS. CHRYSOSTOM: And why, someone will say, if the bath [baptism] takes away all our sins, is it not called the bath of the remission of sins, or the bath of cleansing, rather than the bath of regeneration? The reason is that it does not simply remit our sins, nor does it simply cleanse us of our faults, but it does this just as if we were born anew. For it does create us anew and it fashions us again, not molding us from earth but creating us from a different element, the nature of water. BAPTISMAL INSTRUCTIONS 9.20.[135]

DO NOT RETURN TO SIN AFTER BAPTIZING. CHRYSOSTOM: I have said it before, I say it now, and I shall say it again and again: unless a person has corrected the defects of his character and has developed a facility for virtue, let him not be baptized. For the bath [baptism] can do away with sins previously committed; but there is no small fear or insignificant danger that we may fall again into the same sins, and then the cure becomes a wound for us. For those who sin after baptism, the punishment is proportioned to the greatness of the grace we received in it.

In order, then, that we may not return to our old vomit, let us now instruct ourselves. We must repent and keep far away from our former sins and in this way approach to grace. Hear what John the Baptist says and what the prince of the apostles says to those who are about to receive baptism, for John says,

---

[132]ACW 31:52-53. [133]Ps 51:4. [134]FC 96:39. [135]ACW 31:138.

"Bring forth fruit befitting repentance, and do not begin to say among yourselves, 'We hale Abraham for our father.'"[136] And again, to those who asked him what to do, Peter said, "Repent every one of you and be baptized in the name of the Lord Jesus Christ."[137] But he who repents no longer clings to the same sins of which he repents, and for this reason we are commanded to say, "I renounce you, Satan," in order that we may never return to him.... The bath takes away the sins, but you must correct the habit, so that after the pigments have been daubed on and the royal image shines forth, you may never thereafter blot it out or cause wounds or scars on the beauty that God has given you. BAPTISMAL INSTRUCTIONS 12.21-22, 24.[138]

BAPTISM AND REGENERATION. GREGORY OF NYSSA: But Christ, the repairer of Adam's evildoing, assumes manhood in its fullness, and saves humankind and becomes the type and figure of us all, to sanctify the first fruits of every action and leave to his servants no doubt in their zeal for the tradition. Baptism, then, is a purification from sins, a remission of trespasses, a cause of renovation and regeneration. By regeneration, understand regeneration as conceived in thought, not discerned by bodily sight. For we shall not, according to the Jew Nicodemus and his somewhat dull intelligence, change the old person into a child, nor shall we form anew him who is wrinkled and gray-headed to tenderness and youth, if we bring back the person again into his mother's womb. But we do bring back, by royal grace, him who bears the scars of sin and has grown old in evil habits to the innocence of the babe. For as the child newborn is free from accusations and from penalties, so too the child of regeneration has nothing for which to answer, being released by royal bounty from accountability. And this gift, it is not the water that bestows (for in that case it were a thing more exalted than all creation) but the command of God, and the visitation of the Spirit that comes sacramentally to set us free. But water serves to express the cleansing. For since we hope by washing in water to render our body clean when it is soiled by dirt or mud, so we therefore apply it also in the sacramental action. There it displays the spiritual brightness that is subject to our senses.... Despise not, therefore, the divine bath, nor think lightly of it, as a common thing simply because it makes use of water. For the power that operates is mighty, and wonderful are the things that are wrought by it. For this holy altar too, by which I stand, is stone, ordinary in its nature, in no way different from the other slabs of stone that build our houses and adorn our pavements. But recall that it was consecrated to the service of God and then received the benediction. It is a holy table, an altar undefiled, no longer touched by the hands of all, but of the priests alone, and that with reverence. ON THE BAPTISM OF CHRIST.[139]

THE TEMPLE OF THE HOLY SPIRIT. AUGUSTINE: It goes on in the creed: "And in the Holy Spirit." This Trinity is one God, one nature, one substance, one power, supreme equality, no division, no diversity, perpetual charity. Do you want proof that the Holy Spirit is God? Be baptized, and you will be his temple. The apostle says, "Do you not know that your bodies are the temple of the Holy Spirit in you, whom you have from God?"[140] A temple is what God has, because Solomon the king and prophet was ordered to build a temple for God. If he had built a temple for the sun, or the moon or some star or some angel, wouldn't God have condemned him? So because he built a temple for God, he thereby showed that he worshiped God.... So if our bodies are the temple of the Holy Spirit, what sort of God is it who built a temple for the Holy Spirit? But

---

[136]Lk 3:8. [137]Acts 2:38. [138]ACW 31:179-80. [139]NPNF 2 5:175*. [140]1 Cor 6:19.

yes, it is God. You see, if our bodies are the temple of the Holy Spirit, the one who built a temple for the Holy Spirit is the one who also built our bodies. Observe the apostle saying, "God arranged the body, giving greater honor to the part which lacked it,"[141] when he was speaking of the different parts, so that there should not be divisions within the body. God created our bodies. God created the grass; who created our bodies? How can we prove that God creates the grass? . . . And the apostle says, "Fool, what you sow is not quickened unless it dies; and as for what you sow, it is not the body that is going to be that you sow, but a bare grain, as it may be of wheat or one of the others. But God gives it a body as he wishes, and to each kind of seed its proper body."[142] So if God builds our bodies, if God builds our members and our bodies are the temple of the Holy Spirit, have no doubts that the Holy Spirit is God. And don't add him as a kind of third God, because Father and Son and Holy Spirit are one God. That is how you must believe. SERMON 398.13.[143]

CHRIST GAVE THE HOLY SPIRIT. AUGUSTINE: God takes pleasure in a solemn festivity that is an expression of active piety and of fervent charity. That is, after all, the effect of the presence of the Holy Spirit, as the apostle teaches us when he says, "The charity of God has been poured out in our hearts through the Holy Spirit which has been given to us."[144] So the coming of the Holy Spirit filled 120 men and women gathered together in one place. . . . We now have a pledge of eternal life to come and of the kingdom of heaven. He didn't cheat us of what he had so recently promised, and is he going to cheat us of what we are looking forward to in the future? When people enter into a business contract and wish to have their minds set at rest by financial guarantees, they all, for the most part, receive or give an earnest. And the earnest given creates confidence that the property of which an earnest has already been handed over will in due course follow. The earnest Christ has given us is the Holy Spirit. And the one who could not possibly cheat us has all the same given us security, when he gave us this earnest; even if he hadn't given it, he would most certainly grant us what he has promised. What has he promised us? Eternal life, as the earnest of which he has given us the Holy Spirit. Eternal life is the possession of those who have reached home; the earnest is the reassurance of those who are still on the way there. You see, it is better to call it an earnest than a pledge. I mean, while these two things seem to be much the same as each other, there is still a difference between them that is not to be ignored. Both when a pledge is given and when an earnest is given, the reason it's done is to ensure the fulfillment of a promise. . . . So we have an earnest; let us thirst for the very fountain from which the earnest comes. As an earnest we have a kind of dewfall in our hearts of the Holy Spirit; if any are aware of this sprinkling, they should long for the fountain. Why, after all, do we have an earnest, if not to save us from fainting from hunger and thirst on this journey? We are hungry and thirsty, you see, provided, that is, we acknowledge ourselves to be travelers. Those who are traveling, and know they are traveling, long to reach home; and because they are longing for home, they find the traveling irksome. But if they love traveling, they forget home and don't want to go back. Our true home is not such that we should put anything else before it. SERMON 378.1.[145]

CHILDREN OF GOD. AUGUSTINE: For "the Lord knows those who are his,"[146] and "all who are led by the Spirit of God are sons of God,"[147] children by grace, not by nature. There is but one Son of God, by nature, he

---

[141]Cf. 1 Cor 12:24. [142]1 Cor 15:36-38. [143]WSA 3 10:453-54. [144]Rom 5:5. [145]WSA 3 10:353-54. [146]2 Tim 2:19. [147]Rom 8:14.

who became a son of man, by mercy, for our sake, so that we who are by nature children of mortals might become by grace through him children of God. Remaining immutable in himself, he received from us our nature that in it he might receive us and, while holding firmly to his divinity, he made himself a sharer in our infirmity. His purpose was that we should be transformed into something better by losing our sinfulness and mortality through sharing in his immortality and holiness and by preserving the good he put into our nature through having it fulfilled by the supreme good in the goodness of his nature. For, as we sank into this deep evil through one man's sinning, so we shall rise to that high Good through one Man's winning—the winner of grace being also God. CITY OF GOD 21.15.[148]

GOD IS INTENT ON BRINGING SINNERS TO REPENTANCE. AUGUSTINE: So can any, who find themselves held after baptism in bondage to any of their previous sins, be such enemies to themselves that they still hesitate to change their way of life while there is time, when they are sinning like that and still remaining alive? It's obvious, you see, that because they are persistently sinning like that, they are storing up for themselves wrath on the day of wrath and of the revelation of the just judgment of God. As for the fact, though, that they are still alive, the patience of God is intent on bringing them to repentance.[149] Being therefore entangled in the chains of such death-dealing sins, can they decline to take refuge in the keys of the church, or put it off or hesitate about it, though they can be loosed by them on earth, in order to be loosed in heaven? And can they have the nerve to promise themselves some kind of salvation after this life just because they are called Christians and fail to tremble at that thunderous truth uttered by the Lord, "Not everyone who says to me, 'Lord, Lord,' will enter into the kingdom of heaven; but the one who does the will of my Father who is in heaven, that is the one who will enter into the kingdom of heaven"?[150]

Why, the apostle, writing to the Galatians, comes to the same conclusion, doesn't he, after listing such sins? The works of the flesh, he says, are manifest, which are fornications, impurities, licentious behavior. . . .[151] So let people pass judgment on themselves voluntarily in these matters, while they can, and change their morals for the better; or else, when they no longer can, they will have judgment passed on them, and against their will, by the Lord. And when they have imposed on themselves a sentence of the harshest medicine, but still medicine, let them come to the prelates, by whom the keys in the church are wielded for their benefit; and now beginning, so to say, to be good children and observing the rulings of those who play the role of mother in the church, let them accept from those in charge of the sacraments the manner of making amends required of them. . . . This means that if their sins have not only gravely damaged themselves but have also been such a scandal to others, and if the prelate considers this will be of value to the church, they should not refuse to do their penance in the full knowledge of others, even of the whole congregation; they should not jib at this, not add, through shame, the tumor of conceit to an already mortal and death-dealing wound. SERMON 351.9.[152]

GOD OUR FATHER, THE CHURCH OUR MOTHER. AUGUSTINE: The Son of God, our Lord Jesus Christ, taught us the prayer; and while he, the Lord, as you received and gave back in the creed, is the only Son of God, still for all that he didn't want to be "the one and only." He's the only Son, and he didn't want to be the one and only; he thought it proper to have brothers and sisters. Who, after all, are the ones he tells, "Our Father, who art in heaven"?[153]

---

[148]FC 24:375. [149]Rom 2:4. [150]Mt 7:21. [151]Gal 5:19-21. [152]WSA 3 10:128-29. [153]Mt 6:9.

And who did he want us to call our Father, if not his own Father? Was he in the least jealous of us? Parents sometimes, when they have had one son, or two or three, are afraid to produce any more, in case they condemn them to live by begging. But the inheritance which he promises us is such that many can obtain it without any of them suffering straitened circumstances; that's why he invited the Gentile peoples into his family and why the only Son has innumerable brothers and sisters who can say, "Our Father, who art in heaven."

Those who came before us said this; those who come after us will be saying this. See how many brothers and sisters the only Son has in his grace, sharing his inheritance with those for whom he endured death. We all had our fathers and mothers on earth, of whom we were born to a life of toil and ultimately death; we have found other parents, God our Father and the church our mother, of whom we may be born to eternal life. Let us reflect, beloved, on whose children we have begun to be, and let us live in a way that befits those who have such a Father. Remember that our creator has agreed to be our Father. SERMON 57.2.[154]

SINS LOOSED THROUGH THE KEYS OF THE CHURCH. AUGUSTINE: Here perhaps you will say, "But I have already been baptized in Christ, by whom all my past sins were forgiven. I have become vile in the extreme by going back to my old ways; a dog, revolting to the eyes of God, returning to its vomit."[155] "Where shall I go from his Spirit, and where shall I flee from his face?"[156] . . . And yet the keys of the church are more dependable than the hearts of kings;[157] we are promised that whatever is loosed by these keys on earth is also loosed in heaven.[158] And the humility with which one humbles oneself before the church of God is much more honorable; and a much lighter labor is imposed, and without any risk at all of temporal death, eternal death is avoided. SERMON 351.12.[159]

IN BAPTISM, ALL SINS ARE FORGIVEN. AUGUSTINE: The forgiveness of sins. You have the creed complete in yourselves, when you are baptized. None of you must say, "I did this or that, perhaps it can't be forgiven me." What have you done? How serious was it? Tell me some monstrous sin you've committed, as grave as can be, horrific, which it's horrifying even to think about; you've done whatever you like— have you killed Christ? There is nothing worse than that deed, because there's also nothing better than Christ. How impiously wicked it is to kill Christ! Still, the Jews killed him, and many of them later on believed in him and drank his blood; the sin they had committed had been forgiven them.

When you have been baptized, go on living a good life according to God's commandments, in order to keep your baptism unspoiled to the end. I'm not telling you that you will live here below without sin; but there are venial or pardonable sins, without which this life cannot be lived. Baptism was introduced on account of all sins; on account of the minor sins, without which we cannot exist here, the prayer was introduced. What does the prayer say? Forgive us our debts, just as we too forgive our debtors.[160] We are washed just once by baptism, washed daily by the prayer. But don't commit those sins for which you have to be cut off from the body of Christ, which God preserve you from. I mean, those people you can see here doing penance have committed wicked acts, whether adultery or other frightful deeds; that's why they are doing penance. I mean, if their sins were slight, the daily prayer would be sufficient to blot them out.

So sins are forgiven in the church in three ways: by baptism, by the prayer and by the greater humiliation of penance. Still, God only forgives the sins of the baptized. The sins

---

[154]WSA 3 3:109-10. [155]See 2 Pet 2:22. [156]Ps 139:7. [157]Sir 8:2. [158]Mt 16:19; 18:18. [159]WSA 3 10:132-33. [160]Mt 6:12.

that he first forgives, he forgives only to the baptized. When? When they are baptized. The sins that are forgiven afterward to those who say the prayer, and to the penitents whom he forgives, he forgives those who have been baptized. After all, how can people say "our Father"[161] when they haven't yet been born? As long as they are catechumens, all their sins remain on them. If that's the case with catechumens, how much more with pagans, how much more with heretics? SERMON 398.15-16.[162]

A NEW HUMAN BEING IN BAPTISM. PETER CHRYSOLOGUS: In the forgiveness of sins. What will the one about to be born as a new human being have of the ancient guilt and the old sin? The one who does not believe that his past sins have been forgiven him has doubts about receiving future goods. SERMON 59.15.[163]

GAIN FOR YOURSELF THE PARDON. PETER CHRYSOLOGUS: Gain for yourself the pardon coming from faith, since he is his own worst enemy who does not believe that he is given what the very generous bestower of mercy promises in all his kindness. SERMON 58.13.[164]

FORGIVENESS THROUGH CHRIST AND THE CHURCH. PETER CHRYSOLOGUS: We believe in the forgiveness of sins: since through Christ and the church the one who is born as a new human being will have nothing of the old one. SERMON 60.15.[165]

NO HOPE WITHOUT THE POWER OF FORGIVENESS. AUGUSTINE: "I believe in the forgiveness of sins." If this power were not in the church, there would be no hope; if there were no remission of sins in the church, there would be no hope of future life and of eternal salvation. We give thanks to God who gave this gift to his church. Behold, you are about to come to the sacred font; you will be washed in baptism; you will be renewed in the saving laver of regeneration; when you rise from these waters, you will be without sin. All the sins that in the past haunted you will be wiped out. Your sins will be like the Egyptians following the Israelites, pursuing only up to the Red Sea. What does "up to the Red Sea" mean? Up to the font consecrated by the cross and blood of Christ. For, because that font is red, it reddens. Do you not see how the member of Christ becomes red? Question the eyes of faith. If you see the cross, see the blood too. If you see what hangs on the cross, see what drips down from it. The side of Christ was pierced with a lance and our purchase price flowed forth.[166] Therefore, baptism is signified by the sign of Christ, that is, by the water in which you are immersed and through which you pass, as it were, in the Red Sea. Your sins are your enemies. They follow you, but only to the Red Sea. When you have entered the water, you will escape; they will be destroyed, just as the Egyptians were engulfed by the waters while the Israelites escaped on dry land. And why does Scripture say, "There was not one of them left"?[167] Because, whether you have committed many or few, great or small sins, even the smallest of them has not remained. But since we are destined to live in this world where no one lives without sin, on that account the remission of sin depends not solely on the washing in holy baptism but also on the Lord's daily prayer that you will receive after eight days. In that prayer you will find, as it were, your daily baptism, so that you may give thanks to God who has given to his church this gift that we acknowledge in the creed. Thus, when we have said, "I believe in the holy church," let us add, "and in the remission of sins." SERMON 213.8.[168]

BORN AGAIN IN BAPTISM FOR ETERNAL LIFE. AUGUSTINE: Thus human beings are on the one hand born in the flesh liable to sin and

---

[161]Mt 6:9. [162]WSA 3 10:454-55. [163]FC 109:229. [164]FC 109:224. [165]FC 109:236. [166]See Jn 19:34. [167]Ps 106:11. [168]FC 38:128-29.

death from the first Adam and on the other hand are born again in baptism associated with the righteousness and eternal life of the second Adam. This is what is written in the book of Ecclesiasticus: "Of the woman came the beginning of sin, and through her we all die."[169] Now whether it is said of the woman or of Adam, both statements pertain to the first man; since (as we know) the woman is of the man and the two are one flesh. Thus it is also written: "And the two shall be one flesh." Thus the Lord says, "They are no more two, but one flesh."[170] ON THE MERITS AND FORGIVENESS OF SINS AND ON INFANT BAPTISM 1.21.[171]

OUR SINS ARE FORGIVEN AS A GIFT OF GOD. AUGUSTINE: So what then is grace for grace? By faith we gain God, and seeing that we didn't deserve to be forgiven our sins, by the very fact of receiving such an undeserved gift, that is called grace. What does grace mean? Given gratis. What does given gratis mean? Bestowed, not paid back. If you were owed it, then it was a payment as per invoice, not a grace bestowed on you. If, though, it really was owed you, then you were good; if, however, and this is the truth, you were bad but believed in the one who justifies the godless[172]—what does "justifies the godless" mean if not "makes godly people out of godless ones"—then just think what you had coming to you through the law and what you actually obtained through grace. But having obtained this grace of faith, as a result of your faith you will be just, since the just person lives from faith,[173] and you will gain God by living from faith. When you have gained God by living from faith, you will receive immortality and eternal life as your reward. That too is grace. For what merit, I mean, do you receive eternal life? "For grace." If faith were a grace, you see, and eternal life a kind of payment as per invoice for faith, it does indeed look like God is paying you back eternal life as something owed—but owed to whom? To a believer because you have earned it by faith—but because faith itself is a grace, eternal life too is grace for grace. HOMILIES ON THE GOSPEL OF JOHN 3.9.[174]

PAGANS RIDICULE THE CHRISTIAN CONCEPT OF FORGIVENESS. RUFINUS OF AQUILEIA: As to the forgiveness of sins, it ought to be enough simply to believe. For who would ask the cause or the reason when a prince grants indulgence? When the liberality of an earthly sovereign is no fit subject for discussion, shall human temerity discuss God's largess? For the pagans are prone to ridicule us, saying that we deceive ourselves, fancying that crimes committed in deed can be purged by words. And they say, "Can he who has committed murder be no murderer, and he who has committed adultery be accounted no adulterer? How then shall one guilty of crimes of this sort all of a sudden be made holy?" But to this, as I said, we answer better by faith than by reason. For he is King of all who has promised it. He is Lord of heaven and earth who assures us of it. Would you have me refuse to believe that he who made me a man of the dust of the earth can of a guilty person make me innocent? And that he who when I was blind made me see, or when I was deaf made me hear, or lame walk, can recover for me my lost innocence? And to come to the witness of nature—to kill a man is not always criminal, but to kill of malice, not by law, is criminal. It is not the deed then, in such matters, that condemns me, because sometimes it is rightly done, but the evil intention of the mind. If then my mind, which had been rendered criminal and in which the sin originated, is corrected, why should I seem to you incapable of being made innocent, who before was criminal? For if it is plain, as I have shown, that crime consists not in the deed but in the will, as an evil will, prompted by an evil demon, has made me obnoxious to sin

---

[169]Sir 25:24. [170]Mt 19:5-6. [171]NPNF 1 5:23*. [172]Rom 4:5. [173]Rom 1:17. [174]WSA 3 12:75.

and death, so the will prompted by the good God, being changed to good, has restored me to innocence and life. It is the same also in all other crimes. In this way there is found to be no opposition between our faith and natural reason, while forgiveness of sins is imputed not to deeds, which when once done cannot be changed, but to the mind, which it is certain can be converted from bad to good. A Commentary on the Apostles' Creed 40.[175]

Christ Removes the Sin of the World. Cyril of Alexandria: Emmanuel gave up his soul for us; he died in the flesh. We also were buried together with him when we were baptized. Does this mean that our flesh died in the same way as his did? Hardly. Come, let me explain in what sense we were buried with him in a death like his. Christ died in the flesh in order to remove the sin of the world, but we do not die to the flesh so much as to guilt, as it is written. Thus now we have to break down the power of sin within us by mortifying our earthly members.... As we have died a death like his, so we shall also be conformed to his resurrection, because we shall live in Christ. It is true that the flesh will come to life again, but still we shall live in another way, by dedicating our souls to him and by being transformed into holiness and a kind of glorious life in the Holy Spirit. Explanation of the Letter to the Romans.[176]

Baptism Washes Away Sin and Corruption. John of Damascus: For since Christ made us for incorruption, and we transgressed his saving command, he condemned us to the corruption of death in order that that which is evil should not be immortal. And when in his compassion he stooped to his servants and became like us, he redeemed us from corruption through his own passion. He caused the fountain of remission to well forth for us out of his holy and immaculate side,[177] water for our regeneration, and the washing away of sin and corruption and blood to drink as the hostage of life eternal. And he laid on us the command to be born again of water and of the Spirit,[178] through prayer and invocation, the Holy Spirit drawing near to the water. For since human nature is twofold, consisting of soul and body, he bestowed on us a twofold purification, of water and of the Spirit: the Spirit renewing that part in us which is after his image and likeness, and the water by the grace of the Spirit cleansing the body from sin and delivering it from corruption, the water indeed expressing the image of death but the Spirit affording the promise earnest of life.... The remission of sins, therefore, is granted alike to all through baptism. But the grace of the Spirit is proportional to the faith and previous purification. Now, indeed, we receive the first fruits of the Holy Spirit through baptism, and the second birth is for us the beginning and seal and security and illumination of another life. Orthodox Faith 4.9.[179]

Sin Cut Off in Baptism. John of Damascus: Further, observe that by baptism we cut off all the covering that we have worn since birth, that is to say, sin, and become spiritual Israelites and God's people. Orthodox Faith 4.9-10.[180]

---

[175]NPNF 2 3:559. [176]PG 74:793, 796; ACCS NT 6:157. [177]Jn 19:34. [178]Jn 3:5. [179]NPNF 2 9:78b. [180]NPNF 2 9:79b.

WE LOOK FOR THE RESURRECTION OF THE DEAD

εἰς μίαν, ἁγίαν, καθολικὴν καὶ ἀποστολικὴν ἐκκλησίαν· ὁμολογοῦμεν ἓν βάπτισμα εἰς ἄφεσιν ἁμαρτιῶν· **προσδοκῶμεν ἀνάστασιν νεκρῶν,** καὶ ζωὴν τοῦ μέλλοντος αἰῶνος. Ἀμήν.	Et unam, sanctam, catholicam et apostolicam ecclesiam. Confiteor unum baptisma in remissionem peccatorum; **et expecto resurrectionem mortuorum,** et vitam venturi saeculi. Amen.	We believe in one holy catholic and apostolic Church. We acknowledge one baptism for the forgiveness of sins. **We look for the resurrection of the dead** and the life of the world to come. Amen.

HISTORICAL CONTEXT: Questions on the destiny of the individual are closely connected with the looming problems that concern the final things. We have already seen the results of the patristic reflection on this in the previous chapter. In fact, after the description of the end of the universe and history, questions of great anthropological import arise concerning the future and the state of human beings after death. In this regard the greater part of this section presents how the Fathers viewed the resurrection of the flesh and the immortality of the soul, themes that constitute the center of patristic eschatological reflection.

In the earliest times, faith in the resurrection of the flesh was simply attested and needed no particular explanation. Very soon, however, the renewed cultural circumstances in which the faith was transmitted and the problems deriving from certain deviating doctrinal trends, such as Gnosticism, prompted the Fathers to further investigate this theme, especially from an apologetic point of view.

The passages by the Fathers on the resurrection that we are excerpting are divided into two sections: the first one presents us with texts concerning the resurrection in general; the second presents texts in which the resurrection of bodies and the flesh are discussed.

The first group of passages faces this question in a mostly philosophical sense, relying on the reasonable connection between the omnipotence of God and the resurrection of the dead.[1] The others, by connecting the resurrection of human beings with that of Jesus, emphasize the anthropological and soteriological dimensions of the life and action of Christ.[2] In particular, Tertullian raised his voice against the Gnostics and the Marcionites, asserting the truth of faith in the resurrection of the flesh. He based his reasoning on the work of God, who had the power to create as well as the power to re-create. He also based his argument on the substantial identity of the present body with the resurrected one.[3]

Among the eschatological themes that are connected to the questions concerning the resurrection is the doctrine on the advent of the millennial kingdom, to which we have devoted another selection of patristic passages in this chapter. This doctrine, which is more simply known as millenarianism, circulated among a certain segment of Christianity in the first centuries, even though it was never officially received into the church. It maintains that the universal judgment and the end of the world will be preceded by a future earthly kingdom of one thousand years, which will be entirely new and will be the seat of the heavenly Jerusa-

---

[1]See especially the Apologists, in particular Athenagoras *On the Resurrection of the Dead* 11-25. [2]See Irenaeus *Against Heresies* 5.2.3; 5.31.2. [3]See Tertullian *On the Resurrection* 63.1.

lem descended to earth where the resurrected righteous will reign with Christ, enjoying an immense happiness and abundance of blessings. Many times this theme was connected to the other, which fixed the duration of the world to seven thousand years and had an independent origin.

Deriving from Judaism, millenarianism is traced back in antiquity in the Asiatic milieu to Cerinthus and Papias of Hierapolis in Phrygia,[4] while the key representatives of the Christian millenarianism appear to be Justin, Irenaeus and Tertullian, who established this belief on the basis of Revelation 20:4-6. In any case, the importance of millenarianism in ancient Christian eschatology was not destined to last: very soon Origen would radically criticize this doctrine for the excessive literalism that the millenarists attributed to the passages of Scripture that they quoted.[5]

The last set of selections related to this section of the creed is devoted to the doctrinal positions of Origen. In fact, if on the one hand Origen and his teachings were an object of admiration on the part of many, on the other they were a cause of scandal to the Fathers through nearly the entire patristic age. In particular his conception of the end of the world, namely, the final *apokatastasis* ("recapitulation"), which suggests the idea of a universal salvation and therefore does not admit the eternity of hell and its punishments, was definitively condemned together with other conceptions defined as Origenist by the emperor Justinian in 543. In spite of the contrasting judgments on the figure and the work of Origen, it was impossible to prevent, for instance, the profession of the doctrine of the *apokatastasis* by other thinkers of antiquity as well, as in the case of Gregory of Nyssa, who interpreted the final *apokatastasis* as a restoration of the original condition of the creatures,[6] according to which all the creatures, namely, angels, human beings and demons or spirits, will harmonize one day in goodness.

In conclusion, the passages from the Fathers that are gathered in this section bring to light certain problems inherent in any discussion of eschatological questions. In this regard a modern Christian eschatology cannot help but take into consideration, or at least examine, these abundant and valuable sources.

OVERVIEW: Christ was the first to enjoy the fruit of resurrection that the Lord has promised to everyone (CLEMENT OF ROME). The legend of the Arabian phoenix is a symbol of resurrection (CLEMENT OF ROME). Resurrection is at the same time an essential part of our faith (POLYCARP) and an encouragement of the moral life of the Christian (ARISTIDES). In spite of this, many doubt the resurrection of the flesh and are only barely disposed to believe in a spiritual resurrection (JUSTIN). The faith in the resurrection has nothing to do with the Stoic conception of the eternal return (TATIAN). God made humanity for the sake of the life of those already created, so it is not kindled for a little while and then extinguished (ATHENAGORAS). God the Father is the author of resurrection (THEOPHILUS). On the day of resurrection, all the peoples will live in the harmony of one faith (IRENAEUS), and the souls of the righteous will take back their glorified bodies, while those of the damned will be joined with their diseased bodies (HIPPOLYTUS). It is easier to bring back to life what already existed than to create out of nothing (MINUCIUS FELIX), and it is this faith in the action of God that directs the hope of Christians (TERTULLIAN). The body dies, but not the soul; for this reason at last the body will resurrect, albeit in a spiritual dimension (ORIGEN). The judgment is connected to resurrection, so that the righteous will be resurrected to eternal life, the wicked to eternal damna-

---

[4]This information is provided by Irenaeus, Eusebius of Caesarea and Jerome. [5]Origen *On First Principles* 2.11.2. [6]Gregory of Nyssa *Cathechetical Oration* 26.

tion (APHRAHAT). God, in his omnipotence, is able to perform the resurrection of the body, but the soul also needs to resurrect to a new life from its sinful way of life (AUGUSTINE). In the day of resurrection, a new heaven and earth will rise, so that what had fallen will rise again, and what had died will live again (AMBROSE, CHRYSOLOGUS).

The flesh is the temple of God: as we are called to live in the flesh, so we will return to the flesh (PSEUDO-CLEMENT). Humanity, that is, the soul and the body of human beings, is destined for resurrection (JUSTIN, ATHENAGORAS). The body is the fortress of the soul: now the close union between the soul and the body cannot be dissolved definitively through death, because God has united the soul and the body as the bridegroom and the bride and guarantees resurrection to both (TERTULLIAN). The eucharistic species contain the body and the blood of Christ, and this means that the flesh can also receive the gift of God, that is, eternal life (IRENAEUS). The resurrected body will have a spiritual nature and will be transformed into a vase of honor and benediction (ORIGEN). The body has in itself the seeds of immortality, so that, after being buried, it will be born again at the sound of the trumpet of judgment (APHRAHAT). The body will resurrect, having in itself an eternal dimension, which is difficult to express (CYRIL OF JERUSALEM). The flesh is like a torch from which the light of faith will shine on the day of the judgment (METHODIUS). As the resurrected Christ possesses the same flesh that he had in life, so every human being will have again the body of his youth on the day of resurrection (AUGUSTINE). Since the soul is immortal, it will be the body that is to be clothed with incorruptibility through resurrection (JOHN). Without resurrection there would be no judgment (CHRYSOLOGUS).

According to millenarian teaching, when the resurrection occurs, a kingdom of the righteous will rise in Jerusalem that will last one thousand years, as we read in Ezekiel and Isaiah (JUSTIN). The new heaven and earth will be the signs of an earthly kingdom, which will introduce incorruptibility (IRENAEUS). The new and divinely reconstructed Jerusalem will be the seat of the millenarian kingdom (TERTULLIAN). Not only the prophets of the Old Testament but also the Sibyl has prophesied a millenarian kingdom on earth (LACTANTIUS). Cerinthus, Papias of Hierapolis and Nepos, bishop of Egypt, were millenarists (EUSEBIUS). This doctrine cannot be easily maintained, however, because it is excessively carnal (AUGUSTINE). The millenarian kingdom is a prelude to the entrance to heaven, that is, to the real house of God, and it will cause the corruptible bodies to transform into an angelic shape and beauty (METHODIUS). The real sabbath, that is, the eighth day, will coincide with the seventh millennium of history, when Christ and his elect reign in the flesh (COMMODIAN, VICTORINUS).

Only God knows when the end of the world will happen, in which everything will be purified by the final fire. Then Christ will subject the entire universe and will present it to the Father, together with the devil and his angels (ORIGEN). At the end of time, the work of the devil will be burned and purified by the action of God (GREGORY OF NYSSA). Jerome and Rufinus are accused of following the doctrines of Origen (JEROME, RUFINUS). The ideas of Origen cannot be accepted, especially the final salvation of the devil (AUGUSTINE). In 543, Justinian condemned the Origenist conceptions, considering them to be contrary to faith (EDICT OF 543).

The Resurrection in General

THE LORD DECLARES TO US A RESURRECTION. CLEMENT OF ROME: Let us consider, beloved, how the Lord continually proves to us that there will be a future resurrection, of which he has rendered the Lord Jesus Christ the first fruits by raising him from the dead.

Let us contemplate, beloved, the resurrection that is at all times taking place. Day and night declare to us a resurrection. The night sinks to sleep, and the day arises; the day again departs, and the night comes on. Let us behold the fruits of the earth, how the sowing of grain takes place. The sower goes forth and casts it into the ground, and the seed being thus scattered, though dry and naked when it fell on the earth, is gradually dissolved. Then out of its dissolution the mighty power of the providence of the Lord raises it up again, and from one seed many arise and bring forth fruit. 1 Clement 24.[7]

The Legend of the Phoenix. Clement of Rome: Let us consider that wonderful sign of the resurrection that takes place in eastern lands, that is, in Arabia and the countries round about. There is a certain bird that is called a phoenix. This is the only one of its kind and lives five hundred years. And when the time of its dissolution draws near that it must die, it builds itself a nest of frankincense and myrrh and other spices, into which, when the time is fulfilled, it enters and dies. But as the flesh decays, a certain kind of worm is produced, which, being nourished by the juices of the dead bird, brings forth feathers. Then, when it has acquired strength, it takes up that nest in which are the bones of its parent, and bearing these it passes from the land of Arabia into Egypt, to the city called Heliopolis. And, in open day, flying in the sight of all people, it places them on the altar of the sun, and having done this, hastens back to its former abode. The priests then inspect the registers of the dates and find that it has returned exactly as the five hundredth year was completed. 1 Clement 25.[8]

A Resurrection for Us. Clement of Rome: Do we then deem it any great and wonderful thing for the maker of all things to raise up again those who have piously served him in the assurance of a good faith, when even by a bird he shows us the mightiness of his power to fulfill his promise? For the Scripture says in a certain place, "You will raise me up, and I will praise you,"[9] and again, "I laid down and slept; I awoke, because you are with me,"[10] and again, Job says, "you will raise up this flesh of mine, which has suffered all these things."[11] 1 Clement 26.[12]

The Power of the Word. Clement of Rome: Having then this hope, let our souls be bound to him who is faithful in his promises and just in his judgments. He who has commanded us not to lie will certainly not lie himself; for nothing is impossible with God, except to lie. Let his faith therefore be stirred up again within us, and let us consider that all things are near to him. By the word of his might he established all things, and by his word he can overthrow them. "Who will say to him, 'What have you done?' Or, who will resist the power of his strength?"[13] And he will do everything as he pleases and none of the things determined by him will pass away. All things are open before him, and nothing can be hidden from his counsel. "The heavens declare the glory of God, and the firmament shows his handiwork. Day to day utters speech, and night to night shows knowledge. And there are no words or speeches of which the voices are not heard."[14] 1 Clement 27.[15]

We Should Return to the Word. Polycarp: "For whoever does not confess that Jesus Christ has come in the flesh is antichrist,"[16] and whoever does not confess the testimony of the cross is of the devil; and whoever perverts the oracles of the Lord to his own lusts and says that there is neither a resurrection or a judgment is the firstborn of Satan. Therefore, forsaking the vanity of many, and their false

---

[7]ANF 1:11-12. [8]ANF 1:12. [9]Ps 28:7 (27:7 LXX). [10]Cf. Ps 3:6. [11]Job 19:25-26. [12]ANF 1:12*. [13]Wis 12:12; 11:21. [14]Ps 19:1-3. [15]ANF 1:12. [16]1 Jn 4:3.

doctrines, let us return to the word that has been handed down to us from the beginning, "watching unto prayer"[17] and persevering in fasting; beseeching in our supplications the all-seeing God "not to lead us into temptation,"[18] as the Lord has said: "The spirit truly is willing, but the flesh is weak."[19] EPISTLE TO THE PHILIPPIANS 7.[20]

CHRISTIANS HAVE FOUND THE TRUTH IN GOD. ARISTIDES: But the Christians, O king, while they went about and searched, have found the truth. And, as we learned from their writings, they have come nearer to truth and genuine knowledge than the rest of the nations. For they know and trust in God, the creator of heaven and of earth, in whom and from whom are all things, to whom there is no other god as companion, from whom they received commandments that they engraved upon their minds and observe in hope and expectation of the world that is to come. Therefore they do not commit adultery or fornication, nor do they bear false witness or embezzle what is held in pledge or covet what is not theirs. They honor father and mother and show kindness to those near to them; and whenever they are judges, they judge uprightly. They do not worship idols made in the image of humans; and what they do not want others to do to them, they do not to others; and of the food that is consecrated to idols they do not eat, for they are pure. And their oppressors they appease [lit., comfort] and make them their friends. They do good to their enemies. And their women, O king, are pure as virgins, and their daughters are modest. Their men keep themselves from every unlawful union and from all uncleanness, in the hope of a reward to come in the other world. APOLOGY 15.[21]

HERETICS ATTEMPT TO DISTRACT PEOPLE FROM THE FAITH. JUSTIN MARTYR: Those who maintain the wrong opinion say that there is no resurrection of the flesh, giving as their reason that it is impossible that what is corrupted and dissolved should be restored to the same as it had been. And besides the impossibility, they say that the salvation of the flesh is disadvantageous. They also abuse the flesh, adducing its infirmities, and declare that it only is the cause of our sins, so that if the flesh, they say, rises again, our infirmities also rise with it. And they elaborate such sophistical reasons as the following: If the flesh rises again, it must rise either entire and possessed of all its parts or imperfect. But its rising imperfect argues a lack of power on God's part, if some parts could be saved and others not; but if all the parts are saved, then the body will manifestly have all its members. But is it not absurd to say that these members will exist after the resurrection from the dead, since the Savior said, "They neither marry nor are given in marriage but will be as the angels in heaven"?[22] And the angels, they say, have neither flesh, nor do they eat nor have sexual intercourse; therefore, there will be no resurrection of the flesh. By these and similar arguments they attempt to distract people from the faith. And there are some who maintain that even Jesus appeared only as spiritual, and not in flesh, but presented merely the appearance of flesh: these persons seek to rob the flesh of the promise. FRAGMENTS ON THE RESURRECTION 2.[23]

THE FIRE DESTROYS ALL TRACES OF MY FLESH. TATIAN: And this is why we believe that there will be a resurrection of bodies after the consummation of all things; not the cyclical idea that the Stoics affirm where the same things are produced and destroyed with no purpose in mind. Rather, this is a resurrection once for all, when our periods of existence will come to completion as a consequence solely of the human condition under which human

---

[17]1 Pet 4:7. [18]Mt 6:13. [19]Mt 26:41; Mk 14:38. [20]ANF 1:34-35. [21]ANF 9:276. [22]Mk 12:25. [23]ANF 1:294-95.

beings alone live, in order to pass judgment on them. Nor is sentence on us passed by Minos or Rhadamanthus, before whose death not a single soul, according to the mythic tales, was judged. Rather, the creator, God, becomes the arbiter. And, although you regard us as mere triflers and babblers, this does not bother us since we have faith in this doctrine. For I did not know who I was before I was born and existed only in the potentiality (*hypostasis*) of fleshly matter. But when I was born after my former state of nothingness, I obtained through my birth a certainty of my existence. Similarly, after being born but no longer existing or seen because of death, I will exist again, just as previously I did not exist but was afterward born. Even though fire destroy all traces of my flesh, the world receives the vaporized matter; and though dispersed through rivers and seas or torn in pieces by wild beasts, I am laid up in the storehouses of a wealthy Lord. And, although the poor and the godless have no idea what is stored up for them, our sovereign God will yet restore to its pristine condition the substance that is visible to him alone, when he desires to do so. ADDRESS TO THE GREEKS 6.[24]

GOD CREATED HUMANITY. ATHENAGORAS: But God could not have made humankind in vain, for he is wise, and no work of wisdom is in vain; nor would he have made us for his own use since he is in want of nothing. But to a being absolutely in need of nothing, no one of his works can contribute anything to his own use. Neither, again, did he make humanity for the sake of any of the other works that he has made. For nothing that is endowed with reason and judgment has been created or is created for the use of another, whether greater or less than itself, but for the sake of the life and continuance of the being itself so created. For reason cannot discover any use that might be deemed a cause for the creation of human beings, since immortals are free from want and in need of no help from mortals in order to maintain their existence; and irrational beings are by nature in a state of subjection and perform those services for humans for which each of them was intended but are not intended in their turn to make use of humans: for it neither was nor is right to lower that which rules and leads to the use of the inferior, or to subject the rational to the irrational, which is not suited to rule. Therefore, if humankind has been created neither without cause and in vain (for none of God's works is in vain, so far at least as the purpose of their Maker is concerned) or for the use of the Maker or of any of the works that have proceeded from him, it is quite clear that although, according to the first and more general view of the subject, God made humanity for himself, and in pursuit of the goodness and wisdom that are conspicuous throughout the creation, yet, according to the view that more nearly touches the beings created, he made him for the sake of the life of those created, which is not kindled for a little while and then extinguished. For God has assigned such a life as that to creeping things, I suppose, and birds and fishes, or, to speak more generally, all irrational creatures. But to those who bear on them the image of the Creator, and are endowed with understanding and blessed with a rational judgment, the Creator has assigned perpetual duration, in order that, recognizing their own Maker and his power and skill, and obeying law and justice, they may pass their whole existence free from suffering, in the possession of those qualities with which they have bravely borne their preceding life, although they lived in corruptible and earthly bodies. For whatever has been created for the sake of something else, when that has ceased to be for the sake of which it was created, will itself also appropriately cease to be and will not continue to exist in vain, since, among the works of God, that which is useless can have

---

[24]ANF 2:67*.

no place; but that which was created for the very purpose of existing and living a life naturally suited to it, since the cause itself is bound up with its nature and is recognized only in connection with existence itself, can never admit of any cause that will utterly annihilate its existence. But since this cause is seen to lie in perpetual existence, the being so created must be preserved forever, doing and experiencing what is suitable to its nature. Each of the two parts of its nature contributes what belongs to the nature [as a whole], so that the soul may exist and remain without change in the nature in which it was made and discharge its appropriate functions, presiding over the impulses of the body and judging and measuring what occurs from time to time by the proper standards and measures. It governs the movement of the body—according to the nature it has—toward its appropriate objects, as well as the changes allotted to it that it undergoes, along with the rest of what pertains to the body relating to age or appearance or size at the resurrection. For the resurrection is a species of change, and the last of all, and a change for the better of what still remains in existence at that time. ON THE RESURRECTION 12.[25]

GOD WILL RAISE YOUR FLESH IMMORTAL WITH YOUR SOUL. THEOPHILUS OF ANTIOCH: This is my God, the Lord of all, who alone stretched out the heaven and established the breadth of the earth under it; who stirs the deep recesses of the sea and makes its waves roar; who rules its power and stills the tumult of its waves; who founded the earth on the waters and gave a spirit to nourish it; whose breath gives light to the whole, who, if he withdraw his breath, the whole would utterly fail. By him you speak, O mortal; his breath you breathe, yet you do not know him. And this is your condition, because of the blindness of your soul and the hardness of your heart. But, if you will, you may be healed. Entrust yourself to the Physician, and he will touch the eyes of your soul and of your heart. Who is the Physician? God, who heals and makes alive through his word and wisdom. God by his own word and wisdom made all things, for "by his word were the heavens made, and all the host of them by the breath of his mouth."[26] Most excellent is his wisdom. By his wisdom God founded the earth, and by knowledge he prepared the heavens, and by understanding were the fountains of the great deep broken up, and the clouds poured out their dews. If you perceive these things, O mortal, living chastely, and in a sanctified manner and righteously, you can see God. But before all let faith and the fear of God rule in your heart, and then you will understand these things. When you have put off the mortal and put on incorruption, then you will see God worthily. For God will raise your flesh immortal with your soul. Then, having become immortal, you will see the Immortal, if now you believe on him. Then you will know that you have spoken unjustly against him. TO AUTOLYCUS 1.7.[27]

NOBODY WILL HAVE POWER TO HURT ANYTHING. IRENAEUS: And these things are borne witness to in writing by Papias, the hearer of John and a companion of Polycarp, in his fourth book; for there were five books compiled by him. And he says in addition, "Now these things are credible to believers." And he says that "when the traitor Judas did not give credit to them and put the question, 'How then can things about to bring forth so abundantly be wrought by the Lord?' the Lord declared, 'They who will come to these times will see.'" When prophesying of these times, therefore, Isaiah says, "The wolf also will feed with the lamb, and the leopard will take his rest with the kid; the calf also, and the bull, and the lion will eat together; and a little boy will lead them. The ox and the bear will feed together, and their young ones will agree

---

[25]ANF 2:155*. [26]Ps 33:6. [27]ANF 2:91.

together; and the lion will eat straw as well as the ox. And the infant boy will thrust his hand into the asp's den, into the nest also of the adder's brood; and they will do no harm, nor have power to hurt anything in my holy mountain." And again he says, in recapitulation, "Wolves and lambs will then graze together, and the lion will eat straw like the ox, and the serpent earth as if it were bread; and they will neither hurt nor annoy anything in my holy mountain, says the Lord."[28] I am quite aware that some endeavor to refer these words to the case of savages, both of different nations and various habits, who come to believe, and when they have believed, act in harmony with the righteous. But although this is true now with regard to some who come from various nations to the harmony of the faith, nevertheless in the resurrection of the just the words will also apply to those animals mentioned. For God is not in all things. And it is right that when the creation is restored, all the animals should obey and be in subjection to human beings and revert to the food originally given by God (for they had been originally subjected in obedience to Adam), that is, the produce of the earth. But some other occasion, and not the present, is to be sought for showing that the lion will then feed on straw. And this indicates the large size and rich quality of the fruits. For if that animal, the lion, feeds on straw, of what a quality must the wheat itself be whose straw will serve as suitable food for lions? AGAINST HERESIES 5.33.4.[29]

THE UNRIGHTEOUS WILL RECEIVE THEIR BODIES UNCHANGED. HIPPOLYTUS: Thus far, then, we have spoken on the subject of hades, in which the souls of all are detained until the time that God has determined. And then he will accomplish a resurrection of all, not by transferring souls into other bodies but by raising the bodies themselves. And if, O Greeks, you refuse to give credence to this because you see these bodies in their dissolution, learn not to be incredulous. For if you believe that the soul is originated and is made immortal by God, according to the opinion of Plato, in time, you ought not to refuse to believe that God is able also to raise the body, which is composed of the same elements, and make it immortal. To be able in one thing and to be unable in another is a word that cannot be said of God. We therefore believe that the body also is raised. For if it becomes corrupt, it still is nonetheless not destroyed. For the earth receiving its remains preserves them, and they, becoming as it were seed and being wrapped up with the richer part of earth, spring up and bloom. And that which is sown is sown indeed bare grain; but at the command of God the artificer it buds and is raised arrayed and glorious, but not until it has first died and been dissolved and mingled with earth. Not, therefore, without good reason do we believe in the resurrection of the body. Moreover, if it is dissolved in its season on account of the primeval transgression and is committed to the earth as to a furnace, to be molded again anew, it is not raised the same thing as it is now, but pure and no longer corruptible. And to every body its own proper soul will be given again; and the soul, being endued again with it, will not be grieved but will rejoice together with it, abiding itself pure with it also pure. And as it now sojourns with it in the world right-eously and finds it in nothing now a traitor, it will receive it [the body] again with great joy. But the unrighteous will receive their bodies unchanged, and unransomed from suffering and disease, and unglorified, and still with all the ills in which they died. And whatever manner of persons they were when they lived without faith, as such they will be faithfully judged. AGAINST PLATO, ON THE CAUSE OF THE UNIVERSE 2.[30]

THE BURIED BODY LIKE A TREE IN WINTER. MINUCIUS FELIX: Moreover, it is more

---

[28]Is 11:6-9. [29]ANF 1:563. [30]ANF 5:222.

difficult to begin that which is not than to repeat that which has been. Do you think that if anything is withdrawn from our feeble eyes, it perishes to God? Every body, whether it is dried up into dust, or is dissolved into moisture, or is compressed into ashes or is attenuated into smoke, is withdrawn from us, but it is reserved for God in the custody of the elements. Nor, as you believe, do we fear any loss from the sepulcher, but we adopt the ancient and better custom of burying in the earth. See, therefore, how for our consolation all nature suggests a future resurrection. The sun sinks down and arises, the stars pass away and return, the flowers die and revive again, after their wintry decay the shrubs resume their leaves, seeds do not flourish again, unless they are rotted. Thus the body in the sepulcher is like the trees that in winter hide their verdure with a deceptive dryness. Why are you in a hurry for it to revive and return, while the winter is still raw? We must wait also for the springtime of the body. And I am not ignorant that many, in the consciousness of what they deserve, rather desire than believe that they will be nothing after death. For they would prefer to be altogether extinguished rather than to be restored for the purpose of punishment. And their error also is enhanced both by the liberty granted them in this life and by God's very great patience, whose judgment, the more tardy it is, is so much the more just. OCTAVIUS 34.[31]

THE TERMS BODY AND RESURRECTION.
TERTULLIAN: Meanwhile the Marcionite will exhibit nothing of this kind; he is by this time afraid to say which side has the better right to a Christ who is not yet revealed. Just as my Christ is to be expected, who was predicted from the beginning, so his Christ therefore has no existence, as not having been announced from the beginning. Ours is a better faith, which believes in a future Christ, than the heretic's, which has none at all to believe in.

Touching the resurrection of the dead, let us first inquire how some persons then denied it. No doubt in the same way in which it is even now denied, since the resurrection of the flesh has at all times people to deny it. But many wise people claim for the soul a divine nature and are confident of its undying destiny, and even the multitude worship the dead in the presumption that they boldly entertain that their souls survive. As for our bodies, however, it is manifest that they perish either at once by fire or the wild beasts, or even when most carefully kept by length of time. When, therefore, the apostle refutes those who deny the resurrection of the flesh, he indeed defends, in opposition to them, the precise matter of their denial, that is, the resurrection of the body. You have the whole answer wrapped up in this. All the rest is superfluous. Now in this very point, which is called the resurrection of the dead, it is requisite that the proper force of the words should be accurately maintained. The word *dead* expresses simply what has lost the vital principle, by means of which it used to live. Now the body is that which loses life, and as the result of losing it becomes dead. To the body, therefore, the term *dead* is only suitable. Moreover, as resurrection accrues to what is dead, and *dead* is a term applicable only to a body, therefore the body alone has a resurrection incidental to it. So again the word *resurrection*, or "rising affairs," embraces only that which has fallen down. To rise, indeed, can be predicated of that which has never fallen down but had already been always lying down. But to rise again is predicable only of that which has fallen down; because it is by rising again, in consequence of its having fallen down, that it is said to have rerisen. For the syllable *re* always implies iteration or happening again. We say, therefore, that the body falls to the ground by death, as indeed facts themselves show, in accordance with the law of God. For

---

[31]ANF 4:194.

to the body it was said, "Till you return to the ground, for out of it you were taken; for dust you are, and to dust you will return." That, therefore, which came from the ground will return to the ground. Now that falls down that returns to the ground; and that rises again that falls down. "Since by man came death, by man came also the resurrection."[32] Here in the word *man*, who consists of bodily substance, as we have often shown already, is presented to me the body of Christ. But if we are all so made alive in Christ, as we die in Adam, it follows of necessity that we are made alive in Christ as a bodily substance, since we died in Adam as a bodily substance. The similarity, indeed, is not complete, unless our revival in Christ concurs in identity of substance with our mortality in Adam. AGAINST MARCION 5.9.[33]

THE TRUTH IS WHAT GOD REVEALS.
TERTULLIAN: The resurrection of the dead is the Christian's confidence. By believing it we are what we claim to be. This belief the truth exacts: the truth is what God reveals. But the multitude mocks, reckoning that nothing remains over after death. Yet they offer sacrifices to the deceased, and that with most lavish devotion in accordance with their customs and with foods that are in season, so as to create the supposition that those whom they deny to have any sensation are even conscious of being in need. I however will with better reason mock at the multitude, especially on occasions when they savagely burn up those very deceased whom they presently supply with gluttonous meals, with the same fires both currying favor and provoking hostility. Thus does piety toy with cruelty. Is it sacrifice, or insult, to cremate the cremated? Doubtless at times even philosophers conjoin their own judgment with the multitude. That there is nothing after death is Epicurus's doctrine, and Seneca affirms that after death all things come to an end, including death itself. But it is enough if the not younger judgment of Pythagoras, as well as Empedocles and the Platonists, make the contrary claim that the soul is immortal, yes, even more, assert that it is destined very soon afterward to return into bodies, albeit not the same bodies, nor human bodies only, with the result that Euphorbus is reborn as Pythagoras, and Homer as a peacock. At least they have pronounced that the soul has a corporal recurrence (the alteration of its quality is more tolerable than the denial of it), knocking at truth's door though not entering into its house. Thus not even when it goes astray is the world ignorant of the resurrection of the dead. ON THE RESURRECTION OF THE FLESH 1.[34]

GOD'S WORD SHALL NOT PASS AWAY.
ORIGEN: Let no one, however, suspect that, in speaking as we do, we belong to those who are indeed called Christians but who set aside the doctrine of the resurrection as it is taught in Scripture. For these people can in no way establish, so far as their principles apply, that the stalk or tree that springs up comes from the grain of wheat or anything else (which was cast into the ground). We . . . believe that that which is "sown" is not "enlivened" unless it dies and that the body that is sown is not the future body that will exist. For God gives it a body as it pleases him, raising it in incorruption after it is sown in corruption; and after it is sown in dishonor, raising it in glory; and after it is sown in weakness, raising it in power; and after it is sown a natural body, raising it a spiritual one. Thus we preserve both the doctrine of the church of Christ and the grandeur of the divine promise, proving also the possibility of its accomplishment not by mere assertion but by arguments. We know that although heaven and earth and the things that are in them may pass away, yet his words regarding each individual thing, being, as parts of a whole or species of a genus, the utterances of him who was God the Word, who was in

---

[32]1 Cor 15:21. [33]ANF 3:447-48. [34]TTR 5.

the beginning with God, will by no means pass away. For we desire to listen to him who said, "Heaven and earth will pass away, but my words will not pass away."[35] AGAINST CELSUS 5.22.[36]

THE RESURRECTION CHANGE FROM INDIGNITY TO GLORY. ORIGEN: The present discourse has reminded us of the subjects concerning a future judgment and of retribution and of the punishments of sinners, according to the threats of holy Scripture and the contents of the church's teaching—that is, that when the time of judgment comes, everlasting fire, and outer darkness, and a prison, and a furnace, and other punishments of a similar nature have been prepared for sinners. And so, let us see what our opinions on these points ought to be. But that these subjects may be arrived at in proper order, it seems to me that we ought first to consider the nature of the resurrection, that we may know what that [body] is which will come either to punishment or to rest or to happiness. We have composed other treatises that deal with this question regarding the resurrection, and there we have discussed at greater length and have shown what our opinions were regarding it. But now, also, for the sake of logical order in our treatise, there will be no absurdity in restating a few points from such works, especially since some take offense at the creed of the church, as if our belief in the resurrection were foolish and altogether devoid of sense. These are mainly heretics, who, I think, are to be answered in the following manner. If they also admit that there is a resurrection of the dead, let them answer us this: What died? Was it not a body? It is of the body, then, that there will be a resurrection. Let them next tell us if they think that we are to make use of bodies or not. I think that when the apostle Paul says that "it is sown a natural body, it will arise a spiritual body,"[37] they cannot deny that it is a body that arises, or that in the resurrection we are to make use of bodies. What then? If it is certain that we are to make use of bodies, and if the bodies that have fallen are declared to rise again (for only that which before has fallen can be properly said to rise again), it can be a matter of doubt to no one that they rise again, in order that we may be clothed with them a second time at the resurrection. The one thing is closely connected with the other. For if bodies rise again, they undoubtedly rise to be coverings for us. And if it is necessary for us to be invested with bodies, as it is certainly necessary, we ought to be invested with no other body than our own. But if it is true that these rise again and that they arise "spiritual" bodies, there can be no doubt that they are said to rise from the dead, after casting away corruption and laying aside mortality. Otherwise it will appear vain and superfluous for anyone to arise from the dead in order to die a second time. And this, finally, may be more distinctly comprehended if one carefully considers what the qualities of an animal body are which, when sown into the earth, recovers the qualities of a spiritual body. For it is out of the animal body that the very power and grace of the resurrection educe the spiritual body, when it transmutes it from a condition of indignity to one of glory. ON FIRST PRINCIPLES 2.10.1.[38]

THE MARVEL OF GOD'S WORKS. APHRAHAT: I will teach you about the resurrection of the dead as best as I can, my beloved. For from the beginning God created Adam, molded him from the dust of the earth and raised him up. For if, while Adam was not, he made him from nothing, how much easier now is it for him to raise him up. Look! He is sown in the earth as a seed. For if God should do those things that are easy for us, his works would not appear mighty to us. Look! There are human artisans who make wonderful things, and those who are

---

[35]Cf. Mt 24:35; Mk 13:31. [36]ANF 4:552-53*. [37]1 Cor 15:44. [38]ANF 4:293-94.

not the artisans stand and wonder how they were done, and they view the work of their fellow human beings as something quite difficult. How much more should not the works of God be as a marvel! But for God this was no great thing, that the dead should be quickened. Before seed was sown in the earth, the earth produced that which had not been cast into it. Before it had conceived, it bore in its virginity. How then is this difficult, that the earth should cause to spring up again what had been cast into it, and after conception should bear? And lo! her birth pains are near, as Isaiah said, "Who has seen anything like this and who has heard such things as these—that the earth should travail in one day and a people should be born in one hour?"[39] For Adam unsown sprang up. Conceived, he was born. But look! Now his offspring are sown. They wait for the rain, and then they will spring up. And look! The earth teems with many, and the time of her bringing forth is at hand. DEMONSTRATIONS 8.6.[40]

SINNERS WHO RISE WILL BE DELIVERED TO DEATH. APHRAHAT: And the Lifegiver will come, the destroyer of death, and will bring to nothing death's power over the just as well as the wicked. And the dead will arise with a mighty shout, and Death will be emptied and stripped of all the captivity. And for judgment will all the children of Adam be gathered together, and each will go to the place prepared for him. The risen of the righteous will go to life, and the risen of the sinners will be delivered to death. The righteous who kept the commandment will go and will not come near to judgment in the day that they will rise; as David asked, "And do not bring your servant into judgment";[41] nor will their Lord terrify them in that day. DEMONSTRATIONS 22.15.[42]

DEAD THROUGH SIN. AUGUSTINE: Next, Christ goes on to say, "Amen, amen, I say to you, the hour is coming, and now is here, when the dead will hear the voice of the Son of God, and those who hear will live. For as the Father has life in himself, even so he has given to the Son also to have life in himself."[43] In this text he is not yet speaking of the second resurrection, the corporeal one, which is to come at the end of the world, but of the first, which takes place here and now. It was precisely to set apart the latter that he said, "The hour is coming, and now is here"—surely, a resurrection of souls, not of bodies. For souls, too, have their own sort of death in ungodliness and sin. This was the kind of death those had died of whom our Lord said, "Leave the dead to bury their own dead"[44]—meaning, of course, that the spiritually dead were to bury the corporeally dead.

Thus, it was on account of the former—those dead of soul because of godlessness and sin—that he said, "The hour is coming, and now is here, when the dead will hear the voice of the Son of God, and those who hear will live." "Those who hear" means those who will obey and believe and persevere to the end. Nor did Christ in this text make any distinction between good and bad individuals. It is good for all to hear his voice and to come alive by passing over from the death of sin to the life of grace. It was of death in sin that Paul said, "Therefore all died; and Christ died for all, in order that they who are alive may live no longer for themselves but for him who died for them and rose again."[45]

All, consequently, without a single exception, were dead through sin, original sin or original with personal sin superadded, either by ignorance of, or conscious refusal to do, what is right. And for all these dead souls one living man died—a man utterly free from sin—with the intention that those who come alive by forgiveness of their sins live no longer for themselves but for him who died for

---

[39]Is 66:8. [40]NPNF 2 13:376-77. [41]Ps 143:2 (144:2 LXX). [42]NPNF 2 13:407. [43]Jn 5:25-26. [44]Mt 8:22. [45]2 Cor 5:14-15.

all on account of our sins and rose again for our justification. All this was to the end that, believing in him "who justifies the impious,"[46] we might be rescued from unbelief like those quickened out of death and belong to the first resurrection, which is here and now. For, no one belongs to the first except those who are to be blessed forever. To the second, however, of which Christ is about to speak, belong both the blessed and the damned, as he teaches us. The first resurrection is a resurrection of mercy; the last is to be a resurrection of judgment. Hence the psalm says, "Mercy and judgment I will sing to you, O Lord."[47] CITY OF GOD 20.6.[48]

THE RESURRECTION OF THE FLESH. AUGUSTINE: It is unthinkable that there should be any limits to the Creator's omnipotence in resuscitating and restoring to life every element of any human body that has been devoured by beasts, or consumed by fire, or reduced to dust, or dissolved into liquid or evaporated into air. Nature may have recesses secret enough to hide such elements from our sense, but it has none that can escape the scrutiny or power of the Creator of the universe. And here I may invoke one of the supreme authorities among the pagans. It was Cicero who gave, as best he could, this definition of God: "A spirit unlimited and free, immaterial and immortal, that knows all things and moves all things and is itself endowed with everlasting motion."[49] It is a definition based on the best wisdom of the great philosophers. How, then, if I may use the language of the philosophers, can anything be hidden from a "spirit that knows all things" or escape, ultimately, from one that "moves all things"?

With this in mind, we may now take up the question—usually thought so difficult—of the flesh of a dead person that has become the living flesh of another. To whose body will it belong in the resurrection? There are cases, as history records, and as the unhappy experiences of our own day prove, of people so famished as to be driven to eating dead persons' bodies. And, of course, no one seriously denies that there is here a case of complete digestive assimilation and transformation of one person's flesh into that of another. The fact that the emaciated person fills out is proof enough of where his new flesh came from.

I have already suggested the elements that are needed for the solution of the problem. Whatever flesh the starving person lost by exhalation into the air can be recalled, as I said, by almighty God. And, similarly, the eaten flesh will be restored by God to the one in whom it first became human flesh. This flesh can be looked on as a loan taken by the famished person and, like any other borrowed goods, must be returned to the one from whom it was taken. And, of course, the flesh of the famished person will be restored by the One who can recall even fumes from the air. Even if this lost flesh were completely dissipated so that not a single material particle were to be found anywhere in nature, the Omnipotent could restore it from a source of his own choosing. Of course, we cannot suppose that it could be so completely dissipated. The Truth has said, "Not a hair of your head will perish."[50] It would be absurd, then, to think that so much flesh lost by starvation could perish, while a single hair cannot.

And now, after weighing all these problems and resolving them as best I could, the following conclusions have been reached: first, in the resurrection of the body to eternal life, the size will be that which was reached or would have been reached in each person's maturity; second, there will be an appropriate beauty of the body arising from the harmony of all its parts, and it is a fair supposition that this beauty will be achieved by such a redistribution throughout the body of whatever in any one part was

[46]Rom 4:5. [47]Ps 101:1. [48]FC 24:261-62*. [49]Tusculan *Disputations* 1.127. [50]See Lk 12:7.

out of proportion that, while nothing is lost, the harmony of the whole will be maintained; third, there may be some increase in stature, since beauty will demand a general distribution of what, in any one member, would be an ugly excess; fourth, a good case, however, can be made for the contention that a risen body will be just the same in stature as it was at the time of death, so long as it is admitted that there will be no deformity, no infirmity, no decrepitude, no deficiencies or anything else that would be unbecoming in a realm where the sons of the resurrection and the promise are to be like the angels of God in regard to beatitude, though not, of course, in regard to body and age. CITY OF GOD 22.20.[51]

THE GOOD FIND JOY. AUGUSTINE: All souls then, if I may take this opportunity of giving your graces some instruction, all souls are received when they depart this life in a variety of appropriate ways; there the good find joy, the bad find torment.[52] But when the resurrection takes place, the joy of the good will be amplified, and the torments of the wicked will be more grievous when they are tormented together with the body. The holy patriarchs, prophets, apostles, martyrs, the good among the faithful, have been received in peace; all of them, however, are still to receive what God has promised; the resurrection of the flesh also, you see, has been promised us, the annihilation of death, eternal life with the angels. This is something we are all going to receive together; while the resting in peace, which is given immediately after death, is something we each receive, if we are worthy of it, when we die. The patriarchs were the first to receive it—just see for what a length of time they have been at rest. After them came the prophets, more recently the apostles, much more recently the holy martyrs, every day the good among the faithful. And some have now been at rest like this a long time, others not so long, others for just a few years, others scarcely for a moment. But when they wake up from this sleep, they are all simultaneously going to receive what has been promised. HOMILIES ON THE GOSPEL OF JOHN 49.10.[53]

NO DOUBT FOR CHRISTIANS. AUGUSTINE: Now, as to the resurrection of the body—not a resurrection such as some have had, who came back to life for a time and died again, but a resurrection to eternal life, as the body of Christ rose again—I do not see how I can discuss the matter briefly and at the same time give a satisfactory answer to all the questions that are ordinarily raised about it. Yet that the bodies of all human beings—both those who have been born and those who will be born, both those who have died and those who will die—shall be raised again, no Christian ought to have the shadow of a doubt. ENCHIRIDION 84.[54]

WHAT HAS DIED WILL COME TO LIFE AGAIN. AMBROSE: If the earth and heaven are renewed, why should we doubt that human beings, on account of whom heaven and earth were made, can be renewed? If the transgressor be reserved for punishment, why should not the just be kept for glory? If the worm of sins does not die, how will the flesh of the just perish? For the resurrection, as the very form of the word shows, is this, that what has fallen should rise again, that which has died should come to life again. ON HIS BROTHER SATYRUS 2.87.[55]

SLEEPING AND AWAKENING, DYING AND RISING. PETER CHRYSOLOGUS: "Believe . . . that you can rise in death, you who were nothing before you were living." Or why do you doubt that you will rise, when everything there is in the universe thus rises daily for your benefit? The sun sets and rises; the day is bur-

---

[51]FC 24:470-72*. [52]See Augustine *On the Literal Interpretation of Genesis* 12.32.60-61. [53]*WSA*, forthcoming; cf. NPNF 1 7: 273-74. [54]NPNF 1 3:264. [55]NPNF 2 10:188.

ied and returns; when months, years, seasons, vegetation, seeds pass on, they die; when they return, they come to life from their own death. And so that you might be instructed with an ever-present and familiar example that you will rise again: as often as you sleep and awaken, so often do you die and rise.... It is necessary that the one who rises live forever, because if he did not live forever, he would rise not to life but to death. SERMON 59.16-17.[56]

The Resurrection of the Body

WE MUST PRESERVE THE FLESH AS THE TEMPLE OF GOD. PSEUDO-CLEMENT OF ROME: And let no one of you say that this very flesh will not be judged or rise again. Consider then in what state you were saved, in what circumstances you received sight, if not while you were in this flesh. We must therefore preserve the flesh as the temple of God. For as you were called in the flesh, you will also come to be judged in the flesh. As Christ the Lord who saved us, though he was first a Spirit became flesh and thus called us, so will we also receive the reward in this flesh. Let us therefore love one another, that we may all attain to the kingdom of God. While we have an opportunity of being healed, let us yield ourselves to God who heals us and give to him a recompense. Of what sort? Repentance out of a sincere heart; for he knows all things beforehand and is acquainted with what is in our hearts. Let us therefore give him praise, not with the mouth only, but also with the heart, that he may accept us as children. For the Lord has said, "Those are my brethren who do the will of my Father."[57] 2 CLEMENT 9.[58]

A STATE OF SENSATION. JUSTIN MARTYR: For reflect on the end of each of the preceding kings, how they died the death common to all, which, if it issued in insensibility, would be a godsend to all the wicked. But since sensation remains to all who have ever lived and eternal punishment is laid up (that is, for the wicked), see that you do not neglect to be convinced and to hold as your belief that these things are true. For let even necromancy, and the divinations you practice by faultless children, and the evoking of departed human souls, and those who are called among the magi dream senders and assistant spirits (familiars), and all that is done by those who are skilled in such matters—let these persuade you that even after death souls are in a state of sensation; and those who are seized and cast about by the spirits of the dead, whom all call demoniacs or madmen; and what you repute as oracles, both of Amphilochus, Dodana, Pytho, and as many other such as exist; and the opinions of your authors, Empedocles and Pythagoras, Plato and Socrates, and the pit of Homer, and the descent of Ulysses to inspect these things, and all that has been uttered of a like kind. Such favor as you grant to these, grant also to us, who not less but more firmly than they believe in God; since we expect to receive again our own bodies, though they are dead and cast into the earth, for we maintain that with God nothing is impossible. FIRST APOLOGY 18.[59]

THE SOUL IS INCORRUPTIBLE, THE FLESH CORRUPTIBLE. JUSTIN MARTYR: But, in truth, he has even called the flesh to the resurrection and promises to it everlasting life. For where he promises to save human beings, there he gives the promise to the flesh. For what is a human being but the reasonable animal composed of body and soul? Is the soul by itself a human being? No. But it is a soul of a human being. Would the body be called a human being? No, but it is called the body of a human being. If, then, neither of these is by itself a human being, but that which is made up of the two together is called a human being, and God has called human beings to life and resurrection, he has called not a part but the whole,

---

[56]FC 109:229.   [57]Mt 12:50.   [58]ANF 9:253.   [59]ANF 1:168-69.

which is the soul and the body. Since would it not be unquestionably absurd, if, while these two are in the same being and according to the same law, the one were saved and the other not? And if it is not impossible, as has already been proved, that the flesh be regenerated, what is the distinction on the ground of which the soul is saved and the body not? Do they make God a grudging God? But he is good and will have all to be saved. And by God and his proclamation, not only has your soul heard and believed on Jesus Christ, and with it the flesh, but both were washed, and both wrought righteousness. They make God, then, ungrateful and unjust, if, while both believe on him, he desires to save one and not the other. Well, they say, but the soul is incorruptible, being a part of God and inspired by him, and therefore he desires to save what is peculiarly his own and akin to himself; but the flesh is corruptible and not from him, as the soul is. Then what thanks are due to him, and what manifestation of his power and goodness is it, if he purposed to save what is by nature saved and exists as a part of himself? For it had its salvation from itself; so that in saving the soul, God does no great thing. For to be saved is its natural destiny, because it is a part of himself, being his inspiration. But no thanks are due to one who saves what is his own; for this is to save himself. For he who saves a part of himself saves himself by his own means, lest he become defective in that part; and this is not the act of a good person. For not even when someone does good to his children and offspring does one call him a good person; for even the most savage of the wild beasts do so, and indeed willingly endure death, if need be, for the sake of their cubs. But if someone were to perform the same acts on behalf of his slaves, that person would justly be called good. Therefore the Savior also taught us to love our enemies, since, he says, what thanks do you have? Thus he has shown us that it is a good work not only to love those that are begotten of him but also those that are outside from him. And what he enjoins on us, he himself first of all does. FRAGMENTS ON THE RESURRECTION 8.[60]

THE TWO PARTS OF A PERSON—SOUL AND BODY. ATHENAGORAS: Nor again is it the happiness of soul separated from body, for we are not inquiring about the life or final cause of either of the parts of which humans consist but of the being who is composed of both. For this is true for every person who has a share in this present existence, and there must be some appropriate end proposed for this life. But if it is the end of both parts together—and this can be discovered neither while they are still living in the present state of existence through the numerous causes already mentioned, nor yet when the soul is in a state of separation because the person cannot be said to exist when the body is dissolved, and indeed entirely scattered abroad, even though the soul continue on by itself—it is absolutely necessary that the end of a person's being should appear in some reconstitution of the two together, and of the same living being. And since this necessarily follows, there must by all means be a resurrection of the bodies that are dead or even entirely dissolved. The same human beings must be formed anew, since the law of nature ordains the end not absolutely, nor as the end of any human beings whatsoever, but of the same human beings who passed through the previous life. But it is impossible for the same human beings to be reconstituted unless the same bodies are restored to the same souls. But it is impossible for the same soul to obtain the same body in any other way, and this is possible only by the resurrection because if this takes place, an end befitting the nature of human beings also follows. And we will make no mistake in saying that the final cause of an intelligent life and rational judgment is to be occupied uninterruptedly with those things to

---
[60]ANF 1:297-98.

which the natural reason is chiefly and primarily adapted. Thus we may delight unceasingly in the contemplation of him who is, and of his decrees, notwithstanding that the majority of human beings, because they are affected too passionately and too violently by things below, pass through life without attaining this end. For the large number of those who fail to attain the end that belongs to them does not void the destiny we have in common, since the examination relates to individuals, and the reward or punishment of lives ill or well spent is proportioned to the merit of each. ON THE RESURRECTION 25.[61]

HUMAN THOUGHTS. TERTULLIAN: Come now, let our opponents sever the connection of the flesh with the soul in the affairs of life so that they may be even bolder in separating the two in the rewards of the life to come. Let them deny the flesh and soul's cooperation in what we do so that they may be fairly able to deny also their participation in rewards. The flesh ought not to have any share in the sentence if it had no share in the cause of that sentence. Let the soul alone be called back, if it alone went astray. But nothing of the kind ever happened because the soul did not act alone when it departed from this life any more than it acted alone when it ran through the course of life from which it departed—I mean this present life. Indeed, the soul by itself is so far from conducting the affairs of life on its own that even our thoughts are not isolated from the communion they have with our flesh—however isolated those thoughts may be, however unprecipitated into action by means of the flesh they may be. We know this is the case since whatever is done in the human heart is done by the soul in the flesh and with the flesh and through the flesh. The Lord, in short, when rebuking our thoughts, includes in his censures this aspect of the flesh, the human heart, the citadel of the soul: "Why are you thinking evil in your hearts?"[62] and again, "Whoever looks on a woman to lust after her has already committed adultery with her in his heart."[63] Therefore even the thought, without doing anything or affecting anything, is an act of the flesh. But if you allow that the faculty that rules the senses and that the Greeks call *hegemonikon*[64] has its sanctuary in the brain or in the interval between the eyebrows—or wherever the philosophers are pleased to locate it—the flesh will still be the thinking place of the soul. The soul is never without the flesh, as long as it is in the flesh: it performs no act without the flesh because apart from the flesh the soul does not exist. Consider carefully, too, whether the thoughts are not administered by the flesh, since it is through the flesh that they are distinguished and known externally. Let the soul only meditate some design and the face then gives the indication—the face being the mirror of all our intentions. They may deny all combination in acts, but they cannot deny their cooperation in thoughts. Still they enumerate the sins of the flesh. Surely, then, for its sinful conduct the flesh must be consigned to punishment. But we, moreover, allege against them the virtues of the flesh. Surely then also for its virtuous conduct it deserves a future reward. Again, as it is the soul that acts and impels us in all we do, so it is the function of the flesh to render obedience. Now we are not permitted to suppose that God is either unjust or idle. He would, however, be unjust if he were to exclude from reward the flesh, which is associated in good works. He would also be idle were he to exempt it from punishment when it has been an accomplice in evil deeds. Human judgment is deemed to be the more perfect when it discovers who is responsible for every act and then neither spares the guilty nor begrudges the virtuous their full share of either punishment or praise with the principals who employed their services. ON THE RESURRECTION OF THE FLESH 15.[65]

---

[61]ANF 2:162. [62]Mt 9:4. [63]Mt 5:28. [64]The leading power. [65]ANF 3:555**.

A Marriage of Spirit and Flesh. Tertullian: And so the flesh will rise again—all of it in every person, in its own identity, in its absolute integrity. Wherever it may be, it is in safe keeping in God's presence, through that most faithful "mediator between God and man, the man Jesus Christ."[66] He will reconcile both God to humanity, and humanity to God; the spirit to the flesh, and the flesh to the spirit. He has already united both natures in his own self. He has fitted them together as bride and bridegroom in the reciprocal bond of wedded life. Now, if any should insist on making the soul the bride, then the flesh will follow the soul as her dowry. The soul will never be an outcast, to be kept at home by the bridegroom bare and naked. She has her dowry, her outfit, her fortune in the flesh, which will accompany her with the love and fidelity of a foster sister. But if you think of the flesh as the bride, then in Christ Jesus she has in the contract of his blood received his Spirit as her spouse. Now, what you take to be her extinction, you may be sure is only her temporary retirement. It is not the soul only that withdraws from view. On the Resurrection of the Flesh 63.[67]

At Their Appointed Time. Irenaeus: If the mingled cup and the bread that has been made receives the Word of God and the Eucharist of the blood and the body of Christ is made—and these are the things from which the substance of our flesh is increased and supported—how can they affirm that the flesh is incapable of receiving the gift of God, which is eternal life, when the flesh itself is nourished from the body and blood of the Lord and is one of his members? The blessed Paul declares the same thing in his epistle to the Ephesians: "we are members of his body, of his flesh, and of his bones."[68] He does not speak these words of some spiritual and invisible person, for a spirit has not bones or flesh. Rather, he refers to that dispensation by which the Lord became an actual man, consisting of flesh and nerves and bones—that flesh that is nourished by the cup that is his blood and receives increase from the bread, which is his body. And just as a cutting from the vine planted in the ground bears fruit in its season, or as a grain of wheat falling into the earth and becoming decomposed rises with manifold increase by the Spirit of God, who contains all things, and then, through the wisdom of God, serves for the use of people, and having received the Word of God becomes the Eucharist, which is the body and blood of Christ—in this same way also our bodies, being nourished by it and deposited in the earth and suffering decomposition there, will rise at their appointed time. The Word of God grants them resurrection to the glory of God, even the Father, who freely gives to this mortal immortality and to this corruptible incorruption, because the strength of God is made perfect in weakness. Against Heresies 5.2.3.[69]

Souls Awaiting Resurrection. Irenaeus: The Lord observed the law of the dead so that he might become the first-begotten from the dead. He waited around "in the lower parts of the earth"[70] until the third day and then rose in the flesh afterward, even showing the print of the nails to his disciples,[71] and then ascended to the Father. If all these things occurred, how confused must these people be who allege that "the lower parts" refer to this world of ours but that their inner man, leaving the body here, ascends into the supercelestial place? The Lord "went away in the midst of the shadow of death"[72] to where the souls of the dead were. And yet he arose afterward in the body, and after the resurrection he was taken up into heaven. If this is so, then it is obvious that the souls of his disciples, who tell us that

---

[66]1 Tim 2:5. [67]ANF 3:593-94**. [68]Eph 5:30. [69]ANF 1:528. [70]Eph 4:9. [71]Jn 20:20, 27. [72]Ps 23:4.

these things happened to the Lord, will also go away into the invisible place allotted to them by God and remain there until the resurrection while they wait for that event to occur. Then, when they receive their bodies and rise in their entirety, that is, bodily, just as the Lord arose, they will come in this way into the presence of God. "For no disciple is above the Master, but everyone that is perfect will be as his Master."[73] AGAINST HERESIES 5.31.2.[74]

THE TIME OF RESURRECTION. ORIGEN: The apostolic teaching is that the soul, having a substance and life of its own, shall, after its departure from the world, be rewarded according to what it deserves. It is destined to obtain either an inheritance of eternal life and blessedness if its actions will have procured this for it or to be delivered up to eternal fire and punishments if the guilt of its crimes will have brought it down to this. They also teach that there is to be a time of resurrection from the dead, when this body, which now "is sown in corruption will rise in incorruption," and that which "is sown in dishonor will rise in glory."[75] ON FIRST PRINCIPLES, PREFACE 5.[76]

THE SPIRITUAL CONDITION OF THE BODY. ORIGEN: When, therefore, all rational souls will have been restored to this kind of condition, then the nature of this body of ours will undergo a change into the glory of a spiritual body. For some rational natures have lived in a condition of degradation because of their sins, while others have been called to a state of happiness on account of their merits. But just as we see those same souls, who had formerly been sinful, assisted to a state of happiness after their conversion and reconciliation to God, so we should also consider, with respect to the nature of the body, that the one that we now make use of in a state of mediocrity, corruption and weakness, is not a different body from that which we will possess in incorruption, power and glory. Instead, that same body, when it has cast away the infirmities in which it is now entangled, will be transformed into a condition of glory, being rendered a spiritual body. Thus, what was a vessel of dishonor may, when cleansed, become a vessel of honor and an abode of blessedness. ON FIRST PRINCIPLES 3.6.6.[77]

THE VOICE OF THE TRUMPET. APHRAHAT: Listen, O fool, to the following instruction. Each seed is clothed in its own body. You never sow wheat and yet reap barley. You never plant a vine and yet have it produce figs. Everything grows according to its nature. Thus, the body that was laid in the earth is also the one that will rise again. And concerning the fact that the body is corrupted and wastes away, you ought to be instructed by the parable of the seed. When the seed is cast into the earth, it decays and is corrupted, and from its decay it produces and buds and bears fruit. For the land that is plowed, into which seed is not cast, produces no fruit, even if that land drinks in all the rain. In the same way, the grave in which the dead are not buried will not produce people when the quickening of the dead occurs, although the full voice of the trumpet should sound within it. And if, as they say, the spirit of the just will ascend into heaven and put on a heavenly body, they are in heaven. And he who raises the dead lives in heaven. Then when our Savior comes, whom will he raise up from the earth? And why did he write for us, "The hour will come, and now is, that the dead also will hear the voice of the Son of Man, and they will live and come forth from their tombs"?[78] For the heavenly body will not come and enter into the tomb and again go forth from it. DEMONSTRATIONS 8.3.[79]

READY TO DIE FOR GOD. CYRIL OF JERUSALEM: The root of all good works is the hope

---

[73]Lk 6:40. [74]ANF 1:560. [75]1 Cor 15:42-43. [76]ANF 4:240. [77]ANF 4:347. [78]Jn 5:25, 28, 29. [79]NPNF 2 13:375-76*.

of the resurrection. The expectation of the reward strengthens the soul to undertake good works. Every laborer is ready to endure the toils if he foresees the reward of his toils. But when people weary themselves without seeing any return, their spirit soon fails along with their body. A soldier who expects rewards is ready for war; but no soldier serving an undiscerning king, who bestows no premiums for work done, is ready to die for him. So every soul believing in the resurrection is naturally concerned about itself, but the unbelieving soul abandons itself to perdition. He who believes that the body is destined for resurrection is careful of his robe and does not defile it by fornication. But he who does not believe in the resurrection gives way to fornication, abusing his body as though it were not part of himself. Faith in the resurrection of the dead is a central precept and teaching of the holy catholic church. It is both central and essential. Though denied by many, it is fully confirmed by the truth. Greeks deny it, Samaritans disbelieve it, heretics attack it viciously. Denial takes many forms. Truth is uniform. CATECHETICAL LECTURE 18.1.[80]

THE SPLENDOR OF THE FIRMAMENT. CYRIL OF JERUSALEM: Note particularly how Paul, all but pointing the finger, says, "For this corruptible body must put on incorruption, and this mortal body must put on immortality."[81] For this body will be raised, not in its present weakness; it will be raised the very same body, but by putting on incorruption, it will be transformed, just as iron becomes fire when combined with fire, or rather as the Lord, who raises us, knows. This body, therefore, will rise, but it will not abide in its present condition, but as an eternal body. No longer will it, as now, need nourishment for life or stairs for its ascent, for it will become spiritual, a marvelous thing, beggaring description. "Then will the just," it is said, "shine forth like the sun and the moon and like the splendor of the firmament."[82] God, foreknowing people's unbelief, has given to the smallest worms to emit from their bodies beams of light in the summer, that natural fluorescence might be a parable of what we expect. For he who gives in part can also give wholly; and he who makes the worm shine luminously will much more illumine the just person. CATECHETICAL LECTURE 18.18.[83]

LIKE A TORCH. METHODIUS OF OLYMPUS: And as Thallousa said that there is a chastity of the eyes and of the ears and of the tongue, and so on of the other senses, so here she who keeps inviolate the faith of the five pathways of virtue—sight, taste, smell, touch and hearing—is called by the name of the five virgins, because she has kept the five forms of the senses pure to Christ, as a lamp, causing the light of holiness to shine forth clearly from each of them. For the flesh is truly, as it were, our five-lighted lamp, which the soul will bear like a torch, when it stands before Christ the bridegroom, on the day of the resurrection, showing its faith springing out clear and bright through all the senses, as he taught, saying, "I am come to send fire on the earth; and what will I if it be already kindled?"[84]—meaning by the earth our bodies in which he wished the swift-moving and fiery operation of his doctrine to be kindled. Now the oil represents wisdom and righteousness. For while the soul rains down unsparingly and pours forth these things on the body, the light of virtue is kindled unquenchably, making its good actions shine before people, so that our Father who is in heaven may be glorified. SYMPOSIUM OR THE BANQUET OF THE TEN VIRGINS 6.3.[85]

A DROP OF WATER FOR THE SOUL IN HELL. AUGUSTINE: Now regarding the point . . . that souls after leaving the body are judged, before

---

[80]FC 64:120*. [81]1 Cor 15:53. [82]See Mt 13:43; Dan 12:3. [83]FC 64:130-31. [84]Lk 12:49. [85]ANF 6:330.

they come to that final judgment to which they must submit when their bodies are restored to them and are either tormented or glorified in the very same flesh wherein they once lived here on earth—let me ask you if it really is the case that you were ignorant of this? Who has ever had his mind so obstinately set against the gospel that he did not hear these truths, and after hearing believe them? We hear them, for instance, in the parable of the poor man who was carried away after death to Abraham's bosom and of the rich man who is set forth as suffering torment in hell.[86] But has this man[87] taught you how it was that the soul apart from the body could crave from the beggar's finger a drop of water[88] when he himself confessed that the soul did not require bodily help except for the purpose of protecting the perishing body, which encloses it from dissolution? These are his[89] words: "Is it," asks he, "because the soul craves meat and drink that we suppose material food passes into it?" Then shortly afterwards he says, "From this circumstance it is understood and proved, that the sustenance of meat and drink is not wanted for the soul but for the body, for which clothing also, in addition to food, is provided in a similar way. Thus, the supplying of food seems to be necessary to that nature that is also fitted for wearing clothes." This opinion of his he expounds clearly enough. He, however, adds some illustrative similes, saying, "Now what do we suppose the occupier of a house does on an inspection of his dwelling? If he observe the tenement has a shaky roof, or a nodding wall or a weak foundation, does he not fetch girders and build up buttresses in order that he may succeed in propping up by his care and diligence the fabric that threatened to fall, so that in the dangerous plight of the residence the peril that evidently overhung the occupier might be warded off? From this simile," he says, "see how the soul craves for its flesh, from which it undoubtedly conceives the craving itself." Such are the very lucid and adequate words in which this young person has explained his ideas. He asserts that it is not the soul but the body that requires food. This is, no doubt, out of a careful regard of the soul for the body, as one that occupies a dwelling house and by a prudent repair prevents the downfall with which the fleshly tenement was threatened. Well, now, let him go on to explain to you what probable ruin this particular soul of the rich man was so eager to prevent by propping up, seeing that it no longer possessed a mortal body and yet suffered thirst, and begged for the drop of water from the poor man's finger. Here is a good knotty question for this astute instructor of elderly people to exercise himself on. Let him inquire, and find a solution if he can. For what purpose did that soul in hell beg the sustenance of ever so small a drop of water, when it had no ruinous tenement to support? ON THE SOUL AND ITS ORIGIN 2.4.8.[90]

THE MATURE MEASURE OF THE FULLNESS OF CHRIST. AUGUSTINE: One thing is certain, namely, that Christ rose with the same stature he had when he died. And it would be wrong to say that when the time for the general resurrection comes, anything will be added to the size in which he appeared to his disciples and was known to them, for the sake of making him as tall as the tallest men. On the other hand, if we say that the taller bodies are to be reduced to conform to his size, then much of many bodies would have to perish, contrary to his promise. We are left, therefore, with one conclusion, namely, that each of us will have that size we had in our maturity, even though we die in extreme old age; or we will have that size we would have had in our maturity, in case we died earlier. Thus, we must interpret Paul's words concerning "the mature measure of the fullness of Christ" as meaning, for example,

---

[86]See Lk 16:22-23. [87]Vincentius Victor, who was providing erroneous teaching to Peter the Presbyter, to whom this treatise by Augustine was addressed. [88]Lk 16:24. [89]I.e., Victor's. [90]NPNF 1 5:334.

that the measure of his fullness will be reached when all of his members, the Christian people, will have been added to Christ the head; or the words may mean, if they have reference to the resurrection, that all will rise with bodies neither less nor larger than the size of their mature age, and so in the age and vigor of thirty years—since that is the age reached by Christ and the age that even secular authorities consider the age of maturity and the age beyond which a person declines toward the weakness of old age. That is why Paul did not speak of the measure either of the body or of the stature but of "the measure of the age of the fullness of Christ."[91] CITY OF GOD 22.15.[92]

THE SEX OF WOMEN AFTER THE RESURRECTION. AUGUSTINE: There are some who think that in the resurrection all will be men and that women will lose their sex. This view springs from an interpretation of the texts "Until we all attain to . . . perfect manhood, to the mature measure of the fullness of Christ" and "conformed to the image of the Son of God."[93] The interpretation is based on the fact that the man was made by God out of the slime of the earth, whereas the woman was made from the man. For myself, I think that those others are more sensible who have no doubt that both sexes will remain in the resurrection. After all, there will then be none of that lust that is the cause of shame in connection with sex, and so, all will be as before the first sin, when the man and the woman were naked and felt no shame. In the resurrection, the blemishes of the body will be gone, but the nature of the body will remain. And, certainly, a woman's sex is her nature and no blemish; only, in the resurrection, there will be no conception or childbearing associated with her nature. Her members will remain as before, with the former purpose sublimated to a newer beauty. There will be no concupiscence to arouse, and none will be aroused, but her womanhood will be a hymn to the wisdom of God, who first made her a woman, and to the clemency of God, who freed her from the corruption into which she fell.

Even in the beginning, when woman was made from a rib in the side of the sleeping man, that had no less a purpose than to symbolize prophetically the union of Christ and his church. Adam's sleep was a mystical foreshadowing of Christ's death, and when his dead body hanging from the cross was pierced by the lance, it was from his side that there issued forth that blood and water, which, as we know, signify the sacraments by which the church is built up. "Built" is the very word the Scripture uses in connection with Eve: "He built the rib into a woman,"[94] *aedificavit* ["built"], not *formavit* ["formed"] or *finxit* ["shaped"]. So too Paul speaks of "building up the body of Christ,"[95] which is his church. Therefore, woman is as much the creation of God as man is. If she was made from the man, this was to show her oneness with him; and if she was made in the way she was, this was to prefigure the oneness of Christ and the church.

God, then, who made us man and woman will raise us up as man and woman. This is proved by Christ's own words. He was asked by the Sadducees, who denied the resurrection: "At the resurrection, of which of the seven will she be the wife?" (She had been married by seven brothers in turn, each hoping "to raise up the issue of his brother," as the law prescribed.)[96] Jesus answered, "You err because you know neither the Scripture nor the power of God. For at the resurrection they will neither marry nor be given in marriage but are as the angels of God in heaven." (Notice that he did not say, "The wife you ask about will no longer be a woman but a man.") And when he said they will be "as the angels," he meant like the angels in respect to immortality and beatitude, not like them in being spirits without

---

[91]Eph 4:13.　[92]FC 24:461-62.　[93]Rom 8:29.　[94]Gen 2:22.　[95]Eph 4:12.　[96]See Mt 22:23-30.

bodies, nor like them in the resurrection, since angels had no need of a resurrection, simply because they could not die.

What our Lord said was that in the resurrection, there would be no marriage. He did not say that there would be no women. In the context it would have been an easier answer to the question asked to have said that there would be no women—if that was to be the case in the resurrection. Actually, he affirmed that there would be women when he used the double expression "neither marry" (as men do) nor "be given in marriage" (as in the case of women). In the resurrection, then, there will be those who on earth "marry" and those who "are given in marriage." Only, in heaven there will be no marriage. CITY OF GOD 22.17.[97]

SOUL AND BODY ARE ALWAYS TOGETHER. JOHN OF DAMASCUS: We believe also in the resurrection of the dead. For there will be, in truth, a resurrection of the dead—and by resurrection we mean the resurrection of bodies. For resurrection is the second state of that which has fallen. For the souls are immortal, so how can they rise again? For if they define death as the separation of soul and body, resurrection surely is the reunion of soul and body and the second state of the living creature that has suffered dissolution and downfall. It is, then, this very body, which is corruptible and liable to dissolution, that will rise again incorruptible. For he who made it in the beginning of the sand of the earth does not lack the power to raise it up again after it has been dissolved again and returned to the earth from which it was taken, in accordance with the reversal of the Creator's judgment.

For if there is no resurrection, let us eat and drink. Let us pursue a life of pleasure and enjoyment. If there is no resurrection, how do we differ from the irrational brutes? If there is no resurrection, let us hold the wild beasts of the field happy who have a life free from sorrow. If there is no resurrection, neither is there any God or Providence, but all things are driven and borne along of themselves. For observe how we see most righteous people suffering hunger and injustice and receiving no help in the present life, while sinners and unrighteous people abound in riches and every delight. And who in his right mind would take this for the work of a righteous judgment or a wise providence? There must, therefore, be a resurrection. For God is just and is the one who rewards those who submit patiently to him. Therefore if it is the soul alone that engages in the contests of virtue, it is also the soul alone that will receive the crown. And if it were the soul alone that revels in pleasures, it would also be the soul alone that would be justly punished. But since the soul does not pursue either virtue or vice separate from the body, both together will obtain that which is their just due. ORTHODOX FAITH 4.27.[98]

WE HAVE TO BELIEVE IN THE RESURRECTION. PETER CHRYSOLOGUS: The one who does not believe in the resurrection of the flesh has no faith in what was said above, as the apostle says: "If the dead will not rise, then neither did Christ rise." Whom will God judge and with whom will he reign if the resurrection does not restore to life and to judgment those whom death has removed from the world? SERMON 58.14.[99]

The Millennium

THE CHRISTIAN'S FAITH IN THE EVERLASTING LIFE. JUSTIN MARTYR: And Trypho to this replied, "I remarked to you, sir, that you are very anxious to be safe in all respects, since you cling to the Scriptures. But tell me, do you really admit that this place, Jerusalem, will be rebuilt? Do you expect your people to be gathered together and made joyful with Christ and the patriarchs, and the prophets, both the

---

[97]FC 24:463-65. [98]NPNF 2 9:99. [99]FC 109:224.

people of our nation and other proselytes who joined them before your Christ came? Or have you given way and admitted this in order to have the appearance of overcoming us in the controversies?" Then I answered, "I am not so miserable a fellow, Trypho, as to say one thing and think another. I admitted to you formerly that I and many others are of this opinion and believe that such will take place, as you assuredly are aware. However, on the other hand, I signified to you that many who belong to the pure and pious faith and are true Christians think otherwise. . . . But I and others, who are right-minded Christians on all points, are assured that there will be a resurrection of the dead, and a thousand years in Jerusalem, which will then be built, adorned and enlarged, the prophets Ezekiel and Isaiah and others declare. DIALOGUE WITH TRYPHO 80.[100]

CHILDREN OF THE GOD OF THE RESURRECTION. JUSTIN MARTYR: We have perceived, moreover, that the expression "The day of the Lord is as a thousand years"[101] is connected with this subject. And further, there was a certain man with us, whose name was John, one of the apostles of Christ, who prophesied, by a revelation that was made to him, that those who believed in our Christ would dwell a thousand years in Jerusalem and that thereafter the general and, in short, the eternal resurrection and judgment of all people would likewise take place. Just as our Lord also said, "They will neither marry nor be given in marriage but will be equal to the angels, the children of the God of the resurrection." DIALOGUE WITH TRYPHO 81.[102]

HERETICAL DISCOURSES. IRENAEUS: Inasmuch, therefore, as the opinions of certain orthodox persons are derived from heretical discourses, they are both ignorant of God's dispensations, and of the mystery of the resurrection of the just and of the earthly kingdom that is the commencement of incorruption. By means of this kingdom those who will be worthy become accustomed gradually to partake of the divine nature *(capere Deum)*. Concerning these things, it is necessary to tell them that the righteous must first receive the promise of the inheritance that God promised to the ancestors. They will also reign in this kingdom when they rise again to behold God in this creation that is renovated. The judgment, then, will take place afterward. For it is just that in that very creation in which they toiled or were afflicted, being proved in every way by suffering, they should receive the reward of their suffering. It is just that in the creation in which they were killed because of their love for God that they should be revived again in that very same creation. And that in the creation in which they endured servitude, in that same creation they should reign. AGAINST HERESIES 5.32.1.[103]

THE LIFE EVERLASTING. IRENAEUS: The predicted blessing, therefore, belongs unquestionably to the times of the kingdom when the righteous will rule once they have risen from the dead. At this time the creation, having been renovated and set free, will also become fruitful with an abundance of all kinds of food from the dew of heaven and from the fertility of the earth—just as the elders who saw John, the disciple of the Lord, related that they had heard from him how the Lord used to teach in regard to these times. He would say, The days will come, in which vines will grow, each having ten thousand branches, and in each branch ten thousand twigs, and in each true twig ten thousand shoots, and in each one of the shoots ten thousand clusters, and on every one of the clusters ten thousand grapes, and every grape when pressed will give twenty-five *metretes*[104] of wine. And when any one of the saints will lay hold

---

[100]ANF 1:239. [101]2 Pet 3:8. [102]ANF 1:240. [103]ANF 1:561**.
[104]A *metrete* was the primary liquid measurement of the ancient Greeks. One *metrete* was approximately 9 gallons, or 39.4 liters. Thus the amount of wine mentioned here was around 225 gallons, or 985 liters.

of a cluster, another will cry out, "I am a better cluster, take me; bless the Lord through me." In a similar way the Lord declared that a grain of wheat would produce ten thousand ears, and that every ear should have ten thousand grains and every grain would yield ten pounds of clear, pure, fine flour; and that all other fruit-bearing trees and seeds and grass would produce in similar proportions; and that all animals feeding only on the produce of the earth would become peaceful and live in harmony with each other, and be in perfect subjection to people. AGAINST HERESIES 5.33.3.[105]

THE NEW HEAVEN AND THE NEW EARTH. IRENAEUS: For since there are real human beings, there must also be a real planting (*plantationem*) so that they do not vanish and cease to exist but instead progress among those which have an actual existence. For neither is the substance nor the essence of the creation annihilated (because he who established it is faithful and true). However, "the fashion of the world passes away,"[106] that is, those things among which transgression has occurred, since humankind has grown old in them. And therefore this present fashion has been formed as a temporary measure since God foreknows all things. I have pointed out in the preceding book and have also shown, as far as was possible, the reason for the creation of this world of temporal things. But when this present fashion of things passes away and human beings have been renewed and flourish in an incorruptible state, so as to preclude the possibility of becoming old, then there will be a new heaven and a new earth in which the new humanity will always remain, always having fresh and new conversations with God. And since these things will continue forever without end, Isaiah declares, "For as the new heavens and the new earth which I do make, continue in my sight, says the Lord, so will your seed and your name remain."[107] And as the presbyters say, "Then those who are deemed worthy of an abode in heaven will go there. Others will enjoy the delights of paradise, and others will possess the splendor of the city. For the Savior will be seen everywhere in proportion to the worthiness of those who see him." AGAINST HERESIES 5.36.1.[108]

THE HEAVENLY KINGDOM. TERTULLIAN: But we do confess that a kingdom is promised to us on the earth, although before heaven, only in another state of existence; inasmuch as it will be after the resurrection for a thousand years in the divinely built city of Jerusalem, "let down from heaven,"[109] which the apostle also calls "our mother from above."[110] And, while declaring that our *politeuma*, or citizenship, is in heaven, he predicates of it that it is really a city in heaven. This both Ezekiel had knowledge of and the apostle John beheld. And the word of the new prophecy, which is a part of our belief, attests how it foretold that there would be for a sign a picture of this very city exhibited to view prior to its manifestation. This prophecy, indeed, has been very lately fulfilled in an expedition to the East. For it is evident from the testimony of even heathen witnesses, that in Judea there was suspended in the sky a city early every morning for forty days. As the day advanced, the entire figure of its walls would wane gradually, and sometimes it would vanish instantly. We say that this city has been provided by God for receiving the saints on their resurrection and refreshing them with the abundance of all really spiritual blessings, as a reward for those which in the world we have either despised or lost. For it is both just and God-worthy that his servants should have their joy in the place where they have also suffered affliction for his name's sake. The process for the heavenly kingdom is the following: After its thousand years are over—the period in which is completed the

---

[105]ANF 1:562-63*. [106]1 Cor 7:31. [107]Is 66:22. [108]ANF 1:566-67. [109]Rev 21:2. [110]Gal 4:26.

resurrection of the saints who rise earlier or later depending on what they deserve—the destruction of the world and the conflagration of all things will ensue at the judgment. We will then be changed in a moment into the substance of angels, even by the investiture of an incorruptible nature, and thus will be removed to that kingdom in heaven of which we have now been treating, just as if it had not been predicted by the Creator and as if it were proving Christ to belong to the other god and as if he were the first and sole revealer of it. But now learn that it has been, in fact, predicted by the Creator and that even without prediction it has a claim upon our faith in respect of the Creator. AGAINST MARCION 3.25.[111]

ALL THINGS WILL BE PEACEFUL AND TRANQUIL. LACTANTIUS: The Son of the most high and mighty God will come to judge the living and the dead, as the Sibyl testifies and says, "For then there will be confusion of mortals throughout the whole earth, when the Almighty himself will come on his judgment seat to judge the souls of the living and the dead and all the world." But Christ—after he will have destroyed unrighteousness and executed his great judgment and recalled to life all the righteous who have ever lived from the beginning—will be engaged among people a thousand years and will rule them with the utmost justice. The Sibyl proclaims this in another place, as she utters her inspired predictions: "Hear me, you mortals. An everlasting king reigns." Then they who will be alive in their bodies will not die. Rather, during those thousand years they will produce an infinite multitude, and their offspring will be holy and loved by God. But those who will be raised from the dead will preside over the living as judges. The nations, however, will not be entirely wiped out. Some will be left as a victory for God so that they may be the occasion of triumph for the righteous and may be subjected to perpetual slavery. About the same time the prince of the devils, who is the one who contrives all evil, will be bound with chains and imprisoned during the thousand years of the heavenly rule in which righteousness will reign in the world, so that he may contrive no evil against the people of God. After his coming the righteous will be gathered from all the earth, and once the judgment is completed, the sacred city will be planted in the middle of the earth in which God the builder may dwell together with the righteous as their ruler there. And the Sibyl marks out this city when she says, "And the city that God made, this he made more brilliant than the stars and sun and moon." Then that darkness will be taken away from the world with which the heaven will be overspread and darkened, and the moon will receive the brightness of the sun, nor will it be further diminished. Instead, the sun will become seven times brighter than it now is, and the earth will open its fruitfulness and bring forth most abundant fruits on its own. The rocky mountains will drip with honey, streams of wine will run down, and rivers will flow with milk. In short, the world itself will rejoice and all nature exult, being rescued and set free from the dominion of evil and impiety and guilt and error. Throughout this time beasts will not be nourished by blood or birds by prey; but all things will be peaceful and tranquil. Lions and calves will stand together at the manger, the wolf will not carry off the sheep, the hound will not hunt for prey; hawks and eagles will not injure; the infant will play with serpents. In short, those things will then come to pass that the poets spoke of as being done in the reign of Saturnus. DIVINE INSTITUTES 7.24.[112]

THE KINGDOM OF CHRIST WILL BE AN EARTHLY ONE. EUSEBIUS OF CAESAREA: We have understood that at this time Cerinthus, the author of another heresy, made his appear-

---

[111]ANF 3:342-43. [112]ANF 7:219.

ance. Caius, whose words we quoted above, in the disputation that is ascribed to him, writes as follows concerning this man: "But Cerinthus also, by means of revelations that he pretends were written by a great apostle brings before us marvelous things that he falsely claims were shown him by angels. He says that after the resurrection the kingdom of Christ will be set up on earth and that the flesh dwelling in Jerusalem will again be subject to desires and pleasures. And being an enemy of the Scriptures of God, he asserts, with the purpose of deceiving people, that there is to be a period of a thousand years for marriage festivals." And Dionysius, who was bishop of the parish of Alexandria in our day, in the second book of his work *On the Promises*, where he says some things concerning the Apocalypse of John that he draws from tradition, mentions this same man in the following words: "But they say that Cerinthus, who founded the sect that was named after him, the Cerinthian, desiring reputable authority for his fiction, prefixed the name. For the doctrine that he taught was this: that the kingdom of Christ will be an earthly one." ECCLESIASTICAL HISTORY 3.28.1-4.[113]

MISUNDERSTANDING APOSTOLIC ACCOUNTS. EUSEBIUS OF CAESAREA: The same writer [Papias] also provides other accounts that he says came to him through unwritten tradition, certain strange parables and teachings of the Savior and some other more mythical things. To these belong his statement that there will be a period of some thousand years after the resurrection of the dead and that the kingdom of Christ will be set up in material form on this very earth. I suppose he got these ideas through a misunderstanding of the apostolic accounts, not perceiving that the things said by them were spoken mystically in figures. For he appears to have been of very limited understanding, as one can see from his discourses. But it was due to him that so many of the church fathers after him

adopted a similar opinion, influenced in their own support by the antiquity of the man—as for instance Irenaeus and anyone else who may have proclaimed similar views. ECCLESIASTICAL HISTORY 3.39.11-13.[114]

THE PROMISES OF GOD. EUSEBIUS OF CAESAREA: Besides all these, the two books *On the Promises* were prepared by him.[115] The occasion of these was Nepos, a bishop in Egypt, who taught that the promises to the holy people in the divine Scriptures should be understood in a more Jewish manner and that there would be a certain millennium of bodily luxury on this earth. As he thought that he could establish his private opinion by the Revelation of John, he wrote a book on this subject titled *Refutation of Allegorists*. Dionysius opposes this in his books *On the Promises*. In the first he gives his own opinion of the dogma. In the second he deals with the Revelation of John. He mentions Nepos at the beginning and then writes the following about him: "But since they bring forward a certain work of Nepos, on which they rely confidently, as if it proved beyond dispute that there will be a reign of Christ on earth, I confess that in many other respects I approve and love Nepos, for his faith and industry and diligence in the Scriptures and for his extensive psalmody, with which many of the brethren are still delighted." ECCLESIASTICAL HISTORY 7.24.1-4.[116]

HUMAN SIN AND THE HAPPINESS OF PARADISE. AUGUSTINE: Now those who, on the strength of this passage, got the notion that the first resurrection was to be a bodily one were influenced in this direction mainly by the matter of the thousand years. The notion was that the saints were destined to enjoy so protracted a sabbath of repose, a holy leisure, that

---

[113]NPNF 2 1:160-61. [114]NPNF 2 1:172. [115]That is, Dionysius of Alexandria, a bishop of the third century who died around 265. He was a pupil of Origen. [116]NPNF 2 1:308*.

is, after the labors of the six thousand years stretching from the creation of man, his great sin and merited expulsion from the happiness of paradise into the unhappiness of this mortal life. The interpretation was worked out in the light of the Scripture text: "One day with the Lord is as a thousand years, and a thousand years as one day."[117] Thus, there was supposed to follow on the six thousand years taken as six days a seventh day or sabbath taking up the last thousand and to be given over to the resurrecting saints for celebration.

One might put up with such an interpretation if it included belief in some spiritual delights accruing to the saints from the Lord's company during that sabbath rest. In fact, I myself at one time accepted such an opinion. But when these interpreters say that the rising saints are to spend their time in limitless gourmandizing with such heaps of food and drink as not only go beyond all sense of decent restraint but go utterly beyond belief, then such an interpretation becomes wholly unacceptable save to the carnal-minded. But the spiritual-minded call those who can swallow the literal interpretation of the thousand years Chiliasts (from the Greek *chilias*, "a thousand") or millenarians (from the corresponding Latin word). CITY OF GOD 20.7.[118]

THE LAND OF PROMISE. METHODIUS OF OLYMPUS: Therefore, above all other things, I say to those who love contest, and who are strong-minded, that without delay they should honor chastity as a thing the most useful and glorious. For in the new and indissoluble creation, whoever will not be found decorated with the boughs of chastity will neither obtain rest, because he has not fulfilled the command of God according to the law, nor will he enter into the land of promise, because he has not previously celebrated the Feast of Tabernacles. For only those who have celebrated the Feast of Tabernacles come to the Holy Land, setting out from those dwellings that are called tabernacles until they come to enter into the temple and city of God, advancing to a greater and more glorious joy, as the Jewish types indicate. Like the Israelites, after leaving the borders of Egypt, first came to the Tabernacles and from there, having again set forth, came into the land of promise, so also do we. For I also, taking my journey and going forth from the Egypt of this life, came first to the resurrection, which is the true Feast of the Tabernacles. And there, having set up my tabernacle adorned with the fruits of virtue, on the first day of the resurrection, which is the day of judgment, I celebrate with Christ the millennium of rest that is called the seventh day, even the true sabbath. Then again from there I, a follower of Jesus, "who has entered into the heavens,"[119] as they also, after the rest of the Feast of Tabernacles came into the land of promise—I come into the heavens, not continuing to remain in tabernacles. In other words, my body does not remain as it was before but, after the space of a thousand years, it is changed from a human and corruptible form into an angelic size and beauty. This will be where at last we virgins, when the festival of the resurrection is consummated, will pass from the wonderful place of the tabernacle to greater and better things, ascending into the very house of God above the heavens, as the psalmist says, "in the voice of praise and thanksgiving, among such as keep the holy day."[120] SYMPOSIUM OR THE BANQUET OF THE TEN VIRGINS 9.5.[121]

WHEN SIX THOUSAND YEARS ARE ACCOMPLISHED. COMMODIAN: Adam was the first who fell, and that he might shun the precepts of God, Belial was his tempter by the lust of the palm tree. And he conferred on us also what he did, whether of good or of evil, since he was the head of all that was born from him. And be-

---

[117] 2 Pet 3:8. [118] FC 24:265-66*. [119] Heb 4:14. [120] Ps 42:4. [121] ANF 6:347.

cause of this we die by his means, as he himself, receding from the divine, became an outcast from the Word. We will be immortal when six thousand years are accomplished. The tree of the apple having been tasted, death has entered into the world. By this tree of death we are born to the life to come. INSTRUCTIONS 35.[122]

A THOUSAND YEARS ARE AS ONE DAY. VICTORINUS OF PETOVIUM: And thus in the sixth psalm for the eighth day, David asks the Lord that he would not rebuke him in his anger or judge him in his fury. For this is indeed the eighth day of that future judgment that will pass beyond the order of the sevenfold arrangement. Jesus also, the son of Nave,[123] the successor of Moses, broke the sabbath day; for on the sabbath day he commanded the children of Israel to march around the walls of the city of Jericho with trumpets and declare war against the foreigners. Matthias also, prince of Judah, broke the sabbath, for he killed the prefect of Antiochus the king of Syria on the sabbath and subdued the foreigners by pursuing them. And in Matthew we read how it was written that Isaiah as well as the rest of his colleagues broke the sabbath[124]—that that true and just sabbath should be observed in the seventh millennium. Therefore the Lord attributed to each of those seven days a thousand-year period. For thus went the warning: "In your eyes, O Lord, a thousand years are as one day."[125] Therefore in the eyes of the Lord each period of a thousand years is ordained, for I find that the Lord's eyes are seven.[126] Therefore, as I have narrated, that true sabbath will be in the seventh thousand-year period when Christ will reign with his elect. ON THE CREATION OF THE WORLD.[127]

The Vision of the End—In Light of the Origenist Controversy

THE FINAL PUNISHMENT FOR OUR SINS. ORIGEN: The end of the world, then, and the final consummation will take place when everyone will be subjected to punishment for his sins. This is a time that God alone knows, a time when he will bestow on each one what he deserves. We think, indeed, that the goodness of God, through his Christ, may recall all his creatures to one end, even his enemies that he conquered and subdued. For thus says holy Scripture, "The Lord said, 'Sit at my right hand, until I make your enemies your footstool.' "[128] And if the meaning of the prophet's language here is less clear, we may ascertain it from the apostle Paul, who speaks more openly, thus: "For Christ must reign until he has put all enemies under his feet."[129] But if even that unreserved declaration of the apostle does not sufficiently inform us what is meant by "enemies being placed under his feet," listen to what he says in the following words, "For all things must be put under him." What, then, is this "putting under" by which all things must be made subject to Christ? I am of the opinion that it is this very subjection by which we also wish to be subject to him, by which the apostles also were subject, and all the saints who have been followers of Christ. For the term "subjection," by which we are subject to Christ, indicates that the salvation that proceeds from him belongs to his subjects. This agrees with the declaration of David, "Shall not my soul be subject to God? From him comes my salvation."[130] ON FIRST PRINCIPLES 1.6.1.[131]

THE GOVERNMENT OF THE DEVIL. ORIGEN: It is to be borne in mind, however, that certain beings who fell away from that one beginning of which we have spoken have sunk to such a depth of unworthiness and wickedness as to be deemed altogether undeserving of that training and instruction by which the human race, while in the flesh, are trained and

---

[122]ANF 4:209. [123]That is, Joshua the son of Nun. [124]Mt 12:5. [125]Ps 90:4. [126]See Zech 4:10. [127]ANF 7:342. [128]Ps 110:1. [129]1 Cor 15:25. [130]Ps 62:1. [131]ANF 4:260*.

instructed with the assistance of the heavenly powers. These beings continue, on the contrary, in a state of enmity and opposition to those who are receiving this instruction and teaching. And thus it occurs that the whole of this mortal life is full of struggles and trials, caused by the opposition and enmity of those who fell from a better condition without at all looking back, and who are called the devil and his angels, and the other orders of evil, which the apostle classed among the opposing powers. But whether any of these orders who act under the government of the devil and obey his wicked commands will in a future world be converted to righteousness because they possess the faculty of free will, or whether persistent and inveterate wickedness may be changed by the power of habit into nature, is a result that you yourself, reader, may approve of, if neither in these present worlds that are seen and temporal nor in those that are unseen and are eternal, that portion is to differ entirely from the final unity and fitness of things. But in the meantime, both in those temporal worlds that are seen, as well as in those eternal worlds that are invisible, all those beings are arranged, according to a regular plan, in the order and degree of their merits. Thus some of them in the first, others in the second, some even in the last times—after having undergone heavier and more severe punishments, endured for a lengthened period and for many ages, so to speak—are improved by this stern method of training. They are restored at first by the instruction of the angels and subsequently by the powers of a higher grade. Thus advancing through each stage to a better condition, they reach even to that which is invisible and eternal, having traveled through, by a kind of training, every single office of the heavenly powers. From all of this I make the following inference: every rational nature may, in passing from one order to another, go through each to all and advance from all to each, while made the subject of various degrees of proficiency and failure according to its own actions and endeavors, put forth in the enjoyment of its power of free will. ON FIRST PRINCIPLES 1.6.3.[132]

THE WHOLE WORLD AS AN IMMENSE ANIMAL. ORIGEN: Although the whole world is arranged into offices of different kinds, its condition, nevertheless, is not to be supposed as one of internal discrepancies and discordances. Rather, as our one body is provided with many members and is held together by one soul, so I am of the opinion that the whole world also ought to be regarded as some huge and immense animal that is kept together by the power and reason of God as by one soul. This also, I think, is indicated in sacred Scripture by the declaration of the prophet, "Do not I fill heaven and earth?"[133] says the Lord and again, "The heaven is my throne, and the earth is my footstool"[134] and by the Savior's words, when he says that we are to swear "neither by heaven, for it is God's throne, nor by the earth, for it is his footstool."[135] The words of Paul speak to the same point in his address to the Athenians, when he says, "In him we live, and move, and have our being."[136] For how do we live and move and have our being in God, except by his comprehending and holding together the whole world by his power? And how is heaven the throne of God and the earth his footstool, as the Savior declares, except by his power filling all things both in heaven and earth, according to the Lord's own words? And that God, the Father of all things, fills and holds together the world with the fullness of his power, according to those passages that we have quoted, no one, I think, will have any difficulty in admitting. And now, since the course of the preceding discussion has shown that the different movements of rational beings, and their varying opinions, have brought about

---

[132]ANF 4:261*. [133]Jer 23:24. [134]Is 66:1. [135]Mt 5:34. [136]Acts 17:28.

the diversity that is in the world, we must see whether it may not be appropriate that this world should have a termination like its beginning. For there is no doubt that its end must be sought amid much diversity and variety. This variety, being found to exist in the termination of the world, will again furnish ground and occasion for the diversities of the other world that is to succeed the present. ON FIRST PRINCIPLES 2.1.3.[137]

THE MEASURE OF THE WORLD. ORIGEN: And now I do not understand by what proofs they can maintain their position who assert that worlds sometimes come into existence that are not dissimilar to each other but in all respects equal. For if there is said to be a world similar in all respects to the present, then it will inevitably be the case that Adam and Eve will do the same things that they did before. The same deluge will occur a second time, and the same Moses will again lead a nation numbering nearly six hundred thousand out of Egypt; Judas will also betray the Lord a second time; Paul will keep the garments of those who stoned Stephen a second time; and everything that has been done in this life will be said to be repeated—a state of things that I think cannot be established by any reasoning if souls are actuated by free will and maintain either their advance or regression according to the power of their will. For souls are not driven on in a cycle that returns after many ages to the same round, so as either to do or desire this or that. At whatever point the freedom of their own will aims, to that they direct the course of their actions. For what these persons say is much the same as if one were to assert that if a *medimnus* [measure] of grain were to be poured out on the ground, the fall of the grain would be on the second occasion identically the same as on the first, so that every individual grain would lie for the second time close beside that grain where it had been thrown before. And so, the *medimnus* would be scattered in the same order and with the same marks as formerly occurred. This certainly is an impossible result with the countless grains of a *medimnus*, even if they were to be poured out without ceasing for many ages. Therefore it seems to me impossible for a world to be restored for the second time, with the same order and with the same number of births and deaths and actions. But it may be possible that a diversity of worlds may exist with changes of no unimportant kind, so that the state of another world may be for some unmistakable reasons better, and for others worse and for others again intermediate. But what may be the number or measure of this I confess myself ignorant, although, if any one can tell what this might be, I would gladly learn. ON FIRST PRINCIPLES 2.3.4.[138]

THE FATHER AND THE SON. ORIGEN: But I am astonished how it can be conceived to be the meaning, that he who, while all things are not yet subdued to him, is not himself in subjection, should—at a time when all things have been subdued to him and when he has become king of all people and holds sway over all things—be supposed then to be made subject, seeing he was not formerly in subjection. For these kinds of people do not understand that the subjection of Christ to the Father indicates that our happiness has attained to perfection and that the work undertaken by him has been brought to a victorious termination, seeing he has not only purified the power of supreme government over the whole of creation but presents to the Father the principles of the obedience and subjection of the human race in a corrected and improved condition. If, then, that subjection is held to be good and salutary by which the Son is said to be subject to the Father, it is an extremely rational and logical inference to deduce that the subjection also of enemies, which is said to be made to the Son of God, should be understood as being also

---

[137]ANF 4:269*. [138]ANF 4:272-73*.

salutary and useful. This would be as if, when the Son is said to be subject to the Father, the perfect restoration of the whole of creation is signified. Thus, when enemies are said to be subjected to the Son of God, the salvation of the conquered and the restoration of the lost is understood to consist in that as well. ON FIRST PRINCIPLES 3.5.7.[139]

THE CONSUMMATION OF ALL THINGS. ORIGEN: But our belief is that the Word will prevail over the entire rational creation and change every soul into his own perfection. In this state everyone, by the mere exercise of his power, will choose what he desires and obtain what he chooses. For although, in the diseases and wounds of the body, there are some that no medical skill can cure, yet we hold that in the mind there is no evil so strong that it may not be overcome by the supreme Word and God. For stronger than all the evils in the soul is the Word and the healing power that dwells in him. And this healing he applies, according to the will of God, to every person. The consummation of all things is the destruction of evil, although as to the question whether it will be so destroyed that it can never anywhere arise again, it is beyond our present purpose to say. Many things are said obscurely in the prophecies on the total destruction of evil and the restoration to righteousness of every soul. AGAINST CELSUS 8.72.[140]

THE LAST ENEMY TO BE DESTROYED. ORIGEN: One meaning involves change, and this belongs, as it were, to a way and length that is revealed by the Scripture: "The beginning of a good way is to do justice."[141] For since a "good way" is very great, we must understand that the practical, which is presented by the phrase "to do justice," relates to the initial matters and the contemplative to those that follow. I think its stopping point and goal is in the so-called restoration because no one is left as an enemy then, if indeed the statement is true, "For he must reign until he has put all his enemies under his feet. And the last enemy to be destroyed is death."[142] COMMENTARY ON THE GOSPEL OF JOHN 1.91.[143]

EVERYTHING ADMITS OF CHANGE. ORIGEN: The last enemy, moreover, who is called death, is said on this account to be destroyed, that there may not be anything left that would cause us to mourn when death does not exist, or anything that is adverse when there is no enemy. The destruction of the last enemy, indeed, is to be understood not as if its substance, which was formed by God, is to perish, but because its mind and hostile will, which came not from God but from itself, are to be destroyed. Its destruction, therefore, will not be its nonexistence but in its ceasing to be an enemy and no longer existing as death. For nothing is impossible for the Omnipotent, nor is anything incapable of restoration to its Creator. For he made all things that they might exist, and those things that were made for existence cannot cease to be. This is also why they will admit of change and variety, so as to be placed, according to their merits, either in a better or worse position. But no destruction of substance can befall those things that were created by God for the purpose of permanent existence. For those things that most people agree are believed to perish, the nature either of our faith or of the truth will not permit us to suppose to be destroyed. Finally, our flesh is supposed by ignorant people and unbelievers to be destroyed after death, to such a degree that it retains no remnant at all of its former substance. We, however, who believe in its resurrection, understand that a change only has been produced by death but that its substance certainly remains and that by the

---

[139]ANF 4:343-44*. [140]ANF 4:667*. [141]Prov 16:7 (LXX). [142]1 Cor 15:25-26. [143]FC 80:52.

will of its Creator, and at the time appointed, it will be restored to life. We also believe that a change will take place in it a second time, so that what at first was flesh formed out of earthly soil and was afterwards dissolved by death and again reduced to dust and ashes—"For dust you are," it is said, "and to dust you will return"[144]—will be again raised from the earth and will after this, according to the merits of the indwelling soul, advance to the glory of a spiritual body. ON FIRST PRINCIPLES 3.6.5.[145]

THE HARMONY OF THANKSGIVING. GREGORY OF NYSSA: In the same way when death and corruption and darkness and every other offshoot of evil had grown into the nature of the author of evil, the approach of the divine power, acting like fire and making that unnatural accretion to disappear, thus by purgation of the evil becomes a blessing to that nature, though the separation is agonizing. Therefore even the adversary himself will not be likely to dispute that what took place was both just and salutary, that is, if he will have attained to a perception of the benefit. For this is what occurs even now with those who for their cure are subjected to the knife and their wounds are cauterized. They are angry with the doctors and wince with the pain of the incision. But if recovery of health occurs as a result of this treatment and the pain of the cauterization passes away, they will feel grateful to those who have produced this cure on them. In the same way, when, after long periods of time, the evil of our nature, which now is mixed up with it and has grown with its growth, has been expelled, and when there has been a restoration of those who are now lying in sin in relation to their primal state, a harmony of thanksgiving will arise from all creation, as well from those who in the process of the purgation have suffered chastisement, as well as from those who needed no purgation at all. The great mystery of the divine incarnation bestows these and similar benefits. For in those points in which he was mingled with humanity, passing as he did through all the accidents proper to human nature, such as birth, rearing, growing up and advancing even to the taste of death, he accomplished all the results mentioned previously, freeing both humankind from evil and healing even the introducer of evil himself. For the chastisement, however painful, of moral disease is a healing of its weakness. ADDRESS ON RELIGIOUS INSTRUCTION 26.[146]

THE RESURRECTION OF THE RIGHTEOUS. RUFINUS OF AQUILEIA: These things and many like these you will find in the divine Scriptures concerning the resurrection of the righteous. There will be given to sinners also, as we said above, a condition of incorruption and immortality at the resurrection, that, as God assigns this state to the righteous for perpetuity of glory, so he may assign the same to sinners for prolongation of confusion and punishment. For this also the prophet's words, which we referred to above, state clearly: "Many will rise from the dust of the earth, some to life eternal, and others to confusion and eternal shame."[147] A COMMENTARY ON THE APOSTLES' CREED 47.[148]

THE DIFFERENT POSITIONS OF CHRISTIAN WRITERS. JEROME: It is charged against me that I have sometimes praised Origen. If I am not mistaken, I have only done so in two places: in the short preface (addressed to Damasus) to his homilies on the Song of Songs and in the prologue to my book of Hebrew names. In these passages do the dogmas of the church come into question? Is anything said of the Father, the Son and the Holy Spirit? Or of the resurrection of the flesh? Or of the condition and material of the soul? I have

---

[144]Gen 3:19. [145]ANF 4:346*. [146]NPNF 2 5:153-54. [147]Dan 12:2. [148]NPNF 2 3:562.

merely praised the simplicity of his rendering and commentary, and neither the faith nor the dogmas of the church come in at all. Ethics only are dealt with, and the mist of allegory is dispelled by a clear explanation. I have praised the commentator but not the theologian, the man of intellect but not the believer, the philosopher but not the apostle. But if people want to know my real judgment on Origen, let them read my commentaries on Ecclesiastes, let them go through my three books on the epistle to the Ephesians. They will then see that I have always opposed his doctrines. How foolish it would be to eulogize a system so far as to endorse its blasphemy! The blessed Cyprian takes Tertullian for his master, as his writings prove. Yet, delighted as he is with the ability of this learned and zealous writer, he does not join him in following Montanus and Maximilla. Apollinaris is the author of a most weighty book against Porphyry, and Eusebius has composed a fine history of the church. Yet of these, the former has mutilated Christ's incarnate humanity, while the latter is the most open champion of the Arian impiety. "Woe," says Isaiah, "to those who call evil good and good evil; that put bitter for sweet and sweet for bitter."[149] We must not detract from the virtues of our opponents—if they have any praiseworthy qualities—but neither must we praise the defects of our friends. Each of the cases must be judged on its own merits and not by a reference to the persons concerned. While Lucilius is rightly assailed by Horace for the unevenness of his verses, he is equally rightly praised for his wit and his charming style. LETTER 84.2, TO PAMMACHIUS AND OCEANUS.[150]

ERRORS IN FAITH. AUGUSTINE: And now I must turn from the pagans to deal, however gently, with some of our own tender hearted fellow Christians, who are inclined to feel that there must sooner or later be liberation from hell, if not for all whom the perfect justice of God has judged worthy of its pains, at least for some. Their idea is that after a definite term, differing according to the greater or smaller accumulation of guilt, liberation will come. In this matter, Origen was so moved by pity as to think that even the devil and his angels, after very severe and long-continued pains in proportion to their guilt, would be snatched from the flames to join the company of the holy angels. But Origen has rightly been reproved by the church on more than one account. One was this view of liberation from hell. Among other condemned views was his idea of the ceaseless alternations of blessedness and misery and the unending revolutions of the wheel of the centuries that brought on these goings and returnings of one and the other. Actually, this system that seemed merciful to Origen ceases to be merciful, since it imposes on the saints real miseries and penalties and substitutes for their true and certain joy of everlasting good, unclouded by any fears, a series of false and insecure beatitudes.

Of an altogether different kind is the error of those who are moved by human sympathy to feel that the miseries of people condemned to hell must have an end. They are convinced that happiness will be eternal for all who, sooner or later, are freed from torments. If, however, such a view is good and true merely because it is merciful, then it will be better and truer in proportion to the extension of mercy. Suppose, then, we extend and deepen the well of this mercy to include the condemned angels and say that after many centuries, however protracted, they will finally be freed. For why should that well keep flowing until all humankind is saved and then dry up when it comes to the angels? Those who are moved by mercy do not dare so to stretch their mercy far enough to save even Satan himself. If any should be so bold, his

---

[149]Is 5:20. [150]NPNF 2 6:176.

mercy, at best, would be greater than those who do not, and, therefore, his theory should be truer. But the fact is that the more merciful the theory is, the more it contradicts the words of God, and, therefore, the farther it is from the truth. CITY OF GOD 21.17.[151]

THE ERRORS OF ORIGEN AND PELAGIUS. AUGUSTINE: But what Pelagius added, "Who believes differently is an Origenist," was approved by the judges, because in very deed the church most justly abominates the opinion of Origen, that even they whom the Lord says are to be punished with everlasting punishment, and the devil himself and his angels, after a time, however protracted, will be purged and released from their penalties and will then cleave to the saints who reign with God in the association of blessedness. This additional sentence, therefore, the synod pronounced to be "not opposed to the church," not in accordance with Pelagius but rather in accordance with the gospel, that such ungodly and sinful people will be consumed by eternal fires as the gospel determines to be worthy of such a punishment; and that he is a sharer in Origen's abominable opinion who affirms that their punishment can possibly ever come to an end, when the Lord has said it is to be eternal. Concerning those sinners, however, of whom the apostle declares that "they will be saved, yet so as by fire, after their work has been burned up," inasmuch as no objectionable opinion in reference to them was manifestly charged against Pelagius, the synod determined nothing. Therefore one who says that the ungodly and sinner, whom the truth consigns to eternal punishment, can ever be liberated from there is not inappropriately designated by Pelagius as an Origenist. But . . . one who supposes that no sinner whatever deserves mercy in the judgment of God may be designated by whatever name Pelagius is disposed to give to him, only it must at the same time be quite understood that this error is not received as truth by the church. "For he will have judgment without mercy that has shown no mercy."[152] PROCEEDINGS OF PELAGIUS 10.[153]

AN IMPERIAL EDICT ABOUT THE LAST THINGS. JUSTINIAN THE EMPEROR:

1. Whoever says or thinks that human souls preexisted, that is, that they were previously spirits and holy powers but that, satiated with the vision of God, they turned to evil and in this way the divine love in them died out and they therefore became souls and were condemned to punishment in bodies, will be anathema.

2. If anyone says or thinks that the soul of the Lord preexisted and was united with God the Word before the incarnation and conception of the Virgin, let him be anathema.

3. If anyone says or thinks that the body of our Lord Jesus Christ was first formed in the womb of the holy Virgin and that afterward there was united with it God the Word and the preexisting soul, let him be anathema.

4. If anyone says or thinks that the Word of God has become similar to all heavenly orders, so that for the cherubim he was a cherub, for the seraphim a seraph: in short, like all the superior powers, let him be anathema.

5. If anyone says or thinks that at the resurrection, human bodies will rise spherical in form and unlike our present form, let him be anathema.

6. If anyone says that the heaven, the sun, the moon, the stars and the waters that are above the heavens have souls

---

[151]FC 24:378-79. [152]Jas 2:13. [153]NPNF 1 1:187.

and are reasonable beings, let him be anathema.

7. If anyone says or thinks that Christ the Lord in a future time will be crucified for demons as he was for people, let him be anathema.

8. If anyone says or thinks that the power of God is limited and that he created as much as he was able to handle, let him be anathema.

9. If anyone says or thinks that the punishment of demons and of impious people is only temporary and will one day have an end and that a restoration will take place of demons and of impious people, let him be anathema.

Anathema to Origen and to that Adamantius who set forth these opinions together with his nefarious and execrable and wicked doctrine and to whomsoever there is who thinks thus, or defends these opinions or in any way hereafter at any time will presume to protect them. THE ANATHEMATISMS OF THE EMPEROR JUSTINIAN AGAINST ORIGEN.[154]

---

[154]NPNF 2 14:320.

AND THE LIFE OF THE WORLD TO COME

Blessedness and Condemnation

εἰς μίαν, ἁγίαν, καθολικὴν	Et unam, sanctam, catholicam	We believe in one holy catholic
καὶ ἀποστολικὴν ἐκκλησίαν·	et apostolicam ecclesiam.	and apostolic Church.
ὁμολογοῦμεν ἓν βάπτισμα	Confiteor unum baptisma	We acknowledge one baptism
εἰς ἄφεσιν ἁμαρτιῶν·	in remissionem peccatorum;	for the forgiveness of sins.
προσδοκῶμεν ἀνάστασιν νεκρῶν,	et expecto resurrectionem mortuorum,	We look for the resurrection of the dead
καὶ ζωὴν τοῦ μέλλοντος αἰῶνος. Ἀμήν.	**et vitam venturi saeculi. Amen.**	**and the life of the world to come. Amen.**

Historical Context: We have subdivided this final phrase of the creed into two sections because of the important role that eschatology played in the life of the early church. In this section, we focus on the blessing and condemnation that await believers and unbelievers, respectively, in that life which is to come. In the next section we will focus on the judgment that will accompany Christ's return and the eternal life that believers will enjoy.

Eternal life deriving from the final judgment will have a different development for the righteous and the wicked: the former will be destined to the blessedness of heavenly glory, the latter to eternal damnation. The patristic texts selected in this chapter present the reflections of the Fathers on the nature of blessedness and damnation and on the destiny of Satan and the demons.

Blessedness is often interpreted, especially by the Greek fathers, as a contemplation of God, one and Triune.[1] In this intellectual and mystical vision the long quotation from the second book of *On First Principles* by Origen finds its ideal statement. It suggests that perfect happiness will be reached only in eternal life, when the righteous grasp the reasons of the realities, that is, when they, as pure intelligences, directly contemplate the rational essences.[2] In the Latin context, we have a certain inclination toward a description of the perfect happiness of the blessed, which is in proportion to the merits of each one, as attested by Jerome and Augustine,[3] grounded in faith's reception of grace in Christ. In spite of this, according to Augustine, blessedness essentially remains a vision and enjoyment of God the truth. In this blessedness, there is eternal rest not only for the spirit but for the body as well.[4]

With regard to the fate of the wicked, the general opinion of the Fathers maintains that punishment will be eternal without any possibility of remission. In this regard, the image of the eternal and unquenchable fire, which is in waiting for sinners and demons, recurs, linking this doctrine with the conception of divine justice. With Irenaeus the punishments of hell are recalled also with regard to the fight against the heretics, especially the followers of Marcion, Valentinus, and in general all the Gnostics.[5] Origen opposes this literal vision of eternal punishment, decidedly denying the materiality of the eternal fire and intending it as a sign of purification, so that it is nourished by the sins and is used by the soul to remember its sins and repent.[6] The most delicate point of the reflection of the great Alexandrian will be exactly his refusal

---

[1] See Gregory of Nazianzus *On His Father's Silence*, Oration 16.9.
[2] Origen *On First Principles* 2.11. [3] See the quoted passages: Jerome *Against Jovinianus* 2; Augustine *Sermon* 87. [4] See Augustine *City of God* 22.30.5. [5] See Irenaeus *Against Heresies* 5.26.2.
[6] See Origen *Against Celsus* 5.15.

of the eternity of the punishment, which is connected to the doctrine of the final *apokatastasis*. In the West, we have with Augustine the establishment of certain lines of reflection that will influence the later theological thought on the infernal realities. In particular, he reasserts with force, and in an anti-Origenist position, the eternity of hell and damnation, emphasizing that the infernal fire cannot be purely spiritual, even though, by excluding the mere materiality, the opportunity is left to the believer to form an opinion about the nature of the fire.[7] Finally, Gregory the Great suggests that the damned enter hell immediately after death and their destiny is without any possibility of appeal.[8]

The last group of excerpts related to this section of the creed specifically discusses the destiny of Satan and the demons, on which the great heritage of the thought of Origen and the Origenists weighed. Before them the idea was that the devil and his angels, after being driven out of heaven because they had fallen into sin, continued to act between heaven and earth until their definitive condemnation in the eternal judgment by suffering "death in immortality."[9] In contrast with this idea, Origen with his doctrine of the final *apokatastasis* asserted that in the final conflagration, which would precede the second coming of Christ on earth, Satan and his demons would be purified by the fire of the Logos. All the later Fathers will take a position with regard to this doctrine, underlining the eternal condemnation of the devil and his angels. The final passage, which we have quoted from "On the Orthodox Faith" by John of Damascus, is a synthesis of the patristic demonology, in which, after describing the origin of the devil and his angels, the conclusion is that "after the fall there is no possibility of repentance for the angels anymore, as after death for human beings."

Finally, we must bear in mind that the themes of Christian eschatology that can be known through the texts of the Fathers were strongly influenced by the cosmological and anthropological vision of their times, so that they cause difficulties for the reader of our time. However, this does not excuse us from the effort of penetrating the mentality of the ancient Christian writers. Rather, it is an opportunity to approach themes that are still fundamental in the present day to comprehend Christian faith.

OVERVIEW: The present world is of short duration and transient, whereas the future life will be eternal, great and wonderful (PSEUDO-CLEMENT). God will give to the righteous eternal life, joy, peace, rest and abundance (THEOPHILUS). In particular, God will grant the saints the beatific vision (IRENAEUS), so that they will always be with him, being clothed with eternity (TERTULLIAN). Then their hearts will be purified in order to gain access to the contemplation of God (CLEMENT OF ALEXANDRIA). Following the letter of Scripture, some think that with their resurrection human beings will return to their corporal and material state; but resurrection must be interpreted in a spiritual sense. When Christ returns to earth, he will disclose humankind to himself. The saints will come to know the providential plan of God and therefore will ascend to heaven until they come into contact with eternal, ineffable and unknown realities (ORIGEN). In eternal life the saints will reunite with the patriarchs, the prophets, the apostles and the martyrs (CYPRIAN). Human beings will enjoy prosperity forever (HILARY) and will reach divinization (GREGORY OF NAZIANZUS). The one who is blessed by the Lord will receive eternal life, that is, eternal happiness, which coincides with the seventh age of humanity before the eighth day, the day of the Lord (AUGUSTINE).

---

[7]See Augustine *City of God* 21.9.2. [8]See the two quoted passages from the *Dialogues*. [9]See Tatian *Discourse to the Greeks* 14.

As between the luminaries there is a gradation, so there is gradation among the saints (Aphrahat). The future reserved to the saints in heaven is different according to their merits and virtues (Jerome). Eternal life will be the same for everyone, albeit with a different gradation, as different is the splendor of the sun in comparison with that of the moon and the stars (Augustine).

The bosom of Abraham unanimously receives the souls of the apostles, martyrs and saints (Jerome). The worship of the saints is not like that of the idols or the shadows, because the believer turns to God first of all and then confides in the help and the prayers of those who are already victorious in heaven. For this reason the church extends its limits to heaven, where the saints rule with Christ (Augustine).

Those who corrupt families and, with even more good reason, those who endanger the church of Christ will not inherit the kingdom of God (Ignatius). Eternal damnation will consist in a long series of torments (Martyrdom of Polycarp) in the eternal fire (Letter to Diognetus, Hermas, Pseudo-Clement). In particular, the soul ruined by vices will deserve eternal punishment (Epistle of Barnabas), which will consist in the final expulsion from the church of God (Hermas). The opposition and the refusal of the teaching of the Word of God (Justin, Minucius Felix) lead to the eternal and unquenchable fire (Cyprian), whose nature will be such that it needs no nourishment, because it is pure, fluid and liquid (Lactantius). At the time of resurrection the righteous will receive a heavenly body, like that of angels, whereas the sinners will have a body subject to eternal punishment (Cyril of Jerusalem). The fire can have different meanings: it can, for instance, indicate Christ himself (Gregory of Nazianzus, Gregory of Nyssa). Christians are not indifferent but participates in an interior way in the punishments that the damned pay for their sins (Chrysostom). While the body fears torments, the soul only fears death. Damnation consists in being cut out of the kingdom of God, in being exiled from the city of God and being made an alien from the divine life (Augustine). The resurrection body will be incorruptible (Rufinus). In the future life, a material fire will torment spiritual souls; and the intensity of the punishment will depend on divine justice (Gregory the Great), so that, according to one's sins, there will be a different degree of punishment (Aphrahat).

The demons walk the way of death and persist in death (Tatian). The gods of the nations are demons (Justin). Christ has revealed to Satan his real end (Irenaeus). The cross of Christ has marked its triumph on its enemy, the prince of this world (Origen). Christ will not return before the antichrist has acted on earth by cheating and seducing people. Later, on the day of judgment, the city of the devil with its prophet, the antichrist, will be destroyed, and the devil and his angels will be thrown into the eternal fire (Augustine). The devil and the demons are fallen angels who have no possibility to repent, like the situation of human beings who have died (John).

The Nature of Eternal Blessedness

Sojourning in the Flesh Is Brief and Transient. Pseudo-Clement of Rome: Brothers, willingly leaving our sojourn in this present world, let us do the will of him who called us and not fear to leave this world. For the Lord says, "You will be as lambs in the midst of wolves."[10] And Peter answered and said to him, "What, then, if the wolves will tear in pieces the lambs?" Jesus said to Peter, "The lambs have no cause after they are dead to fear the wolves; and in a similar way, do not fear those who kill you and can do nothing more to you; but fear him who, after you are

---

[10]Mt 10:16.

dead, has power over both soul and body to cast them into hellfire."[11] And consider, brothers, that the sojourn in the flesh in this world is but brief and transient, but the promise of Christ is great and wonderful—which includes the rest of the kingdom to come and of life everlasting. By what course of conduct, then, will we attain these things but by leading a holy and righteous life and by deeming these worldly things as not belonging to us and not fixing our desires on them? For if we desire to possess them, we fall away from the path of righteousness. 2 CLEMENT 5.[12]

BELIEVE IN AND SUBMIT TO GOD. THEOPHILUS OF ANTIOCH: Therefore, do not be skeptical, but believe. I myself also used to not believe that this would take place, but now, having taken these things into consideration, I believe. At the same time, I met with the sacred Scriptures[13] of the holy prophets, who also by the Spirit of God foretold the things that have already happened, just as they came to pass, and the things now occurring as they are now happening and things future in the order in which they will be accomplished. Admitting, therefore, the proof afforded by events happening as predicted, I do not disbelieve. Instead, I believe, obedient to God, whom, if you please, you also submit to, believing him, lest if now you continue unbelieving, you be convinced hereafter, when you are tormented with eternal punishments. These punishments, when they had been foretold by the prophets, were stolen from the holy Scriptures by the later-born poets and philosophers in order to make their doctrines worthy of credit. Yet these also have spoken beforehand of the punishments that are to light on the profane and unbelieving, in order that none would be left without a witness or be able to say, "We have not heard, neither have we known." But you also, if you please, should give reverential attention to the prophetic Scriptures.[14] Then they will make your way plainer for escaping the eternal punishments and obtaining the eternal prizes of God. For he who gave the mouth for speech, and formed the ear to hear and made the eye to see will examine all things and will make a righteous judgment, rendering merited awards to each. To those who by patient continuance in well-doing[15] seek immortality, he will give life everlasting, joy, peace, rest and abundance of good things, which neither eye has seen nor ear heard, nor has it entered into the heart of people to conceive.[16] But to the unbelieving and despisers who do not obey the truth but are obedient to unrighteousness, when they will have been filled with adulteries and fornications, and filthiness, and covetousness and unlawful idolatries, there will be anger and wrath, tribulation and anguish.[17] In the end, everlasting fire will possess such people. Since you said, "Show me your God," this is my God, and I counsel you to fear him and to trust him. TO AUTOLYCUS 1.14.[18]

THE IMMORTALITY OF BELIEVERS. IRENAEUS: The church, though dispersed throughout the whole world, even to the ends of the earth, has received from the apostles and their disciples this faith: It believes in one God, the Father almighty, Maker of heaven, and earth, and the sea, and all things that are in them; and in one Christ Jesus, the Son of God, who became incarnate for our salvation; and in the Holy Spirit, who proclaimed through the prophets the dispensations of God, and the advents, and the birth from a virgin, and the passion, and the resurrection from the dead and the ascension into heaven in the flesh of the beloved Christ Jesus, our Lord, and his future manifestation from heaven in the glory of the Father "to gather all things in one"[19] and to raise up anew all flesh of the whole human race, in order that to Christ

---

[11]Mt 10:28; Lk 12:4. [12]ANF 9:252. [13]See Ps 119:130. [14]Rev 19:10. [15]Rom 2:7. [16]1 Cor 2:9. [17]Rom 2:8-9. [18]ANF 2:93. [19]Eph 1:10.

Jesus, our Lord, and God, and Savior and King, according to the will of the invisible Father, "every knee should bow, of things in heaven, and things in earth, and things under the earth, and that every tongue should confess"[20] to him, and that he should execute just judgment toward all. Thus, he may send "spiritual wickednesses,"[21] and the angels who transgressed and became apostates, together with the ungodly, and unrighteous, and wicked and profane among people, into everlasting fire. But he also may, in the exercise of his grace, confer immortality on the righteous and holy, and those who have kept his commandments and have persevered in his love, some from the beginning of their Christian course and others from the date of their repentance and may surround them with everlasting glory. AGAINST HERESIES 1.10.1.[22]

THOSE WHO SEE GOD ARE IN GOD. IRENAEUS: The prophet set forth these things in a prophetic way. But they did not, as some allege, proclaim that he who was seen by the prophets was a different [God] the Father of all being invisible. Yet this is what those heretics declare, who are altogether ignorant of the nature of prophecy. For prophecy is a prediction of things future, that is, a setting forth beforehand of those things that will be afterwards. The prophets, then, indicated beforehand that God should be seen by humankind. The Lord also says as much: "Blessed are the pure in heart, for they will see God."[23] But in respect to his greatness and his wonderful glory, "no one will see God and live,"[24] for the Father is incomprehensible. But in regard to his love and kindness, and as to his infinite power, even this he grants to those who love him, that is, to see God. This is also what the prophets predicted. "For those things that are impossible with people are possible with God."[25] For a mortal does not see God by his own powers; but when God pleases he is seen by human beings, by whom he wills, and when he wills and as he wills. For God is all powerful, having been seen at that time indeed, prophetically through the Spirit and seen, too, adoptively through the Son. And he will also be seen paternally in the kingdom of heaven, the Spirit truly preparing man in the Son of God and the Son leading him to the Father, while the Father, too, confers on him incorruption for eternal life that comes to every one from the fact of his seeing God. For as those who see the light are within the light and partake of its brilliancy; even so, those who see God are in God and receive of his splendor. His splendor enlivens them. Those, therefore, who see God do receive life. This is why he, although beyond comprehension and boundless and invisible, rendered himself visible and comprehensible and within the capacity of those who believe. He did this so that he might enliven those who receive and behold him through faith. For as his greatness is past finding out, so also his goodness is beyond expression. By his goodness having been seen, he bestows life on those who see him. It is not possible to live apart from life, and the means of life is found in fellowship with God. But fellowship with God is to know God and to enjoy his goodness. AGAINST HERESIES 4.20.5.[26]

GOD HAD POWER TO GRANT PERFECTION TO HUMANKIND. IRENAEUS: And on this account does Paul declare to the Corinthians, "I have fed you with milk, not with meat, for up to this point you were not able to bear it."[27] That is, you have indeed learned of the advent of our Lord as a man. Nevertheless, because of your infirmity, the Spirit of the Father has not as yet rested on you. "For when envying and strife and dissensions are among you, are you not of the flesh and behaving according to human inclinations?"[28] In other words, the Spirit

---

[20]Phil 2:10-11. [21]Eph 6:12. [22]ANF 1:330-31. [23]Mt 5:8. [24]Ex 33:20. [25]Lk 18:27. [26]ANF 1:488-89. [27]1 Cor 3:2. [28]1 Cor 3:3.

of the Father was not yet with them because of their imperfection and the shortcomings of their walk in life. Therefore, the apostle had the power to give them strong meat—for those on whom the apostles laid hands received the Holy Spirit, who is the food of life eternal—but they were not capable of receiving it, because they had the sentient faculties of the soul still feeble and undisciplined in the practice of things pertaining to God. Therefore, in a similar way God had power at the beginning to grant perfection to humankind; but as created, he could not possibly have received it, or even if he had received it, could he have contained it, or containing it, could he have retained it. It was for this reason that the Son of God, although he was perfect, passed through the state of infancy in common with the rest of humankind, partaking of it thus not for his own benefit but for that of the infantile stage of human existence, in order that humanity might be able to receive him. There was nothing, therefore, impossible to and deficient in God, implied in the fact that the human being was not an uncreated being. Rather, this merely applied to him who was lately created, namely, the human being. AGAINST HERESIES 4.38.2.[29]

A WITNESS OF ETERNAL FIRE. TERTULLIAN: Assuredly, since the reason why restoration takes place at all is the appointed judgment, every person must necessarily come forth as the very same person who had once existed so that they may receive God's verdict on the good or evil they deserve. And therefore the body too will appear, for the soul is not capable of suffering without the solid substance (that is, the flesh). Also, it is not right that souls should have to bear all the wrath of God. They did not sin without the body in which they did everything. But how, you say, can a substance that has been dissolved be made to reappear again? Consider yourself, and you will believe in it! Reflect on what you were before you came into existence. Nothing. For if you had been anything, you would have remembered it. You, then, who were nothing before you existed, reduced to nothing also when you cease to be, why may you not come into being again out of nothing, at the will of the same Creator whose will created you out of nothing from the start? Will it be anything new in your case? You who were not, were made. When you cease to be again, you will be made. Explain, if you can, your original creation, and then demand to know how you will be recreated. Indeed, it will be still easier surely to make you what you were once, when the very same creative power made you without difficulty what you never were before. There will be doubts, perhaps, as to the power of God, of him who hung in its place this huge body of our world. He made it out of what had never existed, as if from a death of emptiness and inanity, animated by the Spirit who enlivens all living things—its very self the unmistakable type of the resurrection—so that it might be to you a witness—no, in fact, the exact image of the resurrection. Light, every day extinguished, shines out again, and darkness succeeds light's outgoing with a similar alternation. The defunct stars relive; the seasons, as soon as they are finished, renew their course; the fruits are brought to maturity and then are reproduced. The seeds do not spring up with abundant produce unless they rot and dissolve away—all things are preserved by perishing, all things are refashioned out of death. You, person of nature so exalted, if you understand yourself, taught even by the Pythian words, lord of all these things that die and rise—shall you die to perish evermore? Wherever your dissolution will have taken place, whatever material agent has destroyed you, or swallowed you up, or swept you away or reduced you to nothingness, it will again restore you.

Even nothingness is his who is Lord of all. You ask, will we then be always dying and ris-

---

[29]ANF 1:521.

ing up from death? If so the Lord of all things had appointed, you would have to submit, though unwillingly, to the law of your creation. But, in fact, he has no other purpose than that of which he has informed us. The Reason that made the universe out of diverse elements, so that all things might be composed of opposite substances in unity—of void and solid, of animate and inanimate, of comprehensible and incomprehensible, of light and darkness, of life itself and death—has also disposed time into order by fixing and distinguishing its mode, according to which this first portion of it, which we inhabit from the beginning of the world, flows down by a temporal course to a close; but the portion that succeeds, and to which we look forward, continues forever. When therefore the boundary and limit, that millennial interval, has been passed when even the outward fashion of the world itself—which has been spread like a veil over the eternal economy, equally a thing of time—passes away, then the whole human race will be raised again, to have its dues meted out according as it has merited in the period of good or evil and thereafter to have these paid out through the immeasurable ages of eternity. Therefore after this there is neither death nor repeated resurrections, but we will be the same that we are now and still unchanged—the servants of God, ever with God, clothed with the proper substance of eternity. But the profane, and all who are not true worshipers of God, in a similar way manner will be consigned to the punishment of everlasting fire—that fire that, from its very nature indeed, directly ministers to their incorruptibility. The philosophers are familiar as well as we with the distinction between a common and a secret fire. Thus that which is in common use is far different from that which we see in divine judgments, whether striking as thunderbolts from heaven or bursting up out of the earth through mountaintops. For it does not consume what it scorches, but while it burns it repairs. So the mountains continue ever burning; and a person struck by lighting is even now kept safe from any destroying flame. APOLOGY 48.[30]

REWARD AND HONORS TO THE PERFECT. CLEMENT OF ALEXANDRIA: And this takes place whenever one holds on to the Lord by faith, by knowledge, by love, and ascends along with him to where the God and guard of our faith and love is. This is where at last—because of the necessity for very great preparation and previous training in order both to hear what is said, and for the composure of life and for advancing intelligently to a point beyond the righteousness of the law—it happens that knowledge is committed to those fit and selected for it. It leads us to the endless and perfect end, teaching us beforehand the future life that we will lead, according to God, and with gods, after we are freed from all punishment and penalty that we undergo in consequence of our sins, for salutary discipline.... Knowledge is therefore quick in purifying and fit for that acceptable transformation to the better. With ease it removes the soul to what is akin to the soul, divine and holy, and by its own light conveys human beings through the mystic stages of advancement until it restores the pure in heart to the crowning place of rest; teaching them to gaze on God, face to face, with knowledge and comprehension. For in this consists the perfection of the knowing soul, in its being with the Lord, where it is in immediate subjection to him, after rising above all purification and service. STROMATEIS 7.10.[31]

DIFFERENT OPINIONS ABOUT EVERLASTING LIFE. ORIGEN: Certain persons, then, refusing the labor of thinking, and adopting a superficial view of the letter of the law and yielding rather in some measure to the indulgence of their own desires and lusts, being disciples of the letter alone, are of the opinion

---

[30]ANF 3:53-54**. [31]ANF 2:539.

that the fulfillment of the promises of the future are to be looked for in bodily pleasure and luxury. This is why they especially want to have again, after the resurrection, the kind of bodies that never lack the ability of eating and drinking and performing all the functions of flesh and blood. They do not follow the opinion of the apostle Paul regarding the resurrection of a spiritual body.[32] And consequently they say that after the resurrection there will be marriages and the begetting of children. They imagine that the earthly city of Jerusalem is to be rebuilt, its foundations laid in precious stones and its walls constructed of jasper and its battlements of crystal. They imagine it will have a wall composed of many precious stones like jasper, and sapphire, and chalcedony, and emerald, and sardonyx, and onyx, and chrysolite, and chrysoprase, and jacinth and amethyst.[33] Moreover, they think that the natives of other countries are to be given them as servants for their own pleasure, whom they are to employ either as tillers of the field or builders of walls and by whom their ruined and fallen city is again to be raised up.[34] And they think that they are to receive the wealth of the nations to live on and that they will have control over their riches. They think that even the camels of Midian and Kedar will come and bring gold and incense and precious stones.[35] And these views they think to establish on the authority of the prophets by those promises that are written regarding Jerusalem and by those passages where it also says that those who serve the Lord will eat and drink but that sinners will hunger and thirst; that the righteous will be joyful but that sorrow will possess the wicked.[36] And from the New Testament also they quote the saying of the Savior, in which he makes a promise to his disciples concerning the joy of wine, saying, "From now on, I will not drink of this cup, until I drink it with you anew in my Father's kingdom."[37] ON FIRST PRINCIPLES 2.11.2.[38]

THE BREAD OF LIFE. ORIGEN: Those who receive the representations of Scripture according to the understanding of the apostles entertain the hope that the saints will eat indeed, but that it will be the bread of life that may nourish the soul with the food of truth[39] and wisdom, and enlighten the mind and cause it to drink from the cup of divine wisdom. ON FIRST PRINCIPLES 2.11.3.[40]

THE PURPOSE OF OUR DEEDS. ORIGEN: If these views are not attractive enough to a mind filled with such hoped-for results, let us go back a little, and, irrespective of the natural and innate longing of the mind for the thing itself, let us ask so that we may be able at last to describe, as it were, the very forms of the bread of life, and the quality of that wine and the peculiar nature of the principalities—all in conformity with the spiritual view of things. Now the reason why something is done, or why it is of a special quality, or for a special purpose is an object of investigation to the mind, while the actual work itself is unfolded to view by the agency of the hands as we see, for instance, with tasks usually performed by means of manual labor. In the same way, the reason and the understanding behind those works of God that were created by him, which we see done by him, remains undisclosed. And, just as when our eye sees the products of an artist's labor and the mind then—immediately on perceiving anything of unusual artistic excellence—burns to know what it is made of, or how it was formed or to what purposes it was fashioned; so, in a much greater degree, and in one that is beyond all comparison, does the mind burn with an inexpressible desire to know the reason for what it sees God doing. This desire, this longing, we believe to be unquestionably implanted within us by God. And as the eye

---

[32]See 1 Cor 15:44. [33]Rev 21:19-20. [34]Cf. Is 61:5. [35]Is 61:6. [36]See Is 65:13-16. [37]Mt 26:29. [38]ANF 4:297**. [39]Jn 6:51. [40]ANF 4:297*.

naturally seeks the light and wants to see, and our body naturally desires food and drink, so our mind is possessed with an understandable and natural desire to become acquainted with the truth of God and the causes of things. Now we have received this desire from God, not in order that it should never be gratified or be capable of gratification. Otherwise the love of truth would appear to have been implanted by God into our minds to no purpose if it were never to have an opportunity of satisfaction. This is why, even in this life, those who devote themselves with great labor to the pursuits of piety and religion—even though they might only obtain some small fragments from the numerous and immense treasures of divine knowledge—still, by the very circumstance that their mind and soul are engaged in these pursuits and that in the eagerness of their desire they outstrip themselves, they derive a great advantage. And because their minds are directed to the study and love of the investigation of truth, they are made more fit for receiving the instruction that is to come. . . . Perhaps this is why it is said, "To everyone who has, even more will be given."[41] By this we come to understand that those who possess in this life a kind of outline of truth and knowledge will be given the added beauty of a perfect image in the future. ON FIRST PRINCIPLES 2.11.4.[42]

KNOWLEDGE OF AN UNSPEAKABLE JOY. ORIGEN: He will learn, too, the judgment of divine Providence on each individual thing. He will learn, for instance, that of those events that happen to people, none occur by accident or chance. They occur in agreement with a plan so carefully considered and so amazing that it does not overlook even the number of the hairs on heads—not merely of the saints but perhaps of all human beings. The plan of such providential government extends even to caring for the sale of two sparrows for a denarius, whether sparrows there are understood figuratively or literally. Now, in fact, this providential government is still a subject of investigation, but then it will be fully manifested. All of this leads us to the supposition that it will still be awhile until the worthy and deserving who have departed from this life will learn the reason why things happened on this earth. But once they know all these things, having the grace of that full knowledge, they may then enjoy an unspeakable joy. ON FIRST PRINCIPLES 2.11.5.[43]

SIGNS OF FUTURE EVENTS. ORIGEN: Since a zeal or desire for knowledge of this kind is conceived by us on earth, the full understanding and comprehension of it will be granted after death, if indeed the result should follow according to our expectations. When, therefore, we will have fully comprehended its nature, we will understand in two ways what we saw on earth. This is the kind of view we need to hold, then, regarding this living space in the air. I think, therefore, that all the saints who leave this life will remain in some place situated on the earth that holy Scripture calls paradise. It will be like a place of instruction, and, so to speak, like a classroom or school of souls in which they are to be instructed regarding all the things that they had seen on earth. They also should receive some information about what will happen in the future as even when in this life they had obtained in some degree indications of future events—although "through a glass darkly." All of this will be revealed more clearly and distinctly to the saints in their proper time and place. If anyone indeed is pure in heart, and holy in mind and more practiced in perception, he will by making more rapid progress quickly ascend to a place in the air and reach the kingdom of heaven through those mansions, so to speak, in the various places that the Greeks have termed spheres, that is, globes, but that holy Scripture has called heavens. ON FIRST PRINCIPLES 2.11.6.[44]

---

[41]Mt 25:29. [42]ANF 4:298**. [43]ANF 4:299**. [44]ANF 4:299**.

THE SAINTS WILL KNOW THE CAUSE OF EVERYTHING. ORIGEN: When, then, the saints have reached their celestial living quarters, they will clearly see the nature of the stars one by one and will understand whether they are endued with life or whatever their condition might be. They will also comprehend the other reasons for the works of God that he himself will reveal to them. For he will show to them, as to children, the causes of things and the power of his creation. He will explain why that star was placed in that particular quarter of the sky and why it was separated from another by so great an intervening space. He will explain what, for example, would have been the consequence if it had been nearer or more remote. Or, if that star had been larger than this, he will explain how the totality of things would not have remained the same but all would have been transformed into a different condition of being. And so, when they have finished all those matters that are connected with the stars and with the heavenly revolutions, they will come to those that are not seen or to those whose names only we have heard and to things which are invisible. The apostle Paul has informed us that these are numerous, although what they are or what difference may exist among them, we cannot even conjecture by our feeble intellect. And thus the rational nature, growing by each individual step—not as it grew in this life in flesh and body and soul—but enlarged in understanding and in power of perception, is raised to perfect knowledge as a mind already perfect, no longer at all impeded by those carnal senses but increased in intellectual growth. It ultimately attains perfection as it always gazes purely, and, so to speak, face to face, on the causes of things. It attains such perfection, first of all by that which it ascends to (i.e., the truth), and second, by that which it abides in, having problems and the understanding of things and the causes of events, as the food on which it may feast. For instance, in this life our bodies grow physically to what they are through having a sufficient amount of food in early life that supplies the means of our increasing. But after the due height has been attained, we use food no longer to grow but to live and to be preserved in life by it. In the same way, I also think that the mind, when it has attained perfection, eats and avails itself of suitable and appropriate food in such a degree that nothing ought to be either deficient or superfluous. And in all things this food is to be understood as the contemplation and understanding of God that is of a measure appropriate and suitable to this nature, which was made and created. And it is appropriate that this measure be observed by every one of those who are beginning to see God, that is, to understand him through purity of heart. ON FIRST PRINCIPLES 2.11.7.[45]

WE WILL BE JOYFUL. CYPRIAN: Oh, what and how great will that day be at its coming, beloved brothers, when the Lord will begin to count up his people and to recognize by the inspection of his divine knowledge what each one deserves. He will send the guilty to Gehenna and set on fire our persecutors with the perpetual burning of a punishing fire but will pay to us the reward of our faith and devotion! What will be the glory and how great the joy to be admitted to see God, to be honored to receive with Christ, your Lord God, the joy of eternal salvation and light! To greet Abraham, and Isaac and Jacob, and all the patriarchs, and prophets, and apostles and martyrs! To rejoice with the righteous and the friends of God in the kingdom of heaven, with the pleasure of immortality given to us! To receive there what neither eye has seen nor ear heard, neither has entered into the heart of people! For the apostle announces that we will receive greater things than anything that we here either do or

---

[45] ANF 4:299-300**.

suffer. He says, "The sufferings of this present time are not worthy to be compared with the glory to come hereafter which will be revealed in us."[46] When that revelation will come, when that glory of God will shine on us, we will be as happy and joyful, honored with the condescension of God, as they will remain guilty and wretched who, either as deserters from God or rebels against him, have done the will of the devil so that it is necessary for them to be tormented with the devil himself in unquenchable fire. LETTER 55.10.[47]

EVERYTHING HE DOES WILL PROSPER. HILARY OF POITIERS: Never again will his gift and his statutes be set aside as they were in the case of Adam who, by his sin in breaking the law, lost the happiness of an assured immortality. Now, however, thanks to the redemption brought about by the tree of Life, that is, by the passion of the Lord, all that happens to us is eternal and eternally conscious of happiness by virtue of our future likeness to that tree of Life. For everything they will prosper, occurring no longer amid shift and change or in human weakness, for corruption will be swallowed up in incorruption, weakness in endless life, the form of earthly flesh in the form of God. This tree, then, planted and yielding its fruit in its own season, is what this happy person will resemble, himself being planted in the garden. In this way, what God has planted may remain, never to be rooted up, in the garden where all things done by God will be nurtured to a prosperous result apart from the decay that belongs to human weakness and to time that might otherwise cause it to be uprooted. HOMILIES ON THE PSALMS 1.18.[48]

THE IMAGE OF THE TRINITY. GREGORY OF NAZIANZUS: This is my offering to you, Basil, uttered by the tongue that once was the sweetest of all to you—the tongue of him who was your fellow in age and rank. If this offering is at all worthy of you, it is only thanks to you. For it was from confidence in you that I undertook to speak of you. But if it falls far short of your expectations, what must be our feelings, who are worn out with age and disease and regret for you? Yet God is pleased when we do what we can. Yet may you gaze on us from above, you divine and sacred person. Either, by your entreaties, put a stop to our thorn in the flesh given to us by God for our discipline or prevail on us to bear it boldly and guide all our life toward that which is most for our profit. And if we are translated to eternity, may you receive us there also in your own tabernacle, in order that, as we dwell together and gaze together more clearly and more perfectly on the holy and blessed Trinity, of which we have now in some degree received the image, our longing may at last be satisfied by gaining this compensation for all the battles we have fought and the assaults we have endured. These are the kinds of words we offer on your behalf. Who will there be to praise us, since we leave this life after you, even if we offer any topic worthy of words or praise in Christ Jesus our Lord, to whom be glory forever? Amen. ON BASIL THE GREAT, ORATION 43.82.[49]

ONLY IMMORTAL LIFE IS GENUINELY HAPPY. AUGUSTINE: All people want to be happy; if they want something true, this necessarily means they want to be immortal. They cannot otherwise be happy. In any case, if you ask them about immortality as about happiness, they all answer that they want it. But as long as they despair of immortality, without which true happiness is impossible, they will look for, or rather make up, any kind of thing that may be called, rather than really be, happiness in this life. That person lives happily, as we have said above and established firmly enough, who lives as he wants and does not want anything wrongly. But no one is wrong to

---

[46]Rom 8:18. [47]ANF 5:350**. [48]NPNF 2 9:240-41**. [49]NPNF 2 7:422.

want immortality if human nature is capable of receiving it as God's gift; if it is not capable of it, then it is not capable of happiness either. For a person to live happily, after all, he must live. How can the happy life remain with him if life itself forsakes him as he dies? When it does forsake him, he is without doubt either unwilling for it to do so, or willing, or neither. If he is unwilling, how is this life happy that is in his will without being in his power? If no one is happy by wanting something and not having it, how much less than happy must he be who is being forsaken against his will not by honor, or possessions, or anything else, but by the happy life itself, when he comes to have no life at all? So even if he has no senses left to be unhappy, still as long as he is conscious he is unhappy because he knows that he is losing against his will what he loves more than anything else and what he loves anything else for. So life cannot both be happy and forsake a person against his will, because no one is made happy against his will; thus it would make him unhappy if he had it against his will, so how much more will it do so when it forsakes him against his will? If however it is in accordance with his will that it forsakes him, then how can this life have been a happy one that the person who had it wanted to lose?

The only thing left for them to say is that the happy person is conscious of neither attitude; that is, he is neither willing nor unwilling to be forsaken by the happy life when all life forsakes him at death, because he takes up his position between the two attitudes with a steady equanimity. But then his life can scarcely be the happy one if it does not merit the love of the person it is supposed to make happy. How can the life be happy that the happy person does not love? And how can he really love it if he does not care whether it flourishes or perishes? Unless perhaps the very virtues that we only love for the sake of happiness would dare to persuade us not to love happiness itself. If they do this, then we stop loving them too, when we no longer love the happiness for whose sake alone we loved the virtues. In any case, what will become of the truth of this axiom, so tried, so tested, so clarified, that all people want to be happy, if those who are already happy are neither willing nor unwilling to be so? If they want it, as the truth cries out that they do and as nature compels them to, having this will implanted in it by the supremely good and unchangeably happy creator; if those who are happy do want to be happy, I say, then of course they do not want not to be happy. And if they do not want not to be happy, then without a doubt they do not want their being happy to fade away and cease. They cannot be happy unless they are alive; therefore they do not want their being alive to cease. So anyone who is truly happy or desires to be, wants to be immortal. But a person does not live happily if he has not got what he wants; so it is altogether impossible for a life to be genuinely happy unless it is immortal. Whether human nature is capable of something it confesses to be so desirable is no small question. But if the faith possessed by those to whom Jesus gave the right to become sons of God[50] is to hand, then there is no question at all. ON THE TRINITY 13.8.11–13.9.12.[51]

IT IS IMPOSSIBLE FOR HUMANS TO IMAGINE THE ETERNAL LIFE. AUGUSTINE: And now, with such help as the Lord will grant us, let us try to see what is to be the activity of the saints in those spiritual and immortal bodies in which their flesh is to be alive, not merely with a carnal but with a spiritual life. I speak of activity, although, perhaps, I should rather say calm or repose. To tell the truth, I have no real notion of what eternal life will be like, for the simple reason that I know of no sensible experience to which it can be related. Nor can I say that I have any mental conception of such an activity, for, at

---

[50]Cf. Jn 1:12. [51]WSA 1 5:351-52

that height, what is intelligence or what can it do? In heaven, as Paul assures us, "the peace of God . . . surpasses all understanding."[52] Certainly, it surpasses ours. Maybe it surpasses that of the angels as well. Of course, it does not surpass God's understanding. This much is sure. If the redeemed are to live in the peace of God, they are to live in a peace "which surpasses all understanding." As to ours, there is no doubt at all, and, when Paul says "all understanding" he seems to imply no exception for the angels. We ought, therefore, to take the text to mean that neither human beings nor angels can understand, as God does, that peace which God himself enjoys. Thus, this peace surpasses "all understanding," all except God's. Nevertheless, since we are to be sharers of his peace, commensurate with our capacity to do so, we are to receive, within ourselves in our relations to one another and to God, a supreme degree of peace—whatever that supreme degree for us may be. So, too, the holy angels understand that peace in a way commensurate with their capacity. Human beings on earth, whatever the perfection of understanding they may reach, understand far less than the angels. For we must remember that not even Paul, for all his greatness, could say more than this: "We know in part and we prophesy in part; until that which is perfect has come. . . . We see now through a mirror in an obscure manner, but then face to face."[53]

Face to face—this is how the holy angels, who are called our angels, already see. They are our angels in the sense that, once we have been delivered from the power of darkness, have received the pledge of the Spirit and have been translated to the kingdom of Christ, we will have begun to belong to the angels, with whom we are to be fellow citizens in that holy and supremely satisfying communion that is that city of God about which I have been writing all these pages. The angels, who are God's angels, are our angels in the way that the Christ of God is our Christ. They are God's, because they never deserted God. They are ours, because they have begun to accept us as their fellow citizens. Now, the Lord Jesus said, "See that you do not despise one of these little ones; for, I tell you, their angels in heaven always behold the face of my Father in heaven."[54] In the way, then, that they see, we, also, will one day see. But we do not see in that way yet. That is why Paul said what I have just quoted: "We see now through a mirror in an obscure manner, but then face to face." This implies that there is in store for us a reward for our faith, that Vision that John had in mind when he said, "When he appears, we will be like him, for we will see him just as he is."[55] For, of course, "face" is to be understood not as the kind of face we now have as part of our body but as a manifestation of what God is. CITY OF GOD 22.29.[56]

THE SEVEN DAYS. AUGUSTINE: Who can measure the happiness of heaven, where no evil at all can touch us, no good will be out of reach; where life is to be one long laud extolling God, who will be all in all; where there will be no weariness to call for rest, no need to call for toil, no place for any energy but praise? Of this I am assured whenever I read or hear the sacred song: "Blessed are they that dwell in your house, O Lord; they will praise you forever and ever." Every fiber and organ of our imperishable body will play its part in the praising of God. On earth these varied organs have each a special function, but in heaven function will be swallowed up in felicity, in the perfect certainty of an untroubled everlastingness of joy. Even those muted notes in the diapason of the human organ, which I mentioned earlier, will swell into a great hymn of praise to the supreme Artist who has fashioned us, within and without, in every fiber, and who,

---

[52]Phil 4:7. [53]1 Cor 13:9-12. [54]Mt 18:10. [55]1 Jn 3:2. [56]FC 24:496-98**.

by this and every other of a magnificent and marvelous order, will ravish our minds with spiritual beauty.

These movements of our bodies will be of such unimaginable beauty that I dare not say more than this: There will be such poise, such grace, such beauty as become a place where nothing unbecoming can be found. Wherever the spirit wills, there, in a flash, will the body be. Nor will the spirit ever will anything unbecoming either to itself or to the body.

In heaven, all glory will be true glory, since no one could ever err in praising too little or too much. True honor will never be denied where due, never be given where undeserved, and, since none but the worthy are permitted there, no one will have an unworthy ambition of glory. Perfect peace will reign, since nothing in ourselves or in any others could disturb this peace. The promised reward of virtue will be the best and the greatest of all possible prizes—the very Giver of virtue himself, for that is what the prophet meant: "I will be your God and you will be my people."[57] God will be the source of every satisfaction, more than any heart can rightly crave, more than life and health, food and wealth, glory and honor, peace and every good—so that God, as Paul said, "may be all in all." He will be the consummation of all our desiring—the object of our unending vision, of our unlessening love, of our unwearying praise. And in this gift of vision, this response of love, this paean of praise, all alike will share, as all will share in everlasting life. . . .

There is a clear indication of this final sabbath if we take the seven ages of world history as being "days" and calculate in accordance with the data furnished by the Scriptures. The first age or day is that from Adam to the flood; the second, from the flood to Abraham. (These two "days" were not identical in length of time, but in each there were ten generations.) Then follow the three ages, each consisting of fourteen generations, as recorded in the Gospel of Matthew: the first, from Abraham to David; the second, from David to the transmigration to Babylon; the third, from then to Christ's nativity in the flesh. Thus, we have five ages. The sixth is the one in which we now are. It is an age not to be measured by any precise number of generations, since we are told, "It is not for you to know the times or dates which the Father has fixed by his own authority."[58] After this "day," God will rest on the "seventh day," in the sense that God will make us, who are to be this seventh day, rest in him.

There is no need here to speak in detail of each of these seven "days." Suffice it so say that this "seventh day" will be our sabbath and that it will end in no evening but only in the Lord's day—that eighth and eternal day that dawned when Christ's resurrection heralded an eternal rest both for the spirit and for the body. On that day we will rest and see, see and love, love and praise—for this is to be the end without the end of all our living, that kingdom without end, the real goal of our present life. CITY OF GOD 22.30.[59]

The Degrees of Blessedness

A SUPERIOR REWARD FOR EVERYBODY. APHRAHAT: Furthermore, listen to the apostle, who said, "Every person according to their work will receive their reward."[60] The one who worked only a little will receive according to his negligence. The one who worked quickly will be rewarded according to his speed. And Job also said, "Far be it from God to commit iniquity; and far be it from him to sin. For according to one's works will he reward him, and a man will receive according to his ways."[61] The apostle also said, "Star excels star in brightness. So also is the resurrection of the dead."[62] Therefore know that even when we will enter into life, reward will excel reward, and glory will excel glory and recompense will excel recompense. Degree

---

[57]Lev 26:12. [58]Acts 1:7. [59]FC 24:505-11. [60]1 Cor 3:8. [61]Job 34:10-11. [62]1 Cor 15:41-42.

is higher than degree; and light is better than light in aspect. The sun excels the moon, and the moon is greater than the stars that are with it. And observe that the moon and the stars are also under the power of the sun, and their light is swallowed up in the splendor of the sun. And the sun has power along with the moon and the stars, that it may not abolish the night, which has been separated from the day. And when the sun was created, it was called a luminary. And observe that the sun and the moon and the stars are all called luminaries, but luminary excels luminary. The sun obscures the light of the moon, and the moon likewise darkens the light of the stars, and star excels star in its light. DEMONSTRATIONS 22.19.[63]

THE RIGHTEOUS TOIL TO AVOID LOSS.
JEROME: And if a penny was given to all the laborers, those of the first, the third, the sixth, the ninth and the eleventh hours, and they came first for the reward who were the last to work in the vineyard, even here the persons described do not belong to one time or one age. Rather, from the beginning of the world to the end of it there are different calls and a special meaning attaches to each. Abel and Seth were called at the first hour; Enoch and Noah at the third; Abraham, Isaac, and Jacob at the sixth; Moses and the prophets at the ninth; at the eleventh the Gentiles, to whom the recompense was first given because they believed on the crucified Lord. And inasmuch as it was hard for them to believe, they earned a great reward. Many kings and prophets have desired to see the things that we see, and have not seen them. But the one penny does not represent one reward, but one life and one deliverance from Gehenna. And as by the favor of the sovereign those guilty of various crimes are released from prison, and each one, according to his toil and exertions, is in this or that condition of life, so too the penny, as it were by the favor of our Sovereign, is the discharge from prison of us all by baptism. Now our work is, according to our different virtues, to prepare for ourselves a different future.

So far I have replied to the separate portions of his argument. I will now address myself to the general question. Our Lord says to his disciples, "Whoever would become great among you, let him be least of all."[64] If we are all to be equal in heaven, in vain do we humble ourselves here that we may be greater there. Of the two debtors who owed, one five hundred dollars,[65] the other fifty, he to whom most was forgiven loved most, as the Savior says.[66] "I say to you, her sins which are many are forgiven her, for she has loved much. But to whom little is forgiven, the same loves little."[67] He who loves little and has little forgiven, he will of course be of inferior rank. The householder, when he set out, delivered to his servants his goods: to one five talents, to another two, to another one, to each according to his ability. It is similarly written in another Gospel that a nobleman setting out for a far country to receive for himself a kingdom and a return on his investment called the servants and gave them each a sum of money. One gained ten pounds, another five, and they, each according to his ability and the gain he had made, received ten or five cities. But one had received a talent, or a pound, buried it in the ground, or tied it up in a napkin, and kept it until his master's return. Our first thought is that if, according to the modern Zeno, the righteous do not toil in hope of reward but to avoid the loss of what they already have, he who buried his pound or talent that he might not lose it did no wrong. The caution of him who kept his money is worthy of more praise, then, than the fruitless toil of those who wore themselves out and yet received no reward for their labor. Then observe that the very talent that was taken from the timid or negligent servant was not given to him who had the smaller profit but to him

---

[63]NPNF 2 13:408*. [64]Mt 20:26. [65]Older translations have "pence." [66]Mt 25:15-30. [67]Lk 7:47.

who had gained the most, that is, to him who had been placed over ten cities. If difference of rank is not constituted by the difference in number, why did our Lord say, "He gave to everyone according to his ability"? If the gain of five talents and ten talents is the same, why were not ten cities given to him who gained the least and five to him who gained the most? But that our Lord is not satisfied with what we have but always desires more, he himself shows by saying, "Why did you not give my money to the money changers, so that when I came I might have received it with usury?" The apostle Paul understood this and, forgetting those things that were behind, reached forward to those things that were in front,[68] that is, he made daily progress and did not keep the grace given to him carefully wrapped up in a napkin but his spirit, like the capital of a keen man of business, was renewed from day to day. And if he were not always growing larger, he thought himself growing less. Six cities of refuge are mentioned in the law. They were provided for fugitives who committed involuntary homicides, and the cities themselves belonged to the priests. I should like to ask whether you would put those fugitives among your goats or among our sheep. If they were goats, they would be slain like other homicides and would not enter the cities of God's ministers. If you say they were sheep, they will not possibly be such sheep as can enjoy full liberty and feed without fear of wolves. And it will be plain to you that sheep indeed they are, but wandering sheep: that they are on the right hand but do not stand there: they flee until the high priest dies and, descending into hell, liberates their souls. The Gibeonites met the children of Israel, and although other nations were slaughtered, they were kept as woodsmen and water carriers. And of such value were they in God's eyes that the family of Saul was destroyed for the wrong done to them. Where would you put them? Among the goats? But they were not slain, and they were avenged by the determination of God. Among the sheep? But holy Scripture says they were not of the same merit as the Israelites. You see then that they do indeed stand on the right hand but are of a far inferior grade. Jonathan came between David, the holy man, and Saul, the worst of kings, and we can neither place him among the goat kids because he was worthy of a prophet's love nor among the rams; otherwise we would make him equal to David—this is particularly the case knowing that he was slain. He will, therefore, be among the sheep, but low down. And just as in the case of David and Jonathan, you will be bound to recognize differences between sheep and sheep. "That servant who knew his lord's will and did not make ready or act according to his will will be beaten with many stripes; but he who knew not and did things worthy of stripes will be beaten with few stripes. And to whomever much is given, of him will much be required; and to whom they commit much, of him will they ask the more."[69] Look! More or less is committed to different servants, and according to the nature of the trust, as well as of the sin, is the number of stripes inflicted. AGAINST JOVINIANUS 2.32-33.[70]

NO JEALOUSY OVER UNEQUAL DEGREES OF GLORY. AUGUSTINE: But what's the implication of this that comes next: "In my Father's house there are many lodgings, if not that they were also afraid for themselves"? That's why they had to be told, "Do not let your hearts be troubled."[71] Which of them, after all, would not be afraid, when Peter, more confident and quicker off the mark than the rest, was told, "The cock will not crow until you have denied me three times"?[72] So they were right to be troubled, then, as though they were going to be cut off from him. But on hearing "In my Father's house there are many lodgings; if not, would I have told you that I am on my way to prepare a place

---

[68]See Phil 3:13. [69]Lk 12:47-48. [70]NPNF 2 6:412-13*. [71]Jn 14:1. [72]Jn 13:38.

for you?"⁷³ their troubled hearts are relieved; they are reassured and confident that even after encountering their dangerous temptations, they are going to be lodged in God's house together with Christ. Because even if one is braver than another, one wiser than another, one more just than another, one holier than another, "in my Father's house there are many lodgings." None of them will be turned away from that house, where each of them is going to receive such lodgings as he deserves.

That ten-dollar bill⁷⁴ indeed, which the householder gave instructions was to be given to all those who had worked in the vineyard, was the same for all of them; he made no distinction between those who had worked a shorter time and those who had worked longer. This money, of course, stands for eternal life, in which nobody lives longer than anyone else, because life is not measured out in different proportions in eternity. But the many lodgings represent the varying worth of people's merits in the one common eternal life. "One thing, you see, is the glory of the sun, another the glory of the moon, another the glory of the stars; star after all differs from star in glory; such too is the resurrection of the dead."⁷⁵ Like the stars in heaven, the saints have been allotted lodgings of varying glory in heaven; but in virtue of the same ten-dollar bill for all of them, none is cut off from the kingdom; and in this way "God will be all in all,"⁷⁶ so that since "God is charity,"⁷⁷ charity will ensure that what each has in particular will be common to all. In this way, you see, each one will also have, when he loves it in another, what he does not have himself. And so there will be no jealousy over the unequal degrees of glory, since in all of them will be reigning the unity of charity. HOMILIES ON THE GOSPEL OF JOHN 67.2.⁷⁸

The Communion of Saints

THE LAMB IS PRESENT EVERYWHERE.
JEROME: You say that the souls of apostles and martyrs have their dwelling place in the bosom of Abraham, or in a place where they are refreshed or under the altar of God, and that they cannot leave their own tombs and be present wherever they want. They are, it seems, of senatorial rank and are not subjected to the worst kind of prison and the society of murderers but are kept apart in liberal and honorable custody in the isles of the blessed and the Elysian fields. Will you lay down the law for God? Will you put the apostles in chains so that they are kept in confinement until the day of judgment and are not with their Lord even though it is written concerning them, "they follow the Lamb wherever he goes"?⁷⁹ If the Lamb is present everywhere, the same must be believed respecting those who are with the Lamb. And while the devil and the demons wander through the whole world and with only too great speed present themselves everywhere, are martyrs, after the shedding of their blood, to be kept out of sight shut up in a coffin from which they cannot escape? You say, in your pamphlet, that so long as we are alive we can pray for one another; but once we die, the prayer of no person for another can be heard, and all the more because the martyrs, though they cry for the avenging of their blood,⁸⁰ have never been able to obtain their request. If apostles and martyrs while still in the body can pray for others, when they ought still to be anxious for themselves, how much more must they do so once they have won their crowns and have overcome and triumphed?

A single man, Moses, often wins pardon from God for six hundred thousand armed men.⁸¹ Stephen, the follower of his Lord and the first Christian martyr, entreats pardon for his persecutors⁸²—and you're saying that once

---

⁷³Jn 14:2. ⁷⁴Older translations have "penny." ⁷⁵1 Cor 15:41-42. ⁷⁶1 Cor 15:28. ⁷⁷1 Jn 4:8. ⁷⁸WSA forthcoming; cf. NPNF 1 7:321**. ⁷⁹Rev 14:4. ⁸⁰Rev 6:10. ⁸¹Ex 32:30-35. ⁸²Acts 7:59-60.

they have entered on their life with Christ, will they have less power than before? The apostle Paul[83] says that 276 souls were given to him in the ship; and when, after his dissolution, he has begun to be with Christ, must he shut his mouth and be unable to say a word for those who throughout the whole world have believed in his gospel? Will Vigilantius the live dog be better than Paul the dead lion? I should be right in saying so after Ecclesiastes,[84] if I admitted that Paul is dead in spirit. The truth is that the saints are not called dead but are said to be asleep. This is why[85] Lazarus, who was about to rise again, is said to have slept. And the apostle forbids[86] the Thessalonians to be sorry for those who were asleep. As for you, when wide awake, you are asleep, and asleep when you write, and you bring before me an apocryphal book that, under the name of Esdras,[87] is read by you and those of a similar feather. In this book it is written that after death no one dares pray for others. I have never read the book: for what need is there to take up what the church does not receive? It can hardly be your intention to confront me with Balsamus, and Barbelus, and the Thesaurus of Manichaeus and the ludicrous name of Leusiboras—though possibly because you live at the foot of the Pyrenees and border on Iberia, you follow the incredible marvels of the ancient heretic Basilides and his so-called knowledge, which is actually ignorance—and set forth what is condemned by the authority of the whole world. I say this because in your short treatise you quote Solomon as if he were on your side, though Solomon never wrote the words in question at all; so that, as you have a second Esdras you may have a second Solomon. And, if you like, you may read the imaginary revelations of all the patriarchs and prophets, and, when you have learned them, you may sing them among the women in their weaving shops, or rather order them to be read in your taverns, the more easily by these melancholy ditties to stimulate the ignorant mob to replenish their cups. AGAINST VIGILANTIUS 6.[88]

VICTORS IN THE LIFE TO COME. AUGUSTINE: Faustus also slanders us because we honor the memories of the martyrs saying that we have turned the idols into martyrs for this purpose. I am not moved so much to reply to this slander as to show that, out of a desire to slander us, Faustus himself chose to deviate from the vanities of Mani himself and somehow carelessly to fall into the common and poetic idea of the pagans from which he wants to appear most far removed. For, after he said that we had turned the idols "into martyrs, whom you worship with similar prayers," he said, "You placate with wine and meals the shades of the dead." Are there, then, shades of the dead? We have never heard this in your teachings; we have never read this in your writings. In fact, you used to speak against such views, claiming that the souls of the dead that are evil and less purified either return in cycles or enter into some worse punishments, but that good souls are placed on ships and, sailing in the sky, pass from here into that figment of the imagination, the land of light, for which they died fighting. And in that way no souls are detained around the tombs of their bodies. Where, then, do the shades of the dead come from? What is their substance? What is their place? But out of a desire to speak evil, Faustus forgot what he professed. Or perhaps he dreamed of the shades and dictated this while asleep, and he did not wake up when he read his own words. Christian people, however, celebrate the memorials of the martyrs with religious solemnity both in order to encourage the imitation of them and in order to be united with their merits and helped by their prayers. We do this in such a way, however, that we erect altars to none of the martyrs but to the God of the martyrs, although at the memori-

---

[83]Acts 27:37. [84]Eccl 9:4. [85]Jn 11:11. [86]1 Thess 4:13. [87]2 Esd (4 Ezra) 7:105. [88]NPNF 2 6:419-20.

als of the martyrs. After all, what bishop, while standing at the altar in the places where their holy bodies are buried, ever said, "We offer this to you, Peter or Paul or Cyprian"? Rather, what is offered is offered to God, who crowned the martyrs, but at the memorials of those martyrs he crowned, so that from the suggestive power of those places there may arise a greater feeling to increase our love both for those whom we can imitate and for him by whose help we are able to do so.

We reverence the martyrs, therefore, with that cult of love and fellowship by which we reverence in this life holy men and women of God whose heart we see is ready for great suffering on behalf of the truth of the gospel. But we reverence the martyrs more devoutly the more securely we praise them after all their struggles have been overcome, and also to the extent that we proclaim them with more confident praise when they are already victors in the life to come than when they are still fighting in this life. AGAINST FAUSTUS, A MANICHAEAN 20.21.[89]

THE KINGDOM OF CHRIST. AUGUSTINE: This makes it clear that the mixed kingdom must be the church, such as it exists in its temporal stage, while the unmixed kingdom is the church such as it will be when it is to contain no evildoer. Consequently, the church, even in this world, here and now, is the kingdom of Christ and the kingdom of heaven. Here and now Christ's saints reign with him, although not in the way they are destined to reign hereafter; but the "weeds" do not reign with him, even now, although they grow along with the "wheat" in the church. The only ones who reign with him are those who follow Paul's prescription: "Therefore, if you have risen with Christ, seek the things that are above, where Christ is seated at the right hand of God. Mind the things that are above, not the things that are on earth"[90]—those of whom Paul says in another place that their "citizenship is in heaven."[91] Those alone reign with Christ whose presence in his kingdom is such that they themselves are his kingdom; for, of course, we cannot call the "kingdom of Christ" such people as happen to be in it and will be until all scandals are to be gathered out from it at the world's end but who seek in it "their own interests, not those of Jesus Christ."[92] CITY OF GOD 20.9.[93]

Eternal Damnation

THE CORRUPTERS OF THE CHRISTIAN CHURCH. IGNATIUS OF ANTIOCH: Do not be mistaken, my brothers. Those who corrupt families will not inherit the kingdom of God. If, then, those who do this as respects the flesh have suffered death, how much more will this be the case with anyone who corrupts by wicked doctrine the faith of God, for which Jesus Christ was crucified! Such a person, becoming defiled, will go away into everlasting fire, and so will everyone who listens to him. Do not be mistaken, my brothers. Those who corrupt families will not inherit the kingdom of God. And if those who corrupt mere human families are condemned to death, how much more will those suffer everlasting punishment who endeavor to corrupt the church of Christ, for which the Lord Jesus, the only-begotten Son of God, endured the cross and submitted to death! Whoever "has gotten fat"[94] and "become gross," nullifying his doctrine, will go into hell. In the same way, everyone who has received from God the power of discernment and yet follows an unskillful shepherd and receives a false opinion for the truth will be punished. "What communion has light with darkness? Or Christ with Belial? Or what portion has he who believes with an infidel? or the temple of God with idols?"[95] And in the same way, I say, what communion has truth with

---

[89]*WSA* 1 20:278-79*. [90]Col 3:1-2. [91]Phil 3:20. [92]Phil 2:21. [93]FC 24:276. [94]Deut 32:15. [95]2 Cor 6:14-16.

falsehood? Or righteousness with unrighteousness? Or true doctrine with that which is false? EPISTLE TO THE EPHESIANS 16.[96]

THE GRACE OF CHRIST. MARTYRDOM OF POLYCARP: Looking to the grace of Christ, they despised all the torments of this world, redeeming themselves from eternal punishment by the suffering of a single hour. For this reason the fire of their savage executioners appeared cool to them. For they kept before their view their escape from that fire that is eternal and never will be quenched. They looked forward with the eyes of their heart to those good things that are laid up for those who endure—things "which ear has not heard, nor eye seen, neither have entered into the heart of man"[97] but were revealed by the Lord to them, inasmuch as they were no longer human but had already become angels. And, in a similar way, those who were condemned to the wild beasts endured dreadful tortures, being stretched out on beds full of spikes and subjected to various other kinds of torments, in order that, if it were possible, the tyrant might, by their lingering tortures, lead them to a denial of Christ. MARTYRDOM OF POLYCARP 2.[98]

THE MYSTERIES OF GOD. LETTER TO DIOGNETUS: On the contrary, he who takes on himself the burden of his neighbor; he who, in whatever respect he may be superior is ready to benefit another who is deficient; he who, whatever he has received from God distributes these to the needy—he becomes a god to those who receive his benefits: he is an imitator of God. Then you will see, while still on earth, that God in the heavens rules over the universe; then you will begin to speak the mysteries of God; then you will both love and admire those who suffer punishment because they will not deny God; then you will condemn the deceit and error of the world when you will know what it is to live truly in heaven, when you will despise that which is here esteemed to be death, when you will fear what is truly death which is reserved for those who will be condemned to the eternal fire which will afflict those who are committed to it unto the very end. Then will you admire those who for righteousness' sake endure the fire that is but for a moment and will count them happy when you come to know that fire. LETTER TO DIOGNETUS 10.[99]

THINGS THAT DESTROY THE SOUL. EPISTLE OF BARNABAS: The way of darkness is crooked and full of cursing. It is the way of eternal death and punishment filled with the things that destroy the soul: idolatry, over-confidence, the arrogance of power, hypocrisy, double-heartedness, adultery, murder, rape, pride, transgression, deceit, malice, self-reliance, poisoning, magic, avarice and lack of the fear of God. There are also those along this way who persecute the good, those who hate truth, those who love falsehood, those who don't know the reward of righteousness, those who don't hang on to what is good, those who do not act with justice for the widow and orphan, those who pay no attention to the fear of God, [but incline] to wickedness. Meekness and patience are far from them. They are the kind of people who love vanity, follow after a reward, have no pity for the needy and don't help out when someone else is overcome with work. They are prone to speak evil and are ignorant of the one who made them. They are murderers of children, destroyers of the workmanship of God. They turn away the one who is in need and oppress the afflicted. They are advocates of the rich and unjust judges of the poor, and are in every respect transgressors. EPISTLE OF BARNABAS 20.[100]

PARTAKERS OF THE RIGHTEOUS WORD. HERMAS: "Now the other stones that you saw cast far away from the tower and falling on the public road and rolling from it into pathless

---

[96]ANF 1:56**. [97]1 Cor 2:9. [98]ANF 1:39*. [99]ANF 1:29*.
[100]ANF 1:149**.

places are those who have indeed believed but through doubt have abandoned the true road. Thinking, then, that they could find a better road, they wander and become wretched and enter on pathless places. But those who fell into the fire and were burned are those who have departed forever from the living God. The thought of repentance does not even enter into their hearts because of their devotion to their lusts and to the crimes that they committed. Do you want to know who the others are which fell near the waters but could not be rolled into them? These are they who have heard the word and want to be baptized in the name of the Lord. But when the chastity demanded by the truth comes into their recollection, they draw back and again walk after their own wicked desires." She finished her exposition of the tower. But I, shameless as I yet was, asked her, "Is repentance possible for all those stones that have been cast away and did not fit into the building of the tower, and will they yet have a place in this tower? "Repentance," said she, "is still possible, but in this tower they cannot find a suitable place. But in another and much inferior place they will be laid, and that, too, only when they have been tortured and completed the days of their sins. And the reason they will be transferred is only because they have partaken of the righteous Word. And then only will they be removed from their punishments, when the thought of repenting of the evil deeds that they have done has come into their hearts. But if it does not come into their hearts, they will not be saved because of their hard heart." SHEPHERD, VISION 3.7.[101]

SINNERS WILL BE CONSUMED. HERMAS: But the heathen and sinners, like the withered trees that you saw, will be found to be those who have been withered and unfruitful in that world. They will be burned as wood and thus made public, because their actions were evil during their lives. For the sinners will be consumed because they sinned and did not repent, and the heathen will be burned because they didn't know him who created them. SHEPHERD, SIMILITUDE 4.[102]

ONE BODY OF ONE LOVE. HERMAS: "How, sir," I said, "did they become worse, after having known God?" "The one who does not know God," he answered, "and practices evil receives a certain chastisement for his wickedness. But the one who has known God should do good and stop doing evil. If, then, when he is supposed to be doing good he still does evil, doesn't he appear to do greater evil than the one who does not know God? This is why those who have not known God and do evil are condemned to death. But those who have known God, and have seen his mighty works and still continue in evil will be doubly punished and will die forever. In this way, then, the church of God will be purified. For as you saw the stones rejected from the tower, and delivered to the evil spirits and cast out from there, so they also will be cast out, and]there will be one body of the purified as the tower also became, as it were, of one stone after its purification. A similar thing will happen to the church of God after it has been purified and has rejected the wicked, the hypocrites, the blasphemers, the waverers and those who commit wickedness of different kinds. After these have been cast away, the church of God will be one body, of one mind, of one understanding, of one faith, of one love. And then the Son of God will be very happy and will rejoice over them because he has received his people pure."[103] "All these things, sir," I said, "are great and glorious." SHEPHERD, SIMILITUDE 9.18.[104]

PUNISHMENT FOR THE UNRIGHTEOUS. PSEUDO-CLEMENT OF ROME: For the Lord said, "I come to gather all nations and tongues."[105] This refers to the day of his ap-

---

[101]ANF 2:15*. [102]ANF 2:33*. [103]Eph 5:27. [104]ANF 2:50**. [105]Is 66:18.

pearing when he will come and redeem us—each one according to his works. The unbelievers will see his glory and might and, when they see the empire of the world in Jesus, they will be surprised, saying, "Woe to us, because you existed and we didn't know it, neither did we believe or obey the elders who plainly showed us our salvation." And "their worm will not die, neither will their fire be quenched; and they will be a spectacle unto all flesh."[106] He is talking about the great day of judgment when they will see those among us who were guilty of ungodliness and erred in their estimate of the commands of Jesus Christ. The righteous, having succeeded both in enduring the trials and hating the indulgences of the soul, whenever they witness how those who have swerved and denied Jesus by words or deeds are punished with grievous torments in fire unquenchable, will give glory to their God and say, "There will be hope for him who has served God with his whole heart." 2 CLEMENT 17.[107]

THINGS PROMPTED BY EVIL SPIRITS.
JUSTIN MARTYR: More than all others we are your helpers and allies in promoting peace, seeing that we hold the view that it is just as impossible for the wicked, the covetous and the conspirator to escape God's notice as it is for the virtuous. Each person goes to everlasting punishment or salvation according to the value of his actions. For if everyone knew this, no one would choose wickedness even for a little, knowing that he goes to the everlasting punishment of fire. Instead, he would by all means restrain himself and adorn himself with virtue so that he might obtain the good gifts of God and escape the punishments. There are those who, because of the laws and punishments you impose, try to escape detection when they offend—and they offend, too, under the impression that it is quite possible to escape your detection, since you are only human. However, if those same people learned and were convinced of the fact that nothing, whether actually done or only intended, can escape the knowledge of God, they would by all means live decently in light of the penalties threatened, as even you yourselves will admit. But you seem to be afraid that everyone would become righteous and you would not longer have anyone to punish. Such would be the concern of public executioners but not of good princes. However, as we said earlier, we are persuaded that these things are prompted by evil spirits who demand sacrifices and service even from those who live unreasonably. As for you, however, we presume that you who aim at a reputation for piety and philosophy will do nothing unreasonable. But if you also, like the foolish, prefer custom to truth, do what you have power to do. But rulers who esteem opinion more than truth have only so much power, just like the power robbers have in a desert. The Word himself declares that you will not succeed, and we know there is no ruler more kingly and just than him, after God who begat him. For as all shrink from succeeding to the poverty or sufferings or obscurity of their ancestors, so whatever the Word forbids us to choose, the sensible person will not choose. Our Teacher foretold that all these things would happen—he who is both Son and apostle of God the Father of all and the ruler, Jesus Christ; from whom also we have the name of Christians. For this reason we have become even more sure of all the things he taught us, since whatever he told us ahead of time would happen has in fact happened. Only God can tell about something happening before it happens and then have it occur just as it was foretold. FIRST APOLOGY 12.[108]

LIKE THE FIRES OF VOLCANOES. MINUCIUS FELIX: In the books and poems of the most learned poets there are warnings about that fiery river and about the heat flowing in all

---

[106]Is 66:24. [107]ANF 9:255-56**. [108]ANF 1:166**.

kinds of different turns from the Stygian marsh. These are the kinds of things these poets have delivered to us, prepared for eternal torments and known to them by what they have learned from demons and from the oracles of their prophets. Among their writings even king Jupiter himself is found swearing religiously by the parching banks and the black abyss, along with his worshipers, shuddering with the foreknowledge of the punishment destined to him—nor is there any end to these torments. There the intelligent fire burns the limbs and restores them, feeds on them and nourishes them. Just as the fires of the thunderbolts strike on the bodies and do not consume them and the fires of Mount Aetna and of Mount Vesuvius burn as they glow but are not wasted—so that punishing fire is not fed by the waste of those who burn but is nourished by the unexhausted eating away of their bodies. But no one except a profane individual would hesitate to believe that those who do not know God deserve this torment because they are impious and unrighteous, since it is no less wicked to be ignorant of than to offend the Father of all and the Lord of all. And although ignorance of God is a sufficient enough for punishment—even as knowledge of him helps in securing pardon—yet if we Christians are compared with you, although in some things our discipline is inferior, we will still be found much better than you. For you forbid, and yet commit, adulteries; we are born men only for our own wives. You punish crimes when committed; with us, even to think of crimes is to sin. You are afraid of those who are aware of what you do; we are even afraid of our own conscience alone, without which we cannot exist. And, finally, from your numbers the prison boils over, but there is no Christian there, unless he stands accused because of his religion or he is a deserter. OCTAVIUS 35.[109]

ALL THINGS WILL PASS AWAY LIKE A SHADOW. CYPRIAN: What will then be the glory of faith? What will be the punishment of faithlessness? When the day of judgment comes, what joy will believers have? But what sorrow will unbelievers have that they should have been unwilling to believe here and now that they should be unable to return so that they might believe! An ever-burning Gehenna will burn up the condemned—a punishment that devours with living flames. There is no source for these flames that might run out so that there might at least be some time where they might have either respite or an end to their torments. Souls with their bodies will be reserved in infinite tortures for suffering. Thus the person who here gazed on us for a season will be seen by us forever, and the short joy that those cruel eyes experienced in the persecutions that they made for us will be compensated for by a perpetual spectacle, according to the truth of holy Scripture, which says, "Their worm will not die, and their fire will not be quenched; and they will be for a vision to all flesh."[110] And again: "Then will the righteous stand in great constancy before the face of those who have afflicted them, and have taken away their labors. When they see it, they will be troubled with horrible fear, and will be amazed at the suddenness of their unexpected salvation; and they, repenting and groaning for anguish of spirit, will say within themselves, These are they whom we held for some time in derision, and as a proverb of reproach; we fools counted their life madness, and their end to be without honor. How are they numbered among the children of God, and their lot is among the saints! Therefore we have strayed from the way of truth, and the light of righteousness has not shined upon us, and the sun has not risen upon us. We wearied ourselves in the way of wickedness and destruction; we have gone through deserts where there lay no way; but we have not known the way of the Lord. What has pride profited us, or what good has the

---

[109]ANF 4:195**. [110]Is 66:24.

boasting of riches done us? All those things are passed away like a shadow."[111] The pain of punishment will then be without the fruit of penitence; weeping will be useless and prayer ineffectual. Too late they will believe in eternal punishment who would not believe in eternal life. To Demetrian 24.[112]

The Same Divine Fire Will Supply Bodies with Eternal Nourishment. Lactantius: First of all, therefore, we say that the power of God is so great that he perceives even incorporeal things and manages them as he wants to. For even angels fear God because they can be punished by him in some unspeakable manner. Devils dread him because they are tormented and punished by him. What wonder is it, therefore, if souls, though they are immortal, are nevertheless capable of suffering at the hand of God? For since they have nothing solid and tangible in themselves, they can suffer no violence from solid and corporeal beings. However, because they live in their spirits only, they are capable of being handled by God alone whose energy and substance is spiritual. And yet, the sacred writings also inform us in what manner the wicked are to undergo punishment. For because they have committed sins in their bodies, they will again be clothed with flesh so that they may make atonement in their bodies. And yet it will not be that flesh with which God clothed human beings, like this our earthly body. Rather, it will be indestructible and last forever so that it may be able to hold out against tortures and everlasting fire, the nature of which is different from this fire of ours that we use for the necessary purposes of life and that would go out unless it is sustained by the fuel of some material. That divine fire, however, always lives by itself and flourishes without any nourishment. It has no smoke mixed with it; instead, it is pure, liquid and fluid, kind of like water. For it is not urged upwards by any force, as our fire is, which the taint of the earthly body, by which it is held, and smoke intermingled, compels to leap forth and to fly upwards to the nature of heaven with a tremulous movement. The same divine fire, therefore, with one and the same force and power will both burn the wicked and will form them again, and will replace as much as it will consume of their bodies and will supply itself with eternal nourishment, which the poets transferred to the vulture of Tityus. Thus, it will only burn and affect them with a sense of pain, without however producing any waste from the bodies it burns which instead regain their substance. But when he judges the righteous, he will also try them with fire. Then those whose sins exceed either in weight or in number will be scorched by the fire and burned. But those whom full justice and maturity of virtue has imbued will not perceive that fire, for they have something of God in themselves that repels and rejects the violence of the flame. So great is the force of innocence that the flame shrinks from it without doing harm. Innocence has received a power from God that burns the wicked and is under the command of the righteous. But don't let anyone imagine that souls are immediately judged after death. All are detained in one common place of confinement until the time arrives when the great Judge will investigate what each person deserves. Then those whose piety has been approved will receive the reward of immortality, but those whose sins and crimes have been brought to light will not rise again but will be hidden in the same darkness with the wicked, being destined to certain punishment. Divine Institutes 7.21.[113]

We Have to Be Careful of Our Bodies. Cyril of Jerusalem: We will rise again, and all of us will have eternal bodies, though we won't all have the same bodies. A just person will receive a heavenly body so that he or she is worthy to live with the angels, whereas the sin-

---

[111]Wis 5:1-9. [112]ANF 5:464-65**. [113]ANF 7:216-17**.

ner will receive an eternal body that can never be consumed, though it burns eternally in fire. God is just in both cases in making this kind of arrangement, for nothing is done without the body. We blaspheme with the mouth, with the mouth we pray. We commit fornication through the body, and through the body we preserve our purity. We rob by the hand, by the hand we give alms, and so forth. Since the body has ministered to us in everything, it will share our lot in the hereafter. Therefore, brothers, let us be careful of our bodies and not abuse them as though they were not our own. Let us not say, like the heretics, that the vesture of the body does not belong to us. Instead, let us be concerned for it as our very own. For we must render an account to God of everything we have done through the body. CATECHETICAL LECTURE 18.19-20.[114]

CONQUEROR OF DEATH. GREGORY OF NAZIANZUS: I know the glittering sword and the blade made drunk in heaven, bidden to kill, to bring to naught, to make childless and to spare neither flesh nor marrow nor bones. I know him who, though free from passion, meets us like a bear robbed of her whelps, like a leopard in the way of the Assyrians, not only those of that day but if anyone now is an Assyrian in wickedness. Nor is it possible to escape the might and speed of his wrath when he watches over our impieties or to elude his jealousy, which knows how to devour his adversaries and pursues his enemies to the death. I know the emptying, the making void, the making waste, the melting of the heart and knocking of the knees together. These are the punishments of the ungodly. I do not dwell on the judgments to come, to which indulgence in this world delivers us, as it is better to be punished and cleansed now than to be transmitted to the torment to come. Then it will be the time of chastisement, not of cleansing. He who remembers God here is conqueror of death (as David has most excellently sung). But the departed in the grave do not have the option of confession and restoration. For God has confined life and action to this world and to the future the scrutiny of what has been done. ON HIS FATHER'S SILENCE, ORATION 16.7.[115]

THE LIGHT OF THE RIGHTEOUS IS EVERLASTING. GREGORY OF NAZIANZUS: Let me remind you again about illuminations, as I often do, and what holy Scripture has to say about them.... A light for the righteous has sprung up, and its partner is the joy of gladness. The light of the righteous is everlasting; and you are shining wondrously from the everlasting mountains. This is I think is said to God of the angelic powers that aid our efforts to do good. And you have heard David's words: "The Lord is my light and my salvation, whom shall I fear?"[116] And now he asks that the Light and the Truth may be sent forth for him. Now he gives thanks that he has a share in it, in that the Light of God is marked on him, so that the signs of the illumination given are impressed on him and recognized. There is only one light that we should shun—that light that is the offspring of the dreadful fire. Let us not walk in the light of our fire and in the flame that we have kindled. For I know a cleansing fire that Christ came to send on the earth, and he himself is anagogically called a fire. This Fire takes away whatever is material and of evil habits. This he desires to kindle immediately, because he wants good done for us quickly. He even gives us coals of fire to help us. I also know a fire that does not cleanse but avenges. I'm referring to either that fire of Sodom that he pours down on all sinners, mingled with brimstone and storms, or that which is prepared for the devil and his angels or that proceeds from the face of the Lord and shall burn up his enemies.

The unquenchable fire is even more fearful than these. It is filled with the worm that does

---

[114]FC 64:131**. [115]NPNF 2 7:249-50. [116]Ps 27:1.

not die but is eternal for the wicked. For all these belong to the destroying power, though some may prefer even in this place to take a more merciful view of this fire, worthy of the One that chastises. ON HOLY BAPTISM, ORATION 40.36.[117]

WHICH FIRES CAN BE PUT OUT? GREGORY OF NYSSA: It will be necessary to add to what has been said this remaining statement also: Those good things that are held out in the Gospels to those who have led a godly life are not the kinds of things that can be precisely described. For how is such a description possible with things that "eye has not seen, neither ear heard, neither have entered into the heart of man?"[118] Indeed, the sinner's life of torment presents no equivalent to anything that pains the senses here. Even if some of the punishments in that other world are named in terms that are well known here, the distinction is still not small. When you hear the word fire, you have been taught to think of a fire other than the fire we see, owing to something being added to that fire that we don't have in our fire here. For that fire is never quenched, whereas experience has discovered many ways of quenching fire here. And there is a huge difference between a fire that can be extinguished and one that does not allow itself to be extinguished. That fire, therefore, is something other than the fire we have here. If, again, a person hears the word worm, let not his thoughts, from the similarity of the term, be carried to the creature here that crawls on the ground. For the addition that it "does not die" suggests the thought of another reptile than that known here. Since, then, these things are set before us as expectations concerning the life that follows this one—being the natural outgrowth in the life of each person following his or her own particular disposition, according to the righteous judgment of God—it would be the better part of wisdom not to concern oneself with the present but with that which follows and to lay down the foundations for that unspeakable blessedness during this short and fleeting life. Making prudent choices, they should wean themselves from all experiences of evil now, in their lifetime here, or they will do so hereafter in their eternal reward. ADDRESS ON RELIGIOUS INSTRUCTION 40.[119]

TEARS SPRINGING FROM TRUE AFFECTION. CHRYSOSTOM: Let us then not only wail for the dead but also for those who have died in sins. They deserve wailing; they deserve beating of the breast and tears. For tell me what hope is there, when our sins accompany us there where sins can no longer be removed? As long as they were here, there was perhaps a great expectation that they would change, that they would become better. But when they are gone to hades, where nothing can be gained from repentance—for it is written, "In hell who will give you thanks?"[120]—are they not worthy of our lamentation? Let us wail for those who leave in this way. Let us wail. I hinder you not. Yet do not do so in an unseemly way, not in tearing our hair, or baring our arms, or lacerating our face or wearing black apparel, but only in soul, shedding in quiet the bitter tear. For we may weep bitterly without all that display. And not as in sport only. For the laments that many make are not all that different from a game. Those public mournings do not proceed from sympathy but from display, from emulation and vanity. Many women do this as their craft. Weep bitterly; moan at home when no one sees you. This is the character part of true sympathy. By this you profit yourself too. For one who laments another in such a way will be much more earnest never to fall into the same sins. Sin then will be an object of dread to you. Weep for the unbelievers; weep for those who differ in no way from them, those who leave this world

---

[117]NPNF 2 7:373**. [118]Is 64:4; 1 Cor 2:9. [119]NPNF 2 5:508-9**. [120]Ps 6:5.

without the illumination, without the seal! They indeed deserve our wailing, they deserve our groans; they are outside the palace with the culprits, with the condemned. For, "truly I say to you, unless one is born of water and the Spirit, he will not enter into the kingdom of heaven."[121] Mourn for those who have died in wealth and did not from their wealth think of any solace for their soul, who had power to wash away their sins and would not. Let us all weep for these in private and in public but with propriety, with gravity, not so as to make exhibitions of ourselves. Let us weep for these, not one day, or two, but all our life. Such tears spring not from senseless passion but from true affection. HOMILIES ON PHILIPPIANS 3.[122]

THE TWO DEATHS. AUGUSTINE: Even though in this life there is no flesh that can both feel pain and escape death, nevertheless, in the world to come, flesh will be different from what it is now, and there will be a different kind of death from the death of the body. In regard to this "second death," there will be no question of the soul being incapable of death, since its death will be everlasting. For, once the soul is without God, it will be incapable of escaping the pains of the body. The first kind of death drives an unwilling soul out of the body; the second death holds an unwilling soul in the body. What is common to both deaths is that it is the soul that must reluctantly suffer what the body inflicts.

The real difficulty, then, with unbelievers is that their whole attention is so focused on the fact that, in this life, no flesh that is susceptible of pain can escape bodily death that they overlook the fact that there is a reality higher than the body. That reality is the soul, without whose presence there would be neither life nor movement in the body. What is more, it is a reality that is susceptible of pain and not susceptible of death. Here, in fact, we have the reality that, conscious as it is of pain, it is immortal. And it is this capacity for immortality (already, as we know, inherent in everybody's soul) that, in the world to come, will be present in the bodies of the damned.

Furthermore, if we examine the matter more carefully, we will realize that so-called bodily pain really belongs to the soul. It is the soul, not the body, that is conscious of pain, even though the cause of the pain is present in the body and the pain is felt where the body is injured. So, too, it is the soul that is the source of life and of sensation in the body, even though we speak of "living bodies" and of "bodily sensations." We also speak of "bodies in pain," but, of course, there can be no pain in a body apart from the soul.

What we should say is that "the soul with its body" feels pain in the part of the body where something is happening to cause pain; that "the soul without its body" feels pain (even though the soul is in the body), whenever some cause, however invisible, causes the soul to feel anguish while the body remains uninjured; and that "the soul outside of the body" may feel pain, as in the case of the rich man in hell who cried out, "I am tormented in this flame."[123] On the contrary, even though we might say that "the body with its soul" feels pain, we cannot say that "the body without it soul" feels pain or, still less, that "the body outside of the soul" feels pain. If, then, there is any genuine argument connecting pain and death and reaching the conclusion that, because pain can occur, death is therefore possible, this argument would apply, if at all, to the death of the soul, since it is to the soul rather than to the body that pain pertains. But the fact is that the soul, which more truly feels pain than the body, cannot die. What follows is that there is no basis whatever for arguing that, because bodies in the future life are to be in pain, we therefore must believe that even in the future life they will die. CITY OF GOD 21.3.[124]

---

[121]Jn 3:5. [122]NPNF 1 13:196-97**. [123]Lk 16:24. [124]FC 24:342-43.

The Fire and the Worm. Augustine: There are some who think that both the "fire" and the "worm" here mentioned are meant as pains of the soul rather than of the body. Their argument is that, since those who repent too late and, therefore, in vain (because cut off from the kingdom of God) burn with anguish of soul, the "fire" can be taken very well to symbolize this burning anguish. They quote the words of the apostle: "Who is made to stumble, and I am not inflamed?"[125] They hold that the "worm" also must be taken to mean the soul, as can be seen, they think, in the text: "As a moth eats upon a garment, and a worm upon the wood, so the sadness of a man consumes the heart."[126]

However, those who have no doubt that in hell there will be sufferings for both soul and body hold that the body will be burned in fire while the soul will be gnawed, as it were, by the "worm" of grief. This is certainly a probable enough view, since it is absurd to think that either pain of body or anguish of soul will be lacking there. For me, however, it seems preferable to say that both "fire" and the "worm" apply to the body and that the reason for making no mention in Scripture of the anguish of the soul is that it is implied, though not made explicit. When the body is in such pain, the soul must be tortured by fruitless repentance. Take, for example, this text of the Old Testament: "The vengeance on the flesh of the ungodly is fire and worms."[127] It would have sufficed to say "the vengeance on the ungodly." What, then, could have been the reason for saying "on the flesh of the ungodly," except that both "fire" and "the worm" are to serve as punishment for the body? However, it may be argued that "vengeance on the flesh" was meant to imply that the vengeance is to fall on a person, insofar as he has lived according to the flesh. In support of this interpretation, there are the words of Paul: "For if you live according to the flesh you will die,"[128] words implying that it is because a person lives according to the flesh that he will suffer the "second death." Thus, each of us is free to make his own choice, either attributing "fire" (taken literally) to the body and "the worm" (in a figurative sense) to the soul or attributing both "fire" and "the worm," in their literal meanings, to the body. Suffice it to say that argument enough was given above to prove, first, that living creatures can continue in fire without being consumed and in pain without suffering death; second, that this is in virtue of a miracle of the omnipotent Creator; and, third, that anyone who denies the possibility of this miracle is simply unaware of the Source of all that is wonderful in all natures whatever. This source is God. It is he who made all the natural marvels, great and small, whom I have mentioned. And there is incomparably more that I did not mention. And it is he who embraced all these miracles within a single universe, which is itself the greatest of all these natural miracles. And so, I repeat, each one is free to choose whichever of the two interpretations he finds more satisfactory, namely, that "the worm," too, in its literal sense, applies to the body or that "the worm" is to be taken in a figurative sense to apply to the soul. Which of the two views is true the future reality will soon enough reveal, for then the knowledge of the saints will be in need of no experience of these sufferings but only of that full and perfect wisdom that will suffice to teach them all such truth. For now "we know in part," waiting for the time "when that which is perfect has come."[129] The one thing that we may by no means believe is that bodies in hell will be such that they will be unaffected by any pains inflicted by fire. City of God 21.9.[130]

One and the Same Fire. Augustine: This is the place to ask: How can the wicked spirits suffer by contact with fire, unless the fire, like anguish of soul, is immaterial rather

---

[125]2 Cor 11:29. [126]Prov 25:20. [127]Sir 7:17. [128]Rom 8:13. [129]1 Cor 13:9-10. [130]FC 24:364-66*.

than a material fire that pains by contact, as in the case of the bodies that are there tormented? The answer is: One and the same fire will serve as punishment for both mortals and devils, as we can see from the words of Christ: "Depart from me, accursed ones, into the everlasting fire which was prepared for the devil and his angels."[131] It may be, as scholars have speculated, that the demons have bodies of their own, composed of the kind of dense moist air that we feel, by impact, when the wind is blowing. That such air is highly susceptible to fire can be felt by anyone who is scalded by the steam of a hot bath. Before such steam could scald, it had to be heated; to be active, it had to be passive, that is, to suffer. On the other hand, if one insists that demons have no bodies, there is no call for any elaborate research or any need for fierce debate. It surely is enough to say that by some means, however mysterious, immaterial spirits can be sensitive to the pains of material fire in the same way that human spirits, which are no less immaterial, can be enclosed in their bodily members during life and, in the life to come, will be indissolubly united with their bodies. In the same way, the spirits of demons or, rather, the spirit-demons will be united to the material fires in which they must suffer, however incorporeal and immaterial they may be. This union, of course, will not be such that the spirits are breathed like life into the flames, so as to produce living beings consisting of spirit and matter. Nevertheless, as I have suggested, there will be a real union effected in some mysterious and indescribable manner, so that, although no life will be communicated to the flames, pain will be communicated from the fire. After all, the manner in which our spirits are united with our bodies in order to make us living beings is extraordinarily mysterious and incomprehensible to us, even though we are just such a union. CITY OF GOD 21.10.[132]

NO TORMENTS THAT WE KNOW OF COULD BE COMPARED WITH IT. AUGUSTINE: It is in vain, then, that some—indeed very many—moan about the eternal punishment and perpetual, uninterrupted torments of the lost but say they do not believe it will happen this way. It is not, indeed, that they directly oppose themselves to holy Scripture but, at the suggestion of their own feelings, they soften everything that seems hard and give a milder turn to statements that they think are rather designed to terrify than to be received as literally true. For "has God" they say, forgotten to be gracious? Has he in anger shut up his tender mercies?"[133] Now, they read this in one of the holy psalms. But without doubt we are to understand it as spoken of those who are elsewhere called "vessels of mercy,"[134] because even they are freed from misery not on account of any merit of their own but solely through the pity of God. Or, if the people we speak of insist that this passage applies to all humankind, there is no reason why they should therefore suppose that there will be an end to the punishment of those of whom it is said, "these will go away into everlasting punishment," for this will end in the same way and at the same time as the happiness of those of whom it is said, "but the righteous unto life eternal." But let them suppose, if the thought gives them pleasure, that the pains of the damned are, at certain intervals, in some degree assuaged. For even in this case the wrath of God—that is, their condemnation (for it is this, and not any disturbed feeling in the mind of God that is called his wrath)—remains on them. In other words, his wrath, though it still remains, does not shut up his tender mercies, although his tender mercies are exhibited not in putting an end to their eternal punishment but in mitigating or in granting them a respite from their torments. Notice the psalm does not say, "to put an end to his anger," or, "when his anger is passed

---

[131]Mt 25:41. [132]FC 24:366-67. [133]Ps 77:9. [134]Rom 9:23.

by," but "in his anger."¹³⁵ Now, if this anger stood alone, or if it existed in the smallest conceivable degree—still, to be lost out of the kingdom of God, to be an exile from the city of God, to be alienated from the life of God, to have no share in that great goodness that God has laid up for those who fear him and has worked out for those who trust in him—it would still be a punishment so great that, supposing it was eternal, no torments that we know of could be compared with it even if those torments continued through as many ages as human imagination could conceive. ENCHIRIDION 112.¹³⁶

THE RESURRECTION OF THE RIGHTEOUS AND SINNERS. RUFINUS OF AQUILEIA: This body then, which is now corruptible, will by the grace of the resurrection be incorruptible, and this which is now mortal will be clothed with the virtues of immortality, that, as "Christ rising from the dead dies no more, death has no more dominion over him,"¹³⁷ so those who will rise in Christ will never again feel corruption or death. This is not because the nature of flesh will have been cast off but because its condition and quality will have been changed. There will be a body, therefore, that will rise from the dead incorruptible and immortal—a body not only of the righteous but also of sinners; of the righteous that they may be able ever to abide with Christ, of sinners that they may undergo without end the punishment due to them. A COMMENTARY ON THE APOSTLES' CREED 45.¹³⁸

INCORPOREAL ELEMENTS. GREGORY THE GREAT:

Gregory: If you believe on the basis of God's Word that the souls of the saints are in heaven, you must also believe that the souls of the wicked are in hell. For if eternal justice brings God's chosen ones to glory, does it not follow that it also brings the wicked to their doom? The saints, then, rejoice in bliss, and we cannot but believe that from the day of their death the reprobate burn in fire.

Peter: What reason have we to believe that a physical fire can attack an incorporeal substance?

Gregory: If the incorporeal spirit of a living person is held fast in the body, why should the incorporeal spirit after death not be held fast in corporeal fire?

Peter: In a living person the incorporeal spirit is held in the body because it imparts life to the body.

Gregory: If the incorporeal spirit can be held in the body to which it gives life, why should it not be held for punishment in a place where it endures punishment? When we say that the spirit is held by fire we mean that it is in torment of fire by seeing and feeling. Seeing the fire, it begins to suffer, and when it sees itself attacked by flames it feels the burning. In this way a corporeal substance burns an incorporeal one, because an invisible burn and an invisible pain are received from visible fire. In this physical fire, therefore, the incorporeal mind is tortured with an incorporeal fire that causes pain, although from the words of Scripture we gather that the soul suffers from the burning heat not only through ill sense of sight but also by actually experiencing the pain. We know from Christ's words that the rich man was buried in hell, and his prayer to Abraham declares that his soul was held in fire. "Send Lazarus," he says, "to dip the tip of his finger in water, and cool my tongue; I am tormented in this flame."¹³⁹ Since Christ describes the condemned sinner Dives surrounded by the flames of hell, no one with understanding would deny that the souls of the wicked are held fast in fire.

Peter: The demands of reason and the author-

---

¹³⁵Ps 78. ¹³⁶NPNF 1 3:273**. ¹³⁷Rom 6:9. ¹³⁸NPNF 2 3:561-62*. ¹³⁹Lk 16:24.

ity of Scripture incline me to believe. But left to itself, my mind stubbornly returns to the question, for how can an incorporeal substance be held and tortured by one that is corporeal? This is beyond my comprehension.

Gregory: Tell me this, Peter. Do you think that the apostate spirits who were cast down from their heavenly glory were corporeal or incorporeal?

Peter: Who in his right senses would say that a spirit is corporeal?

Gregory: Well then, would you say the fire of hell is incorporeal or corporeal?

Peter: I am firmly convinced that the fire of hell is corporeal and that bodies are tortured in it.

Gregory: On the last day Christ will say to the wicked, "Go far from me you that are accursed, into that eternal fire which has been prepared for the devil and his angels."[140] If these incorporeal beings, the devil and his angels, are going to be tortured by physical fire, is it incredible that souls should be able to suffer physical torments even before they are again united with the body?

Peter: The point is now clear, and I should not be troubled with further doubts on this question.

DIALOGUES 4.29-30.[141]

THE EVERLASTING JUDGE. GREGORY THE GREAT:

Peter: Surely we do not hold that those who are once plunged into hell will burn there forever?

Gregory: We most certainly do! And that truth stands solid and unshaken. Just as the joys of heaven will never cease, so, too, there is no end to the torments of the damned. For Christ says, "And these will pass on to eternal punishment, and the just to eternal life."[142] Since the promise he made is true, there is no reason to suppose that his threat will prove false.

Peter: What if someone should say: God has merely threatened sinners with eternal punishment to keep them from committing sins?

Gregory: If he makes use of empty threats to keep us from injustice, then the promises he makes to lead us to justice are likewise worthless. But no one in his right mind would entertain such a thought. If God threatened us without ever intending to fulfill his threat, we should have to call him deceitful instead of merciful. And that would be sacrilegious.

Peter: I should like to know whether it is just to inflict an everlasting punishment for a fault that is finite.

Gregory: Your objection would be valid if the supreme Judge were to consider only the deeds people perform without looking into their hearts. To be sure, the sin that a wicked person commits comes to an end when he dies. But would he not be willing to live on endlessly, if that were possible, in order to continue sinning? By not leaving off sinning during his lifetime, he shows his desire to continue in sin forever. The full justice of the Judge, therefore, demands that the wicked, who never wished to be rid of sin during life, should never be without punishment in eternity.

Peter: But a just person does not thrive on cruelty; he has his offending servants punished in order to correct them. The chastisement serves to bring them to better ways. But the wicked condemned to the fires of hell will never correct their wickedness. To what purpose, then, do they burn in hell forever?

Gregory: Almighty God, being a God of love, does not gratify his anger by torturing wretched sinners. However, since he is a God

---
[140]Cf. Mt 25:41. [141]FC 39:225-27. [142]Mt 25:46.

of justice, the punishment of the wicked cannot satisfy him even if it continues eternally. All the wicked condemned to hell are being punished for their wickedness, to be sure. Yet there is another reason why they burn, namely, that the elect may see in God all the joys they experience and may see in the damned all the tortures they escaped. Seeing the terrible punishment for sins that they avoided with God's help, they become all the more conscious of the eternal debt of gratitude they owe God for the graces they received.

Peter: But why are they called saints if they do not pray for their enemies whom they see in torments? Were not the words "pray for your enemies"[143] addressed especially to them?

Gregory: They pray for their enemies at a time when the hearts of their enemies can still produce fruits of repentance and through penance gain salvation. What better prayer could we say for our enemies than that proposed by Paul? "It may be," he says, "that God will enable them to repent, and acknowledge the truth; so they will recover their senses, and shake off the snare by which the devil, till now, has held them prisoners to his will."[144] And how will one pray for one's enemies when these can no longer repent of their evil ways and turn to works of righteousness?

The saints in heaven, therefore, do not offer prayers for the damned in hell for the same reason that we do not pray for the devil and his angels. Nor do saintly people on earth pray for deceased infidels and godless people. And why? Because they do not wish to waste their prayers in the sight of a just God by offering them for souls who are known to be condemned. But if the saints, while still alive and conscious of their own failings, have no compassion on the unjust sinners in hell, if they show no compassion whatever at a time when they realize that their own sins and imperfections are worthy of God's punishment, how much more severely will they look on the torments of the damned

once they are freed from sin and corruption and stand near to their eternal Judge, closely united with him? In their intimate association with the most just of all judges, the force of his severity will penetrate their minds, and they will be utterly displeased with anything that is out of harmony with the least detail of the eternal law. DIALOGUES 4.46.[145]

EVERY PERSON WILL RECEIVE HIS REQUITAL. APHRAHAT: Also in respect of penalty, I say that all people are not equal. One who has done great wickedness is greatly tormented. And one who has offended not so much is less tormented. Some will go into outer darkness, where there is weeping and gnashing of teeth. Others will be cast into the fire, according to what they deserve. For it is not written that they will gnash their teeth or that there is darkness there. Some will be cast into another place, a place where their worm will not die and their fire will not be quenched, and they will became an astonishment to all flesh. In the faces of others the door will be closed, and the Judge will say to them, "I do not know you." And consider that, as the reward for good deeds is not equal for all people, so it is also the case for evil deeds. People will not be judged in only one way. Rather, every person will receive his requital according to what he has done, because the Judge is clothed in righteousness and regards not persons. DEMONSTRATIONS 22.22.[146]

The Fate of Satan and the Demons

THE DEMONS DIE CONTINUALLY. TATIAN: You Greeks acknowledge the dominion of many rather than the rule of one, accustoming yourselves to follow demons as if they were mighty. For as the inhuman robber is

---

[143]Mt 5:44. [144]2 Tim 2:25-26. [145]FC 39:254-57. [146]NPNF 2 13:409*.

accustomed to overpower those like himself by daring, so the demons, going to great lengths in wickedness, have utterly deceived the souls among you that are left to themselves by ignorance and false appearances. These beings do not indeed die easily, for they do not partake of flesh. But while living they practice the ways of death and die themselves as often as they teach their followers to sin. Therefore, what is now their chief distinction, that they do not die like human beings, they will retain when about to suffer punishment. They will not partake of everlasting life so as to receive this instead of death in a blessed immortality. And as we, to whom it now easily happens to die, afterwards receive the immortal with enjoyment, or the painful with immortality, so the demons, who abuse the present life to purposes of wrongdoing, dying continually even while they live, will have hereafter the same immortality like that which they had during the time they lived, but in its nature like that of human beings who voluntarily performed what the demons prescribed to them during their lifetime. And do not fewer kinds of sin break out among human beings owing to the brevity of their lives, while on the part of these demons transgression is more abundant owing to their boundless existence? ADDRESS TO THE GREEKS 14.[147]

PRIEST FOREVER. JUSTIN MARTYR: For your teachers have ventured to refer the passage, "The Lord says to my lord, 'Sit at my right hand, till I make your enemies your footstool,'"[148] to Hezekiah as if he were requested to sit on the right side of the temple when the king of Assyria sent to him and threatened him and he was then told by Isaiah not to be afraid. Now we know and admit that what Isaiah said took place. The king of Assyria did desist from waging war against Jerusalem in Hezekiah's days, and the angel of the Lord killed about 185,000 of the Assyrian army. But it is clear that the psalm does not refer to him. For thus it is written, "The Lord says to my lord, 'Sit at my right hand, till I make your enemies your footstool.' He will send forth a rod of power over Jerusalem, and it will rule in the midst of your enemies. In the splendor of the saints before the morning star have I begotten you. The Lord has sworn, and will not repent. You are a priest forever after the order of Melchizedek."[149] Who does not admit, then, that Hezekiah is no priest forever after the order of Melchizedek? And who does not know that he is not the redeemer of Jerusalem? And who does not know that he neither sent a rod of power into Jerusalem nor ruled in the midst of his enemies but that it was God who averted from him the enemies, after he mourned and was afflicted? But our Jesus, who has not yet come in glory, has sent into Jerusalem a rod of power, namely, the word of calling and repentance meant for all nations over which demons held sway, as David says, "The gods of the nations are demons."[150] And his strong word has prevailed on many to forsake the demons whom they used to serve, and by means of it to believe in the almighty God because the gods of the nations are demons. And we mentioned formerly that the statement, "In the splendor of the saints before the morning star have I begotten you from the womb,"[151] is made to Christ. DIALOGUE WITH TRYPHO 83.[152]

ETERNAL FIRE FOR EVERY KIND OF APOSTASY. IRENAEUS: If therefore the great God showed future things by Daniel and confirmed them by his Son, and if Christ is the stone which is cut out without hands who will destroy temporal kingdoms and introduce an eternal one that includes the resurrection of the just, as he declares, "The God of heaven will raise up a kingdom which will never be destroyed"[153]—let those thus confuted come to their senses who reject the Creator (Demiur-

---

[147]ANF 2:71. [148]Ps 110:1. [149]Cf. Ps 110:1-4. [150]It is unclear to what statement of David Justin is referring. [151]The reference is unclear here as well. [152]ANF 1:240*. [153]Dan 2:44.

gum) and do not agree that the prophets were sent beforehand from the same Father from whom also the Lord came but who assert that prophecies originated from diverse powers. For those things that have been predicted by the Creator alike through all the prophets has Christ fulfilled in the end, ministering to his Father's will and completing his dispensations with regard to the human race. Let those, therefore, who blaspheme the Creator—either by openly expressed words, such as the disciples of Marcion, or by a perversion of the sense of Scripture, as those of Valentinus and all the Gnostics falsely so called—be recognized as agents of Satan by all those who worship God. Through their agency Satan now, and not before, has been seen to speak against God, even him who has prepared eternal fire for every kind of apostasy. For he did not venture to blaspheme his Lord openly of himself. In the beginning, in fact, he led people astray through the instrumentality of the serpent, concealing himself as it were from God. Truly has Justin remarked: Before the Lord's appearance Satan never dared to blaspheme God, inasmuch as he did not yet know his own sentence because it was contained in parables and allegories. But after the Lord had appeared and Satan clearly ascertained from the words of Christ and his apostles that eternal fire had been prepared for him because he apostatized from God of his own free will—and likewise for all who unrepentant continue in the apostasy—Satan now blasphemes the Lord who brings judgment on him by means of such people since he is already condemned. And he imputes the guilt of his apostasy to his Maker, not to his own voluntary disposition. It is the same way with those who break the laws. When punishment overtakes them, they throw the blame on those who frame the laws and not on themselves. In a similar way, those people, filled with a satanic spirit, bring innumerable accusations against our Creator who has both given to us the spirit of life and established a law adapted for all. They will not admit that the judgment of God is just. Therefore they also set about imagining some other Father who neither cares about nor exercises a providence over our affairs—one, in fact, who even approves of all sins. AGAINST HERESIES 5.26.2.[154]

THE GLORY OF THE CROSS. ORIGEN: But since "having put off from himself the principalities and the powers, he made a show of them openly, triumphing over them in the cross,"[155] if any one is ashamed of the cross of Christ, he is ashamed of the dispensation on account of which these powers were triumphed over. And it is fitting that he, who both believes and knows these things, should glory in the cross of our Lord Jesus Christ through which, when Christ was crucified, the principalities—among which, I think, was also the prince of this world—were made a spectacle of and triumphed over before the believing world. And so, when his suffering was at hand he said, "Now the prince of this world has been judged,"[156] and, "Now will the prince of this world be cast out," and, "I, if I be lifted from the earth, will draw all men unto myself,"[157] as he no longer had sufficient power to prevent those going to Jesus who were being drawn by him. COMMENTARY ON THE GOSPEL OF MATTHEW 12.18.[158]

THE SEDUCTIVE ACTION OF SATAN. AUGUSTINE: Thus it is that what is obscure in the words of the apostle has given rise to various conjectures. Yet, of one thing there is no doubt, namely, that he meant Christ will not come to judge the living and the dead until after his adversary, Antichrist, has come to seduce the souls of the dead. And, of course, the fact that those souls are to be seduced is already a part of God's hidden judgment. For, as Paul says, "his coming is according to the working of Satan with all power and signs and

---

[154]ANF 1:555-56**. [155]Col 2:15. [156]Jn 16:11. [157]Jn 12:31-32. [158]ANF 9:461**.

lying wonders and with all wicked deception to those who are perishing."[159] Then it is that Satan will be unbound and, by means of Antichrist, will reveal the full power of his marvelous but seductive action.

There seems to be some ambiguity in the expression "signs and lying wonders." It may be that Satan is to deceive people's senses by means of phantasms whereby they imagine they see wonders that are nonexistent, or, perhaps, true miracles will lead into deception those who ought to believe that miracles can be done only by God but who mistakenly ascribe them to the devil's power, particularly at a time when Satan is to be given unheard-of power. Certainly there were no phantasms when fire fell from heaven and at one sweep destroyed the whole family and all the flocks of holy Job and when the storm broke and destroyed his home and killed his children.[160] Yet, all this was the work of Satan, to whom God had given the power. When the time comes, it will be clear in which sense the "signs and lying wonders" are to be taken. What is certain is that those who have deserved to be seduced will be deceived by the "signs and lying wonders," whatever their nature may be, because "they have not received the love of truth that they might be saved."[161] Nor did Paul hesitate to add: "Therefore God sends them a misleading influence that they may believe falsehood." "God sends" does not imply a mission but a permission. What the devil does is done with his own wicked and malign purpose, but it is permitted by God's just judgment so "that all may be judged who have not believed the truth but have preferred wickedness."

Thus it comes about that judgments both precede and follow the deception. Those who are deceived are antecedently judged by these judgments of God, covertly just and justly covert, by which he has never ceased to judge even since the first sin of his rational creature; and those who are deceived are subsequently judged in a last and overt judgment by Christ Jesus, who is to be the most just of all judges as he was the victim of the most unjust of all judgments. CITY OF GOD 20.19.[162]

THE BOOK OF EACH PERSON'S LIFE. AUGUSTINE: Having spoken thus of the ultimate persecution, John goes on to state succinctly the full punishment that is to be meted out in the last judgment to the hostile city and its prince, the devil. Here are the words: "And the devil who deceived them was cast into the pool of fire and brimstone, where are also the beast and the false prophet; and they will be tormented day and night forever and ever."[163] I have already remarked that the "beast" in this passage can well be the ungodly city. As to the "false prophet," he stands either for Antichrist or the beast's "image," namely, that false-faced faith of which I also spoke.

Next, John picks up again the theme of the last judgment (which is to accompany the second and bodily resurrection of the dead) and describes the manner of its revelation to him: "And I saw a great white throne and the one who sat upon it; from whose face the earth and heaven fled away, and there was found no place for them."[164] Note that he does not say, "one who sat upon it, *and* from his face earth and heaven fled away," because this "flight" had not yet taken place, that is, not before the judgment of the living and the dead. What he says is that he beheld one sitting on the throne "from whose face earth and heaven fled away"—not then, but subsequently. The fact is that it will be after the judgment is completed that heaven and earth will end with the beginning of the new heaven and earth. For it will be by a transformation rather than by a wholesale destruction that this world of ours will pass away. This explains Paul's words: "This world as we see it is passing away. I would have you free from care."[165] It is, to be sure, the visible

---

[159]2 Thess 2:9-10. [160]See Job 1:11, 19. [161]2 Thess 2:10. [162]FC 24:300-301. [163]Rev 20:10. [164]Rev 20:11. [165]1 Cor 7:31-32.

appearance of the world that is destined to pass away, not its nature.

Having said that he saw sitting on the throne One from whose face earth and heaven would later on fly away, John continues, "And I saw the dead, the great and the small, standing before the throne, and scrolls were opened. And another scroll was opened which is the book of each man's life; and the dead were judged out of those things that were written in the scrolls, according to their works."[166] He says he saw scrolls opened, and another scroll, but he makes clear the character of the latter, "which is the book of each man's life." The first scrolls he mentions, then, must represent the holy Scriptures of the Old and New Testaments. These will be opened to show the commandments of God, and the other scroll to show how these commandments were kept or disobeyed by each and every person.

As for this latter scroll, if one considers it materially, it surpasses all powers of thought for size and length. And if it contains the entire life record of all people, how much time would it take to read it? Are we to suppose that there will be an equal number of angels and mortals present in the judgment, and that each person will hear his life record read out by an angel accredited to him for this task? In this supposition, there would not be one book for all but a book for each.

Yet, the Apocalypse wants us to think of one book: "And another scroll was opened," it says. No, the book in question must symbolize some divine action in virtue of which each person will recall his deeds, good or bad, and review them mentally so that, without a moment's delay, each one's conscience will be either burdened or unburdened and thus, collectively and individually, all will be judged at the same moment. And because, in virtue of this divine illumination each person will, so to speak, read the record of his deeds, God's action is called a "book."

Next, John tells what dead people, great and small, are destined for judgment. To do so, he goes back to narrate a detail he had passed by or, better, had momentarily set aside: "And the sea gave up the dead that were in it, and death and hell gave up the dead that were in them." I say he goes back to narrate a detail he had deferred, because, unquestionably, the action of this verse preceded the judgment, even though he speaks of judgment as though it were anterior. From here on, however, he keeps to the sequence of events, and to show the proper sequence he repeats in its proper place what he had already said concerning the judgment of the dead. For, having written "And the sea gave up the dead that were in it, and death and hell gave up the dead that were in them," he reiterates: "And they were judged each one according to their works"—identical with his earlier verse, "And the dead were judged according to their works." CITY OF GOD 20.14.[167]

EVERLASTING PUNISHMENT WILL COME TO AN END. AUGUSTINE: A first question to be asked and answered is: Why has the church been so intolerant with those who defend the view that, however greatly and however long the devil is to be punished, he can be promised ultimately that all will be purged or pardoned? Certainly, it is not because so many of the church's saints and biblical scholars have begrudged the devil and his angels a final cleansing and the beatitude of the kingdom of heaven. Nor is it because of any lack of feeling for so many and such high angels that must suffer such great and enduring pain. This is not a matter of feeling but of fact. The fact is that there is no way of waiving or weakening the words that the Lord has told us that he will pronounce in the last judgment: "Depart from me, accursed ones, into the everlasting fire which was prepared for the devil and his angels."[168] In this way he showed plainly that it is an eternal fire in which the devil and his

---

[166] Rev 20:12. [167] FC 24:286-88. [168] Mt 25:41.

angels are to burn. Then we have the words of the Revelation: "And the devil who deceived them was cast into the pool of fire and brimstone, where also are the beast and the false prophet; and they will be tormented day and night forever and ever."[169] In the one text we have "everlasting," in the other, "forever and ever." These are words that have a single meaning in the divine Scripture, namely, of unending duration.

Thus, it is Scripture, infallible Scripture, that declares that God has not spared them. This is the only reason why it is held as a fixed and unchanging religious truth that the devil and his angels are never to return to the life and holiness of the saints; nor could any more valid or cogent reason be discovered. It is from Scripture that we know that God's sentence implies that he "dragged them down by infernal ropes to Tartarus, and delivered them to be tortured and kept in custody for judgment."[170] They will be received into "everlasting" fire, there to be tortured "forever and ever."

And since this is true of the devil, how can people—whether all or some—be promised an escape, after some indefinitely long period, from this eternity of pain, without at once weakening our faith in the unending torment of the devils? For it is to people that the words will be said: "Depart from me, accursed ones, into the everlasting fire which was prepared for the devil and his angels." Now, if some of these people or all of them are not always to remain in everlasting fire, what ground have we for believing that the devil and his angels are always to remain there? God's sentence will be pronounced on the wicked, both angels and mortals. Can we suppose that it will hold for angels but not for mortals? Yes, but only if people's imaginings have more weight than God's words!

Since this is quite impossible, all those who desire to escape eternal punishment should desist from arguing against God and should rather bow in obedience, while yet there is time, to the command of God. Besides, what kind of imagining is this, to take eternal punishment to mean long-continued punishment and, at the same time, to believe that eternal life is endless, seeing that Christ spoke of both as eternal in the same place and in one and the same sentence: "And these will go into everlasting punishment, but the just into everlasting life."[171] If both are "everlasting," then either both must be taken as long-lasting but not endless or else both must be taken to be unendingly perpetual. For the everlastingness of the punishment and the everlastingness of the life are related as equal to equal. It is highly absurd to say in one and the same sense: "Life everlasting will be endless, but everlasting punishment will come to an end." Therefore, since the eternal life of the saints is to be endless, there can be no doubt that eternal punishment for those who are to endure it will have no end. CITY OF GOD 21.23.[172]

WITHOUT PLENITUDE OF BLESSEDNESS. AUGUSTINE: It is certain, then, that they have known by sight what we have known by faith, in other words, that no holy angel will ever fall from now on. But the devil and his angels, although they were blessed before they fell and did not know that they would fall into misery—there was still something that might be added to their blessedness, if by free will they had stood in the truth until they received that fullness of the highest blessing as the reward of that continuance. In other words, that by the great abundance of the love of God, given by the Holy Spirit, they should absolutely not be able to fall anymore and that they should know this with complete certainty concerning themselves. They did not have this plenitude of blessedness; but since they were ignorant of their future misery, they enjoyed a blessedness that was less, indeed, but still without any defect. For if they had known their future fall

---

[169]Rev 20:10. [170]2 Pet 2:4. [171]Mt 25:46. [172]FC 24:385-87.

and eternal punishment, they certainly could not have been blessed, since the fear of so great an evil as this would compel them even then to be miserable. ON REBUKE AND GRACE 10.27.[173]

THE WICKED PUNISHED. AUGUSTINE: But as for those who, out of the mass of perdition caused by the first man's sin, are not redeemed through the one Mediator between God and humankind, they too will rise again, each with his own body, but only to be punished with the devil and his angels. Now, whether they will rise again with all their diseases and deformities of body, bringing with them the diseased and deformed limbs that they possessed here, it would be labor lost to inquire. We need not weary ourselves speculating about their health or their beauty, which are matters of uncertainty, when their eternal damnation is a matter of certainty. Nor need we inquire in what sense their body will be incorruptible, if it is susceptible to pain; or in what sense corruptible if it is free from the possibility of death. For there is no true life except where there is happiness in life and no true incorruption except where health is unbroken by any pain. When, however, the unhappy are not permitted to die, then, if I may say so, death itself does not die. And where pain without intermission afflicts the soul and never comes to an end, corruption itself is not completed. This is called in holy Scripture "the second death." ENCHIRIDION 92.[174]

THE WORLD OF THE DEVIL AND THE WORLD OF GOD. AUGUSTINE: He will also censure the world about justice, because the prince of this world has already been judged.[175] Who can this be, but the one of whom he says in another place: Behold, the prince of the world is coming, and in me he will find nothing,[176] that is, nothing under his jurisdiction, nothing that is his business, in a word, absolutely no sin at all? This, you see, is what makes the devil the prince of the world. It is not, after all, of heaven and earth, and all that is in them[177] that the devil is prince, which is what "world" means where it says: And the world was made through him; but the world of which the devil is prince is the one of which it goes on to say straight away: And the world did not know him,[178] that is, all unbelieving human beings, of whom the world is full all over the earth. Among them the believing world is groaning, which he through whom the world was made,[179] has chosen from the world;[180] it is about them that he says, The Son of man did not come to judge the world but that the world may be saved through him.[181]

The world judged by him is condemned, the world rescued by him is saved; since like a tree full of leaves and fruit, like a threshing floor full of chaff and grains, so too is the world full of unbelievers and believers. So the prince of this world, then, the prince of this darkness, that is, of unbelievers, from whom the world of those is snatched who are told, "You were once darkness, but now light in the Lord,"[182] the prince of this world about whom he says elsewhere, "Now has the prince of this world been thrown outside,"[183] has certainly been judged, since he has been irrevocably destined to the sentence of everlasting fire. And so it is also about this judgment, by which the prince of this world has been judged, that the world is being censured by the Holy Spirit; since it is being judged with its prince, whom it imitates in its pride and ungodliness.

If God, after all, as the apostle Peter says, did not spare the angels who sinned, but thrusting them down to the pitch-dark dungeons of the underworld, handed them over to be kept for punishment at the judgment,[184] how can the world not be censured

---

[173]NPNF 1 5:483**. [174]NPNF 1 3:266-67*. [175]Jn 16:11. [176]Jn 14:30. [177]See Ps 69:34. [178]Jn 1:10. [179]Jn 1:10. [180]Jn 15:19. [181]Jn 3:17. [182]Eph 5:8. [183]Jn 12:31. [184]2 Pet 2:4.

by the Holy Spirit about this judgment, when it is in the Holy Spirit that the apostle utters these words? Let people accordingly believe in Christ, in order not to be censured about the sin of their unbelief, by which all sins are retained; let them cross over into the number of the faithful, in order not to be censured about the justice of those whom they are not imitating in being justified; let them beware of the future judgment, in order not to be judged with the prince of this world, whom they are imitating in being judged. The rock-hard pride of mortals, you see, in case it should assume that it is going to be spared, has to be terrified by the punishment of the proud angels. HOMILIES ON THE GOSPEL OF JOHN 95.4.[185]

THE UNQUENCHABLE FIRE. JOHN OF DAMASCUS: Concerning the devil and demons: he who from among these angelic powers was set over the earthly realm, and into whose hands God committed the guardianship of the earth, was not made wicked in nature but was good, and made for good ends and received from his Creator no trace whatever of evil in himself. But he did not sustain the brightness and the honor that the Creator had bestowed on him, and of his free choice he was changed from what was in harmony to what was at variance with his nature, and became roused against God who created him and determined to rise in rebellion against him: and he was the first to depart from good and become evil. For evil is nothing else than absence of goodness, just as darkness also is absence of light. For goodness is the light of the mind, and, similarly, evil is the darkness of the mind. Light, therefore, being the work of the Creator and being made good (for God saw all that he made, and behold, they were exceedingly good[186]) produced darkness by his free will. But along with him an innumerable host of angels subject to him were torn away and followed him and shared in his fall. The result was that since they were of the same nature as the angels, they became wicked, turning away by their own free choice from good to evil. And so they have no power or strength against anyone except what God in his dispensation has conceded to them, as for instance, against Job and those swine mentioned in the Gospels. But when God has made the concession they do prevail and are changed and transformed into any form whatever in which they wish to appear. Of the future both the angels of God and the demons are alike ignorant: yet they make predictions. God reveals the future to the angels and commands them to prophesy, and so what they say comes to pass. But the demons also make predictions, sometimes because they see what is happening at a distance and sometimes merely making guesses. Therefore much that they say is false, and they should not be believed, even though they do often, in the way we have said, tell what is true. Besides, they know the Scriptures. All wickedness, then, and all impure passions are the work of their mind. But while the liberty to attack human beings has been granted to them, they do not have the strength to master anyone: for we have it in our power to receive or not to receive the attack. Therefore there has been prepared for the devil and his demons, and those who follow him, fire unquenchable and everlasting punishment. Note, further, that what is death in the case of humans is a fall in the case of angels. For after the fall there is no possibility of repentance for them, just as after death there is no repentance for human beings. ORTHODOX FAITH 2.4.[187]

---

[185]*WSA* forthcoming; cf. NPNF 1 7:370-71**. [186]Gen 1:31. [187]NPNF 2 9:20-21*.

AND THE LIFE OF THE WORLD TO COME
Christ's Return, the Judgment and Eternal Life

εἰς μίαν, ἁγίαν, καθολικὴν καὶ ἀποστολικὴν ἐκκλησίαν· ὁμολογοῦμεν ἓν βάπτισμα εἰς ἄφεσιν ἁμαρτιῶν· προσδοκῶμεν ἀνάστασιν νεκρῶν, καὶ ζωὴν τοῦ μέλλοντος αἰῶνος. Ἀμήν.	Et unam, sanctam, catholicam et apostolicam ecclesiam. Confiteor unum baptisma in remissionem peccatorum; et expecto resurrectionem mortuorum, et vitam venturi saeculi. Amen.	We believe in one holy catholic and apostolic Church. We acknowledge one baptism for the forgiveness of sins. We look for the resurrection of the dead and the life of the world to come. Amen.

HISTORICAL CONTEXT: Both the second and third articles of the Nicene-Constantinopolitan Creed conclude with eschatology. In this second section commenting on "the life of the world to come," we expand on the themes found in the second article in light of the life which is yet to come. The final section of the second article of the Nicene-Constantinopolitan Creed includes the themes of Christian eschatology—namely, Jesus' glorious return to earth, the final judgment and the kingdom of Christ. In this final section of the commentary on this last phrase, we may observe how the complexity of ancient Christian eschatology makes any attempt at schematization quite difficult. Numerous factors influenced the reflection of the Fathers. In fact, the patristic reflection on eschatology takes shape in accordance with historical-cultural shifts, which in turn are influenced by the expansion of Christianity, so that new times and new situations led Christian thinkers to formulate eschatological beliefs in a renewed way, even though they remained substantially faithful to the biblical spirit. New questions constantly arose with regard to the final or last realities, thanks to the meeting of Christianity with Greco-Roman pagan culture, to the influence of Gnosticism and the different Christian heretical movements and to the dramatic experience of persecutions.

We will also notice the variety of language, symbols and images used by the Fathers at least up to Augustine. He was the first who sought to give an organic arrangement to the eschatological questions, influencing most future reflections in this regard. Obviously the main reference of patristic teaching is centered on the Christ event, with all its anthropological and soteriological reflections, so that Christ appears to be the hermeneutical key to any eschatological speech, that is, the crucial element that resolves all questions.

The thematic kernels presented here are four in number: the glorious return of Christ, the final judgment, the intermediate state and eternal life. The Parousia, or Christ's second coming in glory, is the horizon within which all the final events of history find their position, so that history, according to the teaching of Paul,[1] assumes a global meaning that includes the victory of Christ over sin and death, the resurrection of the dead and the judgment. From this point of view the passages from the Fathers reflect the complexity of the envisioned event, highlighting sometimes its most spiritual aspects, sometimes those which are more sensational and grotesque.

The theme of the judgment is closely connected to the Parousia, which is presented

---

[1] See 1 Thess 2:19; 3:13; 4:15; 5:23; 2 Thess 2:1, 8-9; 1 Cor 5:13.

both as a universal and individual event, even though it mostly appears to be universal and final. The judge is Christ, who will separate the good from the bad, destining the former to life and the latter to eternal damnation. We will notice that the Fathers linger on certain particularly terrifying elements of the judgment on which they indulge in graphic detail. It is evident that these reflections offered them the opportunity to call the sinners to a worthy way of life and to deter the believers from a sinful existence.

In the context of the end of the world, the Fathers do not neglect questions concerning the destiny of the individual. They face the theme of the so-called intermediate state, according to which the souls of the dead are in a condition of waiting before the final resurrection, when they will be reunited to their bodies and will fully receive their due reward. In particular, Augustine supposes the existence of a specific judgment for the individual immediately after death, which involves a certain reward, although it is not the definitive one, and without precisely describing the location of this reward.[2]

By presenting certain constant motifs in the early church's heritage of faith, such as Jesus' glorious return, the final judgment and the survival of the individual after death, this chapter reveals the Fathers' efforts to comprehend faith in the first centuries of the Christian age. Despite their disagreements, in the end, the comfort it afforded to those who look forward to that life that is yet to come cannot be overestimated.

Eternal life with God brings an incomparable blessing: communion with God amid the communion of the saints with God and with all who reflect God's holy love. This community embraces both the living faithful and the faithful departed who now enjoy eternal life with God. There is a special union between the faithful on earth and in heaven, enabled by their mutual communion with the one Head and with each other, a communion sustained by prayer, faith, hope and love. The community or fellowship of the saints is a recurrent theme of the New Testament that points to communion with God and communion with all who share God's life. The Son prayed to the Father that the whole community of faith "may be one, as we are one."[3]

The prevailing scriptural term for the final state of the blessed is "eternal life." This life is transmuted into a future life of glory that does not reach full expression until the general resurrection, final judgment and the final destiny of the faithful. The living God permits the new life with God to continue without ceasing. Eternal life brings to completion the work of grace begun in this life, where one is delivered from sin, its roots and consequences, fulfilling God's purpose in creation, redemption and consummation. The transformation begun in faithful baptism does not come to nothing but lives on. The spiritual life begun in penitent faith, imparted in spiritual rebirth, grows by sanctifying grace and lives on by completing grace. The characteristic feature of eternal life is the complete and unending enjoyment of life with God.

In Christian teaching, heaven is both a place and a condition of eternal rest and joy in the Lord. It is "to be present with the Lord."[4] Heaven is where the blessed clearly see God and incomparably enjoy the blessings of divine glory. Heaven is represented as a secure lodging of unutterable glory, joy and peace. Its most prominent features are tranquility, holiness, light, beholding, happiness and the presence of the Lord. What happens in heaven is full and endless participation in God's goodness and happiness. Those "whose names are written in heaven" have "come to God." They are "the spirits of righteous men made perfect."[5] Jesus promised his disciples: "I am going

---

[2]See Augustine *City of God* 13.13.8. [3]Jn 17:11. [4]2 Cor 5:8.
[5]Heb 12:23.

there to prepare a place for you. And if I go and prepare a place for you, I will come back and take you to be with me that you also may be where I am."[6]

OVERVIEW: The second coming of Christ was announced by the prophets of the Old Testament (JUSTIN). The final judgment is connected to Christ's return to the earth, in which the bad will be punished and the good will be saved. Before the end, the Antichrist will ruin the world by what he does (IRENAEUS). The Jews have not understood that Christ's comings to the world are two, and they still wait for the Messiah (TERTULLIAN). When Christ returns to the world, will he still find faith (CYPRIAN)? In the Psalms and the Prophets the faith in the two comings of Christ is well attested (ORIGEN, TERTULLIAN). Christ's return will be glorious, so that it will not be in the humbleness of the first time but in the splendor of divine glory (CYRIL OF JERUSALEM, CHRYSOSTOM). The apostle and all the faithful will participate in the glory of the Lord (HILARY). Then the Son will sit on the right hand of the Father as a sign of their perfect communion (AMBROSE). The parousia will coincide with the judgment (AUGUSTINE, RUFINUS). The angels will pre-announce the return of the Lord and the day of the judgment (LEO).

The judgment will be accompanied by different wonders (DIDACHE). The Lord will judge the living and the dead (EPISTLE OF BARNABAS), destining the righteous to eternal life and the unrighteous to damnation (PSEUDO-CLEMENT). But free will and not fate is the cause of evil: it leads to condemnation in the judgment (JUSTIN). Faith enlightens us about certain facets of the judgment (THEOPHILUS). The judgment is part of the original apostolic heritage of faith (IRENAEUS, TERTULLIAN). Jesus Christ is rightly judge because he is the Lord; rightly Lord, because he is creator; rightly Creator because he is God. That is why the judgment of God will be universal and therefore absolute, final and irrevocable (TERTULLIAN). In spite of it all, the judgment of God will be full of forgiveness and mercy (CYPRIAN). The fear of the judgment leads to a life of perfection, even though a spiritual and not merely material vision of the judgment is necessary (ORIGEN). In this world, the unrighteous seem to live in tranquility and prosperity, but at the end of time the Lord will make justice triumph (CHRYSOSTOM), because the Lord looks into hearts and judges them (CYRIL OF JERUSALEM). The judgment is like a surgical operation, in which the inclination to evil and the sins are taken away from the soul (GREGORY OF NYSSA). For this reason, on the day of judgment all the secrets hidden in our heart will crop up (AMBROSE). The judgment and its accompanying resurrection of the dead were announced already in the Old Testament. When we say, "to judge the living and the dead," we can also mean "to judge the righteous and the sinners" (AUGUSTINE). On the day of judgment, the righteous will shine like the sun among the angels, whereas the unrighteous together with the Antichrist will be damned forever (JOHN).

While there is life, there is a chance to repent (PSEUDO-CLEMENT, CYPRIAN), so that the present time is the best opportunity for our salvation (CHRYSOSTOM). The prayers of friends and relatives were believed to be beneficial to the souls of the dead and can arouse the mercy of God toward sinners (AUGUSTINE, CYRIL OF JERUSALEM). After death, the soul and the body are separated, until they will reunite on the day of the judgment to receive life or eternal damnation (AUGUSTINE). A number of the Fathers believed that before the day of the judgment there would be a period of purgatory when souls are purified from their venial sins committed on earth (GREGORY THE GREAT, CASSIAN). The

---

[6]Jn 14:2-3.

souls, after death, will dwell in an intermediate place for a certain period of time, and there they will comprehend their past and will know their future life (Origen). Before reuniting with the body, the souls suffer punishments or receive solace in that place that is usually called hades (Tertullian). The punishments will be temporary or eternal in proportion to the sins committed in life. It was believed that temporary punishments could be expiated in this life or after death, but in any case before the final judgment (Augustine, Cyprian).

One who has learned the judgments of the Lord should walk in them (Epistle of Barnabas). The Creator and Father of all worlds alone knows the extent and beauty of his gifts. We have to wait for him in order that we may share in his promised gifts (Clement of Rome). At the end of this world, we are delivered from corruption and suffering and deemed worthy of eternal incorruption and of fellowship with God. The Spirit of prophecy speaks of things that are about to happen as if they had already taken place because God already knows they will take place. The Gentiles who have believed on him and have repented of their sins shall receive the inheritance along with the patriarchs and the prophets (Justin). In the exercise of his grace, God will confer immortality on the righteous and holy who have kept his commandments. The Word who glorified his Father while remaining in him did not stand in need of our service when he commanded us to follow him but freely bestowed salvation on those who have faith. He grants to those who follow and serve him life and eternal glory free from death. People therefore shall see God so that they may live, being made immortal by that sight and attaining even unto God. As in the beginning, by means of our first parents, we were all brought into bondage, by being made subject to death; so at last, by means of the new Man, all who have been cleansed and washed from things pertaining to death may come to the life of God. We also await the time prescribed by God for our resurrection. Good things are eternal and without end with God. As in this world some persons participate in the light, and by faith unite themselves with God, but others shun the light and separate themselves from God, the Word of God comes preparing an appropriate dwelling for both (Irenaeus).

Reason [the Logos], which made the universe out of diverse elements, so that all things might be composed of opposite substances in unity, has also disposed time into order. The whole human race shall be raised again. We shall be the same as we are now. The fiery judgment of all that is unworthy of God will then ensue. The faithful shall then be changed in a moment into the substance of angels and so be removed to that kingdom in heaven. There we shall be caught up into the clouds to meet the Lord, and so shall we ever be with the Lord (Tertullian). The kingdom of God is already beginning to be at hand. The reward of life and the rejoicing of eternal salvation is now coming, with the passing away of the world. God promises to the faithful immortality and eternity. In the meantime, we die, passing over to immortality by death. That is not an ending but a transit, and this journey of time being traversed is a passage to eternity. We come without delay and without resistance to the Lord when he calls us (Cyprian). We shall be capable of a life not temporary but ever afterwards abiding and living in Christ (Athanasius). Christ is true life, and our way of life in him is true life. Although at present our days are evil, other days will come, which night does not interrupt. God will be their everlasting light, shining on them with the light of his glory. If the soul is indestructible, its gifts are also indestructible. Those who have fulfilled sufficiently the course of this life will go to their rest. A rest is not given in payment for a debt owed for their works but provided as a grace of the munificent God for those who have hoped in him (BASIL). My life is in exile, and when I hear the voice of the archangel and when I see the transformation of the heavens and the renovation of the universe, my soul will be released (GREGORY OF NAZIANZUS).

There is a great difference between a fire that can be extinguished and one that does not admit of extinction. In the life of each person it must be the part of wisdom not to regard the present, but that which follows after, and by good choices to wean oneself from all experience of evil now in one's lifetime here, hereafter in one's eternal recompense (GREGORY OF NYSSA). In the profession of faith, we are taught to believe also in life eternal. The blessings of life eternal are promised without fail to all who believe. Those who are made free from sin and become servants of God bear the fruits of sanctification toward the goal of eternal life (CYRIL OF JERUSALEM). We no longer are afraid of death after we have learned carefully from this holy initiation that death is not death but a sleep and repose that lasts but for a time. Hell has not been made for the faithful but for the devil and his angels.

The kingdom has been prepared for us before the foundation of the world. Though many wounds are incurable, yet we do not abandon hope (CHRYSOSTOM). The Lord stood revealed in the splendor of his reigning body. We see ourselves as called to become conformed to the glory of his body in the kingdom of the Father (HILARY). By the words of the prophet we are taught not only of his coming and judgment but also of his dominion and kingdom, that his dominion is eternal and his kingdom indestructible. His judgment will be not only for deeds but for thoughts also.

The flesh of the saints is to be changed into such a glorious condition at the resurrection as to be caught up to meet God. He will change the bodies of the righteous into the glory of a spiritual body (RUFINUS). The flesh gains possession of those who are not of the kingdom of God but the devil's kingdom, because when the flesh rises again it will be changed into the kind of body in which there will no longer be any mortal tendency to decay and which therefore will no longer be properly called flesh and blood.

Eternal rest will be ours in the kingdom. Eternal life is the supreme good and eternal death the supreme evil. Since the eternal life of the saints is to be endless, there can be no doubt that eternal punishment for those who are to endure it will have no end. Every fiber and organ of our imperishable body will play its part in the praising of God. The souls in bliss will still possess the freedom of will. In the everlasting city, there will remain in each and every one of us an inalienable freedom of the will, emancipating us from every evil and filling us with every good (AUGUSTINE) as we who have been raised live forever in the city of our God (CHRYSOLOGUS).

The Second Coming of Christ

WHEN CHRIST COMES AGAIN. JUSTIN MARTYR: Since, then, we prove that all things that have already happened had been predicted by the prophets before they happened, we must necessarily believe also that those things that are similarly predicted but have yet to happen will certainly happen. For as the things that have already taken place happened when foretold even though they were unknown, so the things that remain will also happen, even though they are unknown and disbelieved. For the prophets have proclaimed two advents of his: the one that is already past, when he came as a dishonored and suffering Man; but also the second, when, according to prophecy, he will come from heaven with glory, accompanied by his angelic host, when he will also raise the bodies of all who have lived and will clothe those of the worthy with immortality and will send those of the wicked, endued with eternal sensibility, into everlasting fire with the wicked devils. And we will prove that these things also have been foretold as yet to be. By Ezekiel the prophet it was said, "Joint will be joined to joint, and bone to bone, and flesh will grow again; and every knee will bow to the Lord, and every tongue will confess him."[7] And in what kind of sensation and punishment the wicked are to be, hear from what was said in a similar way with reference to this. It is as follows: "Their worm will not rest, and their fire will not be quenched."[8] Then they will repent when it profits them not. And what the people of the Jews will say and do, when they see him coming in glory, has been thus predicted by Zechariah the prophet: "I will command the four winds to gather the scattered children; I will command the north wind to bring them, and the south wind, that it keep not back. And then in Jerusalem there will be great lamentation, not the lamentation of mouths or of lips, but the lamentation of the heart; and they will rend not their garments, but their hearts. Tribe by tribe they will mourn, and then they will look on him whom they have pierced; and they will say, Why, O Lord, have you made us to err from your way? The glory which our fathers blessed has for us been turned into shame."[9] FIRST APOLOGY 52.[10]

THE FINAL JUDGMENT IS CONNECTED TO CHRIST'S RETURN. IRENAEUS: A spiritual disciple of this sort—truly receiving the Spirit of God who was in all the dispensations of God from the beginning, present with humankind and who announced future things, revealed present ones and narrated those in the past—such a person does indeed "judge all, but is himself judged by no one."[11] For he judges the Gentiles, "who serve the creature more than the Creator,"[12] and with a reprobate mind spend all their labor on vanity. And he also judges the Jews who do not accept the word of freedom, nor are they willing to go forth free, although they have a Deliverer present with them. Instead, they pretend, at a time unsuitable for such conduct, to serve God with observances beyond those required by the law, when he stands in need of nothing. They do not recognize the advent of Christ that he accomplished for our salvation, nor are they willing to understand that all the prophets announced his two advents: the first, indeed, in which he became a man subject to stripes, and knowing what it is to bear infirmity, and sat on the foal of a donkey, and was a stone rejected by the builders, and was led as a sheep to the slaughter, and by the stretching forth of his hands destroyed Amalek while he gathered from the ends of the earth into his Father's fold the children who were scattered abroad, and remembered his own dead ones who had formerly fallen asleep and came down to them that he might deliver them. There is also a second advent in which he will come on the clouds, bringing on the day that burns as a furnace and striking the earth with the word of his mouth and killing the impious with the breath of his lips, and having a fan in his hands, and cleansing his floor and gathering the wheat indeed into his barn but burning the chaff with unquenchable fire. AGAINST HERESIES 4.33.1.[13]

CHRIST JESUS WILL COME IN GLORY. IRENAEUS: Many nations of those barbarians who believe in Christ do assent to this faith, having salvation written in their hearts by the Spirit, without paper or ink, and carefully preserving the ancient tradition. They believe in one God, the Creator of heaven and earth, and all things

---

[7]Cf. Ezek 37:7-8; Is 45:23. [8]Is 66:24. [9]Zech 12:3-14; Is 63:17, Is 64:11. [10]ANF 1:180*. [11]1 Cor 2:15. [12]Rom 1:21. [13]ANF 1:506**.

therein, by means of Christ Jesus, the Son of God; who, because of his surpassing love toward his creation, condescended to be born of the Virgin. He himself united humanity through himself to God, and having suffered under Pontius Pilate, and rising again and having been received up in splendor will come in glory, the Savior of those who are saved and the Judge of those who are judged, and sending into eternal fire those who transform the truth and despise his Father and his advent. Those who, in the absence of written documents, have believed this faith are barbarians, so far as regards our language. But as regards doctrine, manner and tenor of life, they are, because of faith, very wise indeed. And they do please God, ordering their conversation in all righteousness, chastity and wisdom. If anyone were to preach to these people the inventions of the heretics, speaking to them in their own language, they would at once stop their ears and flee as far off as possible, not enduring even to listen to the blasphemous address. Thus, by means of that ancient tradition of the apostles, they do not suffer their mind to conceive anything of the doctrines suggested by the portentous language of these teachers, among whom neither church nor doctrine has ever been established. AGAINST HERESIES 3.4.2.[14]

JESUS CHRIST WILL COME AGAIN TO MANIFEST SALVATION. IRENAEUS: All those previously mentioned—although they certainly do with their tongue confess one Jesus Christ—make fools of themselves, thinking one thing and saying another. For their hypotheses vary, as I have already shown, alleging, as they do, that one Being suffered and was born, and that this was Jesus. They also allege, however, that there was another who descended on him, and that this was Christ, who also ascended again. And they argue that he who proceeded from the Demiurge, or he who was dispensational or he who sprang from Joseph was the Being subject to suffering. But on the latter there descended from the invisible and ineffable places the former, whom they assert to be incomprehensible, invisible and impassible. They thus wander from the truth, because their doctrine departs from him who is truly God, being ignorant that his only-begotten Word, who is always present with the human race, united to and mingled with his own creation, according to the Father's pleasure, and who became flesh, is himself Jesus Christ our Lord. This is he who also suffered for us, and rose again on our behalf, and will come again in the glory of his Father to raise up all flesh and in order to make salvation known and to apply the rule of just judgment to all who were made by him. There is therefore, as I have pointed out, one God the Father and one Christ Jesus, who came by means of the whole dispensational arrangements connected with him and gathered together all things in himself. But in every respect, too, he is man, the formation of God. Therefore he took up man into himself, the invisible becoming visible, the incomprehensible being made comprehensible, the impassible becoming capable of suffering and the Word being made man. In this way he summed up all things in himself, so that as in supercelestial, spiritual and invisible things, the Word of God is supreme, so also in visible and corporeal things he might possess the supremacy and, taking to himself the preeminence, as well as constituting himself head of the church, he might draw all things to himself at the proper time. AGAINST HERESIES 3.16.6.[15]

THE LORD WILL COME TO JUDGE THE ANTICHRIST. IRENAEUS: But he indicates the number of the name now, that when this man comes we may avoid him, being aware who he is. The name, however, is suppressed, because it is not worthy of being proclaimed by the Holy Spirit. For if it had been declared by

---

[14]ANF 1:417*. [15]ANF 1:442-43*.

him, he [Antichrist] might perhaps continue for a long period. But now as "he was, and is not, and will ascend out of the abyss, and goes into perdition,"[16] as one who has no existence, so neither has his name been declared, for the name of that which does not exist is not proclaimed. But when this Antichrist will have devastated all things in this world, he will reign for three years and six months and sit in the temple at Jerusalem; and then the Lord will come from heaven in the clouds, in the glory of the Father, sending this man and those who follow him into the lake of fire but bringing in for the righteous the times of the kingdom, that is, the rest, the hallowed seventh day, and restoring to Abraham the promised inheritance, in which kingdom the Lord declared that "many coming from the east and from the west should sit down with Abraham, Isaac and Jacob."[17] AGAINST HERESIES 5.30.4.[18]

Two Advents

TWO ADVENTS OF CHRIST. TERTULLIAN: The Jews too knew that Christ was to come, seeing that it was to them that the prophets used to speak. For even now they are looking out for his arrival, nor is there any greater cause of disagreement between us and them than the fact that they do not believe that he has already come. For as two advents of his have been indicated, the first, which has already been fulfilled (in every predicted detail), in the humility of his human creation, the second, which precedes the end of the world, in the loftiness of the manifested Godhead, they by misunderstanding the first have thought the second, which (having been more clearly prophesied) they expect, to be the only one. It was what their transgression deserved that they should not understand the original advent, for if they had understood, they would have believed, and if they had believed, they would have attained safety. They themselves read it thus written, that they have lost their wisdom and understanding and the use of their eyes and ears. APOLOGY 21.15-16.[19]

FIRST ADVENT IN LOWLINESS, SECOND ADVENT IN GLORY. TERTULLIAN: Our heretic will now have the fullest opportunity of learning the clue of his errors along with the Jew, from whom he has borrowed his guidance in this discussion. Since, however, the blind lead the blind, they fall into the ditch together. We affirm that, as there are two conditions demonstrated by the prophets to belong to Christ, so these two conditions presignified the same number of advents. One of the advents, and that being the first, was to be in lowliness when he had to be led as a sheep to be slain as a victim and to be as a lamb dumb before the shearer, not opening his mouth, and not fair to look on. For, says the prophet, we have announced concerning him, "He is like a tender plant, like a root out of a thirsty ground; he has no form nor comeliness; and we beheld him, and he was without beauty: his form was disfigured,"[20] "marred more than the sons of men; a man stricken with sorrows, and knowing how to bear our infirmity,"[21] "placed by the Father as a stone of stumbling and a rock of offense,"[22] "made by him a little lower than the angels,"[23] declaring himself to be "a worm and not a man, a reproach of men, and despised of the people."[24] Now these signs of degradation suit his first coming quite well, just as the tokens of his majesty do his second advent when he will no longer remain "a stone of stumbling and a rock of offense" but after his rejection become "the chief cornerstone," accepted and elevated to the top place of the temple, even his church, being that very stone in Daniel, cut out of the mountain that was to strike and crush the image of the secular kingdom. Of this advent the same prophet

---

[16]Rev 17:8. [17]Mt 8:11. [18]ANF 1:560*. [19]TA 71. [20]Is 53:2-3. [21]See Is 52:14; 53:3. [22]Is 8:14. [23]Ps 8:5. [24]Ps 22:7.

says, "Behold, one like the Son of man came with the clouds of heaven, and came to the Ancient of days; and they brought him before him, and dominion and glory were given to him as well as a kingdom so that all people, nations, and languages should serve him. His dominion is an everlasting dominion, which will not pass away; and his kingdom is that which will not be destroyed."[25] Then indeed he will have both a glorious form and an unsullied beauty above the sons of mortals. "You are the fairest," says the psalmist, "of the sons of men; grace is poured upon your lips; therefore God has blessed you for ever. Gird your sword upon your thigh, O mighty one, in your glory and majesty!"[26] For the Father, after making him a little lower than the angels, will "crown him with glory and honor" and "put all things under his feet."[27] "Then will they look on him whom they have pierced, and they will mourn for him, tribe after tribe,"[28] because, no doubt, they once refused to acknowledge him in the lowliness of his human condition. He is even a man, says Jeremiah, and who will recognize him? Therefore, asks Isaiah, "Who will declare his generation?"[29]

In Zechariah, as well, Christ Jesus, the true high priest of the Father, in the person of Joshua—no, in fact, in the very mystery of his name—is portrayed in a twofold dress with reference to both his advents. At first he is clothed in sordid garments, that is to say, in the lowliness of suffering and mortal flesh. In this advent, the devil was able to resist him, serving as the instigator of the traitor Judas, not to mention his tempting him after his baptism. Afterwards he was stripped of his first filthy clothing and adorned with the priestly robe and miter and a pure diadem—in other words, with the glory and honor of his second advent. If I may offer, moreover, an interpretation of the two goats that were presented on "the great day of atonement," do they not also provide a figure of the two natures of Christ? They were of similar size and very similar in appearance, owing to the Lord's identity of aspect because he is not to come in any other form, having to be recognized by those by whom he was also wounded and pierced. One of these goats was bound with scarlet and driven by the people out of the camp into the wilderness, amid cursing, and spitting, and pulling and piercing, being thus marked with all the signs of the Lord's own passion. The other, by being offered up for sins and given to the priests of the temple for meat, afforded proofs of his second appearance when (after all sins have been expiated) the priests of the spiritual temple, that is, the church, are to enjoy the flesh, as it were, of the Lord's own grace, while the rest go away from salvation without tasting it. Since, therefore, the first advent was prophetically declared both as most obscure in its types and as deformed with every kind of indignity, but the second advent was declared to be glorious and altogether worthy of God, they [the Jews] would on this very account be (not undeservedly) deceived respecting the more obscure and, at any rate, the more lowly first coming since they confined what they regarded as true to that which they were most easily able both to understand and to believe, in other words, to the second advent. Accordingly, to this day they deny that their Christ has come, because he has not appeared in majesty, while they ignore the fact that he was to come also in lowliness. AGAINST MARCION 3.7.[30]

TAKE TO HEART THE DAY OF THE LORD. CYPRIAN: But in us unanimity is diminished in proportion as the liberality of our deeds is decayed. Then[31] they used to give houses and estates up for sale and, so that they might lay up for themselves treasures in heaven, would present to the apostles the price of them to

---

[25]Dan 7:13-14. [26]Ps 45:2-3. [27]Ps 8:5-6. [28]Zech 12:10. [29]Is 53:8. [30]ANF 3:326-27**. [31]In the first-century church described in Acts.

be distributed for the use of the poor. But now we do not even give the tenths from our patrimony. And while our Lord bids us sell, we rather buy and increase our store. Thus has the vigor of faith dwindled away among us; thus has the strength of believers grown weak. And therefore the Lord, looking to our days, says in his Gospel, "When the Son of man comes, do you think that he will find faith on the earth?"[32] We see that what he foretold has come to pass. There is no faith in the fear of God, in the law of righteousness, in love, in labor. No one considers the fear of what might happen in the future, and no one takes to heart the day of the Lord, and the wrath of God, and the punishments to come on unbelievers and the eternal torments decreed for the faithless. What our conscience would fear—if it believed—it does not fear because it does not believe. But if it believed, it would also listen, and if it listened, it would escape. ON THE UNITY OF THE CHURCH 26.[33]

PROPHECIES SPEAK OF TWO ADVENTS OF CHRIST. ORIGEN: Now it escaped the notice of Celsus, and of the Jew whom he has introduced and of all who are not believers in Jesus, that the prophecies speak of two advents of Christ. The former advent is characterized by human suffering and humility in order that Christ, when he was with the human race, might make known the way that leads to God and might leave no one in this life any ground for excuse in saying that he did not know of the judgment to come. The latter advent is distinguished only by glory and divinity, having no element of human infirmity intermingled with its divine greatness. To quote the prophecies at length would be tedious. Instead I deem it sufficient for the present to quote a part of the forty-fifth psalm, which has this inscription, in addition to others, "A psalm for the beloved," where God is evidently addressed in these words: "Grace is poured upon your lips; therefore God will bless you for ever and ever. Gird your sword on your thigh, O mighty One, with your beauty and your majesty. In your majesty, ride forth prosperously and reign because of your truth, meekness and righteousness; let your right hand lead you marvelously. Your arrows are sharp, O mighty One, in the heart of the enemies of the King; the people will fall under you."[34] But attend carefully to what follows, where he is called God: "Your divine throne endures for ever and ever. Your royal scepter is a scepter of equity; you love righteousness and hate wickedness. Therefore God, your God, has anointed you with the oil of gladness above your fellows."[35] And observe that the prophet, speaking familiarly to God, whose "throne is forever and ever," and "a scepter of righteousness the scepter of his kingdom," says that this God has been anointed by a God who was his God and anointed because he had loved righteousness and hated iniquity more than his companions. And I remember that I pressed the Jew, who was deemed a learned man, very hard with this passage. And he, being perplexed about it, gave such an answer as was in keeping with his Judaistic views, saying that the words "your throne, O God, is forever and ever: a scepter of righteousness is the scepter of your kingdom" are spoken of the God of all things; and these, "you have loved righteousness and hated iniquity, therefore your God has anointed you," refer to the Messiah. AGAINST CELSUS 1.56.[36]

IN HIS SECOND ADVENT, HE WILL COME IN GLORY. CYRIL OF JERUSALEM: We preach not one coming of Christ but a second as well, far more glorious than the first. The first gave us a spectacle of his patience; the second will bring with it the crown of the kingdom of God. In general all things are twofold in our Lord Jesus Christ. His birth is twofold, one born of God before the ages and one born of

---

[32]Lk 18:8. [33]ANF 5:429**. [34]Ps 45:2-5. [35]Ps 45:6-7. [36]ANF 4:421*.

a virgin in the consummation of the ages. His descent is twofold; one descent was lowly, "like the rain upon the fleece,"[37] and the second, his manifest coming, is a descent that has yet to occur. In his first coming he was wrapped in swaddling clothes in the manger; in his second he will be "robed in light as with a cloak."[38] In his first coming he "endured a cross, despising shame";[39] in his second he will come in glory, attended by a host of angels. We do not rest, therefore, in reply to his first coming, but we look also for his second. Just as we said of his first coming, "Blessed is he who comes .in the name of the Lord,"[40] so we will repeat the same at his second coming, saying with the angels in adoration as we meet our Master, "Blessed is he who comes in the name of the Lord." The Savior will come this time, not to be judged but to judge those who then judged him. He who then was silent before his judges will remind those wicked people of their cruelty at the cross and say, "Such and such you did, and I was silent." Then he came by divine condescension, seeking to win over people by his teaching, but this time they will of necessity, whether they want to or not, submit to him as King.[41]

Of these two comings the prophet Malachi says, "And suddenly there will come to the temple the Lord whom you seek";[42] that is one advent. Of the second coming, he says, "And the messenger of the covenant whom you desire. Yes, he is coming, says the Lord of hosts. But who will endure the day of his coming? And who can stand when he appears? For he is like the refiner's fire, or like the fuller's lye. He will sit refining and purifying."[43] In what immediately follows the Savior himself says, "I will draw near to you for judgment, and I will be swift to bear witness against the sorcerers, adulterers, and perjurers."[44] It was with this in view that Paul says in due warning: "But if anyone builds upon this foundation, gold, silver, precious stones, wood, hay, straw—the work of each will be made manifest, for the day of the Lord will declare it, since the day is to be revealed in fire."[45] Paul indicates these two comings also in writing to Titus in these words: "The grace of God our Savior has appeared to all, instructing us, in order that, rejecting ungodliness and worldly lusts, we may live temperately and justly and piously in this world; looking for the blessed hope and glorious coming of our great God and Savior, Jesus Christ."[46] Do you see how he speaks of a first coming, for which he gives thanks, and of second we are to look for? We find the same in the wording of the creed we profess, as delivered to us, that is, to believe in him who "ascended into heaven and sat down on the right of the Father and is to come in glory to judge living and dead, of whose kingdom there will be no end." CATECHETICAL LECTURE 15.1-2.[47]

THE RIGHTEOUS WILL SHINE AS THE SUN. CHRYSOSTOM: But if we will, we also will behold Christ, not as they then on the mount but in far greater brightness. For not thus will he come hereafter. For whereas then, to spare his disciples, he discovered so much only of his brightness as they were able to bear, hereafter he will come in the very glory of the Father, not with Moses and Elijah only, but with the infinite host of the angels, with the archangels, with the cherubim, with those infinite tribes, not having a cloud over his head but even heaven itself being folded up. For as it is with the judges, when they judge publicly, the attendants drawing back the curtains show them to all, even so then likewise all people will see him sitting, and all the human race will stand by, and he will make answers to them by himself; and to some he will say, "Come, you blessed of my Father; for I was an hungered, and you gave me meat";[48] to others, "Well done, you good and faithful servant,

---

[37]See Ps 72:6. [38]Ps 104:2. [39]Heb 12:2. [40]Mt 21:9. [41]See Ps 50:21. [42]Mal 3:1. [43]Mal 3:1-3. [44]Mal 3:5. [45]1 Cor 3:11-13. [46]Tit 2:11-13. [47]FC 64:53-55*. [48]Mt 25:34-35.

you have been faithful over a few things, I will set you over many things."⁴⁹ And again passing an opposite sentence, to some he will answer, "Depart into the everlasting fire that is prepared for the devil and his angels,"⁵⁰ and to others, "O wicked and slothful servants."⁵¹ And some he will "cut asunder" and "deliver to the tormentors," but others he will command to "be bound hand and foot, and cast into outer darkness."⁵² And after the ax the furnace will follow; and all out of the net, that is cast away, will fall therein. "Then will the righteous shine forth as the sun,"⁵³ or rather more than the sun. But so much is said, not because their light is to be so much and no more, but since we know no other star brighter than this, he chose by the known example to set forth the future brightness of the saints. On the mountain too, he spoke in the same way when he said, "He shone as the sun." For the apostles fell down, demonstrating that his light was much brighter by comparison. For had the brightness not been unalloyed but comparable to the sun, they would not have fallen but would easily have borne it. The righteous therefore will shine as the sun, and more than the sun in that time, but sinners will suffer all extremities. Then will there be no need of records, proofs, witnesses. For he who judges is himself all, both witness and proof and judge. For he knows all things exactly, "for all things are naked and opened unto his eyes."⁵⁴ No one will there appear rich or poor, mighty or weak, wise or unwise, bond or free, but these masks will be dashed in pieces, and the inquiry will be into their works only. For if in our courts, when any one is tried as an usurper, or murder, whatever he may be, whether governor, or consul, or what you will, all these dignities fly away, and he that is convicted suffers the utmost penalty; much more will it be so there. HOMILIES ON THE GOSPEL OF MATTHEW 56.7.⁵⁵

THE GREAT CHANGE. HILARY OF POITIERS: He promised also to the apostles participation in this his glory. "So will it be at the end of the world. The Son of man will send forth his angels, and they will gather together out of his kingdom all things that cause stumbling and those who do iniquity, and he will send them into the furnace of fire: there will be weeping and gnashing of teeth. Then will the righteous shine forth as the sun in the kingdom of their Father. He who has ears to hear, let him hear."⁵⁶ Were their natural and bodily ears closed to the hearing of the words so that the Lord should need to admonish them to hear? Yet the Lord, hinting at the knowledge of the mystery, commands them to listen to the doctrine of the faith. In the end of the world all things that cause stumbling will be removed from his kingdom. We see the Lord then reigning in the splendor of his body, until the things that cause stumbling are removed. And we see ourselves, in consequence, conformed to the glory of his body in the kingdom of the Father, shining as with the splendor of the sun, the splendor in which he showed what his kingdom looks like to the apostles, when he was transfigured on the mountain.⁵⁷ ON THE TRINITY 11.38.⁵⁸

Judgment Given to the Son of Man

JUDGMENT IS GIVEN TO THE SON OF MAN. AMBROSE: If our adversaries cannot be turned by kindness, let us summon them before the Judge. To what judge, then, will we go? Surely to him who has the judgment. To the Father, then? No, for "the Father judges no one, for he has given all judgment to the Son."⁵⁹ He has given, that is to say, not out of largess but in the act of generation. See, then, how unwilling he was that you should dishonor his Son—so much so that he even gave him to be your

---

⁴⁹Mt 25:23. ⁵⁰Mt 25:41. ⁵¹Mt 25:26. ⁵²Mt 22:13. ⁵³Mt 13:43. ⁵⁴Heb 4:13. ⁵⁵NPNF 1 10:334. ⁵⁶Mt 13:39. ⁵⁷Cf. Mk 9:2. ⁵⁸NPNF 2 9:214*. ⁵⁹Jn 5:22.

judge. Let us see, then, before the judgment which has the better cause, you or I? Surely it is the care of a prudent party to a suit to gain first the favorable regard of the judge. You honor people—do you not honor God? Which of the two, I ask, wins the favor of the magistrate—respect or contempt? Suppose that I am in error—as I certainly am not. Is Christ displeased with the honor shown him? We are all sinners. Who, then, will deserve forgiveness, the one who renders worship or the one who displays insolence? If reasoning does not move you, at least let the plain aspect of the judgment move you! Raise your eyes to the Judge. See who it is that is seated, with whom he is seated and where. Christ sits at the right hand of the Father. If with your eyes you cannot perceive this, hear the words of the prophet: "The Lord said unto my lord, sit at my right hand."[60] The Son, therefore, sits at the right hand of the Father. Tell me now, you who hold that the things of God are to be judged by the things of this world—say whether you think that he who sits at the right hand is lower? Is it any dishonor to the Father that he sits at the Son's left hand? The Father honors the Son, and you make it to be an insult! The Father would have this invitation be a sign of love and esteem, and you would make it an overlord's command! Christ has risen from the dead and sits at the right hand of God. "But," you object, "the Father said." Good, then hear now a passage where the Father does not speak and the Son prophesies: "Hereafter you will see the Son of man sitting at the right hand of power."[61] This he said with regard to taking back to himself his body—to him the Father said, "Sit at my right hand." If indeed you ask of the eternal abode of the Godhead, he said—when Pilate asked him whether he was the king of the Jews—"For this I was born."[62] And so indeed the apostle shows that it is good for us to believe that Christ sits at the right hand of God, not by command or as any kind of bonus but as God's most dearly beloved Son. For it is written for you: "Seek the things that are above, where Christ is, sitting at the right hand of God; savor the things that are above."[63] This is what it means to savor the things that are above: believe that Christ, in his sitting, does not obey as one who receives a command. He is honored as the well-beloved Son. It is with regard, then, to Christ's body that the Father says, "Sit at my right hand, until I make your enemies your footstool." If, again, you seek to pervert the sense of these words, "I will make your enemies your footstool," I answer that the Father also brings to the Son such as the Son rises up and enlivens. For "no one," Christ says, "can come to me, unless the Father who has sent me draws him, and I will raise him up at the last day."[64] And you say that the Son of God is subject by reason of weakness—the Son, to whom the Father brings people so that he may raise them up in the last day. Does this seem in your eyes to be subjection, I ask, pray you, where the kingdom is prepared for the Father and the Father brings to the Son and there is no place for perversion of words, since the Son gives the kingdom to the Father and none is preferred before him? For inasmuch as the Father renders to the Son, and the Son, again, to the Father, here are plain proofs of love and regard, seeing that they render in this way—the one to the other—so that neither he who receives as it were what was another's nor he that renders loses. Moreover, the sitting at the right hand is no preferment, nor does sitting at the left hand betoken dishonor. There are no degrees in the Godhead, which is bound by no limits of space or time, which are the weights and measures of our puny human minds. There is no disparity of love, nothing that divides the unity. But why roam so far afield? You have looked on everything around you. You have all around seen the Judge. You have noted the angels proclaiming him. They praise, and you revile him! Dominations and

---

[60] Ps 110:1. [61] Mt 26:64. [62] Jn 18:37. [63] Col 3:1-2. [64] Jn 6:44.

powers fall down before him, while you speak evil of his name! All his saints adore him, but the Son of God is adored not, nor the Holy Spirit. The seraphim say, "Holy, holy, holy."[65] ON THE CHRISTIAN FAITH 2.12.100-106.[66]

CHRIST WILL COME TO JUDGE. AUGUSTINE: By the last day or time of divine judgment I mean what the whole church of the true God means when it believes and openly proclaims that Christ will come from heaven to judge the living and the dead. Just how many days this judgment will take we do not know, since even the most casual reader of Scripture knows that the word *day* is often used for "time." And one speaks of "last" or "final" in connection with this particular "day" of divine judgment because, in fact, God is at all times exercising judgment and, therefore, at the present time just as he has been doing from the creation of humankind. For example, he exercised judgment when he expelled our first parents from Eden and drove the perpetrators of the great sin far from the tree of life. And God exercised judgment when he refused to spare the angels who sinned and, especially, their leader who was the cause, by choice, of his own fall and, by envy and hatred, the cause of the fall of humankind. Nor is it without God's high and just judgment that the life of the demons in the air and of people on earth is so miserable, so full of ignorance and anguish. And even had there been no sin to punish, there would have been a place for God's good and righteous judgment in rewarding with eternal felicity all of his national creatures who cling in constancy to him as Lord.

God judges people and angels not only as groups that deserve wretchedness as the wages of the original sin but also as individuals who have freely chosen to do what each has done. When the demons beseech God not to torture them, he may quite justly be more sparing to one and more severe with another according to individual wickedness. So, too, human beings—whether manifestly or hiddenly, whether in this life or later—pay a divinely assessed penalty, each for his or her own personal wrongdoing. And it is right to speak of penalty and reward even though no positively good action can be done without divine help and although there can be no sin of human or angel without a divine permission that is at the same time a perfectly just judgment. For, as Paul says in one place, "Is there injustice with God? By no means!"[67] Again he says, "How incomprehensible are his judgments and how unsearchable his ways!"[68]

In this book, however, as God permits, I will not discuss God's first judgment or those other judgments that are past or those that go on today, but only that last judgment when Christ will come from heaven to judge the living and the dead. This will be a day of judgment in the precise sense that there will be no place for any uncomprehending complaint that this sinner has been blessed or that that good person has been punished. On that day, we will see plainly the true fullness of felicity of all the saints and only of the saints, as we will see the supreme and deserved misery of the wicked and of the wicked alone. CITY OF GOD 20.1.[69]

THE JUDGMENT OF CHRIST. AUGUSTINE: But what we believe as far as Christ's action in the future, when he will come from heaven to judge the living and the dead, has no bearing on the life that we now lead here. For it forms no part of what he did on earth but is part of what he will do at the end of the world. And it is to this that the apostle refers in . . . the passage, "When Christ, who is our life, will appear, then will you also appear with him in glory."[70] ENCHIRIDION 54.[71]

THE LAST JUDGMENT ON EVERYDAY LIFE. RUFINUS OF AQUILEIA: That he will come to

---

[65]Is 6:3. [66]NPNF 2 10:237-38**. [67]Rom 9:14. [68]Rom 11:33. [69]FC 24:250-51. [70]Col 3:4. [71]NPNF 1 3:255*.

judge the living and the dead we are taught by many testimonies of the divine Scriptures. But before we cite what the prophets say on this point, we think it necessary to remind you that this doctrine of the faith would have us concerned daily about the coming of the Judge so that we may frame our conduct in such a way as having to give account to the Judge who is at hand. For this is what the prophet said of the person who is blessed: "He orders his words in judgment."[72] When, however, he is said to judge the living and the dead, this does not mean that some will come to judgment who are still living and others who are already dead. Rather, it means that he will judge both souls and bodies, where by souls are meant "the living" and by bodies "the dead." The Lord also says this in the Gospel: "Fear not them who are able to kill the body but are not able to hurt the soul; but rather fear him who is able to destroy both soul and body in Gehenna."[73] A COMMENTARY ON THE APOSTLES' CREED 33.[74]

THE ANGELS WILL FORETELL CHRIST'S SECOND COMING. LEO THE GREAT: All the children of the church were taught to believe that Jesus Christ will come visibly in the same flesh with which he ascended. They were taught not to doubt that all things are subjected to him on whom the ministry of angels had waited from the first beginning of his birth. For as an angel announced to the blessed Virgin that Christ should be conceived by the Holy Spirit, so the voice of heavenly beings also sang of his being born of the Virgin to the shepherds. As messengers from above were the first to attest his having risen from the dead, so the service of angels was employed to foretell his coming in true flesh to judge the world so that we might understand what great powers will come with him as judge, when such great ones ministered to him even in being judged. SERMON 74.4.[75]

The Judgment of the Living and the Dead

THE SON OF GOD WILL JUDGE. EPISTLE OF BARNABAS: Understand, then, you children of gladness, that the good Lord showed us all these things ahead of time so that we might know to whom we ought to render thanksgiving and praise for everything. If therefore the Son of God, who is Lord all things and who will judge the living and the dead, suffered so that his being stricken might give us life, let us believe that the Son of God could not have suffered except for our sakes. EPISTLE OF BARNABAS 7.[76]

WE MUST BE PERFECT AT THE FINAL HOUR. DIDACHE: Watch over your life. Let your lamps not go out, and let your loins not be ungirded but be ready, for you do not know the hour at which our Lord is coming. You will assemble frequently, seeking what your souls need, for the whole time of your faith will be of no profit to you unless you are perfected at the final hour. In the last days will be multiplied false prophets and corruption and will turn the sheep into wolves, and love will turn into hate. For with the increase of lawlessness they will hate one another and will persecute and betray. And then will appear the world deceiver as a son of God, and he will do signs and wonders, and the earth will be betrayed into his hands, and he will do godless things that have not been done since the beginning of the age. Then human creation will pass into the fire of testing, and many will be caused to stumble and be lost, but those who persevere in their faith will be saved by the curse itself. . . . Not of all the dead, but, as it says, "the Lord will come, and all the holy ones with him." Then the world will see the Lord coming on the clouds of heaven, and all

---

[72]Ps 112:5 (LXX). [73]Mt 10:28. [74]NPNF 2 3:556*. [75]NPNF 2 12:189*. [76]ANF 1:141*.

the holy ones with him, on his royal throne, to judge the world deceiver and to reward each according to his deeds. Then will go away the evil into eternal punishment, but the righteous will enter into life eternal inheriting those things that eye has not seen and ear has not heard and that has not arisen in the heart of mortals. Those things that God has prepared for those who love him. DIDACHE 16.[77]

CHRIST AS THE JUDGE. PSEUDO-CLEMENT OF ROME: Brothers, it is fitting that you should think of Jesus Christ as you do of God—as the judge of the living and the dead. And it does not become us to think lightly of our salvation. For if we think little of him, we will also hope but to obtain little from him. And those of us who hear carelessly of these things, as if they were of small importance, commit sin, not knowing to what we have been called, and by whom and to what place, and how much Jesus Christ submitted to suffer for our sakes. 2 CLEMENT 1.[78]

CHRIST WILL COME AND REDEEM US. PSEUDO-CLEMENT OF ROME: For the Lord said, "I come to gather all nations and tongues." This means the day of his appearing, when he will come and redeem us—each one according to his works. And unbelievers will see his glory and might, and, when they see the governance of the world in Jesus, they will be surprised, saying, "Woe to us, because it was you,[79] and we did not know you and did not believe you and did not obey the elders who show us plainly of our salvation."[80]

And "their worm will not die, neither will their fire be quenched; and they will be a spectacle unto all flesh."[81] He is speaking of the great day of judgment when they will see those among us who were guilty of ungodliness and erred in their estimate of the commands of Jesus Christ. The righteous, having succeeded both in enduring the trials and hating the indulgences of the soul, whenever they witness how those who have swerved and denied Jesus by words or deeds are punished with horrible torments in unquenchable fire will give glory to their God and say, "There will be hope for him who has served God with his whole heart." 2 CLEMENT 17.[82]

CHRIST WILL RAISE US ALSO. POLYCARP: "Therefore, girding up your loins,"[83] "serve the Lord in fear" and truth, as those who have forsaken the vain, empty talk and error of the multitude and "believed in him who raised up our Lord Jesus Christ from the dead and gave him glory"[84] and a throne at his right hand. To him all things in heaven and on earth are subject. Every spirit serves him there. He comes as the judge of the living and the dead. His blood will God require of those who do not believe in him. But he who raised him up from the dead will raise us up also if we do his will, and walk in his commandments and love what he loved, keeping ourselves from all unrighteousness, covetousness, love of money, evil speaking, false witness; "not rendering evil for evil, or railing for railing,"[85] or blow for blow or cursing for cursing but being mindful of what the Lord said in his teaching: "Judge not, that you be not judged;[86] forgive, and it will be forgiven you; be merciful, that you may obtain mercy;[87] with what measure you mete, it will be measured to you again";[88] and once more, "Blessed are the poor, and those who are persecuted for righteousness' sake, for theirs is the kingdom of God." EPISTLE TO THE PHILIPPIANS 2.[89]

REWARDS ACCORDING TO PERSONAL MERITS. JUSTIN MARTYR: But lest some suppose, from what has been said by us, that we say that whatever happens, happens by a fatal necessity, because it is foretold as known beforehand,

---

[77]*GMDD* xxxi-xxxiii. [78]ANF 9:251*. [79]Cf. Jn 8:24, 28; 13:19. [80]Is 66:18. [81]Is 66:24; cf. Mk 9:48. [82]ANF 9:255-56*. [83]1 Pet 1:13; Eph 6:14. [84]1 Pet 1:21. [85]1 Pet 3:9. [86]Mt 7:1. [87]Lk 6:36. [88]Mt 7:2; Lk 6:38. [89]ANF 1:33*.

this too we explain. We have learned from the prophets, and we hold it to be true, that punishments and chastisements and good rewards are rendered according to the merit of each person's actions. Since if it is not so, but instead all things happen by fate, there is nothing at all in our own power. For if it is fated that this person, for example, is good and this other evil, the one who is good merits nothing while the one who is evil should not bear any blame. And again, unless the human race has the power of avoiding evil and choosing good by free choice, they are not accountable for their actions—whatever kind they may be. But we thus demonstrate that it is by free choice that they both walk uprightly and that they stumble. We see the same person making a transition to opposite things. Now, if it had been fated that he were to be either good or bad, he could never have been capable of both the opposites or of so many transitions. But not even would some be good and others bad, since we thus make fate the cause of evil and exhibit it as acting in opposition to itself. Or, that which has been already stated would seem to be true, that neither virtue nor vice is anything but that things are only considered good or evil by opinion which, as the true word shows, is the greatest impiety and wickedness. But this we assert is inevitable fate: that those who choose the good have worthy rewards, and those who choose the opposite have their merited awards. For God did not make human beings like other things such as trees and four-footed creatures that cannot act by choice. For he would be worthy neither of reward or praise if he himself did not choose the good but was created for this end; nor, if he were evil, would he be worthy of punishment, not being evil of himself but being able to be nothing else than what he was made. FIRST APOLOGY 43.[90]

THE FATHER WOULD SUBDUE THE DEVILS. JUSTIN MARTYR: And speaking to the fact that God the Father of all would bring Christ to heaven after he had raised him from the dead and would keep him there until he has subdued his enemies the devils and until the number of those who are foreknown by him as good and virtuous is complete for whose sake he has still delayed the consummation—hear what was said by the prophet David. These are his words: "The Lord said unto my lord, sit at my right hand, until I make your enemies your footstool. The Lord will send to you the rod of power out of Jerusalem; and you will rule in the midst of your enemies. With you is the government in the day of your power, in the beauties of your saints: from the womb of morning I have begotten you."[91] That which he says, "He will send to you the rod of power out of Jerusalem," is predictive of the mighty word that his apostles, going forth from Jerusalem, preached everywhere even though death was decreed against those who teach or even at all confess the name of Christ. We everywhere both embrace and teach it. And if you also read these words in a hostile spirit, you can do no more, as I said before, than kill us, which indeed does no harm to us, but to you and all who unjustly hate us and do not repent, it brings eternal punishment by fire. FIRST APOLOGY 45.[92]

SOULS WORTHY OF GOD NEVER DIE. JUSTIN MARTYR: You are right; for what reason has one for supposing that a body so solid, possessing resistance, composite, changeable, decaying and renewed every day has not arisen from some cause? But if the world is begotten, souls also are necessarily begotten; and perhaps at one time they were not in existence, for they were made because of human beings and other living creatures, if you will say that they have been begotten wholly apart and not along with their respective bodies. "This seems to be correct." "They are not, then, immortal?" "No; since the world has appeared to us to be

---

[90]ANF 1:177*. [91]See Ps 110:1. [92]ANF 1:178*.

begotten." "But I do not say, indeed, that all souls die. For that would truly be a piece of good fortune to the evil souls. What then? The souls of the pious remain in a better place, while those of the unjust and wicked are in a worse place waiting for the time of judgment. Thus some which have appeared worthy of God never die, but others are punished so long as God wills them to exist and to be punished." DIALOGUE WITH TRYPHO 5.[93]

RIGHTEOUSNESS, JUDGMENT AND PUNISHMENT. THEOPHILUS OF ANTIOCH: But what does it matter whether one event comes before or after another? Certainly they were in all these events uttering things that confirmed the prophets. Concerning the burning up of the world, Malachi the prophet foretold, "The day of the Lord comes as a burning oven and will consume all the wicked."[94] And Isaiah: "For the wrath of God is as a violent hailstorm, and as a rushing mountain torrent."[95] The Sibyl, then, and the other prophets—yes, and the poets and philosophers—have clearly taught concerning both righteousness and judgment and punishment. They also taught about providence, that God cares for us, not only for the living among us, but also for those that are dead. Even though when they spoke, they said this unwillingly, for they were being convinced by the truth. And among the prophets indeed, Solomon said of the dead, "There will be healing to your flesh, and care taken of your bones."[96] And David says the same, "The bones which you have broken will rejoice."[97] And in agreement with these sayings was that of Timocles: "The dead are pitied by the loving God." And the writers who spoke of a multiplicity of gods came at length to the doctrine of the unity of God, and those who asserted chance spoke also of providence, and the advocates of impunity confessed there would be a judgment, and those who denied that there is a sensation after death acknowledged that there is. Homer, accordingly, though he had said, "Like fleeting vision passed the soul away,"[98] says in another place, "To hades went the disembodied soul."[99] To AUTOLYCUS 2.38.[100]

JUST JUDGMENT TOWARD ALL. IRENAEUS: The church, though dispersed through the whole world, even to the ends of the earth, has received from the apostles and their disciples this faith: It believes in one God, the Father almighty, Maker of heaven and earth and the sea and all things that are in them; and in one Christ Jesus, the Son of God, who became incarnate for our salvation; and in the Holy Spirit, who proclaimed through the prophets the dispensations of God, and the advents, and the birth from a virgin, and the passion, and the resurrection from the dead and the ascension into heaven in the flesh of the beloved Christ Jesus, our Lord, and his future manifestation from heaven in the glory of the Father "to gather all things in one"[101] and to raise up anew all the flesh of the whole human race, in order that to Christ Jesus, our Lord and God and Savior and King, according to the will of the invisible Father, "every knee should bow, of things in heaven, and things in earth and things under the earth, and that every tongue should confess"[102] to him and that he should execute just judgment toward all. Thus, he may send "spiritual wickednesses,"[103] and the angels who transgressed and became apostates, together with the ungodly, and unrighteous, and wicked and profane among people, into everlasting fire. But he also may, in the exercise of his grace, confer immortality on the righteous and holy and those who have kept his commandments and have persevered in his love. Some have done this from the beginning of their Christian course and others from the date of their repentance, and may surround them with ev-

---

[93]ANF 1:197*. [94]Mal 4:1. [95]Is 30:30. [96]Prov 3:8. [97]Ps 51:8. [98]Homer *Odyssey* 11.222. [99]Homer *Iliad* 16.856. [100]ANF 2:110*. [101]Eph 1:10. [102]Phil 2:10-11. [103]Eph 6:12.

erlasting glory. AGAINST HERESIES 1.10.1.[104]

GRACIOUS TO BELIEVERS, SEVERE TO UNBELIEVERS. IRENAEUS: And it is he who uses the words that it will be more tolerable for Sodom in the general judgment than for those who beheld his wonders and did not believe on him or receive his doctrine.[105] For as he gave by his advent a greater privilege to those who believed on him and who do his will, so also did he point out that those who did not believe on him should have a more severe punishment in the judgment; thus extending equal justice to all and exacting more from those to whom he gives more—more, however, not because he reveals the knowledge of another Father, as I have shown so fully and so repeatedly, but because he has, by means of his advent, poured on the human race the greater gift of paternal grace. AGAINST HERESIES 4.36.4.[106]

EVERLASTING LIFE, EVERLASTING FIRE. TERTULLIAN: Now, with regard to this rule of faith—that we may from this point acknowledge what it is that we defend—it is, you must know, that which prescribes the belief that there is only one God and that he is none other than the Creator of the world who produced all things out of nothing through his own Word, first of all sent forth. We believe that this Word is called his Son, and, under the name of God, was seen "in various ways" by the patriarchs, heard at all times in the prophets, at last brought down by the Spirit and power of the Father into the virgin Mary, was made flesh in her womb, and, being born of her, went forth as Jesus Christ. He then preached the new law and the new promise of the kingdom of heaven and worked miracles. Having been crucified, he rose again the third day. Then having ascended into the heavens, he sat at the right hand of the Father and sent instead of himself the power of the Holy Spirit to lead such as believe. He will come with glory to take the saints to the enjoyment of everlasting life and of the heavenly promises and to condemn the wicked to everlasting fire, after the resurrection of both these classes will have happened, together with the restoration of their flesh. This rule, as it will be proved, was taught by Christ and raises among ourselves no other questions than those that heresies introduce and that make people heretics. PRESCRIPTIONS AGAINST HERETICS 13.[107]

The Inevitability of Judgment

UNBELIEVERS DO NOT ACCEPT THAT GOD WILL JUDGE. TERTULLIAN: Thus we are laughed at when we preach that God will judge. For so do both poets and philosophers place a tribunal in the world below. And if we were to threaten a hell, which is a storehouse of secret fire for subterranean punishment, we are similarly laughed to scorn. For so also is Pyriphlegethon a river among the dead. And if we were to name paradise a place of celestial delight appointed to receive the spirits of the saints, separated from the knowledge of the common world by a sort of wall consisting of that fiery zone, if so, the Elysian Fields have already anticipated the belief. How is it, I ask you, that these things are so similar to the poets and philosophers? Only from our mysteries; if from our mysteries, then, as being taken from the earlier, ours are more reliable and more to be believed, whose copies even find credence; if from their own inventions, our mysteries will then be regarded as copies of the later, which is not borne out by the plan of things, for never does the shadow precede the body or the copy the reality. APOLOGY 47.[108]

CHRISTIANS BELIEVE THAT GOD WILL JUDGE. TERTULLIAN: There are some who, although they do not deny God, yet do not

---

[104]ANF 1:330-31*. [105]See Mt 11:24; Lk 10:12. [106]ANF 1:516*. [107]ANF 3:249*. [108]TA 113.

regard him as one who searches us out and beholds and judges us (in which opinion, of course, they markedly differ from us who cling to that doctrine in fear of the proclaimed judgment). Thus they attempt to honor God by freeing him from the care of watching and the trouble of censuring, not even permitting him to be angry. "For if God is angry," say they, "he is corruptible and passionate; and moreover what is corruptible and passionate is perishable, but God is not perishable." These same persons, however, by their own confession elsewhere say that the soul is divine and God-given. They run up against a testimony of the soul itself which can be retorted against their opinion just given. For if the soul is either divine or bestowed by God, doubtless it knows its giver. If it knows him, it surely fears him as its special benefactor. Does it not fear him whom it would rather have draw near to them than become wrathful? From where does it come then—that natural fear of the soul for God—if God does not know how to be angry? How can he be feared who cannot be offended? What is to be feared except anger? From where does anger arise apart from censure? From where does censure come other than from judgment? And how could judgment occur without power? And who has the supreme power except God alone? From this comes, O soul, your readiness to say from your own inmost knowledge, at all times and places, no one scoffing or objecting, that "God sees all things"; "I leave it to God"; "God will repay"; "God will judge between us." From where does this knowledge come, not being Christian? Moreover, often in the very temples themselves, wreathed with Ceres' fillet, or scarleted with Saturn's cloak or white in Isis' linen, you make supplications to God as judge! You stand under Aesculapius, you deck out Juno in bronze, you bind on Minerva a helmet with dusky ornaments, and yet you do not plead with any one of these deities that are present with you! In your own forum you appeal to a judge in another place: in your own temples you permit another God! O Testimony of truth, which among the very demons makes these a witness for the Christians! ON THE TESTIMONY OF THE SOUL 2.6.[109]

GOD IS NECESSARILY JUDGE. TERTULLIAN: Such for the meanwhile being the broad outlines of those divine powers that God has wrought out in parables as well as expressed in speech, let us now come to his actual edicts and decrees, since this is the way we are at present arranging this division of our subject matter. For we began with the dignity of the flesh, asking whether it is the kind of thing for which, after collapse, salvation is practicable. Thereafter we proceeded to concern ourselves with the power of God, whether it is great enough to be accustomed to confer salvation on a thing that has collapsed. Now, if we have proved both points, I would ask you to raise the question of purpose, whether there is one good enough to establish the resurrection of the flesh as necessary and as indubitably in every way a debt to reason—because it is still possible to suggest that although the flesh is capable of restoration, and although deity is competent to restore it, for all that, restoration will need to have a purpose to justify it. Hear then of its purpose, you who are a disciple of God who is supremely good and also righteous—supremely good in respect of what is his, righteous in respect of what is ours. For if man [humankind] had not become a delinquent, he would have known God only as supremely good, by that nature that is properly his. But now he also experiences him as righteous, by the necessity of his own purpose, yet also supremely good precisely in this that he is also righteous. For while he displays righteousness by aiding that which is good and punishing that which is bad, both the sentences he gives are a tribute to the good,

---

[109]TOTS 20-21.

whether he is exacting vengeance of the one or rewarding the other. But in my books against Marcion you will learn more fully whether this is the whole of what God is. Meanwhile such is our God—necessarily judge because lord, necessarily lord because maker, necessarily maker because God. Hence also that—whatever you may call him—of the heretics is necessarily not judge, for he is not lord, necessarily not lord, for he is not maker, and I suppose then not god, seeing he is neither maker, which God is, nor lord, which a maker is. Therefore since it is most appropriate for one who is God and Lord and Maker to appoint for people judgment concerning precisely this, whether or not he has taken care to acknowledge and respect his Lord and Maker, and since the resurrection will bring that judgment into actuality, this will be the whole purpose, yes, the necessity, of the resurrection, such a provision of judgment as is most appropriate to God. And concerning the ordering of it you have to discern whether the divine censorship presides over the judgment of both the human substances, the flesh no less than the soul: for that which it is fitting should be judged will with good reason also be raised up again. I affirm that God's judgment must be believed to be in the first place plenary and complete, as being by that time final and thereafter everlasting, so that it may in this also be just as not being in any respect defective, and in this also worthy of God that in accord with all his great patience it is plenary and complete. And thus the fullness and completeness of judgment can be assured only by the production in court of the whole person—in fact, that the whole person appears in court in the assemblage of both substances—and consequently he must be made present in both, seeing he needs to be judged as a whole, as assuredly he has not lived except as a whole. Therefore in that state in which he has lived, in that will he be judged, because he has to be judged in respect of his life as he has lived it. For life is the purpose of judgment, and this must be made complete in as many substances as it has employed in living. ON THE RESURRECTION OF THE FLESH 14.[110]

A Just Judgment

THE MERITS OF MARTYRS. CYPRIAN: Let no one cheat himself, let no one deceive himself. The Lord alone can have mercy. He alone can bestow pardon for sins that have been committed against himself. He alone can bear our sins, who sorrowed for us, whom God delivered up for our sins. Human beings cannot be greater than God, nor can a servant remit or forego by his indulgence what has been committed by a greater crime against the Lord. Otherwise the person who has lapsed in this way will have added to his sin, if he is ignorant that it is declared, "Cursed is the man who puts his hope in man."[111] The Lord must be asked. The Lord must be appeased by our atonement, who has said that him who denied him he will deny, who alone has received all judgment from his Father. We believe, indeed, that the merits of martyrs and the works of the righteous are of great help with the Judge, but that will be when the day of judgment will come; when, after the conclusion of this life and the world, his people will stand before the tribunal of Christ. THE LAPSED 17.[112]

BELIEF IN A FUTURE AND JUST JUDGMENT OF GOD. ORIGEN: Some such opinions, we believe, ought to be entertained regarding the divine promises, when we direct our understanding to the contemplation of that eternal and infinite world and gaze on its ineffable joy and blessedness. But as the preaching of the church includes a belief in a future and just judgment of God, which belief incites and persuades people to a good and virtuous life and to an avoidance of sin by all possible means; and as by this it is undoubtedly indicated that

---

[110]*TTR* 37-39. [111]Jer 17:5. [112]ANF 5:442*.

it is within our own power to devote ourselves either to a life that is worthy of praise, or to one that is worthy of censure, I therefore deem it necessary to say a few words regarding the freedom of the will, seeing that this topic has been treated by very many writers in no mean style. And that we may ascertain more easily what is the freedom of the will, let us inquire into the nature of will and of desire. ON FIRST PRINCIPLES 3.1.1.[113]

IN THE AGE TO COME THERE WILL BE REWARDS AND PUNISHMENTS. ORIGEN: Then for some unknown reason Celsus mentions the zeal of those who struggle to the point of death to avoid abjuring Christianity; and as though putting our doctrines on a level with the utterances of priests and initiators in the mysteries, he goes on to say:

Above all, my excellent fellow, just as you believe in eternal punishments, so also the interpreters of the mysteries, the priests and initiators, do the same. You threaten others with these punishments while they threaten you. It is possible to consider which of the two is nearer the truth or more successful. For so far as talk is concerned both sides make equally strong assertions about their own system. But if proofs are required, they point to a lot of distinct evidence and produce works done by certain miraculous powers and oracular utterances and in consequence of oracles of all kinds.

By this he means that both we and the priests of the mysteries are on the same level in our belief in eternal punishments, and he would inquire which of the two are nearer the truth. I would affirm that those are right who are able to make the people who hear what they say live as though these things were real. Jews and Christians are convinced about what they call the age to come and that there are rewards in it for the righteous and punishments for the sinners. Let Celsus and anyone who likes show us who have been convinced about eternal punishments by the priests and initiators of the mysteries. It is probable that the intention of the author of the punishments alleged to exist was not merely to talk about punishments in a casual way but to impress those who hear so that they do all in their power to avoid doing the actions that cause punishments. Moreover, to people who do not give a merely superficial attention to the foreknowledge in the prophecies, they seem to me to be adequate to persuade anyone who reads both with intelligence and with an open mind that there was a divine spirit in those people. Not even the slightest comparison is possible between them and any of the wonderful works to which we are referred, or the miracles done in consequence of oracular utterances or the oracles. AGAINST CELSUS 8.48.[114]

THIS WORLD HAD A BEGINNING AND WILL HAVE AN END. ORIGEN: Accordingly, even if Celsus will not admit it, after many prophets who were reformers of the old Israel, Christ came as reformer of the whole world. He did not need to punish people by the method of the earlier dispensation, with whips and bonds and tortures. For when the sower went forth to sow, his teaching was enough to sow the word everywhere. But if there will be a certain fixed time when the world will be brought to the end that it must necessarily have if it had any beginning, and if it is true that there will be a certain appointed end of the world and after that a righteous judgment of all people, then anyone who constructs a Christian philosophy will need to argue the truth of his doctrines with proofs of all kinds, taken both from the divine Scriptures and from rational arguments. The simpleminded masses, however, who cannot comprehend the complex theology of the wisdom of God, must trust themselves to God and to the Savior of our race and be content simply with the unsupported assertion of

---

[113]ANF 4:302. [114]OCC 487.

Jesus rather than with anything beyond this. AGAINST CELSUS 4.9.[115]

THE SEASON OF THE EXPECTED JUDGMENT DOES NOT REQUIRE TIMES. ORIGEN: And these things will take place whenever that happens that is written in Daniel, "The books were opened and the judgment was set."[116] For a record, as it were, is made of all things that have been spoken and done and thought, and by divine power every hidden thing of ours will be made known and everything that is covered will be revealed,[117] in order that when any one is found who has not "given diligence to be freed from the adversary," he may go in succession through the hands of the magistrate, and the judge and the attendant into the prison, until he pays the very last mite.[118] But when one has given diligence to be freed from him and owes nothing to anyone and already has made the pound ten pounds or five pounds, or doubled the five talents or made the two four, he may obtain the due reward, entering into the joy of his Lord, either being set over all his possessions[119] or hearing the word, "You have authority over ten cities,"[120] or "You have authority over five cities."[121] But we think that these things are spoken of as if they required a long period of time, in order that an account may be made by us of the entire time of our earthly life, so that we might suppose that when the king makes a reckoning with each one of his many servants the matter would require so vast a period of time, until these things come to an end which have existed from the beginning of the world down to the consummation of the age, not of one age but of many ages. But the truth is not so. For when God wished all at once to rekindle in the memories of all everything that had been done by each one throughout the whole time, in order that each might become conscious of his own doings whether good or bad, he would do it by his ineffable power. For it is not with God as it is with us. For if we wish to call some things to remembrance, we require sufficient time for the detailed account of what has been said by us and to bring to our remembrance the things that we wish to remember. But if he wished to call to our memory the things that have been done in this life in order that, becoming conscious of what we have done, we may apprehend for what we are punished or honored, he could do so. But if any one disbelieves the swiftness of the power of God in regard to these matters, he has not yet had a true conception of the God who made the universe, who did not require times to make the vast creation of heaven and earth and the things in them. For, though he may seem to have made these things in six days, there is need of understanding to comprehend in what sense the words "in six days" are said, on account of this, "This is the book of the generation of heaven and earth," etc.[122] Therefore it may be boldly affirmed that the season of the expected judgment does not require times, but as the resurrection is said to take place "in a moment, in the twinkling of an eye,"[123] so I think will the judgment also be. COMMENTARY ON THE GOSPEL OF MATTHEW 14.9.[124]

THE JUSTICE OF GOD MAY BE MADE MANIFEST. CHRYSOSTOM: If you see a sinner being punished, remember the paralytic who passed thirty-eight years on his bed. For listen to what Christ says to that man who had previously been delivered over to his disease because of his sin, "Behold, you are made whole. Sin no more lest a worse thing happen to you."[125] When we are chastened, we pay the penalty of our sins, or else we receive the occasion of crowning if, when we live uprightly, in rectitude, we suffer ill. So whether we live in righteousness or in sins, chastening is a

---

[115]OCC 189-90. [116]Dan 7:10. [117]See Mt 10:26; Lk 12:2. [118]See Lk 12:58-59. [119]See Mt 24:47. [120]Lk 19:17. [121]Lk 19:19. [122]Gen 2:4. [123]1 Cor 15:52. [124]ANF 9:499-500*. [125]Jn 5:14.

useful thing for us. Sometimes it may make us more distinguished and at other times render us more self-controlled. It may even lighten our future punishment for us. For it is possible that one chastened here and bearing it thankfully could experience milder punishment there. We hear Paul saying, "For this reason many are weak and sickly, and some sleep. For if we judged ourselves, we should not be judged. But when we are judged we are corrected by the Lord, that we should not be condemned with the world."[126] Knowing all these things therefore, let us both moralize in this way on the providence of God and stop the mouths of the scornful. And if any of the events that happen exceed our understanding, let us not from this consider that our affairs are not governed by providence. We should instead realize that we only perceive his providence in part, in things incomprehensible. Let us yield to the unsearchableness of his wisdom. For if it is not possible for one not conversant with it to understand one's ability, much more is it impossible for the human understanding to comprehend the infinity of the providence of God. "For his judgments are unsearchable and his ways past finding out."[127]

Nevertheless from the small portions of providence we do see, we can gain a clear and manifest faith about the whole and give thanks to him for everything that happens. For there is even another consideration that cannot be contradicted for those who wish to reflect on the providence of God. For we would ask the scoffers, Is there then a God? If they should say there is not, let us not answer them. For just as it is worthless to answer mad people, so too is it worthless to answer those who say there is no God. For if a ship that only has a few sailors and passengers on it would not be conducted safely for even one mile without the hand that guides it, it is even more the case that a world such as this is, and as populated as it is and composed of so many different elements, would not have continued for as long as it has were there not a certain providence presiding over it, both governing and continually maintaining this whole fabric.

If in humiliation, through the common opinion of all and the experience of affairs, they confess that there is a God, let us say this to them. If there is a God, as indeed there is, it follows that he is just. For if he is not just, neither is he God. And if he is just, he rewards people according to what they deserve.

But we do not see everyone here receiving what they deserve. Therefore it is necessary to hope for some other requital awaiting us, in order that by each one receiving what they deserve, the justice of God may be made known. For this consideration does not only contribute to our wisdom about providence alone, but about the resurrection.

Let us teach others. Let us do due diligence in shutting the mouths of those who rave against the master. Let us ourselves glorify him in all things. For in this way we will win more of his care and enjoy more of his influence and thus be able to escape from real evil and obtain future blessings through the grace and loving-kindness of our Lord Jesus Christ, by whom and with whom be glory to the Father, with the Holy Spirit, now and always, forever and ever. Amen. HOMILIES CONCERNING THE POWER OF DEMONS 1.8.[128]

GOD NEEDS NO EXAMINATION OR PROOFS FOR CONDEMNATION. CYRIL OF JERUSALEM: Let us be fearful, my dear brothers, of God's condemnation. He needs no examination or proofs for condemnation. Do not say, "At night I committed fornication," or "I made use of magical arts," or "I committed a certain other deed, and there was no one at hand." From your own conscience you will be judged, as your conflicting thoughts accuse or defend you, "on the day when God will judge the

---

[126]1 Cor 11:30-32.   [127]Rom 11:33.   [128]NPNF 1 9:185-86**.

hidden secrets of men."[129] The awe-inspiring countenance of the Judge will compel you to speak the truth, or rather, though you are silent, it will convict you. For you will rise clothed in your sins or your just deeds. The Judge himself declared this, (for it is Christ who judges), "For neither does the Father judge any man, but all judgment he has given to the Son";[130] the Father does not deprive himself of his power but judges through the Son. Therefore by the will of the Father the Son judges; for the wills of the Father and the Son are not different but one and the same. What, then, does the Judge say about your bearing or not bearing your deeds? "And before him will be gathered all the nations."[131] In the presence of Christ "every knee should bend of those in heaven, on earth and under the earth."[132] "And he will separate them one from another, as the shepherd separates the sheep from the goats."[133] How does the shepherd do this? Does he seek from a book which is a sheep and which a goat? Or does he decide from the evident facts? Does not the wool manifest the sheep, and the hairy and rough skin the goat? So with you too, once you have been cleansed of your sins, your deeds will be as pure wool, your robe unstained, and you will say always, "I have taken off my robe; how will I put it on?"[134] By your vesture you will be recognized as a sheep. But if you will be found hairy, like Esau, who was shaggy of body and wicked of mind, who lost his birthright for food and sold his prerogative, you will be among those on the left hand. God forbid that anyone present fall from grace or because of evil deeds be found in the ranks of sinners on the left hand! CATECHETICAL LECTURE 15.25.[135]

THE DISEASES OF OUR SOULS ARE SCRAPED AWAY. GREGORY OF NYSSA: Those who use the knife or cautery to remove certain unnatural excrescences in the body, such as cysts or warts, do not bring to the person they are serving a method of healing that is painless, though certainly they apply the knife without any intention of injuring the patient. In the same way, whatever material excrescences that have been sensualized by fellowship with the body's affections and are hardening on our souls are, in the day of the judgment, as it were cut and scraped away by the ineffable wisdom and power of him who, as the Gospel says, "heals those who are sick."[136] For, as he says again, "those who are whole have no need of the physician, but those who are sick."[137] Since, then, there has been inbred in the soul a strong natural tendency to evil, it must suffer, just as the excision of a wart gives a sharp pain to the skin of the body. For whatever contrary to the nature has been inbred in the nature attaches itself to the subject in a certain union of feeling. What is produced then is an abnormal intermixture of our own nature with an alien quality, so that when the separation from this abnormal growth occurs our feelings are hurt and lacerated. ADDRESS ON RELIGIOUS INSTRUCTION 8.[138]

THE CAUSE OF ADAM'S FALL WAS PRIDE. AMBROSE: This law Adam broke, seeking to take for himself what he had not received, so that he might be like his own creator and maker, so that he might claim divine honor. Through disobedience he incurred guilt, and through arrogance he fell into sin. Had he not broken the command and had he been obedient to the heavenly precepts, he would have preserved for his heirs the prerogative of nature and of innocence that was his from birth. But because the authority of the natural law was corrupted and blotted out by disobedience, the written law was determined necessary, that humankind who had lost all might regain at least a part, and he who had lost what was his at birth might know and guard

---

[129]Dan 7:10. [130]Rom 2:15-16. [131]Mt 25:32. [132]Phil 2:10. [133]Mt 25:32. [134]Song 5:3. [135]FC 64:70-71. [136]Mt 9:12. [137]Mt 9:12. [138]NPNF 2 5:141-42**.

at least a part. Since the cause of his fall was pride, and pride sprang from the privilege of his innocence, it was necessary for some law to be passed that would subdue and subject him to God. Now, without the law he was ignorant of sin, and his fault was less when he was ignorant of his fault.[139] Thus, also, says the Lord: "If I had not come and spoken to them, they would have no sin. But now they have no excuse for their sin."[140] LETTER 83.[141]

JUDGMENT ACCOMPANIED BY THE RESURRECTION OF THE DEAD. AUGUSTINE: Now, then, to the matter at hand. When our Savior was rebuking the cities in which he had performed great miracles without their believing in him and was putting foreign cities ahead of them, he said, "But I tell you, it will be more tolerable for Tyre and Sidon on the day of judgment than for you,"[142] and a little further on, addressing another city, he said, "But I tell you, it will be more tolerable for the land of Sodom on the day of judgment than for you."[143] In this text he makes it perfectly clear that the judgment day is to come. In another passage we find: "The men of Nineveh will rise up in the judgment with this generation and will condemn it; for they repented at the preaching of Jonah, and behold, a greater than Jonah is here. The queen of the South will rise up in the judgment with this generation and will condemn it; for she came from the ends of the earth to hear the wisdom of Solomon, and behold, a greater than Solomon is here."[144] This text teaches us two things: first, that judgment will come; second, that it will be accompanied by the resurrection of the dead. For at the time Christ spoke these words concerning the people of Nineveh and the queen of the south he was speaking, of course, about people who had died. And he foretold that these very people would rise again on judgment day. When he said, "They will condemn," he did not mean that they would sit in judgment but only that the other people in question, by comparison with these, will be deservedly damned. Again, in another passage, when he was talking about the present intermingling of good and bad people and the future winnowing out that is to take place on judgment day, he made use of a parable about wheat sown and weeds oversown. Explaining this parable to his disciples, he said, "He who sows the good seed is the Son of man. The field is the world; the good seed, the sons of the kingdom; the weeds, the sons of the wicked one; and the enemy who sowed them is the devil. But the harvest is the end of the world, and the reapers are the angels. Therefore, just as the weeds are gathered up and burned with fire, so will it be at the end of the world. The Son of man will send forth his angels, and they will gather out of his kingdom all who cause scandals and those who work iniquity, and cast them into the furnace of fire, where there will be the weeping and gnashing of teeth. Then the just will shine forth like the sun in the kingdom of their Father. He who has ears to hear, let him hear."[145] In this text, it is true, Christ does not use the words judgment or judgment day. He nevertheless sets forth the reality far more clearly, by means of these descriptions, than if he had done so, and he foretells that judgment is to come at the end of the world. CITY OF GOD 20.5.[146]

FORETOLD IN BOTH TESTAMENTS. AUGUSTINE: There are many other passages of the divinely inspired Scripture that deal with the last judgment, but it would take too long to assemble them all. Suffice it to say that evidence enough has been adduced to prove that the judgment has been foretold in both Testaments. The fact that it is Christ who is to come from heaven as the judge is made less explicit in the Old Testament than in the New. The difficulty is that in the Old Testament,

---

[139]See Rom 7:8. [140]See Jn 15:22. [141]FC 26:465. [142]Mt 11:22. [143]Mt 11:24. [144]Mt 12:41-42. [145]Mt 13:37-43. [146]FC 24:256-57.

when the Lord God says he is to come or when it is stated that the "Lord God will come," it is not obvious that Christ is meant. Now, of course, it is true that the Father, Son and Holy Spirit is each Lord and God; yet that is no reason why one should not attempt to show that, in the relevant texts, it is Christ that is meant. The first proof is this. In the prophetical books, Jesus Christ speaks under the name of the "Lord God" in many passages where there can be no doubt at all that it is Christ who is meant. Hence, when there is a reference to the last judgment, indicating that the "Lord God" is to come, it is at least possible to argue that Christ is meant, even though this is not made explicit. Take, for example, the passage in Isaiah where God says, through the prophet: "Hearken to me, O Jacob, and you Israel when I call. I am he, I am the first, and I am the last. My hand also has founded the earth and my right hand has measured the heavens: I will call them and they will stand together, and all will assemble and all will hear. Who has declared these things? Loving you I will do your will in regard to Babylon, and so take away the seed of the Chaldeans. I, even I, have spoken and called him. I have brought him and I have made his way prosperous. Come near to me and hear this. I have not spoken in secret from the beginning. When these things were done I was there and now the Lord God has sent me and his spirit."[147] Now, it is Jesus Christ who is speaking here as the Lord God; yet this would not have been obvious if he had not added the final words: "And now the Lord God has sent me and his spirit." These words were spoken by Christ in his "form" as a "servant." He used a verb in the past tense to indicate a future event, much as was done in that other text of the same prophet: "He was led as a sheep to the slaughter." Instead of saying "he will be led," he uses a verb in the past tense to indicate a future event, as is frequently the case in the prophecies. . . . The conclusion, then, is that, when we read in the prophetical books that God is to come to pronounce the last judgment, we do not need any indication more specific than the mention of the judgment to realize that it is Christ who is meant. The Father, of course, will judge, but he will do so by means of the coming of the Son of man. Although the Father will manifest himself by his presence, he will not judge anyone, but all judgment he has given to the Son. The Son . . . will manifest himself as a man who is to judge, because it was as a man that he was judged. CITY OF GOD 20.30.[148]

TO JUDGE THE LIVING AND THE DEAD.
AUGUSTINE: Now the expression "to judge the living and the dead" may be interpreted in two ways: either we may understand by the "living" those who at his advent will not yet have died but whom he will find alive in the flesh, and by the "dead" those who have departed from the body or who will have departed before his coming; or we may understand the "living" to mean the righteous and the "dead" the unrighteous; for the righteous will be judged as well as others. Now the judgment of God is sometimes taken in a bad sense, as, for example, "They that have done evil unto the resurrection of judgment,"[149] sometimes in a good sense, as, "Save me, O God, by your name, and judge me by your strength."[150] This is easily understood when we consider that it is the judgment of God that separates the good from the evil and sets the good at his right hand, that they may be delivered from evil and not destroyed with the wicked. And this is why the psalmist cried, "Judge me, O God," and then added, as if in explanation, "and distinguish my cause from that of an ungodly nation."[151] ENCHIRIDION 55.[152]

SOULS UNITED TO INCORRUPTIBLE BODIES.
JOHN OF DAMASCUS: We will therefore rise again, our souls being once more united with

---

[147]Is 48:12-16. [148]FC 24:331-32, 335. [149]Jn 5:29. [150]Ps 54:1. [151]Ps 43:1. [152]NPNF 1 3:255*.

our bodies, now made incorruptible and having put off corruption. We will then stand beside the awful judgment seat of Christ: and the devil and his demons and the man that is his, that is, the Antichrist, and the impious and the sinful will be given over to everlasting fire. It will not be a material fire like our fire but such fire as God would know. But those who have done good will shine forth as the sun with the angels into life eternal, with our Lord Jesus Christ, ever seeing him and being in his sight and deriving unceasing joy from him, praising him with the Father and the Holy Spirit throughout the limitless ages of ages. Amen. ORTHODOX FAITH 4.27.[153]

The Intermediate State of Souls

AS LONG AS THERE IS AN EARTHLY LIFE. PSEUDO-CLEMENT OF ROME: As long, therefore, as we are on earth, let us practice repentance, for we are as clay in the hand of the artisan. If a potter makes a vessel and it becomes distorted or broken in his hands, he makes it over again, unless he throws it into the furnace of fire before he can remake it. In that case, he can no longer find any help for it. In the same way, let us also, while we are in this world, repent with our whole heart of the evil deeds we have done in the flesh so that we may be saved by the Lord while we still have an opportunity to repent. For after we have gone out of the world, there will no further possibility of confessing or repenting for us. Therefore, brothers, by doing the will of the Father and keeping the flesh holy and observing the commandments of the Lord, we will obtain eternal life. For the Lord says in the Gospel, "If you have not kept that which was small, who will commit to you the great? For I say to you that he who is faithful in that which is least is faithful also in much."[154] This, then, is what he means: Keep the flesh holy and the seal undefiled so that you may receive eternal life. 2 CLEMENT 8.[155]

NO REPENTANCE IS TOO LATE. CYPRIAN: Once you have departed from here, there is no longer any place for repentance and no possibility of making satisfaction. Here life is either lost or saved; here eternal safety is provided for by the worship of God and the fruits of faith. Nor let anyone be restrained either by his sins or by his years from coming to obtain salvation. No repentance is too late for the person who still remains in this world. The approach to God's mercy is open, and the access is easy to those who seek and apprehend the truth. Even if you find yourself begging for your sins at the very end of life and at the setting of the sun of time, if you implore God, who is the one and true God, in confession and faith and acknowledge him, pardon is granted to the one who confesses, and saving mercy is given from the divine goodness to the believer. A passage is opened to immortality even in death itself. This grace Christ bestows; this gift of his mercy he confers on us by overcoming death in the trophy of the cross, by redeeming the believer with the price of his blood, by reconciling us to God the Father, by quickening our mortal nature with a heavenly regeneration. If it is possible, let us all follow him; let us be registered in his sacrament and sign. He opens to us the way of life. He brings us back to paradise. He leads us on to the kingdom of heaven. Since he made us the children of God, we will always live with him. We will always rejoice with him, restored by his own blood. We Christians will be glorious together with Christ, blessed of God the Father, always rejoicing with perpetual pleasures in the sight of God and always giving thanks to God. For none can be other than always glad and grateful who, having been once subject to death, has been made secure in the possession of immortality. TO DEMETRIAN 25.[156]

---

[153]NPNF 2 9:101*. [154]Lk 16:10-12. [155]ANF 9:253**. [156]ANF 5:465**.

GOD IS EVERYWHERE BRINGING ABOUT SALVATION. CHRYSOSTOM: Thus whereas he had called the way straight and narrow, in order to soothe our worry on this side of life, he also indicates the great security as well as the great pleasure that is ours—even as he also indicates how precarious and detrimental the opposite course is. For virtue even from things here does have its rewards, as he indicates, just as vice has its penalties. For what I have always been saying I will say now again: that he uses both in dealing with people everywhere in order to bring about the salvation of his hearers on the one hand by stirring them on to virtue or, on the other, by instilling a hatred of vice. Thus, because there would be some who would like what he was saying but would yield no proof of it by their works, he anticipates this and awakens their fears, saying, Although what I said sounds good, hearing is not sufficient for security. There must also be obedience in actions, and the whole lies chiefly in this. And this is where he ends his discourse, leaving the fear at its height in them. He not only exhorted them to be virtuous because of what is coming in the future—speaking of a kingdom, and of heaven, and an unspeakable reward and comfort and innumerable other good things—but also from present realities, indicating the firm and immoveable quality of the Rock. In the same way, he incites a fear of wickedness in them not only from what they can expect in the future—as from the tree that is cut down, and the unquenchable fire, and the not entering into the kingdom and from his saying, "I know you not"—but also from present realities, as for instance when he talks about the house that crashes down. HOMILIES ON THE GOSPEL OF MATTHEW 24.3.[157]

Prayers and Intercession

THE PRAYERS OF FRIENDS AND RELATIVES ARE BENEFICIAL. AUGUSTINE: Nor can it be denied that the souls of the dead are benefited by the piety of their living friends who offer the sacrifice of the Mediator or give alms in the church on their behalf. But these services are of advantage only to those who during their lives have earned such merit, that services of this kind can help them. For there is a manner of life that is neither so good as not to require these services after death nor so bad that such services are of no avail after death. There is, on the other hand, a kind of life so good as not to require them, and again, one so bad that when life is over they render no help. Therefore, it is in this life that all the merit or demerit is acquired that can either relieve or aggravate a person's sufferings after this life. No one, then, should hope that after he is dead he will obtain merit with God that he has neglected to secure here. And accordingly it is plain that the services that the church celebrates for the dead are in no way opposed to the apostle's words: "For we must all appear before the judgment seat of Christ; that every one may receive the things done in his body, according to that he has done, whether it be good or bad,"[158] for the merit that renders such services as I speak of profitable to someone is earned while he lives in the body. It is not to everyone that these services are profitable. And why are they not profitable to all, except because of the different kinds of lives that people lead in the body? When, then, sacrifices either of the altar or of alms are offered on behalf of all the baptized dead, they are thank offerings for the very good, they are propitiatory offerings for the not very bad, and in the case of the very bad, even though they do not assist the dead, they are a species of consolation to the living. And where they are profitable, their benefit consists either in obtaining a full remission of sins or at least in making the condemnation more tolerable. ENCHIRIDION 110.[159]

---

[157]NPNF 1 10:165-66**. [158]See 2 Cor 5:10; Rom 14:10. [159]NPNF 1 3:272-73*.

THE HOLY SACRIFICE IS OF THE GREATEST BENEFIT. CYRIL OF JERUSALEM: Then we commemorate also those who have fallen asleep: first of all, the patriarchs, prophets, apostles and martyrs, that God through their intercessory prayers may accept our supplication. Next we pray also for the holy fathers and bishops who have fallen asleep, and generally for all who have gone before us, believing that this will be of the greatest benefit to the souls of those on whose behalf our supplication is offered in the presence of the holy, the most dread Sacrifice. Let me use an illustration for an argument. For I know that many of you say, "What does it avail a soul departing this world, whether with or without sins, to be remembered at the Sacrifice?" Well, suppose a king banished persons who had offended him, and then their relatives wove a garland and presented it to him on behalf of those undergoing punishment, would he not mitigate their sentence? In the same way, offering our supplications to him for those who have fallen asleep, even though they are sinners, we, though we weave no garland, offer Christ slain for our sins, propitiating the merciful God on both their and our own behalf. MYSTAGOGICAL LECTURES 5.9-10.[160]

A Cleansing

BAD FOR SINNERS, GOOD FOR SAINTS. AUGUSTINE: If we look a little more closely, we will notice that even when a person dies out of faith and loyalty to the truth, he escapes death. His motive in facing a partial death is to escape total death and, above all, a death that is eternal. He suffers the separation of his soul from his body to prevent its separation both from God and his body—to prevent a first death of the whole man which would be followed by a second and eternal death.

Thus, in a word, while people are in the throes of death and death is bringing on disintegration, death is good for no one, but it may become meritorious if suffered to retain or to gain some good. However, when it is a question not of dying but of being dead, then death may well be said to be bad for sinners and good for saints. For the separated souls of the saints are now in peace, while those of the wicked are in pain and will be so until the resurrection of their bodies, when the former will enter into life everlasting and the latter into a second and eternal death. CITY OF GOD 13.8.[161]

A TIME OF CLEANSING. GREGORY THE GREAT: Our Lord says in the Gospel, "Walk while you have the light."[162] By his prophet he says, "In the accepted time I have heard you. In the day of salvation I have helped you."[163] This is what the apostle Paul further explained, saying, "Behold, now is the acceptable time; behold, now the day of salvation."[164] Solomon, likewise, says, "Whatever your hand is able to do, do it instantly. For neither work, nor reason, nor knowledge nor wisdom will be in hell, where you may be headed."[165] David also says, "Because his mercy is for ever."[166] By these sayings it is plain that in the very such state as a person departs out of this life, in that same state he is presented in judgment before God.

But yet we must believe that before the day of judgment there is a purging fire for certain small sins because our Savior has said that "he who speaks blasphemy against the Holy Spirit, that will not be forgiven, neither in this world, nor in the world to come."[167] Out of this sentence we learn that some sins are forgiven in this world and some others may be pardoned in the next. For that which is denied concerning one sin is consequently understood to be granted touching some other. But yet we do not believe this regarding all sin, but yet this, as I said, we have not to believe but only concerning little and very small sins, as, for example, daily idle talk, immoderate laughter,

---

[160]FC 64:197-98. [161]FC 14:308-9. [162]Jn 12:35. [163]Is 49:8. [164]2 Cor 6:2. [165]Eccles 9:10. [166]Ps 118:1. [167]Mt 12:32.

negligence in the care of our family—the sort of offenses that can hardly be avoided, that we know in what sort sin is to be shunned.

I speak here of ignorant errors in matters of no great weight. Indeed, all sins will be punished after death if people do not procure pardon and remission for them in their lifetime. For when Paul says that "Christ is the foundation," he adds, "And if any one build upon this foundation gold, silver, precious stones, wood, hay, stubble: the work of every one, of what kind it is, the fire will try. If any man's work abide which he built thereupon, he will receive reward; if any man's work burn, he will suffer detriment, but himself will be saved, yet so as by fire."[168] For these words may be understood of the fire of tribulation, which people suffer in this world. Yet if any will interpret them as of the fire of purgatory, which will be in the next life, then the interpreter must carefully consider that the apostle said not that he may be saved by fire for any sin that builds on this foundation: iron, brass or lead, that is, the greater sort of sins, as those built on the foundation of iron, brass or lead, and therefore more hard, and consequently not remissible in that place. Rather he speaks here of wood, hay, stubble, that is, little and very light sins, that the fire easily consumes. Yet we have here further to consider, that none can be there purged, no, not for the least sins that be, unless in his lifetime he deserved by faith's virtuous works to find such favor in that place. DIALOGUE 4.41.[169]

THE KINGDOM OF GOD POSSESSED IN PURITY OF HEART. JOHN CASSIAN: For this reason everyone who lives in this body knows that he must be committed to that special task or ministry to which he has given himself in this life as a participant and a laborer, and he ought not to doubt that in that everlasting age he will also be the partner of him whose servant and companion he now wishes to be, according to what the Lord says: "If anyone serves me, let him follow me, and where I am, there also will my servant be."[170] For just as the kingdom of the devil is gained by conniving at the vices, so the kingdom of God is possessed in purity of heart and spiritual knowledge by practicing the virtues. And where the kingdom of God is, there without a doubt is eternal life, and where the kingdom of the devil is, there—it is not to be doubted—are death and hell. Whoever is there cannot praise the Lord, as the prophet says: "The dead will not praise you, Lord, neither will all who go down into hell" (this is doubtless the hell of sin). "But we," he says, "who live"—not to vices or to this world, namely, but to God—"shall praise the Lord, from this time forth and forever. For in death there is no one who is mindful of God. But in hell—the hell of sin—'who will confess' to the Lord?"[171] There is no one. For no one, even if he professed a thousand times that he was a Christian and a monk, confesses God when he sins. No one who does the things that the Lord condemns is mindful of God, nor does he profess in a truthful way that he is the servant of one whose commandments he disdains with reckless obstinacy. The blessed apostle declares that the widow who gives herself to pleasure is in that death when he says, "The widow who gives herself to pleasure is dead while she lives."[172] But there are many who, while living in this body, are dead and are unable to praise God as they lie in hell, and on the other hand there are those who, although dead in the body, bless and praise God in the spirit, in the words of the text: "Spirits and souls of the righteous, bless the Lord."[173] And, "Let every spirit praise the Lord."[174] CONFERENCES 1.14.1-3[175]

PARADISE AS A PLACE OF SPIRITUAL ASCENT. ORIGEN: We are therefore to suppose that the saints will remain there[176] until they

---

[168]1 Cor 3:11-15. [169]DSG 232-34. [170]Jn 12:26. [171]See Ps 115:17-18; 6:5. [172]1 Tim 5:6. [173]See Pr Azar 64 (Dan 3:86 LXX). [174]Ps 150:6. [175]ACW 57:52-53. [176]Origen had previously been speaking of the saints caught up with christ in the air (cf. 1 Thess 4:17) in the space between heaven and earth.

recognize the two ways of government in those things that are performed in the air. And when I say "two ways," I mean this: When we were on the earth, we saw either animals or trees and saw the differences among them and also the very great diversity among human beings. But although we saw these things, we did not understand why they existed. The only thing that was suggested to us from the visible diversity was that we should examine and inquire on what principle these things were either created or arranged so diversely. And a zeal or desire for knowledge of this kind being conceived by us on earth, the full understanding and comprehension of it will be granted after death, if indeed the result should follow according to our expectations. When, therefore, we fully comprehend its nature, we will understand in two ways what we saw on earth. We must hold some kind of view like this regarding this abode in the air. I think, therefore, that all the saints who depart from this life will remain in some place situated on the earth, which holy Scripture calls paradise. It will be like a place of instruction and, so to speak, a classroom or school of souls in which they are to be instructed regarding all the things that they had seen on earth and are to receive also some information respecting things that are to follow in the future, as even when in this life they had obtained in some degree indications of future events, although "through a glass darkly," all of which are revealed more clearly and distinctly to the saints in their proper time and place. If anyone indeed is pure in heart, and holy in mind and more practiced in perception, he will, by making more rapid progress, quickly ascend to a place in the air and reach the kingdom of heaven through those mansions, so to speak, in the various places that the Greeks have termed spheres, that is, globes, but which holy Scripture has called heavens. In each of these spheres he will first see clearly what is done there, and in the second place, will discover the reason why things are done the way they are. Thus he will pass through all the gradations in order, following him who has passed into the heavens, Jesus the Son of God, who said, "I will that where I am, these may be also."[177] And he speaks of this diversity of places when he says, "In my Father's house are many mansions." He himself is everywhere and passes swiftly through all things; nor are we any longer to understand him as existing in those narrow limits in which he was once confined for our sakes, that is, not in that circumscribed body that he occupied on earth when dwelling among us which might make us think that he is enclosed in one single place. ON FIRST PRINCIPLES 2.11.6.[178]

THE SOUL KNOWS JOY AND SORROW.
TERTULLIAN: Why, then, can't you conceive of the soul undergoing punishment and consolation in hades in the interval of waiting for its judgment, in a certain anticipation, either of gloom or of glory? You reply: Because in the judgment of God its situation ought to be safe and secure, nor should there be any inkling beforehand of the award of his sentence. You also say that it is because the soul needs to be covered first by the clothing of its restored flesh which, as the partner of its actions, should also share in the soul's reward.

What, then, is to take place in that interval? Will we sleep? But souls do not sleep even when people are alive. It is indeed the business of bodies to sleep, to which death itself also belongs no less than its mirror and counterfeit sleep.

Or will you have it that nothing is done there toward which the whole human race is attracted and where all our expectation is postponed for safekeeping? Do you think this state is a foretaste of judgment or its actual commencement? Is it a premature encroach-

---

[177]Jn 17:24. [178]ANF 4:299**.

ment on it or the first course in its full ministration? Now really, would it not be the highest possible injustice, even in hades, if all were to be still well with the guilty even there and not well with the righteous even yet? What! Would you have hope be still more confused after death? Would you have it mock us still more with uncertain expectation? Or will it now become a review of our past life and an arranging of judgment, with the inevitable feeling of a trembling fear?

But, again, must the soul always wait for the body in order to experience sorrow or joy? Is it not sufficient, even of itself, to suffer both one and the other of these sensations? How often, without any pain to the body, is the soul alone tortured by ill temper, anger and fatigue? This happens very often unconsciously, even within to itself. How often, too, . . . amid bodily suffering, does the soul seek out for itself some secret joy and withdraw for the moment from the body's annoying society? I am mistaken if the soul is not in the habit, indeed, solitary and alone, of rejoicing and glorifying over the very tortures of the body. Look, for instance, at the soul of Mutius Scoevola as he melts his right hand over the fire. Look also at Zeno's, as the torments of Dionysius pass over it. The bites of wild beasts are a glory to young heroes, as the scars of the bear were on Cyrus. The soul knows full well, then, even in hades how to rejoice and to mourn even without the body since it feels pain in the flesh when it likes, although the body is unhurt, and it also feels joy when it wants to, although the body is in pain. Now if such sensations occur at its will during life, how much more will they happen after death by the judicial appointment of God! Moreover, the soul does not execute all its operations with the assistance of the flesh. The judgment of God pursues even simple thoughts and the slightest choices. "Whoever looks on a woman to lust after her has committed adultery with her already in his heart."[179] Therefore it is most fitting that the soul, without at all waiting for the flesh, should be punished for this lust it has committed without the partnership of the flesh. So, on the same principle, in return for the pious and kindly thoughts that the flesh had no part in helping along, will it without the flesh receive its consolation?

Even in matters done through the flesh, the soul is the first to conceive them, the first to arrange them, the first to authorize them, the first to precipitate them into acts. And even if it is sometimes unwilling to act, it is still the first to treat whatever it means to effect with the help of the body. In no case, indeed, can an accomplished fact be prior to the mental conception of it.

It is therefore quite in keeping with this order of things, that that part of our nature should be the first to have the payback and reward to which they are due on account of its priority. Suppose we understand "the prison" pointed out in the Gospel to be hades.[180] Suppose we also interpret "the uttermost farthing" to mean the very smallest offense that has to be paid back there before the resurrection. If so, no one will hesitate to believe that the soul undergoes in hades some compensatory discipline, without prejudice to the full process of the resurrection, when the reward will be administered also through the flesh.

This point that Paraclete has also pressed home to our attention in most frequent admonitions whenever any of us has admitted the force of his words from a knowledge of his promised spiritual disclosures. And now at last having, as I believe, encountered every human opinion concerning the soul and having tried its character by the teaching of our holy faith, we have satisfied the curiosity that is simply a reasonable and necessary one. As for that which is extravagant and idle, there will always be as great a defect in its information, as there has been exaggeration and self-will in its researches. ON THE SOUL 58.[181]

---

[179]Mt 5:28. [180]See Mt 5:25. [181]ANF 3:234-35**.

GOD DESIRES THAT SINNERS SHOULD DO PENANCE. CYPRIAN: For my own part, I am astonished that there are some who are so obstinate as to judge that no opportunity for penitence ought to be granted to the fallen and who consider that pardon must be denied to those who do penance. And yet it is written, "Remember whence you have fallen, do penance and perform your former good works."[182] Now these words are certainly directed at a person who has undoubtedly fallen and whom the Lord is encouraging to rise up again through good works. For it is also written, "Charity delivers from death,"[183] and there is clearly meant not deliverance from that death that the blood of Christ has quenched once and for all and from which the saving grace of baptism and of our Redeemer has delivered us, but deliverance from that death that afterwards creeps in through sin.

Furthermore, in another passage, an opportunity is indeed granted for penitence, and the Lord actually threatens the person who fails to do penitence: "I have," he says, "many things against you because you allow your wife Jezebel, who declares herself to be a prophetess, to teach and to seduce my servants, to commit fornication and to eat of foods offered in sacrifice, and I gave to her an opportunity to do penitence and she refused to repent of her fornication. See, I will cast her upon a couch, and those who have fornicated with her I will cast into great tribulation unless they do penitence for their deeds."[184] Obviously the Lord would not have encouraged them to do penitence were it not the case that he promises pardon to the penitent. And to this effect in the Gospels he declares, "I say to you that likewise there will be rejoicing in heaven over a sinner who does penitence rather than over ninety-nine just who have no need of penitence."[185]

We read in Scripture: "God did not make death, neither does he take joy in the destruction of the living."[186] Clearly, he who would have no one perish desires that sinners should do penitence and through penitence return again to life. Thus, too, through the prophet Joel he proclaims in these words: "And now the Lord your God says, return to me with all your heart, at the same time with fasting and weeping and mourning, and rend your hearts and not your garments, and return to the Lord your God because he is merciful and loving, slow to anger and full of kindness and he condemns the evil he has inflicted."[187]

Similarly we read in the Psalms of both the strictness and the compassion of God, who is at once menacing and merciful, who punishes that he may correct and when he has corrected saves: "I will visit," he says, "their wicked deeds with the rod and with the lash their iniquities. But my mercy I will not scatter away from them."[188] LETTER 55.22.[189]

The Fire of God

FORGIVENESS IN THE LIFE TO COME. AUGUSTINE: Such is the view of those who hold that the only punishments after death are purgatorial. They think that since water, air and fire are higher elements than earth, one or other of these elements will be used to purge away in expiatory pains whatever stains have been contracted by earthly contacts. When Virgil says, "Some of the souls toss in the winds," he implies punishment inflicted by air; the phrase "whirlpools of the vast sea" indicate water; "some in fire" mentions the punishing element by name. On our part, we admit that some sufferings even in this mortal life are purgative, but only in cases where the sufferers change their ways, not in cases where there is no improvement nor, still less, where sufferings make people worse. All other punishments, whether temporary or everlasting, according to the disposition of divine Providence in

---

[182]Rev 2:5. [183]Tob 4:10. [184]Rev 2:20-22. [185]Lk 15:7. [186]Wis 1:13. [187]Joel 2:12-13. [188]Ps 89:32-33. [189]FC 51:147-48.

individual cases, are inflicted in punishment either for sins past or present or to serve as an exercise in or revelation of virtues. They may be brought about by fellow people or by angels, whether good or bad; although, when a person suffers some evil through the malice or mistake of another person, and this latter sins by reason of the ignorance or the injustice involved in the injury done, God does no wrong since what happens is allowed by his just though hidden judgment. Whether we suffer temporary punishments in this life only or in the life after death, or in both, the sufferings precede that last, severe judgment. However, not all who suffer temporal punishment after death are doomed to the eternal pains that follow the last judgment. For, as I have said, what is not forgiven in this life is pardoned in the life to come, in the case of those who are not to suffer eternal punishment. CITY OF GOD 21.13.[190]

A KIND OF PURGATORIAL FIRE. AUGUSTINE: And it is not impossible that something of the same kind may take place even after this life. It is a matter that may be inquired into and either ascertained or left doubtful as to whether some believers will pass through a kind of purgatorial fire. And in proportion to how they have loved with more or less devotion the goods that perish, they will be less or more quickly delivered from this fire. This cannot, however, be the case for any of those of whom it is said that they "shall not inherit the kingdom of God,"[191] unless after suitable repentance their sins are forgiven them. When I say "suitable," I mean that they are not to be unfruitful in almsgiving. For holy Scripture lays so much stress on this virtue that our Lord tells us beforehand that he will ascribe no merit to those on his right hand except when they abound in generosity and no defect to those on his left hand except when they lack it. Then he will say to the former, "Come, you blessed of my Father, inherit the kingdom," and to the latter, "Depart from me, you cursed, into everlasting fire."[192] ENCHIRIDION 69.[193]

THE TIME BETWEEN DEATH AND FINAL RESURRECTION. AUGUSTINE: During the time that intervenes between one's death and the final resurrection, the soul dwells in a hidden retreat where it enjoys rest or suffers affliction in proportion to the merit it has earned by the life that it led on earth. ENCHIRIDION 109.[194]

Glorification or Destruction

RETRIBUTION FOR EVERYBODY. EPISTLE OF BARNABAS: It is well that he who has learned the judgments of the Lord, as many as have been written, should walk in them. For he who kept these shall be glorified in the kingdom of God, but he who chose other things shall be destroyed with his works. On this account there will be a resurrection, on this account a retribution. EPISTLE OF BARNABAS 21.[195]

THE COMING GIFTS OF THE LORD. CLEMENT OF ROME: How blessed and wonderful, beloved, are the gifts of God! Life in immortality, splendor in righteousness, truth in perfect confidence, faith in assurance, self-control in holiness! And all these fall under the cognizance of our understandings now. What then shall those things be that are prepared for such as wait for him? The Creator and Father of all worlds, the Most Holy, alone knows their extent and their beauty. Let us therefore earnestly strive to be found in the number of those that wait for him, in order that we may share in his promised gifts. But how, beloved, shall this be done? Only if our understanding is focused by faith toward

---

[190]FC 24:372-73. [191]1 Cor 6:10. [192]See Mt 25:31-46. [193]NPNF 1 3:260*. [194]NPNF 1 3:272. [195]ANF 1:149.

God. Only if we earnestly seek the things that are pleasing and acceptable to him. Only if we do the things that are in harmony with his blameless will. And only if we follow the way of truth, casting away from us all unrighteousness and iniquity, along with all covetousness, strife, evil practices, deceit, whispering and evil speaking, all hatred of God, pride and haughtiness, vain glory and ambition. Those who do such things are hateful to God. So also are those who take pleasure in others who do them.[196] 1 Clement 35.[197]

Considered Worthy of Incorruption. Justin Martyr: In the beginning God of his goodness, for our sake, created all things out of unformed matter. If human beings by their works show themselves worthy of this his design, they are deemed worthy and reign in company with him, delivered from corruption and suffering. For as in the beginning he created us when we were not, so do we believe that in a similar way those who choose what is pleasing to him are, on account of their choice, deemed worthy of incorruption and of fellowship with him. First Apology 10.[198]

Promise of Immortality Fulfilled. Justin Martyr: When the Spirit of prophecy speaks of things that are about to happen as if they had already taken place, . . . that this circumstance may afford no excuse to readers for misinterpreting them, we will make even this also quite plain. The things that he absolutely knows will take place, he predicts as if already they had taken place. And that these utterances must be received, you will be able to grasp if you give your attention to them. The words cited above, David uttered fifteen hundred years before Christ became a man and was crucified; and not one of those who lived before him, nor yet of his contemporaries, afforded joy to the Gentiles by being crucified. But our Jesus Christ, being crucified and dead, rose again, and having ascended to heaven, reigned. And joy over those things that were published in his name among all nations by the apostles comes to those who expect the immortality promised by him.[199] First Apology 42.[200]

The Year of Redemption Is Present. Justin Martyr: Those who have persecuted and do persecute Christ, if they do not repent, shall not inherit anything on the holy mountain. But the Gentiles, who have believed on him and have repented of the sins that they have committed, they shall receive the inheritance along with the patriarchs and the prophets. . . . "I [the Lord] speak righteousness and the judgment of salvation. Why are your garments red and your apparel as from the trodden wine press? You are full of the trodden grape. I have trodden the wine press all alone, and of the people there is no one with me. I have trampled them in fury, and crushed them to the ground and spilled their blood on the earth. For the day of retribution has come on them, and the year of redemption is present."[201] Dialogue with Trypho 26.[202]

Conferring Immortality on the Righteous. Irenaeus: He will execute just judgment toward all, sending the "spiritual forces of evil in heavenly places"[203] and the angels who transgressed and became apostates, together with the ungodly, and unrighteous, and wicked and profane among people, into everlasting fire. But, in the exercise of his grace, he will confer immortality on the righteous and holy and those who have kept his commandments and have persevered in his love—some from the beginning of their Christian course, and others from the date of their repentance. And he will surround them with everlasting glory. Against Heresies 1.10.1.[204]

---

[196]Rom 1:32. [197]ANF 1:14*. [198]ANF 1:165*. [199]See Rom 8:16-17; Gal 4:6-7; 1 Pet 1:3-4. [200]ANF 1:176-77*. [201]Is 63:1-4. [202]ANF 1:207. [203]Eph 6:12. [204]ANF 1:330-31*.

GLORY AND COMMUNION WITH GOD.
IRENAEUS: In the beginning, therefore, God formed Adam, not as if he stood in need of humankind, but that he might have someone on whom to confer his benefits. For the Word glorified his Father not alone before Adam but also before all creation, and he remained in him and was himself glorified by the Father, as he himself declared, "Father, glorify me with the glory which I had with you before the world existed."[205] Nor did he stand in need of our service when he ordered us to follow him but instead bestowed salvation on us. For to follow the Savior is to be a partaker of salvation. To follow light is to receive light. But those who are in light do not themselves illumine the light but are illumined and revealed by it. They contribute nothing to it but, receiving the benefit, are illumined by the light. Thus, also, service rendered to God does not profit God, nor has God need of human obedience. But he grants to those who follow and serve him life and incorruption and eternal glory. He bestows benefit on those who serve him, because they do serve him, and on his followers, because they do follow him. But he does not receive any benefit from them; for he is rich, perfect and in need of nothing. But this is why God demands service from us in order that, since he is good and merciful, he may benefit those who continue in his service. For as much as God is in want of nothing, so much does humankind stand in need of fellowship with God. For this is the glory of humanity, to continue and remain permanently in God's service. Therefore the Lord also said to his disciples, "You have not chosen me, but I have chosen you,"[206] indicating that they did not glorify him when they followed him but that, in following the Son of God, they were glorified by him. And again, "I will, that where I am, there they also may be, that they may behold my glory,"[207] not vainly boasting because of this but desiring that his disciples should share in his glory. Isaiah says, "I will bring your seed from the east, and will gather you from the west; and I will say to the north, 'Give up'; and to the south, 'Do not keep back: bring my sons from far away, and my daughters from the ends of the earth'; all, as many as have been called in my name: for in my glory I have prepared, and formed, and made him."[208] Inasmuch as then, "Wherever the carcass is, there shall also the eagles be gathered together."[209] So also do we participate in the glory of the Lord, who has both formed us and prepared us for this, that, when we are with him, we may partake of his glory.

Thus it was, too, that God formed humankind at the first, out of his generosity. He chose the patriarchs for the sake of their salvation. He prepared a people beforehand, teaching the headstrong to follow God. He raised up prophets on earth, accustoming humans to bear his Spirit and to hold communion with God—he himself, indeed, having need of nothing but granting communion with himself to those who stood in need of it. He sketched out like an architect the plan of salvation to those who pleased him. And he did himself furnish guidance to those who beheld him not in Egypt, while to those who became unruly in the desert he promulgated a law very suitable to their condition. Then, on the people who entered into the good land he bestowed a noble inheritance. He killed the fatted calf for those converted to the Father and presented them with the finest robe.[210] Thus, in a variety of ways, he adjusted the human race to an agreement with salvation. On this account also does John also declare in the Revelation, "His voice was like as the sound of many waters."[211] For the Spirit of God is truly like many waters, since the Father is both rich and great. And the Word, passing through all those people,

---

[205]Jn 17:5. [206]Jn 15:16. [207]Jn 17:24. [208]Is 43:5-7. [209]Mt 24:28. [210]See Lk 15:22-23. [211]Rev 1:15.

liberally conferred benefits on his subjects by drawing up in writing a law adapted and applicable to every group among them. AGAINST HERESIES 4.14.1-2.[212]

GOD WILL BE SEEN IN THE KINGDOM OF HEAVEN. IRENAEUS: God is powerful in all things, having been seen at that time indeed, prophetically through the Spirit and seen, too, adoptively through the Son. And he shall also be seen paternally in the kingdom of heaven, the Spirit truly preparing humanity in the Son of God, and the Son leading them to the Father, while the Father, too, confers on them incorruption for eternal life, which comes to everyone from the fact of his seeing God....

Humans therefore shall see God, that they may live, being made immortal by that sight and attaining even to God. This, as I have already said, was declared figuratively by the prophets, that God should be seen by people who bear his Spirit in them and always wait patiently for his coming. AGAINST HERESIES 4.20.5-6.[213]

A CLEANSED LIFE WITH GOD. IRENAEUS: Now in the last days, when the fullness of the time of liberty had arrived, the Word himself did by himself "wash away the filth of the daughters of Zion,"[214] when he washed the disciples' feet with his own hands.[215] For this is the goal of the human race inheriting God; that as in the beginning, by means of our first parents, we were all brought into bondage, by being made subject to death, so at last, by means of the new Man, all who from the beginning were his disciples, having been cleansed and washed from things pertaining to death, should come to the life of God. For he who washed the feet of the disciples sanctified the entire body and rendered it clean. For this reason, too, he administered food to them in a recumbent posture, indicating that those who were lying in the earth were those to whom he came to impart life....

For it was not merely for those who believed on him in the time of Tiberius Caesar that Christ came, nor did the Father exercise his providence for the people only who are now alive, but for all people altogether who, from the beginning, according to their capacity, in their generation have both feared and loved God, and practiced justice and piety toward their neighbors and have earnestly desired to see Christ and to hear his voice. Therefore he shall, at his second coming, first rouse from their sleep all persons of this description and shall raise them up, as well as the rest who shall be judged, and give them a place in his kingdom. AGAINST HERESIES 4.22.1-2.[216]

WE MUST WAIT. IRENAEUS: As our Master did not leave at once, taking flight to heaven, but awaited the time of his resurrection prescribed by the Father—which had also been shown forth through Jonah—and rising again after three days was taken up to heaven; we also should await the time of our resurrection prescribed by God and foretold by the prophets, and so, rising, be taken up, as many as the Lord shall account worthy of this privilege. AGAINST HERESIES 5.31.2.[217]

CAUSE OF THEIR DESTINY. IRENAEUS: All who fly from the eternal light of God, which contains in itself all good things, are themselves the reason why they inhabit eternal darkness, destitute of all good things, having become to themselves the cause of their consignment to an abode of that nature. AGAINST HERESIES 4.39.4.[218]

LIGHT AND BLINDNESS. IRENAEUS: Good things are eternal and without end with God. Therefore the loss of these is also eternal and never-ending. It is the same as occurs in the

---

[212]ANF 1:478-79*. [213]ANF 1:489*. [214]Is 4:4. [215]Jn 13:5. [216]ANF 1:493-94. [217]ANF 1:560-61*. [218]ANF 1:523*.

case of a flood of light: those who have blinded themselves, or have been blinded by others, are forever deprived of the enjoyment of light. It is not, however, that the light has inflicted on them the penalty of blindness; rather, the blindness itself has brought calamity on them. This is why the Lord declared, "He that believes in me is not condemned,"[219] that is, is not separated from God, for he is united to God through faith. . . .

In this world some people become involved with the light and by faith unite themselves with God, but others shun the light and separate themselves from God. Inasmuch as this is the case, the Word of God comes preparing suitable living quarters for both of them. For those indeed who are in the light are in it so that they may derive enjoyment from it and from the good things contained in it. But for those in darkness, they are in it so that they may partake in its calamities. And this is why he says that those on the right hand are called into the kingdom of heaven but that those on the left he will send into eternal fire, for they have deprived themselves of all that is good.

This is why the apostle says, "Because they did not receive the love of God so that they might be saved, therefore God shall also send them the operation of error so that they may believe a lie, that they all may be judged who have not believed the truth but consented to unrighteousness."[220] AGAINST HERESIES 5.27.2–5.28.2.[221]

WE SHALL BE THE SAME THAT WE ARE NOW. TERTULLIAN: The Reason who made the universe out of diverse elements, so that all things might be composed of opposite substances in unity—of void and solid, of animate and inanimate, of comprehensible and incomprehensible, of light and darkness, of life itself and death—has also disposed time into order by fixing and distinguishing its mode, according to which this first portion of it, which we inhabit from the beginning of the world, flows down by a temporal course to a close. But the portion that succeeds, and to which we look forward, continues forever. When, therefore, the boundary and limit, that millennial epoch, has been passed, when even the outward fashion of the world itself—which has been spread like a veil over the eternal economy, equally a thing of time—passes away, then the whole human race shall be raised again, to have its dues meted out according as it has merited in the period of good or evil and thereafter to have these paid out through the immeasurable ages of eternity. Therefore after this there is neither death nor repeated resurrections, but we shall be the same that we are now and still unchanged—the servants of God, ever with God, clothed with the proper substance of eternity; but the profane, and all who are not true worshipers of God, in a similar way shall be consigned to the punishment of everlasting fire—that fire that, from its very nature indeed, directly ministers to their incorruptibility. The philosophers are familiar as well as we with the distinction between a common and a secret fire. Thus that which is in common use is far different from that which we see in divine judgments, whether striking as thunderbolts from heaven or bursting up out of the earth through mountaintops, for it does not consume what it scorches, but while it burns it repairs. So the mountains continue ever burning, and a person struck by lighting is even now kept safe from any destroying flame. A notable proof this is of the eternal fire! A notable example of the endless judgment that still supplies punishment with fuel! The mountains burn and last. How will it be with the wicked and the enemies of God? APOLOGY 48.[222]

---

[219]Jn 3:18-21. [220]2 Thess 2:10-12. [221]ANF 1:556-57**. [222]ANF 3:53-54**.

AN EARTHLY AND HEAVENLY MESSENGER. TERTULLIAN: This is the process concerning the heavenly kingdom: after its thousand years are over—within this period the resurrection of the saints is complete who rise sooner or later according to what they deserve—the destruction of the world and the conflagration of all things at the judgment will ensue. We shall then be changed in a moment into the substance of angels, even by the investiture of an incorruptible nature, and thus be removed to that kingdom in heaven of which we have now been treating, just as if it had not been predicted by the Creator and as if it were proving Christ to belong to the other god and as if he were the first and sole revealer of it. But now learn that it has been, in fact, predicted by the Creator and that even without prediction it has a claim on our faith in respect of the Creator. What appears to be probable to you—when Abraham's seed, after the primal promise of becoming like the multitude of sand on the sea, is destined similarly to an equality with the stars of heaven—are not these the indications both of an earthly and a heavenly dispensation? When Isaac, in blessing his son Jacob, says, "God give you of the dew of heaven, and the fatness of the earth,"[223] are there not in his words examples of both kinds of blessing? Indeed, the very form of the blessing is in this instance worthy of notice. For in relation to Jacob, who is the type of the later and more excellent people, that is to say, ourselves, first comes the promise of the heavenly dew and afterwards that about the fatness of the earth. So we are first invited to heavenly blessings when we are separated from the world, and afterwards we thus find ourselves in the way of obtaining also earthly blessings. And your own gospel likewise says it like this: "Seek first the kingdom of God, and these things shall be added unto you."[224] But to Esau the blessing promised is an earthly one, which he supplements with a heavenly, after the fatness of the earth, saying, "Your dwelling shall be also of the dew of heaven."[225] For the dispensation of the Jews (who were in Esau, the prior of the sons in birth but the later in affection) at first was imbued with earthly blessings through the law and afterwards brought round to heavenly ones through the gospel by faith. Jacob sees in his dream the steps of a ladder set on the earth and reaching to heaven, with angels ascending and descending on it and the Lord standing above. Then we shall without hesitation venture to suppose that by this ladder the Lord has in judgment appointed that the way to heaven is shown to people, whereby some may attain to it and others fall away from it. For why, as soon as he awoke out of his sleep and shook in dread of the spot, does he turn to an interpretation of his dream? He exclaims, "How terrifying is this place!" And then adds, "This is none other than the house of God; this is the gate of heaven!"[226] For he had seen Christ the Lord, the temple of God, and also the gate by which heaven is entered. Now surely he would not have mentioned the gate of heaven if heaven is not a part of the dispensation of the Creator.

But there is now a gate provided by Christ, which admits and conducts to glory. Of this Amos says, "He builds his ascensions into heaven,"[227] certainly not for himself alone but for his people also, who will be with him. "And you shall bind them about you," says he, "like the adornment of a bride."[228] Accordingly the Spirit, admiring such as soar up to the celestial realms by these ascensions, says, "They fly, as if they were kites; they fly as clouds, and as young doves, unto me"[229]—that is, simply like a dove. For we shall, according to the apostle, be caught up into the clouds to meet the Lord (even the Son of Man, who shall come in the clouds, according to Daniel[230]) and so shall we ever be with the Lord, so long as he remains both on the earth and in heaven, who, against

---

[223]Gen 27:28. [224]Lk 12:31. [225]Gen 27:39. [226]Gen 28:12-17. [227]Amos 9:6. [228]Is 49:18. [229]Is 60:8. [230]Dan 7:13.

such as are thankless for both one promise and the other, calls the elements themselves to witness: "Hear, O heaven, and give ear, O earth."[231] Now, for my own part indeed, even though Scripture held out no hand of heavenly hope to me (as, in fact, it so often does), I should still possess a sufficient presumption of even this promise, in my present enjoyment of the earthly gift; and I should look out for something also of the heavenly, from him who is the God of heaven as well as of earth. I should thus believe that the Christ who promises the higher blessings is the Son of him who had also promised the lower ones; who had, moreover, afforded proofs of greater gifts by smaller ones; who had reserved for his Christ alone this revelation of a (perhaps) unheard of kingdom, so that, while the earthly glory was announced by his servants, the heavenly might have God himself for its messenger. You, however, argue for another Christ, from the very circumstance that he proclaims a new kingdom. You ought first to bring forward some example of his beneficence so that I may have no good reason for doubting the credibility of the great promise that you say ought to be hoped for. No, in fact, it is before all things necessary that you should show that a heaven belongs to him, whom you declare to be one who promises heavenly things. As it is, you invite us to dinner but do not point out your house. You assert a kingdom but show us no royal state. Can it be that your Christ promises a kingdom of heaven, without having a heaven? Did he display himself as a man yet without having flesh? O what a phantom from first to last! O hollow pretense of a mighty promise! AGAINST MARCION 3.25.[232]

DO NOT OFFEND CHRIST WITH THE SIN OF UNBELIEF. CYPRIAN: He who has already begun to be a man of God and of Christ must be found worthy of God and of Christ.... For he who fights for God, dearest brothers, ought to acknowledge himself as one who, placed in the heavenly camp, already hopes for divine things. We should not tremble at the storms and whirlwinds of the world, nor should we be disturbed since the Lord had foretold that these would come.... The kingdom of God, beloved brothers, is beginning to be at hand. The reward of life, and the rejoicing of eternal salvation and the perpetual gladness and possession lately lost of paradise are now coming with the passing away of the world. Heavenly things are already taking the place of earthly, and great things of small, and eternal things of things that fade away. What room is there here for anxiety and care? Who, in the midst of these things, is trembling and sad, except he who is without hope and faith? For fear belongs to those unwilling to go to Christ. Those who do not believe that they are about to reign with Christ are unwilling to go to Christ....

"Now let your servant depart in peace, according to your word; for my eyes have seen your salvation."[233] This most assuredly proves and witnesses to the fact that the servants of God, then, have peace and free tranquil repose when, withdrawn from these whirlwinds of the world, we attain the harbor of our home and eternal security, when having accomplished this death we come to immortality. For that is our peace, that is our faithful tranquility, that is our steadfast and abiding and perpetual security....

But no one believes that the things that God promises are true, although he is true whose word to believers is eternal and unchangeable. If a serious and praiseworthy person should promise you anything, you would assuredly have faith in the one who made the promise and would not think that you were going to be cheated and deceived by him whom you knew to be steadfast in his words and his deeds. Now God is speaking with you. And do you faithlessly waver in your unbelieving mind? God promises to you, on your departure from

---

[231]Is 1:2. [232]ANF 3:343-44*. [233]Lk 2:29.

this world, immortality and eternity; and do you doubt? This is not to know God at all. This is to offend Christ, the teacher of believers, with the sin of incredulity. This is for one established in the church not to have faith in the house of faith.

Christ himself, the teacher of our salvation and of our good works, shows us how great the advantage is of leaving this world, who, when his disciples were saddened that he said that he was soon to depart, spoke to them, and said, "If you loved me, you would surely rejoice because I go to the Father."[234] ON MORTALITY 1-7.[235]

CONQUERING AND REIGNING. CYPRIAN: Why do we pray and ask that the kingdom of heaven may come if the captivity of earth delights us? Why with frequently repeated prayers do we entreat and beg that the day of his kingdom can come sooner if our greater desires and stronger wishes are to obey the devil here, rather than to reign with Christ? . . .

For if we believe that Jesus died and rose again, even so God will bring with him those who are asleep in Jesus.[236] He says that those have sorrow in the departure of their friends who have no hope. But we who live in hope, and believe in God and trust that Christ suffered for us and rose again—we who abide in Christ and through him and in him rise again—why either are we ourselves unwilling to depart from this life, or why do we wail and grieve for our friends when they depart as if they were lost when Christ, our Lord and God, encourages us and says, "I am the resurrection and the life: he that believes in me, though he die, yet shall live; and whosoever lives and believes in me shall not die eternally"?[237] If we believe in Christ, let us have faith in his words and promises. And since we shall not die eternally, let us come with a glad security to Christ with whom we are both to conquer and to reign forever.

In the meantime we die. We pass over to immortality by death. No eternal life follows unless it should happen that we depart from this life. That is not an ending but a transit, and this journey of time being traversed, a passage to eternity. Who would not hasten to better things? Who would not crave to be changed and renewed into the likeness of Christ and to arrive more quickly to the dignity of heavenly glory, since Paul the apostle announces and says, "For our conversation is in heaven, from whence also we look for the Lord Jesus Christ, who shall change the body of our humiliation and conform it to the body of his glory."[238] Christ the Lord also promises that we shall be such, when he prays to the Father for us that we may be with him, and that we may live with him in eternal mansions and may rejoice in heavenly kingdoms, saying, "Father, I will that they also whom you have given me be with me where I am, and may see the glory which you have given me before the world was made." [239] He who is to attain to the throne of Christ, to the glory of the heavenly kingdoms, ought not to mourn or lament. Rather, in accordance with the Lord's promise, in accordance with his faith in the truth, he should rejoice in this his departure and translation. . . .

Since the world hates Christians, why do you love that which hates you? And why do you not rather follow Christ, who both redeemed you and loves you? John in his epistle cries and exhorts that we should not follow carnal desires and love the world. "Love not the world," says he, "neither the things which are in the world. If anyone loves the world, the love of the Father is not in him. For all that is in the world is the lust of the flesh, and the lust of the eyes, and the pride of life, which is not of the Father, but of the lust of the world. And the world shall pass away, and the lust thereof; but he who does the will of God abides for ever, even as God abides for ever."[240]

---

[234]Jn 16:28. [235]ANF 5:469-70**. [236]See 1 Thess 4:14. [237]Jn 11:25. [238]Phil 3:21. [239]Jn 17:24. [240]1 Jn 2:15-17.

Rather, beloved brothers, let us be prepared for the whole will of God with a sound mind, with a firm faith, with a robust virtue. Laying aside the fear of death, let us think about the immortality that follows. By not grieving over the departure of those dear to us, let us show ourselves to be what we believe and that when the day of our summons shall arrive, we come without delay and without resistance to the Lord when he calls us....

May God behold this, our eager desire. May the Lord Christ look on this purpose of our mind and faith, he who will give the larger rewards of his glory to those whose desires in respect of himself were greater! ON MORTALITY 18-26.[241]

A PREDESTINED INHERITANCE FOR US. ATHANASIUS: How has he chosen us, before we came into existence, except that, as he says himself, in him we were represented beforehand? How at all, before human beings were created, did he predestine us to adoption, except that the Son himself was "founded before the world," taking on him that economy that was for our sake? How, as the apostle goes on to say, do we have "an inheritance, being predestined," but that the Lord himself was founded "before the world" inasmuch as it was his purpose, for our sakes, to take on himself through the flesh all that inheritance of judgment that lay against us and we subsequently were made children in him? How did we receive it "before the world was," when we were not even in existence but came to exist afterward in time, except that in Christ was stored the grace that has reached us? Therefore also in the judgment, when everyone shall receive according to his conduct, he says, "Come, you blessed of my Father, inherit the kingdom prepared for you from the foundation of the world."[242] How then, or in whom, was it prepared before we came to exist, except in the Lord who "before the world" was founded for this purpose—that we, as built on him, might partake, as well-compacted stones, the life and grace that is from him? This took place, as naturally suggests itself to the religious mind so that, as I said, we, rising after our brief death, may be capable of an eternal life. This is a life of which we were not capable, human as we are, formed of earth. But "before the world" there had been prepared for us in Christ the hope of life and salvation. The Word, on coming into our flesh, was created in flesh as a beginning of ways for his works.[243] This Word has been laid as a foundation according to the Father's will in him before the world existed, as has been said, and before the mountains were settled and before the fountains burst forth. That, though the earth and the mountains and the shapes of visible nature pass away in the fullness of the present age, we on the contrary may not grow old after their pattern but will be able to live after them. For we have the spiritual life and blessing that, before these things, had been prepared for us in the Word according to God's election. Thus, we may be capable of a life that is not temporary but one instead that forever afterward remains and lives in Christ, since, even before this, our life had been founded and prepared in Christ Jesus. DISCOURSES AGAINST THE ARIANS 2.22.76.[244]

INDESTRUCTIBLE GIFTS. BASIL THE GREAT: "Who is the man that desired life: who loved to see good days?"[245] If anyone wishes life, he says, he does not live this common life, which brute beasts also live, but the true life that is not cut short by death. "For now," it is said, "you have died and your life is hidden with Christ in God. When Christ, your life, shall appear, then you too will appear with him in glory."[246] Therefore, Christ is, in truth, life, and our way of life in him is true life. In a similar way, also, the other days are good that the

---

[241]ANF 5:473-75**. [242]Mt 25:34. [243]See Prov 8:22. [244]NPNF 2 4:389-90**. [245]Cf. Ps 34:12. [246]Col 3:3-4.

prophet set forth in the promise. "Who is the man that desired life: who loved to see good days?" For the days of this life are evil, since this life, being the measure of the world—concerning which there is the saying, "The whole world is in the power of the evil one"[247]—is made quite like the nature of the world that it measures. But these days are parts of this time. Therefore, the apostle says, "Making the most of your time, because the days are evil."[248] Likewise Jacob says, "The days of my pilgrimage are short and wretched."[249] We are not, then, in life but in death. And so the apostle prayed, saying, "Who will deliver me from the body of this death?"[250] There is, however, a certain other life, to which these words call us; and, although at present our days are evil, yet some others are good, which night does not interrupt; for God will be their everlasting light, shining on them with the light of his glory.[251] Consequently, when you hear of the good days, do not think that your life here is set forth in the promises. In fact, these are the destructible days, which the sensible sun produces, but nothing destructible could suitably be a gift for the indestructible. Now, if the soul is indestructible, its gifts are also indestructible. "This world as we see it is passing away."[252] HOMILY 16 ON PSALM 33 9.[253]

WE WILL TURN INTO OUR REST. BASIL THE GREAT: "Turn, O my soul, into your rest: for the Lord had been bountiful to you."[254] The brave contestant applies to himself the consoling words, very much like to Paul, when he says, "I have fought the good fight, I have finished the course, I have kept the faith. For the rest, there is laid up for me a crown of justice."[255] These things the prophet also says to himself: Since you have fulfilled sufficiently the course of this life, turn into your rest, "for the Lord has been bountiful to you." For eternal rest lies before those who have struggled through the present life observant of the laws, a rest not given in payment for a debt owed for their works but provided as a grace of the munificent God for those who have hoped in him. HOMILY 22 ON PSALM 114.[256]

THE HEAVENLY TRUTH OF EARTHLY DREAMS. GREGORY OF NAZIANZUS: I believe the words of the wise, that is, that every fair and God-beloved soul, when it leaves here and is set free from the bonds of the body, at once enjoys a sense and perception of the blessings that await. That which darkened it has been purged away or laid aside—I know not how else to term it—and feels a wondrous pleasure and exultation and goes rejoicing to meet its Lord. It has escaped as it were from the grievous poison of life here and shaken off the fetters that bound it and held down the wings of the mind. It thus enters into the enjoyment of the bliss laid up for it of which it even now has some conception. Then, a little later, it receives its kindred flesh that once shared in its pursuits of things above, from the earth that both gave and had been entrusted with it, and in some way known to God, who knit them together and dissolved them, enters with it on the inheritance of the glory there. And, as it shared through their close union in its hardships, so also it bestows on it a portion of its joys, gathering it up entirely into itself and becoming with it one in spirit and in mind and in God, the mortal and mutable being swallowed up by life.

Hear at least how the inspired Ezekiel talks about the knitting together of bones and sinews, how after him Paul speaks of the earthly tabernacle and the house not made with hands, the one to be dissolved, the other laid up in heaven, alleging absence from the body to be presence with the Lord and bewailing his life in it as an exile, and therefore longing for and hurrying toward his release. Why am I

---

[247]1 Jn 5:19. [248]Eph 5:16. [249]Cf. Gen 47:9. [250]Rom 7:24. [251]Cf. Rev 22:5. [252]1 Cor 7:31. [253]FC 46:263-64*. [254]Ps 116:7. [255]2 Tim 4:7-8. [256]FC 46:356-57.

fainthearted in my hopes? Why behave like a mere creature of a day? I await the voice of the archangel, the last trumpet,[257] the transformation of the heavens, the transfiguration of the earth, the liberation of the elements, the renovation of the universe.[258] Then shall I see Caesarius himself, no longer in exile, no longer laid on a bier, no longer the object of mourning and pity but brilliant, glorious, heavenly, such as in my dreams I have often beheld you, dearest and most loving of brothers, pictured thus by my desire, if not by the very truth. ON HIS BROTHER CAESARIUS, ORATION 7.21.[259]

THE CHANGE IS NECESSARY FOR ALL SINNERS. GREGORY OF NYSSA: For that change in our life that takes place through regeneration will not be change if we continue in the state in which we were. I do not see how it is possible to deem one who is still in the same condition and in whom there has been no change in the distinguishing features of his nature to be any other than he was. It is palpable to everyone that it is for a renovation and change of our nature that the saving birth is received. And yet human nature does not of itself admit of any change in baptism. Nor does the reason, or the understanding, or the scientific faculty or any other peculiar characteristic of humankind become a subject for change. Indeed, the change would be for the worse if any one of these properties of our nature were exchanged away for something else. If, then, the birth from above is a definite refashioning of the human being, and yet these properties do not admit of change, it is a subject for inquiry what that is in human beings, by which the grace of regeneration is perfected. It is evident that when those evil features that mark our nature have been obliterated a change to a better state takes place. . . . The person whom he has unjustly treated, the one whom he has falsely accused, the one whom he has forcibly deprived of his property, these, as far as they are concerned, see no change in him though he has been washed in the laver of baptism. . . . If, then, you have received God, if you have become a child of God, make known in your disposition the God that is in you, make known in yourself him that begot you. This relationship to God of the one born in this way must be exhibited by the same marks whereby we recognize God. ADDRESS ON RELIGIOUS INSTRUCTION 40.[260]

A FIRE THAT DOES NOT ADMIT OF EXTINCTION. GREGORY OF NYSSA: How is that possible with things which "eye has not seen, neither ear heard, neither have entered into the heart of man?"[261] Indeed, the sinner's life of torment presents no equivalent to anything that pains the sense here. Even if some one of the punishments in that other world are named in terms that are well known here, the distinction is still not small. When you hear the word fire, you have been taught to think of a fire other than the fire we see, owing to something being added to that fire that in this there is not; for that fire is never quenched, whereas experience has discovered many ways of quenching this; and there is a great difference between a fire that can be extinguished, and one that does not admit of extinction. That fire, therefore, is something other than this. If, again, a person hears the word worm, let not his thoughts, from the similarity of the term, be carried to the creature here that crawls on the ground; for the addition that it "does not die" suggests the thought of another reptile than that known here. Since, then, these things are set before us as to be expected in the life that follows this, being the natural outgrowth according to the righteous judgment of God, in the life of each, of his particular disposition, it must be the part of the wise not to regard the present but that which follows after, and to lay down the foundations for that unspeakable blessedness during

---

[257]See 1 Cor 15:52. [258]See 2 Pet 3:10. [259]NPNF 2 7:236-37*. [260]NPNF 2 5:507-8. [261]Is 64:4; 1 Cor 2:9.

this short and fleeting life and by a good choice to wean themselves from all experience of evil, now in their lifetime here, hereafter in their eternal recompense. Address on Religious Instruction 40.[262]

How to Obtain Eternal Life. Cyril of Jerusalem: In this holy catholic church receiving instruction and behaving ourselves virtuously, we shall attain the kingdom of heaven and inherit eternal life. For this we endure all toils, that we may be made partakers of life from the Lord. For ours is no trifling aim. Our endeavor is for eternal life. Therefore in the profession of the faith, after the words, "and in the resurrection of the flesh," that is, of the dead (of which we have discoursed), we are taught to believe also "in the life eternal," for which as Christians we are striving.

The real and true life then is the Father, who through the Son in the Holy Spirit pours forth as from a fountain his heavenly gifts to all. Through his love the blessings of the life eternal are promised without fail. We must not disbelieve the possibility of this, but having an eye not to our own weakness but to his power, we must believe that "for with God all things are possible," and that this is possible and that we may look for eternal life. Daniel declares, "And of the many righteous shall they shine as the stars forever and ever."[263] And Paul says, "And so shall we be ever with the Lord"[264] for "being forever with the Lord" implies the life eternal. But most plainly of all the Savior says in the Gospel, "And these shall go away into eternal punishment, but the righteous into life eternal."[265]

There are many evidences of life eternal. When we desire to gain this eternal life, the sacred Scriptures suggest to us the ways of gaining it. Because of the length of our discourse, the texts we now set before you shall be but few. The rest are left to the search of the diligent. They declare at one time that this gain is by faith. For it is written, "He that believes in the Son has eternal life."[266] What follows? He again says, "Truly, truly, I say unto you, he that hears my word and believes him that sent me has eternal life."[267] At another time, it is by the preaching of the gospel. He says that "he who reaps receives wages, and gathers fruit for life eternal."[268] At another time, it is by martyrdom and confession in Christ's name. For he says, "he that hates his life in this world shall keep it unto life eternal."[269] And again, by preferring Christ to riches or relations: "Everyone that has forsaken brothers or sisters"[270] shall inherit eternal life. Moreover, it is by keeping the commandments, you shall not commit adultery, you shall not kill,[271] and the rest that follow; as he answered to him that came to him and said, "Good Master, what shall I do that I may have eternal life?"[272] But further, it is by departing from evil works and henceforth serving God; for Paul says, But now being made free from sin, and having become servants to God, you have your fruit unto sanctification, and the end which is eternal life.[273]

And the ways of finding eternal life are many, though I have passed over them by reason of their number. For the Lord in his loving-kindness has opened not one or two only but many doors, by which to enter into the life eternal, that, as far as lay in him, all might enjoy it without hindrance. This is why we have, for the present, spoken as much as we have concerning eternal life, which is the last doctrine of those professed in the faith and its termination, which life may we all, both teachers and hearers, by God's grace enjoy! Catechetical Lecture 18.28-31.[274]

The Earthly Death Is But a Sleep. Chrysostom: This same thing happens in the case of our soul. Whenever grace comes

---

[262]NPNF 2 5:508-9. [263]Dan 12:3 (LXX). [264]1 Thess 4:17. [265]Mt 25:46. [266]Jn 3:36. [267]Jn 5:24. [268]Jn 4:36. [269]Jn 12:25. [270]Mt 19:29. [271]Mt 19:16-18. [272]Mk 10:17. [273]See Rom 6:22. [274]NPNF 2 7:141.

and drives out the darkness from our mind, we learn the exact nature of things; what frightened us before now becomes contemptible in our eyes. We no longer are afraid of death after we have learned carefully from this holy initiation that death is not death but a sleep and repose that lasts but for a time. Nor are we afraid of poverty or disease or any such misfortune, because we know that we are on our way to a better life, which is impervious to death and destruction and is free from all such inequality. BAPTISMAL INSTRUCTIONS 12.12.[275]

PARTAKERS OF THE KINGDOM OF HEAVEN. CHRYSOSTOM: Let us then turn to him, my beloved friend, and execute the will of God. For he created us and brought us into being that he might make us partakers of eternal blessings, that he might offer us the kingdom of heaven, not that he might cast us into hell and deliver us to the fire; for this was made not for us but for the devil: but for us the kingdom has been destined and made ready in ancient times. And by way of indicating both these truths he says to those on the right hand, "Come you blessed of my Father inherit the kingdom prepared for you from the foundation of the world," but to those on the left "Depart from me, you cursed, into fire everlasting prepared"; he no longer says "for you" but "for the devil and his angels."[276] Thus hell has not been made for us but for him and his angels; but the kingdom has been prepared for us before the foundation of the world. LETTER TO THE FALLEN THEODORE 1.9.[277]

THE THINGS OF THE EVERLASTING WORLD. CHRYSOSTOM: Here indeed both good and evil things have an end that will happen very quickly. But there, both are coextensive with immortal ages and in their quality differ unspeakably from the things that now are. LETTER TO THE FALLEN THEODORE 1.9.[278]

THE GUIDE OF SOUL AND MIND. CHRYSOSTOM: Not only the bodily wounds work death, if they are neglected, but also those of the soul. And yet we have arrived at such a pitch of folly as to take the greatest care of the former and to overlook the latter. Although in the case of the body it naturally often happens that many wounds are incurable, yet we still do not abandon hope, but even when we hear the physicians constantly declaring that it is not possible to get rid of this suffering by medicines, we still persist in pleading with them to devise at least some slight alleviation. But in the case of souls, where there is no incurable malady—for it is not subject to the necessity of nature—here, as if the infirmities were strange to us, we are negligent and despairing. And where the nature of the disorder might naturally plunge us into despair, we try everything possible as if there were great hope of restoration to health. But where there is no occasion to renounce hope, we desist from efforts and become as heedless as if matters were desperate; so much more account do we take of the body than of the soul. . . .

"For my counsels," we read, "are not as your counsels nor my ways as your ways; but far as is the heaven from the earth, so far are my thoughts from your mind, and my counsels from your counsels." At times we admit to our favor household servants when they have often offended against us, on their promising to become better, and place them again in their former positions and sometimes even grant them greater freedom of speech than before. God does this even more. For if God had made us in order to punish us, you might well have despaired and questioned the possibility of your own salvation, but if he created us for no reason other than his own good will and with a view to our enjoying everlasting blessings, and if he does and contrives everything for this end, from the first day until the present time, what is there that can ever cause you to doubt? LETTER TO THE FALLEN THEODORE 1.15.[279]

---

[275]ACW 31:176. [276]Mt 25:34, 41. [277]NPNF 1 9:97. [278]NPNF 1 9:98. [279]NPNF 1 9:105-6*.

THOSE TO WHOM MUCH IS FORGIVEN.
CHRYSOSTOM: If the confession of sins brings so much consolation, much more does the endeavor to wash them away by means of our deeds. For if this was not the case, but those who had once swerved from the straight path were forbidden to return to it again, perhaps no one, except a few persons whose numbers would be easily counted, would ever enter the kingdom of heaven; but as it is we shall find the most distinguished among those who have fallen. For those who have exhibited much vehemence in evil things will also in turn exhibit the same in good things, being conscious what great debts they have incurred, which Christ also declared when he spoke to Simon concerning the woman: "For do you see," says he, "this woman? I entered into your house, you gave me no water for my feet; but she has washed my feet with her tears, and wiped them with the hairs of her head. You gave me no kiss, but she since the time I came in has not ceased to kiss my feet. You did not anoint my head with oil, but she has anointed my feet with ointment. Therefore I say to you: her sins which are many are forgiven; for she loved much; but to whom little is forgiven, the same loves little. And he said unto her, your sins are forgiven."[280] LETTER TO THE FALLEN THEODORE 1.15.[281]

THE GATES OF HEAVEN WILL OPEN TO US.
CHRYSOSTOM: When the kingdom of heaven is set before you—that office that has none to supersede you in it—and God tells you to take not a part of a corner of the earth but the whole of heaven entirely, are you hesitating, and reluctant, and gaping after money and forgetful that if the parts of that heaven that we see are so fair and delightful, how great must the upper heaven be, and the heaven of heaven? But since we have as yet no means of seeing this with our bodily eyes, ascend in your thought, and, standing above this heaven, look up to that heaven beyond this, into that height without bounds, into that Light surcharged with awe, into the crowds of the angels, into the endless ranks of archangels, into the rest of the incorporeal Powers. And then lay hold again of the image we have of that place after coming down from above and make a sketch of the estate of a king with us, as his men in gold armor, and his pairs of white mules proudly decked with gold, and his chariots set with jewels and his snow-like cushions, and the spangles that flutter about the chariot, and the dragons shaped out in the silken hangings, and the shields with their gold bosses, and the straps that reach up from these to the rim of them through so many gems and the horses with the gilded trappings and the gold bits. But when we see the king we immediately lose sight of all these. For he alone turns our eyes to him, and to the purple robe, and the diadem, and the throne, and the clasp and the shoes, all that splendor of his appearance. After gathering all these things together then with accuracy, then again remove your thoughts from these things to things above and to that awful day in which Christ is coming. For then you will not see any pairs of mules, or golden chariots or dragons and shields, but things that are big with a mighty awe and strike such amazement that the very incorporeal Powers are astonished. For the "powers of the heavens," he says, "shall be shaken."[282] Then is the whole heaven thrown open, and the gates of those concaves unfold themselves, and the only-begotten Son of God comes down, not with twenty, not with a hundred men for his bodyguard, but with thousands, ten thousands of angels and archangels, cherubim and seraphim and other powers, and with fear and trembling shall everything be filled while the earth is bursting itself up, and all of the people that were ever born, from Adam's birth up to that day, are rising from the earth, and all are caught up.[283] HOMILIES ON ROMANS 14.28.[284]

---

[280]Lk 7:44-48. [281]NPNF 1 9:106. [282]Mt 24:29. [283]See 1 Thess 4:17. [284]NPNF 1 11:450*.

DEATH IS ONLY A NAME OF ETERNAL LIFE. HILARY OF POITIERS: The true faith in God would pass unrewarded if the soul was destroyed by death and quenched in the extinction of bodily life. Even unaided reason pleaded that it was unworthy of God to usher humankind into an existence which has some share of his thought and wisdom, only to await the sentence of life withdrawn and of eternal death. . . .

In a calm assurance of safety did my soul gladly and hopefully take its rest and feared so little the interruption of death that death seemed only a name for eternal life. And the life of this present body was so far from seeming a burden or affliction that it was regarded as children regard their alphabet, sick people their illness, shipwrecked sailors their swim, young people the training for their profession, future commanders their first campaign; that is, as an endurable submission to present necessities, bearing the promise of a blissful immortality. And further, I began to proclaim those truths in which my soul had a personal faith, as a duty of the episcopate that had been laid on me, employing my office to promote the salvation of all. ON THE TRINITY 1.9.14.[285]

CONFORMED TO CHRIST'S BODY IN THE KINGDOM OF GOD. HILARY OF POITIERS: Nor are the Gospels silent concerning the glory of his present reigning body. It is written that the Lord said, "Truly, I say to you that there are some standing here who shall not taste of death till they see the Son of man coming in his kingdom. And it came to pass, after six days Jesus took with him Peter and James and John his brother and led them up into a high mountain apart. And Jesus was transfigured before them, and his face shone like the sun, and his garments became as snow."[286] Thus was shown to the apostles the glory of the body of Christ coming into his kingdom, for in the fashion of his glorious transfiguration the Lord stood revealed in the splendor of his reigning body.

He promised also to the apostles the participation in this his glory, "So shall it be in the end of the world. The Son of man shall send forth his angels, and they shall gather together out of his kingdom all things that cause stumbling, and those who do iniquity, and he shall send them into the furnace of fire: there shall be the weeping and gnashing of teeth. Then shall the righteous shine forth as the sun in the kingdom of their Father. He that has ears to hear, let him hear."[287] Were their natural and bodily ears so closed to the hearing of the words that the Lord should need to admonish them to hear? Yet the Lord, hinting at the knowledge of the mystery, commands them to listen to the doctrine of the faith. In the end of the world all things that cause stumbling shall be removed from his kingdom. We see the Lord then reigning in the splendor of his body, until the things that cause stumbling are removed. And we see ourselves, in consequence, conformed to the glory of his body in the kingdom of the Father, shining as with the splendor of the sun, the splendor in which he showed the apostles what his kingdom looked like, when he was transfigured on the mountain.

He shall deliver the kingdom to God the Father, not in the sense that he resigns his power by the delivering but that we, being conformed to the glory of his body, shall form the kingdom of God. It is not said, "He shall deliver up his kingdom," but "he shall deliver up the kingdom,"[288] that is, deliver up to God us who have been made the kingdom by the glorifying of his body. He shall deliver us into the kingdom, as it is said in the Gospel, "Come, you blessed of my Father, inherit the kingdom prepared for you from the foundation of the world."[289] The just shall shine like the sun in the kingdom of their Father, and the Son shall deliver to the Father, as his kingdom,

---

[285]NPNF 2 9:42, 44. [286]Mt 16:28–17:2. [287]Mt 13:40-43. [288]1 Cor 15:24. [289]Mt 25:34.

those whom he has called into his kingdom, to whom also he has promised the blessedness of this mystery, "Blessed are the pure in heart, for they shall see God."[290] While he reigns, he will remove all things that cause stumbling, and then the just shall shine as the sun in the kingdom of the Father. Afterwards he will deliver the kingdom to the Father, and those whom he has handed to the Father, as the kingdom, shall see God. He himself witnesses to the apostles what kind of kingdom this is: "The kingdom of God is within you."[291] Thus it is as king that he shall deliver up the kingdom, and if any ask, Who it is that delivers up the kingdom, let him hear, "Christ is risen from the dead, the first fruits of those who sleep; since by man came death, by man came also the resurrection of the dead."[292] ON THE TRINITY 11.37-39.[293]

A KINGDOM WITHOUT END. RUFINUS OF AQUILEIA: If you want to know with even greater certainty who this Lord is of whom these things are said, listen to what the prophet Daniel foretells: "I saw," he says, "in the vision of the night, and, behold, one like the Son of man coming with the clouds of heaven, and he came nigh to the Ancient of Days, and was brought near before him; and there was given to him dominion, and honor, and a kingdom. And all peoples, tribes, and languages shall serve him. And his dominion is an eternal dominion which shall not pass away, and his kingdom shall not be destroyed."[294] By these words we are taught not only of his coming and judgment but of his dominion and kingdom. We are taught that his dominion is eternal and his kingdom indestructible, without end, just as it says in the creed, "and of his kingdom there shall be no end." Therefore, anyone who says that Christ's kingdom shall one day have an end is very far from the faith. Yet it behooves us to know that the enemy likes to counterfeit this salutary advent of Christ with cunning in order to deceive the faithful. In the place of the Son of man who is looked for as coming in the majesty of his Father, the enemy prepares the son of perdition with miracles and lying signs so that instead of Christ he may introduce Antichrist into the world. The Lord warned the Jews beforehand in the Gospels about him, "Because I have come in my Father's name, and you didn't receive me, another will come in his own name, and you will receive him."[295] . . . For this reason, therefore, this "delusion" is told to us ahead of time by the words of prophets, evangelists and apostles, in case anyone should mistake the coming of Antichrist for the coming of Christ. But as the Lord says, "When they shall say unto you, lo, here is Christ, or lo, he is there, do not believe it. For many false Christs and false prophets shall come and shall seduce many."[296] But let us see how he has pointed out the judgment of the true Christ: "As the lightning shines from the east unto the west, so shall the coming of the Son of man be."[297] When, therefore, the true Lord Jesus Christ shall come, he will sit and set up his throne of judgment. As also he says in the Gospel, "He shall separate the sheep from the goats,"[298] that is, the righteous from the unrighteous; as the apostle writes, "We must all stand before the judgment seat of Christ, that everyone may receive the awards due to the body, according to deeds done, whether they be good or evil."[299] Moreover, the judgment will be not only for deeds but for thoughts also, as the same apostle says: "Their thoughts mutually accusing or else excusing one another, in the day when God shall judge the secrets of men."[300] A COMMENTARY ON THE APOSTLES' CREED 34.[301]

THE RIGHTEOUS SHALL SHINE AS THE SUN. RUFINUS OF AQUILEIA: Thus there is much

---

[290]Mt 5:8. [291]Lk 17:21. [292]1 Cor 15:20-21. [293]NPNF 2 9:213-14*. [294]Dan 7:13-14. [295]Jn 5:43. [296]Mt 24:2. [297]Mt 24:27. [298]Mt 25:32. [299]2 Cor 5:10. [300]Rom 2:15-16. [301]NPNF 2 3:556-57*.

that exists in proof of the profession that we make in the creed when we say "the resurrection of this flesh." As to the addition "this," you can see how consonant it is with all that we have cited from the divine books. What else does Job signify in the place that we explained above, "He will raise again my skin, which is now draining this cup of suffering,"[302] that is, which is undergoing these torments? Does he not plainly say that there will be a resurrection of this flesh, this, I mean, which is now undergoing the extremity of trials and tribulations? Moreover, when the apostle says, "This corruptible must put on incorruption, and this mortal must put on immortality,"[303] are not his words those of one who in a manner touches his body and places his finger on it? This body then, which is now corruptible, will by the grace of the resurrection be incorruptible, and this that is now mortal will be clothed with virtues of immortality so that, as "Christ rising from the dead dies no more, death has no more dominion over him,"[304] so those who shall rise in Christ shall never again feel corruption or death—not because the nature of flesh will have been cast off but because its condition and quality will have been changed. There will be a body, therefore, that will rise from the dead incorruptible and immortal, not only of the righteous but also of sinners. The bodies of the righteous will rise so that they may always be able to abide with Christ; the bodies of sinners will rise so that they may undergo without end the punishment due to them.

That the righteous will always abide with Christ our Lord we have proved above where we have shown that the apostle says, "Then we who are alive and remain shall be caught up together with them in the clouds to meet Christ in the air, and so shall we ever be with the Lord."[305] And do not marvel that the flesh of the saints is to be changed into such a glorious condition at the resurrection as to be caught up to meet God, suspended in the clouds and borne in the air, since the same apostle, setting forth the great things that God bestows on those who love him, says, "Who shall change our vile body that it may be made like unto his glorious body."[306] It is in no way absurd then, if the bodies of the saints are said to be raised up into the air, seeing that they are said to be renewed after the image of Christ's body, which is seated at God's right hand. But this also the holy apostle adds, speaking either of himself or of others of his own place or merit, "He will raise us up together with Christ and make us sit together in the heavenly places."[307] Thus, since God's saints attested these promises and an infinite number like them concerning the resurrection of the righteous, it will now not be difficult to believe those also which the prophets have foretold, namely, that "the righteous shall shine as the sun and as the brightness of the firmament in the kingdom of God."[308] For who will think it difficult that they should have the brightness of the sun and be adorned with the splendor of the stars and of this firmament, for whom the life and conversation of God's angels are being prepared in heaven or who are represented as being hereafter to be conformed to the glory of Christ's body? In reference to this glory, promised by the Savior's mouth, the holy apostle says, "It is sown as an animal body; it will rise a spiritual body."[309] For if it is true, as it certainly is true, that God will follow through on his promise to associate every one of the righteous and of the saints in companionship with the angels, it is certain that he will change their bodies also into the glory of a spiritual body. A COMMENTARY ON THE APOSTLES' CREED 45-46.[310]

WE BELIEVE IN LIFE EVERLASTING. AUGUSTINE: We also believe in the resurrection

---

[302]Job 19:26-27 (LXX). [303]1 Cor 15:53. [304]Rom 6:9. [305]1 Thess 4:17. [306]Phil 3:21. [307]Eph 2:6. [308]Mt 13:43. [309]1 Cor 15:44. [310]NPNF 2 3:561-62*.

of the flesh, which has already taken place in Christ, so that the body might also hope for what has first taken place with the head. The head of the church is Christ; the body of Christ is the church. Our head rose again, ascended into heaven. Where the head is, there too are the members. How will the resurrection of the flesh occur? In case anyone should assume it will happen in the same way as it did with Lazarus, to show that that is not how it will be, there is added, *in life everlasting.* May God bring you to new birth; may God preserve and protect you; may God bring you finally to himself, who is himself that very life everlasting. SERMON 398.17.[311]

FLESH AND BLOOD. AUGUSTINE: We would inquire, as best we could, according to the Scriptures, what kind of life the just are going to have in the resurrection. So we lingered so long on the first part, where we dealt with the dead rising again, as you no doubt remember, that there was no time to deal with the second question, and thus we were forced to put it off until today....

"I have the power," Christ said, "to lay down my life, and I have the power to take it up again. Nobody can take it from me."[312] Great indeed the power by which he was willing to die. The reason, you see, he did by lovingkindness what he was also able by power not to do, was to lay the foundation for us of resurrection; so that the mortal element that he carried around for our sakes would both die, because we are going to die; and would rise again to immortality, so that we might hope for immortality....

The apostle said, "Flesh and blood cannot gain possession of the kingdom of God by inheritance."[313] He was speaking correctly; you see, it is not the place of flesh to possess but to be possessed. After all, it is not your body that possesses anything, but your soul that possesses things through the body, just as it also possesses the body itself. So if the flesh rises again in such a way as to be owned, not to own, to be possessed, not to possess, what is so surprising about flesh and blood not possessing the kingdom of God, because it will of course be possessed itself?

The flesh, you see, gains possession of those who are not the kingdom of God but the devil's kingdom; and that is why they are enslaved to the pleasures of the flesh.... So when we have risen again, the flesh will not be carrying us, but we shall be carrying it. If it is we who are carrying it, it is we who shall not be possessed by it, because now that we have been delivered from the devil's grip, we are the kingdom of God....

So then, that we are to rise again has already been said; and that we rise again to the life of the angels, we have heard from the Lord; but in what specific form we are to rise again, he has shown us himself in his own resurrection. It is because that specific form, however, will have no tendency to decay that the apostle says, "But this I must say, brothers, that flesh and blood shall not gain possession by inheritance of the kingdom of God; nor shall what is perishable gain possession by inheritance of imperishability"[314] to show that by the expression "flesh and blood" he wished us to understand the tendency to decay of a mortal and merely soul-animated body....

But if this perishable thing puts on imperishability and this mortal thing puts on immortality, there will no longer be any perishable flesh. So if there is no more perishable flesh, all mention of perishing and decay in flesh and blood will fall away; even proper mention of flesh and blood will fall away, because these are words that imply mortality. And if that is the case, it is true both that the flesh will rise again and that because it is changed and becomes imperishable, "flesh and blood shall not gain possession of the kingdom of God."... So even in this respect

---

[311]WSA 3 10:455. [312]Jn 10:18. [313]1 Cor 15:50. [314]1 Cor 15:50.

flesh and blood are unable to gain possession of the kingdom of God, because when the flesh rises again it will be changed into the kind of body in which there will no longer be any mortal tendency to decay and that therefore will no longer be properly called flesh and blood. . . .

"Do not be surprised at this, that the hour is coming in which all who are in the grave will hear his voice; and those who have done good will come forth to the resurrection of life; but those who have done evil to the resurrection of judgment."[315] . . . Here, though, where he is referring to those who are going to rise again in the body, he does not say, "They will hear his voice, and those who hear will come forth." After all, they will all hear the last trumpet and come forth, because we shall all rise again. But because "we shall not all be changed,"[316] he goes on to say, "Those who have done good to the resurrection of life; but those who have done evil, to the resurrection of judgment." And so above, where it is a matter of coming to life again through faith according to the spirit, they all come to life again to the same life of the same sort; their life is not divided into the two kinds of blessed and wretched, but they all belong on the same good side. And that is why, after saying "those who hear shall live" he did not add, "those who have done good, for eternal life, but those who have done evil, for eternal punishment." You see, he wished this simple expression "shall live" to be taken in a good sense only, in the same way as he had said earlier on, "has made the passage from death to life;" and he did not say to what life, because to come to life again from death through faith cannot be to a bad life. . . .

In the end, that reclining in the kingdom will be eternal rest; the fare at that banquet will be unchangeable divine truth; that feasting on it will be eternal life, that is, the actual knowledge of the truth. Because "this," he said, "is eternal life, that they may know you, the one true God, and the one you have sent, Jesus Christ."[317] SERMON 362.1-30.[318]

TO OBTAIN ETERNAL LIFE. AUGUSTINE: Eternal life is the supreme good and eternal death the supreme evil, and we should live rightly in order to obtain the one and avoid the other. Hence the scriptural expression, "the just man lives by faith"[319]—by faith, for the fact is that we do not now behold our good and, therefore, must seek it by faith; nor can we of ourselves even live rightly, unless he who gives us faith helps us to believe and pray, for it takes faith to believe that we need his help. CITY OF GOD 19.4.[320]

MEMBERS OF THE BODY OF CHRIST BY BAPTISM. AUGUSTINE: Another view of freedom from eternal punishment is that of those who do not extend the promise of impunity to all human beings but only to those who, by reason of baptism, are members of the body of Christ. As for these, it does not matter how they have lived or whether they were heretics or great sinners. The argument for the view is found in the text, "This is the bread that comes down from heaven, so that if anyone eats of it he will not die. I am the living bread that has come down from heaven. If anyone eats of this bread he shall live forever."[321] Therefore, in this view, all those baptized must be saved from eternal death and must reach, whenever it may be, life eternal. CITY OF GOD 21.19.[322]

ETERNAL PUNISHMENT FOR EVILDOERS. AUGUSTINE: The fact is that there is no way of waiving or weakening the words that the Lord has told us that he will pronounce in the last judgment: "Depart from me, accursed ones, into the everlasting fire which was prepared for the devil and his angels."[323] In this way

---

[315]Jn 5:28-29. [316]1 Cor 15:51 (Vg). [317]Jn 17:3. [318]WSA 3 10:241-69. [319]Gal 3:11. [320]FC 24:194-95. [321]Jn 6:50-51. [322]FC 24:382. [323]Mt 25:41.

he showed plainly that it is an eternal fire in which the devil and his angels are to burn. Then we have the words of the Apocalypse: "And the devil who deceived them was cast into the pool of fire and brimstone, where also are the beast and the false prophet; and they will be tormented day and night forever and ever."[324] In the one text we have "everlasting," in the other, "forever and ever." These are words that have a single meaning in the divine Scripture, namely, of unending duration.

Thus, it is Scripture, infallible Scripture, that declares that God has not spared them. This is the only reason why it is held as a fixed and unchanging religious truth that the devil and his angels are never to return to the life and holiness of the saints; nor could any more valid or cogent reason be discovered. It is from Scripture that we know that God's sentence implies that he "dragged them down by infernal ropes to Tartarus, and delivered them to be tortured and kept in custody for judgment."[325] They will be received into "everlasting" fire, there to be tortured "forever and ever."

And since this is true of the devil, how can people—whether all or some—be promised an escape, after some indefinitely long period, from this eternity of pain, without at once weakening our faith in the unending torment of the devils? For it is to people that the words will be said: "Depart from me, accursed ones, into the everlasting fire which was prepared for the devil and his angels." Now, if some of these people or all of them are not always to remain in everlasting fire, what ground have we for believing that the devil and his angels are always to remain there? God's sentence will be pronounced on the wicked, both angels and mortals. Can we suppose that it will hold for angels but not for mortals? Yes, but only if people's imaginings have more weight than God's words! Since this is quite impossible, all those who desire to escape eternal punishment should desist from arguing against God and should rather bow in obedience, while there is still time, to the command of God. Besides, what kind of imagining is this, to take eternal punishment to mean long-continued punishment and, at the same time, to believe that eternal life is endless, seeing that Christ spoke of both as eternal in the same place and in one and the same sentence: "And these will go into everlasting punishment, but the just into everlasting life."[326] If both are "everlasting," then either both must be taken as long-lasting but not endless or else both must be taken to be unendingly perpetual. For the everlastingness of the punishment and the everlastingness of the life are related as equal to equal. It is highly absurd to say in one and the same sense: "Life everlasting will be endless, but everlasting punishment will come to an end." Therefore, since the eternal life of the saints is to be endless, there can be no doubt that eternal punishment for those who are to endure it will have no end. CITY OF GOD 21.23.[327]

ONE WHO RISES SHOULD LIVE FOREVER. PETER CHRYSOLOGUS: It is necessary that the one who rises live forever, because if he did not live forever, he would rise not to life but to death. SERMON 59.17.[328]

THE PERFECT GLORY IN HEAVEN. AUGUSTINE: Who can measure the happiness of heaven, where no evil at all can touch us, no good will be out of reach; where life is to be one long laud extolling God, who will be all in all; where there will be no weariness to call for rest, no need to call for toil, no place for any energy but praise. Of this I am assured whenever I read or hear the sacred song: "Blessed are they that dwell in your house, O Lord: they shall praise you forever and ever."[329] Every fiber and organ of our imperishable body will play its part in the praising of God. On earth these

---

[324]Rev 20:10. [325]2 Pet 2:4. [326]Mt 25:46. [327]FC 24:385-87. [328]FC 109:229. [329]Cf. Ps 84:4.

varied organs have each a special function, but in heaven function will be swallowed up in felicity, in the perfect certainty of an untroubled everlastingness of joy. . . . In heaven, all glory will be true glory, since no one could ever err in praising too little or too much. True honor will never be denied where due, never be given where undeserved, and, since none but the worthy are permitted there, no one will have an unworthy ambition of glory. Perfect peace will reign, since nothing in ourselves or in any others could disturb this peace. The promised reward of virtue will be the best and the greatest of all possible prizes—the very Giver of virtue himself, for that is what the prophet meant: "I will be your God and you shall be my people."[330] God will be the source of every satisfaction, more than any heart can rightly crave, more than life and health, food and wealth, glory and honor, peace and every good so that God, as Paul said, "may be all in all."[331] He will be the consummation of all our desiring—the object of our unending vision, of our unvarying love, of our unwearying praise. And in this gift of vision, this response of love, this paean of praise, all alike will share, as all will share in everlasting life. . . .

The souls in bliss will still possess the freedom of will, though sin will have no power to tempt them. They will be more free than ever so free, in fact, from all delight in sinning as to find, in not sinning, an unfailing source of joy. . . .

Our will will be as ineradicably rooted in rectitude and love as in beatitude. It is true that, with Adam's sin, we lost our right to grace and glory, but, with our right, we did not lose our longing to be happy. And, as for freedom, can we think that God, who certainly cannot sin, is therefore without freedom? The conclusion is that, in the everlasting city, there will remain in each and all of us an inalienable freedom of the will, emancipating us from every evil and filling us with every good, rejoicing in the inexhaustible beatitude of everlasting happiness, unclouded by the memory of any sin or of sanction suffered, yet with no forgetfulness of our redemption or any loss of gratitude for our Redeemer. CITY OF GOD 22.30.[332]

---

[330]Lev 26:12. [331]1 Cor 15:28. [332]FC 24:505-8.

Conclusion of the Ancient Christian Doctrine Series

Thomas C. Oden
General Editor

Ancient Christian Doctrine is a commentary on the Nicene Creed. Here the major issues of early Christian theology have been organized and presented as a phrase-by-phrase commentary on the classic creed. The creed formed an authoritative consensual basis for drawing together the entire narrative meaning of Old and New Testament Scripture into a simple memorizable affirmation of baptismal faith.

Our purpose in the Ancient Christian Doctrine series has been single-minded: to set in order a consensual compendium of classic doctrinal interpretations organized around the key phrases of the Nicene-Constantinopolitan (Nicene) Creed. The result is a five-volume patristic compendium of classic doctrinal definitions focused on carefully assessing the truth claims of each phrase of the creed and the whole faith it confesses.

We have examined each phrase of the creed as it was understood by the leading teachers of the ancient church viewed as a concise summary of the whole biblical narrative as interpreted by the apostles. We have included comments on these key phrases as they were under discussion both prior to and after the time of Constantine, when the received confession of baptismal faith was under Arian challenge and was firmly defined for subsequent Christian orthodoxy in the first two ecumenical councils at Nicaea and Constantinople (325 and 381).

The predecessor of this series is the twenty-nine-volume Ancient Christian Commentary on Scripture (ACCS). It has spawned numerous other projects (Ancient Christian Texts, the Ancient Christian Devotional series and the Center for Early African Christianity). That massive commentary, produced between 1993 and 2009, has elicited many requests that it be followed by a doctrinal series organized around familiar themes of the central loci of Christian teaching. This series on Ancient Christian Doctrine has followed closely on the methods and outcomes of the huge digital database created by the ACCS.

Interpreters have been selected from the leading figures of the patristic period (95-750). They span from Clement of Rome to Bede the Venerable—from the end of the New Testament to the mid-eighth century. These doctrinal treasures all depend on scriptural interpretations that we have mined and organized as a commentary on the most authoritative doctrinal confession of the early church.

Baptismal Teaching

Historically, each phrase of the creed was committed to memory by those seeking to be baptized. For each phrase the church fathers looked for its full meaning and implications. Thus to learn the meaning and import of each phrase of the baptismal confession is to learn the meaning of the baptism by which the faithful enter into the community of faith and new life in Christ. In this way we have reviewed the classic order of teaching of Christian doctrine as it arose out of prebaptismal teaching practice based on consensual scriptural exegesis.

Those commissioned to prepare persons for baptism had a consistent goal: Bring this lofty teaching into consistent unity. By this means they provided care of souls for the worshiping community. The mentor for baptism was called the catechist. The primary catechists for children are their parents. A catechumen is one who receives catechetical instruction, whose task is to make interconnected sense out of the creed to the learner.

Each phrase has a history of debate concerning its meanings and consequences. Each part must be consistent with the whole confession that brings the believer fittingly to the Lord's table. Each must be carefully defended against distortions and misinterpretations.

Christian teaching is baptismal teaching. Christian theology came into being to explain Christian baptism. The earliest summaries of Christian theology were lectures to prepare people for baptism. Our organization of key themes of Christian teaching depends on this thought sequence of the most influential early summaries by its greatest teachers: Cyril of Jerusalem (*Catechetical Lectures*), Gregory of Nyssa (*Address on Religious Instruction*), John Chrysostom (*Baptismal Instructions*) and Augustine (*Catechizing the Uninstructed* and *On Faith and the Creed*). These early creedal summaries are the best condensed statements of Christian faith and the most reliable way to learn the heart of faith.

Tested Intergenerational, Ecumenical Teaching Arises Out of Baptismal Teaching

All who join in the praise of the worshiping community have a right and a responsibility to know the meaning of their baptism. The purpose of this series is to clarify the ancient ecumenical faith into which Christians of all times and places are still being baptized.

This is why the most ecumenical of all creeds over the longest period of time has also been the church's best teaching summary. It brings together the whole scope of scriptural wisdom into a single, short, memorable confession. It has been most widely received as a summary of scriptural truth because it has repeatedly proven itself as the most tested and reliable means of teaching the heart of scriptural faith.

Christians all over the world still appeal to the most ecumenical of all ancient creeds, the Nicene Creed, as the most reliable rule of baptismal faith. This is why we employ this interconnected means to bring together the best thinking of early Christian teachers. This series has brought together the classic arguments about what each of these phrases meant and how they have been textually grounded in sacred Scripture.

This is not a systematic theology by typical modern standards, but rather a feast of classic patristic wisdom that precedes and conditions all systematic theology. These defining texts form the substantive doctrinal basis of all subsequent systematic theology and Christian dogmatic reasoning. They constitute a teaching guide to the earliest layers of classic Christian formulations of ecumenically received orthodox doctrine.

The First Word of the Creed: Learning to Say "Credo"
The room for private opinion among Christians is vast, provided those opinions are not repugnant to the core of faith. Nothing is required of any believer other than faith in grace as revealed in Scripture.

The formal confession of that faith that is necessary for salvation has been affirmed consensually by the Christian community over time in the articles of faith that have been continually received by common ecumenical consent.

Christians who first said credo ("I believe," or in Greek *pisteuomen*, "we believe") did not do so lightly but at the risk of their lives under threat of persecution. Only those who were prepared to sacrifice their lives for their belief were considered valid apostolic witnesses. To them believers listen attentively.

The Nicene Creed remains the most authoritative common confession of worldwide Christians. It is the most fitting framework for this series. Like all ancient baptismal confessions, it is set forth in three phases or articles corresponding with the three Persons of the one God attested in Scripture. Those baptized are expected to understand what it means to believe in God the Father almighty, in God the Son and in God the Spirit.

The core of this summary teaching appeared in Matthew 28:19-20 in the words to be spoken at baptism, where the resurrected Lord concluded his earthly teaching with this summary charge: "Go therefore and make disciples of all nations, baptizing them in the name of the Father and of the Son and of the Holy Spirit, teaching them to observe all that I have commanded you; and lo, I am with you always, to the close of the age." In this way, Jesus forever linked baptizing and teaching with the promise of his continuing presence. Implicitly included in the instructions for baptism is the charge to teach its significance.

Condensing the Whole Faith to a Short Confession
The believer keeps close to the center of that faith delivered by the apostles, that faith "which has been built up strongly out of all the Scriptures. . . . In order that the soul should not be starved in ignorance, the church has condensed the whole teaching of the faith in a few lines. This summary I wish you both to commit to memory when I recite it and to rehearse it with all diligence among yourselves, not writing it out on paper but engraving it by the memory on your heart. . . . Keep this as a provision through the whole course of your life, and beside this receive no alternative teaching, even if we ourselves should change and contradict our present teaching."[1]

---

[1]Cyril of Jerusalem *Catechetical Lecture* 5.12.

In this series we have followed the classic exposition of this simple faith as it unfolds logically through five steps:

Volume 1: *We Believe in One God*—the knowledge of God the Father; the triune God revealed in creation, providence and human history (Gerald L. Bray, Latimer Trust and Samford University).

Volume 2: *We Believe in One Lord Jesus Christ*—the coming of God the Son, the incarnate God, one person in two natures (John Anthony McGuckin, Union Theological Seminary and Columbia University).

Volume 3: *We Believe in the Crucified and Risen Lord*—the revelation of divine love, the reconciling work of Jesus Christ, his earthly ministry, death and resurrection (Mark Edwards, Christ Church, Oxford).

Volume 4: *We Believe in the Holy Spirit*—the ministry of God the Spirit, the person and work of the Holy Spirit in justification, salvation and the holy life (Joel Elowsky, Drew University).

Volume 5: *We Believe in One Holy Catholic and Apostolic Church*—the triune God in the church and in history, the glory of God in the community of faith as manifested throughout the whole of history (Angelo Di Berardino, Augustinian Patristic Institute of Rome).

Canon and Creed

The creed is at heart a confession of the cumulative meaning of the prayers, liturgy and common acts of confession of the whole Christian community of all times and places. It expresses the common sense of the faithful about what the revelation of God in Scripture narrates and proclaims.

This consensus set the boundaries for the shared confession of the worldwide faithful. Many ideas were able to be freely examined within these boundaries, but some were out of bounds. When advocates of these nonconsensual views turned up purported texts by alleged apostles, they were judged and rejected in relation to the consensus that had emerged firmly from the earliest communities of faith as expressed in their baptismal confessions, which became the rule of faith *(regula fidei)* for the worshiping community, the trustworthy instruction by which the boundaries of scriptural teaching could be marked out.

The New Testament canon is the list of books authorized to be read in the early church in addition to the Hebrew Scriptures. It was necessary to define these books consensually in order to defend the apostolic consensus against other floating documents that were contrary to the liturgy and hymns and catechetics and scripture of the apostolic preaching. It closed the door against later documents claiming apostolic authorship. It definitively identified those documents most widely acknowledged as fit from the beginning for reading in Christian worship and fully trustable as doctrine. The four Gospels and the letters of Paul were from the outset widely agreed on as apostolic texts, and all others were carefully examined as to apostolic claims. As this list of books became ever more clearly defined, the basis became clearer on which both consensual (orthodox) and nonconsensual (heretical) readings of the written Word could be assessed. Out of this canonical consensus flowed continuing productions of liturgical expression, scriptural commentary, early theological treatises and moral discourse.

The most elitist of all false claimants to Christian truth were the Gnostics, who were contemptuous of the naive consensus of uninformed believers and who were never even interested in gaining the hearts of ordinary believers. Yet the ordinary believers could easily see that these later speculations did not match the authenticity and beauty and clarity of the original apostolic witnesses.

In Slow Motion

We have looked at the phrases of the creed in slow motion, to carefully show their biblical grounding, to challenge distortions of scriptural teaching and to provide a plausible cohesion for the worshiping life of the baptized community. It offers the reader direct access to the patristic writers in their own unvarnished language, not squeezed through the sieve of modern demythologizing interpreters. It brings the great early teachers into direct contact with the mind of the present reader. Here we discover their most resilient comments on the most crucial confessional statements of the ancient baptismal creed. This is not just a casual exercise for theological voyeurs or for dilettantes who want to fly to the Nile for a cruise. Rather, it is a window into the earliest Christian reflection on the most decisive points of saving faith.

There is an emerging awareness among Catholic, Protestant and Orthodox laity that vital ecumenical orthodox teaching stands in urgent need of deeper grounding in its most consensual classic Christian sources. These sources emerged many centuries prior to ideological and historical critical orientations that have dominated so much theological study in our time. Today's communities of prayer, praise and service are being steadily drawn toward these earliest Christian ecumenical sources for spiritual formation. These worshiping communities are asking for primary source texts of spiritual formation that are accessible in ordinary language form, well-grounded in reliable critical scholarship and designed for practical use.

The reason the consensual interpreters of canonical Scripture were called Fathers is that they were widely regarded by ordinary lay Christians as trustable fathers in the faith who presented not their own inventive speculations but the truth of the apostolic testimony as consensually viewed from Spain to India, from Ethiopia to Britain. In its journey through history Christianity has honored those consensual ecumenical teachers who by common consent were reliably led by the Spirit in their transmission of apostolic teaching.

A Long-Delayed Task

It has been a long time since any deliberate attempt has been made to produce this sort of consensual ecumenical doctrinal compendium.

We have offered here the first full-scale early Christian commentary on the Nicene Creed. Future work in orthodox apologetics will be intently referring to these sources. We have brought together a distinguished international network of Protestant, Catholic and Orthodox scholars, editors and translators of the highest quality and reputation to accomplish this design. We hope this will provide a model for the study of the history of doctrine as creedal commentary.

The varied audiences of this collection (lay, clergy and academic) are much broader than the highly technical and specialized scholarly field of patristic studies as conceived in the West. They are not limited to the Western university scholar concentrating on the study of the history of the transmission of the text or to those with highly focused interests in textual morphology or historical critical issues or comparative cultural studies. Though these remain crucial concerns for specialists, they are not the burning interest of the Ancient Christian Doctrine series. The editors welcome all who want to think with the early church about the plain sense, theological wisdom and moral and spiritual meaning of the most central Christian doctrines and texts most honored as authoritative by believers of all times, cultures and places. These texts have fed the fertile imagination of the global faithful for two millennia. Only in an ancillary way do we have in mind as our particular audience the esteemed guild of Western patristic academicians, whom we expect carefully to assess our translations and methods utilizing the rigorous standards, which we welcome. If these brilliant texts find their way to the hearing of ordinary lay readers to serve them practically, we expect they also will be advantageously utilized where pertinent by academics in Scripture studies, hermeneutics, church history, historical theology and homiletics.

Common Ground

This series expresses and actively develops a lively ecumenical undertaking. Under this classic textual umbrella, it brings together Christians who have long distanced themselves from each other by competing historical memories. Under this aegis these texts gather traditional Catholics with Protestant evangelicals and Eastern Orthodox with Pentecostals. How is it that such varied Christians are able to find common dogmatic inspiration in these classic sources? Why are these texts and studies so intrinsically ecumenical, so broadly catholic in their cultural range? Because all of these modern ecclesial traditions have an equal right to appeal to the earliest apostolic traditions of teaching. All of these traditions can, without a sacrifice of intellect, draw modestly together to study the same texts most common to them all. These classic texts have decisively shaped the wider subsequent history of doctrine in global Christianity.

Surprisingly, the most extensive new emergent audience for patristic studies is found among the expanding worldwide audience of evangelical readers who are now burgeoning out of a history that has often been somewhat lacking in historically awareness. This is a tradition that has often been caricatured as hermeneutically challenged and critically backward. But we are now witnessing Baptist and Pentecostal laity who are rediscovering the history of the Holy Spirit. Both evangelicals and Catholics are recognizing their need for doctrinal resources that go far beyond those that have been made available to them in either the pietistic or historical critical traditions.

Scripture Texts in Concert as Judge of the Interpreter

Modern secularizing theology has a persistent habit of mind: I come to judge the text. The text does not form me; I form an opinion of the text. I am there to criticize the alleged divine Word. By this means a tight control is exercised over the legitimacy of the Scripture text by the interpreter. This habit is based on a much more endemic pattern of modern chauvinism that views later critical sources as intrinsically more credible than earlier. This prejudice tends to view the biblical text primarily through historical-critical lenses that are absolutely accommodative to contemporary culture. The critic does not assume the truth of Scripture as revelation, as do the patristic texts, nor does he even consider submitting personally to the categorical moral requirement of the revealed text in obedience to its truth claims.

The purpose of catechesis in the patristic period was the opposite: to seek the revealed truth the Scriptures convey to those who were already ready and penitently prepared to seek to put it into practice. The seeker will not even approach an elementary discernment of the meaning of the sacred text if he is not ready to hear it as divine address. They practiced the Word in order to hear it.

OUTLINE OF CONTENTS

We Believe in One Holy Catholic and Apostolic Church: The Church   **1**
    The Preexistent Church and Its Visible Foundation by Christ   7
    Images of the Church   15
    The Church as the Body of Christ   23
    The Church as Bride of Christ   34
    The Church as Mother   40
    The Church as a Ship   50

We Believe in One Holy Catholic and Apostolic Church:
    One Holy Catholic and Apostolic   **54**
    The Unity of Christians and of the Whole Church   59
    The Church, a Community of Believers, Is Holy   69
    The Church Is Catholic, Bringing Salvation to All   72
    The True Catholic Church Is Apostolic   77

We Acknowledge One Baptism   **87**
    Baptism That Occurred Before Christ's Death and Resurrection   92
    The Living Water of Baptism   93
    Rebirth, Illumination and Eucharist   97
    The Baptismal Seal   100
    The Remission of Sins   101
    Regeneration   101
    Baptism and the Holy Spirit   104
    One Baptism   106
    Infant Baptism   107
    Blood Baptism   109
    Baptism as Type   110

For the Forgiveness of Sins   **112**
    You Are God's Temple   116

Adoption into the Family of God	117
The Forgiveness of Sins	124

We Look for the Resurrection of the Dead — 139

The Resurrection in General	141
The Resurrection of the Body	153
The Millennium	161
The Vision of the End—In Light of the Origenist Controversy	167

And the Life of the World to Come: Blessedness and Condemnation — 175

The Nature of Eternal Blessedness	177
The Degrees of Blessedness	188
The Communion of Saints	191
Eternal Damnation	193
The Fate of Satan and the Demons	206

And the Life of the World to Come: Christ's Return, the Judgment and Eternal Life — 214

The Second Coming of Christ	218
Two Advents	221
Judgment Given to the Son of Man	225
The Judgment of the Living and the Dead	228
The Inevitability of Judgment	232
A Just Judgment	234
The Intermediate State of Souls	241
Prayers and Intercession	242
A Cleansing	243
The Fire of God	247
Glorification or Destruction	248

LIST OF ANCIENT AUTHORS AND TEXTS CITED

Abercius
Ancient Roman Funeral Inscription

Acts of Paul and Thecla

Acts of Peter

Acts of Thomas

Alexander of Alexandria
Epistles on the Arian Heresy

Ambrose
Jacob and the Happy Life
Letters
On His Brother Satyrus
On the Christian Faith
On the Sacraments

Ambrosiaster
Commentary on 1 Corinthians
Commentary on Paul's Epistles

Aphrahat
Demonstrations

Aristides
Apology

Athanasius
Defense of the Nicene Definition
Discourses Against the Arians
Letter to Serapion

Athenagoras
On the Resurrection

Augustine
Against Faustus, a Manichaean
Against the Letter of the Manichaeans
City of God
Enchiridion
Expositions of the Psalms
Homilies on the Gospel of John
On Baptism
On Continence
On Faith and the Creed
On the Literal Interpretation of Genesis
On the Merits and Forgiveness of Sins and on Infant Baptism
On the Morals of the Catholic Church
On the Soul and Its Origin
On the Trinity
Predestination of the Saints
Proceedings of Pelagius
Sermons

Basil the Great
Concerning Baptism
Homilies
On the Holy Spirit

Caesarius of Arles
Sermons

Cassian, John
Conferences

Chrysostom
Baptismal Instructions
Homilies
Letter to the Fallen Theodore

Clement of Alexandria
Christ the Educator
Exhortation to the Greeks
Stromateis

Clement of Rome
1 Clement

Commodian
Instructions

Constitutions of the Holy Apostles

Cyprian
The Dress of Virgins
Jealousy and Envy
The Lapsed
Letters
On Morality
On the Unity of the Church
To Demetrian

Cyril of Alexandria
Explanation of the Letter to the Romans
Letters

Cyril of Jerusalem
Catechetical Lectures
Mystagogical Lectures
Sermons

Didache

Didymus the Blind
Commentary on Zechariah

Ephrem the Syrian
Carmina Nisibena
Commentary on Tatian's Diatessaron
Homilies
Hymns
Memre of Holy Week
On Epiphany

Epistle of Barnabas

Epistula Apostolorum

Eusebius of Caesarea
Ecclesiastical History

Firmilian of Caesarea
Letters

Fulgentius of Ruspe
On the Incarnation

Gregory of Nazianzus
On Basil the Great, Oration 43
On His Brother Caesarius, Oration 7
On His Father's Silence, Oration 16
On Holy Baptism, Oration 40

Gregory of Nyssa
Address on Religious Instruction
On the Baptism of Christ

Gregory the Great
Dialogues
Homilies on the Gospels
Letters

Hegesippus
(via Eusebius, Ecclesiastical History)

Hermas
Shepherd, Mandate
Shepherd, Similitude
Shepherd, Vision

Hilary of Poitiers
Homilies on the Psalms
On the Trinity

Hippolytus
Against Plato, On the Cause of the Universe
Apostolic Tradition
Treaties on Christ and Antichrist

Ignatius of Antioch
Epistle to the Ephesians

Epistle to the Magnesians
Epistle to the Smyrneans
Epistle to the Trallians

Inscriptions
Third and Fourth Century

Irenaeus
Against Heresies
Proof of the Apostolic Teaching

Jerome
Against Jovinianus
Commentary on the Epistle to the Ephesians
Homilies
Letters

John of Damascus
Orthodox Faith

Justin Martyr
Dialogue with Trypho
First Apology
Fragments on the Resurrection

Justinian the Emperor
The Anathematisms of the Emperor Justinian Against Origen

Lactantius
Divine Institutes
On Baptism

Leo the Great
Sermons

Letter to Diognetus

Liturgy of Saint Basil

Liturgy of the Blessed Apostles

Martyrdom of Polycarp

Macus
Funeral Inscription from Rome

Melito of Sardis
On Pascha

Methodius of Olympus
Symposium or The Banquet of the Ten Virgins

Minucius Felix
Octavius

Munnulus of Girba
(via the Seventh Council of Carthage Under Cyprian)

Niceta of Remesiana
Explanation of the Creed

Novatian
In Praise of Purity

Odes of Solomon

Origen
Against Celsus
Commentary on the Epistle to the Romans
Commentary on the Gospel of John
Commentary on the Gospel of Matthew
Commentary on the Song of Songs
Exhortation to Martyrdom
Homilies
On First Principles

Pacian of Barcelona
Letters
On Baptism

Papias of Hierapolis
(via Eusebius, Ecclesiastical History)

Pelagius
Commentary on Romans

Peter Chrysologus
Sermons

Polycarp
Epistle to the Philippians

Pseudo-Clement of Rome
2 Clement
Epistle to James
Pseudo-Clementine Homilies

Rufinus of Aquileia
A Commentary on the Apostles' Creed

Tatian
Address to the Greeks

Tertullian
Against Marcion
Apology
The Chaplet
On Baptism
On Idolatry
On Modesty
On Monogamy
On Prayer
On Repentance
On the Resurrection of the Flesh
On the Soul
On the Testimony of the Soul
Prescriptions Against Heretics
To the Martyrs

Theodore of Mopsuestia
Commentary on the Gospel of John
Fragment on 1 Corinthians
Pauline Commentary from the Greek Church

Theodoret of Cyr
Commentary on the First Epistle to the Corinthians

Theophilus of Antioch
To Autolycus

Treatise on Rebaptism

Victorinus of Petovium
Commentary on the Apocalypse
On the Creation of the World

Vincent of Lérins
Commonitory

Biographical Sketches & Short Descriptions of Select Anonymous Works

This listing is cumulative, including all the authors and works cited in this series to date.

Abba John (date unknown). Noted monk in John Cassian's *Conferences* who presided over a coenobitic community in the desert of Scetis and was sought out for his wisdom.

Abba Moses (c. 332-407). Moses the Ethiopian or Moses the Black. He began as a house slave of a government official, later dismissed for robbery, a life he continued after his dismissal. After his conversion, he became a monk of Scetis and then a priest trained by Isidore the Priest. He retired to Petra where he was martyred with seven others by barbarian invaders.

Abba Pior (d. 373). An Egyptian desert father. He left his family while still a boy. His sister sought him out fifty years later, trying to persuade him to return from his life of solitude, but she was unsuccessful. He was known as a generous monk who was willing to put up with much discomfort, living in a horrible cell that no one who followed after him could stand to live in.

Abraham of Nathpar (fl. sixth-seventh century). Monk of the Eastern Church who flourished during the monastic revival of the sixth to seventh century. Among his works is a treatise on prayer and silence that speaks of the importance of prayer becoming embodied through action in the one who prays. His work has also been associated with John of Apamea or Philoxenus of Mabbug.

Acacius of Beroea (c. 340-c. 436). Syrian monk known for his ascetic life. He became bishop of Beroea in 378, participated in the council of Constantinople in 381, and played an important role in mediating between Cyril of Alexandria and John of Antioch; however, he did not take part in the clash between Cyril and Nestorius.

Acacius of Caesarea (d. c. 365). Pro-Arian bishop of Caesarea in Palestine, disciple and biographer of Eusebius of Caesarea, the historian. He was a man of great learning and authored a treatise on Ecclesiastes.

Acts of Paul and Thecla (second century). A story about a disciple of Paul known for her continence and miraculous deliverances from martyrdom. Originally a part of *The Acts of Paul*, the work was judged a forgery by Tertullian who opposed its use in the advocacy of female preaching and baptizing. Nonetheless, the work was widely popular and translated into several languages.

Acts of Peter (c. 190). An apocryphal account of the apostle's life and ministry, including his conflicts with Simon Magus and his death via inverted crucifixion.

Acts of Thomas (c. 225). A widely circulated apocryphal account of the missionary and wonderworking activities of Thomas, which includes the earliest report of the apostle's martyrdom in India.

Adamantius (early fourth century). Surname of Origen of Alexandria and the main character in the dialogue contained in *Concerning Right Faith in God*. Rufinus attributes this work to Origen. However, trinitarian terminology, coupled with references to Methodius and allusions to the fourth-century Constantinian era bring this attribution into question.

Adamnan (c. 624-704). Abbot of Iona, Ireland, and author of the life of St. Columba. He was influential in the process of assimilating the Celtic church into Roman liturgy and church order. He also wrote *On the Holy Sites*, which influenced Bede.

Alexander of Alexandria (fl. 312-328). Bishop of Alexandria and predecessor of Athanasius, on whom he exerted considerable theological influence during the rise of Arianism. Alexander excommunicated Arius, whom he had appointed to the parish of Baucalis, in 319. His teaching regarding the eternal generation and divine substantial union of the Son with the Father was eventually confirmed at the Council of Nicaea (325).

Ambrose of Milan (c. 333-397; fl. 374-397). Bishop of Milan and teacher of Augustine who defended the divinity of the Holy Spirit and the perpetual virginity of Mary.

Ambrosiaster (fl. c. 366-384). Name given to the author of an anonymous Pauline commentary once thought to have been composed by Ambrose.

Ammonas (fourth century). Student of Antony the Great and member of a colony of anchorite monks at Pispir in Egypt. He took over leadership of the colony upon Antony's death in 356. He was consecrated by Athanasius as bishop of a small unknown see. He died by 396. Fourteen letters and eleven sayings in the Apophthegmata Patrum are attributed to him, although it is unlikely that all of the identified sayings are his.

Ammonius (c. fifth century). An Aristotelian commentator and teacher in Alexandria, where he was born and of whose school he became head. Also an exegete of Plato, he enjoyed fame among his contemporaries and successors, although modern critics accuse him of pedantry and banality.

Amphilochius of Iconium (b. c. 340-345; d. c. 398-404). An orator at Constantinople before becoming bishop of Iconium in 373. He was a cousin of Gregory of Nazianzus and active in debates against the Macedonians and Messalians.

Anastasius I of Antioch (d. 598/599). Patriarch of Antioch (559-570 and 593-598), exiled by Justinian II and restored by Gregory the Great. His writing significantly influenced later theologians, though only his five-part treatise on orthodox belief survives in its entirety.

Anastasius of Sinai (d. c. 700). Abbot of the monastery of St. Catherine. He argued against various heresies in his dogmatic and polemical works. His main treatise, the *Hodegos* or "Guide," is primarily an attack on monophysism.

Andreas (c. seventh century). Monk who collected commentary from earlier writers to form a catena on various biblical books.

Andrew of Caesarea (early sixth century). Bishop of Caesarea in Cappadocia. He produced one of the earliest Greek commentaries on Revelation and defended the divine inspiration of its author.

Andrew of Crete (c. 660-740). Bishop of Crete, known for his hymns, especially for his "canons," a genre which supplanted the *kontakia* and is believed to have originated with him. A significant number of his canons and sermons have survived and some are still in use in the Eastern Church. In the early Iconoclastic controversy he is also known for his defense of the veneration of icons.

Antony (or Anthony) the Great (c. 251-c. 356). An anchorite of the Egyptian desert and founder of Egyptian monasticism. Athanasius regarded him as the ideal of monastic life, and he has become a model for Christian hagiography.

Aphrahat (c. 270-350; fl. 337-345). "The Persian Sage" and first major Syriac writer whose work survives. He is also known by his Greek name Aphraates.

Apollinaris of Laodicea (310-c. 392). Bishop of Laodicea who was attacked by Gregory of Nazianzus, Gregory of Nyssa and Theodore for denying that Christ had a human mind.

Aponius/Apponius (fourth-fifth century). Author of a remarkable commentary on Song of Solomon (c. 405-415), an important work in the history of exegesis. The work, which was influenced by the commentaries of Origen and Pseudo-Hippolytus, is of theological significance, especially in the area of Christology.

Apostolic Constitutions (c. 381-394). Also known as *Constitutions of the Holy Apostles* and thought to be redacted by Julian of Neapolis. The work is divided into eight books, and is primarily a collection of and expansion on previous works such as the *Didache* (c. 140) and the *Apostolic Traditions*. Book 8 ends with eighty-five canons from various sources and is elsewhere known as the *Apostolic Canons*.

Apringius of Beja (mid sixth century). Iberian bishop and exegete. Heavily influenced by Tyconius, he wrote a commentary on Revelation in Latin, of which two large fragments survive.

Arator (c. 490-550). Roman subdeacon appointed by Pope Vigilius. From Liguria, Italy, he served as an imperial ambassador for the Gothic court prior to his appointment as subdeacon. A poet at heart, his *De actibus apostolorum*, a poetic paraphrase and allegorical expansion of the book of Acts, was popular in the Middle Ages.

Arethas of Caesarea (c. 860-940). Byzantine scholar and disciple of Photius. He was a deacon in Constantinople, then archbishop of Caesarea from 901.

Aristides (second century). Christian philosopher and early apologist. Reputed to be from Athens, he wrote his *Apologia*, addressed either to Hadrian or Antoninus Pius, to defend the Christian understanding of God against that of the barbarian, Greek and Jewish traditions.

Arius (fl. c. 320). Heretic condemned at the Council of Nicaea (325) for refusing to accept that the Son was not a creature but was God by nature like the Father.

Armenian Liturgy (c. fourth or fifth century). Ancient Christian liturgy based in part on Syrian rites used by early missionaries to Armenia and similar in structure to the old rite of Antioch. The Armenian liturgy also incorporates unique elements and influences from a variety of traditions. The invention of a national script in the fifth century allowed for the translation of the liturgy into Armenian.

Arnobius of Sicca (d. c. 327). Teacher of rhetoric at Sicca Veneria in Numidia in North Africa and opponent of Christianity, he converted late in life and became an apologist for the faith he formerly opposed. According to Jerome, Arnobius's one extant work, *Against the Nations*, was written at the request of his bishop, who wanted proof that his conversion was genuine. It was probably composed during the persecution under Diocletian.

Arnobius the Younger (fifth century). A participant in christological controversies of the fifth century. He composed *Conflictus cum Serapione*, an account of a debate with a monophysite monk in which he attempts to demonstrate harmony between Roman and Alexandrian theology. Some scholars attribute to him a few more works, such as *Commentaries on Psalms*.

Asterius the Homilist (late fourth-early

fifth century). Author of thirty-one homilies on Psalms 1–15 and 18, abbreviated versions of which are preserved under the name of John Chrysostom. This otherwise unknown preacher, sometimes identified with Asterius of Amasea and Asterius the Sophist, lived in or near Antioch.

Athanasian Creed (c. fourth or fifth century). One of the three ecumenical creeds in Western Christianity. Also known as the *Quicumque vult*, it expounds in great detail the doctrines of the Trinity and Incarnation. Traditionally attributed to Athanasius, the creed's origin and date are now disputed; it likely arose in Southern Gaul.

Athanasius of Alexandria (c. 295-373; fl. 325-373). Bishop of Alexandria from 328, though often in exile. He wrote his classic polemics against the Arians while most of the eastern bishops were against him.

Athenagoras (fl. 176-180). Early Christian philosopher and apologist from Athens, whose only authenticated writing, *A Plea Regarding Christians*, is addressed to the emperors Marcus Aurelius and Commodus, and defends Christians from the common accusations of atheism, incest and cannibalism.

Augustine of Hippo (354-430). Bishop of Hippo and a voluminous writer on philosophical, exegetical, theological and ecclesiological topics. He formulated the Western doctrines of predestination and original sin in his writings against the Pelagians.

Babai (c. early sixth century). Author of the *Letter to Cyriacus*. He should not be confused with either Babai of Nisibis (d. 484) or Babai the Great (d. 628).

Babai the Great (d. 628). Syriac monk who founded a monastery and school in his region of Beth Zabday and later served as third superior at the Great Convent of Mount Izla during a period of crisis in the Nestorian church.

Bardesanes (154-222). Philosopher who sought to reconcile Christian thought with contemporary astrological theories, while rejecting Zoroastrian determinism. His ideas, including arguments against the Marcionites, were recorded by a disciple in the *Book of the Laws of the Lands*. He also wrote 150 doctrinal hymns.

Basil of Seleucia (fl. 444-468). Bishop of Seleucia in Isauria and ecclesiastical writer. He took part in the Synod of Constantinople in 448 for the condemnation of the Eutychian errors and the deposition of their great champion, Dioscurus of Alexandria.

Basil the Great (b. c. 330; fl. 357-379). One of the Cappadocian fathers, bishop of Caesarea and champion of the teaching on the Trinity propounded at Nicaea in 325. He was a great administrator and founded a monastic rule.

Basilides (fl. second century). Alexandrian heretic of the early second century who is said to have believed that souls migrate from body to body and that we do not sin if we lie to protect the body from martyrdom.

Bede the Venerable (c. 672/673-735). Born in Northumbria, at the age of seven he was put under the care of the Benedictine monks of Saints Peter and Paul at Jarrow and given a broad classical education in the monastic tradition. Considered one of the most learned men of his age, he is the author of *An Ecclesiastical History of the English People*.

Benedict of Nursia (c. 480-547). Considered the most important figure in the history of Western monasticism. Benedict founded many monasteries, the most notable found at Montecassino, but his lasting influence lay in his famous Rule. The Rule outlines the theological and inspirational foundation of the monastic ideal while also legislating the shape and organization of the cenobitic life.

Besa the Copt (fifth century). Coptic monk, disciple of Shenoute, whom he succeeded as head of the monastery. He wrote numerous letters, monastic catecheses and a biography of Shenoute.

Book of Steps (c. 400). Written by an anonymous Syriac author, this work consists of thirty homilies or discourses which specifically deal with the more advanced stages of growth in the spiritual life.

Braulio of Saragossa (c. 585-651). Bishop of Saragossa (631-651) and noted writer of the Visigothic renaissance. His *Life* of St. Aemilianus is his crowning literary achievement.

Byzantine Order. Eastern rite incorporating diverse local traditions from throughout the empire. Byzantine liturgy, which fused into a more standard order in the late Middle Ages, is marked by a variety of rich cultural influences, especially lyrical and mystical elements.

Caesarius of Arles (c. 470-543). Bishop of Arles renowned for his attention to his pastoral duties. Among his surviving works the most important is a collection of 238 sermons that display an ability to preach Christian doctrine to a variety of audiences.

Callistus of Rome (d. 222). Pope (217-222) who excommunicated Sabellius for heresy. It is very probable that he suffered martyrdom.

Cassia (b. c. 805; d. between 848 and 867). Nun, poet and hymnographer who founded a convent in Constantinople.

Cassian, John (360-432). Author of the *Institutes* and the *Conferences*, works purporting to relay the teachings of the Egyptian monastic fathers on the nature of the spiritual life which were highly influential in the development of Western monasticism.

Cassiodorus (c. 485-c. 580). Founder of the monastery of Vivarium, Calabria, where monks transcribed classic sacred and profane texts, in Greek and Latin, preserving them for the Western tradition.

Chromatius (fl. 400). Bishop of Aquileia, friend of Rufinus and Jerome and author of tracts and sermons.

Clement of Alexandria (c. 150-215). A highly educated Christian convert from paganism, head of the catechetical school in Alexandria and pioneer of Christian scholarship. His major works, Protrepticus, Paedagogus and the Stromata, bring Christian doctrine face to face with the ideas and achievements of his time.

Clement of Rome (fl. c. 92-101). Pope whose *Epistle to the Corinthians* is one of the most important documents of subapostolic times.

Commodian (probably third or possibly fifth century). Latin poet of unknown origin (possibly Africa, Syria, Rome or Gaul) whose two surviving works suggest chiliast and patripassionist tendencies.

Constantine (d. 337). Roman emperor from 306, with his fellow-emperor Licinius. The two proclaimed religious tolerance in the *Edict of Milan* in 313, allowing Christianity to be practiced freely. He became sole emperor in 324 and sought to preserve the unity and structure of the church for the good of the state. Constantine issued decrees against schisms and summoned the Council of Nicaea (325) to settle the Arian controversy.

Constitutions of the Holy Apostles. See *Apostolic Constitutions*.

Cosmas of Maiuma (c. 675-c. 751). Adopted son of John of Damascus and educated by the monk Cosmas in the early eighth century. He entered the monastery of St. Sabas near Jerusalem and in 735 became bishop of Maiuma near Gaza. Cosmas in his capacity as Melodus ("Songwriter") is known for his canons composed in honor of Christian feasts. An alternate rendering of his name is Kosmas Melodos.

Council of Chalcedon (451). The fourth of seven ecumenical councils. The council was summoned by Emperor Marcian in response to a controversy over the person and nature of Christ. The Definition of Chalcedon, informed by Leo's *Tome*, affirmed the statements of Nicaea (325) and Constantinople (381) while further defining the relationship between the two natures in the one person of Christ as unmixed, unchangeable, indivisible and inseparable. The Oriental Orthodox Church refused to accept Chalcedon's definition of the faith, preferring to stay with the *miaphysite* Christology of Cyril of Alexandria.

Council of Constantinople (381). The second ecumenical council, convened by Theodosius I to unify the Eastern Church. The council endorsed the Nicene Creed of 325, expanding it at certain controverted points in order to answer to challenges from, among others, the Eunomians and Pneumatomachians who denied the divinity of the Holy Spirit, while also condemning the Apollinarian denial of Christ's full humanity.

Council of Rome (382). Called by Damasus in response to the Council of Constantinople, this gathering affirmed the Council of Constantinople while also seeking to establish the primacy of the Roman see. The first three chapters of the *Decretum Gelasianum*, which list a hierarchy of authoritative sources and a biblical canon, may have been produced by this council.

Council of Toledo (447). Affirmed the earlier Council of Toledo I (400) and the liturgical practice already established in the West of including the procession of the Spirit from the Father *and the Son (filioque)*, which had been added to the recitation of the creed by some in the West in order to combat the heresy of Arianism which subordinated the Son to the Father.

Cyprian of Carthage (fl. 248-258). Martyred bishop of Carthage who maintained that those baptized by schismatics and heretics had no share in the blessings of the church.

Cyril of Alexandria (375-444; fl. 412-444). Patriarch of Alexandria whose extensive exegesis, characterized especially by a strong espousal of the unity of Christ, led to the condemnation of Nestorius in 431.

Cyril of Jerusalem (c. 315-386; fl. c. 348). Bishop of Jerusalem after 350 and author of Catechetical Homilies.

Cyril of Scythopolis (b. c. 525; d. after 557). Palestinian monk and author of biographies of famous Palestinian monks. Because of him we have precise knowledge of monastic life in the fifth and sixth centuries and a description of the Origenist crisis and its suppression in the mid-sixth century.

Damasus of Rome (c. 304-384). Appointed pope in 366, following a conflict with Ursinus settled by Valentinian I. Damasus solidified the authority of Rome, attacked heresy using councils and strategic partnerships, promoted the cult of the martyrs, and commissioned Jerome's production of the Vulgate.

Diadochus of Photice (c. 400-474). Antimonophysite bishop of Epirus Vetus whose work *Discourse on the Ascension of Our Lord Jesus Christ* exerted influence in both the East and West through its Chalcedonian Christology. He is also the subject of the mystical *Vision of St. Diadochus Bishop of Photice in Epirus*.

Didache (c. 140). Of unknown authorship, this text intertwines Jewish ethics with Christian liturgical practice to form a whole discourse on the "way of life." It exerted an enormous amount of influence in the patristic period and was especially used in the training of catechumen.

Didascalia Apostolorum (Teaching of the Twelve Apostles and Holy Disciples of Our Savior) (early third century). A Church Order composed for a community of Christian converts from paganism in the northern part of Syria. This work forms the main source of the first six books of the *Apostolic Constitutions* and provides an important window to view what early liturgical practice may have looked like.

Didymus the Blind (c. 313-398). Alexandrian exegete who was much influenced by Origen and admired by Jerome.

Diodore of Tarsus (d. c. 394). Bishop of Tarsus and Antiochene theologian. He authored a great scope of exegetical, doctrinal and apologetic works, which come to us mostly in fragments because of his condemnation as the predecessor of Nestorianism. Diodore was a teacher of John Chrysostom and Theodore of Mopsuestia.

Dionysius of Alexandria (d. c. 264). Bishop

of Alexandria and student of Origen. Dionysius actively engaged in the theological disputes of his day, opposed Sabellianism, defended himself against accusations of tritheism and wrote the earliest extant Christian refutation of Epicureanism. His writings have survived mainly in extracts preserved by other early Christian authors.

Dorotheus of Gaza (fl. c. 525-540). Member of Abbot Seridos's monastery and later leader of a monastery where he wrote *Spiritual Instructions*. He also wrote a work on traditions of Palestinian monasticism.

Dracontius (fifth century). Latin poet and legal scholar. During imprisonment (484-c. 496) for angering the ruler of Carthage, Dracontius produced his *Satisfactio* and *Laudes Dei*, which explore, in particular, biblical themes of mercy.

Egeria (or Etheria, Aetheria) (fourth century). Possible name for the author of an *Itinerary* or pilgrimage diary that records valuable details on early liturgy, traditions, and church and monastic structure. Through letters to her religious community, likely in Gaul, Egeria describes a journey (c. 381-384) to Egypt, Palestine and Asia Minor.

Ennodius (474-521). Bishop of Pavia, a prolific writer of various genre, including letters, poems and biographies. He sought reconciliation in the schism between Rome and Acacius of Constantinople, and also upheld papal autonomy in the face of challenges from secular authorities.

Ephrem the Syrian (b. c. 306; fl. 363-373). Syrian writer of commentaries and devotional hymns which are sometimes regarded as the greatest specimens of Christian poetry prior to Dante.

Epiphanius of Salamis (c. 315-403). Bishop of Salamis in Cyprus, author of a refutation of eighty heresies (the *Panarion*) and instrumental in the condemnation of Origen.

Epiphanius the Latin. Author of the late fifth-century or early sixth-century Latin text *Interpretation of the Gospels*, with constant references to early patristic commentators. He was possibly a bishop of Benevento or Seville.

Epistle of Barnabas. See *Letter of Barnabas*.

Epistula Apostolorum (mid second century). A self-purported letter of doubtful authenticity from the apostles to the churches of the world that emphasizes the divinity and sonship of Jesus along with his childhood miracles.

Ethiopian Liturgy. Liturgical rite similar to the rite of Alexandria. Ethiopian liturgy has evolved since the introduction of Coptic liturgy to Ethiopia, traditionally by St. Frumentius in the fourth century. Significant Eastern and Jewish influences were added over time.

Eucherius of Lyons (fl. 420-449). Bishop of Lyons c. 435-449. Born into an aristocratic family, he, along with his wife and sons, joined the monastery at Lérins soon after its founding. He explained difficult Scripture passages by means of a threefold reading of the text: literal, moral and spiritual.

Eugippius (b. 460). Disciple of Severinus and third abbot of the monastic community at Castrum Lucullanum, which was made up of those fleeing from Noricum during the barbarian invasions.

Eunomius (d. 393). Bishop of Cyzicyus who was attacked by Basil and Gregory of Nyssa for maintaining that the Father and the Son were of different natures, one ingenerate, one generate.

Eusebius of Caesarea (c. 260/263-340). Bishop of Caesarea, partisan of the Emperor Constantine and first historian of the Christian church. He argued that the truth of the gospel had been foreshadowed in pagan writings but had to defend his own doctrine against suspicion of Arian sympathies.

Eusebius of Emesa (c. 300-c. 359). Bishop of Emesa from c. 339. A biblical exegete and writer on doctrinal subjects, he displays some semi-Arian tendencies of his mentor Eusebius of Caesarea.

Eusebius of Gaul, or Eusebius Gallicanus (c. fifth century). A conventional name for a collection of seventy-six sermons produced in Gaul and revised in the seventh century. It contains material from different patristic authors and focuses on ethical teaching in the context of the liturgical cycle (days of saints and other feasts).

Eusebius of Vercelli (fl. c. 360). Bishop of Vercelli who supported the trinitarian teaching of Nicaea (325) when it was being undermined by compromise in the West.

Eustathius of Antioch (fl. 325). First bishop of Beroea, then of Antioch, one of the leaders of the anti-Arians at the council of Nicaea. Later, he was banished from his seat and exiled to Thrace for his support of Nicene theology.

Euthymius (377-473). A native of Melitene and influential monk. He was educated by Bishop Otreius of Melitene, who ordained him priest and placed him in charge of all the monasteries in his diocese. When the Council of Chalcedon (451) condemned the errors of Eutyches, it was greatly due to the authority of Euthymius that most of the Eastern recluses accepted its decrees. The empress Eudoxia returned to Chalcedonian orthodoxy through his efforts.

Evagrius of Pontus (c. 345-399). Disciple and teacher of ascetic life who astutely absorbed and creatively transmitted the spirituality of Egyptian and Palestinian monasticism of the late fourth century. Although Origenist elements of his writings were formally condemned by the Fifth Ecumenical Council (Constantinople II, A.D. 553), his literary corpus continued to influence the tradition of the church.

Eznik of Kolb (early fifth century). A disciple of Mesrob who translated Greek Scriptures into Armenian, so as to become the model of the classical Armenian language. As bishop, he participated in the synod of Astisat (449).

Facundus of Hermiane (fl. 546-568). African bishop who opposed Emperor Justinian's postmortem condemnation of Theodore of Mopsuestia, Theodoret of Cyr and Ibas of Ebessa at the fifth ecumenical council. His written defense, known as "To Justinian" or "In Defense of the Three Chapters," avers that ancient theologians should not be blamed for errors that became obvious only upon later theological reflection. He continued in the tradition of Chalcedon, although his Christology was supplemented, according to Justinian's decisions, by the theopaschite formula *Unus ex Trinitate passus est* ("Only one of the three suffered").

Fastidius (c. fourth-fifth centuries). British author of *On the Christian Life*. He is believed to have written some works attributed to Pelagius.

Faustinus (fl. 380). A priest in Rome and supporter of Lucifer and author of a treatise on the Trinity.

Faustus of Riez (c. 400-490). A prestigious British monk at Lérins; abbot, then bishop of Riez from 457 to his death. His works include *On the Holy Spirit*, in which he argued against the Macedonians for the divinity of the Holy Spirit, and *On Grace*, in which he argued for a position on salvation that lay between more categorical views of free will and predestination. Various letters and (pseudonymous) sermons are extant.

The Festal Menaion. Orthodox liturgical text containing the variable parts of the service, including hymns, for fixed days of celebration of the life of Jesus and Mary.

Filastrius (fl. 380). Bishop of Brescia and author of a compilation against all heresies.

Firmicus Maternus (fourth century). An anti-Pagan apologist. Before his conversion to Christianity he wrote a work on astrology (334-337). After his conversion, however, he criticized paganism in *On the Errors of the Profane Religion*.

Firmilian of Caesarea (fl. c. 230-c. 268). Influential bishop of Caesarea in Cappadocia. He studied under Origen and became involved in the controversies over the return of the lapsed into the church and rebaptism, having

written to Cyprian concerning the latter issue.
First Creed of the Council of Antioch (341). Eastern bishops' response to charges of Arianism from Western leaders. At a gathering that marked the dedication of the Golden Church at Antioch, the bishops put forth four creeds as alternatives to the Nicene formula.
Flavian of Chalon-sur-Saône (d. end of sixth century). Bishop of Chalon-sur-Saône in Burgundy, France. His hymn Verses on the Mandate in the Lord's Supper was recited in a number of the French monasteries after the washing of the feet on Maundy Thursday.
Fructuosus of Braga (d. c. 665). Son of a Gothic general and member of a noble military family. He became a monk at an early age, then abbot- bishop of Dumium before 650 and metropolitan of Braga in 656. He was influential in setting up monastic communities in Lusitania, Asturia, Galicia and the island of Gades.
Fulgentius of Ruspe (c. 467-532). Bishop of Ruspe and author of many orthodox sermons and tracts under the influence of Augustine.
Gaudentius of Brescia (fl. 395). Successor of Filastrius as bishop of Brescia and author of twenty-one Eucharistic sermons.
Gennadius of Constantinople (d. 471). Patriarch of Constantinople, author of numerous commentaries and an opponent of the Christology of Cyril of Alexandria.
Germanus of Constantinople (c. 640-c. 733). Patriarch of Constantinople (715-730). He wrote the *Historia Ecclesiastica*, which served for centuries as the explanation of the divine liturgy of the Byzantine Church, written during the outbreak of the great iconoclastic controversies in Eastern Christianity. One of the leading theologians of the Sixth Ecumenical Council (680-681), which condemned monothelitism.
Gerontius (c. 395-c. 480). Palestinian monk, later archimandrite of the cenobites of Palestine. He led the resistance to the council of Chalcedon.
Gildas (sixth century). British monk and historian. His major work is *De excidio Britanniae*, a history focused on the pagan invasion of Britain and the vices of contemporary Britons. Fragments of letters and a Penitential are also attributed to Gildas.
Gnostics. Name now given generally to followers of Basilides, Marcion, Valentinus, Mani and others. The characteristic belief is that matter is a prison made for the spirit by an evil or ignorant creator, and that redemption depends on fate, not on free will.
Gospel of Peter (late second century). An early apocryphal writing with Docetic aspects that likely originated in Syria. It was referred to by Serapion (c. 190) and Origen, though only one section survives in an eighth-century manuscript.
Gospel of Philip (second or third century). A Gnostic collection of sayings, including several attributed to Jesus, on the process of salvation. This Coptic document, discovered at Nag Hammadi, is probably unconnected with the *Gospel of Philip* cited by Epiphanius.
Gospel of Truth (second century). One of the Coptic texts found at Nag Hammadi. This Gnostic treatise discusses the nature, ministry and death of Jesus, and includes several unique speculations. Some scholars have connected it with the second-century Gnostic Valentinus. Irenaeus referred to it disparagingly as the so-called *Gospel of Truth*, which he found to be in conflict with the four canonical Gospels.
Gregory of Elvira (fl. 359-385). Bishop of Elvira who wrote allegorical treatises in the style of Origen and defended the Nicene faith against the Arians.
Gregory of Narek (950-1003). Armenian monk, philosopher, mystic and poet who lived in the monasteries of Narek (greater Armenia, now Turkey). He wrote a mystical interpretation of the Song of Songs and the Armenian Prayer book and liturgy. The latter, which he authored in his mature years, he referred to as his "last testament."
Gregory of Nazianzus (b. 329/330; fl.

372-389). Cappadocian father, bishop of Constantinople, friend of Basil the Great and Gregory of Nyssa, and author of theological orations, sermons and poetry.

Gregory of Nyssa (c. 335-394). Bishop of Nyssa and brother of Basil the Great. A Cappadocian father and author of catechetical orations, he was a philosophical theologian of great originality.

Gregory of Tours (c. 538-594). Bishop of Tours elected in 573. Gregory produced hagiographical and historical works. His *Historia Francorum*, a fragmentary yet valuable source, begins with creation and highlights sixth-century Gaul.

Gregory Thaumaturgus (fl. c. 248-264). Bishop of Neocaesarea and a disciple of Origen. There are at least five legendary *Lives* that recount the events and miracles which led to his being called "the wonder worker." His most important work was the *Address of Thanks to Origen*, which is a rhetorically structured panegyric to Origen and an outline of his teaching.

Gregory the Great (c. 540-604). Pope from 590, the fourth and last of the Latin "Doctors of the Church." He was a prolific author and a powerful unifying force within the Latin Church, initiating the liturgical reform that brought about the Gregorian Sacramentary and Gregorian chant.

Hegemonius (fl. early fourth century). Author of *Acta disputationis*, traditionally believed to have been written in fourth-century Syria. This work is a fictitious debate between a Mesopotamian bishop and a Manichaean.

Hegesippus (second century). An author, possibly of Jewish descent, who served as a source for Eusebius and is best known for five books of anti-Gnostic polemic.

Heracleon (fl. c. 145-180). Gnostic teacher and disciple of Valentinus. His commentary on John, which was perhaps the first commentary to exist on this or any Gospel, was so popular that Ambrose commissioned Origen to write his own commentary in response, providing a more orthodox approach to the Fourth Gospel.

Hesychius of Jerusalem (fl. 412-450). Presbyter and exegete, thought to have commented on the whole of Scripture.

Hilary of Arles (c. 401-449). Archbishop of Arles and leader of the Semi-Pelagian party. Hilary incurred the wrath of Pope Leo I when he removed a bishop from his see and appointed a new bishop. Leo demoted Arles from a metropolitan see to a bishopric to assert papal power over the church in Gaul.

Hilary of Poitiers (c. 315-367). Bishop of Poitiers and called the "Athanasius of the West" because of his defense (against the Arians) of the common nature of Father and Son.

Hippolytus (fl. 222-245). Recent scholarship places Hippolytus in a Palestinian context, personally familiar with Origen. Though he is known chiefly for *The Refutation of All Heresies*, he was primarily a commentator on Scripture (especially the Old Testament) employing typological exegesis.

Horsiesi (c. 305-c. 390). Pachomius's second successor, after Petronius, as a leader of cenobitic monasticism in Southern Egypt.

Hyperichius (c. fifth century). A monk known only from his *Exhortation to the Monks*, 160 statements in Greek on monastic virtues, and the collection *Sayings of the Fathers*, which quotes eight of these exhortations.

Ignatius of Antioch (c. 35-107/112). Bishop of Antioch who wrote several letters to local churches while being taken from Antioch to Rome to be martyred. In the letters, which warn against heresy, he stresses orthodox Christology, the centrality of the Eucharist and unique role of the bishop in preserving the unity of the church.

Irenaeus of Lyons (c. 135-c. 202). Bishop of Lyons who published the most famous and influential refutation of Gnostic thought.

Isaac of Nineveh (d. c. 700). Also known as Isaac the Syrian or Isaac Syrus, this monastic writer served for a short while as bishop of Nineveh before retiring to live a secluded monastic life. His writings on ascetic subjects survive in the form of numerous homilies.

Isaiah of Scete (late fourth century). Author of ascetical texts, collected after his death under the title of the *Ascetic Discourses*. This work was influential in the development of Eastern Christian asceticism and spirituality.

Isho'dad of Merv (fl. c. 850). Nestorian bishop of Hedatta. He wrote commentaries on parts of the Old Testament and all of the New Testament, frequently quoting Syriac fathers.

Isidore of Pelusium (d. c. 440). Egyptian ascetic. Born to a prominent Egyptian family in Alexandria, he left behind his wealth to live on a mountain near Pelusium, and was often consulted by church and civic leaders alike, such as Cyril of Alexandria and Theodosius II, for his wisdom and his counsel of moderation. Many of his letters also have come down to us, some of which provide keen insight into the interpretation of Scripture.

Isidore of Seville (c. 560-636). Youngest of a family of monks and clerics, including sister Florentina and brothers Leander and Fulgentius. He was an erudite author of comprehensive scale in matters both religious and sacred, including his encyclopedic *Etymologies*.

Jacob of Nisibis (d. 338). Bishop of Nisibis. He was present at the council of Nicaea in 325 and took an active part in the opposition to Arius.

Jacob of Sarug (c. 450-c. 520). Syriac ecclesiastical writer. Jacob received his education at Edessa. At the end of his life he was ordained bishop of Sarug. His principal writing was a long series of metrical homilies, earning him the title "The Flute of the Holy Spirit."

Jerome (c. 347-420). Gifted exegete and exponent of a classical Latin style, now best known as the translator of the Latin Vulgate. He defended the perpetual virginity of Mary, attacked Origen and Pelagius and supported extreme ascetic practices.

John Chrysostom (344/354-407; fl. 386-407). Bishop of Constantinople who was noted for his orthodoxy, his eloquence and his attacks on Christian laxity in high places.

John of Antioch (d. 441/42). Bishop of Antioch, commencing in 428. He received his education together with Nestorius and Theodore of Mopsuestia in a monastery near Antioch. A supporter of Nestorius, he condemned Cyril of Alexandria, but later reached a compromise with him.

John of Apamea (fifth century). Syriac author of the early church who wrote on various aspects of the spiritual life, also known as John the Solitary. Some of his writings are in the form of dialogues. Other writings include letters, a treatise on baptism, and shorter works on prayer and silence.

John of Carpathus (c. seventh/eighth century). Perhaps John the bishop from the island of Carpathus, situated between Crete and Rhodes, who attended the Synod of 680/81. He wrote two "centuries" (a literary genre in Eastern spirituality consisting of 100 short sections, or chapters). These were entitled *Chapters of Encouragement to the Monks of India* and *Chapters on Theology and Knowledge* which are included in the *Philokalia*.

John of Damascus (c. 650-750). Arab monastic and theologian whose writings enjoyed great influence in both the Eastern and Western Churches. His most influential writing was the *Orthodox Faith*.

John the Elder (c. eighth century). A Syriac author also known as John of Dalyatha or John Saba ("the elder") who belonged to monastic circles of the Church of the East and lived in the region of Mount Qardu (northern Iraq). His most important writings are twenty-two homilies and a collection of fifty-one short letters in which he describes the mystical life as an anticipatory experience of the resurrection life, the fruit of the sacraments of baptism and the Eucharist.

John the Monk. Traditional name found in *The Festal Menaion*, believed to refer to John

of Damascus. See John of Damascus.
Joseph of Thebes (fourth century). One of the desert fathers of Scetis, also known as Abba Joseph, who taught the most important virtue of a monk was to remain in complete submission to a spiritual father in total renunciation of one's own will.

Joseph's Bible Notes (Hypomnestikon) (fourth or fifth century). A pastiche of biblical and historical questions drawn from various writers, including the Jewish historian, Josephus. It was believed to have been written by Josephus Christianus, derived from the brief poem appended at the end of the book, but the author ultimately is unknown. It evidences an Alexandrian Christology.

Josephus, Flavius (c. 37-c. 101). Jewish historian from a distinguished priestly family. Acquainted with the Essenes and Sadducees, he himself became a Pharisee. He joined the great Jewish revolt that broke out in 66 and was chosen by the Sanhedrin at Jerusalem to be commander-in-chief in Galilee. Showing great shrewdness to ingratiate himself with Vespasian by foretelling his elevation and that of his son Titus to the imperial dignity, Josephus was restored his liberty after 69 when Vespasian became emperor.

Julian of Eclanum (c. 385-450). Bishop of Eclanum in 416/417 who was removed from office and exiled in 419 for not officially opposing Pelagianism. In exile, he was accepted by Theodore of Mopsuestia, whose Antiochene exegetical style he followed. Although he was never able to regain his ecclesiastical position, Julian taught in Sicily until his death. His works include commentaries on Job and parts of the Minor Prophets, a translation of Theodore of Mopsuestia's commentary on the Psalms, and various letters. Sympathetic to Pelagius, Julian applied his intellectual acumen and rhetorical training to argue against Augustine on matters such as free will, desire and the locus of evil.

Julian the Arian (c. fourth century). Antiochene, Arian author of *Commentary on Job*, and probably a follower of Aetius and Eunomius. The 85 *Apostolic Canons*, once part of the *Apostolic Constitutions*, and the Pseudo-Ignatian writings are also attributed to him.

Justin Martyr (c. 100/110-165; fl. c. 148-161). Palestinian philosopher who was converted to Christianity, "the only sure and worthy philosophy." He traveled to Rome where he wrote several apologies against both pagans and Jews, combining Greek philosophy and Christian theology; he was eventually martyred.

Justinian the Emperor (482-565). Emperor of Byzantium, 527-565. As the second member of the Justinian Dynasty, he instituted an ambitious, though failed, restoration of the Byzantine Empire. He sought theological unity through a politicized Christianity that persecuted perceived heretics and apostates along with Jews and pagans. Many of his writings are extant, including twenty-one letters and four dogmatic works.

Lactantius (c. 260-c. 330). Christian apologist removed from his post as teacher of rhetoric at Nicomedia upon his conversion to Christianity. He was tutor to the son of Constantine and author of *The Divine Institutes*.

Leander (c. 545-c. 600). Latin ecclesiastical writer, of whose works only two survive. He was instrumental in spreading Christianity among the Visigoths, gaining significant historical influence in Spain in his time.

Leo the Great (regn. 440-461). Bishop of Rome whose *Tome to Flavian* helped to strike a balance between Nestorian and Cyrilline positions at the Council of Chalcedon in 451.

Letter of Barnabas (c. 130). An allegorical and typological interpretation of the Old Testament with a decidedly anti-Jewish tone. It was included with other New Testament works as a "Catholic epistle" at least until Eusebius of Caesarea (c. 260/263-340) questioned its authenticity.

Letter to Diognetus (c. third century). A refutation of paganism and an exposition of the Christian life and faith. The author of this letter is unknown, and the exact identity of its recipient, Diognetus, continues to elude patristic scholars.

Liturgy of St. Basil (fourth century and onward). The liturgical collections of the Byzantine liturgy containing an anaphora attributed to Basil the Great. The liturgy has evolved considerably over the centuries.

Liturgy of St. James. A liturgy adopted throughout the East, including by the Syrian Orthodox Church. Traditionally attributed to St. James the bishop of Jerusalem, it survives in both Greek and Syriac versions.

Liturgy of St. Mark (fourth century). Traditional Eucharistic liturgy of the Alexandrian Church. First adopted by the Egyptian Melchites, its extant manuscripts are based on an early Egyptian text, and forms of the rite are still used by the Coptic and Ethiopian Churches.

Liturgy of the Blessed Apostles (first or second century). One of the earliest Christian liturgies. Attributed to Addai (Addaeus) and Mari (Maris), Christian missionaries to Edessa and surrounding areas of Syria, the liturgy was also celebrated in Mesopotamia and Persia. It was likely used in the Syrian church and was also taken up later by the Nestorians.

Liturgy of the Coptic Jacobites (sixth century). Liturgy of the West Syrian Church named after the monophysite Jacob Baradaeus (d. 578) who used this rite, in the Coptic language, to solidify the hierarchy of monophysitism. Many of the anaphorae can be traced back in their basic structure the church of Jerusalem in apostolic times.

Liturgy of the Hours (third century). Early liturgy for prayers throughout the day. The church community, especially monastics, offered prayer at set times of the day: morning prayer, prayers of terce (third hour), sext (sixth hour) and none (ninth hour) that correspond to the hours of Christ's crucifixion and death. Evening prayer was associated with the nighttime rest of the world itself. More elaborate and extended divisions of the hours followed that included Lauds, Prime, Terce, Sext, None, Vespers and Compline, reflective of a theology of time that celebrates the rhythm of life as God's people communicate with him.

Lucifer (d. 370/371). Bishop of Cagliari and vigorous supporter of Athanasius and the Nicene Creed. In conflict with the emperor Constantius, he was banished to Palestine and later to Thebaid (Egypt).

Luculentius (fifth century). Unknown author of a group of short commentaries on the New Testament, especially Pauline passages. His exegesis is mainly literal and relies mostly on earlier authors such as Jerome and Augustine. The content of his writing may place it in the fifth century.

Macarius of Egypt (c. 300-c. 390). One of the Desert Fathers. Accused of supporting Athanasius, Macarius was exiled c. 374 to an island in the Nile by Lucius, the Arian successor of Athanasius. Macarius continued his teaching of monastic theology at Wadi Natrun.

Macrina the Younger (c. 327-379). The elder sister of Basil the Great and Gregory of Nyssa, she is known as "the Younger" to distinguish her from her paternal grandmother. She had a powerful influence on her younger brothers, especially on Gregory, who called her his teacher and relates her teaching in *On the Soul and the Resurrection*.

Manichaeans. A religious movement that originated circa 241 in Persia under the leadership of Mani but was apparently of complex Christian origin. It is said to have denied free will and the universal sovereignty of God, teaching that kingdoms of light and darkness are coeternal and that the redeemed are particles of a spiritual man of light held captive in the darkness of matter (see Gnostics).

Marcellus of Ancyra (d. c. 375). Wrote a refutation of Arianism. Later, he was accused of Sabellianism, especially by Eusebius of Caesarea. While the Western church declared him orthodox, the Eastern church excommunicated him. Some scholars have attributed to him certain works of Athanasius.

Marcion (fl. 144). Heretic of the mid second century who rejected the Old Testament and much of the New Testament, claiming that the Father of Jesus Christ was other than the Old Testament God (see Gnostics).

Marius Victorinus (b. c. 280/285; fl. c. 355-363). Grammarian of African origin who taught rhetoric at Rome and translated works of Platonists. After his conversion (c. 355), he wrote works against the Arians and commentaries on Paul's letters.

Mark the Hermit (c. sixth century). Monk who lived near Tarsus and produced works on ascetic practices as well as christological issues.

Martin of Braga (fl. c. 568-579). Anti-Arian metropolitan of Braga on the Iberian peninsula. He was highly educated and presided over the provincial council of Braga in 572.

Martyrdom of Polycarp (c. 160). A letter written shortly after the death of the eighty-six-year-old bishop of Smyrna which provides, in sometimes gruesome detail, the earliest account Christian martyrdom outside of the New Testament.

Martyrius. *See* Sahdona.

Maximinus (the Arian) (b. c. 360-65). Bishop of an Arian community, perhaps in Illyricum. Of Roman descent, he debated publicly with Augustine at Hippo (427 or 428), ardently defending Arian doctrine. Besides the polemical works he wrote against the orthodox, such as his *Against the Heretics, Jews and Pagans*, he also wrote fifteen sermons that are considered much less polemical, having been previously attributed to Maximus of Turin. He is also known for his twenty-four *Explanations of Chapters of the Gospels*.

Maximus of Turin (d. 408/423). Bishop of Turin. Over one hundred of his sermons survive on Christian festivals, saints and martyrs.

Maximus the Confessor (c. 580-662). Palestinian-born theologian and ascetic writer. Fleeing the Arab invasion of Jerusalem in 614, he took refuge in Constantinople and later Africa. He died near the Black Sea after imprisonment and severe suffering, having his tongue cut off and his right hand mutilated. He taught total preference for God and detachment from all things.

Melito of Sardis (d. c. 190). Bishop of Sardis. According to Polycrates, he may have been Jewish by birth. Among his numerous works is a liturgical document known as *On Pascha* (ca. 160-177). As a Quartodeciman, and one involved intimately involved in that controversy, Melito celebrated Pascha on the fourteenth of Nisan in line with the custom handed down from Judaism.

Methodius of Olympus (d. 311). Bishop of Olympus who celebrated virginity in a Symposium partly modeled on Plato's dialogue of that name.

Minucius Felix (second or third century). Christian apologist who was an advocate in Rome. His *Octavius* agrees at numerous points with the *Apologeticum of Tertullian*. His birthplace is believed to be in Africa.

Montanist Oracles. Montanism was an apocalyptic and strictly ascetic movement begun in the latter half of the second century by a certain Montanus in Phrygia, who, along with certain of his followers, uttered oracles they claimed were inspired by the Holy Spirit. Little of the authentic oracles remains and most of what is known of Montanism comes from the authors who wrote against the movement. Montanism was formally condemned as a heresy before by Asiatic synods.

Muratorian Fragment (second century). Earliest known list of New Testament books, preserved in an eighth-century manuscript. The document is missing its first lines yet includes all but five books of the final canon. It also discusses various contested writings, several of which are clearly rejected.

Nemesius of Emesa (fl. late fourth century). Bishop of Emesa in Syria whose most important work, *Of the Nature of Man*, draws on several theological and philosophical sources and is the first exposition of a Christian anthropology.

Nestorius (c. 381-c. 451). Patriarch of Constantinople (428-431) who founded the heresy which says that there are two persons, divine and human, rather than one person truly united in the incarnate Christ. He resisted the teaching of theotokos, causing Nestorian churches to separate from Constantinople.

Nicetas of Remesiana (fl. second half of fourth century). Bishop of Remesiana in Serbia, whose works affirm the consubstantiality of the Son and the deity of the Holy Spirit.

Nilus of Ancyra (d. c. 430). Prolific ascetic writer and disciple of John Chrysostom. Sometimes erroneously known as Nilus of Sinai, he was a native of Ancyra and studied at Constantinople.

Novatian of Rome (fl. 235-258). Roman theologian, otherwise orthodox, who formed a schismatic church after failing to become pope. His treatise on the Trinity states the classic Western doctrine.

Odes of Solomon (early second century). A collection of forty-two pseudo-Solomonic poems containing commentary on the liturgy of a Judeo-Christian community in Syria. The poems are permeated with soteriological concerns, though they never mention the name Jesus.

Oecumenius (sixth century). Called the Rhetor or the Philosopher, Oecumenius wrote the earliest extant Greek commentary on Revelation. Scholia by Oecumenius on some of John Chrysostom's commentaries on the Pauline Epistles are still extant.

Olympiodorus (early sixth century). Exegete and deacon of Alexandria, known for his commentaries that come to us mostly in catenae.

Optatus (fourth century). Bishop of Milevis in North Africa. He wrote a treatise against Donatism. These six books emphasize the uniqueness of the Catholic Church and include a list of documents on the Donatist controversy.

Origen of Alexandria (b. 185; fl. c. 200-254). Influential exegete and systematic theologian. He was condemned (perhaps unfairly) for maintaining the preexistence of souls while purportedly denying the resurrection of the body. His extensive works of exegesis focus on the spiritual meaning of the text.

Pachomius (c. 292-347). Founder of cenobitic monasticism. A gifted group leader and author of a set of rules, he was defended after his death by Athanasius of Alexandria.

Pacian of Barcelona (c. fourth century). Bishop of Barcelona whose writings polemicize against popular pagan festivals as well as Novatian schismatics.

Palladius of Helenopolis (c. 363/364-c. 431). Bishop of Helenopolis in Bithynia (400-417) and then Aspuna in Galatia. A disciple of Evagrius of Pontus and admirer of Origen, Palladius became a zealous adherent of John Chrysostom and shared his troubles in 403. His *Lausaic History* is the leading source for the history of early monasticism, stressing the spiritual value of the life of the desert.

Papias of Hierapolis (c. early second century). Bishop of Hierapolis in Phrygia who may have known the apostle John. Through his writings, which are extant only in fragments preserved in Eusebius's *Ecclesiastical History*, Papias influenced later theologians including Irenaeus, Hippolytus and Victorinus, and provided an important witness to traditions about the origins of the Gospels.

Paschasius of Dumium (c. 515-c. 580). Translator of sentences of the Desert Fathers from Greek into Latin while a monk in Dumium.

Paterius (c. sixth-seventh century). Disciple of Gregory the Great who is primarily responsible for the transmission of Gregory's works to many later medieval authors.

Patrick (d. c. 492). Saint known as the apostle to Ireland. Born in Britain and later kidnapped at the age of sixteen by pirates, Patrick was taken to Ireland where he worked as a shepherd. He later returned to Britain and undertook training in Gaul and possibly also Lerins for the apostolate. According to tradition, he was consecrated a bishop and returned to northern Ireland in 432 where he preached the gospel and established his see at Armagh, which was extended to the continent via Irish missionaries. His two works that survive are *Epistle to the Soldier Coroticus* and *Confession*, written toward the end of his life. His feast day is March 17.

Paulinus of Milan (late 4th-early 5th century). Personal secretary and biographer of Ambrose of Milan. He took part in the Pelagian controversy.

Paulinus of Nola (355-431). Roman senator and distinguished Latin poet whose frequent encounters with Ambrose of Milan (c. 333-397) led to his eventual conversion and baptism in 389. He eventually renounced his wealth and influential position and took up his pen to write poetry in service of Christ. He also wrote many letters to, among others, Augustine, Jerome and Rufinus.

Paulus Orosius (b. c. 380). An outspoken critic of Pelagius, mentored by Augustine. His *Seven Books of History Against the Pagans* was perhaps the first history of Christianity.

Pelagius (c. 354-c. 420). Contemporary of Augustine whose followers were condemned in 418 and 431 for maintaining that even before Christ there were people who lived wholly without sin and that salvation depended on free will.

Peter Chrysologus (c. 380-450). Latin archbishop of Ravenna whose teachings included arguments for adherence in matters of faith to the Roman see, and the relationship between grace and Christian living.

Peter of Alexandria (d. c. 311). Bishop of Alexandria. He marked (and very probably initiated) the reaction at Alexandria against extreme doctrines of Origen. During the persecution of Christians in Alexandria, Peter was arrested and beheaded by Roman officials. Eusebius of Caesarea described him as "a model bishop, remarkable for his virtuous life and his ardent study of the Scriptures."

Philip the Priest (d. 455/56) Acknowledged by Gennadius as a disciple of Jerome. In his *Commentary on the Book of Job*, Philip utilizes Jerome's Vulgate, providing an important witness to the transmission of that translation. A few of his letters are extant.

Philo of Alexandria (c. 20 B.C.-c. A.D. 50). Jewish-born exegete who greatly influenced Christian patristic interpretation of the Old Testament. Born to a rich family in Alexandria, Philo was a contemporary of Jesus and lived an ascetic and contemplative life that makes some believe he was a rabbi. His interpretation of Scripture based the spiritual sense on the literal. Although influenced by Hellenism, Philo's theology remains thoroughly Jewish.

Philoxenus of Mabbug (c. 440-523). Bishop of Mabbug (Hierapolis) and a leading thinker in the early Syrian Orthodox Church. His extensive writings in Syriac include a set of thirteen *Discourses on the Christian Life*, several works on the incarnation and a number of exegetical works.

Phoebadius of Agen (d. c. 395). Bishop of Agen whose *Contra arianos* attacked the 357 pro-Arian formula of Sirmium. Phoebadius was the last leader induced to sign the formula of Ariminum in 359, a compromise widely viewed as an Arian triumph.

Photius (c. 820-891). An important Byzantine churchman and university professor of philosophy, mathematics and theology. He was twice the patriarch of Constantinople. First he succeeded Ignatius in 858, but was deposed in 863 when Ignatius was reinstated. Again he followed Ignatius in 878 and remained the patriarch until 886, at which time he was removed by Leo VI. His most important theological work is *Address on the Mystagogy of the Holy Spirit*, in which he articulates his opposition to the Western filioque, i.e., the procession of the Holy Spirit from the Father and the Son. He is also known for his Amphilochia and Library (Bibliotheca).

Poemen (c. fifth century). One-seventh of the sayings in the *Sayings of the Desert Fathers* are attributed to Poemen, which is Greek for shepherd. Poemen was a common title among early Egyptian desert ascetics, and it is unknown whether all of the sayings come from one person.

Polycarp of Smyrna (c. 69-155). Bishop of Smyrna who vigorously fought heretics such as the Marcionites and Valentinians. He was the leading Christian figure in Roman Asia in the middle of the second century.

Possidius (late fourth-fifth century). A member of Augustine's monastic community at Hippo from 391, then bishop of Calama in Numidia sometime soon after 397. He fled back to Hippo when Vandals invaded Calama in 428 and cared for Augustine during his final illness. Returning to Calama after the death of Augustine (430), he was expelled by Genseric, Arian king of the Vandals, in 437. Nothing more is known of him after this date. Sometime between 432 and 437 he wrote *Vita Augustini*, to which he added *Indiculus*, a list of Augustine's books, sermons and letters.

Potamius of Lisbon (fl. c. 350-360). Bishop of Lisbon who joined the Arian party in 357, but later returned to the Catholic faith (c. 359?). His works from both periods are concerned with the larger Trinitarian debates of his time.

Primasius (fl. 550-560). Bishop of Hadrumetum in North Africa (modern Tunisia) and one of the few Africans to support the condemnation of the Three Chapters. Drawing on Augustine and Tyconius, he wrote a commentary on the Apocalypse, which in allegorizing fashion views the work as referring to the history of the church.

Proclus of Constantinople (c. 390-446). Patriarch of Constantinople (434-446). His patriarchate dealt with the Nestorian controversy, rebutting, in his *Tome to the Armenian Bishops*, Theodore of Mopsuestia's Christology where Theodore was thought to have overly separated the two natures of Christ. Proclus stressed the unity of Christ in his formula "One of the Trinity suffered," which was later taken up and spread by the Scythian monks of the sixth century, resulting in the theopaschite controversy. Proclus was known as a gifted preacher and church politician, extending and expanding Constantinople's influence while avoiding conflict with Antioch, Rome and Alexandria.

Procopius of Gaza (c. 465-c. 530). A Christian exegete educated in Alexandria. He wrote numerous theological works and commentaries on Scripture (particularly the Hebrew Bible), the latter marked by the allegorical exegesis for which the Alexandrian school was known.

Prosper of Aquitaine (c. 390-c. 463). Probably a lay monk and supporter of the theology of Augustine on grace and predestination. He collaborated closely with Pope Leo I in his doctrinal statements.

Prudentius (c. 348-c. 410). Latin poet and hymn writer who devoted his later life to Christian writing. He wrote didactic poems on the theology of the incarnation, against the heretic Marcion and against the resurgence of paganism.

Pseudo-Clementines (third-fourth century). A series of apocryphal writings pertaining to a conjured life of Clement of Rome. Written in a form of popular legend, the stories from Clement's life, including his opposition to Simon Magus, illustrate and promote articles of Christian teaching. It is likely that the corpus is a derivative of a number of Gnostic and Judeo-Christian writings. Dating the corpus is a complicated issue.

Pseudo-Dionysius the Areopagite (fl. c. 500). Author who assumed the name of Dionysius the Areopagite mentioned in Acts 17:34, and who composed the works known as the *Corpus Areopagiticum* (or *Dionysiacum*). These writings were the foundation of the apophatic school of mysticism in their denial that anything can be truly predicated of God.

Pseudo-Macarius (fl. c. 390). An anonymous

writer and ascetic (from Mesopotamia?) active in Antioch whose badly edited works were attributed to Macarius of Egypt. He had keen insight into human nature, prayer and the inner life. His work includes some one hundred discourses and homilies.

Quodvultdeus (fl. 430). Carthaginian bishop and friend of Augustine who endeavored to show at length how the New Testament fulfilled the Old Testament.

Rabanus (Hrabanus) Maurus (c. 780-856). Frankish monk, theologian and teacher, student of Alcuin of York, then Abbot of Fulda from 822 to 842 and Archbishop of Mainz from 848 until his death in 856. The author of poetry, homilies, treatises on education, grammar, and doctrine, and an encyclopedia titled On the Nature of Things, he also wrote commentaries on Scripture, including the books of Kings and Esther. Though he is technically an early medieval writer, his works are included as they reflect earlier thought.

Riddles in the Apocalypse (eighth century). Commentary on Revelation of unknown authorship. *De Enigmatibus ex Apocalypsi* in Latin, the commentary explores the enigmatic symbolism of the book. It is contained in the one volume commentary known as the *Irish Reference Bible*, or *Das Bibelwerk* which dates from the late eighth century (see also CCL 7:231-95).

Romanus Melodus (fl. c. 536-556). Born as a Jew in Emesa not far from Beirut where after his baptism later he later became deacon of the Church of the Resurrection. He later moved to Constantinople and may have seen the destruction of the Hagia Sophia and its rebuilding during the time he flourished there. As many as eighty metrical sermons (*kontakia*, sg. *kontakion*) that utilize dialogical poetry have come down to us under his name. These sermons were sung rather than preached during the liturgy, and frequently provide theological insights and Scriptural connections often unique to Romanus. His Christology, closely associated with Justinian, reflects the struggles against the Monophysites of his day.

Rufinus of Aquileia (c. 345-411). Orthodox Christian thinker and historian who nonetheless translated and preserved the works of Origen, and defended him against the strictures of Jerome and Epiphanius. He lived the ascetic life in Rome, Egypt and Jerusalem (the Mount of Olives).

Sabellius (fl. 200). Allegedly the author of the heresy which maintains that the Father and Son are a single person. The patripassian variant of this heresy states that the Father suffered on the cross.

Sahdona (fl. 635-640). Known in Greek as Martyrius, this Syriac author was bishop of Beth Garmai. He studied in Nisibis and was exiled for his christological ideas. His most important work is the deeply scriptural *Book of Perfection* which ranks as one of the masterpieces of Syriac monastic literature.

Salvian the Presbyter of Marseilles (c. 400-c. 480). An important author for the history of his own time. He saw the fall of Roman civilization to the barbarians as a consequence of the reprehensible conduct of Roman Christians. In *The Governance of God* he developed the theme of divine providence.

Second Letter of Clement (c. 150). The so called *Second Letter of Clement* is an early Christian sermon probably written by a Corinthian author, though some scholars have assigned it to a Roman or Alexandrian author.

Sedulius, Coelius (fl. 425-450). Author of the *Paschale carmen*, a poem in five books, which focuses on the miraculous character of Christ's suffering. Sedulius learned philosophy in Italy and was later converted to Christianity by the presbyter Macedonius. He has at times been confused with the poet Sedulius Scotus (ninth century). He is also known for the similarly themed *Paschale opus*, among other works.

Seventh Council of Carthage Under Cyprian (256). One of many Carthaginian councils convened in response to the controversy surrounding rebaptisms. All bishops present, including Cyprian, deemed that baptism administered by heretics was invalid and necessitated rebaptism, a position later revised by Augustine.

Severian of Gabala (fl. c. 400). A contemporary of John Chrysostom, he was a highly regarded preacher in Constantinople, particularly at the imperial court, and ultimately sided with Chrysostom's accusers. He wrote homilies on Genesis.

Severus of Antioch (fl. 488-538). A monophysite theologian, consecrated bishop of Antioch in 522. Born in Pisidia, he studied in Alexandria and Beirut, taught in Constantinople and was exiled to Egypt.

Shenoute (c. 350-466). Abbot of Athribis in Egypt. His large monastic community was known for very strict rules. He accompanied Cyril of Alexandria to the Council of Ephesus in 431, where he played an important role in deposing Nestorius. He knew Greek but wrote in Coptic, and his literary activity includes homilies, catecheses on monastic subjects, letters, and a couple of theological treatises.

Shepherd of Hermas (second century). Divided into five *Visions*, twelve *Mandates* and ten *Similitudes*, this Christian apocalypse was written by a former slave and named for the form of the second angel said to have granted him his visions. This work was highly esteemed for its moral value and was used as a textbook for catechumens in the early church.

Sibylline Oracles (second century B.C.-second century A.D.) An apocryphal collection of Greek prophecies. Spanning the second century B.C. to the second century A.D., the collection is the product of Christian redaction of Jewish adaptations and expansions of pagan Greek oracles.

Socrates (Scholasticus) (c. 380-450). Greek historian and lawyer from Constantinople. His *Ecclesiastical History*, meant to continue the work of Eusebius, comprises seven books, each covering the reign of one emperor between 306 and 439.

Sulpicius Severus (c. 360-c. 420). An ecclesiastical writer from Bordeaux born of noble parents. Devoting himself to monastic retirement, he became a personal friend and enthusiastic disciple of St. Martin of Tours.

Symeon the New Theologian (c. 949-1022). Compassionate spiritual leader known for his strict rule. He believed that the divine light could be perceived and received through the practice of mental prayer.

Syncletica (fifth century). Egyptian nun known from collected sayings and a fifth-century *Life*. Syncletica began ascetic practices in her parents' Alexandria home and after their death retired to desert life. Until succumbing to illness in her eighties, she was a spiritual leader to women who gathered to learn from her piety.

Synesios of Cyrene (c. 370-c. 413). Bishop of Ptolemais elected in 410. Born of a noble pagan family, Synesios studied in Alexandria under the neoplatonist philosopher Hypatia. His work includes nine hymns that present a complex Trinitarian theology with neoplatonic influences.

Synod of Alexandria (362). A gathering of Egyptian bishops and Nicene delegates, called by Athanasius after the death of Constantius. The synod published a letter that expressed anti-Arian agreement on Trinitarian language.

Tarasius of Constantinople (d. 806). Patriarch of Constantinople from 784. Tarasius promoted reconciliation between Eastern and Western churches. At his urging Empress Irene II called the Second Council of Nicaea (787) to address debates over iconoclasm.

Tatian (second century). Christian apologist from the East who studied under Justin in Rome, returning to his old country after his mentor's martyrdom. Famous for his Gospel harmony, the *Diatessaron*, Tatian also wrote *Address to the Greeks*, which was a defense of Christianity addressed to the pagan world.

Tertullian of Carthage (c. 155/160-225/250; fl. c. 197-222). Brilliant Carthaginian apologist and polemicist who laid the foundations of Christology and trinitarian orthodoxy in the West, though he himself was later estranged from the catholic tradition due to its laxity.

Theodore of Heraclea (d. c. 355). An anti-Nicene bishop of Thrace. He was part of a team seeking reconciliation between Eastern and Western Christianity. In 343 he was excommunicated at the council of Sardica. His writings focus on a literal interpretation of Scripture.

Theodore of Mopsuestia (c. 350-428). Bishop of Mopsuestia, founder of the Antiochene, or literalistic, school of exegesis. A great man in his day, he was later condemned as a precursor of Nestorius.

Theodore of Tabennesi (d. 368) Vice general of the Pachomian monasteries (c. 350-368) under Horsiesi. Several of his letters are known.

Theodoret of Cyr (c. 393-466). Bishop of Cyr (Cyrrhus), he was an opponent of Cyril who commented extensively on Old Testament texts as a lucid exponent of Antiochene exegesis.

Theodotus the Valentinian (second century). Likely a Montanist who may have been related to the Alexandrian school. Extracts of his work are known through writings of Clement of Alexandria.

Theophanes (775-845). Hymnographer and bishop of Nicaea (842-845). He was persecuted during the second iconoclastic period for his support of the Seventh Council (Second Council of Nicaea, 787). He wrote many hymns in the tradition of the monastery of Mar Sabbas that were used in the *Paraklitiki*.

Theophilus of Alexandria (d. 412). Patriarch of Alexandria (385-412) and the uncle of his successor, Cyril. His patriarchate was known for his opposition to paganism, having destroyed the Serapeion and its library in 391, but he also built many churches. He also was known for his political machinations against his theological enemies, especially John Chrysostom, whom he himself had previously consecrated as patriarch, ultimately getting John removed from his see and earning the intense dislike of Antioch Christians. He is, however, venerated among the Copts and Syrians, among whom many of his sermons have survived, although only a few are deemed authentically his. His *Homily on the Mystical Supper*, commenting on the Last Supper, is perhaps one of his most well known.

Theophilus of Antioch (late second century). Bishop of Antioch. His only surviving work is *Ad Autholycum*, where we find the first Christian commentary on Genesis and the first use of the term Trinity. Theophilus's apologetic literary heritage had influence on Irenaeus and possibly Tertullian.

Theophylact of Ohrid (c. 1050-c. 1108). Byzantine archbishop of Ohrid (or Achrida) in what is now Bulgaria. Drawing on earlier works, he wrote commentaries on several Old Testament books and all of the New Testament except for Revelation.

Third Council of Constantinople (681). The Sixth Ecumenical Council, convoked by Constantine IV to resolve the Monothelite controversy. The council's decree affirmed the doctrine that Christ's two natures correspond to two distinct wills and two energies.

Treatise on Rebaptism (third century). An anonymous treatise arguing, possibly against Cyprian, that those receiving baptism by heretics in the name of Jesus ought not be rebaptized.

Tyconius (c. 330-390). A lay theologian and exegete of the Donatist church in North Africa who influenced Augustine. His *Book of Rules* is the first manual of scriptural interpretation in the Latin West. In 380 he was excommunicated by the Donatist council at Carthage.

Valentinian Exposition (second century). A type of secret catechism for those who were to be initiated into the Valentinian version of gnosis. It provided an exposition of the origin of creation and was also concerned with the process of how our salvation is achieved in light of the myth of Sophia. There are references to the sacramental rituals of baptism and the Eucharist and also early evidences of the disagreements and theological controversies that existed among Valentinian theologians.

Valentinus (fl. c. 140). Alexandrian heretic of the mid second century who taught that the material world was created by the transgression of God's Wisdom, or Sophia (*see* Gnostics).

Valerian of Cimiez (fl. c. 422-439). Bishop of Cimiez. He participated in the councils of Riez (439) and Vaison (422) with a view to strengthening church discipline. He supported Hilary of Arles in quarrels with Pope Leo I.

Venantius Fortunatus (c. 530-c. 610). Latin poet. In 597 Venantius was appointed bishop of Poitiers, where he had served the community of former queen Radegunde since 567. His works include lives of saints and two hymns that were soon incorporated into Western liturgy.

Verecundus (d. 552). An African Christian writer, who took an active part in the christological controversies of the sixth century, especially in the debate on Three Chapters. He also wrote allegorical commentaries on the nine liturgical church canticles.

Victorinus of Petovium (d. c. 304). Latin biblical exegete. With multiple works attributed to him, his sole surviving work is the *Commentary on the Apocalypse* and perhaps some fragments from *Commentary on Matthew*. Victorinus expressed strong millenarianism in his writing, though his was less materialistic than the millenarianism of Papias or Irenaeus. In his allegorical approach he could be called a spiritual disciple of Origen. Victorinus died during the first year of Diocletian's persecution, probably in 304.

Vincent of Lérins (d. before 450). Monk who has exerted considerable influence through his writings on orthodox dogmatic theological method, as contrasted with the theological methodologies of the heresies.

Walafridius (Walahfrid) Strabo (808-849). Frankish monk, writer and student of Rabanus Maurus. Walafridius was made abbot of the monastery of Reichenau in 838 but was exiled in 840, when one of the sons of Emperor Louis the Pious—to whom Walafridius was loyal—invaded Reichenau. He was restored in 842 and died in 849. His writings include poetry, commentaries on scripture, lives of saints and a historical explanation of the liturgy. Though he is technically an early medieval writer, his works are included

Zephyrinus (d. 217). Bishop of Rome from 199 to 217. Renewed his predecessor Victor's condemnation of the adoptionism being taught in Rome by Theodotus of Byzantium and re-admitted the excommunicated modalist bishop Natalius upon the latter's repentance, but as a layperson. Much of what we know about him is from the work of Hippolytus, whose negative opinion of Zephyrinus may have been colored by his antagonism toward Zephyrinus's successor, Callistus. The epistles attributed to Zephyrinus are now considered spurious (part of the so-called False Decretals of the ninth century) but are included as possibly reflecting earlier thought.

Timeline of Writers of the Patristic Period

Location / Period	British Isles	Gaul	Spain, Portugal	Rome* and Italy	Carthage and Northern Africa
2nd century				Clement of Rome, fl. c. 92-101 (Greek)	
				Shepherd of Hermas, c. 140 (Greek)	
				Justin Martyr (Ephesus, Rome), c. 100/110-165 (Greek)	
				Tatian (Rome/Syria), 2nd cent. (Greek)	
				Muratorian Fragment, 2nd cent. (Latin [orig. Greek])	
				Valentinus the Gnostic (Rome), fl. c. 140 (Greek)	
				Hegesippus, 2nd cent. (Greek)	
		Irenaeus of Lyons, c. 135-c. 202 (Greek)			
				Marcion (Rome), fl. 144 (Greek)	
				Heracleon, 145-180 (Greek)	
				Zephyrinus (Rome), regn. 199-217	Tertullian of Carthage, c. 155/160-c. 225 (Latin)
3rd century				Callistus of Rome, regn. 217-222 (Latin)	
				Minucius Felix of Rome, fl. 218-235 (Latin)	
				Hippolytus (Rome, Palestine?), fl. 222-235/245 (Greek)	
				Novatian of Rome, fl. 235-258 (Latin)	Cyprian of Carthage, fl. 248-258 (Latin)
					Seventh Council of Carthage Under Cyprian, 256 (Latin)
					Treatise on Rebaptism, 3rd cent. (Latin)
				Victorinus of Petovium, 230-304 (Latin)	

*One of the five ancient patriarchates

Timeline of Writers of the Patristic Period

Alexandria* and Egypt	Constantinople* and Asia Minor, Greece	Antioch* and Syria	Mesopotamia, Persia	Jerusalem* and Palestine	Location Unknown
Philo of Alexandria, c. 20 B.C. - c. A.D. 50 (Greek)				Flavius Josephus (Rome), c. 37-c. 101 (Greek)	
Basilides (Alexandria), 2nd cent. (Greek)	Polycarp of Smyrna, c. 69-155 (Greek)	Ignatius of Antioch, c. 35-107/112 (Greek)			
	Martyrdom of Polycarp, c. 160 (Greek)	*Didache* (Egypt?), c. 100 (Greek)			
Letter of Barnabas (Syria?), c. 130 (Greek)	Aristides, 2nd cent. (Greek)	*Odes of Solomon* (perhaps also Palestine or Egypt), early 2nd cent. (Syriac/Aramaic)			
Gospel of Truth (Egypt?), 2nd cent. (Coptic/Greek)	Papias of Hierapolis, c. early 2nd cent. (Greek)				*Second Letter of Clement* (spurious; Corinth, Rome, Alexandria?) c. 150, (Greek)
Valentinian Exposition, 2nd cent. (Greek)					
Theodotus the Valentinian, 2nd cent. (Greek)	Athenagoras (Greece), fl. 176-180 (Greek)				
Epistula Apostolorum, mid 2nd cent. (Greek [Coptic/Ethiopic])					
	Melito of Sardis, d. c. 190 (Greek)				
	Acts of Paul and Thecla, 2nd cent. (Greek)	*Gospel of Peter*, late 2nd cent. (Greek)			
Clement of Alexandria, c. 150-215 (Greek)	*Acts of Peter*, c. 190 (Greek)	Theophilus of Antioch, c. late 2nd cent. (Greek)			
	Montanist Oracles, late 2nd cent. (Greek)				
Sabellius (Egypt), 2nd-3rd cent. (Greek)		*Gospel of Philip* (Syria, Egypt?) 2nd or 3rd cent. (Coptic/Greek)			
Letter to Diognetus, 3rd cent. (Greek)		Bardesanes, 154-222 (Syriac)			
		Acts of Thomas, c. 225 (Syriac)	Mani (Manichaeans), c. 216-276 (Persian/Syriac)		Pseudo-Clementines 3rd cent. (Greek)
Origen (Alexandria, Caesarea of Palestine), 185-254 (Greek)	Firmilian of Caesarea, fl. c. 230-c. 268 (Greek)	*Didascalia Apostolorum*, early 3rd cent. (Syriac)			
	Gregory Thaumaturgus (Neocaesarea), fl. c. 248-264 (Greek)				
Dionysius of Alexandria, d. 264/5 (Greek)					
	Methodius of Olympus (Lycia), d. c. 311 (Greek)				

Timeline of Writers of the Patristic Period

Location	British Isles	Gaul	Spain, Portugal	Rome* and Italy	Carthage and Northern Africa
Period					
4th century		Lactantius, c. 260-330 (Latin)			
				Firmicus Maternus (Sicily), fl. c. 335 (Latin)	Arnobius of Sicca, d. c. 327 (Latin)
			Hosius of Cordova, d. 357 (Latin)	Marius Victorinus (Rome), fl. 355-363 (Latin)	
			Potamius of Lisbon, fl. c. 350-360 (Latin)	Eusebius of Vercelli, fl. c. 360 (Latin)	
		Hilary of Poitiers, c. 315-367 (Latin)	Gregory of Elvira, fl. 359-385 (Latin)	Lucifer of Cagliari (Sardinia), d. 370/371 (Latin)	
				Damasus of Rome, c. 304-384 (Latin)	Optatus of Milevis, 4th cent. (Latin)
				Ambrosiaster (Italy?), fl. c. 366-384 (Latin)	
				Filastrius of Brescia, fl. 380 (Latin)	
			Pacian of Barcelona, 4th cent. (Latin)	Faustinus (Rome), fl. 380 (Latin)	
			Prudentius, c. 348-c. 410 (Latin)	Faustus of Riez, fl. c. 380 (Latin)	
					Isaiah of Scete, late 4th cent. (Greek)
		Egeria, 4th cent. (Latin)		Gaudentius of Brescia, fl. 395 (Latin)	Paulus Orosius, b. c. 380 (Latin)
		Phoebadius of Agen, d. c. 395 (Latin)			
		Athanasian Creed, c. 4th or 5th cent. (Latin)		Ambrose of Milan, c. 333-397; fl. 374-397 (Latin)	Augustine of Hippo, 354-430 (Latin)
					Synesios of Cyrene (Alexandria, Cyrene), c. 370-c. 413 (Greek)
5th century	Fastidius (Britain), c. 4th-5th cent. (Latin)	*Joseph's Bible Notes*, 4th or 5th cent. (Latin)		Paulinus of Milan, late 4th-early 5th cent. (Latin)	Possidius, late 4th-5th cent. (Latin)
		Sulpicius Severus (Bordeaux), c. 360-c. 420/425 (Latin)		Rufinus (Aquileia, Rome), c. 345-411 (Latin)	
		John Cassian (Palestine, Egypt, Constantinople, Rome, Marseilles), 360-432 (Latin)		Chromatius (Aquileia), fl. 400 (Latin)	
				Aponius, fl. 405-415 (Latin)	Luculentius, 5th cent. (Latin)
	Sedulius, Coelius, fl. 425-450 (Latin)	Vincent of Lérins, d. 435 (Latin)		Pelagius (Britain, Rome), c. 354-c. 420 (Greek)	
		Valerian of Cimiez, fl. c. 422-449 (Latin)		Maximus of Turin, d. 408/423 (Latin)	Quodvultdeus (Carthage), fl. 430 (Latin)
		Eucherius of Lyons, fl. 420-449 (Latin)		Paulinus of Nola, 355-431 (Latin)	
		Hilary of Arles, c. 401-449 (Latin)		Peter Chrysologus (Ravenna), c. 380-450 (Latin)	Dracontius, 5th cent. (Latin)
				Julian of Eclanum, 386-454 (Latin)	

*One of the five ancient patriarchates

Timeline of Writers of the Patristic Period

Alexandria* and Egypt	Constantinople* and Asia Minor, Greece	Antioch* and Syria	Mesopotamia, Persia	Jerusalem* and Palestine	Location Unknown
	Constantine, d. 337 (Greek)		Hegemonius, fl. early 4th cent. (Greek)		
Antony, c. 251-355 (Coptic /Greek)	Theodore of Heraclea (Thrace), fl. c. 330-355 (Greek)	Eustathius of Antioch, fl. 325 (Greek)	Aphrahat (Persia) c. 270-350; fl. 337-345 (Syriac)	Eusebius of Caesarea (Palestine), c. 260/263-340 (Greek)	Commodian, c. 3rd or 5th cent. (Latin)
Peter of Alexandria, d. c. 311 (Greek)	Marcellus of Ancyra, d. c. 375 (Greek)	Eusebius of Emesa, c. 300-c. 359 (Greek)			
Arius (Alexandria), fl. c. 320 (Greek)	Epiphanius of Salamis (Cyprus), c. 315-403 (Greek)	Ephrem the Syrian, c. 306-373 (Syriac)	Jacob of Nisibis, fl. 308-325 (Syriac)		
Alexander of Alexandria, fl. 312-328 (Greek)	Basil (the Great) of Caesarea, b. c. 330; fl. 357-379 (Greek)	Julian the Arian, c. 4th cent. (Greek)			
Pachomius, c. 292-347 (Coptic/Greek?)	Macrina the Younger, c. 327-379 (Greek)	First Creed of the Council of Antioch, 341 (Greek)			
Theodore of Tabennesi, d. 368 (Coptic/Greek)	Apollinaris of Laodicea, 310-c. 392 (Greek)				
Athanasius of Alexandria, c. 295-373; fl. 325-373 (Greek)	Gregory of Nazianzus, b. 329/330; fl. 372-389 (Greek)	Nemesius of Emesa (Syria), fl. late 4th cent. (Greek)			Maximinus, b. c. 360-365 (Latin)
Abba Pior, d. 373 (Coptic/Greek)	Gregory of Nyssa, c. 335-394 (Greek)	Diodore of Tarsus, d. c. 394 (Greek)		Acacius of Caesarea (Palestine), d. c. 365 (Greek)	
Horsiesi, c. 305-390 (Coptic/Greek)		John Chrysostom (Constantinople), 344/354-407 (Greek)		Cyril of Jerusalem, c. 315-386 (Greek)	
Macarius of Egypt, c. 300-c. 390 (Greek)	Amphilochius of Iconium, c. 340/345- c. 398/404 (Greek)				
Abba John, date unknown (Coptic/Greek)	Evagrius of Pontus, 345-399 (Greek)	*Apostolic Constitutions*, c. 375-400 (Greek)			
Didymus (the Blind) of Alexandria, 313-398 (Greek)	Eunomius of Cyzicus, fl. 360-394 (Greek)	*Didascalia*, 4th cent. (Syriac)			
		Theodore of Mopsuestia, c. 350-428 (Greek)		Diodore of Tarsus, d. c. 394 (Greek)	
Tyconius, c. 330-390 (Latin)	Pseudo-Macarius (Mesopotamia?), late 4th cent. (Greek)	Acacius of Beroea, c. 340-c. 436 (Greek)		Jerome (Rome, Antioch, Bethlehem), c. 347-420 (Latin)	
Joseph of Thebes, 4th cent. (Coptic/Greek)	Nicetas of Remesiana, d. c. 414 (Latin)	Asterius the Homilist (Antioch), late 4th- early 5th (Greek)			
Ammonas, 4th cent. (Syriac)		*Book of Steps*, c. 400 (Syriac)			
Abba Moses, c. 332-407 (Coptic/Greek)		Severian of Gabala, fl. c. 400 (Greek)			
Theophilus of Alexandria, d. 412 (Greek)	Socrates (Scholasticus), c. 380-450 (Greek)				
Palladius of Helenopolis (Egypt), c. 365-425 (Greek)	Proclus of Constantinople, c. 390-446 (Greek)		Eznik of Kolb, fl. 430-450 (Armenian)	Philip the Priest (d. 455/56)	
	Nestorius (Constantinople), c. 381-c. 451 (Greek)				
Cyril of Alexandria, 375-444 (Greek)	Basil of Seleucia, fl. 440-468 (Greek)			Hesychius of Jerusalem, fl. 412-450 (Greek)	
Isidore of Pelusium, d. c. 440 (Greek)		Nilus of Ancyra, d. c. 430 (Greek)		Euthymius (Palestine), 377-473 (Greek)	
Hyperichius, c. 5th cent. (Coptic/Greek)	Diadochus of Photice (Macedonia), 400-474 (Greek)	John of Antioch, d. 441/2 (Greek)			

Timeline of Writers of the Patristic Period

Location / Period	British Isles	Gaul	Spain, Portugal	Rome* and Italy	Carthage and Northern Africa
5th century (cont.)		Eusebius of Gaul, 5th cent. (Latin)			
		Prosper of Aquitaine, c. 390-c. 463 (Latin)		Leo the Great (Rome), regn. 440-461 (Latin)	
		Salvian the Presbyter of Marseilles, c. 400-c. 480 (Latin)		Arnobius the Younger (Rome), fl. c. 450 (Latin)	
		Gennadius of Marseilles, d. after 496 (Latin)		Ennodius (Arles, Milan, Pavia) c. 473-521 (Latin)	
				Epiphanius the Latin, late 5th-early 6th cent. (Latin)	
6th century		Caesarius of Arles, c. 470-543 (Latin)	Paschasius of Dumium (Portugal), c. 515-c. 580 (Latin)	Eugippius, c. 460- c. 533 (Latin)	Fulgentius of Ruspe, c. 467-532 (Latin)
				Benedict of Nursia, c. 480-547 (Latin)	Verecundus, d. 552 (Latin)
	Gildas, 6th cent. (Latin)		Apringius of Beja, mid-6th cent. (Latin)		Primasius, fl. 550-560 (Latin)
			Leander of Seville, c. 545-c. 600 (Latin)	Cassiodorus (Calabria), c. 485-c. 540 (Latin)	Facundus of Hermiane, fl. 546-568 (Latin)
		Gregory of Tours, c. 538-594 (Latin)	Martin of Braga, fl. 568-579 (Latin)	Arator, c. 490-550 (Latin)	
		Flavian of Chalon-sur-Saône, fl. 580-600 (Latin)	Isidore of Seville, c. 560-636 (Latin)	Gregory of Agrigentium, d. 592 (Greek)	
7th century			Braulio of Saragossa, c. 585-651 (Latin)	Gregory the Great (Rome), c. 540-604 (Latin)	
			Fructuosus of Braga, d. c. 665 (Latin)	Paterius, 6th/7th cent. (Latin)	
		Venantius Fortunatus (Gaul, Italy), c. 530-c. 610 (Latin)			
8th-12th century	Adamnan, c. 624-704 (Latin)				
	Bede the Venerable, c. 672/673-735 (Latin)	Rabanus Maurus (Frankish), c. 780-856 (Latin)			
	Riddles in the Apocalypse, 8th cent. (Latin)	Walafridius Strabo (Frankish), 808-849 (Latin)			

*One of the five ancient patriarchates

Timeline of Writers of the Patristic Period

Alexandria* and Egypt	Constantinople* and Asia Minor, Greece	Antioch* and Syria	Mesopotamia, Persia	Jerusalem* and Palestine	Location Unknown
Syncletica, 5th cent. (Coptic/Greek)					
Ammonius of Alexandria, c. 460 (Greek)	Gennadius of Constantinople, d. 471 (Greek)	Theodoret of Cyr, c. 393-466 (Greek)		Gerontius of Petra c. 395-c. 480 (Syriac)	
Poemen, 5th cent. (Greek)		Pseudo-Victor of Antioch, 5th cent. (Greek)			
Besa the Copt, 5th cent. (Sahidic)		John of Apamea, 5th cent. (Syriac)			
Shenoute, c. 350-466 (Coptic)					
Olympiodorus, early 6th cent. (Greek)	Andrew of Caesarea (Cappadocia), early 6th cent. (Greek)	Philoxenus of Mabbug (Syria), c. 440-523 (Syriac)	Jacob of Sarug, c. 450-520 (Syriac)	Procopius of Gaza (Palestine), c. 465-530 (Greek)	Pseudo-Dionysius the Areopagite, fl. c. 500 (Greek)
	Oecumenius (Isauria), 6th cent. (Greek)	Severus of Antioch, c. 465-538 (Greek)	Babai, early 6th cent. (Syriac)	Dorotheus of Gaza, fl. 525-540 (Greek)	
	Romanus Melodus, fl. c. 536-556 (Greek)	Mark the Hermit (Tarsus), c. 6th cent. (4th cent.?) (Greek)		Cyril of Scythopolis, b. c. 525; d. after 557 (Greek)	
	Justinian the Emperor, 482-565 (Greek)	Anastasius I of Antioch, d. 598/599 (Latin)	Abraham of Nathpar, fl. 6th-7th cent. (Syriac)		(Pseudo-) Constantius, before 7th cent.? (Greek)
	Maximus the Confessor (Constantinople), c. 580-662 (Greek)		Babai the Great, c. 550-628 (Syriac)		
Anastasius of Sinai (Egypt, Syria), d. c. 700 (Greek)					Andreas, c. 7th cent. (Greek)
	Germanus of Constantinople, c. 640-c. 733 (Greek)	Sahdona/Martyrius, fl. 635-640 (Syriac)	Isaac of Nineveh, d. c. 700 (Syriac)		
	Andrew of Crete, c. 660-740 (Greek)	John of Damascus (John the Monk), c. 650-750 (Greek)			
	John of Carpathus, 7th-8th cent. (Greek)			Cosmas Melodus, c. 675-751 (Greek)	
	Tarasius of Constantinople, d. 806 (Greek)		John the Elder of Qardu (north Iraq), 8th cent. (Syriac)		
	Theophanes (Nicaea), 775-845 (Greek)		Isho'dad of Merv, d. after 852 (Syriac)		
	Cassia (Constantinople), c. 805-c. 848/867 (Greek)				
	Photius (Constantinople), c. 820-891 (Greek)				
	Arethas of Caesarea (Constantinople/Caesarea), c. 860-940 (Greek)				
	Gregory of Narek, 950-1003 (Armenian)				
	Symeon the New Theologian (Constantinople), 949-1022 (Greek)				
	Theophylact of Ohrid (Bulgaria), 1050-1126 (Greek)				

Author/Writings Index

Abercius, 60
Acts of Paul and Thecla, 109
Acts of Peter, 99
Acts of Thomas, 100
Alexander of Alexandria, 85
Ambrose, 21, 36, 101, 120, 128, 152, 225, 238
Ambrosiaster, 116, 120, 128, 129
Aphrahat, 149, 150, 157, 188, 206
Apostolic Constitutions. See Constitutions of the Holy Apostles
Aristides, 143
Athanasius, 85, 256
Athenagoras, 144, 154
Augustine, 7, 8, 9, 10, 13, 14, 15, 16, 20, 27, 28, 29, 30, 31, 33, 38, 39, 40, 41, 51, 66, 67, 68, 70, 75, 85, 101, 107, 108, 109, 110, 117, 120, 121, 122, 132, 133, 134, 135, 136, 137, 150, 151, 152, 158, 159, 160, 165, 172, 173, 185, 186, 187, 190, 192, 193, 201, 202, 203, 208, 209, 210, 211, 212, 227, 239, 240, 242, 243, 247, 248, 264, 265, 266, 267
Basil the Great, 104, 116, 256, 257
Caesarius of Arles, 10
Cassian, John, 244
Chrysostom, 18, 21, 25, 64, 65, 103, 104, 116, 117, 120, 129, 130, 131, 200, 224, 236, 242, 259, 260, 261
Clement of Alexandria, 7, 13, 23, 44, 45, 61, 69, 84, 98, 99, 118, 181
Clement of Rome, 77, 141, 142, 248
Commodian, 166
Constitutions of the Holy Apostles, 51, 73
Cyprian, 16, 17, 35, 36, 46, 47, 48, 61, 62, 63, 64, 107, 116, 184, 197, 222, 234, 241, 247, 254, 255
Cyril of Alexandria, 117, 138
Cyril of Jerusalem, 69, 74, 97, 99, 101, 119, 157, 158, 198, 223, 237, 243, 259
Didache, 94, 228
Didymus the Blind, 20, 26
Ephrem the Syrian, 16, 22, 36, 64, 75, 84, 106
Epistle of Barnabas, 94, 124, 194, 228, 248
Epistula Apostolorum, 73
Eusebius of Caesarea, 43, 164, 165
Firmilian of Caesarea, 16
Fulgentius of Ruspe, 35
Gregory of Nazianzus, 185, 199, 257
Gregory of Nyssa, 132, 171, 200, 238, 258
Gregory the Great, 20, 44, 52, 53, 204, 205, 243
Hegesippus (via Eusebius), 78
Hermas. *See Shepherd* of Hermas
Hilary of Poitiers, 185, 225, 262
Hippolytus, 50, 108, 146
Ignatius of Antioch, 7, 59, 72, 78, 193
Inscriptions, 109. *See* Abercius and Macus
Irenaeus, 11, 12, 41, 60, 61, 79, 80, 81, 106, 107, 117, 118, 126, 145, 156, 162, 163, 178, 179, 207, 219, 220, 231, 232, 249, 250, 251
Jerome, 25, 27, 34, 48, 171, 189, 191
John of Damascus, 138, 161, 213, 240
Justin Martyr, 9, 51, 95, 97, 98, 125, 126, 143, 153, 161, 162, 196, 207, 218, 229, 230, 249
Justinian the Emperor, 173
Lactantius, 16, 17, 20, 164, 198
Leo the Great, 9, 228
Letter to Diognetus, 194
Liturgy of Saint Basil, 64, 75
Liturgy of the Blessed Apostles, 73
Macus, 49

Martyrdom of Polycarp, 72, 73, 194
Melito of Sardis, 101
Methodius of Olympus, 9, 24, 37, 38, 48, 49, 158, 166
Minucius Felix, 146, 196
Munnulus of Girba, 49
Niceta of Remesiana, 74, 128
Novatian, 36
Odes of Solomon, 106
Origen, 8, 10, 17, 21, 23, 24, 34, 35, 84, 92, 96, 108, 110, 111, 116, 118, 119, 127, 128, 148, 149, 157, 167, 168, 169, 170, 181, 182, 183, 184, 208, 223, 234, 235, 236, 244
Pacian of Barcelona, 22, 26, 75, 103, 105, 128
Papias of Hierapolis (via Eusebius), 77
Pelagius, 117
Peter Chrysologus, 40, 42, 52, 72, 136, 152, 161, 267

Polycarp, 142, 229
Pseudo-Clement of Rome, 8, 35, 50, 96, 124, 153, 177, 195, 229, 241
Rufinus of Aquileia, 71, 137, 171, 204, 227, 263
Shepherd of Hermas, 7, 18, 19, 42, 59, 94, 124, 125, 194, 195
Tatian, 143, 206
Tertullian, 16, 24, 34, 43, 45, 46, 50, 78, 81, 82, 83, 92, 93, 96, 98, 101, 106, 126, 127, 147, 148, 155, 156, 163, 180, 221, 232, 233, 245, 252, 253
Theodore of Mopsuestia, 27, 117, 123
Theodoret of Cyr, 25
Theophilus of Antioch, 69, 95, 145, 178, 231
Treatise on Rebaptism, 69
Victorinus of Petovium, 19, 167
Vincent of Lérins, 48, 76

Scripture Index

Genesis
1:11, 66
1:20, 66
1:24, 66
1:27, 8
1:28, 37
1:31, 213
2:4, 236
2:16, 12
2:21-22, 38
2:22, 160
2:23, 26, 121
2:23-24, 25
2:24, 29, 33, 39
3:19, 102, 171
6:9, 51
22:18, 14
27:15, 21
27:22, 21
27:27, 20
27:28, 253
27:39, 253
28:12-17, 253
47:9, 257

Exodus
32:30-35, 191
33:20, 179

Leviticus
8:3, 74
16:3-22, 110
26:12, 188, 268

Deuteronomy
4:10, 74
9:10, 74
32:6, 118
32:15, 193

Judges
13:18, 76

1 Kings
11:31, 62

1 Chronicles
16:22, 99

Job
1:11, 209
1:19, 209
14:4-5, 108
19:25-26, 142
19:26-27, 264
31:33-34, 65
34:10-11, 188

Psalms
2:7-8, 123
3:5, 33
3:6, 142
6:5, 200, 244
8:5, 221
8:5-6, 222
16:5, 123
19:1-3, 142
19:4, 29
22:1, 32
22:7, 221
22:16-18, 32
22:27, 14
23:4, 156
25:4, 20
26:5, 71, 74
26:8, 74
26:12, 74
27:1, 199
28:7, 142
29:2, 27
33:6, 145
34:5, 28
34:12, 256
35:18, 74
42:4, 166
43:1, 240
45:2, 40
45:2-3, 222
45:2-5, 223
45:6-7, 223
45:9, 34
45:12, 22, 128
50:13, 110
50:21, 224
51:4, 131
51:7, 104
51:8, 231
51:11, 119
54:1, 240
57:5, 15
62:1, 167
68:26, 74
69:34, 212
72:6, 224
74:2, 8
77:9, 203
80:10, 24
82:1, 20
82:6, 99, 119
82:6-7, 117
84:4, 267
89:32-33, 247
89:37, 3
90:4, 167
101:1, 151
104:2, 224
105:15, 48
106:11, 136
109:3, 7
110:1, 167, 207, 226, 230
110:1-4, 207
110:3, 123
112:5, 228
113:3, 40
115:17-18, 244
116:7, 257
118:1, 243
119:130, 178
121:6, 24
127:1, 17
128:3, 22, 26
139:7, 135
143:2, 150
147, 14, 15
149:1, 74
150:6, 244

Proverbs
1:20-21, 61
3:8, 231
3:34, 59
8:22, 256
9:10, 118
16:7, 170
25:20, 202

Ecclesiastes
3:2, 97
9:10, 243

Song of Solomon
4:8, 34, 37
4:12-13, 16
5:3, 238
5:15, 37
5:16, 37
6:8, 22
6:8-9, 35
6:9, 22, 71

Isaiah
1:2, 45, 254
1:16, 39
1:16-20, 125
4:4, 251

Scripture Index

5:20, *172*
6:3, *227*
8:14, *221*
11:6-9, *146*
30:30, *231*
32:17-18, *120*
40:6, *30*
43:5-7, *250*
45:23, *219*
48:12-16, *240*
49:8, *243*
49:18, *34, 253*
50:5, *27*
52:7, *29*
52:14, *221*
53:2-3, *221*
53:3, *221*
53:8, *222*
53:9, *22*
54:5, *5*
54:9, *95*
59:7, *64*
60:1-4, *49*
60:8, *253*
60:17, *77, 81*
61:1, *100*
61:3, *100*
61:5, *182*
61:6, *182*
63:1-4, *249*
63:17, *219*
64:4, *200, 258*
64:11, *219*
65:13-16, *182*
66:1, *168*
66:8, *150*
66:12-13, *44*
66:18, *195, 229*
66:22, *163*
66:24, *196, 197, 219, 229*

Jeremiah
2:13, *12, 103*
7:11, *8*
17:5, *234*
23:24, *168*
31:8, *93*

Lamentations
4:20, *51*

Ezekiel
37:7-8, *219*
47:12, *94*

Daniel
2:44, *207*
7:10, *236, 238*
7:13, *253*
7:13-14, *222, 263*
12:2, *171*
12:3, *158, 259*

Joel
2:12-13, *247*

Amos
9:6, *253*

Haggai
2:5, *120*

Zechariah
4:10, *167*
12:3-14, *219*
12:10, *222*

Malachi
1:11, *74, 116*
3:1, *224*
3:1-3, *224*
3:5, *224*
4:1, *231*

Baruch
3:37, *120*

Prayer of Azariah
64, *244*

Sirach
7:17, *202*
8:2, *135*
25:24, *137*
34:25, *63*

Tobit
4:10, *247*

Wisdom of Solomon
1:5, *67*
1:13, *247*
5:1-9, *198*
11:21, *142*
12:12, *142*

Matthew
2:16, *109*
3:3, *106*
3:6, *94*
3:11, *87, 105, 110*
4:19, *11, 85*
5:8, *179, 263*
5:11-12, *28*
5:25, *246*
5:28, *155, 246*
5:34, *168*
5:35, *34*
5:44, *206*
6:9, *134, 136*
6:12, *28, 42, 107, 119, 135*
6:13, *143*
7:1, *229*
7:2, *229*
7:21, *67, 134*
8:11, *221*
8:22, *150*
8:24, *6, 51*
9:4, *155*
9:12, *238*
9:15, *5*
10:16, *177*
10:26, *236*
10:28, *178, 228*
11:11, *93*
11:19, *21, 118*
11:22, *239*
11:24, *232, 239*
11:27, *82*
12:5, *167*
12:30, *36*
12:32, *243*
12:41-42, *239*
12:42, *22*
12:50, *153*
13:37-43, *239*
13:39, *225*
13:40-43, *262*
13:43, *158, 225, 264*
14:29, *51*
16:18, *74, 75*
16:19, *70, 135*
16:28—17:2, *262*
18:8, *25*
18:10, *187*
18:18, *135*
18:20, *24*
18:22-25, *113*
19:5-6, *39, 137*
19:6, *33*
19:16-18, *259*
19:28, *119*
19:29, *259*
20:26, *189*
21:9, *224*
21:13, *8*
22:13, *225*
22:23-30, *160*
23:3, *67*
24:2, *263*
24:23-24, *14*
24:27, *263*
24:28, *250*
24:29, *261*
24:35, *149*
24:45-46, *81*
24:47, *236*
25:15-30, *189*
25:23, *225*
25:26, *225*
25:29, *183*
25:31-46, *248*
25:32, *238, 263*
25:34, *11, 256, 260, 262*
25:34-35, *224*
25:41, *7, 11, 203, 205, 210, 225, 260, 266*
25:46, *205, 211, 259, 267*
26:28, *28, 113*
26:29, *182*
26:39, *112*
26:41, *143*
26:42, *112*
26:64, *226*
28:19, *49, 82, 92*
28:19-20, *271*
28:20, *14*

Mark
1:2, *106*
1:8, *110*
5:30-31, *29*
5:42, *39*
9:2, *225*
9:48, *229*
10:17, *259*
10:38, *110*
12:25, *143*
13:31, *149*
14:13, *93*
14:36, *112*
14:38, *143*
16:15-16, *87*

Luke
2:29, *254*
3:4, *106*
3:7, *111*
3:8, *128, 132*

313

3:16, *110*	1:33, *110*	12:47, *108*	5:31, *113*	7:24, *257*
3:17, *96*	2:19, *129*	13:5, *251*	7:59-60, *191*	8:13, *202*
5:4-8, *11*	3:3, *104*	13:10, *93*	8:14-17, *88, 90*	8:14, *120, 133*
6:36, *229*	3:4, *122*	13:19, *229*	8:37, *106*	8:15, *112*
6:38, *229*	3:5, *92, 96, 97, 105,*	13:38, *190*	9:3-5, *2*	8:16, *120*
6:40, *157*	*108, 111, 125,*	14:1, *190*	9:4, *29, 39*	8:16-17, *249*
7:15, *39*	*138, 201*	14:2, *191*	9:6, *92*	8:17, *22, 123*
7:30, *102*	3:13, *122*	14:2-3, *216*	9:18, *87, 92*	8:18, *185*
7:44-48, *261*	3:16, *116*	14:6, *9*	10:43, *113*	8:29, *99, 160*
7:47, *189*	3:17, *212*	14:26-27, *116*	10:44-48, *90*	9:14, *227*
8:45, *29*	3:29, *5*	14:30, *212*	11:15-17, *90*	9:23, *203*
10:12, *232*	3:36, *259*	15:1, *20*	11:17, *87*	10:10, *108*
12:2, *236*	4:14, *116*	15:5, *20*	13:38, *113*	10:15, *29*
12:4, *178*	4:20-23, *116*	15:5-8, *2*	14:23, *56*	11:33, *227, 237*
12:7, *151*	4:36, *259*	15:16, *250*	17:28, *168*	12:3, *12*
12:31, *253*	5:14, *236*	15:19, *212*	19:1-6, *90*	12:4-5, *4*
12:47-48, *190*	5:22, *225*	15:22, *239*	19:5-6, *88*	12:5, *2*
12:49, *42, 158*	5:24, *259*	16:11, *208, 212*	19:41, *69*	12:11, *27*
12:50, *110*	5:25, *157*	16:28, *255*	20:17, *56*	14:10, *242*
12:58-59, *236*	5:25-26, *150*	16:33, *85*	22:10, *92*	14:15, *92*
14:26, *110*	5:28, *157*	17:3, *266*	22:16, *87, 113*	15:29, *105*
15:7, *247*	5:28-29, *266*	17:5, *250*	27:37, *192*	
15:22-23, *250*	5:29, *85, 157, 240*	17:11, *215*		**1 Corinthians**
16:10-12, *241*	5:43, *263*	17:21, *55*	**Romans**	1:1, *65*
16:22-23, *159*	5:46, *64*	17:24, *245, 250,*	1:17, *137*	1:2, *55*
16:24, *159, 201,*	6:44, *226*	*255*	1:21, *219*	1:13, *28*
204	6:50-51, *266*	18:37, *226*	1:32, *249*	1:24, *116*
17:21, *263*	6:51, *28, 182*	19:23-24, *62*	2:4, *134*	1:30, *28, 116*
18:8, *36, 223*	6:53, *28*	19:34, *3, 38, 136,*	2:7, *178*	2:9, *178, 194, 200,*
18:27, *179*	7:37, *118*	*138*	2:8-9, *178*	*258*
19:17, *236*	7:37-39, *67*	20:20, *156*	2:15-16, *238, 263*	2:15, *219*
19:19, *236*	8:24, *229*	20:21-23, *113*	4:5, *137, 151*	3:1, *2*
20:36, *34, 122*	8:28, *229*	20:27, *156*	5:5, *133*	3:2, *179*
22:10, *93*	8:35, *98*	21:4, *52*	5:14, *33*	3:3, *128, 179*
23:43, *110*	8:56, *64*	21:5, *52*	5:18, *109*	3:6-7, *20*
24:46, *14*	10:18, *265*	21:6, *11*	6:3, *87, 119*	3:8, *188*
24:46-47, *14*	10:30, *36, 45*	21:8, *52*	6:3-4, *101*	3:9, *20*
24:47, *14, 113*	11:11, *192*		6:4, *104, 106*	3:11, *17*
	11:25, *255*	**Acts**	6:4-5, *104*	3:11-13, *224*
John	11:44, *39*	1:5, *111*	6:6, *104, 105*	3:11-15, *244*
1:10, *212*	12:25, *259*	1:7, *188*	6:9, *39, 204, 264*	3:13, *105*
1:12, *106, 123, 186*	12:26, *244*	2:2-4, *68*	6:22, *259*	3:16, *116*
1:12-13, *112*	12:31, *212*	2:38, *87, 113, 132*	6:23, *117*	3:17, *70, 75*
1:13, *112, 121*	12:31-32, *208*	3:19, *113*	7:5, *105*	3:22, *118*
1:14, *39, 122*	12:35, *243*	4:27, *101*	7:8, *239*	4:15, *105*

Scripture Index

5:1-13, *113*
5:13, *214*
6:10, *248*
6:15, *2, 24, 30*
6:17, *2*
6:19, *132*
7:31, *163, 257*
7:31-32, *209*
9:13, *110*
10:17, *2, 29, 66, 68*
11:1, *104*
11:3, *39*
11:7, *15*
11:14, *76*
11:16, *23*
11:19, *77*
11:24, *28*
11:30-32, *54, 237*
12:3, *67*
12:12, *2, 4, 25*
12:14, *26*
12:14-26, *4*
12:21, *25*
12:23, *26*
12:24, *133*
12:27, *29, 33, 41, 68*
12:27-31, *1*
12:28, *12, 61, 70, 81*
13:9-10, *202*
13:9-12, *187*
13:10, *9*
15:20-21, *263*
15:21, *148*
15:24, *262*
15:25, *167*
15:25-26, *170*
15:28, *191, 268*
15:36-38, *133*
15:41-42, *188, 191*
15:42-43, *157*
15:44, *149, 182, 264*
15:45, *48*

15:47, *106*
15:49, *106*
15:50, *265*
15:51, *38, 266*
15:52, *236, 258*
15:53, *158, 264*
15:54, *42*

2 Corinthians
2:5-11, *113*
5:8, *215*
5:10, *242, 263*
5:14-15, *150*
5:17, *103*
6:2, *243*
6:7-8, *70*
6:14-16, *193*
6:16, *116*
11:1-3, *5*
11:2, *5, 23, 40, 41*
11:2-4, *41*
11:29, *202*

Galatians
2:9, *18*
3:7, *9*
3:11, *266*
3:27, *17, 99, 103*
4:5, *112*
4:6-7, *249*
4:7, *123*
4:19, *48*
4:21-24, *46*
4:26, *46, 69, 163*
4:31, *46*
5:16-17, *27*
5:19-21, *134*
5:22, *117*
6:1, *113*

Ephesians
1:3-14, *3*
1:4, *76*
1:4-5, *8*

1:5, *99*
1:7, *113*
1:10, *12, 178, 231*
1:22, *4*
1:22-23, *2*
2:6, *128, 264*
2:11-22, *11*
2:13-17, *116*
2:20, *17, 22*
3—4, *59*
3:9-10, *3*
3:10, *22*
3:14-17, *48*
3:18, *5*
3:19, *116*
4:4, *31*
4:4-5, *107*
4:5, *64*
4:6, *118*
4:9, *156*
4:11, *20*
4:12, *160*
4:13, *160*
4:13-15, *23*
4:16, *4*
4:22-24, *128*
5:8, *99, 212*
5:14, *7*
5:15-32, *5*
5:16, *257*
5:23, *1, 26, 30*
5:24, *27*
5:25, *69*
5:25-27, *42*
5:26, *87*
5:26-27, *37*
5:27, *22, 26, 39, 55, 103, 195*
5:28-29, *121*
5:28-32, *25*
5:29-32, *1*
5:30, *22, 26, 103, 156*
5:31, *34, 37*
5:31-32, *29, 33, 36,*

39, 46
6:12, *179, 231, 249*
6:14, *229*

Philippians
1:1, *55*
2:10, *238*
2:10-11, *179, 231*
2:21, *193*
3:1, *32*
3:10-11, *104*
3:13, *190*
3:13-14, *40*
3:20, *122, 193*
3:21, *99, 255, 264*
4:7, *187*

Colossians
1:1, *55*
1:14, *113*
1:18, *2, 4, 33*
1:20, *75*
1:24, *2, 4, 29, 39*
1:26, *3*
2:10, *34*
2:11, *104*
2:11-12, *104*
2:15, *208*
2:19, *2*
3:1-2, *193, 226*
3:3-4, *256*
3:4, *227*
3:10, *128*

1 Thessalonians
1:4-5, *120*
2:19, *214*
3:13, *214*
4:13, *192*
4:14, *255*
4:15, *214*
4:17, *244, 259, 261, 264*
5:23, *214*

2 Thessalonians
2:1, *214*
2:8-9, *214*
2:9-10, *209*
2:10, *209*
2:10-12, *252*
3:14, *113*

1 Timothy
1:20, *113*
2:2, *70*
2:5, *52, 156*
3:15, *20, 22, 23, 70, 74, 103*
3:16, *21*
4:14, *56*
5:6, *244*
5:17, *56*
5:22, *56*
6:20, *56*

2 Timothy
1:6-7, *56*
1:7, *120*
1:11, *29*
2:17, *128*
2:19, *133*
2:20, *22, 26*
2:25-26, *206*
4:3, *56*
4:7-8, *257*

Titus
1:5, *56*
1:16, *67*
2:11-13, *224*
3:5, *39, 87, 103*

Hebrews
2:12, *74*
3:6, *20*
3:14, *99*
4:13, *225*

4:14, *166*
6:4-6, *103*
9:13, *110*
10:4, *110*
10:22, *120*
10:32, *103*
12:2, *224*
12:23, *215*

James
2:13, *173*
4:6, *59*
5:14-16, *113*

1 Peter
1:3-4, *249*
1:13, *229*
1:21, *229*
2:5, *17, 21*
2:9, *55*
3:9, *229*
3:20, *95*
3:20-21, *6, 16*
3:21, *16, 104, 105, 113*
4:7, *143*
5:5, *59*

2 Peter
2:4, *211, 212, 267*
2:22, *135*
3:8, *162, 166*
3:10, *258*

1 John
1:8, *28, 119*
2:1, *116*
2:15-17, *255*
3:2, *187*
3:14, *120*
4:3, *142*
4:8, *117, 191*
4:16, *117*
5:8, *36*
5:19, *257*

Revelation
1:15, *250*
2:5, *247*
2:20-22, *247*
6:9, *110*
6:10, *51, 191*
7:4, *19*
14:4, *191*
17:8, *221*
19:10, *178*
20:4, *110*
20:4-6, *140*
20:10, *209, 211, 267*
20:11, *209*
20:12, *210*
21:1-11, *5*
21:2, *163*
21:19-20, *182*
22:5, *257*